# EXACTLY THE W
## WHEN YOU

With our extensive crossword _____, _____ comprehensive special reference sections, and our exclusive Word Finder, *The Dell Crossword Dictionary* ends your down-and-across search for stumpers like these:

1. Temple birds
2. Addams Family handyman?
3. Belted hunter
4. Nice name?
5. Cassino cash

Answers:

1. Owls (See Colleges & Universities.)
2. Thing
3. Orion (Look up "hunter.")
4. Nom (Look up "French Words.")
5. Lira (See Nations Information, Italy.)

## QUANTITY SALES

Most Dell books are available at special quantity discounts when purchased in bulk by corporations, organizations, or groups. Special imprint, messages and excerpts can be produced to meet your needs. For more information, write to: Dell Publishing, 1540 Broadway, New York, NY 10036. Attention: Director, Special Markets.

## INDIVIDUAL SALES

Are there any Dell books you want but cannot find in your local stores? If so, you can order them directly from us. You can get any Dell book currently in print. For a complete up-to-date listing of our books and information on how to order, write to: Dell Readers Service, Box DR, 1540 Broadway, New York, NY 10036.

# THE DELL
# CROSSWORD
# DICTIONARY

### ORIGINALLY COMPILED BY
### KATHLEEN RAFFERTY

### REVISED, UPDATED, AND EXPANDED BY
### WAYNE ROBERT WILLIAMS

**A Dell Book**

Published by
Dell Publishing
a division of
Random House, Inc.
1540 Broadway
New York, New York 10036

If you purchased this book without a cover you should be aware that this book is stolen property. It was reported as "unsold and destroyed" to the publisher and neither the author nor the publisher has received any payment for this "stripped book."

Copyright © 1950, 1960, 1984, 1994 by Dell Publishing
Copyright © renewed 1978 by Dell Publishing

All rights reserved. No part of this book may be reproduced or transmitted in any form or by any means, electronic or mechanical, including photocopying, recording, or by any information storage and retrieval system, without written permission of the Publisher, except where permitted by law.

Dell® is a registered trademark of Random House, Inc. and the colophon is a trademark of Random House, Inc.

ISBN: 0-440-21871-3

Printed in the United States of America

Published simultaneously in Canada

Dell reissue: August 2002

20  19  18  17

# ABOUT THIS BOOK . . .

Kathleen Rafferty compiled and edited *The Dell Crossword Dictionary* 44 years ago. It continues to this day to be the cross-word puzzle solver's ultimate reference source.

It was designed to be a portable book in which one could find the answers to put into those few remaining unfilled squares and complete every crossword. Although much has changed in the world of crossword puzzles in the last 44 years, completely filling in every square in a puzzle is still the solver's goal.

Crossword puzzles have evolved over the years. They have improved along with the skills of the people constructing them. Most contemporary constructors try to avoid using obscure, obsolete, and archaic words. The emphasis has shifted from puzzles full of little-known words to puzzles with clever clues for interesting and challenging words. However, one person's inter-esting word may be another person's obscure word. The need for a reference source to help solve crossword puzzles remains.

This book is many reference books combined into a single, easy-to-carry volume. It is a dictionary, thesaurus, almanac, encyclopedia, gazetteer, word finder, and much more. This new edition, while maintaining its convenient size, has been expand-ed to include more information. This was accomplished by reor-ganizing the material and eliminating redundancies. Many new facts have been added and some outdated information has been removed.

The format of the book remains the same. There are still three basic sections: Clues & Definitions, Special Sections, and the Word Finder. (For more information on Clues & Definitions and the Word Finder, see the introductions on pages 8 and 247.) One important change in this edition concerns alphabetization. The original dictionary used the word-by-word alphabetizing method. In this book the method used is letter-by-letter. This method is the one used in most dictionaries. When alphabetizing single words, both methods are the same. In this book, however, there are many multi-word items alphabetized and it is here where the difference between the two methods comes into play. In the letter-by-letter method, alphabetization progresses letter by letter and stops when you reach a comma. Spaces between words, hyphens, and abbreviation periods are disregarded. When two or more items are identical up to the comma, the words following the commas are used to alphabetize them.

The Special Sections have been greatly expanded in this new edition of *The Dell Crossword Dictionary*. The largest single addition is the Name Finder. The names of thousands of famous people are cross-referenced by first and last names. When you know a person's first name but not his last, the Name Finder is the only reference source you need. As an additional helpful feature, each name is accompanied by a code letter to indicate the person's profession. (See page 136 for an introduction to the Name Finder.)

The Special Sections that you have relied on in the past have been updated and expanded. Many new ones have been added, including: Animals, Constellations & Stars, Sports Teams, and more.

All three- and four-letter words found in the Clues & Definitions section and every one of the Special Sections are cross-referenced from the Word Finder.

It is impossible to pack more information into a book which is already full. Some things had to be removed. Deciding what to keep, what to eliminate, and what to add has not been easy. The goal in creating this edition was to make the "ultimate reference source" even better for you, the crossword puzzle solver.

All the Best,

Wayne Robert Williams

# CONTENTS

# CLUES & DEFINITIONS

Crossword Puzzle clues and definitions are arranged alphabetically letter by letter, as explained in the introduction. Each clue is accompanied by a word or words in capital letters. These are some possible answers to the clue.

That is simple enough, however, the clue in the crossword puzzle you are solving will not always be expressed in the same way as it is listed here. To attempt to list all the different ways that constructors and editors might choose to write a clue would be a daunting task indeed.

A logical method has been determined to avoid the redundancy of listing the same clues over and over in different wordings. This space would be better used by more clues for other answer words. In general, clues are listed with the primary word of a clue first. This results in many inverted clues of the type "deer, red." The clue in the puzzle you are solving may read "Red deer," but you won't find it listed both ways here. Space is at a premium. Of course, exceptions abound. It is not always easy to determine which is the primary word in a clue. Many clues are still listed more than once with slightly different wording.

When your clue is a single word, you may find your answer word immediately. Then again, perhaps not. The English language is full of synonyms. Constructors and editors often stretch their imaginations to the limit. Don't give up if your answer is not listed with the clue word when you find it. Try looking up some of the answer words listed with the clue word. This may lead you to the correct answer.

If the answer you are seeking is not in this section you may find it in one of the other sections of this book. Become familiar with the information in the Special Sections. By fully utilizing all of the sections of this book, you should be able to find the answers for most clues.

# A

9

a Adam, son of ....ABEL, CAIN, SETH
adapt ...............FIT; SUIT; ADJUST,
.........................TAILOR; FASHION
Addams Family butler.........LURCH
Addams Family cousin ...............ITT
Addams Family hand............THING
adder, common......................ASP
addict .....................................USER
addition.......................ADDENDUM
addition to a bill ...................RIDER
add on .....................AFFIX, ANNEX;
.........................................ATTACH
adept .....ABLE; EXPERT, MASTER
adequate...................FAIR; AMPLE;
.........................................ENOUGH
adhere...........BOND, KEEP, OBEY;
.................CLING, STICK; CLEAVE
adhesive.........GUM; GLUE; PASTE
adjust...........FIX, SET; SUIT, TUNE;
.............ADAPT; ATTUNE, TAILOR
adjutant ..................AIDE; SECOND
adjutant bird .HURGILA, MARABOU
admonish...............CHIDE, SCOLD;
........................REBUKE; UPBRAID
adolescence .........TEENS, YOUTH;
.........................................NONAGE
adorable ...............................CUTE
Adriana, servant of .................LUCE
Adriatic seaport...........................BARI
adroit..............DEFT, NEAT; SLICK;

b ............CLEVER, FACILE, NIMBLE
adulterate ..................DOPE, LOAD;
.....................DEBASE, DOCTOR
advantage .....EDGE, JUMP, ODDS,
....SAKE; FAVOR, START; PROFIT
advisor, female ..................EGERIA
Aeëtes, daughter of............MEDEA
Aegeus, wife of ..................MEDEA
Aeneas, wife of .................CREUSA
Aeneid author........VERGIL, VIRGIL
aerial bomb, guidable...........AZON;
.........................................RAZON
Aesir gods ..........TYR; FREY, LOKI,
........ODIN, THOR; FRIGG, FREYA,
..............BRAGI, WODEN; BALDER
Aeson, half-brother of..........PELIAS
Aeson, son of .......................JASON
affectionate ..............FOND, WARM;
........................LOVING, TENDER
affirm .........AVER; POSIT; ASSERT
affirmative .............AYE, YEA, YEP,
..............YES; OKAY, SURE, YEAH
afflict..............PAIN, RACK; CURSE
affluence ................EASE; RICHES,
.......................................WEALTH
affray ........BRAWL, FIGHT, MELEE
Afghan title ..................AMIR, KHAN
afresh .......................ANEW; AGAIN
African bast fiber........................IYO
Afr. bustard variety .................KORI

c Afr. cattle breed ...................SANGA
Afr. cereal grass.......................TEFF
Afr. cotton garment .......TOB; TOBE
Afr. ground squirrel ..............XERUS
Afr. hornbill...............................TOCK
Afr. milletlike grass...............FUNDI
Afr. plant ................................ALOE
Afr. ravine .............................DONGA
Afr. scrubby tree .....................BITO
Afr. soldier...........................ASKARI
Afr. tableland .....KAROO; KARROO
Afr. thorn-bush stockade .......BOMA
Afr. worm ...................................LOA
Afrikaans ................................TAAL
Afrikaner .................................BOER
aft ..........................REAR; ASTERN
after awhile ............................ANON
aftermath ..........ROWEN; EFFECT,
.....................RESULT; OUTCOME
afterward .................................THEN
again............................BIS; ANEW;
.....................AFRESH, ENCORE
against .........CON; ANTI; CONTRA,
.....................VERSUS; ABUTTING
agalloch ....................ALOESWOOD
Agamemnon, brother of.MENELAUS
Agamemnon, daughter of.ELECTRA
Agamemnon, parents of...AEROPE,
.......................................ATREUS
Agamemnon, son of........ORESTES

d agate stone........................ACHATE
agave fiber......TULA; ISTLE, IXTLE
age....................EON, ERA; RIPEN;
........................MATURE, PERIOD
aged ..............OLD; ANILE; SENILE
agency .................MEANS; MEDIUM
agent ........................REP; FACTOR
aggregate ...........ALL, SUM; MASS;
..........TOTAL; GARNER, GATHER
agitate .......................MOVE, STIR;
.................CHURN, SHAKE, SHIFT
agitated state ...............FUNK, SNIT
agitation.............DITHER, FLURRY,
.....................TUMULT; TURMOIL
agnomen ..................NAME; EPITHET
agree .....GIBE; ASSENT, CONCUR
agreement.MISE, PACT; ACCORD,
....TREATY; CONCORD, ENTENTE
agriculture goddess ...........CERES;
.....................VACUNA; DEMETER
Agrippina, son of...................NERO
ahead .................EARLY; LEADING
aid ..................ABET, HAND, HELP;
............ASSIST, RELIEF, SUCCOR
Aïda's love....................RADAMES
aim ...................END; GOAL, MARK;
..........INTENT, OBJECT, TARGET
air.......AURA, MOOD, TUNE, WIND
air-conditioning abbreviation .....BTU
aircraft, motorless ...............GLIDER

*a* airfoil, vertical .............................FIN
Air Force mascot ...............FALCON
air passage..................FLUE, VENT
airplane .......................JET; FLIGHT
airport, Boston .....................LOGAN
airport, Chicago ...................OHARE
airport, Washington D.C. ...DULLES
airport marker .......................PYLON
airship.................................BLIMP
air supply.........................AERATOR
airy .........GAUZY, LIGHT; BREEZY,
.....................JAUNTY; VAPOROUS
ait ........................................ISLE
Ajax, father of .................TELAMON
akin ..............COGNATE, RELATED
alarm ..........FEAR; ALERT, PANIC
.........SCARE; TOCSIN; WARNING
alas ..................ACH, HEU, OCH
alas, Irish...........OHONE; OCHONE
Alaska glacier .........................MUIR
alb: archaic...........................AUBE
albatross, sooty ...................NELLY
*Alceste* composer ...............GLUCK
alcohol, solid.....................STEROL
alcoholic drink .......GIN, RUM, RYE;
........GROG, OUZO, RAKI; VODKA;
......BRANDY, COGNAC, GRAPPA,
...PERNOD, SCOTCH; BOURBON,
.................WHISKEY, TEQUILA
Alcott heroine .....AMY, MEG; BETH
*b* alcove...................NICHE; RECESS
alder tree, Scot. .....................ARN
ale, sour.............................ALEGAR
ale, strong ..................NOG; NOGG
ale mug .............................TOBY
alert ..................................WARN
alewife.....POMPANO; MENHADEN
Alexandrian theologian .........ARIUS
Alexander, erroneous victory site of.
.....................................ARBELA
Alexander, father of ............PHILIP
Alexander, tutor of........ARISTOTLE
Alexander, victory site of........IRBIL,
.....................ISSUS; GRANICUS
Alexander's kingdom .....MACEDON
alfalfa ...........LUCERN; LUCERNE
Alfonso's queen .......................ENA
alga, Jap. food ......................NORI;
.....................LAVER; AMANORI
alga, one-celled..................DIATOM
algae, fan-shaped...............PADINA
algarroba tree ......................CAROB
Algerian governor ....................DEY
Algonquian language .............CREE
Ali Baba's word .................SESAME
alienate........................ESTRANGE;
.................................DISAFFECT
align ...............ALLY, LINE; RANGE;
...................LEAGUE; FEDERATE
alkali ....................LYE, REH; USAR

alkaloid, stimulating ........CAFFEINE *c*
allanite ................................CERINE
allay ...EASE, CALM, LULL; QUIET,
...............STILL; SETTLE, SOOTHE
allegory, religious ............PARABLE
Aleppo resident....................SYRIAN
alleviate ....................EASE; ALLAY;
.....................LESSEN; ASSUAGE
alley ...................MIB, MIG; LANE
Alley Oop, girlfriend of............OOLA
alliance .....PACT; UNION; LEAGUE
alliance, Pac. ........................SEATO
alliance, Western ...................NATO
alligator, S. A. ..................CAIMAN
alligator in "Pogo" ...............ALBERT
alligator pear ...................AVOCADO
allot ..............GIVE, METE; ASSIGN
allotment ........LOT; PART; QUOTA,
...........SHARE; RATION; PORTION
allow...............LET; ADMIT; PERMIT,
.....................SUFFER; SANCTION
allowance ...........LOT; ODDS, PART;
.............QUOTA, SHARE; RATION
alloy .................................MIX
alloy, aluminum-copper........DURAL
alloy, copper-tin................BRONZE,
.........................................OROIDE
alloy, copper-zinc................BRASS,
.........................................OROIDE
alloy, iron-nickel .................INVAR
alloy, lead-tin .............CALIN, TERNE *d*
alloy, nickel-copper ............MONEL
alloy, non-ferrous ......TULA; NIELLO
allspice..............................PIMENTO
allure ..........DRAW, PULL; CHARM,
...............TEMPT; APPEAL, ENTICE
allusion ................................HINT
almond-flavored drink .......ORGEAT
almost ...ABOUT, ANEAR; NEARLY
alms box or chest...................ARCA
aloe .................................AGAVE
aloe derivative .....................ALOIN
aloe fiber ...............................PITA
alone ..................BUT; ONLY, SOLO
alone on stage..........SOLA; SOLUS
along.......................WITH; BESIDE
alp.........................................PEAK
Alp, Fr. ..............................BLANC
alpaca ................................PACO
alphabet, Arabic ....AYN, DAD, DAL,
....JIM, KAF, KHA, LAM, MIM, NUN,
..QAF, SAD, SIN, THA, WAW, ZAY;
.................ALIF, DHAL, SHIN; GHAYN
alphabet, Greek (in order) ...ALPHA,
.................BETA, GAMMA, DELTA,
...................EPSILON, ZETA, ETA,
...................THETA, IOTA, KAPPA,
..LAMBDA, MU, NU, XI, OMICRON,
..PI, RHO, SIGMA, TAU, UPSILON,
.................PHI, CHI, PSI, OMEGA

a  alphabet, Hebrew............HET, KAF;
...........MEM, NUN, SIN, TAV, VAV;
..............YOD; AYIN, BETH, KOPH;
..........RESH, SHIN, TETH; ALEPH,
...............GIMEL, LAMED, SADHE,
...............ZAYIN; DALETH, SAMEKH
alphabet, spoken (in order) .ALPHA,
..........BRAVO, CHARLIE, DELTA,
..........ECHO, FOX-TROT, GOLF,
........HOTEL, INDIA, JULIET, KILO,
..............LIMA, MIKE, NOVEMBER,
..............OSCAR, PAPA, QUEBEC,
..........ROMEO, SIERRA, TANGO,
.....UNIFORM, VICTOR, WHISKEY,
..................X-RAY, YANKEE, ZULU
Alps .....................................TYROL
Alps pass ............................CENIS
Altar constellation ....................ARA
altar end of a church..............APSE
altar screen ...................REREDOS
altar shelf ......................GRADIN;
.....................GRADINE, RETABLE
altar side curtain ................RIDDEL
altar top ...........................MENSA
alternate .............FILL-IN, ROTATE;
...................................STAND-IN
alternatives..............................ORS
alumni ................................GRADS
always ............................E'ER; EVER
amadou .................................PUNK
b  amass ...........................HOARD;
..................GARNER, GATHER
amateur ...........TYRO; NOVICE
Amazon cetacean genus ..........INIA
Amazon region people.............TUPI
Amazon tributary.............APA, ICA;
...............JURUA, NEGRO, PURUS
...........................XINGU; JAPURA;
...................MADEIRA, TAPAJOS
ambassador ........ENVOY; LEGATE
amend ..................ALTER; REVISE
amends, make .....................ATONE
ament....................IDIOT, MORON
American, to a Brit. ...............YANK
Amer. nighthawk ......................PISK
Amer. patriot...............HALE, OTIS;
.......................ALLEN; REVERE
ammunition ..............AMMO, SHOT
ammunition wagon...........CAISSON
among............MID; AMID; AMIDST
Amon-Re, wife of...................MUT
amorous stare.........................LEER
amphibian genus......HYLA; ANURA
amphitheater.......................ARENA
amulet ...........CHARM; FETISH
amuse ...............................DIVERT
analyze .............ASSAY; DISSECT
analyze grammatically .........PARSE
ancestral spirit, P. I. ...........ANITO
ancestral spirits, Rom. .........LARES

anchor..............................FIX, TIE;  c
.............................MOOR; KEDGE
anchor part ...........................FLUKE
anchovy sauce........................ALEC
ancient .......................OLD; AGED
ancient times................ELD; YORE
and...............................TOO; ALSO,
.................................PLUS, WITH
Andes' cold higher region ......PUNA
Andes grass ............................ICHU
Andes mountain basin ...........HOYA
andiron .................................DOG
and not....................................NOR
Andromache, husband of..HECTOR
Andy Capp, wife of...................FLO
anecdotes....................ANA; TALES
anent ....................ABOUT; BESIDE
anesthetic ...................GAS; ETHER
Angel of Death ...................AZREAL
anger .........IRE; WRATH; ENRAGE
anger, fit of.................SNIT; PIQUE;
...........................................TEMPER
angle .............BEND, BIAS, TURN,
...............VIEW; SLANT; OUTLOOK
angle, 57° ...........................RADIAN
angle of a leafstalk ...................AXIL
Anglo-Saxon god of peace ........ING
A.-S. king ..............................INE
A.-S. letter..........EDH, ETH; YOGH
A.-S. slave ............................ESNE
angry ......................HOT, MAD;  d
...............................SORE; IRATE
animal, draft ..........................OXEN
animal, giraffelike ..................OKAPI
animal, undersized................RUNT
animal and plant life .............BIOTA
animal body ............................SOMA
animal's leg on coat of arms....GAMB
animals of an area ..............FAUNA
animal sound.......BAY, LOW, MOO;
.........BARK, BRAY, HOWL, ROAR,
........YAWP, YELP, YOWL; BLEAT,
..............GRUNT, NEIGH, SNORT
animal trail......RUN; SLOT; SPOOR
animated: music ..................ANIME
ankle(s) ..................TARSI, TALUS;
..............................................TARSUS
Annapolis student.................PLEBE
annas, sixteen ....................RUPEE
annatto seeds or tree ......ACHIOTE
anneal ...........TEMPER; TOUGHEN
annex ...................ADD, ELL; WING;
.............................................ATTACH
annihilate ........................DESTROY
announce....CALL, PAGE; HERALD
annoy......................IRK, TRY, VEX;
...................RILE; PEEVE, TEASE
annuity, form of .................TONTINE
annul........................UNDO, VOID;
.........................CANCEL, REVOKE

12

*a* anoint..............................OIL; ANELE
another .......................NEW; AGAIN
answer, have the ..................KNOW
ant ......................EMMET; PISMIRE
ant, stinging ...........................KELEP
Antarctic bird....................PENGUIN
antecedent......PRIOR, ANCESTOR
antelope.....................GNU, KOB;
..........GUIB, KOBA, KUDU, ORYX,
......................POKU, PUKU, TORA;
...............................ADDAX, BONGO,
...............ELAND, ORIBI; RHEBOK
antelope, Indian .......SASIN; NILGAI
antelope, large Afr. ............IMPALA
antelope, Siberian .................SAIGA
antelope, small Afr. ............DUIKER
antelope, tawny .....................ORIBI
antenna ................HORN, PALP;
............................AERIAL, FEELER
anthracite ...............................COAL
anthracite, inferior quality.......CULM
anti-aircraft fire ......................FLAK
antic............DIDO; CAPER, PRANK
antiseptic ...CLEAN, IODIN, SALOL;
.............................CRESOL, IODINE
antitoxin(s)...............SERA; SERUM
antler point....SNAG, TINE; PRONG
anvil, small............................TEEST
anvil of the ear ......................INCUS
anxiety .....CARE; ANGST, WORRY

*b* aoudad ...................................ARUI
apathy.................ENNUI; PHLEGM
aperture ...........GAP; HOLE, SLOT,
...........VENT; OPENING, ORIFICE
aphasia, motor.....ALALIA, MUTISM
aphorism ....................SAW; RULE;
...........................ADAGE, MAXIM
Aphrodite, lover of .................ARES;
................................ANCHISES
Aphrodite, mother of ............DIONE
Aphrodite, son of ..............AENEAS
Aphrodite to Romans...........VENUS
apiece .....................................EACH
apocopate .............................ELIDE
Apocrypha, books of the.......TOBIT;
..................BARUCH, DANIEL,
.....................ESDRAS, ESTHER,
...................JUDITH, WISDOM;
............MANASSEH; MACCABEES
Apollo, birthplace of .............DELOS
Apollo, mother of ....LETO; LATONA
Apollo, sacred valley of........TEMPE
Apollo, sister of ...DIANA; ARTEMIS
Apollo, son of.............................ION
Apostles ...............................JOHN,
..........JUDE (THADDEUS); JAMES,
................JUDAS, PETER, SIMON;
..........ANDREW, PHILIP, THOMAS
......(DIDYMUS); MATTHEW (LEVI);
........MATTHIAS; BARTHOLOMEW

*c* apparent ................CLEAR, PLAIN;
.........................PATENT; EVIDENT,
.....................VISIBLE; MANIFEST
apparition ..............BOGY; GHOST,
...........SHADE, SPOOK; SHADOW,
.............................SPIRIT, WRAITH;
...............PHANTOM, SPECTER
appear .........LOOK, LOOM, SEEM;
...............ARISE, ISSUE; EMERGE
appearance ................LOOK, MIEN;
...........................IMAGE; ADVENT,
.......................ASPECT; ARRIVAL
appease ...................................CALM;
.........................PACIFY, SOOTHE;
....................PLACATE, SATISFY
appellation .................NAME; TITLE
append ......................ADD; ANNEX
appendage........ARM; FORK, LIMB;
....................................BRANCH
appendage, caudal ....................TAIL
appetizer ...........................CANAPE
applaud ..................................CLAP
applause, thunderous ...........ROAR
apple.......................ROME; PIPPIN
apple acid.............................MALIC
applelike tree .........................SORB
apples, crushed .................POMACE
apple seed....................................PIP
apple tree genus ...............MALUS
appoint ..........GEAR, MAKE, NAME

*d* apportion ,.................GIVE, METE;
............................ALLOT, ALLOW;
.....................ASSIGN; ALLOCATE
appraise....RATE; ASSAY, GAUGE,
.............JUDGE, VALUE; ASSESS
apprise ......TELL; ADVISE, NOTIFY
approach ........NEAR, PLAN, TACK
appropriate ...........APT, FIT; RIGHT
approve ..........................ÓKAY, PASS
approved ...............................OK'D
approves..............................OK'S
apricot, Jap. ...............................UME
apricot, Korean.......................ANSU
apricots, Afr. dried................MEBOS
apropos.....GERMANE; RELEVANT
apteryx ....................................KIWI
aptitude ..........BENT, GIFT; FLAIR,
..........KNACK; TALENT; FACULTY
aquamarine ..........................BERYL
Arab ..................GAMIN; SEMITE
Arab cloak, sleeveless..............ABA
Arab drink, beerlike ....BOSA, BOZA
Arab state of bliss ....................KEF
Arabian chief.....................SAYYID
Arabian chieftain .......AMIR, EMIR
Arabian domain ................EMIRATE
Arabian judge .....CADI, KADI, QADI
"Arabian Nights" dervish..........AGIB
Arabian nomad..................BERBER
Arabian Sea gulf ...................ADEN

a
Arabic alphabet..........See alphabet.
Arabic jinni, evil.....AFRIT; AFREET, ............................AFRITE, EFREET
Arabic script..........NESKI; NESKHI, ............................................NASKHI
Arabic script, angular ...........CUFIC, ............................................KUFIC
arachnid.........MITE, TICK; SPIDER
Arawakan language ..............TAINO
arbiter.................JUDGE; UMPIRE; .........................................REFEREE
arch, pointed ..........OGEE; OGIVE; ............................................LANCET
archangel............URIEL; MICHAEL
archbishop ........................PRIMATE
Archbishop of Canterbury..BECKET
archer, famous Gr. ...........TEUCER
archer, famous Swiss .............TELL
archer in Eng. ballad .............CLYM
archetype ......MASTER; ORIGINAL
archfiend .............................SATAN
architect's drawing, full-scale ..................................................EPURE
architectural style ...............DORIC, ..........IONIC; GOTHIC; GEORGIAN
Arctic.......NORTH, POLAR; FRIGID
Arctic AF base ....................THULE
Arctic dog........HUSKY; SAMOYED
Arctic gull genus ...................XEMA
Arctic plain .......................TUNDRA

b
ardor ..........FIRE, ZEAL; FERVOR; ...........................................PASSION
areca.....................................BETEL
arene derivative ......................ARYL
Ares, mother of ......................HERA
Ares, sister of..........................ERIS
ares, ten .............................DECARE
Argo crewman ...............MOPSUS, .....................TIPHYS; ANCAEUS, .................................POLYDEUCES
Argonauts, leader of the.......JASON
Argonauts, ship of the ...........ARGO
argument.........ROW; CASE, SPAT; ...............FIGHT, POINT; DEBATE
arhat .....................................LOHAN
aria...........AIR; SOLO, SONG, TUNE
arias ...........................................SOLI
aridity, having.......................XERIC
Arikara people .........................REE
arise...........DAWN, FLOW; BEGIN, ..........START; APPEAR, EMERGE
arista .......................................AWN
Ark's landing place ...........ARARAT
armadillo, Braz. ..TATU; DASYPUS
armadillo, six-banded ........PELUDO
armadillo, small ....................PEBA
armadillo, three-banded .........APAR
armadillo, twelve-banded TATOUAY
armor, body .....................CUIRASS
armor, buttocks ...................CULET

c
armor, chain ............................MAIL
armor, horse ...........................BARD
armor, leg ...........................GREAVE
armor, Rom. cuirass ..........LORICA
armor, thigh .........CUISSE, TUILLE
armor, throat ....................GORGET
armor bearer.....................ARMIGER
army ........HOST; CROWD, FLOCK; ..................LEGION; MULTITUDE
army group ..........................CADRE
army provisioner .................SUTLER
aromatic herb.....DILL, MINT, SAGE
aromatic seed..........ANISE, CUMIN
aromatic substance ............BALSAM
aromatic weed.....................TANSY
around .......BACK, OVER; ABOUT, ........................ROUND; THROUGH
arouse ........STIR; WAKEN; EXCITE
arpeggio..........................ROULADE
arraign ............ACCUSE, CHARGE, ......................INDICT; INCULPATE
arrange .............................FIX, SET
arrangement .......ORDER; LAYOUT
array.................LOT, SET; GROUP
arrest.........NAB; BUST, HALT, ...............................STOP; COLLAR
arrest writ ...........................CAPIAS
arris............................PIEN; PIEND
arrow ...........DART; POINTER
arrow, fit string to an ..............NOCK

d
arrowroot ....................................PIA
arrowshaped....................HASTATE
arroyo, broad .......................HONDO
arsenic trisulfide ............ORPIMENT
art............CRAFT, GUILE, KNACK
Artemis, mother of .................LETO
Artemis, twin of.................APOLLO
Artemis, victim of.................ORION
artery, largest.......................AORTA
artery of the neck ...........CAROTID
artful .........SLY; DEFT, FOXY, WILY
arthritis, form of.....................GOUT
Arthur, foster brother of............KAY
Arthurian lady ...........ENID; ELAINE
article .............................THE; ITEM.
articulated joint ...................HINGE
artifice............PLOY; FEINT, TRICK
artificial fishing fly ..................HERL
artificial language.......................IDO
artless....................................NAIVE
art medium, diluted................WASH
art movement.........................DADA
art with acid, create ...............ETCH
artwork, pasted ...............COLLAGE
arum plant ...TARO; AROID, CALLA
Aryan ..........................MEDE, SLAV
asafetida ................................HING
ascent.......CLIMB, GRADE, SLOPE
ascetic, ancient....................ESSENE
asceticism, Hindu ..................YOGA

14

a ascorbic acid..................VITAMIN C
ash seed ...........................SAMARA
ashy pale................................LIVID
Asia Minor, ancient city in......MYRA
Asia Minor region ................AEOLIA
Asiatic evergreen.....................BAGO
askew...............AWRY; CROOKED
aspect.CAST, FACE, LOOK, VIEW;
............ANGLE, SLANT; VISAGE
ass, wild .............KIANG; ONAGER
assail ............HIT; ABUSE, BESET;
...................REVILE, STRIKE
Assam hills............................NAGA
assault ...............STORM; ATTACK
assault, prolonged................SIEGE
assayer ..............................TESTER
assaying cup ........................CUPEL
assemble ...CALL, MEET; MUSTER
assembly ......GROUP; CONGRESS
assembly, A.-S. GEMOT; GEMOTE
assembly, Hawaiian...................HUI
assembly, S. Afr. Boer .........RAAD
assert ..........AVER, AVOW, HOLD;
..........CLAIM; ALLEGE; DECLARE
assess ............TAX; LEVY; VALUE
assets, liquid .......................CASH
asseverate............................AVER
assimilate...ABSORB, DIGEST
assistance .........AID; HAND, HELP;
...................RELIEF, SUCCOR
b assistant ..............................AIDE
assistant, military.....................ADC
associate ........ALLY, CHUM, MATE
association, trade ................GUILD
assuage.................CALM, EASE;
...................ALLAY; SOFTEN;
..............SOOTHE; RELIEVE
asterisk ................................STAR
astern ...............AFT; ABAFT
astringent ..............SOUR; ACERB,
...................ACRID, HARSH;
...................BITTER; ACERBIC
astringent fruit.......................SLOE
asylum ............HAVEN; REFUGE
Atahualpa, King ....................INCA
Atalanta, husband of.......MILANION
atap palm ..............................NIPA
atelier...............................STUDIO
Athabaskan language ...........HUPA
Athamas, daughter of ..........HELLE
Athamas, first wife of......NEPHELE
Athamas, second wife of ..........INO
Athamas, son of ...........PHRIXUS
Athena ..............................PALLAS
Athena, Rom. ...............MINERVA
Athena, title of .....................ALEA
Athenian.............................ATTIC
Athenian demagogue ..........CLEON
Athens, first king of.........CECROPS
Athens, last king of .........CODRUS

atom, parts of an ...............GLUON, c
.........QUARK; PROTON; NEURON
atomic number..........See page 245.
atomic physicists .......BOHR, RABI,
...................UREY; FERMI, PAULI
atomic submarines .............SKATE,
.........SARGO; TRITON; NAUTILUS
at once: pharmacy ..................STAT
attach ...................FIX; CLIP, MOOR
attack ..............................HIT; PLAN,
...................TACK; COURSE
attack, mock .........................FEINT
attempt ......................TRY; STAB;
...................TRIAL; EFFORT
attendant, hunter's...GILLY; GILLIE
attention .........HEED, MARK, NOTE
attention-getting sound ..........AHEM
attest ...................SWEAR; VERIFY
attic ......................LOFT; GARRET
Attica resident-alien ............METIC
Attila ..........................ATLI; ETZEL
Attila's followers ...................HUNS
attitude..........POSE; STANCE
Attorney General, Clinton's....RENO
attribute................................TRAIT;
...................CREDIT, IMPUTE
attune .............FIX, SET; ADJUST
auction ..................................SALE
audience,................GATE; PUBLIC;
...................HEARING
auditory.................OTIC; AURAL d
auger .................................BORER
augment ...WAX; GROW; SWELL
augur.............DIVINE; PROPHESY
augury ..............OMEN; PORTEND
auk, razor-billed .....................ALCA
auricle ..................................EAR
auricular ..................OTIC; EARED
aurochs ..................URUS; WISENT
aurora ..........................EOS; DAWN
auspices ..............................AEGIS
Australasian harrier-hawk ......KAHU
Austral. shrub genus..............HOYA
Austral. boomerang .............KILEY,
...................KYLIE
Austral. cockatoo ................GALAH
Austral. gum tree ...................KARI;
...................TUART, KARRI
Austral. marsupial .....TAIT; KOALA;
...................NUMBAT, WOMBAT;
...................KANGAROO
Austral. timber tree ...............PENDA
author ..................MAKER, WRITE
author, boys' .........ALGER, HENTY
author, nature stories...........SETON
author, unknown ...................ANON
authoritative .............TRUE; VALID;
...................MIGHTY; OFFICIAL
authority ................POWER, RIGHT
automaton .........................ROBOT

15

a automaton, Jewish legend ..GOLEM
ave .................................................HAIL
avena......................................OAT
avenge .............................REPAY
avenger: Heb. ...................GOEL
average ...................PAR; MEAN;
.................................NORM; USUAL;
...................COMMON, MEDIAN
averse ................................LOATH
Avernal ...................INFERNAL
Avernus...............................HELL
Avesta division ...............YASHT
avid.........KEEN; EAGER; GREEDY
avifauna(e) ....BIRD; BIRDS; ORNIS
___ Aviv.....................................TEL
avocado, Mex. ......................COYO

c avoid..........DUCK, SHUN; DODGE,
................ELUDE, EVADE; ESCAPE
avouch....AVER, AVOW, HOLD
await judgment.......................PEND
aware, be ..............................KNOW
aweto .................................WERI
awkward ................BULKY, INEPT;
...........CLUMSY, GAUCHE, UNEASY
awn .....................................ARISTA
awned.........................ARISTATE
awry ....................AMISS, WRONG
axilla ........................................ALA
axillary ...................................ALAR
axis deer ..........CHITAL; CHEETAL
Ayatollah's predecessor.........SHAH
Aztec spear......................ATLATL

# B

Babism founder.......................BAB
Babist.......................................BABI
babul tree pods ...................GARAD
baby carriage.......................PRAM
Babylonia, part of .............SUMER
Babylonian's neighbor ......ELAMITE
Bacchanalian cry................EVOE
bacchante ........................MAENAD
b Bacchus, follower of............SATYR
Bacchus, son of ................COMUS
back, of the.........................DORSAL
backbone ................CHINE, SPINE
back door........................POSTERN
back of the neck ....................NAPE
back talk ...............GUFF, SASS
backward .................................FRO
bacon, cover meat with .........BARD
bacteria-free ...................ASEPTIC
badge, Jap. family .................MON
badger...................................BAIT
badgerlike animal...............RATEL
badgers, Old World.............MELES
baffle .....................BALK, FOIL;
.................STUMP; STYMIE;
..............THWART; CONFOUND
bagatelle .............................TRIFLE
bag net.................................FYKE
bagpipe hole ..........................LILL
bagpipe pipe ....DRONE; CHANTER
bagpipe sound ...................SKIRL
bailiff, old Eng. .................REEVE
baize fabric.........DOMET; DOMETT
baker bird...........................HORNERO
baking chamber............KILN, OAST
balance...................................REST;
....................POISE; OFFSET,
......................STASIS, STEADY
balance, sentence.............PARISON

d Balance, The .......................LIBRA
balancing weight ..............BALLAST
Balder, killer of......................LOKI
Balder, wife of.....................NANNA
baldness.......................ALOPECIA
ball, yarn or thread.................CLEW
ballad .......................................LAY
ballet jump...........................JETE
ballet skirt ..............................TUTU
ballet turn ..................FOUETTE
balloon basket ................NACELLE
balm of Gilead ...................BALSAM
balsalike wood.................BONGO
balsam ...............FIR; TOLU; RESIN
Balt .......................................ESTH
Baltic Finn .............................VOD
Balto-Slav ..............................LETT
Baluchistan people .......MARI, REKI
Bambi author.....................SALTEN
Bambi rabbit ..............THUMPER
Bambi's cousin ...................GOBO
bamboo ................................REED
bamboo shoots, pickled.......ACHAR
banal ....................BLAND, INANE,
............................VAPID; CLICHE,
..................JEJUNE; INSIPID
banana, kind of....................PLANTAIN
banana, Polynesian ...................FEI
banana genus ......................MUSA
band...............BELT, BEVY, GANG,
.........GIRD, PACK, RING; CORPS,
.............GROUP, STRIA, TROOP;
......................LEAGUE, STRIPE
band: Arch. .........................FASCIA
band, muscle or nerve ........TAENIA
bandages, inferior.................BATT
bandicoot ...................................RAT
banish......EXILE, EXPEL; DEPORT

*a* bank................HEAP, HILL, LUMP,
................MASS, PILE; MOUND,
................STACK; DEPOSIT
bank of a river, of the .....RIPARIAN,
................LITTORAL
bankrupt ................BUST
bank shot................CAROM
bank transaction................LOAN
banner.......FLAG, JACK; COLORS,
................ENSIGN; PENNANT;
................STANDARD, STREAMER
banter .........JEST, JOSH; CHAFF
Bantu language ................ILA
Bantu people................GOGO
Bantu-speaking people ......PONDO;
................MPONDO
baptismal basin ................FONT
baptism font................LAVER
bar................ROD; STOP; BLOCK,
................COURT, SHAFT;
................IMPEDE; OBSTRUCT
bar, legally ................ESTOP
bar, topmast ................FID
barb, feather................HERL
barbarian ................BOOR; YAHOO;
................VULGAR
Barbary ape................MAGOT
barber ................SHAVER, TONSOR
Barber of Seville................FIGARO
Barbie's boyfriend................KEN
*b* bare................BALD, MERE, NUDE;
................NAKED, STRIP; EXPOSE,
................REVEAL, SIMPLE
bargain ..BUY; DEAL, PACT, SALE;
................DICKER, HAGGLE
barge, heavy................HOY
bark................BAY, YAP, YIP; SNAP
bark, lime tree ..........BAST; BASTE
bark, medicinal ................COTO;
................CORTEX
bark, paper mulberry ..............TAPA
bark, rough exterior................ROSS
barking................LATRANT
bark remover................ROSSER
barometric line................ISOBAR
barracuda ............SENET; SENNET
barracuda, small ................SPET
barrelmaker ................COOPER
barrel slat ................STAVE
barren land................USAR
*Bartered Bride, The* character................
................HANS, MUFF; AGNES,
................KEZAL, MARIE, MISHA
base................LOW; FOOT, MEAN,
................ROOT, VILE; CHEAP;
................SORDID; SQUALID
base, arch. ..........SOCLE; PLINTH
base, attached at the ........SESSILE
baseball equipment................BAT;
................BALL, MITT

baseball error................MUFF *c*
baseball hit................BUNT
baseball hose?................SOX
baseball team................NINE
bashful ................COY, SHY; TIMID
basin, broad structural ..........TALA
basis................ROOT; REASON;
................FOOTING
basket................GOAL; SCORE
basketball team................FIVE
Basse-Normandie city............CAEN
bath cake ................SOAP
baton ................STICK
batrachian................FROG, TOAD
batter ................RAM; BEAT, DRUB,
................MAUL; PUMMEL
battery plate................GRID
battle................ANZIO, CRECY;
................ACTIUM, MIDWAY,
................VERDUN; BULL RUN,
................IWO JIMA; HASTINGS,
................NORMANDY
battle, Amer. Rev..........CONCORD
battle, Civil War ................SHILOH
battle, King Arthur's last ....CAMLAN
battle, WW I ................MARNE,
................SOMME, YPRES
battle-ax ................TWIBILL
"Battle Hymn of the Republic" writer
................HOWE
bauble ................BEAD *d*
bay ................COVE, HOWL;
................BIGHT, INLET
bay tree ................LAUREL
bay window................ORIEL
bazaar........FAIR, SOUK; MARKET
beach................SHORE; STRAND
beach cabin................CABANA
beads, prayer................ROSARY
beak ................NEB, NIB; BILL
beam................RAY; SMILE, STRUT
bean ................SOY, URD; LIMA
bean, field ................PINTO
bean, kidney................HARICOT
bean, pleasant-smelling.......TONKA
bean, poisonous..............CALABAR
bean tree ................CATALPA
bear ................CARRY, FETCH,
................STAND, YIELD;
................STOMACH; TOLERATE
bear, Australian................KOALA
bear constellation................URSA
bearded seal ................MAKLUK
beard of grain ..........AWN; ARISTA
bearing................MIEN; HEADING
bearing plate ................GIB
bear's-ear................AURICULA
bear witness ........VOUCH; ATTEST
beast of burden................ASS;
................BURRO, LLAMA

17

*a* beat ...........WHIP; METER, PULSE,
............................THROB, THUMP;
............................HAMMER, THRASH
beater, mortar ............................RAB
Beatles, the.........JOHN (LENNON),
........................PAUL (McCARTNEY;
........................RINGO (STARR);
..............GEORGE (HARRISON)
Beatles' record label.......:....APPLE
beat rapidly ..............PANT; THROB
beat up ..................................LICK
beaver oil ..........................CASTOR
beaver skin ..........................PLEW
beche-de-mer ..............TREPANG
beckon .....COURT, TEMPT; INVITE
bed....................................COT, KIP;
..................................DOSS; FLOOR;
..............................BOTTOM, PALLET
Bedouin headband cord .........AGAL
bee, male ..........................DRONE
beechnuts, fallen ....................MAST
beefwood, Australian............BELAH
beefwood, Polynesian ..............TOA
beehive, straw ......................SKEP
bee house ...............HIVE; APIARY
beer..............................ALE; BOCK,
................MEAD, SUDS; LAGER,
......................STOUT; PORTER
beer ingredient ...........HOPS, MALT
beer mug ................................STEIN
*b* bees, of ...............................APIAN
Beethoven, birthplace of........BONN
beetle...................................DOR
beetle, click ......................ELATER
beetle, sacred....................SCARAB
bee tree .......LINDEN; BASSWOOD
befall ..................................HAP
before ......ERE, PRE; EVER, ONCE
beget ......................SIRE; SPAWN;
..........................................FATHER
*Beggar's Opera* dramatist ........GAY
begin ......................OPEN; START;
........................................EMBARK
beginner ................TIRO, TYRO
beginning ..............BASIC; INITIAL;
..........................................GENESIS
beginning at........................FROM
behind .........AFT; AFTER; ASTERN
behold!......................ECCE; VOILA
beige shade ..........................ECRU
being ..................................ENTITY
being, abstract .....ESSE; ENTIA
being, essential......................ENS
belch ..................................BURP
beleaguerment ......................SIEGE
Belem's state........................PARA
belief.........CREED, FAITH, TENET
believe ..............................CREDIT
believe, formerly....................TROW
bell, alarm ..........................TOCSIN

bell, sound of a......................TOLL
bellow..........................BAWL, YELL
bellowing ..............................AROAR
bell's tongue ..................CLAPPER
bell tower.....BELFRY; CAMPANILE
below: naut. ..........................ALOW
belt......................HIT; GIRD, SASH,
..............................ZONE; CLOUT
belt, sword or bugle ..........BALDRIC
bench ......................PEW; SETTLE
bend ................SNY; FLEX, GENU;
........................STOOP; FLEXURE
benediction ..BENISON; BLESSING
benefactor ........................PATRON
benefit ......................BOON; AVAIL
Bengal people ..............KOL; KOHL
*Ben Hur*, author of ........WALLACE
Ben Hur's rival................MESSALA
Benjamin, firstborn of.............BELA
bent....................ARCED, BOWED;
........................ANGLED, TALENT;
........................................CROOKED
*Beowulf* monster............GRENDEL
bequeath..............................WILL
Bermuda grass ......................DOOB
Bern's river....................AAR; AARE
berserk ......................AMOK, WILD
beseech..............PRAY; ENTREAT
besides .....TOO, YET; ALSO, ELSE
bestow......................AWARD; CONFER
betel leaf concoction.....PAN; BUYO
betel nut ............................BONGA
betel palm ............ARECA; PINANG
betoken ..............................DENOTE
betroth, formerly....................AFFY
bevel......................................SLANT
bevel a ship's timber ............SNAPE
bevel out ..............................REAM
bevel to join........................MITER
beverage..............DRINK, QUAFF;
........................LIQUOR; POTABLE
beverage, Australian ..............KAVA
beverage, hot wine and lemon..........
..........................................NEGUS
beverage, malt ......................BEER
beverage, Mex. ......................CHIA
beverage, Paraguayan...........MATE
Bible..........................See page 196.
bicarbonate ............................SODA
bice blue ..........................AZURITE
bicker ..................................CAVIL
bicycle built for two ...........TANDEM
biddy......................................HEN
Big Apple ..............................NYC
big casino ............................TEN
Bihar India, city in...................GAYA
bikini top ..............................BRA
bile ......................................GALL
bill .........DUN, NEB; BEAK; CHECK
bill, soft part of a......................CERE

18

a billiard shot.............BANK; BREAK,
.....................CAROM, MASSE
bill of fare.................MENU; CARTE
billow.......BULGE, SURGE, SWELL
binary digits.............................BITS
bind..................TAPE, WRAP;
.....................PINCH, SWATH
biography .............LIFE; MEMOIRS
bird...................AUK, KEA, MEW,
.............OWL, TIT; CHAT, COOT,
.........DOVE, DUCK, ERNE, GULL,
...............HAWK, IBIS, KITE, KIWI,
.........LARK, LOON, MERL, RAIL,
.....SMEW, SORA; SWAN, TEAL,
....TERN, WREN; BOOBY, CRAKE,
..CRANE, EAGLE, EGRET, FINCH,
...........GOOSE, GREBE, HERON,
.............MACAW, MURRE, OUZEL,
......PEWIT, PIPIT, ROBIN, SNIPE,
.....STILT, STORK, SWIFT, VIREO;
......ARGALA, AVOCET, BARBET,
.....CANARY, CONDOR, CUCKOO,
........CURLEW, DARTER, DUNLIN,
......GANNET, GROUSE, HOOPOE,
.........LINNET, MAGPIE, MARTIN,
.........ORIOLE, OSPREY PETREL,
.........PIGEON, PLOVER, PUFFIN,
.........SHRIKE, THRUSH, TOUCAN,
.....................TOWHEE, TURKEY,
bird, Arctic............BRANT; FULMAR
b bird, black....................ANI, CROW,
.......................ROOK; RAVEN
bird, blue.................................JAY
bird, extinct.................MOA; DODO
bird, flightless........EMU; EMEU,
.................KIWI, RHEA, WEKA;
.................OSTRICH, PENGUIN
bird, hunting.......................FALCON
bird, mythical............................ROC
bird, S.A. game..................GUAN
bird, talking.........................MYNA;
...................MYNAH; PARROT
bird, unfledged....................EYAS
bird, US national.................EAGLE
bird, web-footed........DUCK, LOON;
...................................GOOSE
bird, West Indies.....................TODY
bird flesh...............................FOWL
bird house................................COTE
bird in Pers. poetry.............BULBUL
bird life.................................ORNIS
bird's beak.......................NEB, NIB
bird's cry.....................CAW, COO;
.....................CHIRP, TWEET
birds of a region..................ORNIS;
.......................................AVIFAUNA
biretta....................................CAP
birth, at...................................NEE
birth, of ...............................NATAL
birthmark.MOLE; NEVUS; NAEVUS

birthmarks...............................NEVI c
birthstones .........January-GARNET
.....................February-AMETHYST
.....................March-BLOODSTONE
.................................April-DIAMOND
.............................May-EMERALD
.............June-PEARL (alexandrite)
.............................July-RUBY
.........August-SARDONYX (peridot)
.................September-SAPPHIRE
.............October-OPAL (tourmaline)
.............November-TOPAZ (citrine)
....December-TURQUOISE (zircon)
birthwort, Eur. ................CLEMATIS
bishop ...........................PRELATE
bishop of Rome.....................POPE
bishopric....................................SEE
bishop's attendant............VERGER
bishop's hat.......................MITER
bishop's title, Eastern ............ABBA
*Bismarck* sinker....................HOOD
bistro.......................................CAFE
bite.................NIP; EDGE, GNAW;
.............................STING; MORSEL
bitter............ICY; ACRID; ACERBIC
bitter drug ...............................ALOE
bitter vetch................................ERS
bivalve mollusk......CLAM; MUSSEL
bivouac...................................CAMP
bizarre.................................OUTRE
black....................JET; EBON, INKY; d
.............EBONY, RAVEN, SABLE
black and blue.......................LIVID
blackbird.....CROW, MERL; RAVEN
blackbird, Eur. ......................OUZEL
black buck of India ................SASIN
black cuckoo .............................ANI
blackfish.........TAUTOG: TAUTAUG
black measles.........................ESCA
Blackmore heroine................LORNA
Black Sea arm........................AZOV
blacksmith's block..................ANVIL
blacksnake .........................RACER
blackthorn fruit........................SLOE
blanch...................PALE; BLEACH;
.......................................ETIOLATE
blanket, horse.....................MANTA
blanket, S.A...................PONCHO,
.......................................SERAPE
blast-furnace stone ..............TYMP
blaubok ................................ETAAC
bleach....................PALE; BLANCH;
.......................................ETIOLATE
bleaching vat ...........................KIER
bleak......GRIM; HARSH; GLOOMY
bled.........................................RAN
blemish .....FLAW; FAULT; DEFECT
blesbok ..................................NUNNI
bless.........SAIN; THANK; HALLOW
bless: Yidd. ..........................BENSH

19

## blessing / bookbinding style

a blessing..BOON; GRACE; THANKS
blight..........DASH; BLAST, WRECK
blind cetacean........................SUSU
blind god, Teutonic .HOTH; HODER
blind in falconry.......................SEEL
blindness............................CECITY
blister ...............BLEB; EXCORIATE
block ...............BAR; CLOG; IMPEDE
blockhead..........ASS; DOLT, JERK
block of wood..........................NOG
blood, liquid part of...............SERUM
bloodcurdling..........GORY; SCARY
blood of the gods .................ICHOR
blood pigment ........................HEME
blood sucker........................LEECH
blood-sucking parasite .............TICK
blood vessel............................VEIN
blood vessel, main..............AORTA
bloody........................................GORY
blouse, long............................TUNIC
blow ...............GUST, JOLT, PUFF,
.............SWAT; BLAST; EXPLODE
blow, heavy ...........................THUD
blubber, strip ...................FLENSE
blue..................................SAD; RACY
Bluebeard, wife of ..............FATIMA
bluebonnet ...........................LUPINE
blue bull of India ..................NILGAI
blue color..................NAVY; SMALT
blue dye ...................................WOAD
b "Blue Eagle"...............................NRA
blue flag ....................................IRIS
blue-footed petrel......................TITI
bluegrass, Kentucky .................POA
blue gray ................MERLE, SLATE
blue-green .................AQUA, BICE,
.............................TEAL; EMAIL
blue mineral ...........................IOLITE
blue-pencil ...............................EDIT
blue pointer shark.................MAKO
bluff ............FOOL; COZEN, TRICK
bluish-white metal...................ZINC
blunder ........................................ERR
blunt.............CURT, DULL; GRUFF
blurt out .....................................BLAT
blush ...................FLUSH; REDDEN
boa, ringed ...........................ABOMA
boast........................BRAG, CROW,
.................................HAVE; VAUNT
boastful air ..........................PARADO
boat.ARK, HOY, TUB, TUG; DORY,
.......PUNT, YAWL; CANOE, SKIFF,
.........SLOOP; CAÏQUE, CUTTER,
........DINGHY, DUGOUT, GALLEY;
.....................PINNACE, PIRAGUA
boat, back of a ......................STERN
boat, Chin. ........................SAMPAN
boat, dispatch.........................AVISO
boat, fishing....................DOGGER;
..............................................CORACLE

c boat, flat-bottomed .SCOW; BARGE
boat, freight ......................LIGHTER
boat, Inuit................KAYAK, UMIAK
boat, It. ............................GONDOLA
boat, mail ............................PACKET
boat, Malay ..............................PROA
boat, Nile ............................SANDAL
boat, North Sea....................COBLE
boat, racing .........SCULL, SHELL
boat, river .............BARGE, FERRY
boat, three-oared .............RANDAN
boat deck ................POOP; ORLOP
boat front ....................BOW; PROW
boatswain .............................BO'S'N
bobbin ...........PIRN, REEL; SPOOL
Bobbsey Twins .............NAN; BERT
bobwhite .................................COLIN
bodice support........................BUSK
body ....................BULK; CORPUS
body, trunk of the ...............TORSO
body, zoological....................SOMA
body of laws ..........CODE; CODEX
body of people ......CORPS, FORCE
Boer general ........................BOTHA
bog........................FEN; MIRE,
............................QUAG; MARSH
boil ...........................MOIL, STEW;
................................CHURN; SEETHE
boil down ..........................DECOCT
Bolero composer .................RAVEL
boll weevil ..........................PICUDO
Bolshevik leader ................LENIN
bolt ..................RUN; GULP; SCOOT
bombastic.......TURGID; OROTUND
bombyx .....................SILKWORM
bond .................TIE; PACT; STICK;
............................................ADHERE
Bond movie ........................DR. NO
bondsman..............SERF; VASSAL
bondsman's money .................BAIL
bone: Gr. .................................OSTE
bone, ankle ..........................TALUS
bone, arm ...............................ULNA
bone, breast ...................STERNUM
bone, ear .................ANVIL, INCUS;
....................STAPES, HAMMER;
...................MALLEUS, STIRRUP
bone, jaw ......................MANDIBLE
bone, leg....FEMUR, TIBIA; FIBULA
bone, of..................................OSTEAL
bone, pelvic ...........................ILIUM
bone, skull.........NASAL; MASTOID;
.................PARIETAL, TEMPORAL
bones .....................................OSSA
bone scraper.........................XYSTER
bonnet monkey ..................MUNGA
bonnyclabber.........................SKYR
bony ....................................OSTEAL
book......TOME; PRIMER, VOLUME
bookbinding style...................YAPP

20

*a* bookkeeping entry..DEBIT; CREDIT
booklet.........................BROCHURE
book of devotions...............MISSAL
book of feasts, Cath. ............ORDO
book of hours.......................HORA
book of maps......................ATLAS
book palm .......................TALIERA
boom times.............................UPS
boor..................OAF; CLOD, LOUT
boot....................................KICK
boot, Inuit sealskin...............KAMIK
booth...................KIOSK, STALL;
............................................CUBICLE
booty ..............LOOT, PELF, SWAG
booty, take ........................REAVE
borax, crude .....................TINCAL
Borden calf........................ELMO
Borden cow........................ELSIE
border ...............RIM; ABUT, BRIM,
............................EDGE; VERGE
bore ........TIRE; WEARY; CALIBER
bore, tidal..........................EAGRE
boredom..............................ENNUI
boredom indication ................YAWN
born ......................................NEE
borough ..............................BURG
bosh ..........................ROT, POSH
boss.......HEAD; ORDER; HONCHO
boss on a shield ..................UMBO
botanist ................GRAY; MENDEL
*b* botch..FLUB, HASH, MESS, MUFF
bother ..............ADO, BUG, NAG,
.........VEX; FUSS, TO-DO; PEEVE;
...........................TEASE; HARASS,
.......................MOLEST, PESTER
bottle, glass ......................CARAFE
bottle, liquor ......................FLASK
bottle, oil and vinegar .........CRUET
bottom, river or sea................BED
boundary................EDGE; MARCH;
.............................................BORDER
bounder .................................CAD
bounds ...............AMBIT, JUMPS
bouquet .............................AROMA
Bovary, Madame ...............EMMA
bovine animal .COW; BULL; STEER
bovines ...................COWS, OXEN;
........................STEER; CATTLE
bow, Oriental .....................SALAAM
bower ..................................ARBOR
bowfin ...................AMIA; MUDFISH
bowling alley .........................LANE
bowling score ........SPARE; STRIKE
box.............................BIN; CUFF;
...............................SPAR; CHEST
box, ecclesiastic .....................ARCA
box, metal .....................CANISTER
boxfish ..............................CHAPIN
boxing decision ......................TKO
boxing glove, Rom. ...........CESTUS

boxing weapon .......................FIST *c*
box-opener .....................PANDORA
box sleigh .............................PUNG
boy .................LAD; TYKE; YOUTH
"Boy King" .............................TUT
BPOE member .........................ELK
brace ...............TWO; PAIR; TRUSS
bracer...................................TONIC
brag .......................BOAST, VAUNT
brahma bull............................ZEBU
Brahman rules ....................SUTRA
braid ..................PLAIT, QUEUE
brain layer ...........................OBEX
brain opening ........................PYLA
brain ridge(s) ...........GYRI; GYRUS
brain tissue(s) ...........TELA; TELAE
branch ..............ARM; LIMB, TWIG
branched .........................RAMOSE
branches: biol. ......................RAMI
branchia ................................GILL
brant, common ....................QUINK
brassard ......................ARMBAND
brassie .................................CLUB
*Brave Bulls* author................LEA
brawl ................MELEE; FRACAS
Brazilian nutritious drink .......ASSAI
Braz. red .........................ROSET
Braz. heron ..........................SOCO
Braz. rubber tree ..........ULE; HULE
Braz. tree .................APA; ANDA
Brazos, city on the ..............WACO *d*
breach ......................GAP; RIFT;
...........................CLEFT; HIATUS
bread, hard crisp ....................RUSK
break....................REST, SNAP;
...............................PAUSE, SPLIT
breakers .................................SURF
breakwater.............PIER; BARRIER
breast ...................BUST; BOSOM
breath, audible ........................SIGH
breathe rapidly........GASP, PANT
breathing, harsh ...RALE; STRIDOR
breath of life, Hindu ............PRANA
breech-cloth, Polynesian .......MALO
breed ........................REAR, SIRE;
...............................BEGET, RAISE
breeding establishment.........FARM
Bremen's river....................WESER
breviary.........................SUMMARY
brewer's vat ............................TUN
brewing, one ........................GYLE
bribe .......................SOP; GRAFT
brick, sun-dried ..................ADOBE
brick carrier ...........................HOD
bricklayer .........................MASON
bridal wreath ......................SPIREA
bridge ..................................SPAN
bridge, floating ...............PONTOON
bridge, Mississippi.................EADS
bridge call .....................BID; PASS

*a*

| | |
|---|---|
| bridge holding | TENACE |
| bridge maneuver | FINESSE |
| bridge part | TRESTLE |
| brief | CURT; TERSE |
| brigand | LATRON |
| Brigham Young U. site | PROVO |
| bright | APT; NITID; SMART, VIVID |
| bright-colored fish | BOCE, OPAH; TANG; TETRA; WRASSE |
| brilliance | ECLAT |
| bring | TOTE |
| brisk: music | ALLEGRO |
| bristle | SETA |
| bristly | SETOSE |
| Britain, ancient | CELT, PICT |
| Brit. conservative | TORY |
| Briton, ancient | CELT |
| Britons, ancient tribe of | ICENI |
| broadbill duck | SCAUP |
| broadcast | AIR |
| broken seed coats | BRAN |
| Brontë heroine | EYRE |
| bronze Roman money | AES |
| brood | FRET, MOPE; WORRY; LITTER |
| brook, small | RILL |
| broom of twigs | BESOM |
| brothel keeper | BAWD; MADAM |
| brother | FRA; FRIAR |

*b*

| | |
|---|---|
| brown | TAN; SEPIA; UMBER, RUSSET, SIENNA, SORREL |
| brown, dull yellowish | DRAB |
| brown, pale | ECRU |
| brown, yellowish | BRAN; ALOMA, PABLO |
| Browning poem, girl in a | PIPPA |
| brown sugar, low-grade | PANELA |
| brow of a hill: Scot. | SNAB |
| browse | LOOK; GRAZE |
| Brünhilde, mother of | ERDA; ERDE |
| brusque | BLUNT, TERSE |
| Brythonic | CORNISH |
| Brythonic sea god | LER |
| bubble in glass | BLEB |
| Buddha's birth country | INDIA |
| Buddha's sacred tree | PIPAL |
| Buddha's title | GAUTAMA |
| Buddhist liturgical language | PALI |
| Buddhist monk | LAMA |
| Buddhist monk in Nirvana | ARHAT, LOHAN |
| Buddhist sacred city | LHASA |
| Buddhist sacred mountain | OMEI |
| Buddhist scripture | SUTRA |
| Buddhist sect | ZEN |
| Buddhist shrine | DAGOBA |
| buds, pickled | CAPERS |
| buffalo, Indian | ARNA |

*c*

| | |
|---|---|
| buffalo pea | VETCH |
| buffet | SLAP, TOSS |
| buffoon | FOOL; CLOWN; JESTER, MUMMER |
| build | ERECT |
| building wing | ELL |
| bulb, edible | SEGO; CAMASS |
| bulblike stem | CORM |
| bulk | HEFT, MASS |
| bull, sacred Eg. | APIS |
| bullet size | CALIBER |
| bull fighter | TORERO; MATADOR |
| bullring | CORRIDA |
| bullring cheer | OLE |
| bully | HECTOR |
| bulrush | TULE |
| Bulwer-Lytton heroine | IONE |
| bunch | TUFT; GROUP |
| bunch grass | STIPA |
| bundle | BALE, PACK; PACKET |
| bundle of twigs | FAGOT |
| bundling machine | BALER |
| bungle | BOTCH |
| bungling action | MUFF |
| bunting | FLAGS |
| buoy | MARKER |
| buoy, kind of | CAN, NUN, NUT; BELL, SPAR |
| buoyancy | FLOTAGE |
| burbot | LING |

*d*

| | |
|---|---|
| Burchell's zebra | DAUW |
| burden | LOAD, ONUS; WEIGHT |
| burglar | YEGG |
| burial place | TOMB; CRYPT |
| Burmese capital, ancient | AVA |
| burn | BLAZE, STING; SCORCH |
| burn incense | CENSE |
| burning bush: Biblical | WAHOO |
| burning desire? | ARSON |
| burnish | RUB |
| burrowing animal | MOLE; RATEL |
| bury | INTER |
| bushel quarter | PECK |
| bushy clump: Brit. | TOD |
| business | TRADE |
| business symbol | LOGO |
| buss | KISS |
| *Bus Stop* playwright | INGE |
| bustle | ADO; TO-DO |
| but | YET; ONLY; STILL |
| but also | NAY |
| butcher's frame | GAMBREL |
| butter, Indian | GHEE |
| butterfly | PAPAW, SATYR, SNOUT; CALIGO, IDALIA; BUCKEYE |
| butterfly's kin | MOTH |
| butter tree | SHEA |
| butter tub | FIRKIN |

22

a buttocks..........PRAT, RUMP, TUSH
button, detachable.................STUD
bygone days ...............AGO; YORE

Byron poem ...........................LARA c
Byzantine ......................INTRICATE
Byzantine capital ...............NICAEA

# C

*C*, mark under a ...............CEDILLA
caama, S. Afr. .......................FOX
cabal....................................PLOT;
...............COTERIE, PLOTTERS
cabaret, small.....................BOITE
cabbage .................KAIL, KALE
cabbage, type of ................SAVOY
cabinet, open ................ETAGERE
cactus fruit, edible ...........COCHAL
Caddoan Indian .....................REE
cadence count................HEP, HUP
Cadmus, daughter of ..............INO
Caen's river .......................ORNE
Caesar, slayer of ...............CASCA;
.................BRUTUS; CASSIUS
Cain, brother of .....................ABEL
Cain, land of ........................NOD
Cain, son of ......................ENOCH
Cain, victim of ......................ABEL
cake, rich ..........................TORTE
calamity ...............WOE; DISASTER
b calcium oxide..,......................LIME
calf meat ............................VEAL
caliber................BORE; DIAMETER
calico horse........................PINTO
California, southern ...............BAJA
California base or fort...............ORD
California motto .................EUREKA
California wine county ............NAPA
caliph...........................ALI, IMAM
call ...................................CRY, DUB;
............WAKEN; MUSTER
call forth ................EVOKE; ELICIT
calling ............METIER; VOCATION
Calliope, sister of ................ERATO
Callisto, son of ...................ARCAS
*Call of the Wild, The* dogs.....BUCK;
...................................SPITZ
call to cows ........................SOOK
calm .............COOL, EVEN; QUIET,
...............STILL; GENTLE, PLACID,
.....SERENE, SETTLE; TRANQUIL
calorie................................THERM
calumniate .......MALIGN; SLANDER
calumny ...............LIBEL; SLANDER
Calvinist...........................GENEVAN
calyx leaf ...........................SEPAL
cam ...................................TAPPET
cambric..........................PERCALE
cambric grass ....................RAMIE
came down with ......................GOT

camel, female ......................NAGA
camel, Indian .....................OONT
camel hair cloth or robe ...........ABA
Camelot lady .........................ENID
cameo stone .......................ONYX
camera lens......................ZOOM
camera platform ..................DOLLY
*Camille* dramatist ..............DUMAS
Canada goose ................OUTARDE
canal, Afr. ..........................SUEZ
canal, Canadian.............WELLAND
canal, Eur. ...........................KIEL
canal, Latin Amer. ...........PANAMA
canal, New York ...............ERIE
canal bank .........................BERM
canary yellow....................MELINE
canasta collection ...........SEVENS
canasta play ........................MELD
cancel........DELE; ANNUL, ERASE
candid .....................OPEN; FRANK
candidates, list of ...............SLATE d
candle ............DIP; TEST; TAPER
candle element ......................WICK
candle holder ..................SCONCE;
.................................GIRANDOLE
candlelight .............................GLIM
candlenut tree ........................AMA
candle wick, snuffed............SNAST
cane ................................RATTAN
canine animal ................DOG, FOX;
.................WOLF; DINGO, HYENA
Canio, wife of......................NEDDA
cannabis.................HEMP; GRASS
canna plant......................ACHIRA
cannon ....................BIT; MORTAR
canoe, Central Amer. ........BONGO,
...................................BUNGO
canoe, Malay ......................PROA
canoe, Maori seagoing ..........WAKA
canon ......................LAW; CODE
canonical hour .........SEXT; LAUDS,
...............NONES, PRIME;
.................MATINS, TIERCE
canopy ....................COPE; TESTER
cant ..........................TILT; ARGOT,
.............................IDIOM, SLANT
cant hook .........................PEAVEY
*Cantique de Noel* composer ..ADAM
canvas............DUCK, TUKE; SAILS
canvasback duck .................SCAUP
canvas piece ..........................TARP

23

a canvas shelter .......................TENT
 cape .............................COD, MAY;
 ...................................HORN, NESS
 cape, fur...........................PALATINE
 cape, Pope's .........FANON, ORALE
 Capek character..................ROBOT
 caper...............DIDO, LEAP; ANTIC
 caprice ...................WHIM; FANCY
 captain, Melville's...................AHAB
 captain, Muslim ship's...RAIS, REIS
 captain's boat ............................GIG
 capture...................BAG, NAB;
 ...................................NET; SEIZE
 capucine ...........................MELINE
 car ..........................AUTO; COUPE,
 ...........................SEDAN; VEHICLE
 car, classic ..............................REO
 caracallike animal ..................LYNX
 caravel of Columbus ...NINA; PINTA
 carbolic acid .......................PHENOL
 carbon, powdery ......................SOOT
 card....................ACE; JACK, KING,
 ................TREY; DEUCE, JOKER,
 ......................KNAVE, QUEEN
 card game..........GIN, LOO; BRAG;
 .............MONTE, OMBRE, POKER,
 .............RUMMY, WHIST; BRIDGE,
 ........CASINO, ECARTE, EUCHRE,
 ....HEARTS; BEZIQUE, CANASTA,
 ......................PIQUET; PINOCHLE;
b ......................SOLITAIRE
 card game, gambling .............FARO
 card game, three-handed ......SKAT
 card in Euchre, high ..........BOWER
 card-reader's card...............TAROT
 cards, high...................HONORS
 card wool ...................TUM; TEASE
 care, anxious......................CARK
 careen.............LEAN, TILT; LURCH
 career ..........................CALLING
 care for .......................LIKE, LOVE,
 ...........................RECK, TEND
 caress..........................PET; TOUCH
 cargo.............LOAD; PORTAGE
 cargo, load..............................LADE
 *Carmen* composer .................BIZET
 carnation ...............................PINK
 carnelian .............................SARD
 carol .......................................NOEL
 Caroline Islands group ..........TRUK
 carol singer, Eng. ..................WAIT
 carom ............BOUNCE; RICOCHET
 carousal .....ORGY; BINGE, SPREE
 carouse ...............................REVEL
 carp .....................................CAVIL
 carp, Jap. .................................KOI
 carp, red-eyed .....................RUDD
 carpet, Afghan ...................HERAT
 carpet, Caucasian .....BAKU, KUBA;
 ....................SHIRVAN; KARISTAN

c carpet, Indian .......................AGRA
 carpet, Pers..........SEHNA, SENNA
 carriage .......................GIG; DRAY,
 .........HACK, MIEN, PRAM, SADO,
 ................TRAP; BUGGY, COACH,
 ....................COUPE, POISE, SULKY;
 .........CALASH, FIACRE, HANSOM,
 ....................LANDAU, SURREY,
 ....................TROIKA; BEARING,
 ....................CARIOLE, DROSHKY,
 ....................HACKNEY, PHAETON
 carriage, Fr. ........................FIACRE
 carried away ...........................GAGA
 Carroll heroine .......................ALICE
 carrot-family plant..................ANISE
 carrot ridges ...........................JUGA
 carry .........................LUG; TOTE
 carry over water ...................FERRY
 cart, heavy .............................DRAY
 carte .....................................MENU
 Carthage, of .........................PUNIC
 Carthage, queen of .................DIDO
 cartograph ...............................MAP
 *Casablanca* characters ...........SAM;
 ...................................ILSA, RICK
 case, grammatical...............DATIVE
 case, needle ...........................ETUI
 cask ...............KEG, TUB, TUN
 cassava .....................JUCA, YUCA
 cassia leaves ......................SENNA
d caste, cattle rearing.................AHIR
 caste, gardener.......................MALI
 caste, low .............KOLI, PARIAH
 caste, Tamil merchant .......CHETTY
 caster ...............CRUET; ROLLER
 casting mold..............................DIE
 cast metal ............................INGOT
 cast off ....................MOLT, SHED
 Castor, killer of.........................IDAS
 Castor, mother of.....................LEDA
 castor bean poison ...............RICIN
 cat.................MANX, PUSS; KITTY,
 ............TABBY; CALICO, KITTEN,
 ....................MOUSER, TOMCAT;
 ...............BURMESE, CHESHIRE,
 ....................SIAMESE
 cat, Afr. ...............CIVET, GENET
 cat, Amer. ..........................PUMA;
 ...................COUGAR, OCELOT
 cat, castrated male ...................GIB
 cat, spotted.........PARD; MARGAY,
 ............................OCELOT
 cat, tailless............................MANX
 catalog ...................LIST; RECORD
 catalufa ..................................SCAD
 catapult...............................ONAGER
 cataract .................................FALLS
 catch ...............NAB; HOOK, SNAG,
 ...............................TRAP; SNARE
 catchword ................CUE; SLOGAN

a caterpillar, N. Z. .......WERI; AWETO
catfish, armor-plated ...........DORAD
cat genus ................................FELIS
cathedral ...........................MINSTER
cathedral, Fr. ..................CHARTRES
cathedral city, Eng. ....................ELY
cathedral passage ...............SLYPE
Catholic, Eastern....UNIAT; UNIATE
Catholic tribunal .....................ROTA
catkin ...................................AMENT
cat's cry....................MEW; MEOW;
......................MIAOU, MIAOW
cat's-paw...DUPE, TOOL; STOOGE
cattail .....................................TULE
cattle, largest type of ............GAUR
cattle breed..........ANGUS, DEVON;
.........DEXTER, JERSEY, SUSSEX;
..............GUERNSEY, HEREFORD,
................LONGHORN, HOLSTEIN
cattleman........COWBOY, DROVER
Caucasian wild goat ................TUR
Caucasian language....ANDI, AVAR
Caucasian Muslim ....................LAZ
Caucasus people .....SVAN; OSSET
caucho tree....................ULE; HULE
caudal appendage ...................TAIL
caulk lightly .......................CHINSE
cause ...............MOTIVE, REASON;
....................................CRUSADE
caustic ...........ACERBIC, CUTTING,
b ....................MORDANT; SCATHING
caustic poison ....................PHENOL
cauterize..............................SEAR
cauterizing agent ...................MOXA
caution .........CARE, HEED, WARN;
..............................ALERT; REGARD
cautious ..................WARY; CHARY
Cavalleria Rusticana heroine...LOLA
cavalryman, Pol. ..................UHLAN
cavalryman, Turk. or Alg. ...............
...................SPAHI; SPAHEE
cave explorer..............SPELUNKER
cavern.................................GROTTO
caviar......................................ROE
caviar fish .......SHAD; STURGEON
cavil...................CARP; OBJECT
cavity, sinus ....................ANTRUM
cavity in a rock............VUG; VUGG,
....................................VUGH; GEODE
cavy, spotted .........................PACA
cavy, wild..............................APEREA
cease.............HALT, STOP; AVAST
Cecrops, daughter of ..........HERSE
cedar, Himalayan...............DEODAR
celebrated ..........FAMED, NOTED;
................EMINENT; RENOWNED
ceiling, build a .........................CEIL
cell, reproductive.............GAMETE
cella .........................................NAOS
cellular substance ..................LININ

Celt ........................................GAEL c
Celt, legendary ...........ITH; MILED
Celtic ..........ERSE, MANX; WELSH
Celtic church center ...............IONA
Celtic land measure ..............COLP;
............................................COLLOP
cement ....................LUTE; PUTTY;
.......................................SOLDER
cenobite....................................MONK
cenote ......................................WELL
censure..................BLAME, FAULT
center............HUB; CORE; HEART
center, farthest away from ...DISTAL
center, toward .....................ENTAD
centerpiece ....................EPERGNE
centesimal unit.........................GRAD
centessimi, 100 .......................LIRA
central ............KEY, MID; PIVOTAL
central line ................................AXIS
central points ...........................FOCI
century plant .........AGAVE, YUCCA
century plant fiber ....................PITA
cereal, cooked ...................FARINA
cereal grain or grass ......OAT, RYE;
........................WHEAT; MILLET
cereal grass, E. Indian...........MAND
................................RAGI; RAGGEE
cereal spike....................COB, EAR
ceremonial chamber, Pueblo ...KIVA
Ceres, mother of....................OPS
certificate, money.................SCRIP d
cerulean ...........AZURE; SKY-BLUE
cervine animal......................DEER
cesspool ................................SUMP
cetacean...................ORC; WHALE;
................NARWHAL; PORPOISE
Ceylon ..........................SRI LANKA
Ceylonese fishing boat...........DONI;
.............................................DHONI
Ceylonese langur.................MAHA
chafe .................RUB; FRET, GALL
chaff.................................BANTER
chaffinch................CHINK, SPINK
chain, form into a ..........CATENATE
chain, nautical .........................TYE
chair...........................HEAD, SEAT
chair, portable ......................SEDAN
chair part ...................RUNG; SPLAT
chaise .......................................GIG
chalcedony .............ONYX; AGATE;
................JASPER; CAT'S-EYE
chalcedony, red......................SARD
chalice, ecclesiastical....................
..................AMA; AMULA, CALIX
chalice, holy .........................GRAIL
chalice veil, Eastern church......AER
chalky silicate..........................TALC
challenge ...................DARE, DEFY
chamber ..............ROOM; CAMERA
chance .................HAP, LOT; LUCK

25

a chances ........................LOTS, ODDS
chancy ..............................IFFY; RISKY
change...........FLUX, VARY; ALTER
change: music.....................MUTA
change the decor.....................REDO
channel, television .........ABC, AMC,
.BBC, CBC, CBS, CNN, HBO, MTV,
.NBC, PBS, TBS, TNT, USA; ESPN
Channel Islands ....SARK; JERSEY;
.............ALDERNEY, GUERNSEY
channel marker......................BUOY
channels.................MEDIA, STRIA
chant.................................INTONE
chanticleer .............................COCK
chantry ...............................CHAPEL
chaos ....................MESS; SNARL
Chaos, son of....................EREBUS
chapel, private................ORATORY
chapel, sailor's................BETHEL
chaperon, Sp. .....................DUENA
chaplet ...........ANADEM, WREATH
character .........NATURE, SYMBOL
characteristic ........................TRAIT
charge ....................FEE; COST;
.....................DEBIT; INDICT
charged particle .......................ION
charger ...............................STEED
charge solemnly ................ADJURE
chariot race site ................CIRCUS
charity ..................................ALMS
b Charlemagne, father of .........PEPIN
charm, magic .........JUJU; SPELL;
.....................AMULET, GRI-GRI
Charon's payment...................OBOL
Charon's river ..........................STYX
chart .......................................MAP
Charybdis, partner of..........SCYLLA
chasm ..................................ABYSS
chaste....................PURE; VESTAL
Chateaubriand heroine .........ATALA
chatter .............GAB, YAP; PRATE
chatterbox .................PIET; MAGPIE
cheat ............CON; BILK; COZEN
cheater's notes............CRIB, PONY
check .........REIN, STEM; BRAKE
cheek, lower ...........................JOWL
cheek bone ............................MALAR
cheer ...........OLE, RAH; BRAVO
cheerless ....................SAD; DRAB
cheese ...........BLEU, BRIE, EDAM;
..........GOUDA, GRANA; ROMANO
.................BOURSIN, CHEDDAR,
.................GRUYÈRE, RICOTTA;
.............MUENSTER, PARMESAN
cheeselike ......................CASEOUS
chela .....................................CLAW
chemical compound.............AMIDE,
.......AMINE, ESTER, IMIDE, IMINE
chemical salt ..........ESTER, NITER
chemist's pet......................ALUDEL

c cherish .........FOSTER; TREASURE
cherry red ............................CERISE
chess finale ...........................MATE
chess move ......................CASTLE
chess piece ...............KING, PAWN,
..............................ROOK; QUEEN;
.......................BISHOP, KNIGHT
chess situation..................CHECK
chestnut, sweet Eur. .......MARRON
chest sound ............................RALE
chew ...........BITE, GNAW; CHOMP
chewink ...........................TOWHEE
chide ...................SCOLD; BERATE
chief ...........HEAD, MAIN; LEADER
chief, Native Amer. .........SACHEM
chilblain .................................KIBE
child ...............................KID, TOT;
.................BABE, BABY, TYKE
child, unruly ............................BRAT
child of the streets ................GAMIN
child's seat ..............................LAP
Chilean timber tree ................PELU;
.................................KOWHAI
Chilean volcano .................LASCAR
.................................LLAIMA
chills and fever .....AGUE; MALARIA
chimney pipe...........................FLUE
China grass............................RHEA
China in poetry .................CATHAY
Chin. boat ..............................JUNK
d Chin. chairman......................MAO
Chin. character (longevity).....SHOU
Chin. dynasty........HAN, SUI, YIN;
.....................CH'IN, CHOU, HSIA,
.....................MING, SUNG,
.....................T'ANG, TSIN, YUAN;
.................CH'ING, SHANG; MANCHU
Chin. flour...............................MEIN
Chin. idol.................................JOSS
Chin. people, ancient ...........SERES
Chin. plant ...........UDO; GINSENG
Chin. poet .............................LI PO
Chin. secret society ...............TONG
Chin. silk cloth .................PONGEE
Chin. stringed instrument ...........KIN
Chin. warehouse ...................HONG
Chin. wormwood paste ..........MOXA
Chin. yellow ...............................SIL
chinin .................................COYO
chinook salmon.......................TYEE
chip .......................................NICK
chipmunk...........................HACKEE
chipmunks, cartoon......CHIP, DALE
chip of stone..........SPALL; GALLET
chirp...................TWEET; TWITTER
chocolate source .................CACAO
choice ..........BEST, FINE; CREAM,
.................ELECT, ELITE; SELECT
choke ........................GAG; RETCH
choler ..................IRE; BILE, RAGE

a  choose ..............OPT; PICK; ELECT
   chop .............AXE, CUT, HEW, LOP
   chopped ..............................HEWN
   chop up...............................MINCE
   chord, three-toned................TRINE
   chore ........................JOB; DUTY
   Chosen nation ....................KOREA
   Christmas .......NOEL, XMAS, YULE
   Christmas scene ..............CRECHE
   chromosome positions.............LOCI
   chronicles ........................ANNALS
   chrysalis .............................PUPA
   chrysanthemum .......................MUM
   chrysanthemum, Jap. .............KIKU
   church, Scot. ........................KIRK
   church bench .........................PEW
   church calendar...................ORDO
   church center .....................NAVE
   church contribution ..............TITHE
   church council .....................SYNOD
   church court .........................ROTA
   church dignitary.....................POPE;
   .....................BISHOP, PRIEST;
   .............PRELATE; CARDINAL
   church dish .........................PATEN
   church leader .....................ELDER
   church part...............APSE, NAVE
   church property ...................GLEBE
   church reader .....................LECTOR
   church recess .......................APSE
b  church vessel .................AMA, PYX;
   ..........................................AMULA
   church worker ..SEXTON, VERGER
   cibola ................................ONION
   cicatrix ................................SCAR
   cigar.....................CLARO, SMOKE;
   ......................CORONA, STOGIE;
   .........................................CHEROOT
   cigarette: Brit. slang.................FAG
   cigarfish................................SCAD
   cinchona bark...................QUININE
   cincture ................................BELT
   cinnamon, kind of................CASSIA
   cipher ..................................ZERO
   cipher system .......................CODE
   Circe, home of....................AEAEA
   circle............................LOOP, RING
   circle of light ..........HALO; NIMBUS
   circle segment ........................ARC
   circuit ..........LAP; AMBIT, ORBIT
   circular motion .......................GYRE
   circular plate .........................DISK
   circular turn ..........................LOOP
   circular saw .........................EDGER
   circumference measure ..................
   ...............................GIRT; GIRTH
   Cisco Kid's horse .................DIABLO
   cistern ..............................BAC, VAT
   cite.....................................QUOTE
   *Citizen Kane* sled ...........ROSEBUD

c  citrus fruit ..................LIME; LEMON;
   ..........................................ORANGE
   city, of a ....................CIVIC, URBAN
   city, Philistines' ...................EKRON
   City, Queen .................CINCINNATI
   City of a Hundred Towers......PAVIA
   City of Bridges .................BRUGES
   City of God .......................HEAVEN
   City of Kings ...........................LIMA
   City of Lights ........................PARIS
   City of Luxury ...................SYBARIS
   City of Masts.....................LONDON
   City of Rams .....................CANTON
   City of Refuge ...........MEDINA
   City of Saints................MONTREAL
   City of the Prophet .............MEDINA
   City of the Seven Hills ...........ROME
   City of the Violet Crown .....ATHENS
   City of Victory ......................CAIRO
   city political division ................WARD
   city slicker ............................DUDE
   civet, Asiatic ............ZIBET; ZIBETH
   civet, lesser .........................RASSE
   civetlike animal ...................GENET
   Civil War commander...............LEE;
   .....................POPE; EWELL, GRANT,
   ...........................MEADE, SCOTT,
   ...........SYKES; CUSTER, HOOKER;
   .............FORREST, JACKSON
   civil wrong ............................TORT
d  claim ...........ASSERT, DEMAND
   clam, razor.........................SOLEN
   clamor.........................DIN; NOISE
   clan .............GEN; SEPT; TRIBE
   clan, Gr. ............................GENOS
   clan leader .........................ALDER
   clarinet socket ......................BIRN
   clash ....................JAR; COLLIDE
   clasp .........................GRIP, HOLD,
   ..............HOOK; GRASP; CLENCH;
   ..........................................EMBRACE
   class...............ILK; CASTE, GENUS;
   .....................GENERA; SPECIES
   classifieds .............................ADS
   classify..........RANK, RATE, SORT,
   ..................................TYPE; GRADE
   claw ..........NAIL; CHELA, TALON
   claw, ornamental...............GRIFFE
   clay ....................ARGIL, LOESS
   clay, baked ...............................TILE
   clay, porcelain .....................KAOLIN
   clay, potter's .......................ARGIL
   clayey soil .....BOLE, MALM, MARL;
   ..........................................GAULT
   clay mineral .....................NACRITE
   clay molding plate ...................DOD
   clay-pigeon shooting ............SKEET
   clay plug ...............................BOTT
   cleansing agent ...................BORAX
   clear .......NET, RID; LUCID; LIMPID

a cleave ..........................REND, RIVE;
.............................CLING, SPLIT
cleaving tool ..........................FROE
Clemenceau's nickname .......TIGRE
clement ..................................MILD
Cleopatra's attendant ............IRAS
Cleopatra's needle............OBELISK
Cleopatra's serpent...................ASP
clergyman..............................ABBE;
..........................CANON, PADRE;
..........................VICAR; CURATE;
..........................PRIEST, RECTOR
clergyman, Coptic ..................ANBA
cleric, opposite of ...................LAIC
clerical cap ........................BIRETTA
clerical seats ....................SEDILIA
clever ..........................APT; ARCH
click beetle ........................ELATER
climb ....................SCALE; ASCENT
climbing pepper .....................BETEL
climbing plant ......IVY; VINE; LIANA
cling ....................STICK; ADHERE
clingfish ...........................SUCKER
Clio, sister of.......................ERATO
clip ........................CUT, MOW;
.............................SNIP; SHEAR
clique.......................................SET
cloak ..................WRAP; CAPOTE;
.................................MANTLE
cloak, woman's .................DOLMAN
b clock, shipshaped ....................NEF
clogs, wooden .................PATTENS
cloister ......................MONASTERY
*Cloister Hearth* author .........READE
close...........................NEAR, NIGH;
...........................SEAL, SHUT
closing measure in music ......CODA
cloth ..................................FABRIC
cloth, apronlike ..........................BIB
cloth, old wool ................CHEYNEY
clothe ........................TOG; VEST
clothes moth ........................TINEA
clothing ........DUDS, GARB, GEAR,
.........................TOGS; RAIMENT
cloth made from bark.............TAPA
cloth measure, former...............ELL
cloth scrap...............................RAG
cloud..................CIRRUS, NIMBUS;
.................CUMULUS, STRATUS
cloud, luminous .................NIMBUS
cloudiness .........FOG; FILM, HAZE,
.................MIST, MURK; BRUME
clouds, broken......................RACK
cloudy ...................DULL; LOWERY
clout..............HIT; SWAT; WHACK
clown ............APER, GOOF, ZANY;
.............................JOKER; JESTER
cloy .............................PALL, SATE
club, shaped like a ...........CLAVATE
clumsy...................INEPT; OAFISH

cluster ...................................TUFT c
cluster of fibers .........................NEP
cluster pine.....................PINASTER
coach, Turk. .........................ARABA
coach dog....................DALMATIAN
coagulate.......................GEL; CLOT
coagulated substance............CRUD
coal, heat-treated...................COKE
coal, live ..............................EMBER
coal, size of ..........EGG, NUT, PEA
coal cart .................................CORF
coal dust .......COOM, SMUT, SOOT
coalition ..............UNION, MERGER
coal refuse..................CULM, SLAG
coal scuttle ..............................HOD
coarse ................CRUDE, ROUGH;
.................................GRITTY
coastal bird .................GULL, TERN
coastal region of India............GHAT
coat .....................................LAYER
coat, animal...FUR; PELT; PELAGE
coat, soldier's .........................TUNIC
coat with alloy ......................TERNE
cob .......................................SWAN
cobbler...................................SUTOR
cobra, Eg. ..............................HAJE
cobra, Hindu ..........................NAGA
cobra, hoodless ..................MAMBA
cocaine source .......................COCA
cockatoo, Australian ............GALAH
cockboat ...................................TUG d
coconut, dried.....................COPRA
coconut fiber...........................COIR
cocoon insect .........................PUPA
cod, young ........................SCROD
code.........................LAW; CIPHER
code breaker ............................KEY
codfish, small Eur. .................POOR
codfish, of ..........................GADOID
Coeus, daughter of .................LETO
coffee ....................................JAVA
coffee, brew.............................PERK
coffee and chocolate ..........MOCHA
coffee cup stand ......................ZARF
coffin stand ..............................BIER
cognizant ...........................AWARE
cognomen.............NAME; EPITHET
cohere .......BOND; STICK; CLEAVE
coil ...............WIND; TWINE, TWIST
coin, cut edges of .....................NIG
coin, reverse side of .............VERSO
coincide......................JIBE; AGREE
coin money .............................MINT
colander................................SIEVE
cold...........................ALGID, GELID;
.................................FRIGID
cold mountain wind of Peru....PUNA
coldwater trout .....................CISCO
cole ____ ..............................SLAW
collect.................AMASS; GARNER

28

*a* collection of sayings ................ANA
college common ....................QUAD
college entrance exams..........SATS
college organization, briefly ....FRAT
colleges ....................See page 200.
colloquialism ........................IDIOM
colonize ..............................SETTLE
colonnade, Gr. ........................STOA
color ........................HUE; SHADE;
................................................REDDEN
color, change ................DYE; TINT
color, splash of ......................BLOB
Colorado park........................ESTES
colorless................................DRAB
color slightly ................TINT; TINGE
columbite, variety of..........DIANITE
Columbus, birthplace of ......GENOA
Columbus, port of................PALOS
Columbus, ship of .......NINA; PINTA
column, Gr. .............DORIC, IONIC
column, Buddhist......................LAT
columns, arranged in .......TABULAR
coma ...................................TRANCE
combat, knight's ..................JOUST
combat scene ......................ARENA
comb horses.......................CURRY
combination ............BLEND, UNION
comb wool ................CARD; TEASE
come back........................RECUR
comedian's foil ..................STOOGE
*b* come down with ......................GET
comedy ..............................FARCE
*Comedy of Errors* servant ......LUCE
come forth............ISSUE; EMERGE
comfort................EASE; SOLACE;
................................................CONSOLE
command..............SWAY; ORDER,
..............................SKILL; BEHEST;
.....................BIDDING, MASTERY
commander, Eg. ..............SIRDAR
command to horses ................GEE;
............................HAW, HUP
commercial award, TV ............CLIO
commission, military ..........BREVET
commodity ..........................STAPLE
common .........VULGAR; GENERAL
common man ........................PLEB
commonplace ..........BANAL, TRITE
commotion........ADO; STIR, TO-DO
commune, Dutch ......................EDE
communion cup ......................AMA
communion dish ..................PATEN
communion table ..................ALTAR
commute..............................RIDE
compact .......LEAN; SPARE, THICK
companion......PAL; MATE; SPOUSE
company ..............FIRM; GUEST
company image ......................LOGO
comparative conjunction ........THAN
compassion ..................PITY, RUTH

compass direction .........EBN, EBS, *c*
.........ENE, ESE, NBE, NBW, NNE,
.........NNW, SBE, SBW, SSE, SSW,
................WBN, WBS, WNW, WSW
compel....................MAKE; FORCE;
.....................COERCE; OBLIGE
compendium ................SYLLABUS
compensate ..............PAY; REPAY;
................................................OFFSET
competed................................RAN
competent ............................ABLE
complacent..........................SMUG
complain ..............BEEF; GRIPE,
...................WHINE; GROUCH;
................................................GRUMBLE
complete ....................ALL; FULL;
........................TOTAL, WHOLE
comply ......................MIND, OBEY
composition ..........ESSAY, THEME
composition, musical ............OPUS;
..............:ETUDE, MOTET, RONDO,
................................SUITE; SONATA;
..............CONCERTO, SYMPHONY
computer, load a ....................BOOT
computer chip ........................ROM;
.....................PROM; EPROM
computer choices ..................MENU
computer input......................DATA
computer operator..................USER
computer terminals ..................PCS
comrade-in-arms ..................ALLY *d*
conceal ............HIDE, MASK, VEIL
concede ..........OWN; AVOW, GIVE;
.................ADMIT, GRANT, YIELD
conceive............VISION; PICTURE
concern ......CARE, FIRM; REGARD
concerning............................IN RE;
.....................ABOUT, ANENT
concert halls..........................ODEA
conch ...................................SHELL
conciliate ............................ATONE
conciliatory gift..........................SOP
concise ................................BRIEF,
.....................SHORT, TERSE
concluding passage: music ...CODA
concoct....................................BREW
concur ....................JIBE; AGREE
condescend............DEIGN, STOOP
condiment....SALT; CURRY, SPICE
condition ...............STATE; STATUS
condition in agreement ....PROVISO
conduct....................LEAD; GUIDE
conductor ......................MAESTRO
conductor's stick ..................BATON
conduit ....................MAIN; DRAIN,
................................................SEWER
cone filled with explosives .PETARD
cone of silver ..........................PINA
confabulate.......CHAT, CHIN, TALK
confection ............CANDY; COMFIT

a confection, nut ..................PRALINE
  confederate ..........................ALLY
  Confederate soldier .................REB
  confederation.....................LEAGUE
  conference......................PALAVER
  confess ....................AVOW; ADMIT
  confession of faith ..............CREDO
  confidence ...............FAITH, TRUST
  confine .........................PEN; CAGE
  confined.............................PENT
  confront ......................FACE, MEET
  confused, make.................,.ADDLE
  confusion .................MESS; BABEL
  congealed dew ....................RIME
  conger ................................EEL
  congregate ..........MEET; GATHER
  coniferous tree ......FIR, YEW; PINE;
  ...........................CEDAR; SPRUCE
  conjunction ..........AND, BUT, NOR
  connect .............JOIN, LINK; UNITE
  connected series of writings.........
  ...................................CATENA
  connecting strip of land ....ISTHMUS
  connection .........................NEXUS
  connective tissue ................FASCIA
  connubial .........................MARITAL
  conquer ......................BEAT, BEST;
  .....................................MASTER
  conqueror of Mexico .........CORTES
  .....................................CORTEZ

b Conrad's *Victory* heroine ........LENA
  conscript............DRAFT; DRAFTEE
  consecrate.........................BLESS
  consecrated ..........HOLY; OBLATE
  consecrated places, Gr. .......HIERA
  consequence .RESULT; OUTCOME
  Conservative, Brit. .................TORY
  consider ...................DEEM, RATE;
  .........................TREAT; REGARD
  consonant, hard ...............FORTIS
  consonant, unaspirated .........LENIS
  consonant, voiceless .............SURD
  conspire ...............................PLOT
  Constantine, birthplace of .........NIS
  constellations............See page 207.
  constrictor.................BOA; ABOMA
  container .......BOX, CAN, JAR, TIN,
  ......TUB, URN, VAT; CASE, CASK,
  ...........PAIL, SACK, VASE; CRATE
  contemporary, briefly ..............MOD
  contempt, show ..................SNEER
  contend ..................VIE; COPE
  contest ...............................BOUT
  contest, ancient Gr. ..............AGON
  contingencies .........................IFS
  continue .................LAST; ENDURE
  contort ...................WARP; TWIST
  contraction, poetic ........E'EN, 'ERE,
  ..................O'ER, OFT', 'TIL, 'TIS;
  ..............................NE'ER, 'TWAS

c contraction, pronoun.....HE'D, HE'S,
  .....................I'LL, IT'S, I'VE, WE'D;
  ..........HE'LL, IT'LL, SHE'D, SHE'S,
  .................................WE'LL, WE'RE,
  ................WE'VE, YOU'D; SHE'LL,
  .............THEY'D, YOU'LL, YOU'RE;
  .......................THEY'LL, THEY'RE
  contradict .................DENY; REBUT
  ...................................NEGATE
  contrition .......................REMORSE
  contrive ..................MAKE; DEVISE
  control.......................REIN; STEER
  conundrum.........ENIGMA, RIDDLE
  convert to Judaism ..............GER
  convex moldings....................TORI
  convoy ...........................ESCORT
  coney .......................PIKA; RABBIT
  cook...................................CHEF
  cook food.....................FRY; BAKE,
  .......................BOIL, STEW; BROIL,
  ..............................ROAST, SAUTE
  cook in cream .......................SHIRR
  cooking pot .............................OLLA
  cool .....................................ICE
  copal ....................ANIME, ELEMI
  copper ...............................CENT
  Copperfield, Mrs. .................DORA
  copper yellow....................MELINE
  copse..................................HOLT
  copse, prairie .......................MOTTE

d copy .................APE, FAX; MODEL;
  ...................................ECTYPE
  coral element ......................POLYP
  cord .................LINE, ROPE, WIRE
  cord, Bedouin's......................AGAL
  cordage fiber...........COIR, ERUC,
  ............FERU, HEMP, IMBE, JUTE;
  ..............................ABACA, SISAL
  cordage tree ...........................SIDA
  Cordelia, father of...................LEAR
  core ........................PITH; HEART
  core, casting mold ....COPE, DRAG;
  .................................NOWEL
  cork, extract of .....................CERIN
  cork, shallow ......................SHIVE
  Cork County port ..................COBH
  cork helmet.............TOPI; TOPEE
  corkwood ..........................BALSA
  corn.....................................BULB
  cormorant, Afr. ..................DUIKER
  corn, hulled .....................HOMINY
  cornbread...........................PONE
  corn crake bird .......................RAIL
  corner .........NOOK, TREE; ANGLE;
  ...................................RECESS
  cornerstone ......................QUOIN
  corn extract.............................ZEIN
  cornice support ..................ANCON
  corn lily ..................................IXIA
  cornmeal ..............................MASA

*a* cornmeal drink ..................POSOL;
........................POSOLE, POZOLE
cornu ........................................HORN
corolla part............................PETAL
coronation stone, Scot. ......SCONE
corpulent ....................FAT; OBESE
correct............FIX; TRUE; RIGHT
correlative ...............................NOR
correspond....JIBE; AGREE, TALLY
corridor...................................HALL
corrode ........................EAT; RUST
corrupt .................VENAL; VITIATE
corrupt with money ...............BRIBE
corsair ..................................PIRATE
corset bone ............................BUSK
cortege ..............................RETINUE
corundum ............................EMERY
cos lettuce ......................ROMAINE
Cossack ................................TATAR
Cossack chief..................ATAMAN,
..................................HETMAN
cosset ....................PET; PAMPER
costa ........................................RIB
coterie .....................................SET
cotillion attendee......................DEB
cotton, SW US......................PIMA
cotton fabric ..........................LAWN;
....................DENIM; MADRAS
cotton fabric, coarse ...........SURAT
cotton flannel .....DOMET; DOMETT

*b* cotton gum tree..................TUPELO
cotton machine ........................GIN
cotton tree .............................SIMAL
cottonwood ...........................ALAMO
cougar ................PUMA; PANTHER
council, ecclesiastical ..........SYNOD
council, A.-S. king's ..............WITAN
counsel...................................REDE
counselor..........................MENTOR
count .................TOTAL; NUMBER
counter ...........BAR; COMPUTER
counter current.......................EDDY
countermand ....................REVOKE
counterpart.......MATCH; VIS-A-VIS
countersink ...........................REAM
counting frame ...................ABACUS
country bumpkin......RUBE; YOKEL
county: Danish.........................AMT
county: Eng. .........................SHIRE
county: Swed. ..........................LAN
couple....................TWO; PAIR
courage ..........HEART, NERVE,
..............PLUCK; METTLE, SPIRIT
course .............WAY; ROAD, TACK
course, complete....................CYCLE
course, meal ........SALAD, ENTREE
course, part of a ...........LAP, LEG
course, school: Abbr. .......ALG, BIO,
....................LIT, SCI; CHEM, TRIG
court .......................................WOO

court, A.-S. .......GEMOT; GEMOTE *c*
court, church ...........................ROTA
court, inner ...........PATIO; ATRIUM
court, old Eng. .......................LEET
court action .............................SUIT
court cry .....................OYES, OYEZ
court hearing..........................OYER
courtly....................................AULIC
court order ...........................ARRET
court panel ............................JURY
court proceeding ...................TRIAL
courtship area, grouse's...........LEK
Cousteau's ship .............CALYPSO
cover, take ............................HIDE
cover, took ..............................HID
covey .....................BEVY; BROOD
cow........BOSSY, BULLY; HECTOR
coward ...............................CRAVEN
cowboy, S. A. ....................GAUCHO
cowboy's leg covering ........CHAPS
cowboy's nickname ......TEX: BUCK
cowfish....................................TORO
cowl.......................................HOOD
cows .......................................KINE
cow shelter .............................BYRE
coxcomb...................FOP; DANDY
coy .................SHY; TIMID; FLIRTY
coypu ...................................NUTRIA
cozy .....................SNUG; HOMEY
cozy spot.......................DEN; NEST

crab genus.............................MAJA *d*
crack .......SNAP; CHINK; CREVICE
crackpot ....................NUT: LOONY
craft.......................ART; TRADE
craftsman...........................ARTISAN
crafty.......SLY; CAGY, FOXY, WILY
craggy hill ...............................TOR
cramp.....................................KINK
crane, ship's .......................DAVIT
cranial nerves ........................VAGI
crape fern ...........................TODEA
cravat....................................TIE
crave ....ASK, BEG; LONG; DESIRE
craw .............................MAW; CROP
crayon .................CHALK; PASTEL
craze........................FAD; MANIA
crazy..........LOCO, WILD; LOONY
cream ....................................ELITE
created...................................MADE
credit transfer system .............GIRO
creek ........................KILL, RILL
creep along .............................INCH
creeper......................................IVY
Cremona craftsman ..............AMATI
crescent moon's point ...........CUSP
crescent-shaped ...............LUNATE
crescent-shaped figure...........LUNE
crescent-shaped mark .......LUNULA
crest .................TOP; COMB, PEAK
crest, mountain ...................ARETE

31

*a* Cretan princess ................ARIADNE
crew............................GANG, TEAM
cribbage pin or score .............PEG
cribbage term ...............NOB; NOBS
cricket .................................GRIG
cricket field parts..........ONS; OFFS
cricket term .............BYE; OVER;
.......................................YORKER
Crimean river.......................ALMA
criminal.............................FELON
crimp..................................CURL
crimson ...............................RED
cringe and flatter..................FAWN
crippled ....................HALT, LAME
criticize .........CARP, ZING; CAVIL
crocodile of India ................GAVIAL
Croesus, land of .................LYDIA
crony .............PAL; CHUM; BUDDY
crooked.....................AWRY, BENT
crookneck squash ...........CUSHAW
crooner.............VALLEE; SINATRA
crop .......................MAW; CRAW
crops, raise ........................FARM
cross ....................SPAN; IRATE;
................................TRAVERSE
cross, crude wooden ...........ROOD
cross, Eg. ...........................ANKH
crossbeam ........................TRAVE
crossbill bird .....................LOXIA
cross-examine .....................GRILL

*b* cross hairs ......................RETICLE
cross oneself .......................SAIN
crosspiece ...............BAR; RUNG
cross stroke .......................SERIF
cross threads .........WEFT, WOOF
crow .........BRAG, ROOK; CRAKE
crow, Brit. ....................JACKDAW
crowd.............PRESS; THRONG
crown ...............CAP; PATE; TIARA;
..................................DIADEM
crown, pope's triple ...........TIARA
crown of Osiris ....................ATEF
crucial point.......................CRUX
crucible ..........TRIAL; ORDEAL
crucifixion letters ......................INRI
crude ...................RAW; ROUGH;
....................................COARSE
crude metal .........................ORE
cruel person .....................SADIST
cruet.................AMA; CASTER
cruising ..............................ASEA
crumbled, easily ...............FRIABLE
Crusader's foe .................SARACEN
crush ...........MASH; SUBDUE
crustacean ...........CRAB; ISOPOD,
...................SHRIMP; LOBSTER
cry .......SOB; HOWL, MOAN, WAIL,
...........................WEEP; LAMENT
cry, mournful.......................YOWL
cry, Australian ...................COOEE

*c* cry for silence in court ...........OYES,
.......................................OYEZ
crystal-clear ....................PELLUCID
Cuban dance ....................CONGA;
...................................HABANERA
Cuban secret police ...........PORRA
cubic decimeter....................LITER
cubicle ........................CELL; STALL
cubic measure ......................CORD
cubic meter ........................STERE
cubitus ...............................ULNA
cuckold...........................RAM, TUP
cuckoo, black colonial ...............ANI
cuckoo, Oriental ........KOEL, KOIL
cuckoopint .........................ARUM
cucumber ................CUKE, PEPO
cud ...................QUID; RUMEN
cuddly................................CUTE
cudgel......................CLUB, DRUB;
...............................STAVE, STICK
cue .....................................HINT
cue, music.........................PRESA
cuirass, Rom. .....................LORICA
cull ......................GLEAN; SELECT
culmination ................END; ACME,
.............................APEX, PEAK
cultivate land ......HOE; PLOW, TILL
culture medium ...................AGAR
cunning.......................SLY; WILY;
.........................SHARP, SLICK

*d* cup, assaying .....................CUPEL
cupbearer of the gods .............HEBE;
...................................GANYMEDE
Cupid.........................AMOR, EROS
cupola................................DOME
cup stand of metal, coffee ......ZARF
cup to hold a gem ........DOP; DOPP
cur ..........................DOG; MUTT
curassow ..............................MITU
curdling powder.................RENNET
cure....................................HEAL
cure-all...............ELIXIR; PANACEA
curl ....................COIL, FRIZ, WIND;
.......................................FRIZZ
currency ...................See page 213.
curse ..................................CUSS
curt ..................TERSE; BRUSQUE
curve ..................ARC, BOW, ESS;
................................BEND; SINUS
curved in..........................CONCAVE
curved out ......................CONVEX
curved plank .........................SNY
cushion.................PAD; HASSOCK
Cushitic lang. ...........KAFA, SAHO;
...............................GALLA, KAFFA
custard ................................FLAN
custard apple ...................ANNONA
custard cake......................ECLAIR
Custer's horse ......................VIC
custody ...........................CHARGE

a custom.....................LAW; WONT;
.......................HABIT, USAGE
customer ...........................PATRON
customs ...............................MORES
cut .................HEW, LOP, MOW;
.................DOCK, HACK, KERF;
.................REAP, SLIT, SNEE;
.........SEVER, SHEAR; CLEAVE
cut, deep ...............................GASH
cut down ...................................FELL
cut of beef .........RIB; LOIN, RUMP;
.................CHUCK, FLANK, PLATE,
.................ROUND, SHANK, STEAK

cut out ...................................EXCISE c
cutting tool ......................ADZ, AXE,
.........................................HOB, SAW
cuttlefish ...............................SQUID
cuttlefish fluid ..........................INK
cylinder.....................................TUBE
cylinder, moving.................PISTON
cylindrical ............................TERETE
cyma .......................................GOLA
Cymbeline, daughter of .....IMOGEN
Cymru.....................................WALES
Cymry.....................................WELSH
cyst ...........................................WEN

# D

Dadaist .......ARP; ERNST, GROSZ,
.................TZARA; DUCHAMP
Daedalus, son of ...............ICARUS
dagger..........DIRK, SNEE; BODKIN
dagger, Scot. ......................SKEAN
dagger, thin.....................STILETTO
daily.....................................DIURNAL
dais ...................................ESTRADE
daisy, type of .........MOON; OXEYE;
.................................SHASTA
Dallas sch. ..............................SMU
b dam.........................................WEIR
dam, US .............OAHE; HOOVER;
.................FORT PECK, OROVILLE
damage.......HARM, HURT; INJURY
Damascus river......................ABANA
Damon, friend of ...............PYTHIAS
damp...............WET; DANK; MOIST
damselfish ..........................PINTANO
dance ......HOP, JIG; FRUG, PONY,
....REEL; GALOP, GAVOT, POLKA,
.................RUMBA, TANGO, TWIST
dance, Israeli ........................HORA
dance, school ...........HOP; PROM
dance, stately old ..............MINUET,
.................................PAVANE
dance company .................A.B.T.;
.................KIROV; BOLSHOI;
.................................MOISEYEV
dancer/choreographer ..........AILEY,
.................HINES, KELLY, PETIT,
..........THARP; ALONSO, ASHTON,
.........BEJART, BOLGER, CASTLE,
.........DUNCAN, FOKINE, GRAHAM,
.........VALOIS, VEREEN; ASTAIRE,
.................DE MILLE, FONTEYN,
.................JOFFREY, MARKOVA,
.................NUREYEV, PAVLOVA
dance step ..............PAS; CHASSE;
.................................GLISSADE
dancing girl, Eg. ....................ALMA

dancing girl, Jap. ...............GEISHA
dandy.....................FOP; DUDE, TOFF
Danish astronomer ............BRAHE
Danish king............KNUT; CANUTE
Danish physicist....................BOHR
dank ...............WET; DAMP; MOIST
Dante's patron ....................SCALA
Danube, city on the ...............ULM;
.................................LINZ, WIEN
Danube, old name of ............ISTER
Danube tributary ...........INN, OLT;
.................................ISAR, PRUT d
daring ......................BOLD; BRAVE
dark ...............DIM; INKY; BLACK,
.........DUSKY, MURKY; GLOOMY
dark and threatening, appear.LOUR
dark wood..............................EBONY
Darwin's ship .....................BEAGLE
___ Darya River .......................AMU
dash .......BRIO, DART, ELAN, FLIT,
.................HINT; SCOOT; HASTEN
date, Rom. ...............IDES; NONES
date, specific............................DAY
*David Copperfield* character ...........
.................DORA, HEEP; DARTLE
David's captain ........................JOAB
David's commander.............AMASA
David's daughter .................TAMAR
David's father.........................JESSE
David's son ......................SOLOMON
David's wife .........................MICHAL
dawn: poetically ....................MORN
dawn goddess .........EOS; AURORA
day: Heb. ...............................YOM
day, specified ........................DATE
Dayak people.........................IBAN
Dayak short sword .............PARANG
daybreak ...............................DAWN
daydream ..........................REVERIE
day's march............................ETAPE
dead .......LATE, NUMB; DEFUNCT

*a* dead, abode of the ...............HELL;
.........................HADES, SHEOL
deadly....................FATAL; LETHAL
deadly sins, seven,..............ENVY;
...................LUST; ANGER, PRIDE;
.......................SLOTH; GLUTTONY;
.........................COVETOUSNESS
dealer.........MONGER; MERCHANT
dealer, cloth .....................DRAPER
dearth ...............................WANT
death deity, Rom. ................MORS
death notice, briefly ..............OBIT
death rattle...........................RALE
debauchee .........RAKE, ROUE
debris, rocky .......................SCREE
debts, have ...........................OWE
decade ...................................TEN
decamp...................ELOPE, LEAVE
decay ..................ROT; SPOIL;
.................................PUTREFY
decay, dental ...................CARIES
deceit...........SHAM, WILE; FRAUD;
.......................GUILE; DUPLICITY
deceive .......................BILK, DUPE;
.......................FOOL, GULL; TRICK;
...............MISLEAD; HOODWINK
decelerate .............SLOW; RETARD
deception .............................HOAX
decibels, ten ..........................BEL
decimal unit ...........................TEN
*b* deck, ship's ...........POOP; ORLOP
declaim ......................RANT, RAVE;
.........................ORATE; RECITE
declaration in whist............MISERE
declare .....................AVER, AVOW;
..........................STATE; AVOUCH
declare, in card games...........MELD
decline .............EBB; SINK, WANE;
................................REFUSE
declivity...................SCARP, SLOPE
decorate ...................DECK; ADORN
decorated wall part ..............DADO
decorous .............STAID; DEMURE
decoy ...................LURE; PLANT
decrease ..................EBB; WANE;
.......................LESSEN, RECEDE
decree .............ACT; FIAT; CANON,
.........................EDICT; ORDAIN
decree, Russ. .....................UKASE
decree of a court................ARRET
deduce ..................INFER, JUDGE;
.................GATHER; CONCLUDE
deed ..........ACT; GESTE; EXPLOIT
deeds.....................................ACTA
deep-fat fried ......................RISSOLE
deer, Andean .......................PUDU
deer, Asian.......................SAMBAR
deer, barking....................KAKAR,
.....................KAKUR; MUNTJAC
deer, female.........DOE, ROE; HIND

deer, Indian .............................AXIS *c*
deer, Jap. .............................SIKA
deer, Kashmir....................HANGUL
deer, male ..................BUCK, STAG
deer, red ......................ROE; HART
deer, S. A. .......................GEMUL;
.........................GUEMAL, HUEMUL
deer, spotted .........KAKAR; CHITAL
deer, young ...........................FAWN
deerlike ............................CERVINE
deer track..............................SLOT
defamation .............................LIBEL
defeat ............BEST, ROUT; CRUSH
defeat in chess......................MATE
defect......................FLAW, LACK
deference .......................RESPECT
defiant shout ............................YAH
defraud ..........BILK, GULL; CHEAT
defy ..............DARE; CHALLENGE
degrade................ABASE, LOWER;
.................................DEBASE
degrading...........................MENIAL
degree ..................GRADE, STAGE
degree, ultimate ......................NTH
deity ....................................GOD
delay ...............LAG; STAY; DALLY,
.............TARRY; DETAIN; HOLDUP
delicate ................................FINE
delicate pattern, having a .......LACY
delight......................JOY; CHEER;
.........................PLEASE, RELISH *d*
demand .......NEED; CLAIM; INSIST
demeanor......................AIR; MIEN;
.........................STYLE; MANNER;
...................BEARING, CONDUCT
Demeter, daughter of............CORA
Demeter's other name ..........IOULO
demigod................................HERO
demolish ....RAZE, RUIN; FLATTEN
demolish: Brit. .........................RASE
demon ...........IMP; DEVIL, FIEND
demon, Muslim .........DJINN, JINNI;
.................................DJINNI
demonstrative pronoun ..........THAT;
............................... THIS, WHOM;
.........................THESE, THOSE
den .................DIVE, LAIR; HAUNT
denary ....................................TEN
denial ...................NAY; REFUSAL;
.................................NEGATION
Dennis the Menace's dog ......RUFF
denomination.........................SECT
denote ...................MEAN, SHOW;
.................................INDICATE
dense .......CRASS, THICK; STUPID
dental tool ........................SCALER
deny ...............NEGATE; GAINSAY
depart................DIE; QUIT; LEAVE
departed.........GONE, LEFT, WENT
departure ...........................EXODUS

34

| | |
|---|---|
| dependent............WARD; CHARGE | devaluate ...........LOWER; REDUCE |
| depict........LIMN, SHOW; RENDER | deviate ..........ERR, VEER; STRAY; |
| depict sharply ......................ETCH | ...............WANDER; DIVERGE |
| deplore ..................RUE; REGRET, | devil ......................DEMON, SATAN |
| ..................REPENT; CENSURE, | devilfish .,........................MANTA |
| ..................................CONDEMN | Devon river ...............................EXE |
| deposit, alluvial.......DELTA, GEEST | devotee ........................................FAN |
| deposit, caked .......................CRUD | devotion, nine-day ..........NOVENA |
| deposit, clayey ......................MARL | devoutness ...........................PIETY |
| deposit, geyser .................SINTER | dewlap....................................JOWL |
| deposit, mineral ..........ORE; LODE | dexterity...........SKILL; AGILITY |
| deposit, river ..........ALLUVIUM | diadem.....................................TIARA |
| depravity...................................VICE | diagonal....................................BIAS |
| depressed .........LOW, SAD; DOWN | dialect........IDIOM, LINGO; PATOIS |
| depressed state....................FUNK | diamond, industrial................BORT |
| depression .............DENT; FOVEA | Diana.................................ARTEMIS |
| deprivation ............................LOSS | Diana, mother of ................LATONA |
| depute .........APPOINT; DELEGATE | diaper .......................................DIDY |
| deputy ...........AGENT; SECOND | diaphanous................THIN; SHEER |
| derby ...................................BOWLER | diatribe .......SCREED; HARANGUE |
| deride......................GIBE, MOCK; | Dickens, illustrator of .............PHIZ |
| ..................SCOFF, TAUNT | Dickens character ............PIP, TIM; |
| derrick ............CRANE; STEEVE | ...............DORA, GAMP, HEEP; |
| descendant...........................SCION | ........DROOD, FAGIN; DORRIT |
| descendants, male side .........GENS | Dickens pseudonym .................BOZ |
| desert, Afr. ..........NAMIB; NUBIAN, | die away........................FADE, FAIL |
| ..................SAHARA; KALAHARI | *Die Fledermaus* girl .............ADELE |
| desert, Asian .....LUT; GOBI, THAR; | *"Dies ___"*.....................................IRAE |
| ..................................KARA-KUM | diet...........................................FARE |
| desert, Australian .............GIBSON | differ.................VARY; DISAGREE |
| desert, California ...............MOJAVE | difference, solar/lunar year ..EPACT |
| desert, Chilean ...............ATACAMA | different................OTHER; DIVERS |
| desert date..............................BITO | difficulty..................RUB; RIGOR; |
| deserter......................................RAT | ....................STRIFE; TROUBLE |
| desert plant .........AGAVE; CACTUS | dig ...........................GRUB; DELVE |
| deserve ............EARN; MERIT | dignitary......................................VIP |
| design......................IDEA, PLAN; | dike.........................................LEVEE |
| ..........MOTIF; LAYOUT, SCHEME | dilatory...................SLOW; TARDY |
| desire .....................YEN; URGE, | dilemma.................FIX, JAM; SPOT |
| ..................WANT, WISH; CRAVE | dilute ........................THIN; WATER |
| desire, strong..................HUNGER | dim, become ........BLEAR; DARKLE |
| desirous....................................FAIN | diminish..................EBB; ABATE; |
| desolate .................BLEAK, WASTE | ....................................REDUCE |
| despoil.......................................RUIN | dingle ..............DALE, DELL, GLEN |
| despot ...........TYRANT; DICTATOR | dinner jacket ............TUX; TUXEDO |
| dessert...........PIE; CAKE; SWEET; | Dioscuri .............CASTOR, POLLUX |
| ..................MOUSSE, TRIFLE | dip :...............DAP; DUNK, LADE |
| destiny ........DOOM, FATE; KARMA | diplomacy .................................TACT |
| destroy......................RAZE, RUIN; | diplomat........ENVOY; CONSUL; |
| ..........LEVEL, SMASH, WRECK | ...................................ATTACHE |
| detail ............FACT, ITEM; POINT | dipping in water ......................BATH |
| detain ...................SEIZE; ARREST | direct ..........LEAD; FRANK, GUIDE; |
| detection device....RADAR, SONAR | ..................LINEAL; FIRSTHAND |
| detective ..........................TEC; DICK | direct a helmsman .................CONN |
| determination ...........WILL; RULING | direct attention ......................REFER |
| determine .....RULE; JUDGE, LIMIT; | dirge.............................LINOS, LINUS |
| ..................DECIDE; RESOLVE | dirigible .................................BLIMP |
| detest ....................HATE; LOATHE | dirk.........................SNEE; DAGGER |
| dethrone................OUST; DEPOSE | dirty lock of wool ......................FRIB |
| detonator ......................CAP; FUZE | disable ...............................CRIPPLE |

35

a disappear gradually ...............FADE;
...................................EVANESCE
disapproval, express......BOO; HISS
disavow .................DENY; RECANT
disburse .........PAY; DEAL; SPEND
discernment .............WIT; ACUMEN
discharge....................EMIT, FIRE,
...................................SACK; SHOOT
disciple .............................APOSTLE
disciple in India....................CHELA
disciplinarian .................MARTINET
disclaim ................................DENY
disclose .................BARE; REVEAL
disconcert ..............FAZE; ABASH;
................CHAGRIN, MORTIFY
discord...............CLASH; DISSENT
discourse .......HOMILY, SPEECH
discourse, art of.............RHETORIC
discover ..........................SEE, SPY;
...............................FIND; LEARN
discriminate ......................SECERN
discussion ...............................TALK
discussion group .................FORUM
disease, fungal.....................ERGOT
disease, grape-vine...............ESCA;
...............ERINEUM, ERINOSE
disease, imaginary.................CRUD
disease, plant..........SMUT; SCALD
disease, skin............POX; ECZEMA
disease, tropical..................SPRUE
b disease spreader.................GERM;
................VECTOR; CARRIER
disembark ..............................LAND
disencumber ............................RID
disengage ...............................FREE
disfigure .................MAR; DEFACE
disgrace .........SHAME; IGNOMINY
disguise...........MASK, VEIL; CLOAK
...............COVER; COSTUME
dish ....................................PLATE
dish, Hawaiian .........................POI
dish, highly seasoned.............OLIO;
..........................................OLLA
dish, hominy ......................POSOL;
................POSOLE, POZOLE
dish, Hung. .....................GOULASH
dish, It. ...........PASTA; RAVIOLI;
...............GNOCCHI, LASAGNA
dish, main .........................ENTREE
dish, meat............STEW; RAGOUT
dish, Mex. ........................TAMALE
dish, stemmed ...............COMPOTE
dishearten ....................LET DOWN;
........................................DISPIRIT
dishonor.........SHAME; OBLOQUY
disinclined.........................AVERSE
disinfectant .......CRESOL, PHENOL
disk, ice hockey.....................PUCK
disk, metal ........................PATEN
dislocate ........MOVE, SLIP; SHAKE

dismal........................SAD; BLEAK;
...................DREARY, GLOOMY
dismantle .................RAZE; LEVEL;
......................................DESTROY
dismay ...............................DAUNT,
...................SHAKE, SHOCK;
...............APPALL, HORRIFY
dismiss ...............FIRE; REFUSE,
..........................................REJECT
dismiss from a job ...........AXE, CAN
dismounted..............................ALIT
disorder .................MESS; CHAOS;
...............ANARCHY, TURMOIL
disorderly retreat....................ROUT
disparaging .............................SNIDE
disparaging remark...................SLUR
dispatch....................SEND; HASTE
dispatch a dragon ......................SLAY
dispatch boat.........................AVISO
dispelled ..............................GONE
display .....................AIR; SHOW;
...............ARRAY; EVINCE
display area, bird's.....LEK; BOWER
display proudly....................VAUNT
displease ...........................OFFEND
disposed ..................APT; GIVEN;
...................PRONE; LIABLE,
..................LIKELY; INCLINED
disposition ............MOOD; TEMPER
dispossess ....ROB; STRIP; DIVEST
disprove .................BELIE; REFUTE
disputable ............................MOOT
dissertation ......THESIS; TREATISE
dissonant ...........................ATONAL
distance, to or from a...............AFAR
distant ............................FAR, YON;
...........................YOND; REMOTE
distilling vessel..................MATRASS
distinctive air .............AURA, MIEN;
........................................CACHET
distress signal............................SOS
distribute ...............DEAL, SORT;
..............GROUP, SHARE, STREW
district........AREA, ZONE; REGION
disturb........................VEX; FRET;
...................ANNOY, UPSET;
...................RUFFLE; DERANGE
disturbance..................FUSS, STIR;
...................UPROAR, RUMPUS,
........................................TUMULT
ditch................FOSS, RINE, FOSSE,
.........SHUCK; TRENCH; DISCARD
ditch, water-filled....................MOAT
ditto .....................................SAME
divan .....................................SOFA
dive .................DEN; HEADER
dive bomber ........................STUKA
diverge ...................FORK; STRAY;
...................SWERVE; DEVIATE
diverse...................MIXED; VARIED

*a* divest .........................ROB; STRIP;
.........................EXPOSE; DEPRIVE
divide ...................FORK; BREAK;
..............SEVER, SPLIT; BRANCH;
.........................................SEPARATE
*Divine Comedy* author .........DANTE
divine favor..............................GRACE
divine revelation, Heb. .......TORAH
divine utterance.................ORACLE
divinity ..................................DEITY
divorce, Muslim...................TALAK
"Dixie" composer..............EMMETT
___ *dixit* ..................................IPSE
dizzy, be ...............................SWIM
DNA element ......................CODON
docile ........MEEK, TAME; GENTLE
Dr. Jekyll's other self.............HYDE
doctrine .................DOGMA, TENET
documents, wicker box for ..............
.........................................HANAPER
doe .......................HIND; FEMALE
dog ......................CANIS; CANINE
dog, breed of..........PUG; CHOW;
.............BOXER; HOUND, HUSKY;
.............SPITZ; BEAGLE, BORZOI;
..........BRIARD, COLLIE, POODLE,
.........................SALUKI, SETTER;
.........................SPANIEL, TERRIER
dog, Cracker Jacks..............BINGO
dog, Greyfriars'..................BOBBY
*b* dog, Hungarian ........PULI; KUVASZ
dog, John Brown's ...................RAB
dog, RCA Victor.................NIPPER
dog, Sputnik..........................LAIKA
dog, Welsh ..........................CORGI
dog, wild Australian ............DINGO
dog, wild Indian...................DHOLE
dog-fisher.............................OTTER
dog in movies .........ASTA, TOTO;
.........................BENJI; LASSIE;
.........................RIN TIN TIN
dog in the *Odyssey* ...........ARGOS
dogma ..................................TENET
dog salmon ...........................KETA
dog sound ..........YIP; BARK, RUFF
.................WOOF, YELP; GROWL
dog star.................................SIRIUS
dogwood .............................CORNEL
dole .................RELIEF; WELFARE
dolphin ............................DORADO
dolt.............................ASS, OAF;
.........................CLOD; DUNCE
domain .........AREA; FIELD, REALM
Dombey's suitor, Miss..........TOOTS
dome, small ......................CUPOLA
domestic....................MAID; LOCAL
domesticated.........................TAME
dominion ..................RULE, SWAY;
.........................POWER, TITLE;
.........................COMMAND

domino ......................CAPE, MASK *c*
*Don Carlos*, princess in .........EBOLI
Don Juan, mother of ................INEZ
donkey...........ASS; MOKE; BURRO
donkey's call...........................BRAY
doom ..............................CONDEMN,
.........................................DESTINE
door ....................ENTRY; PORTAL
doorkeeper, Masonic .............TILER
door part .....................JAMB, SASH,
.........................SILL; LINTEL
door section...........................PANEL
dorado .................CUIR, DOLPHIN
dormant .............ASLEEP, LATENT
dormouse, large Eur. .............LOIR
dots, paint with .................STIPPLE
dotted with (figures) .............SEME
double .........................DUAL, TWIN;
.........................................BINARY
double-curved molding .........CYMA,
.........................................GOLA
double dagger ......................DIESIS
double salt............................ALUM
double tooth .......................MOLAR
doubletree ........................EVENER
dowel.........................................PIN
down ...................SAD; FUZZ; EIDER
down, facing .......................PRONE
down quilt .........................DOVET
drag...........LUG, TOW, TUG; HAUL
drain..................SAP; SEWER; *d*
.........................................DEPLETE
Dravidian language.....MALE, NAIR,
.........................TODA; NAYAR, TAMIL
draw ............TIE; PULL; DEPICT,
.........................................SKETCH
draw forth ...........................EDUCE
draw from...........................DERIVE
drawing curve ...................SPLINE
drawing room .......................SALON
draw out...................ATTENUATE
draw tight..............................FRAP
dreadful ..................................DIRE
*Dream Girl* playwright.............RICE
dregs .....................LEES; DROSS
drench ..................WET; SOAK;
.........................DOUSE, SOUSE
dress .................GARB; CLOTHE
dress, ball ............................GOWN
dressed...................................CLAD
dried up ..................................SERE
drift .........FLOW; MOUND; INTENT
drill ........................BORE; TRAIN
drill piece .................................BIT
drink ...................SIP; GULP, SWIG;
.........................QUAFF; IMBIBE;
.........................................BEVERAGE
drink, almond-flavored ......ORGEAT
drink, Christmas .....NOG; WASSAIL
drink, fermented honey ..........MEAD

*a*    drink, hot...............................TODDY
drink, hot milk ....................POSSET
drink, palm .............................NIPA
drink, rum or gin and spices ..........
................................................BUMBO
drink, small ..............NIP, PEG, SIP;
...............................DRAM, SLUG
drink, soft ...........ADE, POP; SODA
drink, whiskey ...................STINGER
drinking bowl, large .............MAZER
drinking vessel ........................CUP,
.................MUG; TOBY; JORUM,
...........................STEIN; TANKARD
drink of liquor ...........NIP; BRACER
drink of the gods...............NECTAR
drive ...............RUN; PROD, PUSH,
...............ROAD; IMPEL, PILOT,
...............................VIGOR; PROPEL,
......................THRUST; CRUSADE
drive away ............SHOO; DISPEL
drive back ..........REPEL; REPULSE
drivel ...................DROOL; SLAVER
driver, reckless ........................JEHU
drizzle..........MIST; SMUR; MIZZLE
droll ............ZANY; COMIC, FUNNY
dromedary, swift................MEHARI
drone ..........BEE, BUM, DOR, HUM
droop .................SAG; FLAG, LOLL,
..................................WILT; SLOUCH
drooping ...................................ALOP

*b*    drop ........................DAB; DRAM,
................FALL; DEPTH, LOWER,
...........................SLUMP; CANCEL,
...........................PLUNGE; GLOBULE
drop, one ...............................MINIM
dropsy............EDEMA; ANASARCA
dross...................................SLAG;
..........................SPRUE; SCORIA
drought-tolerant legume ........GUAR
drove ......................HERD, RODE
drove of horses....................ATAJO
drowse .......................................NOD
drudge ...........SLOG, TOIL; GRIND
drug ......................DOPE; OPIATE
drum, small..........TABOR; TABRET
drumbeat ..........................TATTOO;
..................................RAT-A-TAT
drumbeat, double .................FLAM
drum-call to arms ...............RAPPEL
drunkard ...........SOT; LUSH, WINO,
.......................RUMMY, SOUSE,
.........TOPER; BARFLY; BOOZER;
......................TIPPLER, TOSSPOT
drunk driving: Abbr. .........DUI, DWI
dry ............................................ARID
dry, as wine..................SEC; BRUT;
...............................................SECCO
dry-goods dealer ...............DRAPER
dry riverbed...........................WADI
dub .........................NAME; KNIGHT

*c*    duck ...................STOOP; CROUCH
duck, Arctic ...........................EIDER
duck, breed of .......PEKIN, ROUEN;
................................................MALLARD
duck, diving ..........................SMEW
duck, fresh-water ...................TEAL
duck, male ...........................DRAKE
duck, N. Amer. .......................COOT
duck, ring-necked scaup .....DOGY
duck, river....................SHOVELER
duck, sea ...............EIDER, SCAUP;
................................................SCOTER
duck eggs, Chin. ..................PIDAN
duck lure...............................DECOY
duct, anatomical ...........VAS; VASA
dude ..........................FOP; DANDY
dueling, prove a claim by ...........
................................................DERAIGN
dugout canoe ...................PIROGUE
dugout canoe with outrigger BANCA
duke's domain ....................DUCHY
dulcimer ..........................CIMBALOM
dulcimer, Pers. ...................SANTIR
dull...............................DRY, LOGY;
..............BLUNT, PROSY; BORING
dullard .............OAF; BOOR, DODO
dull color.........DUN; DRAB; TERNE
dull finish .............................MATTE
dull silk fabric ........................GROS
Dumas hero .......................ATHOS;

*d*    .................ARAMIS; PORTHOS;
................................................D'ARTAGNAN
dunderhead.....BOZO, FOOL, JERK
dung beetle .........DOR; SCARAB
dunlin bird ...............................STIB
dupe.........................USE; SUCKER
duration......................SPAN, TIME
dusk........................EVE; SUNSET
dusky ...........DIM; DARK; SWART
Dutch cheese........................EDAM
Dutch coin, old.......................DOIT
Dutch commune .......................EDE
Dutch courage...................LIQUOR
Dutch painter ...........HALS; STEEN
duty.....................CHORE; TARIFF
dwarf..........RUNT; STUNT, TROLL
dwell................................BIDE, LIVE
dwelling ...............................ABODE
dye, blue ..............................WOAD
dye, indigo..............................ANIL
dye, red...................AURIN, EOSIN;
................................................ANNATTO
dye, yellow ...............WELD, WOLD
dye gum ..................................KINO
dyes, any ................................FUCI
dyes containing nitrogen..........AZO
dyewood tree..........................TUI
dynamite inventor ................NOBEL
dynasty, first Chin. ................HSIA
dynasty, It. .........................SAVOY

38

# E

a eager.........AGOG, AVID; ARDENT
eagle, sea.....................ERN; ERNE
eagle of the Bible ...................GIER
eagle's nest ...............AERY, EYRY;
.....................AERIE, EYRIE
eaglestone............................AETITE
ear.......................LUG; HANDLE
ear, of the ..................OTIC; AURAL
earache .........................OTALGIA
ear canal ...............................SCALA
ear cavity ...........................UTRICLE
ear inflammation ....................OTITIS
earnest..............GRAVE, SOBER,
.........STAID; PLEDGE, SOMBER;
.....................SERIOUS, SINCERE
Earp brothers......................WYATT;
.........................MORGAN, VIRGIL
ear prominence ................TRAGUS
ear shell ..........ORMER; ABALONE
ear stone ........OTOLITE, OTOLITH
earth .................DIRT, LOAM, SOIL
earth, fine-grained ................CLAY
earth, wet .....................BOG, MUD;
.............................MIRE, MUCK
earth deposit in rock cavities .GUHR
earthenware maker ..........POTTER
earthly .............................TERRENE
b Earth personified .........GAEA, GAIA
earthquake ........SEISM; TEMBLOR
earthquake shock ............TREMOR
East.........ASIA; LEVANT, ORIENT
Easter ...............................PASCH
Eastern Catholic.....UNIAT; UNIATE
Eastern Orthodox synod .....SOBOR
E. Indian dye tree ..................DHAK
E. Indian fruit....................DURIAN
E. Indian herb ...............PIA; SOLA;
.........................TOPEE; SESAME
E. Indian red dye root............CHAY,
.................CHOY; CHAYA, CHOYA
E. Indian palm........................NIPA
E. Indian tanning tree ...........AMLA;
.............................EMBLIC
E. Indian term of address ......SAHIB
E. Indian timber tree ......SAL; TEAK
E. Indian tree, large ...........SIRIS;
.............................LEBBEK
east of Eden country ................NOD
east wind .............................EURUS
easy....................LAX; COZY,
.....................SOFT; FACILE,
.............GENTLE, SMOOTH
easy gait ...............................LOPE
easy job ..................SNAP; CINCH,
.........................SINECURE
eat ..............................SUP; DINE
eat away ...........................ERODE

c eaten away ..........................EROSE
eating away .....................CAUSTIC,
.............................ERODENT
eating dirt or clay .........GEOPHAGY
eccentric person .........GINK, KOOK
eccentric piece, rotating ...........CAM
ecclesiastic ......................PRELATE
ecru .......................................BEIGE
edge .................HEM, LIP, RIM;
.................HONE, WHET; BLADE,
.............................BRINK, STING;
.................BORDER; ADVANTAGE
edging ...................................PICOT
edging, make............................TAT
edible mushroom....................CEPE
edible root..........OCA, YAM; TARO;
.............................CASSAVA
edict .........LAW; DECREE, NOTICE
Edison's middle name.............ALVA
edit ...................REVISE, REDACT
Edomite city ............................PAU
Edomite king ...........................BELA
educated ....................LETTERED,
.............................LITERATE
educe ....................EVOKE; ELICIT
eel, marine ........................CONGER
eel, small ...............................GRIG
d eel, young............................ELVER
eelworm .................................NEMA
effeminate mannerisms .........CAMP
effervescence ..........................FIZZ
effervescent, make ...........AERATE
effigy .......................IDOL; DUMMY
effluvium .................AURA; VAPOR;
.............................MIASMA
effort..........CHORE, PAINS, TRIAL
effusive .............................GUSHING
eft .......................................NEWT
egg .......................................OVUM
egg, fertilized .........................ZOON
egg, insect ................................NIT
egg dish............................OMELET
egg drink................................NOG
eggs..............................OVA, ROE
eggs, fertilized ..........................ZOA
egg-shaped .............................OVAL;
.............................OVATE, OVOID
egg white, raw .......................GLAIR
ego .......................................SELF
Egyptian bird ............................IBIS
Eg. capital, former .............THEBES
Eg. Christian ...........................COPT
Eg. city, ancient ....................SAIS
Eg. cobra ...............................HAJE
Eg. crown.................................ATEF
Eg. god of pleasure ..................BES
Eg. king..............MENES; RAMSES

39

a
Eg. paper ......................PAPYRUS
Eg. Pharaoh, briefly .................TUT
Eg. sacred bird .........................IBIS
Eg. sacred bull .........................APIS
eight ....................OCTAD, OCTET
eight days after feast .............UTAS
eight notes..........................OCTAVE
Eire legislature .........................DAIL
eject ...............EMIT, OUST, SPEW
elaborate ...........................ORNATE
Elam's capital ..........................SUSA
eland .............................ANTELOPE
Elbe tributary ...............EGER, ISER
elbow ...................................ANCON
El Cid's horse ..................BABIECA
El Cid's sword ..................COLADA
elder ...................................SENIOR
eldest, in law ........................EIGNE
electric catfish .......................RAAD
electric force unit .....................VOLT
electric reluctance unit .............REL
electric unit..................AMP, MHO,
.........................OHM; FARAD,
.........................HENRY; AMPERE
electrified particle......................ION
electrode .........ANODE; CATHODE
electromagnet .......................RELAY
electron tube.....................TRIODE;
.........................KLYSTRON
elegance............................GRACE

b
elegant ..................FINE, POSH
elegist ....................................POET
elements, chemical...See page 245.
elemi .....................ANIME, COPAL
elephant, flying ..................DUMBO
elephant, Indian...................HATHI
elephant prod....................ANKUS
elevated ground ..................MESA
elevated ground, slightly.....RIDEAU
elevation of mind...........ANAGOGE
elevator, Brit. ..........................LIFT
elf .........................PIXIE; SPRITE
Elia ......................................LAMB
elicit ....................................EDUCE
elide ...............DELE, OMIT, SLUR
eliminate ................RID; DELETE,
.........................REMOVE
Elixir of Love, The heroine ....ADINA
elk, Amer. ...........MOOSE; WAPITI
elk hide .................................LOSH
elliptical .....................OVAL; OVOID
elm seed ..........................SAMARA
elongated ........................PROLATE
else ..............OTHER; OTHERWISE
elude ....................DODGE, EVADE
elude with sudden turns ..........JINK
emanation ............................AURA
embankment.....DAM; BUND, DIKE;
.........................LEVEE
embellish .................GILD; ADORN

c
embellished, overly ...........ORNATE
ember............................ASH; COAL
emblem..............BADGE; INSIGNIA
emblem of authority ..............MACE
embrace ...................HUG; CLASP;
.........................EMBODY, TAKE ON;
.........................SQUEEZE
emend.....................................EDIT
emerald ............BERYL; SMARAGD
emerge.........LOOM; ARISE, ISSUE
emetic ................................IPECAC
eminent...............................NOTED
emit.......................................VENT
emmer..................................SPELT
emmet......................................ANT
emphasis ..........ACCENT, STRESS
empire ..................................REALM
employ................USE; HIRE; PLACE
employees ....STAFF; PERSONNEL
employer ...................BOSS, USER
emporium.................MART; STORE
empty ....................BARE, IDLE,
.........................VAIN, VOID; CLEAR;
.........................HOLLOW, VACANT
emulate .................COPY; MODEL;
.........................FOLLOW; PATTERN
enamelware ......................LIMOGES
enchantress ..........CIRCE, MEDEA
encircle ......................GIRD, RING
encircled area................ENCLAVE

d
encircling band......................ZONE
enclose ......................HEM; CAGE,
.........................COOP, RING
enclosure ......PEN; YARD; ATRIUM
encomium..........PRAISE; TRIBUTE
encompass .........CIRCLE, ENGIRD
encounter ..............MEET; CLASH,
.........................RUN-IN
encountered ............................MET
encourage ..........CHEER; FOSTER
end ....................TIP; GOAL, REAR,
.........................STOP, TAIL;
.........................CEASE; FINALE, FINISH
end: music ...............................FINE
endearment ............HON; BABE,
.........................BABY; DEAR; HONEY,
.........................SUGAR; DARLING
endeavor ....TRY; ESSAY; EFFORT
ending, comparative.........-IER, -IOR
ending, superlative..................-EST
endow ...............ENDUE; INVEST
end result ......................PRODUCT
endure ...........BEAR, LAST; ABIDE
energy ........PEP, VIM, ZIP; FORCE
.........................POWER, STEAM, VIGOR
energy unit....................ERG, RAD
engage ......HIRE, MESH; PLEDGE
engaged .................................BUSY
engender ..............MAKE; SPAWN;
.........................EFFECT

a engine, fixed part of an ......STATOR
engine, gun the .........................REV
engine, rotary ...................TURBINE
English daisy......................GOWAN
Eng. dramatist .......SHAW; ORTON;
.........................PEELE; DRYDEN;
..................STOREY; SHERIDAN
Englishman in India..................RAJ
Eng. poet...............GRAY; AUDEN;
..........BLAKE, BYRON, CAREW;
.........DONNE, ELIOT; SPENDER;
......COLERIDGE; WORDSWORTH
Eng. royal house .....YORK; TUDOR
Eng. spa ..........BATH; MARGATE
Eng. spy .............................ANDRE
Eng. statesman ...........EDEN, PITT
engraver's tool ......................BURIN
engrossed...............................RAPT
enigma ................PUZZLE, RIDDLE
enlarge ...............................GROW;
..........................SWELL; DILATE,
.....................EXPAND; MAGNIFY
enlarge a hole ......................REAM
enmity...........ANIMUS; ANIMOSITY
Enoch, father of .....................CAIN
ensign ..................................FLAG
ensnare ........................NET; TRAP
entangle ...................WEB; SNARL
enter ...................BEGIN; ENROLL,
.................TAKE UP; PENETRATE

b entertain ..............AMUSE; DIVERT
enthusiasm ............ELAN; ARDOR,
.............VERVE; SPIRIT; PASSION
enthusiastic.................AVID; RABID
entice .............................BAIT, LURE,
.................TOLE; TEMPT; ALLURE
entrance ....DOOR, GATE; PORTAL
entrance, ceremonial .............ARCH
entrance, mine .......................ADIT
entreat ......................PRAY; PLEAD
entry, single ............................ITEM
entwine ...............WEAVE; ENLACE
enumerate .................LIST; COUNT
envelop ...................WRAP; ENFOLD
environment...........SCENE; MILIEU
envoy .....................................AGENT
envoy, pope's.....................LEGATE
envy ....................................COVET;
...................................BEGRUDGE
epic poetry.............EPOS; EPOPEE
epoch...................AGE, ERA; TIME;
...................................PERIOD
equal ....................TIE; EVEN, PEER
equality .......................PAR; PARITY
equilibrium ........STASIS; BALANCE
equine ..........ASS; HORSE, ZEBRA
equip ......................FIT, RIG; GEAR;
.....................OUTFIT; FURNISH
equitable ...........EVEN, FAIR, JUST
equivocate...........HEDGE; PALTER

c era................................AGE; TIME;
...................................EPOCH; PERIOD
eradicate ...............ERASE, PURGE
erase......UNDO; CLEAR; REMOVE
erect ........REAR; RAISE; UPRIGHT
ergo ....................................HENCE
ergs, ten million ...................JOULE
Eris, brother of.......................ARES
ermine, summer...................STOAT
Eros .....................................CUPID
erotic .....................................SEXY
errand boy .............................PAGE
error ............SLIP; LAPSE; MISCUE
error in print.............................TYPO
error list ...............................ERRATA
Esau .....................................EDOM
Esau, brother of ...................JACOB
Esau, father-in-law of ............ELON
Esau, grandson of ................OMAR
Esau, home of .......................SEIR
Esau, wife of .........................ADAH
escape ....................FLEE; DODGE,
.........................ELUDE; DECAMP,
.......................FLIGHT; EVASION
eschew....................................SHUN
Eskimo ...........................See Inuit.
esoteric ...........DEEP; PROFOUND
Esperanto, modified..................IDO
espy ...................SEE; SPY; SIGHT;

d ...........................................GLIMPSE
esquire .............................ARMIGER
essay ..............TRY; TEST; PAPER,
..........................THEME; ATTEMPT;
.................................ENDEAVOR
essence, rose ........................ATTAR
essential part...............CORE, PITH
establish .................BASE; FOUND
established value ......................PAR
estate, landed ......................MANOR
estate manager.................STEWARD
esteem ...................HONOR, PRIZE
ester, hydroid acid ...............IODINE
ester, oleic acid.................OLEATE
estimate ...................RATE; GAUGE;
..................................RECKON
estrade...................................DAIS
estuary ......................................RIA
Eternal City...........................ROME
eternity.........AGE, EON; INFINITY
ether compound ...................ESTER
ethereal.........AIRY; FILMY; SHEER
Ethiopian Christian language .GEEZ
Eth. Danakil people ...............AFAR
Eth. king's title ...................NEGUS
Eth. prince .............................RAS
Ethiopic .................................GEEZ
eucalyptus eater...................KOALA
eucalyptus secretion....LAAP, LERP
eucalyptus tree ......................YATE

*a*
Eucharist case ........................PYX
Eucharist cloth .....................FANON
Eucharist spoon ....................LABIS
Eucharist wafer ....................HOST
eulogy ................................ELOGE
euphemistic oath ......DANG, DARN,
.........DRAT, GOSH, HECK, JEEZ
euphorbia .........................SPURGE
eureka red..........................PUCE
Euripedes play ............MEDEA;
.................BACCHAE, ORESTES;
..................................ALCESTIS
European iris ......................ORRIS
Eur. kite ...................GLED; GLEDE
Eur. porgy ........................PARGO
Eurydice, husband of .....ORPHEUS
Eurytus, daughter of ..............IOLE
evade .......DODGE, ELUDE, SHIRK
evaluate ...............RATE; ASSESS
evangelist ..................LUKE, MARK
Evans, Mary Ann ..................ELIOT
Eve, grandson of..................ENOS
even.................TIE; FLAT; EQUAL,
.............LEVEL, PLANE; STEADY;
...............................UNVARYING
even if ..............................THOUGH
evening party ....................SOIREE
evening prayers ..............VESPERS
ever ..................................ALWAYS
evergreen ...........FIR, YEW; PINE;

*b*
..............CAROB, CEDAR, OLIVE,
.............SAVIN; CALABA, LAUREL,
.................SABINE, SPRUCE
evergreen bean ..................CAROB
evergreen genus ..................OLAX
evict...................................OUST
evident ....................CLEAR, PLAIN;
...................PATENT; VISIBLE
evil...................................BAD, MAL
evil god, Eg. ...............SET; SETH
evil intent, in law....DOLUS, FRAUD
evil spirit, Hindu ...................ASURA
evolve ...........UNFOLD; DEVELOP
exacerbate .....................IRRITATE
exact ......................EVEN, TRUE;
.........BLEED; DEMAND, EXTORT,
..........SQUARE, STRICT; PRECISE
examine ...........QUIZ, TEST, VIEW;
...........ASSAY, CHECK; INSPECT
excavate ........DIG; PION; DREDGE
excavated..............................DUG
excavation, mine ..........PIT; STOPE
exceed............TOP; BEST; OUTDO
exceedingly: music .................TRES
excellence.............MERIT; VIRTUE
excellent ..................A-ONE; PRIME
except...............................BUT; SAVE
excess .......GLUT; LUXUS, SPARE;
......................NIMIETY, SURPLUS
excess of solar year .............EPACT

*c*
exchange premium, discount ..AGIO
exchequer ......................FISC, FISK
excite ...................ELATE, ROUSE;
.......................................AROUSE
excited ......................AGOG; MANIC
excitement, public ...............FUROR
exclamation .........ACH, A-HA, BAH,
..............FIE, HAH, HEY, HOI, HUH,
.........OCH, O-HO, PAH, TCH, TSK,
.......TUT, UGH, WOW, YOW; ALAS,
....................PHEW, WHOA; ALACK
exclamation, Fr. ......................HEIN
exclamation, Ger. .................HOCH
exclamation, Irish ................ADAD,
..............AHEY; ARRAH; OCHONE
exclamation, It........................UFA
exclamation, Scot. ...................OCH
exclamation of disdain ..........POOH
exclamation of disgust ............PISH
exclamation of pain .....OUCH, YIPE
exclamation of relief ............WHEW
exclamations of delight ...AHS, OHS
exclamations of doubt ...........HAHS
exclude .....................BAR; DEBAR;
.......................EXCEPT; PROHIBIT
exclusive ...............SOLE; FANCY;
............CHOICE, SELECT, SINGLE
exclusive group ......................ELITE
exclusively ..............................ONLY
excoriate ...................DRUB, FRET,
.....................LASH; CHAFE;
....................ABRADE, SCATHE
excrement ...........DUNG; MANURE
excuse ...........PLEA; REMIT, SPARE
execrated ...............CURST, SWORE
exemplar...........MODEL; PATTERN
exertion ................................DINT
exhaust.........SAP; TIRE; DEPLETE
exigency ................................NEED
exist .....................................LIVE
existing ...................ALIVE, BEING
exit ......................LEAVE; DEPART,
.................................EGRESS

*d*
___ *ex machina*....................DEUS
expand .................GROW; DILATE;
.......................DISTEND, ENLARGE
expanse ...................SEA; SWEEP;
.....................SPREAD; BREADTH
expatriate .............................EXILE
expectation ...........................HOPE
expedite.................................EASE;
.....................HURRY; HASTEN
expedition.............................SAFARI
experienced emotions ............FELT
expert ...................................ADEPT;
.......................MASTER, WIZARD
expiate ................................ATONE
explain ..................SOLVE; DEFINE
explode .........POP; BLOW; BURST,
............................ERUPT; DEBUNK

a exploit ...................USE; DEED,
...............................FEAT; STUNT
explorer Ericson ......................LEIF
explosive letters ......................TNT
explosive sound ...................BOOM
expose..........................AIR; BARE,
...........................SHOW; DISPLAY
expression, local ..................IDIOM
expressionless...............WOODEN
expunge....DELE; ERASE; DELETE
extend ....................GROW; SWELL,
.........WIDEN; EXPAND, SPREAD;
................LENGTHEN, ELONGATE
extensive...............AMPLE, BROAD
extent..................RANGE, REACH,
.......................SCOPE; DEGREE,
.....................LENGTH; MEASURE
external covering.......HIDE, HUSK,
..............PEEL, PELT, RIND, SKIN
extirpate ................CLEAR, ERASE
extort.......BLEED, EXACT, GOUGE

extra ...............NEW; MORE, VERY; c
................ADDED, OTHER, SPARE
extract.....................DRAW; ELICIT
extraneous .......ALIEN; FOREIGN
extra page ..........................INSERT
extreme ...........................ULTRA
exudate plant .....GUM, LAC; RESIN
exude...............EMIT, OOZE, REEK
exult .........CROW; ELATE, GLORY
eye ..........ORB, SEE; GLIM, OGLE
eye, of the .............................OPTIC
eye cosmetic ......KOHL; MASCARA
eye inflammation...........STY; IRITIS
eyelash(es) ...............CILIA; CILIUM
eye layer...................................UVEA
eye of a bean ......................HILUM
eye of an insect ...............STEMMA;
...................................OCELLUS
eye part ....IRIS; CORNEA, RETINA
eye socket.............................ORBIT
eye-worm, Afr. ..........................LOA

# F

Fabian Soc. member G.B.S.; SHAW
fable ...............MYTH, TALE, YARN;
...........................STORY; LEGEND
b _Fables in Slang_ author..............ADE
fable writer ...........................AESOP
fabled .......................LEGENDARY
fabric.....BAFT DUCK, LAWN, SILK,
.......TAPA, TUKE; CREPE, MOIRE,
.......ORLON, RAYON; CANVAS
fabric, angora....................MOHAIR
fabric, bleeding .................MADRAS
fabric, camel's hair.............CAMLET
fabric, coarse cotton ............SURAT
fabric, corded ...............REP; REPP;
.........................................PIQUE
fabric, cotton .............LENO, MULL;
................DENIM, MANTA, SCRIM;
......................CALICO, CRETON,
.......................NANKIN, PENANG;
................NANKEEN; CRETONNE
fabric, curtain ..............NET; SCRIM
fabric, feltlike...........................BAIZE
fabric, figured ..................DAMASK;
...........................................PAISLEY
fabric, fuzzy .............................FELT
fabric, knitted ......................TRICOT
fabric, light wool .................ALPACA
fabric, lustrous ....POPLIN, SATEEN
fabric, mourning....................CRAPE
fabric, net..............TULLE; MALINE
fabric, plaid............MAUD; TARTAN
fabric, printed.......................BATIK
fabric, ribbed ..........CORD; PIQUE

fabric, satin .............PEKIN; ETOILE
fabric, sheer.......................GAUZE;
...................................ORGANZA
fabric, silk ..........SURAH; PONGEE, d
...........................................SAMITE
fabric, stiff ...........................WIGAN
fabric, striped.......DORIA; MADRAS
fabric, thick .............................DRAB
fabric, thick silk ....................GROS
fabric, twilled wool .............SERGE
fabric, upholstery .........BROCATEL;
...............................BROCATELLE
fabric, velvetlike finished......PANNE
fabric, wool .............FELT; SERGE;
....................MERINO; STAMMEL
fabric, worsted ...............ETAMINE
fabricate ...............................MAKE
fabric from remnants ..........MUNGO
fabric stretcher....................TENTER
face .................DIAL, LOOK, MEET;
............FRONT; FACADE, VISAGE
facet, gem ...............BEZEL, CULET
face with stone .....................REVET
facile .....................................EASY
facing of a glacier.................STOSS
fact.......................DATUM; DETAIL
faction.............SECT, SIDE; CABAL
factor.........................PART; DETAIL
factory.....................................PLANT
faculty .....KNACK, RIGHT; TALENT
fade ................DIE, DIM; WITHER
_Faerie Queene_ iron man ......TALUS
_Faerie Queene_ lady.................UNA

43

*a* Faerie Queene writer ......SPENSER
failure ........................DUD; BUST,
........................FLOP; DEFEAT
fainting ........................SYNCOPE
fair ........................JUST; CLEAR;
........................IMPARTIAL
fairway, piece of the ..............DIVOT
fairy ........................ELF, FAY; PERI;
........................PIXIE; SPRITE
fairy king ........................OBERON
fairy queen ..............MAB; TITANIA
faith, article of ........................TENET
faithful ..............TRUE; LOYAL;
........................STAUNCH
falcon ........................SAKER; MERLIN
falcon, Asian ....LAGGAR, LUGGAR
falcon, female ........................LANNER
falcon, Indian ........................SHAHIN
falcon, male ........................SAKERET
fall ..................DROP, PLOP; SPILL
fallacy ..............ERROR; IDOLUM
fallacies ........................IDOLA
fall back ........................RETREAT
fallow deer ........................ADDRA
fall short ........................FAIL
false excuse .....LIE; SUBTERFUGE
false friend ........IAGO; TRAITOR
false fruit of a rose ..................HIP
false god ........................IDOL
Falstaff's follower ..................NYM

*b* fame ..................ECLAT, KUDOS,
........................RENOWN, REPUTE
famed ........................NOTED
familiar ..............BRAZEN, VERSED;
........................ROUTINE; INTIMATE
family, Ferrara ........................ESTE
family, Florentine ..................MEDICI
family, Genoese ........................DORIA
family member ..............DAD, MOM,
..............POP, SIS; AUNT, MAMA,
..............PAPA; UNCLE; COUSIN
famous...GREAT, KNOWN, NOTED
fan ..............ROOTER; SUPPORTER
fan, swinging.......PUNKA; PUNKAH
fanatical..................RABID, ULTRA;
........................EXTREME, RADICAL
fancy ..............IDEA, WHIM; SWANK
fancy dresser..............FOP; DUDE
fanfare ........................TANTARA
fare ..................DIET, FEND, FOOD;
..............GET BY, SHIFT; MANAGE
farewell........AVE; VALE; SO LONG
farewell, Brit. ........................TA-TA
farinaceous ........................MEALY
farinaceous food ..................SAGO;
........................SALEP; FARINA
farm, tenant ........................CROFT
farmer ........................GRANGER
farmer, Soviet........................KULAK
farm group ........................GRANGE

farmyard, S. Afr. ..................WERF    *c*
Faroe Islands magistrate ......FOUD,
........................FOWD
Farouk, father of ..................FUAD
fashion .........FORM, MAKE, MODE,
........................MOLD; MODEL, STYLE
fasten .......PIN; BOLT, LOCK, NAIL,
.......SEAL, TACK; RIVET; ATTACH
fasten: naut. ......BELAY; BATTEN
fastener................NUT, PIN; BRAD,
..............CLIP, HASP, NAIL, SNAP,
........................STUD; CLASP, RIVET;
........................CLEVIS, COTTER
fastener, wire........................STAPLE
fastener, wood........................FID,
........................PEG; DOWEL
fastening........................LATCH
fastening post: naut. ..............BITT;
........................BOLLARD
fastidious........................FUSSY
........................PICKY; DAINTY
fast month ........................RAMADAN
fast period, Rom. Cath. ..........LENT
fat ........................LARD, OILY,
..................SUET; OBESE, STOUT,
........................THICK; PORTLY
fat, animal........................TALLOW
fat, liquid part of..................OLEIN
fat, of........................SEBACEOUS
fat, solid part of................STEARIN

fatal ........................DEADLY,    *d*
........................LETHAL, MORTAL
fate ..............LOT; DOOM; KISMET
fateful ........................DIRE
Fate in Gr. mythology..........MOIRA
Fates, The Three ..........CLOTHO;
..................ATROPOS; LACHESIS
father .....DAD, POP; SIRE; BEGET,
..............DADDY, PADRE; PRIEST
father: Arabic ................ABU; ABOU
father: Heb. ........................ABBA
father's side kinship..........AGNATE
fathom ........................GRASP,
........................PROBE, SOUND
fatigue.........TIRE; DRAIN, WEARY
Fatima, husband of....................ALI
fatty ........................ADIPOSE
fatty gland secretion ..........SEBUM
fatuous........................INANE
faucet ...........TAP; COCK; SPIGOT
fault finder ........................MOMUS
faulty ........................BAD; FLAWED
faux pas ..............ERROR, GAFFE
favor .........GAIN; GRACE, HONOR
favorable vote ..................AYE, YES
favorite ........................PET; IDOL
fawn color................................FAON
fawning favorite..................MINION
FDR's coin ........................DIME
FDR's dog ........................FALA

a fear ...................DREAD; HORROR,
.........................PHOBIA, TERROR
fearful .......DIRE; AWFUL; AGHAST
feast..................DEVOUR, RELISH,
.........................SPREAD; BANQUET
Feast of Lanterns (Jap.) ...........BON
Feast of Tabernacles (Heb.) ...........
..................................................SUKKOT
feather ......PENNA, PINNA, PLUME
feathered scarf .........................BOA
feather grass..........................STIPA
feather palms .......................EJOO;
..................................................GOMUTI
feathers, molt ...........................MEW
feathers, soft ...........DOWN; EIDER
federal agent...........G-MAN, T-MAN
federal agents .........G-MEN, T-MEN
feeble .......................PUNY, WEAK;
...........FAINT, MUTED; TENUOUS
feel ................................AIR; GROPE,
.........................SENSE, THINK,
.............TOUCH, YEARN; FINGER
...........INTUIT, HANDLE; BELIEVE
feeler...................PALP; ANTENNA
feet, having .......................PEDATE
feet, of ...................................PEDAL
feign.............................ACT; FAKE,
.........................SHAM; PUT ON
feline ..........................................CAT
b fellow ..........BUB, BUD, GUY, JOE,
.........................LAD, MAC, PAL;
.....................CHAP, CHUM, GENT;
.........................BLOKE, BUDDY
female....GAL; DAME, DOLL, GIRL,
...................LADY, LASS; BROAD,
.............CHICK, WENCH, WOMAN
female insect...........................GYNE
fence, steps over a.................STILE
fence, sunken and hidden.....HA-HA
fence of shrubs....................HEDGE
fence of stakes ................PALISADE
fencing guard position ..........SIXTE;
.........................OCTAVE, QUARTE,
.........................QUINTE, TIERCE,
.................SECONDE, SEPTIME
fencing hit ...........................PUNTO
fencing sword ..............EPEE, FOIL;
..................................................SABER
fencing term ....................TOUCHE
fencing thrust ......LUNGE; REMISE;
.................PASSADO, RIPOSTE
ferment ...................................YEAST
fern, climbing..........................NITO
fern, edible.............................TARA
fern "seed"............................SPORE
fern spore cluster(s) ..............SORI;
..................................................SORUS
Ferrara patron of the arts........ESTE
ferrum......................................IRON
ferryman ...........................CHARON

fertilizer .................MARL; GUANO;    c
..................................................MANURE
fertilizer, banned ......................DDT
fertilizer ingredient..................UREA
fervent.......KEEN; FIERY; ARDENT
fervor.................ZEAL, ZEST; ARDOR
fester..........ROT; DECAY; RANKLE
festival .........................FAIR, FETE,
.........................GALA; FIESTA
festival, Creek Indian.............BUSK
festival, Gr. .................AGON; DELIA
fetal membrane ......................CAUL
fetish ....................OBI; JUJU, OBIA,
.................ZEMI; CHARM; GRI-GRI
fetter.............GYVE, IRON; CHAIN;
.................SHACKLE; HANDCUFF
feudal benefice .........................FEU
feudal estate .................FEUD, FIEF
feudal land .....................BENEFICE
feudal tenant ......................VASSAL
fever, intermittent .................AGUE;
..................................................TERTIAN
feverish ...........................FEBRILE
fez .................................TARBOOSH
fiber ..........................PITA; RAFFIA,
.................STAPLE, THREAD
fiber, bark ...TAPA; OLONA, TERAP
fiber, cordage ...........COIR, FERU,
.................HEMP, IMBE, JUTE;
..................................ABACA, SISAL
fiber, hat or basket .................DATIL    d
fiber, textile ............................SABA
fiber, woody ...........................BAST
fiberboard substance ......BAGASSE
fiber from palms ....................ERUC
fiber knot .................................NEP.
fiber plant......ISTLE, IXTLE, RAMIE
fiber plant, Braz. .................CAROA;
..................................................PINGUIN
fiber plant, E. Indian...............SUNN
fibers, knotted .........................NOIL
fiddle, medieval ....GIGA; GIGUE
fiddler crab genus ....................UCA
field...................LEA; ACRE, AREA;
.............CROFT, REALM; DOMAIN
field deity.........................PAN; FAUN
field stubble ........................ROWEN
fight..........FRAY; MELEE; BATTLE
fight, two-man .........................DUEL
figurative usage ...................TROPE
figure ...................................SOLID
figure, five-sided ..........PENTAGON
figure, four-sided ........TETRAGON
figure, multi-sided...........POLYGON
figure, oval .......................ELLIPSE
figure, six-sided..............HEXAGON
figure, ten-sided ..............DECAGON
figure of speech ..................TROPE;
.................SIMILE; METAPHOR
figure with equal angles.....ISOGON

45

a
| | |
|---|---|
| Fijian chestnut | RATA |
| Fijian sarong | SULU |
| filament | HAIR; FIBER |
| filament, plant | ELATER |
| filament of flax | HARL; HARLE |
| filch | STEAL, SWIPE |
| file | ROW; LINE, RANK, TIER; QUEUE; COLUMN |
| file, coarse | RASP |
| file, three-square single-cut | CARLET |
| filefish | LIJA |
| filled completely | SATED; REPLETE |
| fillet | BONE, ORLE, ORLO |
| fillip | PROD, PUSH, SPUR |
| film, green | PATINA |
| film yeast | FLOR |
| filthy | VILE |
| filthy lucre | PELF |
| finale: music | CODA |
| finch | LINNET, SISKIN |
| finch, Eur. | TARIN, SERIN |
| finch, S. Afr. | FINK |
| find fault | CARP; CAVIL |
| fine, as a line | LEGER |
| fine, punish by | AMERCE |
| fine, record of | ESTREAT |
| finesse | ART; SKILL |
| finger | DIGIT, THUMB; TOUCH; PINKIE; MINIMUS, POINTER |

b
| | |
|---|---|
| finger cymbals | CASTANETS |
| finger inflammation | FELON; WHITLOW |
| fingerless glove | MITT; MITTEN |
| finger nail half-moon | LUNULA |
| fingerprint pattern | WHORL |
| finger-throwing game | MORA |
| finisher | EDGER, ENDER |
| finishing tool | REAMER |
| Finland, in Finnish | SUOMI |
| Finnish steam bath | SAUNA |
| firearm | GUN; RIFLE; MAUSER, PISTOL; CARBINE; REVOLVER |
| fire basket (torch) | CRESSET |
| fire bullet | TRACER |
| firecracker | PETARD |
| fired clay | TILE |
| firedog | ANDIRON |
| fire god | VULCAN |
| fire opal, Fr. | GIRASOL |
| fireplace | GRATE; INGLE; HEARTH |
| fireplace side shelf | HOB |
| firewood bundle | FAGOT |
| fireworks | GERB; GERBE |
| firm | FAST; STEADY; COMPANY, STAUNCH |

c
| | |
|---|---|
| firmament | SKY |
| firn | NEVE |
| firs' genus, true | ABIES |
| first | PRIME; INITIAL |
| first, went | LED |
| first appearance | DEBUT |
| firstborn | ELDEST, SENIOR |
| firstborn, in law | EIGNE |
| first day of the month, Rom. | CAL, KAL; CALENDS |
| First Ladies, US | See page 190. |
| first miracle site | CANA |
| first part in a duet | PRIMO |
| first place, took | WON |
| first principles | ABCS |
| first-rate | ACE; A-ONE |
| fish | ANGLE, TRAWL, TROLL |
| fish, alligator | GAR |
| fish, ancient | ELOPS |
| fish, aquarium | GUPPY, LOACH, MOLLY, TETRA; GOURAMI |
| fish, Atl. | TAUTOG; ESCOLAR, TAUTAUG |
| fish, bait | CHUB |
| fish, boned | FILLET |
| fish, bony | CARP; TELEOST |
| fish, butterfly | BLENNY; CHITON |
| fish, carplike | DACE, RUDD |
| fish, Caspian Sea | STERLET |

d
| | |
|---|---|
| fish, codlike | CUSK, HAKE, LING, TUSK |
| fish, colorful | BOCE, OPAH |
| fish, cyprinoid | IDE; ORFE |
| fish, dolphin | MAHI-MAHI |
| fish, elongated | EEL, GAR; PIKE |
| fish, flat | DAB, RAY; SOLE; BRILL, FLUKE; FLOUNDER |
| fish, Florida freshwater | TARPON |
| fish, game | BASS; TROUT |
| fish, garden pond | KOI |
| fish, Great Lakes | CISCO, PERCH |
| fish, Hawaiian | AKU |
| fish, herringlike | SHAD |
| fish, hook for | GIG; GAFF; DRAIL |
| fish, linglike | COD |
| fish, mackerellike | CERO; TINKER |
| fish, nest-building | ACARA |
| fish, N. Z. | IHI |
| fish, parasitic | REMORA |
| fish, perchlike | DARTER |
| fish, piece of | FILLET |
| fish, silvery | MULLET |
| fish, sparoid | SARGO |
| fish, spiny | GOBY; PERCH |
| fish, sucker | PEGA; REMORA |

a fish, tropical ......................GUASA,
................................SARGO, SNOOK;
.......................ROBALO; GROUPER
   fish, young ...............................FRY
   fish by trolling ......................DRAIL
   fish cleaner .......................SCALER
   fish eggs................................ROE
   fisherman's hut, Orkney .........SKEO
   fish from a boat...................TROLL
   fishhook line-leader ..............SNELL
   fishhook point........................BARB
   fishing line ......SNELL, TRAWL
   fishing line cork .........BOB; BOBBIN
   fishing line, multihooked ....SPILLER
   fishing trip, Scot. herring .....DRAVE
   fish net .................SEINE, TRAWL;
........................................SPILLER
   fish-pitching prong........PEW; GAFF
   fish-poison tree ......................BITO
   fish sauce ...............................ALEC
   fish sign..............................PISCES
   fish sperm .............................MILT
   fish trap ...............................WEIR
   fish whisker .......................BARBEL
   fish with bait on the surface .....DAP,
.............................................DIB
   fissure .......................RIFT, RIMA;
................BREAK, CHINK, CLEFT,
..............................CRACK, SPLIT
   fissures, full of ...................RIMOSE

b fist...........................NEAF; NIEVE
   fit............APT; RIPE, SUIT; ADAPT
   fit for cultivation .................ARABLE
   fit of sulks....................FUNK, HUFF
   fit of temper.................SNIT; PIQUE
   fit to drink...........................POTABLE
   five, group of.....................PENTAD
   five-dollar bill ....................FIN, VEE
   five-franc piece .......................ECU
   five of trump ........................PEDRO
   fixed charge ...........................FEE
   fix or fixed............................SET
   flaccid ...................................LIMP
   flag ...........................TIRE; ENSIGN
   flag, military.......................GUIDON
   flag's corner ......................CANTON
   flank ....................................SIDE
   flap ......................................TAB
   flaring edge ...............LIP; FLANGE
   flat .................DRAB, DULL, EVEN;
...............................LEVEL, PLANE,
..............................STALE; INSIPID
   flat-bottomed boat.....DORY, PUNT,
...............................SCOW; BARGE
   flatten .................LEVEL; SMOOTH
   flatter ...................SUIT; BECOME;
.........................................BLANDISH
   flattery, Irish....................BLARNEY
   flavor...........LACE, TANG; AROMA,
...............................SAPOR; SEASON

flax, soak................................RET c
   flee......................LAM, RUN; BOLT
   fleece ...................WOOL; SWINDLE
   fleet............FAST, NAVY; ARMADA
   fleet, merchant ..................ARGOSY
   fleur-de-lis ............................LILY
   flexible ...........................AGILE;
...........................PLIANT, SUPPLE
   flight, Mohammed's ...........HEJIRA
   flightless birds, of ...............RATITE
   flight organ ...........................WING
   Flintstones characters ...........DINO,
................................FRED; BETTY,
..........................WILMA; BAM BAM,
.........................BARNEY; PEBBLES
   flip .....................SCAN, SKIM, TOSS
   flit.....................FLY, GAD; FLUTTER
   float ...............BUOY, RAFT, WAFT
   floating ...............................NATANT
   floating masses of weeds ......SUDD
   floating wreckage ...........FLOTSAM
   flock, small ...........................COVEY
   flock of fowl in flight ...............SKEIN
   flock of quail .........................BEVY
   flock of swans .......................BANK
   flog .................BEAT, LASH, WHIP
   flood .......................SEA; EAGRE,
.............................SPATE; DELUGE;
..........................FRESHET, TORRENT
   floodgate ..................CLOW; SLUICE
   floor covering .......MAT, PAD, RUG; d
...........................................CARPET
   flora and fauna .....................BIOTA
   floral leaf ...............BRACT, SEPAL
   Florentine family ..................MEDICI
   Florida tree .............................MABI
   flounder ..........DAB; SOLE; FLUKE;
...........................PLAICE, WALLOW
   flourish, musical ..............ROULADE
   flour sieve ..........................BOLTER
   flow...............................RUN; FLUX
   flower, Easter...........................LILY
   flower, fall ..........ASTER; COSMOS
   flower, field .........................GOWAN
   flower, new ..............................BUD
   flower, Oriental ...................LOTUS
   flower, showy ........................CALLA
   flower cluster .......CYME; ANADEM,
...........................................RACEME
   flower holder...........................VASE
   flower part .............PETAL, SEPAL;
..........................CARPEL, SPADIX
   flower spike .......................AMENT
   flow out ........................EMIT; SPILL
   fluctuate ............................WAVER
   fluent ...................................GLIB
   fluff of yarn ............................LINT
   fluid(s), medical .......SERA; SERUM
   fluidity unit ...............................RHE
   flume ...................SHUTE; SLUICE

a flunk.................................................FAIL
flushed............................................RED
flute, ancient.................................TIBIA
flute, small....................................FIFE
flutter......................FLAP, LUFF,
.............................WAVE; HOVER
fly ............................SOAR, WING;
.......................GLIDE; AVIATE
fly, Afr. ...............................TSE-TSE
fly, artificial..............................HARL
fly, small.................GNAT; MIDGE
fly agaric..........................AMANITA
flycatcher.........ALDER, PEWEE;
...................................PHOEBE
flying ........................................VOLANT
*Flying Dutchman* girl ...........SENTA
flying fox.......................KALONG
flying lemur......................COLUGO
flying saucer ...........................UFO
foam................SUDS; LATHER
fodder, store ...................ENSILE
fodder building ....................SILO
fog.......................DAZE, HAZE,
.................MIST, MURK; GLOOM;
.................STUPOR; OBSCURE
foist...............................FOB; IMPOSE
fold..........PLY; RUGA; PLEAT;
...................CREASE, DOUBLE
folded like a fan ................PLICATE
fold of skin ...........................PLICA

b folds, arrange in ................DRAPE
folio ..................................PAGE
folk dance, Slavic ................KOLO
folklore monster..................TROLL
folkways ...........................MORES
follow ................DOG; TAIL;
..........ENSUE, TRACE; COMPLY,
.....................PURSUE, SHADOW
foment............................ABET
fondle ...................PET; CARESS
font ..................LAVER, STOUP
food ..............EATS, FARE, MEAT,
..............MENU; MANNA; ALIMENT
food, bit of.............................ORT
food, provide with................CATER
food, soft ..................................PAP
food, unappetizing.................SLOP
food for animals..............FORAGE
food forbidden Israelites ........TREF;
.................TEREFA; TEREFAH
food of the gods................AMRITA;
.................................AMBROSIA
fool ..................ASS; DOLT, DUPE,
................JERK, SIMP; BLUFF;
.......COZEN, IDIOT, NINNY, TRICK
foolish............DAFT, ZANY; INANE,
.................SILLY; ASININE
fool's bauble ..................MAROTTE
fool's gold.............................PYRITE
foot, animal's .................PAD, PAW

c foot, Gr. poetic ......................IONIC
foot, having a ....................PEDATE
foot, poetic ...........IAMB; ANAPEST
foot, two-syllable............SPONDEE;
...................................TROCHEE
foot, verse .........................DACTYL
footless .................APOD; APODAL
footlike structure .....................PES
foot part, horse's .............PASTERN
foot soldier ...........................PEON
foot soldier, Irish ......KERN; KERNE
footstalk, leaf or flower .........STRIG
footstool...................MORA, POUF;
.................HASSOCK, OTTOMAN
for ........................................PRO
forage plant ..................ALSIKE,
.................LUCERN; ALFALFA
forage plant, Indian ...............GUAR
foramen.................................PORE
foray .....................................RAID
forbidden .................TABU; TABOO;
............................,.........BANNED
Forbidden City......................LHASA
forbidding ..........................STERN
force................VIM; CREW, TEAM;
.........CORPS, POWER; COERCE,
.......COMPEL, DURESS, ENERGY;
..................................PRESSURE
force, unit of ........................DYNE
foreboding ...........................OMEN

d forefather..............................SIRE
forehead...............................BROW
forehead, of the ..............METOPIC
foreigner in Hawaii ...............HAOLE
foreign in origin ................EXOTIC
foreign trade discount ............AGIO
foremost part................BOW, VAN;
...................................FRONT
foremost segment of an insect.........
...................................ACRON
foreordain ........................DESTINE
foreshadow .........................BODE
forest, Braz. .........................MATTA
forestall ................AVERT, DETER;
...................................PREVENT
forest clearing .....................GLADE
forest ox ............................ANOA
forests, of ......................SYLVAN;
..................................NEMORAL
forest warden ..................RANGER
foretell...............AUGUR; PREDICT
foretoken ............................OMEN
forever, in poetry ..............ETERNE
for fear that..............................LEST
forfeit ........................DROP, LOSE
forgetfulness fruit .................LOTUS
forgetfulness water .............LETHE
forgive .................REMIT; EXCUSE,
...................................PARDON
forgiving ...........................CLEMENT

48

a forgo ........................WAIVE, YIELD;
........................................ABANDON
formation, military ..........ECHELON
former ........................................ERST
formerly ....................................ONCE
formic acid source ......................ANT
formula ..........RECIPE; EQUATION
forsaken ....................................LORN
for shame ...................................FIE
fort ....................REDAN; CITADEL
fort, US military..............DIX, ORD;
........................KNOX, SILL; BLISS,
........................BRAGG; EUSTIS
forth ............................................OUT
forthwith....................................NOW
fortification........REDAN; REDOUBT
fortification, ditchside.........ESCARP
fortification, slope ..................TALUS
fortification of felled trees ....ABATIS
fortified place, Irish.............LIS; LISS
fortify ..............................ARM, MAN
forward ....................PERT; AHEAD,
........................SASSY; FOSTER;
................PROMOTE, REROUTE
foul-smelling ............OLID; FETID
........................REEKY; FOETID
found ............................ESTABLISH
foundation ..................BASE; BASIS
four, group of ....................TETRAD
four-inch measure ..................SPAN
b fourth estate ........................PRESS
fowl ...............HEN; CAPON, POULT
fowl's gizzard, etc. ..............GIBLET
fox, Afr. desert ....................FENNEC
fox, S. Afr. ............ASSE; CAAMA
fox-hunters' coats ..................PINKS
Fox River tribe ........................SAUK
fraction ............PART; DECIMAL
*Fra Diavolo* composer .........AUBER
fragment of pottery ..............SHARD
fragrant ..........................SCENTED;
........................................REDOLENT
frail piece ...............................WISP
frame, supporting.............TRESTLE
framework ..............................TRUSS
France, once ........................GAUL
franchise ............VOTE; CHARTER
Franciscan....................MINORITE
frank............................................OPEN;
................CANDID, HONEST
Frankenstein's assistant .........IGOR
frankincense..................OLIBANUM
fraud ........................................SHAM
fraught ....................................LADEN
fray.........................................MELEE
free..........RID; GRATIS; UNLOOSE
freebooter................................PIRATE
freedman in Kentish law..........LAET
freedom, briefly ..........................LIB
free-for-all.................FRAY; MELEE

freeman, A.-S. ....................CEORL c
freight car ......................GONDOLA
French art group ....DADA; FAUVES
Fr. artist....................DORE, DUFY,
................GROS; COROT, DEGAS,
..........MANET, MONET; BRAQUE,
........................RENOIR; CHAGALL,
........................MATISSE, UTRILLO
Fr. author .........SUE; GIDE, HUGO,
....................LOTI, ZOLA; CAMUS,
........................DUMAS, RENAN,
........................VERNE; RACINE,
........................SARTRE; COCTEAU
Fr. business abbreviation ..........CIE
Fr. chalk ..................................TALC
Fr. coin, old ..............................SOU
Fr. detective force..............SURETE
Fr. dramatist ......................RACINE
Fr. ecclesiastical city .............SENS
Fr. explorer.........CABOT; CARTIER
Fr. exclamation ........................HEIN
Fr. fort, Battle of Verdun .........VAUX
Fr. general..............FOCH; HOCHE
................GAMELIN; DEGAULLE
Fr.-Ger. region......................SAAR
Fr. historic provinces ............FOIX,
........................NICE; ANJOU, AUNIS,
..............BEARN, BERRY, CORSE,
........................MAINE; ALSACE,
........................ARTOIS, MARCHE,
........................POITOU, SAVOIE d
Fr. lace-making town ..........CLUNY
Fr. marshal................NEY; MURAT
Fr. meat dish ........................SALMI
Fr. months (in order)........JANVIER,
........................FEVRIER, MARS,
........................AVRIL, MAI,
................JUIN, JUILLET, AOUT,
..............SEPTEMBRE, OCTOBRE,
..............NOVEMBRE, DECEMBRE
Fr. philosopher ....................COMTE
Fr. premier, former................LAVAL
Fr. priest ....................ABBE, PERE
Fr. pronoun.............CES, ILS, MES,
................TOI, UNE; ELLE; ELLES
Fr. psychologist ....................BINET
Fr. revolutionary ..................MARAT
Fr. sculptor ..........................RODIN
Fr. singer .................PIAF; SABLON
Fr. soldier ..............................POILU
Fr. soprano..........PONS; CALVE
Fr. statesman ........................COTY
FRENCH WORDS:
........after................................APRES
........again ............................ENCORE
........airplane............................AVION
........alas ................................HELAS
........all ........................TOUS, TOUT
........among ..........................ENTRE
........arm....................................BRAS

#### French words (article / read)

a FRENCH WORDS: *continued*

| | |
|---|---|
| article | LAS, LES, UNE |
| at the home of | CHEZ |
| aunt | TANTE |
| baby | BEBE |
| back | DOS |
| bacon | LARD |
| bath | BAIN |
| be, to | ETRE |
| beach | GREVE, PLAGE |
| beast | BETE |
| before | AVANT |
| between | ENTRE |
| bitter | AMER |
| black | NOIR |
| blue | AZUR, BLEU |
| bridge | PONT |
| but | MAIS |
| cabbage | CHOU |
| cake | GATEAU |
| carefully groomed | SOIGNE |
| carriage | FIACRE; VOITURE |
| case or box | ETUI |
| chicken | POULET; POUSSIN |
| child | ENFANT |
| cloud | NUE; NUAGE |
| cock (rooster) | COQ |
| cup | COUPE, TASSE |
| dance, formal | BAL |
| daughter | FILLE |

b

| | |
|---|---|
| dear | CHER |
| deed | FAIT |
| devil | DEMON; DIABLE |
| dirty | SALE |
| donkey | ANE; BAUDET |
| down with | A BAS |
| dream | REVE; SONGE |
| duke | DUC |
| dungeon | CACHOT |
| east | EST |
| egg | OEUF |
| enamel | EMAIL |
| encore! | BIS |
| equal | EGAL |
| evening | SOIR |
| evil | MAL |
| father | PERE |
| fear | PEUR |
| finally | ENFIN |
| fingering | DOIGTE |
| fire | FEU |
| five | CINQ |
| friend, female | AMIE |
| friend, male | AMI |
| friends | AMIS |
| game(s) | JEU; JEUX |
| gift | DON; CADEAU |
| God | DIEU |
| good | BON |
| good-bye | ADIEU; AU REVOIR |

c

| | |
|---|---|
| gravy | JUS |
| gray | GRIS |
| ground | TERRE |
| hall | SALLE |
| handle | ANSE; MANCHE |
| head | CHEF, TETE |
| health | SANTE |
| here | ICI |
| his | SES |
| hour | HEURE |
| house | MAISON |
| husband | MARI; EPOUX |
| idea | IDEE |
| in | DANS |
| is | EST |
| island | ILE |
| kind | SORTE |
| king | ROI |
| lamb | AGNEAU |
| land | TERRE |
| laugh | RIRE |
| laughter | RISEE |
| law | LOI; DROIT |
| leather | CUIR |
| left | GAUCHE |
| lily | LIS |
| little | PEU; EXIGU |
| lively | GAI, VIF; VIVANT |
| lodging place | GITE |
| low | BAS |

d

| | |
|---|---|
| maid | BONNE |
| mail | POSTE |
| mask, black velvet | LOUP |
| me | MOI |
| milk | LAIT |
| mine | A MOI |
| mother | MERE |
| mount | MONT |
| museum | MUSEE |
| nail | CLOU; ONGLE |
| name | NOM |
| near | PRES; PROCHE |
| night | NUIT |
| no | NON |
| nose | NEZ |
| nothing | RIEN; NEANT |
| on | SUR |
| one | UNE |
| our | NOUS |
| out | HORS; DEHORS |
| over | SUR |
| pork | PORC |
| pout | MOUE |
| pretty | JOLI; JOLIE |
| queen | REINE |
| quickly | VITE |
| rabbit | LAPIN |
| railway station | GARE |
| raw | CRU |
| read | LIRE |

## a FRENCH WORDS: *continued*

| | |
|---|---|
| rifle range | TIR |
| riot | EMEUTE |
| river | RIVIERE |
| roast | ROTI; ROTIR |
| salt | SEL; SALE |
| school | ECOLE, LYCEE |
| sea | MER; MARIN |
| senior | AINE |
| servant | BONNE |
| she | ELLE |
| sheath | ETUI |
| sheep | MOUTON |
| shelter | ABRI |
| shine | LUIRE; LUSTRE |
| shooting match | TIR |
| sickness | MALADIE |
| silk | SOIE |
| small | MENU; PETIT |
| soldier | SOLDAT |
| some | DES |
| son | FILS |
| soul or spirit | AME |
| spring | PRINTEMPS |
| star | ETOILE |
| state | ETAT |
| storm | ORAGE |
| summer | ETE |
| there! | VOILA |
| they | ILS; ELLES |

## b

| | |
|---|---|
| thirty | TRENTE |
| thou | TOI |
| too much | TROP |
| towards | VERS |
| under | SOUS |
| upon | SUR |
| us | NOUS |
| very | TRES |
| vineyard | VIGNE |
| wall | MUR |
| water(s) | EAU; EAUX |
| wave | ONDE; VAGUE |
| well | BIEN |
| wine | VIN |
| winter | HIVER |
| with | AVEC |
| without | SANS |
| wolf | LOUP |
| woods | BOIS |
| yes | OUI |
| yesterday | HIER |
| you | TOI; VOUS |
| your | VOTRE |
| frenzied | AMOK |
| frequently | OFTEN |
| fresh | NEW; NOVEL |
| freshet | FLOOD, SPATE |
| freshwater worm | NAID, NAIS |
| Freud, translator of | BRILL |
| Freudian concepts | IDS |

## c

| | |
|---|---|
| Freudian stage | ANAL |
| friar | FRA; MONK |
| friar, mendicant | SERVITE |
| friction-reduction device | GIB |
| Friendly Islands | TONGA |
| friends | CIRCLE, CLIQUE |
| friendship | AMITY |
| frigate bird, Hawaiian | IOA, IWA |
| Frigg, husband of | ODIN |
| fright | FEAR; DREAD, PANIC |
| frighten | ALARM, SCARE |
| frill, neck | RUFF; JABOT |
| fringe benefit | PERK |
| fringe of curls or bangs | FRISETTE |
| frisk | PLAY, ROMP; |
| | SEARCH |
| frog genus | RANA |
| frogs, of | RANINE |
| frolic | LARK, PLAY, ROMP; |
| | CAPER, SPORT, SPREE |
| from head-to-foot | CAP-A-PIE |
| front | HEAD, FORE; |
| | FACADE, FACING |
| frontier post | FORT |
| frontiersman | BOONE; CARSON; |
| | CROCKETT |
| frost | ICE; HOAR, RIME |
| froth | FOAM; SPUME |
| frown | GLARE, SCOWL; |
| | GLOWER |

## d

| | |
|---|---|
| frugal | THRIFTY, PRUDENT |
| fruit | FIG; IMBU, LIME, |
| | PEAR, PLUM, UGLI; APPLE, |
| | BERRY, CACAO, GRAPE, |
| | GUAVA, ICACO, ILAMA, |
| | LEMON, OLIVE, PEACH, |
| | PRUNE; BANANA, |
| | DAMSON, DURIAN, FEIJOA, |
| | JUJUBE, LITCHI, LOQUAT, |
| | MEDLAR, ORANGE, |
| | PIPPIN, QUINCE, RAISIN, |
| | SAPOTE; TANGELO |
| fruit, Afr. | AKEE; ACKEE |
| fruit, decay of overripe | BLET |
| fruit, dry | ACHENE |
| fruit, fleshy | POME |
| fruit, hard-shelled | NUT; GOURD |
| fruit, interior of a | PITH, PULP |
| fruit, lemonlike | CITRON |
| fruit, plumlike | SLOE |
| fruit, pulpy | UVA; DRUPE |
| fruit, southern | PAPAW |
| fruit, tropical | DATE; MANGO |
| fruit, vine | MELON |
| fruit, yellow tropical | PAPAYA |
| fruit dish | COMPOTE |
| fruiting spike | EAR |
| fruit of a maple | SAMARA |
| frustrate | STYMIE, THWART |
| fry lightly | SAUTE |

a fuel .........................GAS, LOG, OIL;
.....................................COAL, COKE
fuel, rocket ................................LOX
fuel, turf.................................PEAT
fuel ship ............................TANKER
Fugard heroine .....................LENA
fugue theme ...........................DUX
fulcrum, oar's .....................THOLE
full...............................PLENARY
Fulton's steamboat ......CLERMONT
fume .......................REEK; SMOKE
fun...............................SPORT
function ............USE; ROLE, WORK
function, trigonometric .............SINE;
.........................COSINE, SECANT
fundamental .........................BASIC
funeral bell .........................KNELL

funeral music .......................DIRGE c
funeral notice .........................OBIT
funeral oration......................ELOGE
funeral pile..........................PYRE
fungus..........................AGARIC
fungus, edible....MOREL; TRUFFLE
fungus, white-spored........AMANITA
fur, in Heraldry ......................VAIR
Furies, Gr. .....................ERINYES
Furies, Rom. .....................DIRAE
Furies, the.....ALECTO; MAGAERA;
.....................................TISIPHONE
furlongs, eight .........................MILE
furtive ...................SLY; SNEAKY
fury ..........................................IRE
furze .......................WHIN; GORSE
fuss ............ADO; TO-DO; BOTHER

# G

gabi .........................TARO
gadget ......................GIZMO
Gaelic ...............ERSE; CELTIC
Gaelic poem, division of a ......DUAN
gaff ..........................SPAR
gain.......GET, WIN; EARN; PROFIT
gait .................LOPE, PACE, TROT;
b ........................CANTER, GALLOP
Galahad, mother of .............ELAINE
Galatea's beloved..................ACIS
Galilee town ...........................CANA
gallery, art..............................SALON
gallery, open....................LOGGIA
galley.........................BIREME;
.....................TRIREME, UNIREME
galley, fast....................DROMOND
gallop, rapid .....................TANTIVY
gallop slowly .........................LOPE
gal of song .........................SAL
Galsworthy heroine ..............IRENE
Galway Bay isles..................ARAN
gamble..................WAGER; BET; RISK;
.....................WAGER; CHANCE;
.....................HAZARD; VENTURE
gambling, legal: Abbr. ..............OTB
gambling game, bingolike ......KENO
gambling location ..............CASINO
gambol.................DIDO; CAPER
game.......FUN; PLAY; SPORT;
.......PLUCKY; GALLANT, VALIANT
game, Basque...................PELOTA
game, dice .........................LUDO
game, equipmentless ..............TAG
game, guessing....MORA; CANUTE
gamecock.........................STAG
gamekeeper.....................RANGER
game of skill............POOL; CHESS

game piece ...........................MAN
gaming cubes .......................DICE
Ganda dialect .......................SOGA
Ganges boat .......................PUTELI
gangplank ..........................RAMP
gangrene precursor..............NOMA
gangster.........MUG; HOOD; THUG
gangster's gal.......................MOLL d
gap ...................HIATUS, LACUNA
gap, hedge ...........MUSE; MEUSE
gardening tool ........................HOE;
.....................................RAKE; SPADE
garden invader ......................WEED
garden plot..............................BED
garland ...................LEI; ANADEM;
.....................................CHAPLET
garment..........COAT, ROBE, SLIP;
.................CLOAK, DRESS, SHIFT;
.................SHIRT, SKIRT, TUNIC;
.................BLOUSE, JACKET
garment, Anglican bishop's.........
.....................................CHIMERE
garment, Arab .........................ABA
garment, fitted ..................REEFER;
.....................................LEOTARD
garment, Hindu .......SARI; BANYAN
garment, Jewish high priest's.........
.....................................EPHOD
garment, loose ....CYMAR; CAMISE
garment, Malay...................SARONG
garment, Muslim women's.......IZAR
garment, N. Afr. ..........HAIK; HAICK
garment, outer.................CAPOTE;
.....................................PALETOT
garment, Polynesian ............PAREU
garment, priest's .........ALB; COPE;
.....................................AMICE, STOLE

a garment, rain ......................PONCHO
garment, Renaissance.........SIMAR,
.................................................SYMAR
garment, scarflike ................TIPPET
garment, Turk. .................DOLMAN
garment, woman's.............BODICE,
.................................................MANTUA
garnishment ..............................LIEN
garret ........................................ATTIC
gas......................................FUEL; BLAST
gas, charge with ...................AERATE
gas, inert .............ARGON, XENON
gas, radioactive......RADON, NITON
gas apparatus...................AERATOR
gas for colored lights ............NEON
gastropod .............WHELK; LIMPET
gate.......................................PORTAL
gate, water .........................SLUICE
gateway ..................................PYLON
gateway, Buddhist temple ...TORAN
gateway, Chin. commemorative......
.................................................PAI-LOU
gateway, Jap. ........................TORII
gateway, Pers. ..........................DAR
gateway, Shinto shrine ..........TORII
gather ....................MASS; AMASS,
..........................GLEAN; ACCRUE,
......................GARNER, MUSTER
gather in bundles ...............SHEAVE
gaucho's device........BOLA; BOLAS
b Gaul, ancient people of ..........REMI
gaunt..........................................THIN;
......................SPARE; SKINNY
gazelle .....................................ARIEL
gazelle, Afr. .............ADMI, MOHR;
................ADDRA, KORIN, MHORR
gazelle, Asian .............................AHU
gazelle, Pers. ...........................CORA
gazelle, Tibetan.........................GOA
gear ............................RIG; EQUIP;
..........................OUTFIT, TACKLE
gear-shift position ...................PARK
gear tooth ...................................COG
gear wheels, smaller of two .PINION
gee whiz ..................GOSH; GOLLY
Gelderland city...........................EDE
gelid ..............................ICY; COLD
gem ..............JADE, ONYX, OPAL,
...................RUBY, SARD; AGATE,
............PEARL; GARNET, SPINEL;
................EMERALD, PERIDOT
Gemini's immortal half ......POLLUX
Gemini's mortal half ..........CASTOR
gem weight ...........................CARAT
gender........................SEX; MALE;
......................FEMALE, NEUTER
genealogy representation .......TREE
generation ..................................AGE
genetic letters .................DNA, RNA
genie, Eg. ................................HAPI

c gentle ........................EASY, MEEK,
.....................MILD, TAME; DOCILE,
...........................PACIFY, TENDER
genuflect.................................KNEEL
geode .............VUG; VUGG, VUGH
geological epoch .....................BALA,
..........ECCA, LIAS, MUAV; ERIAN,
.........UINTA; EOCENE; PLIOCENE
geological formation .........TERRAIN
geological vein angle .............HADE
geometrical line ..................LOCUS;
...............................................SECANT
geometric solid .......................CONE,
...............................CUBE; PRISM
geometry rule .................THEOREM
geophagy....................................PICA
Geraint, wife of ........................ENID
germ ..........................BUG; VIRUS;
...............................................MICROBE
Germanic gods...........................TIU;
.............................DONAR, WODEN
German admiral.........................SPEE
Ger. article .............DAS, DER, EIN
Ger. bacteriologist .................KOCH
Ger. conjunction .......................UND
Ger.-Czech region ...........SUDETEN
Ger. district of old ....................GAU
Ger. dive bomber .................STUKA
Ger. emperor...........................OTTO
Ger. highway.................AUTOBAHN
Ger. industrial valley .............RUHR d
Ger. John ................................HANS
Ger. landscape painter ........ROOS
Ger. name prefix .......................VON
Ger. philosopher......KANT; HEGEL
Ger. physicist............OHM; ERMAN
Ger. theologian ......................ARND
Ger. title ..........VON; GRAF; PRINZ
Ger. toast...............................HOCH
GERMAN WORDS:
A....................................EIN; EINE
above ...................................UBER
again ..............................WIEDER
alas.......................ACH; WEHE
ass or donkey ......................ESEL
beer....:..................................BIER
blood....................................BLUT
count.....................................GRAF
eat .......................................ESSEN
eight ....................................ACHT
evening..............................ABEND
everything........................ALLES
four .......................................VIER
gentleman.............................HERR
hall ........................................SAAL
hall, great ............................AULA
heaven...............................HIMMEL
hunter ...............................JAGER
I ...........................................ICH
ice .........................................EIS

**a GERMAN WORDS: continued**

iron ....................................EISEN
league ...........................BUNDNIS
love ..................................LIEBE
mind .............................GEMUT
Mrs. ...................................FRAU
nation or people .................VOLK
never ...................................NIE
new ....................................NEU
no ....................................NEIN
noble ..............................EDEL
old ..................................ALT
one ..........................EIN; EINE
out ..................................AUS
soft ..................................LEISE
song ..................................LIED
spirit ..............................GEIST
state ................................STAAT
steel ..............................STAHL
storm ............................STURM
stress ............................DRANG
than ..................................ALS
the ..................DAS, DER, DIE
three ..............................DREI
thunder ......................DONNER
town ..............................STADT
us ..................................UNS
very ....................ECHT, SEHR
with ..................................MIT
without ............................OHNE

**b** you .........IHR, SIE; DICH, EUCH
your ....................IHR; DEIN,
.....................EUER, EURE, IHRE
germfree ....ASEPTIC; ANTISEPTIC
get by, barely ......................EKE
get out! ....SCAT, SHOO; SCRAM
ghastly ....................DIRE, GRIM;
..........AWFUL, LURID; MACABRE;
..............................GRUESOME
ghost ..................SHADE, SPOOK;
....................SHADOW, SPIRIT,
....................WRAITH; SPECTER
ghost, Indian ......................BHUT
giant ...........HUGE; JUMBO, TITAN
giant, Norse ........................YMIR
giant, rock-throwing bronze ...TALOS
giant killed by Apollo ..............OTUS
*Giant* ranch ......................REATA
giants, Biblical ............ANAK, EMIM
gibbon, Malay ......................LAR
gift ..................TALENT; PRESENT
gift giver ............................DONOR
gift recipient ......................DONEE
gig ..................................NAPPER
Gilgit language ....................SHINA
gills, four ............................PINT
gilt ....................................DORE
gin ....................................TRAP
gingerbread tree ..................DOOM
ginkgo tree ............................ICHO

**c** giraffelike animal ..................OKAPI
girasol ................................OPAL
girder ................................TRUSS
girdle ..................OBI; CEST, SASH
girl ..............FOX, GAL, SIS; CHIT,
..........DAME, MAID, MISS; BROAD,
..............CHICK, HONEY; MAIDEN
Girl Scouts founder ..................LOW
girth, saddle ......................CINCH
gist ..................................NUB; PITH
give, legally ......................REMISE
give up .........CEDE; WAIVE, YIELD
glacial chasm ................CREVASSE
glacial pinnacle ....................SERAC
glacial snow field .........FIRN, NEVE
glacial stage, last Eur. ........WURM
glacial trough ......................DORR
gladly, once ..........................FAIN
gland ............PINEAL; ADRENAL,
..................................THYROID
glass ......................LENS; MIRROR
glass, blue ..........................SMALT
glass, bubble in ....................BLEB
glass, partly fused ..FRIT; PARISON
glass, super-transparent .......UVIOL
glass-furnace mouth ...........BOCCA
glass ingredient ................SILICON
glassmaker ......................GLAZIER
glassmaker's oven ................LEHR
glassy ..............................HYALINE
glazier's tack ......................BRAD
gleam ................................GLINT
glide ............................SKIM, SLIP;
..............................SKATE, SLIDE
globe ..................ORB; SPHERE
gloomy ..................DARK, DOUR;
..................GLUM, GRUM; MURKY;
..........................DREARY, SULLEN
"Gloomy Dean" ......................INGE
glove ..................................MITT
glove leather ....KID; NAPA; SUEDE
glower ....................LOUR; SCOWL
glowing ..................ROSY; RUDDY;
..................................ARDENT
glut ..................CLOY, SATE;
..................GORGE; EXCESS;
..............SURFEIT, SURPLUS
gnarl ..................................KNUR
gnat, small ........................MIDGE
gnome ..........................GREMLIN
gnome in Germanic folklore ......
..................................KOBOLD
go ................RUN; WEND; DEPART
goad ............PROD, SPUR, URGE;
..............IMPEL; INCITE; PROVOKE
goal ..................AIM, END;
........................SCORE; TARGET
goa powder ..................ARAROBA
goat, Alpine mountain ..............IBEX
goat, Asian ............JAGLA, SEROW

54

goat, wild .....................TAHR, THAR
goat antelope, Himalayan....GORAL
goat god...................................PAN
goatsucker, large ...............POTOO
gob ....................TAR, WAD; LUMP;
............CLUMP; SAILOR, SEAMAN
go back ............................REVERT
goblet, medieval ................HANAP
goblin ..................................PUCK
goby, small ........................MAPO
Gods and Goddesses .....................
..................................See page 198.
Goethe heroine ................MIGNON
Goethe work .......FAUST; EGMONT
golconda .............................MINE
gold, of ...............................AURIC
golden ............................AUREATE
Golden Fleece keeper .......AEETES
Golden Fleece seeker ..........JASON
golden oriole..........................PIROL
golden oriole, Eur. .............LORIOT
golden-touch king ..............MIDAS
gold leaf, imitation ..........ORMOLU
golf attendant .......CADDY; CADDIE
golf ball holder...........................TEE
golf ball position .........................LIE
golf club ....................IRON, WOOD;
.......................BAFFY, CLEEK,
.......................SPOON, WEDGE;
.........DRIVER, MASHIE, PUTTER;
..........................BRASSIE, NIBLICK
golf club, part...............TOE; HEEL;
.......................HOSEL, SHAFT
golf course, part..............TEE; TRAP;
..........GREEN, ROUGH; BUNKER,
.......................DOGLEG; FAIRWAY
golf hole ...............................CUP
golf score .....PAR; BOGIE, EAGLE;
.......................BIRDIE
golf shot ..........CHIP, HOOK, LOFT;
........PUTT; DRIVE, PITCH, SLICE
golf stroke, ground-striking .....BAFF
gomuti ..............................ARENGA
gondolier's song.........BARCAROLE
gone ..........OUT; AWAY; PASSED
gone by.............AGO; PAST, YORE
gonfalon .............................BANNER
"Good Queen Bess" ...........ORIANA
goods ................................WARES;
.......................THINGS; EFFECTS
goose, male ......................GANDER
goose, sea ..........................SOLAN
goose, wild...........................BRANT
gooseberry...............................FABE
goose call ............................HONK
goose genus ........................ANSER
gorge ......................GLUT; CHASM;
.......................RAVINE; SATIATE
Gorgons, The..MEDUSA, STHENO;
.......................EURYALE

Gorgons' parent .....................CETO;
.......................PHORCYS
gorse........................WHIN; FURZE
Gottfried, sister of ..................ELSA
gourd rattle .......................MARACA
gourmet............................EPICURE
government patronage..........PORK
governor, Pers. ..................SATRAP
governor, Turk. .......................BEY
grace ..................ADORN; PRAYER
graceful.................................EASY;
.......................FLUID; ELEGANT
Graces, aka ....................CHARITES
Graces, father of The ............ZEUS
Graces, mother of The EURYNOME
Graces, The........AGLAIA, THALIA;
.......................EUPHROSYNE
grackle ......................DAW; MYNAH
grade ......................MARK, RANK,
.......................RATE, STEP; CLASS,
.......................SCORE; CALIBER
grade, mediocre ......................CEE
gradient ..............................SLOPE
graduation attire ..........CAP; GOWN
Graf ___ .............................SPEE
graft .................FIX; BRIBE; SCION
grain .......................OAT, RYE;
................SEED, WALE; DURRA,
................SPELT, WHEAT; MILLET
grain, coarse .........................SAMP
grain, ground ........................GRIST
grain beetle larva .............CADELLE
grain husk ............................BRAN
grain stalks ..........................HAULM
grammatically dissect ..........PARSE
grampus ..................................ORC
grange ..................................FARM
grant .....CEDE; AWARD; CONFER;
.......................CONCEDE; TRANSFER
granular snow .............FIRN, NEVE
grape ...................UVA; MUSCAT
................CATAWBA, CONCORD
grape, white ......................MALAGA
grape disease......................ESCA
grapefruit ..........................POMELO
grape genus ...........................VITIS
grape juice ..........................MUST
grape juice, unfermented .......STUM
grape refuse ........................MARC
*Grapes of Wrath, The* family ..JOAD
grape syrup ................DIBS, SAPA
graphite ...................KISH; KEESH
grasp ......................SEE, GRIP;
..............RANGE, SEIZE; CLENCH,
.......................CLUTCH, FATHOM
grass ..................BENT, HEMP,
.......................REED; SEDGE;
.......................DARNEL; TIMOTHY
grass, Andes ...........................ICHU
grass, blue ...............................POA

a grass, range ........................GRAMA
grass, sour ........................SORREL
grasshopper.............................GRIG
grassland.........................SAVANNAH
grasslands, S. Afr. ................VELDT
grasslands, western ............RANGE
grass stem .............................CULM
grass tuft ..........................HASSOCK
grate .............JAR; RASP; SCRAPE
gratify ......................SATE; PLEASE
grating ..................................GRILLE
gratuitous..................................FREE
gratuity ........................................TIP
grave ...........DIRE; SOBER; STAID;
........................SEVERE, SOMBER
gravestone(s).......STELE; STELAE
Gray, botanist ..........................ASA
gray, mole ............................TAUPE
gray and black plaid ............MAUD
grayish ..................................ASHEN
grayish-brown............DUN; TAUPE
grayish-reddish brown ..........KAFFA
gray kingbird ........................PIPIRI
gray parrot, Afr. ......................JAKO
graze ..........................SKIM, SKIP;
.......................BRUSH, CAROM;
....................GLANCE; RICOCHET
grease...........................OIL; LARD
greater ..................MORE; MAJOR
Greece .................................HELLAS
b greedy..................AVID; PIGGISH
Greek ..................................HELLENE
Greek alphabet ..........See alphabet.
Gr. amphora ........................PELIKE
Gr. assembly ........................AGORA
Gr. athletic contest ...............AGON
Gr. author .............ZENO; AESOP;
...............HOMER, PLATO, TIMON;
.........HESIOD, PINDAR, SAPPHO,
....STRABO, THALES; PLUTARCH
Gr. city ..................................POLIS
Gr. city, ancient......ELIS; SPARTA
Gr. colony in Asia Minor .........IONIA
Gr. column ...............DORIC, IONIC
Gr. commonalty .................DEMOS
Gr. community ........................DEME
Gr. dialect ...........................AEOLIC
Gr. festival city....................NEMEA
Gr. garment .........................CHITON
Gr. goddess of night ................NYX
Gr. hero ...............AJAX; JASON
Gr. market place ..................AGORA
Gr. mythical flyer...................ICARUS
Gr. pastoral poet ....................BION
Gr. patriarch .........................ARIUS
Gr. priest ...............................MYST
Gr. quadrennial festival..........DELIA
Gr. sculptor ........................PHIDIAS
Gr. shield .............................PELTA
Gr. township ........................DEME

c green .............BICE, JADE; BERYL,
..............FRESH, OLIVE; RESEDA;
.................EMERALD, UNTRIED
green, pale grayish .........CELADON
Green Bay tribe ......................SAUK
green chalcedony...............JASPER
green cheese.................SAPSAGO
green chrysolite .................PERIDOT
Green Hornet's valet .............KATO
green in heraldry ....................VERT
Greenland town ........ETAH; THULE
*Green Mansions* bird-girl........RIMA
Green Mountain hero............ALLEN
greeting...........AVE; HAIL; SALUTE
grief ........................WOE; SORROW
grimalkin ....................................CAT
grinding tooth ......................MOLAR
groom, Indian.....SAIS, SICE, SYCE
groove .......RUT; GRIND; ROUTINE
grooved ..............LIRATE; STRIATE
grope ........................................FEEL
gross ......................................CRASS
grotesque figure ..................MAGOT
ground grain ...........................MEAL
groundhog .........................MARMOT
groundnut .................SOJA; APIOS
group...........BAND, BODY, CREW;
................TEAM; BATCH, CROWD;
.......................ASSORT, GATHER
grouper .....................................MERO
d grouse........................PTARMIGAN
grove of trees ......................COPSE
grow .................WAX; RAISE;
.................................INCREASE
growl ......................GNAR; SNARL
grub ........................FOOD; LARVA
grudge ....................................SPITE
gruel, maize ...........................ATOLE
gruesome ........GRISLY; MACABRE
guard ..................................SENTRY
Gudrun, husband of.................ATLI
guenon monkey.....................MONA
guest house .............................INN
Guinea tree ...........................MORA
guide .............LEAD; PILOT, STEER
guiding rule .........................MOTTO
Guido's note .........................E LA
guild of merchants .............HANSE
guillemot ...............COOT; MURRE
guilty.............NOCENT; CULPABLE
guinea fowl, young.................KEET
guinea pig............................CAVY
gulf, Med. ...........................TUNIS
gulf, southeast Asian .........TONKIN
gulf of the Ionian Sea .............ARTA
gull .......................MEW; SKUA,
.................................TERN, XEMA
gullet..........................MAW; CRAW
gullible person .............SAP; DUPE;
........................CHUMP; SUCKER

a  Gulliver's Travels author .......SWIFT
   Gulliver's Travels race ......YAHOOS
   gulls, of.................................LARINE
   gully, Afr. ..............................DONGA
   gulp.........................................SWIG
   gum ......................RESIN; BALATA
   gum, astringent .......................KINO
   gum arabic ..........................ACACIA
   gumbo......................................OKRA
   gum resin .............ELEMI, LOBAN,
   ...........................................MYRRH

gum tree, Central Amer. ........TUNO
gun: slang .....................GAT, ROD;
   ...............................IRON; PIECE;
   .....................HEATER, ROSCOE
gun-barrel cleaner ..................SWAB
gusto .....................ZEST; RELISH
guy-rope ....................STAY, VANG
gymnastics move .......................KIP
gypsum, kind of .................GESSO;
   ...................................SELENITE
gypsy ....................ROM; ROMANY

# H

H................................................AITCH
habit .............RUT; WONT; USAGE
habitation ..................LIFE; ABODE
habituate .................................INURE
habituated ................................USED
hackney coach: Fr. ............FIACRE
had been ..................................WAS
Hades...........................DIS; HELL;
   ........................ORCUS, PLUTO,
   ..................SHEOL; TARTARUS
Hades, area near ..............EREBUS
Hades ferryman.................CHARON
Hades river...............STYX; LETHE;
b  ...................................ACHERON
hag ......................CRONE, WITCH
haggard ....................WAN; GAUNT;
   ....................................DRAWN
Haggard novel .........................SHE
hail............................AVE; LAUD;
   ........................EXTOL, GREET;
   ....................SALUTE; ORIGINATE
hail, naut. ...............AHOY; AVAST
hair, animal........FUR; MANE; PELT
hair, false.............RUG; WIG; FALL;
   ....................................TOUPEE
hair, remove...................DEPILATE
hair, rigid..................................SETA
hair, quantity of..................CURL,
   .................HANK; LOCK; BANGS,
   ...........................SHOCK; TRESS
hairdo .............AFRO; COIF; SHAG;
   .................BANGS, BRAID, PLAIT;
   ...................CHIGNON, PAGEBOY
hair dressing..................POMADE
hair knot.................BUN; CHIGNON
hairnet.................................SNOOD
hair shirt...............................CILICE
hair splitter.............................PART
hairy .................COMOSE, PILOSE
Haitian voodoo deity ................LOA
Halcyone, husband of ..........CEYX
half ..................................MOIETY
half-boot.................................PAC

half dozen................................SIX
halfpenny, Brit. ........................MAG
half-way....................................MID
hallow ....................................BLESS
halo .....AURA; CORONA; NIMBUS;
   ...................AUREOLA, AUREOLE
halt ..............LAME, STOP; CEASE
Ham, son of ............................CUSH
Hamite ..............BERBER, SOMALI
Hamite people of Eth. ...........SAHO
Hamitic language.......AGAO, AGAU
hamlet..........BURG, DORP, TOWN
Hamlet's castle .............ELSINORE
Hamlet's friend.................HORATIO  d
Hamlet's jester .................YORICK
Hamlet's love ....................OPHELIA
hammer ................KEVEL; POUND
hammer, heavy ........................MAUL
hammer, large ..................SLEDGE
hammer, lead..........................MADGE
hammer, tilt........................OLIVER
hammerhead part.....................PEEN
hamper ...................CRAMP; FETTER;
   ....................................TRAMMEL
hand ..................AID, PUD; MANUS
hand, clenched........................FIST
hand, whist ........................TENACE
handbill .................................FLIER
handcuff........................MANACLE
handle ..............EAR, LUG, PAW;
   ...................ANSA, HILT, KNOB;
   .............HELVE, TREAT; MANAGE
handle, scythe....................SNATH,
   ...................SNEAD; SNATHE
handle roughly .......................MAUL
hand of cards, abandon a.......FOLD
handsome man ......HUNK; ADONIS
handwriting ............................SCRIPT
handwriting on the wall .........MENE,
   .............MENE, TEKEL, UPHARSIN
hang ...................................LOOM;
   ....................HOVER; DANGLE,
   ...................IMPEND; SUSPEND

57

a hang fire .....................PEND, SLOW
hankering ......................YEN; ITCH
Hannibal's defeat, site of ........ZANA
Hannibal victory, site of a .CANNAE
happen ...............OCCUR; BEFALL,
.....................BETIDE, CHANCE
happening ...........................EVENT
harangue ................RANT, RAVE;
.................TIRADE; DIATRIBE
Haran, son of ...........................LOT
harass ........NAG; BESET; PESTER
harbinger .........................HERALD
harbor ..........................BAY; COVE,
.........................PORT; HAVEN;
.................REFUGE; SHELTER
harden ...............GEL, SET; INURE
hardwood......ASH, OAK; HICKORY
Hardy heroine ..........................TESS
hare, immature ................LEVERET
hare genus ..........................LEPUS
harem ........ZENANA; SERAGLIO
harem guard .....................EUNUCH
harem room ...............................ODA
harlot of Jericho ...................RAHAB
harm ........................BANE, HURT;
.........................DAMAGE, INJURE
harmony..............TUNE; ACCORD;
.................BALANCE, CONCORD
harp, ancient triangular ......TRIGON
Harp constellation ..................LYRA
b harp guitar key .....................DITAL
Harpies, The.....AELLO; CELAENO,
.................OCYPETE, PODARGE
harrow .................LOOT; PLUNDER
harrow blade..........................DISC
Harrow's rival .........................ETON
hartebeest ...............TORA; KAAMA
harvest ...................................REAP
harvest goddess .......................OPS
hashish .......................KEF; KEEF,
.......................KHAT; BHANG
hasty pudding ......................SEPON
hat.................FEZ, TAM; BERET,
..............BUSBY, DERBY, TOQUE;
.......BOATER, BONNET, BOWLER,
........CALASH, CAPOTE, CASTOR,
......CLOCHE, FEDORA, MOBCAP;
.....................PILLBOX, STETSON
hat, straw .TOYO; MILAN; PANAMA
hat, sun.....................................TERAI
hatred........ODIUM, CONTEMPT
hautboy..................................OBOE
haven ..............ASYLUM, REFUGE;
.................RETREAT; SANCTUARY
Hawaiian bird, extinct............MAMO
Haw. bird, red-tailed..............KOAE
Haw. dance ...........................HULA
Haw. farewell/greeting .........ALOHA
Haw. feast ...............................LUAU
Haw. food..................................POI

c Haw. garland ............................LEI
Haw. goddess of fire ...............PELE
Haw. goose ..............................NENE
Haw. gooseberry.....................POHA
Haw. governor, first................DOLE
Haw. honeycreeper ..................IIWI
Haw. loincloth ........................MALO
Haw. porch ............................LANAI
hawk .....................KITE; PEDDLE
hawk, fish.........................OSPREY
hawk, leash for a ...................LUNE
hawk, unfledged .....................EYAS
hawk-headed god of Egypt .HORUS
hawk's cage ............................MEW
hawthorn, Eng. .........................MAY
hay, spread to dry ....................TED
haystack ..................................RICK
hazard ......................RISK; PERIL;
.................CHANCE, DANGER
hazelnut.............................FILBERT
head ...........................NOB; BEAN,
.................LEAD; BRAIN, CHIEF,
.................FROTH; LEADER,
.................NOGGIN, NOODLE
head, crown of the .................PATE
head-and-shoulders art ..........BUST
head covering...............CAP, HAT,
.......................TAM; HOOD, VEIL;
.................BERET, SCARF, SHAWL
headdress, bishop's.................MITER
d headdress of hair, elaborate ..POUF
headgear, brimless.................TOQUE
headgear, clerical ...........BERETTA,
.........................................BIRETTA
headgear, military .....KEPI; SHAKO;
.........................................HELMET
headgear, Muslim ........TARBOOSH
headgear, Turk. ........................FEZ
headland........CAPE, NESS; POINT
headstrong ........................TOUGH;
.................DOGGED, MULISH;
.........................STUBBORN
health resort ..............................SPA
heap ...............MASS, PILE; STACK
hear .........................HEED; LISTEN
hear ye! ...................OYES, OYEZ
heart...................CORE; CENTER
heart auricle(s)........ATRIA; ATRIUM
heart contraction............SYSTOLE
heartless ...........CRUEL; CALLOUS
heart problem ....................ANGINA
heat.......................................WARM
heat, sexual ......................ESTRUS
heath ......................................MOOR
heathen .................................PAGAN
heathen god.............................IDOL
heather ....................................LING
heath evergreen....................ERICA
heating apparatus, old............ETNA
heavenly .............EDENIC, URANIC

58

a heavenly being...................ANGEL;
.................................SERAPHIM
Hebrew alphabet........See alphabet.
Heb. descendant ......................JEW
Heb. measure .........OMER; EPHAH
Heb. month, ancient.................ABIB
Heb. zitherlike instrument ......ASOR
heckle .....................RAZZ; TAUNT
Hector, mother of .............HECUBA
Hecuba, husband of .............PRIAM
hedge plant .......................PRIVET
heed .............CARE, HEAR, OBEY;
.........................LISTEN, NOTICE
heel of the foot.......................CALX
height..........APEX, PEAK; SUMMIT
heir.............................SON; SCION;
..................HERITOR, LEGATEE
Helen of Troy, lover of...........PARIS
Helen of Troy, mother of........LEDA
helical ...............................SPIRAL
Helios ...................................SUN
Helios, daughter of...............CIRCE
hell ......................HADES, SHEOL
Hellespont swimmer........LEANDER
helmet, 15th-century .........SALLET
helmet, medieval ...............ARMET;
.................................HEAUME
helmet, Rom. .....................GALEA
helmetshaped.................GALEATE
helm position..........................ALEE

b helmsman ...........................PILOT
Heloise, husband of .......ABELARD
help ....................AID; ABET, BACK,
.............................HAND; ASSIST,
.........................RELIEF, SUCCOR
helper.............................CAD; AIDE
Helvetic..............................SWISS
hem in ..............................BESET
hemp, broken fibers of............TOW
hemp, Afr. bowstring .................IFE
hemp, Manila ....................ABACA
hemp shrub............................PUA
hemp stalk .............................HARL
hen ........................BIDDY, LAYER
hence ........................OFF, AWAY;
.............................THEREFORE
Henry IV, birthplace of .............PAU
hep ..................................ON TO
Hera, son of..........................ARES
herald............................PRESAGE;
...........ANNOUNCE, PROCLAIM
heraldic bearing........ORLE; FILLET
herald's coat ....................TABARD
herb ...................LEEK, MINT,
..................MOLY, WORT; TANSY;
..................YARROW; OREGANO
herb, aromatic ......BASIL; DITTANY
herb, bitter.................RUE; ALOE
herb, umbel family.................ANISE
herb, forage ......................SULLA

c herb, medicinal.........ALOE; SENNA
herb, S. A. ...............................ANU
herbaceous plant, broad-leaved ......
...............................................FORB
herb of grace ............................RUE
Hercules, captive of ................IOLE
Hercules, father of .................ZEUS
Hercules, horse of ................ARION
Hercules, monster slain by ..HYDRA
Hercules, mother of ....ALCMENE
Hercules, wife of.....................HEBE
herd .........................PROD; DRIVE
hereditary factor....................GENE
hereditary property .................UDAL
heretic, 4th-Century ............ARIUS
heretofore .......................ERENOW
Hermes, mother of .................MAIA
Hermes, son of .......................PAN
Hermes, wife of.....................HERSE;
.................CHIONE; AGLAUCUS
hermit.............................RECLUSE;
..............................ANCHORITE
hermit, pre-Islamic.................HANIF
Hero, love of...................LEANDER
heroic .......................EPIC; EPICAL
heroic poem ...........................EPOS
heroic song of Iceland............EDDA
heron .................EGRET; BITTERN
herring, lake ..........................CISCO
herring, small Eur. .................SPRAT
herring, young ..........BRIT; BRITT
herring barrel........................CADE
hesitate ...................HALT; PAUSE,
..........................WAVER; DITHER,
...........................FALTER, TEETER
hesitation sounds.......................ERS
Hesperides, one of the ........AEGLE
Hezekiah, mother of .................ABI
Hi and Lois, child of .....DOT; DITTO
hiatus .....................GAP; LACUNA
hickory tree........................NOGAL
hidden.............ARCANE, BURIED,
.......................COVERT, SECRET,
.......................VEILED; CLOAKED
hide .....................VEIL; CACHE
hide, undressed........................KIP
hide of an animal ..........PELT, SKIN
hide thong...........................RIEM
Highlander.............................SCOT
high point..........TOP; APEX, PEAK;
.............................CREST; ZENITH
highway ................PIKE; ROUTE
highwayman ..LADRON; LADRONE
"Highwayman, The" poet .....NOYES
hike .........................CLIMB, TRAMP
hill, broad.................LOMA, LOMITA
hill, crest of a.........................BROW
hill, flat-topped .......................MESA
hill, isolated ............................BUTTE
hill, S.Afr. .................................KOP

*a* hill formed by a glacier .........PAHA,
...................................................KAME
hillock: Brit. ...........................TUMP
hillside, Scot. .........................BRAE
hilltop .....................................KNAP
hilt of a sword.........HAFT; HANDLE
Himalayan monkshood .............ATIS
hind...................ROE; BACK, REAR
hindrance.....................BAR; SNAG;
.............................BLOCK; HURDLE;
...................................BARRICADE
Hindu, low caste .....................KORI
Hindu ascetic ...........YOGI; FAKIR
Hindu breath of life ..............PRANA
Hindu era ...............................YUGA
Hindu essence of being .............SAT
Hindu garment......................SARI
Hindu gentleman .....................BABU
Hindu god of love ..................KAMA
Hindu good spirit .....................DEVA
Hindu holy man ...............SADHU;
...................................................SADDHU
Hindu magic.........................MAYA
Hindu mendicant...................NAGA
Hindu philosophy .....................YOGA
Hindu poet .........................TAGORE
Hindu prince.............RAJA; RAJAH
Hindu princess ......................RANA
Hindu queen.........RANI; RANEE
Hindu sacred writings.............VEDA
*b* Hindu sect.........JAIN, SIKH; JAINA
Hindu slave.............................DAS
Hindu scripture.....................AGAMA
...................................................TANTRA
Hindustani language ..URDU; HINDI
Hindu stringed instrument.......BINA,
...................................................VINA; SITAR
Hindu teacher .......................GURU
Hindu term of respect............SAHIB
Hindu title .................................SRI
Hindu widow's suicide........SUTTEE
hint ................TIP; CLUE; POINTER
hip.......................COXA, ILIA
hip, of the .............................ILIAC
hip, once .................................HEP
Hippocrates, birthplace of.......KOS
hippodrome .........................ARENA
hipster.....................................CAT
hire.......................LET; RENT;
...................ENGAGE; CHARTER
hired carriage ......................HACK
history .....................LORE, PAST
hit .........JAB; BASH, BIFF, CUFF,
..................WHAP, WHOP; PUNCH
hitherto .....................................YET
hit on the head.............BOP; BEAN,
...................................................CONK, COSH
hive of bees .........................SKEP
hoard.....................AMASS, STORE
hoarder .................................MISER

hoarfrost...............................RIME
hoary .....................OLD; GRAY
hoax........RUSE; FRAUD; CANARD
hobgoblin .................PUCK; SPRITE
hock .....................PAWN, WINE
hock of a horse .............GAMBREL
hodgepodge ...........OLIO; JUMBLE,
...................................MEDLEY; VARIETY
hog, female .............................GILT
hog, wild.................................BOAR
hog deer.................................AXIS
hog plum, W. Indian ...AMRA, JOBO
hog's guts...............................HASLET
hoist .....................................HEAVE
hold.........................GRIP, KEEP;
...................................GRASP; CLUTCH;
...................................CONTAIN, POSSESS
hold back .............................DETER
hold fast: naut. .....................BELAY
holding device ..........VISE; TONGS
hole.....................FIX; LAIR,
...................................RENT, VENT; CAVITY;
...................................ORIFICE, RUPTURE
hole for molten metal ...........SPRUE
hole-in-one.................................ACE
holidays, Rom. ....................FERIA
hollow .............IDLE, SINK; EMPTY;
...................................CAVITY; CONCAVE
holly .............ASSI, HOLM; YAUPON
holm oak.....................ILEX; HOLLY
holy water font .....................STOUP
homage...................................HONOR
home .................ABODE, HAVEN,
...................................HOUSE; REFUGE;
...................................HABITAT; DWELLING
homestead: Brit. ....................TOFT
homeopath school founder HERING
Homer.........................................KOR
Homer, epic by .....................ILEAD;
...................................................ODYSSEY
"Home Sweet Home" poet ...PAYNE
hominy ...................................SAMP
homosexuals.........................GAYS
honey ...........................MEL; MELL
honey-badger .......................RATEL
honeybee .......................DESERET
honey buzzard .......................PERN
honeycomb, like a .............FAVOSE
honey drink .........................MEAD
honey-eater bird ...........IAO; MOHO
honey possum .........................TAIT
honor .......................HAIL; EXALT,
...................................KUDOS; ESTEEM,
...................................HOMAGE, REPUTE
honorarium .................................TIP
honorary commission ........BREVET
Honshu bay ...............................ISE
Honshu city......................GIFU
Honshu seaport..........KOBE, KURE
hooded garment..................PARKA

a

hoodoo .....................JINX
hoodwinked............HAD; CONNED;
...............................SWINDLED
hoofbeat .....................CLOP
hook, large ................CLEEK
hooked .........HAMATE; FALCATE
Hoover Dam lake .................MEAD
hopscotch stone .............PEEVER
Horeb, Mount...................SINAI
horizontal timber .................LINTEL
horn.........................CORNU
horn, crescent moon ............CUSP
horn, Heb. ..................SHOFAR
hornblende .................EDENITE
homless stag.................POLLARD
hors d'oeuvre ..................CANAPE
horse .........................COB, NAG;
....................MOUNT, STEED;
................EQUINE, JENNET;
...............CHARGER, MUSTANG
horse, Australian ..............WALER
horse, brown................BAY; ROAN;
...............................SORREL
horse, draft...................SHIRE
horse, female ................MARE
horse, male ................STALLION
horse, piebald ................PINTO
horse, Polish wild .............TARPAN
horse, small ..............PONY
horse, spirited ...............STEED

b

horse, young ..........COLT, FOAL
horse blanket...................MANTA
horse-collar part..............HAME
horse disease ...............SPAVIN
horsehair....................SETON
horse-mackerel ..............SCAD
horsemanship.................MANEGE
horses, goddess of.............EPONA
horseshoe gripper............CALK
horse-shoeing stall..............TRAVE
horse sound....................NEIGH;
...............NICKER, WHINNY
horse's sideways tread .........VOLT
Horus, mother of ..................ISIS
Hosea, wife of...................GOMER

c

host..........ARMY; HORDE, WAFER
hostelry ......................INN
hot-air chamber.................OVEN
hot spring, eruptive ..........GEYSER
Hottentot ......................NAMA
hourly .......................HORAL
house...................HOME; VILLA;
..................COTTAGE, MANSION;
......................RESIDENCE
household gods...................LARES
housetop ..................ROOF
Howdy Doody's original name ........
...............................ELMER
howl ............BAY; WAIL; ULULATE
howler monkey .......MONO; ARABA
hubbub.....DIN; CLAMOR, TUMULT
hue ........................COLOR,
...................SHADE, TINGE
huge .......VAST; JUMBO; MASSIVE
Huguenot leader..............ADRETS
hull......................POD; HUSK
humble ......MEEK; ABASE, LOWLY
hummingbird.............AVA; TOPAZ
humorist.......................WIT
humpback salmon ..HADDO, HOLIA
Hung. dog ....................PULI
Hung. hero ...........................NAGY
Hung. playwright...............MOLNAR
Hung. violinist......................AUER
Huns, king of the ........ATLI; ETZEL;
...............................ATTILA

d

hunter .................ORION; NIMROD
hunting cry ...........TO-HO; YOICKS;
......................TALLY-HO
huntress............DIANA; ATALANTA
hup count ......................ONE
hurry .........................HIE; HASTEN
hurt.............HARM, PAIN; INJURE
hurtful ......................MALEFIC
husk, cereal.............................BRAN
hut, crude Mex. ...................JACAL
hymn..................ODE; SONG
hypnotic state ..................TRANCE
hypocritical remarks.......JAZZ, JIVE
hyson .........................TEA

**I**

Iago, wife of..........................EMILIA
Ibsen character.............ASE; NORA
ice, slushy...................SISH; LOLLY
ice block, glacial .................SERAC
Icelandic tale ...................EDDA
ice mass .....................BERG, FLOE
icy...........................GELID
idea, start of an ...................GERM
ideal .............................. UTOPIAN

identical.......EVEN, SAME; EQUAL,
...........................EXACT; PRECISE
idiot........................FOOL; MORON;
...............................CRETIN
idle .................LAZE, LOAF
idolatrous............................PAGAN
Idumaea ...............................EDOM
if ever..............................ONCE
if not..........................ELSE

*a* ignoble...............LOW; BASE, VILE;
.........................COMMON, VULGAR
ignominy ........SHAME; DISHONOR
ignorant.........................UNAWARE
ignore ....................SNUB; SLIGHT;
....................................NEGLECT
illness ....................FLU; COLD;
....................................DISEASE
illuminated...................................LIT
illumination unit ........................LUX
illusion ..........MIRAGE; CHIMERA;
..................FANTASY, FIGMENT
ill-will..................SPITE; RANCOR
image .......COPY, IDOL; REPLICA
image, religious ...........ICON, IKON
imbibe ...........................NIP; DRINK
imitate ......................APE; COPY,
..............................MOCK; MIMIC
imitation ...............FAKE; MIMESIS
imitation gems ......................PASTE
immature seed ...................OVULE
immediately .....NOW; ANON, ASAP
immense..................HUGE, VAST;
............................GIANT; TITANIC
.................................COLOSSAL
immerse ...........DIP; DUCK, DUNK;
............................DOUSE, SOUSE
imou pine ...............................RIMU
impair.......................MAR; HARM,

*b* ............................HURT; BLEMISH,
.......................TARNISH, VITIATE
impart.........LEND, TELL; CONVEY,
.......................................REPORT
impartial .....................FAIR, JUST;
........................................NEUTRAL
impede...................BAR; BLOCK;
.................HAMPER, HINDER;
..................................OBSTRUCT
impel ........MOVE; DRIVE; PROPEL
impertinent...........................PERT;
.................SASSY; BRAZEN;
.................FORWARD; IMPUDENT
implement, pounding..........PESTLE
implement, worker's ..............TOOL
implied...................TACIT; UNSAID
import...........SENSE; MEANING
important...............VITAL; URGENT
importune..............BESET, HARRY;
.................HOUND; BADGER;
...................HARASS, PESTER
impose ........LEVY; FOIST, WREAK
impost................................TAX
imposture ...............RUSE; TRICK
impoverish ...........RUIN; DEPLETE;
...............................BANKRUPT
Impressionist painter .........DEGAS,
..........MANET, MONET; RENOIR
imprison..................JAIL; IMMURE
improve .....HELP; AMEND, RALLY;
...................BETTER; UPGRADE

*c* improvise music .....................VAMP
impudence..........LIP; GUFF, SASS;
.................BRASS, CHEEK, NERVE
impudent person ...................SNOT
impurities, layer of ..............SCUM
inactive .......................IDLE; INERT
inadequate ..........WEAK; SCANTY;
..................SKIMPY; WANTING
in addition .........TOO; ALSO, PLUS
in agreement .......AS ONE; UNITED
inborn .................INBRED, NATIVE
incense ..................................JOSS
incense ingredient......GUM; SPICE;
.................................STACTE
incentive ..................PROD, SPUR;
......................FILLIP; IMPETUS
incessantly .....EVER; ENDLESSLY
inch, .001 of an ........................MIL
incinerate ..............BURN; CREMATE
incite ..........GOAD, SPUR; ROUSE
inclination................BENT, CANT,
..................TILT; SLOPE; TALENT;
..............................GRADIENT
inclined.....................APT; PRONE
inclined way .............................RAMP
incompletely .........................SEMI
inconsiderable .....PETTY; PALTRY;
.................TRIVIAL; PICAYUNE
increase.....................HIKE, RISE;
..............................BOOST, RAISE

*d* incursion....................RAID; FORAY
indentation, small ....DING, POCK
India, minstrel of .....................BHAT
Indian aborigine.....................GOND
Indian coin, former...................PICE
Indian corn ...........................MAIZE
Indian dance drama..................RAS
Indian deer............................SAMBAR
Indian fried wheat cake ..........PURI
Indian ground salt.....REH; USAR
Indian intoxicant ..................SOMA
Indian lady....................................BIBI
Indian nursemaid...................AYAH
Indian ox..................................ZEBU
Indian servant ......................MATY
Indian tenant farmer..............RYOT
Indian wild ox ...........................GAUR
indict..............CHARGE; ARRAIGN
indifferent .............ALOOF; STOLID
indigo plant................................ANIL
indistinct, make...........................BLUR
indite ...........PEN; WRITE; SCRIBE
individual ..................ONE; SELF
Indo-Chin. people.............LAO, TAI;
.................................SHAN
Indo-Eur.................................ARYAN
indolent...,.......IDLE, LAZY; OTIOSE
induce...................CAUSE, SPAWN
industrial arts class ...............SHOP
industrial fuel........................COKE

*a* ineffectual...................VAIN, WEAK;
................................FUTILE; IMPOTENT
inelastic......................................LIMP
inert............................................IDLE
infatuation ..........................PASSION
infection's liquid matter.............PUS
inflexible .............RIGID; ADAMANT
inflict.............FOIST, VISIT, WREAK
inflorescence .....RACEME, SPADIX
influence .................................SWAY;
............................AFFECT, EFFECT,
............................IMPACT, WEIGHT
information............................DATA
informer: slang ......................NARK
ingenuous ...........NAIVE; ARTLESS
inheritor................HEIR; LEGATEE
initiate .........OPEN; BEGIN; START
injure................MAR; HARM; HURT
injured remark........................OUCH
injury ............LESION, TRAUMA
inlaid decoration ..................BUHL;
............................BOULE; BOULLE
inlet ...................BAY, RIA; FJORD
inlet, Dutch ..............................ZEE
inlet, Orkneys ..........................VOE
inn ...........KHAN, SERAI; HOSTEL,
.........................POSADA; HOSPICE
inn, Turk. .........................IMARET
in name only ...................NOMINAL
innards ..................................GUTS
*b* inner ................INSIDE; VISCERAL
inn in *The Canterbury Tales*........
........................................TABARD
innkeeper ......................PADRONE;
...................................BONIFACE
inquisitive ............................NOSY
insane ...........MAD; LOCO; CRAZY
insect .........ANT, BEE, BUG, DOR,
.............FLY; FLEA, GNAT, MITE;
..........................APHID, EMESA;
.........BEETLE, CADDIS, CICADA,
.........MANTIS; PLOIARIA
insect, adult..........................IMAGO
insect, immature ..................PUPA;
....................LARVA; INSTAR
insect, stinging......................WASP
insect body.......................THORAX
insect order......................DIPTERA
insertion mark ......................CARET
inset.....................................PANEL
insidious ...........SLY; ALLURING
insincere talk.................CANT, JIVE
insipid......................DULL, FLAT;
.................BANAL, BLAND, INANE,
..........................VAPID; JEJUNE
insist...........PROD, URGE; PRESS
inspire............STIR; AROUSE,
..........INHALE, KINDLE, PROMPT
install .....................SEAT; INSTATE
instance...............CASE; EXAMPLE

instant .......................WINK; TRICE; *c*
...........................................MOMENT
instigate ....SPUR; ROUSE; KINDLE
instruct................BRIEF; EDUCATE
instrument, ancient Chin. ..........KIN
instrument, Heb. .............TIMBREL
instrument, Jap. 3-stringed .............
...........................................SAMISEN
instrument, lyrelike Afr. ......KISSAR
instrument, naut. .........PELORUS,
...........................................SEXTANT
instrument, Sp. .............CASTENET
instrument, surveying ...TRANSIT
instrument, three-stringed ...............
...........................................BANDORE
insulate ......SECLUDE; SEPARATE
insult ...................CAG; OFFEND;
...........................................AFFRONT
insurgent ............................REBEL
intact ...................SOUND, WHOLE
intellect .................MIND; REASON
inter............................................BURY
interdict ....................BAN; FORBID
interferometer ...................ETALON
interlock ...................LINK, MESH
international pact............ENTENTE
interpret.............READ; RENDER
intersect.................MEET; CROSS
interstice, small.................AREOLA
intervening, in law .............MESNE
interweave ..........TWINE; RADDLE *d*
in the know.........................AWARE
in the matter of .....................IN RE
in the past .............................ONCE
in this place ..........................HERE
intimidate ........AWE, COW; DAUNT
intone .....................................CHANT
intoxicated ..........................DRUNK
intricate...............................KNOTTY;
.........................COMPLEX, TANGLED
intrigue .................................CABAL
introduce ........BROACH; PRESENT
Inuit boat ..............................KAYAK
Inuit boot ..........................MUKLUK
Inuit coat .............................PARKA
Inuit house ...........................IGLOO
Inuit sealskin boot ..............KAMIK
Inuit settlement .......................ETAH
Inuit woman's knife ...................ULU
inundation ............FLOOD, SPATE
...................DELUGE; CATARACT
inveigle ......LURE; TEMPT; ENTICE
inventor, elevator ....................OTIS
inventor, sewing machine .....HOWE
inventor, steam engine ..........WATT
inventor's rights.................PATENT
invest .................ENDOW, ENDUE;
.........................CLOTHE, ORDAIN
investigate .............DELVE, PROBE
investigator......................TRACER

*a* invite....................ASK, BID; COURT
involve............ENTAIL; PERTAIN
Io, father of......................INACHUS
iodine source .........................KELP
ion, negative ..........................ANION
ion, positive ......................CATION
Ionian city ...........................TEOS
iota.............................JOT; MITE
Iranian, northern ...................KURD
Iranian of central Asia............SART
irascible ...............SURLY, TESTY
irate .................ANGRY; ENRAGED
Ireland ......................EIRE, ERIN
iridescent gem .......................OPAL
iris, layer of the.......................UVEA
iris root ...................................ORRIS
Irish assembly ..........................DAIL
Irish church ...................................KIL
Irish clan, ancient.....................SEPT
Irish competitive meet .............FEIS;
............................................AENACH
Irish crowning stone .........LIA FAIL
Irish dramatist .....SYNGE; BECKET
Irish-Gaelic .................................ERSE
Irish king's home ...................TARA
Irish nobleman ........................AIRE
Irish poet ..............................COLUM;
....................MOORE, YEATS
Irish rebel group .........................IRA
Irish sweetheart ......................AGRA
*b* Irish writing.............OGAM, OGUM;
..................................................OGHAM
iron, of...................................FERRIC
iron disulfide ........................PYRITE
ironic ..........................................WRY
iron lung ............................CUIRASS
ironwood ....................................ACLE
irony .....................................SATIRE
irrigation ditch .......FLUME; SLUICE
irritate.................VEX; GALL, RILE;
..............ANNOY, CHAFE; NETTLE
irritating sensation ...................ITCH
Irtysh, city on the ...................OMSK
Isaac, son of.......................EDOM;
........................ESAU; JACOB
Ishmael, mother of .............HAGAR
Ishmael, son of ...................DUMAH
isinglass ....................................MICA
Isis, husband/brother of .......OSIRIS
island ..................AIT, CAY, KEY;
..........HOLM, ISLE; ATOLL, ISLET
island, Aleutian ......................ADAK;
..................ATTU; KISKA, UMNAK;
..............................................TANAGA
island, Argyll...........................IONA
island, Australian ...........TASMANIA
island, Azores ........................FAIAL
island, Baltic.........................ALAND
island, Brit. .................MAN; SARK;
.............................WIGHT; JERSEY

island, Canadian ..DEVON, BANKS; *c*
..................BAFFIN; SOMERSET;
..........................................VANCOUVER
island, Caribbean .................CUBA;
..........................ARUBA; TOBAGO;
..................ANTIGUA; DOMINICA
island, Chin. ...........................HIANAN;
..........................................QUEMOY
island, Cyclades............KEA; KEOS
island, Dodecanese ..................KOS;
..................CASO, LERO, SIMI
island, E. Indies............BALI, JAVA;
.........TIMOR; BORNEO, MADURA;
..................CELEBES, SUMATRA
island, Fr. ...........TAHITI; CORSICA
island, Great Barrier ..............OTEA
island, Gr. ............CORFU, CRETE,
..........................NAXOS, PAROS;
..................LESBOS, RHODES
island, Hawaiian ........MAUI, OAHU;
..................KAUAI, LANAI; NIIHAU;
..............................................MOLOKAI
island, Ionian ........................ZANTE
island, Irish ............................ARAN
island, It. ......ELBA; CAPRI; SICILY
island, Jap. ....HONSHU, KYUSHU;
..................IWO JIMA; OKINAWA
island, gulf of Riga ...............OESEL
island, N. Z. .............................NIUE
island, Pac. .............................GUAM;
..............NAURU, SAMOA, TONGA; *d*
..............BIKINI, EASTER, KODIAK,
..........................MIDWAY, TAHITI;
..............................................VANUATU
island, Philippine .........CEBU, JOLO;
..................LEYTE, LUZON, PANAY,
.....SAMAR; NEGROS; MINDORO,
..................PALAWAN; MINDANAO
island, Rhode Island ............BLOCK
Island, Scot. ...........HOY; SKYE,
..................UIST, YELL; ARRAN,
..................................ISLAY, LEWIS
island, Tanzania ....................PEMBA
island in the Firth of Clyde......BUTE
isolate..................................SECLUDE
Islamic leader's title ............SAYYID
Israelite tribe ........DAN, GAD; LEVI;
.............ASHER, JUDAH; REUBEN;
.....SIMEON; EPHRAIM, ZEBULUN;
..................ISSACHAR, BENJAMIN,
..................MANASSEH, NAPHTALI
issue..............EMANATE, PUBLISH
isthmus...................................NECK
Italian, ancient......OSCAN; SABINE
It. actress ...............................DUSE
It. coins ....................................LIRE
It. commune ............................ESTE
It. composer .........VERDI; ROSSINI
It. family ..................................ESTE;
..................CENCI, DORIA; MEDICI

64

*a* It. finger-throwing game ........MORA
It. painter....................RENI; LIPPI;
.........CRESPI, GIOTTO; DA VINCI
It. poet...................DANTE, TASSO;
.....................................ARIOSTO
It. violinmaker......................AMATI
It. wine................................ASTI
ITALIAN WORDS:
   alley................................CALLE
   dear.....................CARA, CARO
   dough..........................PASTA
   eight..............................OTTO
   enough..........................BASTA
   evening...........................SERA
   field.............................CAMPO
   fly off, to.....................VOLARE
   goat.............................CAPRA
   hand..............................MANO
   harbor..........................PORTO
   harp..............................ARPA
   hatred............................ODIO
   hello or good-by................CIAO
   lady...............DAMA; SIGNORA
   lake..............................LAGO
   leader............................DUCE

*c* love...................................AMORE
mother...........................MADRE
mountain summit...............CIMA
nine..................................NOVE
one......................................UNO
Rome................................ROMA
seven..............................SETTE
shore................................LIDO
six.......................................SEI
street...................VIA; STRADA
three...................................TRE
time....................ORA; TEMPO
today.................................OGGI
tomorrow.......................DOMANI
tour or drive.......................GIRO
two.....................................DUE
very.................................MOLTO
voice................................VOCE
well.................................BENE
with....................................CON
yesterday...........................IERI
itch.................................PSORA
itemize...............................LIST
ivory, elephant's..................TUSK
ivory nut..........................TAGUA

# J

*b* jab...............POKE, PROD; PUNCH
jackal, N. Afr. ..........................DIEB
jackal genus.........................THOS
jackdaw, Scot. ........................KAE
jacket...................ETON; BOLERO
jacket, armored....................ACTON
jacket, Malay.........................BAJU
jacket, record....................SLEEVE
jackfish.................................SCAD
jackfruit...............JACA; KATHAL
jack in cribbage.......................NOB
jack-in-the-pulpit.......ARAD; AROID
Jackson heroine...............RAMONA
Jacob, brother of.......EDOM, ESAU
Jacob, wife of.........LEAH; RACHEL
jaeger gull..............................SKUA
jagged line.....:...................ZIG ZAG
jaguarundi's color phase........EYRA
jai alai.............................PELOTA
jai alai arena..................FRONTON
jai alai racket......................CESTA
Jamaican dance music.............SKA
Japanese admiral.....................ITO
Jap.-Amer. .........................ISSEI,
....................KIBEI, NISEI; SANSEI
Jap. apricot...........................UME
Jap. cedar............................SUGI
Jap. cherry............................FUJI
Jap. clogs.............................GETA

*d* Jap. decorative alloy..........MOKUM
Jap. deer..............................SIKA
Jap. drama........................KABUKI
Jap. drink............................SAKE
Jap. elder statesman.........GENRO
Jap. Emperor's title.............TENNO;
.......................................MIKADO
Jap. festival..........................BON
Jap. fish................................TAI
Jap. food paste....................MISO
Jap. game of forfeits...............KEN
Jap. garment........HAORI; KIMONO
Jap. hat material....................TOYO
Jap. lute...............................BIWA
Jap. national park....................ASO
Jap. news agency................DOMEI
Jap. parliament.......................DIET
Jap. persimmon.....................KAKI
Jap. plane.............................ZERO
Jap. plant, celerylike................UDO
Jap. poisonous fish...............FUGU
Jap. prefecture........................KEN
Jap. raw fish........SUSHI; SASHIMI
Jap. rural community.............MURA
Jap. sash..............................OBI
Jap. self-defense..................JUDO
Jap. Shinto deity...................KAMI
Jap. ship............................MARU
Jap. shrub............................HAGI

a

| | |
|---|---|
| Jap. sliding door | FUSUMA |
| Jap. stock exchange | NIKKEI |
| Jap. sword | CATAN; CATTAN |
| Jap. town | MACHI |
| Jap. vegetable | UDO; GOBO |
| Jap. volcano | FUJI |
| Jap. wrestling | SUMO |
| Jap. writing system | KANA |
| Jap. zither | KOTO |
| Japheth, son of | GOMER |
| jar | BUMP, EWER, JOLT, OLLA; CLASH, CRUSE |
| jargon | CANT; ARGOT; PATOIS |
| jar ring | LUTE |
| Jason, father of | AESON |
| Jason, first wife of | MEDEA |
| Jason, second wife of | CREUSA |
| Jason, teacher of | CHIRON |
| Jason, uncle of | PELIAS; ATHAMAS |
| Jason's ship | ARGO |
| jaunty | AIRY; DEBONAIR |
| Javanese carriage | SADO |
| Javanese language, ancient | KAVI, KAWI |
| Javanese poison tree | UPAS |
| javelin, Afr. | ASSEGAI |
| javelin, Rom. | PILUM |
| jazz | JIVE |
| jazz solo | LICK, RIFF |

b

| | |
|---|---|
| jazz style | BOP; SWING |
| jeer | MOCK; SCOFF, TAUNT |
| Jehoshaphat, father of | ASA |
| Jehovah | GOD |
| Jehovah, Heb. | YAHWEH |
| jejune | DULL; BANAL, BLAND, INANE, VAPID; PUERILE |
| jelly, meat | ASPIC |
| jelly base | PECTIN |
| jelly fruit | GUAVA |
| jeopardize | RISK; MENACE; IMPERIL; ENDANGER |
| Jericho, land opposite | MOAB |
| jersey, woolen | SINGLET |
| Jerusalem in poetry | ARIEL |
| jest | FUN; JOKE, JOSH, QUIP |
| jester | MIME; BUFFOON |
| jet, fast | SST |
| Jetsons, dog of the | ASTRO |
| jetty | PIER; BLACK, EBONY, SOOTY, WHARF |
| Jew | HEBREW, SEMITE |
| jewelry setting | PAVE |
| jewels, adorn with | BEGEM |
| jewfish | MERO; GROUPER |
| Jewish ascetic, ancient | ESSENE |
| Jewish evil demon | SHEDU |
| Jewish feast | SEDER |
| Jewish holiday | PURIM; SUKKOT; SUKKOTH |

c

| | |
|---|---|
| Jewish law | TALMUD |
| Jewish marriage contract | KETUBAH |
| Jewish offering | CORBAN, KORBAN |
| Jewish prayer book | MAHZOR, SIDDUR; MACHZOR |
| Jewish scholar | RAB |
| Jewish teacher | RABBI |
| Jewish title of honor | GAON |
| Jezebel, husband of | AHAB |
| jinx | HEX; CURSE, SPELL |
| Joan of Arc's victory, site of | ORLEANS |
| job, soft | SNAP; SINECURE |
| Job's-tears | COIX |
| jog | TROT; NUDGE |
| John, Gaelic | IAN |
| John, Irish | SEAN |
| John, Russ. | IVAN |
| johnny-cake | PONE |
| join | WED; LINK, SEAM, WELD; MERGE, UNITE; ATTACH |
| joining bar | YOKE |
| joint | HIP; KNEE, NODE; HINGE |
| joint, corner | MITER, MITRE |
| joint, wood | RABBET |
| joint part | TENON; MORTISE |
| joke | GAG; JAPE, JEST, JOSH, QUIP; CAPER, PRANK |
| joker | WAG, WIT; CARD |
| Jones, of Wall Street | DOW |
| Joseph, father of | JACOB |
| Joseph, nephew of | TOLA |
| Joshua tree | YUCCA |
| jostle | JOG; BUMP; ELBOW |
| jot | IOTA; TITTLE |
| journey | RIDE, TOUR, TREK, TRIP; TRAVEL |
| joy | CHEER; RELISH; DELIGHT |
| joyous | GLAD |
| Judah, city in | ADAR, ENAM |
| Judah, son of | ONAN |
| Judaism scriptures | TORAH |
| judge | DEEM, RATE; ARBITER |
| judge in Hades | MINOS |
| judges' bench | BANC |
| judge's chambers | CAMERA |
| judgment in Fr. law | ARRET |
| judicial assembly | COURT |
| jug, large beer | RANTER |
| jug, wide-mouthed | EWER |
| jug shaped like a man | TOBY |
| juice | SAP |
| jujitsu | JUDO |
| Juliet, betrothed of | PARIS |
| Juliet, family of | CAPULET |

d

a jumble .....................MESS; CHAOS;
............................................MUDDLE
jump ...........................HOP; BOLT;
.................LEAP; BOUND, VAULT;
...........................HURDLE, SPRING
jumping rodent...................JERBOA
juncture, line of .....................SEAM
June bug .................................DOR
June 6, 1944 ........................D-DAY
*Jungle Book, The* python ..........KAA
*Jungle Book, The* boy .......MOWGLI
jungle clearing, temporary .....MILPA
junior's transportation .............BIKE
juniper ....................GORSE, SAVIN
juniper, desert.....................RETEM

juniper, Eur. ...........................CADE    c
juniper tree, Biblical ..EZEL; RETEM
Jupiter.....................................JOVE
Jupiter, wife of ............HERA, JUNO
jurisdiction..............SWAY; POWER
jurisdiction, old-Eng. ....SOC; SOKE
jurisprudence............................LAW
jury .......................................PANEL
jury list ...............................VENIRE
just ...................EVEN, FAIR; VALID
just about................................MUCH
Jutland cape ..........................SKAW
Jutelander .............................DANE
jutting rock................................TOR
juxtapositon, place in.........APPOSE

# K

kangaroo, male ...............BOOMER
kangaroo, young...................JOEY
Katzenjammer Kids....HANS; FRITZ
kava bowl............................TANOA
Keats poem .......................LAMIA;
................HYPERION, ISABELLA
keel......................................CARINA
keel, at right angles to the ...ABEAM
keel, kind of ...............................FIN
b keel, part of a .........................SKEG
keen....................AVID; ACUTE,
......................SHARP; ASTUTE
keep ........................HOLD, MIND,
..............OBEY, SAVE; CHECK,
........................STORE; COMPLY,
........................RETAIN; OBSERVE
keepsake ...........................TOKEN;
.........MEMENTO; SOUVENIR
Kemo ____ ..........................SABE
Kentucky coffee tree ..........CHICOT
kernel.......................................NUT
ketone, liquid ...................ACETONE
kettledrum ...........NAKER; ATABAL;
...........................................TIMPANI
key ...............ISLE; MAIN; PIVOTAL
keyed up............................AGOG
key fruit ............................SAMARA
key notch ............................WARD
key part____ ...........................BIT
Keystone ____ ....................KOPS
Khond language.....................KUI
kick.......................................BOOT
kid, undressed ...................SUEDE
kidney bean .............................BON
kidneys, of the ...................RENAL
killer whale .............................ORCA
kiln................................OAST, OVEN
kiloliter ...............................STERE
kilt, drawers under a............TREWS

kind .................ILK; SORT; GENRE;
.......................HUMANE; SPECIES
kindly ..................................BENIGN
kindness ..............................LENITY
kindred......AKIN; AGNATE, ALLIED
...................CONNATE, RELATED
king .........................................REX
king, Amalekite .....................AGAG
king, Midianite .......................REBA
king, Phrygian .....................MIDAS    d
king, rich .........................CROESUS
king, Spartan .......AGIS; LEONIDAS
King Arthur, court of........CAMELOT
King Arthur, father of ...........UTHER
King Arthur, fool of .........DAGONET
King Arthur, lance of ...............RON
King Arthur, land of ...........AVALON
King Arthur, magician of .....MERLIN
King Arthur, mother of .......IGRAINE
King Arthur, queen of ..GUINEVERE
King Arthur, sword of ...EXCALIBUR
kingfish ...................................CERO
king of Crete .......................MINOS
king of Athens ...............CECROPS
king of elves ......................ERLKING
king of Israel ...........AHAB, ELAH,
...................OMRI, SAUL; NADAB
king of Judah...............ASA; AHAZ
.........................AMON; UZZIAH
king of Judea...................HEROD
king of Naples ...................MURAT
king of Naples, Shak. ......ALONSO
king of Persia.....................CYRUS
king of the Visigoths............ALARIC
king's bodyguard.............THANE
king's yellow...............ORPIMENT
Kipling hero...............................KIM
Kipling poem ...............MANDALAY
____ Kippur .............................YOM

kismet ...............................FATE
kiss ........BUSS; SMACK; SMOOCH
kitchen, ship's ...................GALLEY
kitchen tool............CORER, RICER;
.............................................GRATER
kitchen worker ..........CHEF, COOK
kittiwake ............................GULL
kitty, feed the .....................ANTE
knave ...........JACK; ROGUE
knave of clubs .......................PAM
kneecap.......................PATELLA
Knievel, daredevil ..............EVEL
knife.............SHIV, STAB; BLADE
..................MACHETE; STILETTO
knife, Burmese.............DAH, DAO
knife, Inuit woman's .................ULU
knife, P. I.............................BOLO
knife, Scot. .......................SNEE
knife, single-edged...........BOWIE
knife, surgical ................SCALPEL
knife dealer .....................CUTLER
knight..........See also Round Table.
knight ........................SIR; RITTER;
..................................TEMPLAR
knight, heroic ...................PALADIN
knight's mantel ................TABARD

knight's wife ..........................DAME
knitting stitch...........................PURL
knob: anatomical.................CAPUT
knoblike ............................NODAL
knoblike ornament ...............KNOP
knockout................................KAYO
knot......BOW; MILE, NODE, SNAG;
..........................GNARL, NODUS
knot, insecure ..................GRANNY
knot in wood ........................KNAR
knots, types of ....HITCH; BOWLINE
..............................SHEEPSHANK
knot in fiber....................NEP; NOIL
knot in wood ..............BURL, KNUR
knot lace .................................TAT
know ........................KIN; WIST
kopecks, 100 ......................RUBLE
Koran chapter..........SURA; SURAH
Koran scholars.................ULEMA
Korea, once ...................CHOSEN
Korean apricot........................ANSU
Korean president, former .......RHEE
Korean soldier........................ROK
Kronos, wife of .....................RHEA
kurrajong tree ...................CALOOL
Kwa language ......IBO; IGBO, AGNI

# L

Laban, daughter of ..............LEAH
label ...........TAG; BRAND; MARKER
*La Boheme* heroine................MIMI
Labrador tea ........................LEDUM
labyrinth ..............................MAZE
lac ......................................RESIN
lace, Fr. ..........CLUNY; ALENCON
lace, square mesh background.........
..............................................FILET
lacerate.....................RIP; TEAR
laces' tip ...........................AGLET
lack .....................NEED, WANT
lack of power .....................ATONY
Laconian clan group .................OBE
ladderlike ........................SCALAR
ladle .....................................BAIL
*Lady of the Lake* outlaw ..........DHU
lagoon .................................LIMAN
lake .....................................MERE
lake, Afr. salt ......................SHATT
lake, Blue Nile source............TANA
lake, California-Nevada .......TAHOE
lake, Irish ...........................LOUGH
lake, Italian ........COMO; AVERNUS
lake, mountain.......................TARN
lake, Scot. .........................LOCH
lake, Zaire-Rwanda ...............KIVU
lake near Sea of Galilee .....MEROM

Lakes, Great ..........................ERIE;
.......................HURON; ONTARIO;
..................MICHIGAN, SUPERIOR
Lake Tahoe trout ...................POGY
lama, head ...........................DALAI
lamb, birth a ........................YEAN
lamb, holy ...........................AGNUS
lamb, young ....................COSSET
Lamb's pen name....................ELIA
Lamb stew .......................HARICOT
Lamech, ancestor of...............CAIN
Lamech, son of.........NOAH; JUBAL
lament ...........KEEN, WAIL, WEEP;
...........................GRIEVE, PLAINT
lamp black...........................SOOT
lamprey ....................................EEL
lance, short............................DART
lance head, blunted ...........MORNE
Lancelot's beloved ...........ELAINE
lancewood ........................CIGUA
land, church ........................GLEBE
landed .........................LIT; ALIT
landfill area ........................DUMP
landing place.............................KEY;
......................DOCK, PIER, QUAY;
....................LEVEE, WHARF
land in law ...........................SOLUM
land measure ......ARE, ROD; ACRE

68

a landscape, home .................LAWN,
.............................YARD; GARDEN
language, Aramaic..............SYRIAC
language, Bantu ....................EFIK
language, early It. ...............OSCAN
language, Eg. ....................COPTIC
language, Finn. ...................UGRIC
language, Gilgit ...................SHINA
language, Indic......................HINDI
language, Indo-Chin. .......LAI, LAO,
.............................MRU, PWO; AMOY,
.............................BODO, GARO,
.............................LOLO, NAGA, SHAN
language, Indo-Chin. extinct .AHOM
language, Kashmir ...............SHINA
language, Mossi ....................MOLE
language, Niger-Congo..........KWA;
.............................................AKAN
language, N. Afr. ..............BERBER
language, Semitic ...............ARABIC
language, S. Afr. ...................TAAL
language of Jesus ...........ARAMAIC
language of the P. I. .....TAGALOG
languish ..........FLAG, PINE, WANE;
.............................WEAKEN, WITHER
langur, Ceylonese.................MAHA
Laomedon, father of................ILUS
Laomedon, son of............PRIAM;
.............................................TITHONUS
Laos aborigine ..............KHA, YUN

b lapel(s) ...............REVER; REVERS
Lapp sled............................PULKA
larboard ..............................APORT
large ......................BIG; HUGE;
.............................JUMBO, BROAD;
.............................SIZABLE, WEIGHTY
large intestine beginning(s) ...CECA;
.............................................CECUM
lariat ...........ROPE; LASSO, RIATA
larva.....................................GRUB
larva, fly ..................................BOT
lascivious ..............................LEWD
lash ...........................TIE; WHIP
lasso ..........ROPE; RIATA; LARIAT
last ..........FINAL; OMEGA; ENDURE
last but one ............PENULTIMATE
*Last Days of Pompeii* character ......
.............................................IONE
last Imam ............................MAHDI
last section ..........................FINALE
late ..........DEAD; TARDY; RECENT
lateen-rigged boat................DHOW;
.............................................MISTIC
latent ..........ABEYANT, DORMANT
lateral....................................SIDE
lath .........................SLAT; STRIP
LATIN WORDS:
abbot...............................ABBAS
about ............CIRCA; CIRCITER
above ...............SUPER, SUPRA

c across.................................TRANS
after......................................POST
all .......................OMNIS, TOTUS
alone ...................UNUS; SOLUS
and others: Abbr. ..............ET AL.
around .............CIRCA; CIRCUM
art.........................................ARS
as far as ...............................QUA
at the age of ...........AET; AETAT
backwards.....................RETRO
before .................ANTE, PRAE
behold! .............................ECCE
believe ...........................CREDO
below.................INFRA; SUBTER
bird......................................AVIS
book...................CODEX, LIBER
blessed .........................BEATUS
bronze ................................AES
but .....................SED; PRAETER
cattle ................BOVES, PECUS
country .....................RUS; RURI
cup .....................................CALIX
custom ..............................USUS
day........................................DIES
divination by lots...............SORS
divine law .............................FAS
door .................IANUA; OSTIUM
earth .................SOLUM, TERRA
egg........................................OVUM
eight.....................................OCTO
error.................................LAPSUS d
evil .....................MALUM; MALUS
field .................AGER; CAMPUS
fire........................................IGNIS
first ...................................PRIMUS
fish .....................................PISCIS
force......................................VIS
god.......................................DEUS
goddess..............................DEA
gold...................................AURUM
good ....BONA; BONUM, SALUS
grandfather ........................AVUS
he .......................................ILLE
head..............CAPUT; VERTEX
high ....................ALTE; ALTUS
himself.................................IPSE
hours..............................HORAE
ivory..................................EBUR
journey.................................ITER
knee ..................................GENU
lamb ...............................AGNUS
land.....................................AGER
learned ...........................DOCTUS
life........................VITA; ANIMA
lo .........................................ECCE
love..............AMO, AMAS, AMAT
man ..........................VIR; HOMO
mark....................................NOTA
mine ...................................MEUS
mountain ..........................MONS

*a* LATIN WORDS: *continued*

| | |
|---|---|
| name | NOMEN |
| not | NON; HAUD |
| once | SEMEL |
| or | AUT |
| other | ALIUS |
| over | SUPER, SURPA |
| pardon | VENIA |
| peace | PAX; OTIUM |
| pin | ACUS |
| pledge | PIGNUS |
| power | VIS |
| property | BONA |
| quickly | CITO |
| rate of interest | USURA |
| right | FAS, IUS; DEXTER |
| same | IDEM; EADEM |
| same place, in the | IBID |
| scarcely | VIX |
| see | VIDERE |
| side | LATUS |
| speaks, he or she | LOQ |
| surety | VAS |
| table | MENSA |
| tail | CAUDA |
| that is (to say) | ID EST |
| thing | RES |
| this one | HIC, HOC; HAEC |
| thus | ITA, SIC |
| throat | FAUCES, GUTTUR |
| *b* tooth | DENS |
| twice | BIS |
| under | SUB |
| unless | NISI |
| use, to | USUS |
| vein | VENA |
| voice | VOX |
| water | AQUA |
| we | NOS |
| well | BENE; PUTEUS |
| where | UBI |
| within | INTRA |
| without | SINE |
| wool | LANA |
| wrong | MALE; FALSUS |
| year | ANNO |
| laugh | CACKLE, GUFFAW, HEEHAW, TITTER; CHORTLE, CHUCKLE |
| laughable | RISIBLE |
| laughing | RIANT |
| laughing, of | GELASTIC |
| laughter sound | YUK; TEE-HEE |
| laughter sounds | HA'S, HO'S; YUKS |
| laurel | BAY; DAPHNE |
| lava | LATITE, SCORIA |
| lavender, Eur. | ASPIC |
| law | JURE, RULE; CANON, EDICT |
| law, Rom. | JUS, LEX |

| | |
|---|---|
| law excluding women from reign | *c* SALIC |
| lawful | LEGAL, LICIT |
| lawgiver, Gr. | DRACO, MINOS, SOLON |
| lawgiver, Heb. | MOSES |
| law of Moses | TORAH |
| lawyer | LEGIST |
| lay | PUT; DITTY |
| layer | PLY; LAMINA; PROVINE, STRATUM |
| layer of wood | VENEER |
| layers | STRATA |
| layman, of | LAIC |
| lazar | LEPER |
| lazy | IDLE; OTIOSE; INDOLENT, SLOTHFUL |
| LBJ's beagles | HER, HIM |
| lead, pellets of | SHOT |
| lead, pencil | GRAPHITE |
| lead, white | CERUSE |
| lead-colored | LIVID |
| leader, fishing | SNELL |
| leader, Rom. | DUX |
| lead ore | GALENA |
| lead telluride | ALTAITE |
| leaf, fern | FROND |
| leaf, flower | BRACT, SEPAL |
| leaf appendage | STIPEL |
| leaf-cutting ant | ATTA; PARASOL |
| leaf division | LOBE *d* |
| leaf-miner beetle | HISPA |
| leaf of a book | PAGE; FOLIO |
| leaf vein | RIB |
| league, trading | HANSE |
| Leah, father of | LABAN |
| Leah, son of | LEVI |
| lean | CANT; GAUNT, SPARE |
| Leander's love | HERO |
| Leaning Tower city | PISA |
| lean-to | SHED |
| leap | LUNGE, VAULT |
| leap, horse's | CURVET |
| leaping | SALTANT |
| Lear, daughter of | REGAN; GONERIL; CORDELIA |
| Lear, faithful follower of | KENT |
| learned | ERUDITE; LETTERED |
| learned person | SAGE; PEDANT, SAVANT |
| learning | LORE |
| least bit | RAP |
| leather, glove | KID; MOCHA, SUEDE |
| leather, kind of | ELK; BOCK |
| leather, prepare | TAN, TAW |
| leather, soft | NAPA; ALUTA |
| leatherfish | LIJA |
| leather flask, Gr. | OLPE |

*a* leatherneck ........................MARINE
leather thong, hawk-restraining.......
.............................................BRAIL
leatherwood.............................TITI
leave .............QUIT, EXIT; DEPART
leave destitute ...................STRAND
leaven....................................YEAST
leave of absence, school......EXEAT
leave-taking ......................CONGE
leavings ...........DREGS; RESIDUE
Lebanese port .....................TYRE
ledge, fort...............BERM; BERME
ledger entry.........................ITEM;
.............................DEBIT; CREDIT
lee, opposed to ...................STOSS
leer.......................................OGLE
Leeward island ..................NEVIS
left, turn.................................HAW
left-hand page ...................VERSO
leftover table scrap .................ORT
leg, front of the ..................SHIN
legal action .........RES; CASE, SUIT
legal claim ............................LIEN
legal delays........................MORAE
legal injury ............................TORT
legal offense ......................DELICT
legal order............................WRIT
legal profession..............BAR, LAW
legal prosecution......................SUIT
legal title..............................DEED
*b* legatee...................................HEIR
leg covering, ancient.........PEDULE
legend ....................LORE, MYTH,
.............................SAGA, TALE
leg ends ...............................FEET
legion division, Rom. ......COHORT
legislate...............................ENACT
legislature ...............DIET; SENATE
legislature, Sp. .................CORTES
leg joint, animal's .................HOCK
leglike part ............................CRUS
leg of mutton or lamb...........GIGOT
leg part ..................SHIN; SHANK
legs, shapely ......................GAMS
legume .............PEA, POD; BEAN
leisure ........EASE, REST; REPOSE
lemur ......................MAKI; INDRI,
.............................LORIS; AYE-AYE
lemur, Afr. .......................GALAGO
lemur, flying ....................COLUGO
lemur, ruffed ..........................VARI
lens-shaped aggregate .........AUGE
leopard's bane ..................ARNICA
lepidopteran insect ...............MOTH
lepton, charged ...................MUON
Lesbos poet .........................ARION
less .................FEWER, MINUS
less: music ..........................MENO
lessen.................ABATE; MITIGATE
let ...............HIRE; LEASE; PERMIT

lethal .................FATAL; MORTAL *c*
lethargic..................DOPY; DOPEY
lethargy ....................................COMA;
.............................STUPOR, TORPOR
let it stand ...............................STET
letter ......................NOTE; EPISTLE,
.............................................MISSIVE
letter, curved .........CEE, ESS, GEE
letter, forked.............................WYE
letter, hooked...............................JAY
letter of resignation ..............DEMIT
letters, slanted ...................ITALICS
lettuce, kind of........COS; ICEBERG
.............................................ROMAINE
let up ......................ABATE, LAPSE
Levantine ketch ......................SAIC
levee .......................................DIKE
level ............EVEN, RAZE; PLANE
leveling device .........................SHIM
lever .........PRY; PEAVEY, TAPPET
levy ...............TAX; CESS; IMPOST
liability...................................DEBT
liana ...........................CIPO, VINE
liang .......................................TAEL
liar ....................................ANANIAS
Liberal precursor, Brit. ..........WHIG
library component.................BOOK
librettist von Hofmannsthal ....HUGO
lichen ....................................MOSS
lie.............FIB; CANARD, REPOSE
liegeman .............................VASSAL *d*
lie in wait..................................LURK
lieu .....................................STEAD
life ....................TERM; BIOTA;
.............................ENTITY, PERSON
life, brought to .......................BORN
lifeless ........BLAH, DULL; AMORT,
.............................AZOIC, INERT
life prolonger.........................ELIXIR
life story, brief ..................BIO; VITA
lifetime ....................................AGE
lifted and threw .....................HOVE
ligament................................BOND
light..................AIRY, LAMP; KLIEG
light, as a line.....................LEGER
light, circle of .........HALO; NIMBUS
light, science of...................OPTICS
light-bulb filler.....................ARGON
light gas................................NEON
light ring.........................CORONA
light unit ..........LUMEN; HEFNER
lighter, lamp............................SPILL
lighter, make ...................LEAVEN
lighthouse .........................PHAROS
ligulate ...............................LORATE
likely ......................................APT
likeness ...............IMAGE; REPLICA
lily.....................LYS; ALOE, ARUM,
.............................SEGO; CALLA; CAMASS
Lily Maid of Astolat ..............ELAINE

limb ....................ARM, LEG; MANUS
limber .........................................LITHE
limestone, grainy.................OOLITE
limestone, soft .........MALM; CHALK
lime tree ....................TEIL; LINDEN
limicoline bird........SNIPE; PLOVER
limit ............TERM; BOUND, STINT
limn .....................................DESCRIBE
line.................................ROW; RANK;
...............QUEUE, TRADE, WARES;
.................................................WRINKLE
line, move in a ..........................FILE
line, naut. .........EARING; MARLINE
line, waiting .........................QUEUE
linear measure, old Texas......VARA
line in mathematics ...........VECTOR
linen, fine .....................LAWN; TOILE
linen, household ................NAPERY
linen tape, braid.....................INKLE
linen-thread fiber ....................FLAX
line on a letter.........................SERIF
lines, marked with ...............RULED;
.................................................STRIATED
lines, of..................................LINEAR
lines, telescope-lens .........RETICLE
line with stone.........STEEN, STEIN,
.................................................STEYN
linger ..........WAIT; TARRY; LOITER
lingo .....................ARGOT; PATOIS
lingua....................................GLOSSA
link................TIE; BOND; BRIDGE
linnet .......................................TWITE
linseed oil source ...................FLAX
lion ...................................LEO; SIMBA
lionet ...........................................CUB
lion group ................................PRIDE
lion killed by Hercules .......NEMEAN
lion of God ..................................ALI
lip ornament .........................LABRET
lips, of the .............................LABIAL
liquefy ........................MELT; THAW
liqueur ...................................CREME
liquid, lose ..................DRIP, LEAK,
.................................................OOZE, SEEP
liquid, without ...................ANEROID
liquor .........GIN, RUM, RYE; GROG
liquor, malt................ALE; PORTER
liquor, Oriental...................ARRACK
liquor, P. I. ...............................VINO
liquor, Russ. ........................VODKA
liquor, sugar-cane ................TAFFIA
Lisbon's river .......................TAGUS
lissome ................................SVELTE
list ...........................TILT; ROSTER;
.............CATALOG; ENUMERATE
listed thing ...............................ITEM
listen................HARK, HEAR, HEED
list-ending abbreviation ............ETC
listless.................MOPY; LANGUID
listlessness ...........ENNUI; APATHY

list of candidates...................SLATE
list of persons ......PANEL; ROSTER
literary collection ......................ANA
literate ........LEARNED; LETTERED
little: music...............................POCO
"Little Boy Blue" poet ..............FIELD
*Little Caesar* gangster.............RICO
little casino................................TWO
little chief hare.........................PIKA
Little Joe on dice....................FOUR
liturgy ........................................RITE
lively ..............PERT, SPRY; BRISK;
.......................KINETIC; ANIMATED
lively: music..............VIVO; DESTO;
.................................................ANIMATO
lively person...........................GRIG
lively song ...............................LILT
live oak ................................ENCINA
liver, of the........................HEPATIC
lixiviate .................................LEACH
lizard .......................GILA; GECKO,
.............GUANA, SKINK; IGUANA
lizard, Amer. ........................ANOLE
lizard, Caribbean.......................UTA
lizard, large......................MONITOR
lizard, myth. ......................BASILISK
lizard, old world ......................SEPS
lizard, small ...............................EFT
lizard, starred ...................AGAMA
lizardlike ............................SAURIAN
llamalike animal ................ALPACA
load ............................LADE, ONUS
loam .......................................LOESS
loam, Indian ........................REGUR
loath......................................AVERSE
loathe.......................HATE; ABHOR
lobster box ...............................CAR
local ..............NARROW; LIMITED
locale........................................SITE
locality ......AREA; LOCUS; VENUE
location ...........SITE, SPOT; PLACE
lock....................CURL; TRESS
lockjaw ..............................TETANUS
locks, Panama Canal .........GATUN
locust....................ACACIA, CICADA
locust, N. Z. .........................WETA
lodestone .........................MAGNET
lodge, soldier's .....................BILLET
lofty ...........................................TALL
log, spin a floating ....................BIRL
loge ........................................STALL
logger's implement ............PEAVEY
logrolling tournament...........ROLEO
log splitter ..........................WEDGE
Lohengrin, wife of ....................ELSA
loincloth, Polynesian ..............MALO
Loire, city on the ...................BLOIS
Loki, daughter of .......................HEL
Loki, son of...............................NARE
Loki, wife of..........................SIGYN

a lollapalooza............................LULU
London district.........................SO-HO
long............PINE; CRAVE, YEARN
long ago.......................ELD; YORE
longing............................YEN; ACHE
long journey.......TREK; ODYSSEY
long live!....................VIVA, VIVE
look.................................SEE; CAST,
....................FACE, VIEW; WATCH;
....................REGARD; OBSERVE
look after.....................MIND, TEND
look at.................EYE; SCAN, VIEW
look narrowly...PEEK, PEEP, PEER
look slyly.....................LEER, OGLE
loom, heddles of a................CAAM
loon, kind of..........................DIVER
loop, edging........................PICOT
Loop trains...............................ELS
loose.............................LAX; FREE;
....................SLACK, UNTIE;
....................WANTON; RELEASE
loose coat.......................PALETOT
loosen....................UNDO; UNTIE
loose robe.............SIMAR, SYMAR
lop.............................SNED; PRUNE
Lord High Executioner in *Mikado*
....................................KOKO
lord, Scot. ...........................LAIRD
lorica...............................CUIRASS
*Lorna Doone* character...........RIDD
b lot, .......................................FATE
Lot, father of.......................HARAN
Lot, son of..........................MOAB
loud: music.........................FORTE
loudness measure.................PHON
loudspeaker, high..........TWEETER
loudspeaker, low.............WOOFER
loud-voiced person.........STENTOR
Louisiana county.................PARISH
Louisiana people..............CREOLE
lounge.....................LOAF, LOLL
love.......ZERO; AMORE; PASSION
love apple.........................TOMATO
love feast.............................AGAPE
lover...................................ROMEO

*Love's Labour's Lost* constable........ c
....................................DULL
love song, dawn.....................ALBA
loving.................FOND; AMATORY
low..................MOO; BASE, DEEP
Lowell, poetess.........................AMY
lower...................ABASE; DEBASE,
....................................NETHER
lower intestine(s).........ILEA; ILEUM
lowest deck..........................ORLOP
lowest part of a base..........PLINTH
lowest point...........................NADIR
low pasture................................ING
loyal...........................LEAL, TRUE;
....................................STAUNCH
loyalist, Brit. ...........................TORY
lozenge.............PASTIL, ROTULA,
....................TROCHE; PASTILLE
lucky stroke.........................FLUKE
lugubrious...............SAD; WOEFUL
lukewarm.............................TEPID
lumberman.......................SAWYER
lumberman's boot......................PAC
lumberman's hook.............PEAVEY
luminaire.............................LAMP
luminary..................................STAR
lump...............NUB, WAD; CLOT
luncheon.............................TIFFIN
luncheon meat, canned.........SPAM
lurch...................................CAREEN
lure............................BAIT; DECOY d
luster..................GLOSS, SHEEN
lusterless....................DIM; MATTE
lustrous................................NITID
lute, flat-backed....................CITOLE
luxuriant.....................LUSH, RANK,
....................RICH; PLUSH;
....................PROFUSE, RIOTOUS
luxuriate..................................BASK
Luzon people...............................ATA
Lynette's knight...............GARETH
lynx, Afr. ......................SYAGUSH
lynx, Pers. ......................CARACAL
lyric muse............................ERATO
Lytton heroine.........................IONE

# M

macaque, crab-eating..............KRA
macaque, pigtailed.................BRUH
macaque monkey..........RHESUS
macaw, military..........ARA; ARARA
mace-bearer.....................BEADLE
macerate.................RET; STEEP
machine, finishing.............EDGER
machine, hummeling.........AWNER
machine, ore-processing...VANNER

machine, rubber...........EXTRUDER
machine, sorting...............GRADER
machine gun.............BREN, STEN
machine part.............CAM; PAWL;
....................................TAPPET
mackerel.............................WAHOO
mackerel, young...................SPIKE
mackerel net.....................SPILLER
Madagascar mammal.........LEMUR

73

a madam......................MUM; MA'AM
madder................................RUBIA
madder, Indian ...............MUNJEET
madness ..........MANIA; DEMENTIA
mafura tree ..........................ROKA
magazine, cheap ...................PULP
maggot................................LARVA
Magi, gifts of the .....GOLD; MYRRH
Magi, the .....GASPAR; MELCHIOR;
.....................................BALTHAZAR
magic................................SORCERY
magic, of black .................GOETIC
magic, W. Indian ................OBEAH
magic dragon .........................PUFF
magician ..................WIZ; MAGE;
.............................MAGUS; WIZARD
magician, King Arthur's ......MERLIN
magic stone .......................AGATE
magic word......................PRESTO,
.......................SESAME, SHAZAM
magistrate, Athenian ........ARCHON
magistrate, It. ......................DOGE
magistrate, Orkney or Shetland .......
...........................FOUD, FOWD
magistrate, Rom. ...............AEDILE,
.......................CONSUL; PRAETOR
magnanimous......BIG; GENEROUS
magnate ...........MOGUL; TYCOON
magnifying glass....................LENS
Magog, partner of ...................GOG

b magpie ................PIET; NINUT
___ Mahal................................TAJ
Mahatma, the ...................GANDHI
mah-jongg piece ......................TILE
mahogany, Sp. ......CAOBA; QUIRA
mahogany tree, Indian ...........TOON
maid ..........................LASS; BONNE
maid, lady's ......................ABIGAIL
maid, Oriental ......................AMAH
maiden ...............FIRST; DAMSEL
maiden name lead-in ................NEE
maid-of-all-work .................SLAVEY
mail................................POST, SEND
main point......................NUB; CRUX,
.................................GIST, PITH
maintain .....AVER, HOLD; ASSERT
maize................................CORN
maize bread ..............................PIKI
major: music.........................DUR
majority ................................MOST
major third: Gr. music ........DITONE
make ................CREATE, RENDER
make fast: naut. .....................BELAY
make happy......................ELATE
makeover..............................REDO
malarial fever ..........................AGUE
Malay canoe ...........................PROA
Malay dagger ......................KRIS
Malay gibbon............................LAR
Malay law .............................ADAT

c Malay sarong ...........................KAIN
Malay title of respect ..............TUAN
male ........MACHO, MANLY; VIRILE
male cat ...........................GIB, TOM
malefic.....................................EVIL
male person..........BOY, GUY, LAD,
.................MAN, SON; CHAP, JOCK,
.................STUD; BLOKE, HE-MAN
male swan ................................COB
malic acid source ...APPLE, GRAPE
malign.......................SLUR; VILIFY
malignant..................VILE; NASTY;
..............................................DEADLY
malleable...............SOFT; DUCTILE
malleable metal .........................TIN
mallet .......................MALL; GAVEL
maltreat................................ABUSE
mammoth .............................GIANT
man ......................BUB, GUY, MAC;
..........................................FELLOW
man, rich..........NABOB; CROESUS
manger ..................CRIB; CRECHE
mangle .........IRON, MAUL; PRESS
mango fruit, wild ......................DIKA
mania ..................RAGE; CRAZE;
...........................................LUNACY
manifest.................SHOW; OVERT;
...........................................EVINCE
Manila hemp .........................ABACA
manner................AIR, HOW, WAY;
.................MIEN, MODE; METHOD

d manor ...........................DEMESNE
man's name: Abbr. ......EDW, GEO,
.................JAS, JOS; CHAS, THOS
mantle ..................................CAPE
manure ................................DUNG
Maori hen .............................WEKA
map.................................CHART
map, builder's........................PLAT
map collection.......................ATLAS
maple fruit or seed ...........SAMARA
maple genus ..........................ACER
map on a map ......................INSET
mar................DAMAGE; TARNISH
marble......MIB, MIG, TAW; AGATE,
.........................AGGIE; SHOOTER
marble, It. ......CARRARA, CIPOLIN
March King .........................SOUSA
margin ..........................RIM; EDGE
marine snail ........................WHELK
mark..........DUPE, SIGN; BRAND,
.............GRADE; NOTICE, STIGMA
mark, diacritical....................TILDE;
.........................................MACRON
mark, short vowel................BREVE
market............MART, SELL, VEND;
.........................STORE; RIALTO
market, Indonesian ..............PASAR
market, Oriental ...........SUQ; SOUK
marketplace ......................BAZAAR

a marketplace(s), Rom. ...........FORA;
.................................................FORUM
  mark of omission..................CARET
  marmalade tree ................SAPOTE
  marquisette ............................LENO
  marriage notice ....................BANNS
  marriage settlement............DOWRY
  marriage vows ....................TROTH
  marrow..................................PITH
  marry..........................WED; UNITE
  Mars, Gr. ..............................ARES
  marsh...........................BOG, FEN;
  ...............LIMAN, SWALE, SWAMP
  marsh elder ..............................IVA
  marsh gas ........................METHANE
  marsh hen...................COOT, RAIL
  marsh mallow ...................ALTHAEA
  marsh marigold...............COWSLIP
  marsh plant..............REED; SEDGE
  marsh tea ..........................LEDUM
  marshy ..............................HELODES
  marsupial ...........KOALA; NUMBAT,
  ...................WOMBAT; OPOSSUM;
  .............KANGAROO; PHALANGER
  martyr, first Christian.......STEPHEN
  marvel...........WONDER; MIRACLE
  Marx Brothers..................CHICO,
  ............GUMMO, HARPO, ZEPPO;
  .......................................GROUCHO
  Mascagni heroine ..................LOLA
b mashie..................CLUB, IRON
  masjid..............................MOSQUE
  mask .......VEIL; COVER; SHROUD
  mask, half............................DOMINO
  mass..................GOB, WAD; BULK,
  ...............HEAP; MOUND, SWARM
  mass, amorphous......BLOB, GLOB,
  ...................................GLOP, PULP
  mass book ..........................MISSAL
  mass meeting ......................RALLY
  master stroke........................COUP
  masticate.............................CHEW
  mastic bully ........................ACOMA
  mast support............................BIBB
  mat, ornamental ..................DOILY
  match ..............FIT; TWIN; EQUAL
  match, friction........................FUSEE
  match, wax ..........................VESTA
  matgrass.................................NARD
  mature...............AGE; RIPE; RIPEN
  Mau Mau country ................KENYA
  maxilla....................................JAW
  maxim .......SAW; ADAGE, GNOME,
  .............................MOTTO; SAYING
  Mayan year ..................TUN; HAAB
  meadow...................................LEA
  meadow mouse ......................VOLE
  meager................................SCANT
  meal.................................REPAST
  meal, boiled ..........................MUSH

c meal, fine ............................FARINA
  meal, light ............................BEVER
  meal course ............SOUP; SALAD;
  .......................ENTREE; DESSERT
  meaning .............SENSE; IMPORT,
  .......................INTENT; OBJECTIVE
  meantime ..........................INTERIM
  meat................HAM, RIB; BEEF,
  .........CHOP, LOIN, PORK, RUMP;
  ......................VEAL; FILET, STEAK
  meat on a skewer................KEBAB
  meat roll, fried..................RISSOLE
  Mecca, pilgrimage to .............HAJJ
  Mecca pilgrim ..............HAJI; HAJJI
  Mecca pilgrim's garb............IHRAM
  Mecca shrine........................KAABA
  mechanical man ....................ROBOT
  mechanics, branch of........STATICS
  mechanics of motion .....DYNAMICS
  meddle ...........................TAMPER;
  .....................................INTERFERE
  Medea, father of................AEETES
  medical picture ......................X-RAY
  medicinal bark ......................COTO
  medicinal herb.........ALOE; IPECAC
  medicinal plant....................SENNA
  medicinal tablet................TROCHE
  medicine man ....................SHAMAN
  medieval dawn love song .......ALBA
  medieval poem ..........................LAY
d medieval society .................GUILD
  Mediterranean reedy grass.....DISS
  medlar..................................MISPEL
  medley..................................OLIO
  Medusa, father of ..........PHORCYS
  Medusa, mother of..................CETO
  Medusa, slayer of ...........PERSEUS
  meet .................SIT; ABUT; GREET
  meeting ..............TRYST; SESSION
  meeting, political ..............CAUCUS
  melancholy ....................SAD; BLUE
  melodious..........................ARIOSO
  melody ..................AIR; ARIA, TUNE
  melon ..................PEPO; CASSAVA
  melted ...............................MOLTEN
  melt together ..........................FUSE
  membrane ......WEB; TELA; VELUM
  memento ...............................RELIC
  memorandum ..........................NOTE
  memorial post, Indian ..........TOTEM
  memory, of ...................MNEMONIC
  memory method ......................ROTE
  Memphis, chief god of ...........PTAH
  Memphis, Tenn. street.........BEALE
  mend .............................FIX, SEW;
  ...............................DARN; REPAIR
  mendacious person..................LIAR
  mendicant friar............CARMELITE
  Menelaus, wife of ................HELEN
  menhaden fish .....................POGY

75

*a*
Menotti hero.........................AMAHL
Menotti heroine ...................AMELIA
men's party...........................STAG
mentally confused..................GAGA
mention .................................SITE
menu item...............................DISH
merchandise .........WARE; WARES
merchant ............................TRADER
merchant, rich Indian..............SETH
merchant ship ..................ARGOSY
Mercury, Gr. ....................HERMES
Mercury's wand...........CADUCEUS
mercy ..................................GRACE;
...............................CLEMENCY
mere......................BARE; SCANT
merely...................JUST, ONLY
merganser duck...SMEW; GARBILL
merge...............MIX; FUSE; BLEND
merit ................EARN; VALUE;
...............................VIRTUE
merriment ...............................GLEE
*Merry Widow* composer .......LEHAR
mesh......................NET, WEB;
...............................ENGAGE
Mesopotamian city .................URFA
mesquite bean flour ...........PINOLE
metal, bar of...........................INGOT
metal, coat with ......PLATE, TERNE
metal, white................TIN; ZINC
metal alloy.............BRASS, INVAR;

*b*
...............................MONEL; BRONZE
metal-decorating art ............NIELLO
metal disk ...........................MEDAL
metal dross............................SLAG
metal filings ..........................LEMEL
metal fissure.........................LODE
metal leaf ..............................FOIL
metallic rock ...........................ORE
metallic sound ............DING, PING,
...............................TING; CLINK
metal mixture........................ALLOY
metal refuse .......................SCORIA
metal spacer in printing ..........SLUG
metal suit ...............................MAIL
metal sulfide, impure ............MATTE
metalware, lacquered ............TOLE
metalwork, god of ..............VULCAN
meteor, exploding ..............BOLIDE
meter, one-millionth of a ....MICRON
meters, one hundred square ....ARE
method ........................HOW, WAY;
...............................PLAN; ORDER
Methuselah, grandson of .......NOAH
Metis, lover of ...................SELENE
metrical rhythm.....................ICTUS
metrical unit...........................MORA
metric measure ......................ARE;
...............GRAM, KILO; LITER,
...............................METER, STERE;
...............DECARE; HECTARE

*c*
metropolis .............................CITY
metropolitan........................URBAN
mew .......................................GULL
Mex. Indian ............................SERI
Mex. medicinal plant ............JALAP
Mex. mush..........................ATOLE
Mex. painter ......................RIVERA
Mex. peninsula.......................BAJA
Mex. persimmon ............CHAPOTE
Mex. plant oil .........................CHIA
Mex. president ......................DIAZ;
...............ALEMAN, CALLES,
...............MADERO; GORTARI
Mex. resin tree ...................DRAGO
Mex. slave............................PEON
Mex. spiny tree................RETAMA;
...............................PALOVERDE
Mex. wind instrument.........CLARIN
Mex. yucca............................DATIL
MGM lion ..............................LEO
microbe ...............................GERM
microspores ......................POLLEN
midday..................................NOON
middle ....................MEAN; MESNE;
...............CENTER, MEDIAN
middling .............................SO-SO
Midgard Serpent, slayer of the ......
...............................THOR
midge ...................................GNAT
midwife, Indian ......................DHAI
mien .........AIR; MANNER; ASPECT

*d*
might............................MAY; SWAY;
...............................POWER, VIGOR
mignonette..........GREEN; RESEDA
migratory worker.....................OKIE
Milanion, wife of.............ATALANTA
mild............................MEEK, SOFT,
...............................TAME; BLAND;
...............................DOCILE, GENTLE
mile, naut. ...........................KNOT
milestone ............................STELE
milfoil ...............................YARROW
military cap..............................KEPI
military command..............AT EASE
military flag.......................GUIDON
military group ........CADRE, CORPS
military maneuvers...........TACTICS
milk, coagulated....................CURD
milk, curdled ...................CLABBER
milk, part of.......SERUM; LACTOSE
milk, of.............................LACTIC
milk, watery part of ...............WHEY
milk coagulator ...................RENNIN
milk protein ........................CASEIN
mill, primitive hand .............QUERN
millrace ................................LADE
millstone support........RIND, RYND
millwheel bucket ......................AWE
Milton, masque by ..............COMUS
Milton's rebel angel................ARIEL

a mime ........................................APER

mimosa ...............................ACACIA

mind .............CARE, TEND; BRAIN

mine, narrow vein of a .........RESUE

mine-cutter ...................PARAVANE

mine entrance ...........................ADIT

mine incline ...........................DOOK

mine-laying soldier ............SAPPER

mine passageway ....BORD; STULM

mineral, blue .......................IOLITE

mineral, gun-powder .............NITER

mineral, lustrous .....................SPAR

mineral, raw .............................ORE

mineral, soft ...........................TALC

mineral, transparent ...............MICA

mineral salt............................ALUM

mineral spring ...........................SPA

mineral tar ..............................BREA

mineral waste ...................GANGUE

mine roof support....................NOG

Minerva, Gr. .....................ATHENA

mine shaft drain pit .............SUMP

mine stair......................LOB; LOBB

Ming's planet....................MONGO

minim ....................................DROP

mining tool .............................GAD

minister, Muslim ....................VIZIR

mink, Amer. .........................VISON

minority, legal .................NONAGE

Minos, daughter of .........ARIADNE

b Minotaur, slayer of the ....THESEUS

minstrel ...............................RIMER

minstrel, medieval ...........GOLIARD

minstrel, Norse ...................SKALD

mint............COIN; FORTUNE

mint herb ..............................SAGE

minus ....................................LESS

minute ...........................WEE; TINY;

........................SMALL; LITTLE

mischievous sprite .................PUCK

misplaced ..............................LOST

misplay..............ERROR; RENEGE

misrepresent ..........BELIE, COLOR;

...................FALSIFY, PERVERT

missile .................................DART

missile, guided ........JUNO, NIKE,

...................SCUD, THOR; ATLAS,

............TITAN; BOMARC; JUPITER;

...................PERSHING, REGULUS

mist .................FILM, HAZE, MURK

mistake ................BONER, ERROR

mistakes, list of ..................ERRATA

mite..................................ACARID

mitigate ........EASE; ABATE, ALLAY

mix .............................STIR; BLEND;

................................MINGLE

mixer .....................................DANCE

mixture....................OLIO; BLEND

mixture, mineral .................MAGMA

mock..............APE; SHAM; FARCE

mock blow............................FEINT c

mock orange ...................SYRINGA

model, perfect ...............PARAGON

moderate....................EASY, MILD;

........................ABATE; EASE UP,

........................GENTLE, RELENT

modernist ................................NEO

modest.........................SHY; MEEK;

........................TIMID; CHASTE,

........................DEMURE, HUMBLE

modify .......VARY; ALTER, EMEND;

........................CHANGE, TEMPER

Mogul emperor....................AKBAR

Mohammed, adopted son of.......ALI

Mohammed, birthplace of ...MECCA

Mohammed, daughter of....FATIMA

Mohammed, mule of ...........FADDA

Mohammed, supporters of....ANSAR

Mohammed, tomb city of ....MEDINA

Mohammed, uncle of ..........ABBAS

Mohammed, wife of.............AISHA

Mohammedanism ................ISLAM

Mohawk, city on the .............UTICA

Mohicans, last of the ..........UNCAS

moiety ...................................HALF

moist ..............WET; DAMP, DANK,

........................DEWY; HUMID

moisture, morning ..................DEW

molasses ........................TREACLE

molasses rum ..........TAFIA; TAFFIA

mold ......................MODEL, SHAPE d

molding................OGEE; REEDING

molding, concave ...............CONGE;

........................SCOTIA; CAVETTO

molding, concave and convex ......

..................CYMA, GOLA; DUCINE

molding, convex ...................BEAK;

........................OVOLO, TORUS;

........................ASTRAGAL

molding, edge of ...................ARRIS

molding, flat ..........FILLET, REGLET

molding, square ..................LISTEL

molding clay ...........................PUG

moldy.................................MUSTY

mole(s) ...................:.NEVI; NEVUS

........................NAEVUS

mole, Old World ...................TALPA

molelike mammal...............DESMAN

mollusk .................CLAM; CHITON,

........................MUSSEL; ABALONE

mollusk, bivalve ...............SCALLOP

mollusk, chambered .......NAUTILUS

mollusk, gastropod ................SNAIL

mollusk, largest ...................CHAMA

molt .......................................SHED

molten rock..............LAVA; MAGMA

moment ........................JIFF; TRICE

monad ........................ATOM, UNIT

monastery church ............MINSTER

monetary units ..........See page 213.

77

*a* money.............CASH, GELT, JACK,
..........................KALE; BREAD,
...........BUCKS, DOUGH; DINERO,
.....................MAZUMA, MOOLAH;
................CABBAGE; SIMOLEONS
money, borrowed ...................LOAN
money, bronze ...........................AES
money, medieval .....................ORA
money, Native Amer. ......WAMPUM
money, put in .......................INVEST
money, shell ......SEWAN; SEAWAN
money certificate ......BOND; SCRIP
money drawer ...........................TILL
money exchange fee..............AGIO
moneylender ......................USERER
money reserve .......................FUND
Mongol .............................TARTAR
Mongol, Buddhist................ELEUT;
.....................................KALMUCK
Mongol dynasty.....................YUAN
Mongol tent ...........................YURT
mongoose, crab-eating .........URVA
mongrel .......................CUR; MUTT
monitor lizard ........................URAN
monk ............................FRA; FRIAR;
.....................................CENOBITE
monk, Buddhist...................ARHAT
monk, Eng. ...........................BEDE
monk, head .........................ABBOT
Monkees movie .....................HEAD
*b* monkey ............................APE, SAI;
........CHACMA, GIBBON, GRIVET,
.....................GUENON, RHESUS,
.....................SIMIAN; MACAQUE;
................CAPUCHIN, MANDRILL,
..........MARMOSET; ORANGUTAN
monkey, Madagascar ..........LEMUR
monkey, S. A. .................SAKI, TITI
monkey puzzle ............ARAUCARIA
monk settlement, E. Orthodox .........
..................................SKETE
monk's hood ........................COWL
monolith .........................MENHIR
monopoly ............................TRUST
monopoly, international......CARTEL
monster...................OGRE; BEAST
monster, man-bull .........MINOTAUR
monster, 100-eyed ..............ARGUS
monster in Gr. myth .........CHIMERA
monster slain by Hercules ...HYDRA
month, Hindu ................PUS; ASIN;
.................JETH, MAGH; AGHAN,
..............................ASARH, CHAIT;
.........SAWAN; BHADON, KARTIK;
.......................PHAGUN; BAISAKH
month, Islamic ......................RABI;
...............RAJAB, SAFAR, JUMADA,
.................SHA'BAN; RAMADAN,
.................SHAWWAL; MUHARRAM;
.............................DHU'L-QA'DAH

month, Jewish ...........ADAR, ELUL, *c*
......................IYAR; NISAN, SIVAN;
..............KISLEV, SHEBAT, TISHRI,
......................TAMMUZ; HESHVAN
month, Muslim fast........RAMADAN
month abbreviation ........APR, AUG,
...........DEC, FEB, JAN, JUL, JUN,
.........MAR, NOV, OCT, SEP; SEPT
monument stone .................CAIRN;
.....................DOLMEN; CROMLECH
moons........See planets & satellites.
moon flower..........................DAISY
moon goddess .................ASTARTE
moon valley ...........................RILLE
moon vehicle: Abbr. ..............LEM
mop .......................................SWAB
morass ...........FEN; MIRE; MARSH;
.....................TANGLE; QUAGMIRE
moray ......................................EEL
more..........ALSO; ADDED, EXTRA,
.............................STILL; BETTER
more!........................BIS; ENCORE
More's island ......................UTOPIA
more than enough ...TOO; EXCESS
more than 50% .....................MOST
morning glory .................IPOMOEA
morning prayer ...................MATINS
morning song .....................AUBADE
Moroccan Berber ....................RIFF
Moroccan ...............................MOOR
moron .........FOOL; IDIOT; CRETIN *d*
morose ...........DOUR, GLUM; SULLEN
morsel ............BIT; CRUMB; TIDBIT
mortar................BOWL; CANNON
mortar ingredient ......LIME, SAND;
..............................WATER; CEMENT
mortar instrument ...............PESTLE
mortar mixer................................RAB
mortar tray...............................HOD
mortise insert......................TENON
Mosaic law........................TORAH
mosaic piece(s)................SMALTI,
.........................SMALTO; TESSERA
Moscow department store ......GUM
Moselle tributary....................SAAR
Moses, brother of .............AARON
Moses, father-in-law of ......JETHRO
Moses's death mountain........NEBO
Moses's spy in Canaan ........CALEB
Moslem..........................See Muslim.
mosque ...........................MASJID
mosque in Jerusalem ...........OMAR
mosque student ..................SOFTA
mosquito genus ...............AEDES
mossbunker fish ..................POGY;
..................................MENHADEN
most...............MAX; VERY; EXTRA
moth...........LUNA; EGGER, TINEA
motherless calf .....................DOGIE
mother of gods .......................RHEA

a  mother-of-pearl ....................NACRE
mother-of-pearl shell .......ABALONE
mother's side, related on......ENATE
motionless .................INERT, STILL
motive.................CAUSE; REASON
motor, race the .........................REV
mound .....................HEAP, LUMP,
...........................PILE; STACK
mound, manmade protective..TERP
mountain, Afr. .........................JAJA;
...........................KILIMANJARO
mountain, Alps .....................BLANC
mountain, Ant. .......SHINN, TYREE
mountain, Biblical.................NEBO;
.............HOREB, SINAI; ARARAT
mountain, Canary Islands......TEIDE
mountain, fabled Hindu .........MERU
mountain, Gr. .................HELICON
mountain, N. Z. ......................COOK
mountain, Sp. .....................ANETO
mountain, Swiss .....................DOM;
.................CASTOR; JUNGFRAU;
.....................MATTERHORN
mountain, Yukon .................LOGAN
mountain ash .........SORB; ROWAN
mountain climbing gear........PITON
mountain crest .....................ARETE
mountain in Thessaly ...........OSSA;
.....................................PELION
mountain lion .........................PUMA
b  mountain mint .......................BASIL
mountain on Crete .....................IDA
mountain pass ...........................COL
mountain pass in the Alps.....CENIS
mountain pass in India...........GHAT
mountain peak.............................ALP
mountain pool........................TARN
mountain range, Eur. .............ALPS
mountain range, Fr.-Swiss......JURA
mountain range, Ger. ............HARZ
mountain recess .....................CWM
mountains, Asian ...................ALTAI
mountain spinach ................ORACH
mountains, US .........BEAR, BONA,
.................HOOD, YALE; EVANS;
.........ANTERO, CASTLE, ELBERT;
........................HUNTER, WILSON;
.................FORAKER, HARVARD
.....LA PLATA, RAINIER, WHITNEY
Mount of Olives ...................OLIVET
mourn.................GRIEVE; LAMENT
mournful .................SAD; RUEFUL,
...................WOEFUL; UNHAPPY
mourning band....................CRAPE
mouse, field .........................VOLE
mousebird .............COLY; SHRIKE
mouse-spotter's cry ..................EEK
mouth, away from the ........ABORAL
mouth, of the .........................ORAL
mouth, river .........................DELTA

c  mouth, tidal river....................FIRTH
mouthlike orifice .................STOMA
mouth open.........................AGAPE
mouthpiece .............REED, BOCAL;
...........................................LAWYER
move ...........STIR; SHIFT, TOUCH;
.....................AFFECT; RELOCATE
move a camera.........................PAN
move back ...............EBB; RECEDE
move little by little ...................INCH
movement, biological ............TAXIS
movement, capable of ........MOTILE
movement in music ...............MOTO
move to and fro .........................WAG;
.............................FLAP, SWAY
move up and down ....................BOB
movies...............................CINEMA
movies, XXX-rated.................PORN
moving part .........................ROTOR
mow.........................................CUT
mowed strip.........................SWATH
Mowgli, friend of .................BALOO
muck.........................GOO; OOZE;
...............................GRIME, SLIME
mud, stick in the .....................MIRE
mud deposit .............................SILT
muddle.................MESS; TURMOIL
muddy, make ......................ROIL
mudfish ...................AMIA; BOWFIN
mudhole.................................PULK
d  mud volcano .........................SALSE
mug...........................FACE; STEIN;
..............................................NOGGIN
mug, small.............................TOBY
mulberry-bark cloth ...............TAPA
mulberry-flavored wine........MORAT
mulberry of India .......................AAL
mulct .....................FINE; AMERCE
mullet, red................................SUR
multiform .........................DIVERSE
multiplicand .....................FACIEND
multiplier ..........................FACIENT
multitude .................HOST; HORDE
munch ...............................CHOMP
mundane.........................PROSAIC,
...........................................WORLDLY
Munich's river .........................ISAR
Munsters, dragon of the .........SPOT
murder.................OFF; KILL, SLAY
murder by suffocation ..........BURKE
murderer, first .........................CAIN
murmur .................BUZZ; GOSSIP,
........................MUMBLE, RUMBLE
muscle ..................THEW; SINEW
muscle, kind of .................TENSOR;
...................ERECTOR, LEVATOR
muscle, like ............................MYOID
muscular spasm .........................TIC
Muse of astronomy.............URANIA
Muse of comedy .................THALIA

a Muse of dance .......TERPSICHORE
Muse of epic song .........CALLIOPE
Muse of erotic poetry ...........ERATO
Muse of history ........................CLIO
Muse of hymns ........POLYHYMNIA
Muse of lyric poetry .........EUTERPE
Muse of tragedy ........MELPOMENE
Muses, nine ....................PIERIDES
musette .................................OBOE
museum head ................CURATOR
mush ....................ATOLE, SEPON
mushroom ............................MOREL
mushroom cap ....................PILEUS
mushroom stalk ....................STIPE
music, as written in ..................STA
music, choral ....................MOTET;
.........................................CANTATA
music, Indian ..........................RAGA
musical beat............................TAKT
musical direction .................TACET
musical instrument (brass).......SAX;
...............TUBA; BUGLE; CORNET;
.....................ALPHORN, CLARION,
....................HELICON, TRUMPET;
.....................................TROMBONE
musical instrument (keyboard)..........
.........................ORGAN, PIANO;
.....................CLAVIER; CALLIOPE
musical instrument (percussion) ......
....................DRUM, GONG; BELLS,
b ..............CONGA, TABOR, VIBES;
........CHIMES, CYMBAL, NAGARA,
....................TAM-TAM; CELESTA;
....................MARACAS, MARIMBA,
....................TIMPANI; TRIANGLE
musical instrument (string) ......OUD;
.............BASS, HARP, LUTE, LYRE,
....................VIOL; BANJO, CELLO,
...............DOBRO, REBEC, SITAR,
...............VIOLA; FIDDLE, GUITAR,
.............................VIOLIN, ZITHER;
..................BANDORE, UKULELE;
..................DULCIMER, MANDOLIN

musical instrument (woodwind)........ c
.............FIFE, OBOE, PIPE; FLUTE;
....SHAWM; BASSOON, OCARINA,
......................PANPIPE, PICCOLO,
....................WHISTLE; CLARINET
musical work ..........................OPUS
music character .DOT; REST, CLEF
music drama .......................OPERA
music for nine ....................NONET
music for three..........................TRIO
music for two ..........................DUET
music interval ...................TRITONE
music lines ...........................STAFF
music student's piece ..........ETUDE
music symbols, old ............NEUME
music terminology.....See page 233.
Musketeer ...........ATHOS; ARAMIS;
..............PORTHOS; D'ARTAGNON
Muslim, branch of ......SHI'A; SUNNI
Muslim, strict....................WAHABI
Muslim call to prayer ........... AZAN
Muslim deity........................ALLAH
Muslim fast....................RAMADAN
Muslim festival..................BAIRAM
Muslim fiat............................IRADE
Muslim fourth caliph................ALI
Muslim guide in Pak. or India .....PIR
Muslim holy city..................MECCA
Muslim holy man...................IMAM
Muslim judge .........................CADI,
.................................KADI, QADI d
Muslim marriage, temporary ..MUTA
Muslim nymph ......................HOURI
Muslim prayer .........SALAH, SALAT
Muslim pulpit......MIMBAR, MINBAR
Muslim sacred book ............KORAN
Muslim sect ...........SUNNI, SHIITE
Muslim theologians..............ULEMA
mussel, freshwater.................UNIO
musteline animal.OTTER, WEASEL
mutilate ..................................MAIM
muttonfish ..............................SAMA
mysterious........ARCANE, OCCULT

# N

nab .......................GRAB; ARREST
NaCl .......................................SALT
nail ...........................CLAW, TACK;
..................................SPIKE, TALON
nail, thin.................................BRAD
nail with a hole ......................SPAD
nakedwood tree......................MABI
namaycush ............................TROUT
name ................DUB; TERM; TITLE
named .............CALLED, DUBBED,
.............................................YCLEPT

namely........................................VIZ
Naomi, daughter-in-law of ......RUTH
naos......................................CELLA
nap-raising device ..............TEASEL
nap-raising machine .................GIG
Napoleon, brother-in-law of.MURAT
Napoleon, isle of ....................ELBA
Napoleon, marshal of ..............NEY
Napoleon, victory site of ........JANA,
.............................................LODI
Narcissus, lover of ................ECHO

*a* narcotic...................DOPE, DRUG;
..................HEROINE, OPIATE
narcotic shrub ........................COCA
narrate ....................TELL; RECITE,
...................RELATE, REPORT
narrow..................TIGHT; INSULAR
nation, of a..........................STATAL
National Socialist, Ger. ...........NAZI
native .....................RAW; CRUDE;
..................................ENDEMIC
natural..................................BORN
natural talent .........................FLAIR
nature ...........HUMOR; ESSENCE
nature goddess .................CYBELE
nature-story writer...............SETON
nautical...............................MARINE
nautical cry ..............AHOY; AVAST
Navaho dwelling .................HOGAN
navy jail.................................BRIG
Navy mascot..........................GOAT
near ...........NIGH; ABOUT, CLOSE
nearest................NEXT; PROXIMAL
nearsightedness.................MYOPIA
nearsighted person ............MYOPE
neat...............................TIDY, TRIM;
..................................SPRUCE
necessitate ........................ENTAIL;
..................................REQUIRE
neck, nape of the.................NUCHA
neckline shape..........................VEE;
*b* ...........................BOAT, CREW
necktie ................................CRAVAT
neckwear .......BOA; FICHU, STOLE
nee.......................................BORN
need .....................WANT; REQUIRE
needle ...................PROD; BODKIN
needle case .............................ETUI
needlefish ...............................GAR
needleshaped ...................ACUATE
negation, particle of ................NOT
negative ......................NAY; NOPE
negatives ............................NOES
neglect ....................OMIT, SNUB;
..................SHIRK; IGNORE,
...................SLIGHT; DISREGARD
negligent ...................LAX; REMISS
negotiate...........................FIX, SET;
..................CLEAR; SETTLE;
..................................ARRANGE
neighborhood, dilapidated......SLUM
Nelson, victory site of.............NILE
nemesis...............................BANE
Neptune's spear .............TRIDENT
nerve cell.............AXON; NEURON
nerve layers, brain's.............ALVEI
nervous..................EDGY; JUMPY,
..................TENSE; UNEASY
nervous disease ...............CHOREA
nest, eagle's...........................AERIE
Nestor, mother of ..................TYRO

*c* net.........................................MESH;
..................CLEAR, SEINE
netlike ...............................RETIARY
network....................WEB; RETE
Nevada resort .......................RENO
new ........................NOVEL; RECENT
New Mexico art colony ...........TAOS
News agency, Eng. ........REUTERS
News agency, Jap. ..............DOMEI
News agency, Soviet ..............TASS
newspaper....................RAG; POST;
..................PRESS; GAZETTE,
..................................JOURNAL
news piece ..............................ITEM
news service ...........................UPI
newt ......................EFT; TRITON
new wine ...............................MUST
New York harbor island..........ELLIS
New Zealand bird ........HUIA, KAKI,
..................PEHO, RURU
N. Z. evergreen.......................TAWA
N. Z. honeyeater .......................TUI
N. Z. native people ...............MAORI
N. Z. parrot..............................KAKA
N. Z. rail bird.........................WEKA
N. Z. tree ................KAURI, NGAIO;
..................................TOTARA
N. Z. woody vine .......................AKA
niche ..............ALCOVE, RECESS
Nichols' hero ............................ABIE
*d* nickel-steel alloy...............INVAR
Nick's dog...............................ASTA
Nick's wife................................NORA
nicotinic acid ......................NIACIN
nictitate ...............................WINK
niggardly ...........MEAGER, STINGY
nigh .......................................NEAR
nightingale, Pers. ............BULBUL
nightjar ................................POTOO
Nile island ..............................RODA
Nile sailboat......................CANGIA
nimble ....................SPRY; AGILE
nimbus....................................HALO
nimrod ................................HUNTER
nine, group of ...................ENNEAD
nine, music for .....................NONET
nine inches ...........................SPAN
nipple .....................................TEAT
Nisan, in old Hebrew................ABIB
niton ...................................RADON
nitrogen, once .....................AZOTE
No: Russ. ...............................NYET
Noah, landing place of.......ARARAT
Noah, son of ...............HAM; SHEM;
..................................JAPHETH
noble, female .......................DAME,
..................LADY; QUEEN;
..................DUCHESS; COUNTESS,
..................BARONESS, PRINCESS
noble, Ger. ...........GRAF; RITTER

a noble, male ...............DUKE, EARL;
......................KING, LORD, PEER;
.............BARON, COUNT; KNIGHT,
......................PRINCE; BARONET,
..................MARQUIS; VISCOUNT
nocturnal mammal .....BAT; LEMUR
nod..............................BOW; BECK;
.........................................ASSENT
Nod, land west of .................EDEN
node....................KNOB, KNOT;
.........................................NODUS
nod off ................................SLEEP
nomad ......................WANDERER
nomadic people of the Nile .....BEJA
nomenclature ..................NAMES
nominal value ..........................PAR
nominate............................NAME
non-cleric........................LAY; LAIC
nonchalant ...............CALM, COOL,
..................EVEN; COLLECTED
non-Jew(s) ................GOY; GOYIM
nonsense ................BOSH, BUNK,
....................CRAP, GUFF, TOSH;
.........................BILGE; BUNKUM,
.........................PIFFLE; BLATHER
nonsensical talk ......................BLAH
noose ...................................LOOP
Normandy landing................D-DAY
Norse destiny goddess..........NORN
Norse epic............................EDDA
b Norse letter ..........................RUNE
Norseman ..............DANE; SWEDE
Norse mythical hero................EGIL
North, Mrs.........................PAMELA
N. Afr. people ..................BERBER
North Carolina college..........ELON
North Carolinian ..........TARHEEL
North Caucasian language .......UDI;
........................AVAR; UDIC; UDISH
northern ...........................BOREAL
northern Scand. ....................LAPP
northernmost land ..............THULE
North Sea, river into the..........DEE;
.........................TAY; ELBE, TEES;
.........................FORTH; HUMBER
North Sea boat ....................COBLE
North Sea inlet ....................WASH
North Star ........................POLARIS
Northumberland river............TYNE
Norwegian coin ......................ORE
Norwegian composer ..........GRIEG
Norwegian king......................OLAF
Norwegian novelist..........HAMSUN
nose .................SNOOP; SCHNOZ
nose, having a large ..........NASUTE
nose, having a snub..........SIMOUS
nosegay ...............................POSY
nose opening(s)......NARES, NARIS
nostrils, of the....................NARIAL,
.........................................NARINE

c _____ Nostrum (Mediterranean)..........
.........................................MARE
not at home ...........................OUT
notch..................KERF, NICK, NOCK
notched........................SERRATED
note ...............CHIT, MEMO, TONE;
.....................REMARK, RENOWN
note, Guido's high ..................E LA
note, Guido's low ...............GAMUT
note, half..........................MINIM
notes in Guido's scale ..........ELAMI
not ever, in poetry .................NE'ER
nothing ...................NIL, NIX; NULL,
.............................ZERO; NIHIL
not in style .................OUT; PASSE
notion....................................IDEA
notion, capricious ..................WHIM
not long ago ......................LATELY
not moving...........INERT; STATIC
not one......................NARY, NONE
notorious .......................INFAMOUS
not so great.............LESS; FEWER
notwithstanding .........................YET
nought ....................ZERO, NULL
noun form ............................CASE
nourish ...................FEED; FOSTER
nourished ...............................FED
Nova Scotia ....................ACADIA
novelty ....................TOY; BAUBLE
novice .........................TIRO, TYRO
d nucha ...............................NAPE
nudge ...............JOG; POKE, PROD
nuisance ...............PEST; BOTHER
nullify ...........................NEGATE
nullify, legally ........................VOID
number, irrational .................SURD
number, whole ................INTEGER
number under ten ..................DIGIT
numerous...........................MANY;
.........................LEGION, MYRIAD
nun, Franciscan ..................CLARE
nun, head........................ABBESS
nun's dress ..........................HABIT
nurse, Oriental ......................AMAH
nurse, Slavic ........................BABA
nursemaid, Indian ................AYAH
nut ...........COLA, KOLA; ALMOND,
.........................CASHEW, LITCHI
nut, hickory .........................PECAN
nut, pine ...........................PINON
nutlike drupe .......................TRYMA
nutmeg husk .......................MACE
nutria ..................................COYPU
nutriment ............FOOD; ALIMENT
nuts ..................CRAZY; WHACKO
nymph, fountain ..................EGERIA
nymph, laurel ...................DAPHNE
nymph, mountain................OREAD
nymph, Muslim ....................HOURI
nymph, water .......................NAIAD

# O

oaf.............CLOD, LOUT; LUMMOX
oak, California ...................ENCINA
oak, dried fruit of ...............CAMATA
oak, evergreen......................HOLM
oak moss..........................EVERNIA
oakum, seal with ..................CAULK
oar.............ROW; BLADE; PROPEL
oar at stern ...........................SCULL
oasis, N. Afr. .........................WADI
oat genus ............................AVENA
oath, euphemistic........GAD; DARN,
.............................DRAT; PHOOEY,
..................................SHUCKS
oath, old-fashioned .................EGAD
oath, say under .................DEPOSE
obeisance, show......................BOW
obey..........................HEED, MIND
object..........................ITEM; THING
objection, petty .....................CAVIL
objective .........................AIM; GOAL
object of art..........................CURIO
obligation ........DEBT, DUTY, ONUS
oblique..............BIASED; SLANTED
obliterate..............ERASE; EFFACE
oblivion ..................LETHE, LIMBO;
.............................................ESCAPE
obscure ..................DIM; FAINT,
b   ..........MURKY, VAGUE; BLEARY
obscure, render .................DARKLE
observe .......SEE; NOTE; BEHOLD,
.................REMARK; CELEBRATE
obstinate .......TOUGH; STUBBORN
obtain .........GET; GAIN; PROCURE
obtained ......................GOT; TOOK
obvious ..................OPEN; PATENT
obvious, not........................SUBTLE
occasional .........RARE; SCARCE;
.................UNUSUAL; SPORADIC
Occident ...............................WEST
occipital protuberance(s)..........INIA;
.............................................INION
occupant........TENANT; RESIDENT
occupation ..........................TRADE
occupied................................BUSY
occupy.....FILL; ENGAGE; PEOPLE
occurrence ..........................EVENT
oceanic ...........................PELAGIC
oceanic tunicate ........SALP; SALPA
ocean motion..............TIDE, WAVE
octopus..................POULP; POULPE
Odin, brother of ......................VILI
Odin, grandfather of ............NANNA
Odin, home of ...............VALHALLA
Odin, son of ........TYR; THOR, VALI
odor ......................AROMA, SCENT
Odysseus .......................ULYSSES
Odysseus, companion of ELPENOR

Odyssey beggar .....................IRUS
Odyssey singer .....................SIREN
Oedipus, father of .................LAIUS
Oedipus, mother of .........JOCASTA
off .........................................AWAY
offend ...............................AFFRONT
offense.........................SIN; CRIME
offer ...........................BID; TENDER
offhand..............................CASUAL
office, R.C. curia ..................DATARY
office holders...........................INS
officer, church .....................BEADLE
officer, Scot. court ...............MACER
officer, Scot. municipal.........BAILIE
officer, minor Rom. .............LICTOR
officer, synagogue ............PARNAS
officer, university ...DEAN; BURSAR
office worker's skill ...............STENO
official, Muslim court .............HAJIB
official, Rom. .........EDILE; AEDILE;
.............................................TRIBUNE
official, subordinate............SATRAP
offspring .........BABY, CION, SONS;
..............................HEIRS; SCION
ogygian .................................AGED;
.................ANCIENT; PRIMEVAL
Ohio college town .....................ADA
oil ...............FAT; LARD, SUET
oil, beetle .............................MELOE
oil, cruet .............................AMPULLA
oil, of...................................OLEIC
oil, orange .........................NEROLI
oil, put on .............................ANOINT
oil, rose ..................................ATTAR
oil bottle .............................CRUET
oilfish................................ESCOLAR
oil-yielding tree......................TUNG
oily ketone .............................IRONE
ointment ...................BALM, NARD;
.............SALVE; CERATE, POMADE
okay.................ROGER; APPROVE
Okefenoke possum .............POGO
okra dish............................GUMBO
old.........................................AGED
Old Curiosity Shop girl ............NELL
old Eng. militia......................FYRD
old Eng. gold piece ...............RYAL
old Eng. rune .........................WEN
old Gr. coin...........OBOL; OBOLUS
old Irish counterfeit coin...........RAP
old Pers. money ..................DARIC
old Sp. gold coin .................DOBLA
old-timer...................COOT, FOGY;
.............................................CODGER
old times ...................ELD; YORE
old-womanish ......................ANILE
oleaginous ...............................OILY

oleic-acid salt ........................OLEATE
oleoresin ................................ANIME,
..............................ELEMI; BALSAM
olive color................................DUNE;
..................................TWINE; ANAMITE
olive genus .............................OLEA
Olympus, mount near............OSSA
Olympus, region near...........PIERIA
omen ..............AUGURY; PORTENT
omentum, great ........................CAUL
omission in a word .............ELISION
omit ................DROP, PASS, SKIP
omit in pronunciation .............ELIDE
onager......................................ASS
one ............BUCK, UNIT; SINGLE
one, music for .........................SOLO
one-base hit ........................SINGLE
one behind another...........TANDEM
one-eighth troy ounce............DRAM
one-eyed giant .................CYCLOPS
one-horse carriage .................SHAY
one hundred square meters .....ARE
one hundred thousand rupees .........
..................................................LAKH
O'Neill heroine .......................ANNA
one-spot ...................................ACE
onion, Welsh .........................CIBOL
onion, Sp. .............................CIBOLA
onionlike plant...........LEEK; CHIVE;
..............................................SHALLOT
only.................MERE, SAVE, SOLE
onward ...........AHEAD; FORWARD
ooze ..............LEAK, SEEP; EXUDE
open .....................AJAR; OVERT
opening.............GAP; HOLE, RIFT,
....................SLOT, VENT; HIATUS
opening, skin.........................PORE
opera, Beethoven...............FIDELIO
opera, Bellini.......................NORMA
opera, Bizet ......................CARMEN
opera, Delibes.....................LAKME
opera, Gounod .....................FAUST
opera, Massenet ....MANON, THAIS
opera, Puccini....................TOSCA;
...............................TURANDOT
opera, Strauss...................SALOME;
...............................................ELEKTRA;
...................ARABELLA, CAPRICIO
opera, Verdi ..........AIDA; ERNANI,
...................OTELLO; FALSTAFF;
..........DON CARLOS, RIGOLETTO
opera, Wagner ....................RIENZI
opera hat..............................GIBUS
opera heroine ..........AIDA, ELSA,
...................MIMI; SENTA; ISOLDE
opera house, Milan .........LA SCALA
opera star .............................DIVA
operate ...................RUN; MANAGE
operated ....................................RAN
opium poppy seed..................MAW

opossum rat......................SELVA
opponent .......FOE; ENEMY, RIVAL
opportune ..........................TIMELY
opportunity ........................CHANCE
opposed, one .........................ANTI
opposite......................COUNTER,
................REVERSE; CONTRARY
opposite extremities .............POLES
Ops, daughter of .................CERES
Ops, husband of................SATURN
optical glass..........................LENS
optical illusion ...................MIRAGE
optimistic................................ROSY
oracle, Gr. ...........DELOS; DELPHI
orange-red stone ...................SARD
orator ...................................RHETOR
orbit point .......APOGEE; PERIGEE
orchid tuber ..........................SALEP
ordain ...........DECREE, IMPOSE
order...............................BID; FIAT;
...............................EDICT; DECREE
order, put in .............TIDY; SETTLE
ordinance .................................LAW
ore deposit ...........................LODE
ore of iron...........................OCHER
organ, seed-bearing..............PISTIL
organ control .........................STOP
organism, one-celled ........AMOEBA
organism, simple..................MONAD
organization .............CLUB; GUILD,
.........SETUP; LEAGUE; SOCIETY
organ pipe .............................REED
organ prelude ....................VERSET
organ stop.............................SEXT;
.....................DOLCAN; CELESTE,
...................MELODIA; DIAPASON
orgy ............................BINGE, FLING,
......................SPREE; RAMPAGE
Orient.......................................EAST
Oriental ................................ASIAN
Oriental nursemaid .............AMAH
Oriental plane tree.............CHINAR
Oriental potentate ....................AGA
Oriental sailing ship .............DHOW
Oriental servant ..................HAMAL
orifice ...................PORE; STOMA
origin ....................SEED; SOURCE
original ...........NEW; FIRST, PRIME
original sinner .......................ADAM
originate .................ARISE, BEGIN,
...............................START; INVENT
Orinoco tributary......................ARO
oriole, golden .....................LORIOT
ornament ............TRIM; ADORN
ornament, curly .................SCROLL
ornamental border ...............DADO
ornamental grass ..............EULALIA
ornamental nailhead...............STUD
ornament in relief.............EMBOSS
Orpheus, destination of .......HADES

a Orpheus, instrument of ..........LYRE
orris .............................................IRIS
oscillate ...................SWAY; SWING
osier ......................................WITHE
Osiris, brother of .........................SET
Osiris, wife/sister of .....................ISIS
ostentation ...............................POMP
ostrich, S. A. .............................RHEA
ostrichlike bird ..........................EMU
Othello, foe of...........................IAGO
otherwise ..................................ELSE
otic ...........................................AURAL
otter, common Indian...............NAIR
otter brown color...............LOUTRE
Ottoman ...................................TURK
ottoman ..........POUF; HASSOCK
Ottoman court.....................PORTE
Ottoman official ....................PASHA
Ottoman peasant..................RAYA;
.................................................RAYAH
Our Gang dog ..........................PETE
Our Gang girl .........................DARLA
Our Mutual Friend character.WEGG
oust ....................EJECT, EVICT
out-and-out....................ARRANT
outbreak ...................................RIOT
outburst, sudden ....................SPATE
outcast .................LEPER; PARIAH
outcome ...........RESULT, UPSHOT
outcry.....................................CLAMOR
b outer portion of Earth ..............SIAL
outfit...........KIT, RIG; GEAR, SUIT
outfit, unusual ........................GETUP
outlet.......................VENT; SOCKET
outline................DRAFT; SKETCH;
...................CONTOUR, PROFILE
outlook .............VISTA; PROSPECT
outmoded .............................PASSE
out of the way.......................ASIDE

ova...........................................EGGS c
oval .................................ELLIPTICAL
oven .........................KILN, OAST
oven, annealing....................LEHR
over......................ATOP, DONE;
.............ABOVE, AGAIN, ENDED;
.......ACROSS, AROUND, UNDULY
overact ...............................EMOTE
overcoat...........LODEN; ULSTER;
....................................PALETOT
overdue payment...........ARREARS
overflow .............GLUT; SURPLUS
overjoy ...............................ELATE
overly fond of, act...................DOTE
overnice person........................PRIG
overshadow................TOP; BEST;
..............................PASS; EXCEL,
..........................OUTDO; BETTER
overshoes......................GALOSHES
overskirt.........................PANIER
overt.......................................OPEN
over there...............YON; YONDER
overwhelm ........................FLOOD;
....................DELUGE, ENGULF
ovule .......................................SEED
ovum .......................................EGG
owl, horned ...........................BUBO
owl's cry ...............................HOOT
own up to .............................AVOW
ox, extinct wild ......................URUS
ox, forest .............................ANOA d
ox, long-haired .......................YAK
Oxford ...................................OXON
Oxford fellows .......................DONS
oxide ......................................CALX
oxidize .................................RUST
oyster, young ..........................SPAT
oysterfish........TAUTOG; TAUTAUG
Oz books author ...................BAUM

# P

pace ..........WALK; SPEED, TEMPO
pachyderm ....................ELEPHANT
pacify ....................CALM; GENTLE,
.......................SOOTHE; PLACATE
pack ...................JAM, WAD; STOW
pack animal...............ASS; BURRO,
........................LLAMA; SUMPTER
pack down...................RAM; TAMP
pad ......................BLOCK; TABLET
padded jacket under armor .ACTON
padnag ...................TROT; AMBLE
Padua, town near ...................ESTE
pagan god..............................IDOL
page ...........................CALL, LEAF
pageantry ..............................POMP

page number ...........................FOLIO
Pagliacci characters............BEPPE,
.............................CANIO, NEDDA,
.............................TONIO; SILVIO
pain .............ACHE, PANG; AGONY
pain, causing ....................ALGETIC
pain reliever ....OPIATE; ANODYNE
paint ................COLOR; TEMPERA
paint, face .............................ROUGE
painting, wall.........................MURAL
painting style .........................GENRE
pair .................DUO; DUAD, DUET,
.............DYAD, MATE; TWOSOME
pairing ................................MATING
pair of horses ............SPAN, TEAM

a Pakistani woman.................BEGUM
palanquin, Jap. .....................KAGO
palanquin bearer..................HAMAL
palate, soft .........................VELUM
pale ............................WAN; ASHY;
.............................ASHEN, PASTY
pale color............................PASTEL
pale-colored .......................MEALY
Pallas................................ATHENA
pallid ...................................PALE
palm ....................COCO; TALIPOT
palm, Asian.........ARENGA, BETEL
palm, betel .........................ARECA
palm, book .........................TALIERA
palm, Braz. ............DATIL, ASSAI
palm, climbing....................RATTAN
palm, N. Z. .......................NIKAU
palm, nipa ...............ATAP; ATTAP
palm, sago ........................GOMUTI
palmetto...............................SABAL
palm fiber ...........DATIL; RAFFIA
palm juice, fermented............SURA
palm liquor ................BENO, BINO,
................NIPA, TUBA; TODDY
palm starch ..........................SAGO
palp ...................................FEELER
pamper...............................COSSET
pamphlet ............................TRACT
pan, Chin. .............................WOK
panacea ..............................ELIXIR
b Panama, former name of....DARIEN
panel of jurors...................VENIRE
pangolin, five-toed .............MANIS
panic ................FEAR; ALARM;
..................................TERRIFY
pannier...............................DOSSER
pant.....................................GASP
pantry.............AMBRY; LARDER,
.................SPENCE; BUTTERY
papal cape..........................FANON
papal church.....................LATERAN
papal court.................SEE; CURIA
papal letter ...........................BULL
papal scarf ..........................ORALE
papal seal ...........................BULLA
paper, thin crisp .................PELURE
paper base............................PULP
paper folded once ...............FOLIO
paper measure..........REAM; QUIRE
paper mulberry ....................KOZO
paper mulberry bark ............TAPA
paper size ............................DEMY;
.........................FOLIO, SEXTO;
.....................OCTAVO, QUARTO
papyrus...............................SEDGE
par ................NORM; AVERAGE
par, one under.....................BIRDIE
par, two under......................EAGLE
Para, Brazil, capital of..........BELEM
para-aminobenzoic acid .........PABA

c parade.................MARCH, STRUT;
.....................FLAUNT, REVIEW
paradise, earthly ...................EDEN
paradisiacal .......................EDENIC
parasite ..............................LEECH
parasitic insect......................MITE;
.........................LOUSE; ACARID
parasitic insects ....................LICE
parasitic plant.......MOSS; DODDER
Parcae...............................FATES
Parcae, the .............NONA; MORTA;
.................................DECUMA
parcel of land ..........................LOT
parchment, book ...............FOREL;
..................................FORREL
pardon .............REMIT; CONDONE
pardon, general ...............AMNESTY
pare ......................................PEEL
pari-mutuel machine ...............TOTE
Paris, father of ....................PRIAM
Paris, first bishop of ..............DENIS
Paris, wife of ....................OENONE
Paris art exhibit....................SALON
parish head .......................RECTOR
Paris subway......................METRO
Paris thug ..........................APACHE
Parkinson's disease drug ...L-DOPA
parlay ............................PALAVER
Parliamentary report.......HANSARD
paroxysm ..................FIT; SPASM
d parrot ...................EOS, KEA; LORY
parrotfish ............................LORO
parry ...................FEND; EVADE;
..................................COUNTER
Parsee priest.......................MOBED
Parsee scripture................AVESTA
parsley camphor.....APIOL; APIOLE
parsonage ...........................MANSE
parson bird ..........POE, TUI; KOKO
part ............ROLE, SOME; BREAK,
.................PIECE, SEVER, SHARE;
..................CLEAVE; ELEMENT
participle ending .......................-ING
particle.................BIT, JOT; DROP;
................MITE; GRAIN; TITTLE
particle, electrically charged ......ION
particle in cosmic rays.........MESON
particular..............................ITEM
partlet .......................HEN; BIDDY
part of speech.............NOUN, VERB
party, wild ............................BASH
parvenu .........................UPSTART
pasha.......................................DEY
pass .....................SEND; THROW;
................ELAPSE; OVERTAKE
passable .................OKAY, SO-SO
passage ...............TEXT; SECTION;
..................................TRANSIT
passage, bastion ............POSTERN
passage, covered..............ARCADE

86

a passageway.................HALL; AISLE
pass a rope through.............REEVE
pass between peaks.................COL
pass on.........................DIE; RELAY
pass over..........OMIT; SKIP; ELIDE
Passover..............................PASCH
Passover meal.....................SEDER
passport stamp........................VISA
past...................AGO; OVER, YORE
pasteboard...........................CARD
pastoral.............................IDYLLIC
pastry............FLAN, TART; ECLAIR
pasture..................................LEA
pasture, low...........................ING
pasty...............................DOUGHY
patella................................ROTULA
path: mathematics.............LOCUS
path of a planet......................ORBIT
pathos.................................PITY
pathos, false....................BATHOS
patriarch's title, Heb. .............NASI
patron...............................CLIENT
patron saint of sailors.............ELMO
pattern.................HABIT, MOTIF;
.....................DESIGN; EMULATE
pattern, large square...........DAMIER
pattern, recurring.................CYCLE
Paul, apostle.........................SAUL
Paul, birthplace of..............TARSUS
paulownia tree.........................KIRI

b pause............HALT, REST; BREAK
pause in poetry..............CAESURA
paver's mallet...........................TUP
pavilion.................................TENT
paving stone................FLAG, SETT
paw.............................PUD; FOOT
pawl.....................................DETENT
pawn....................................HOCK
pay.........................REMIT, WAGES
pay, fixed........................STIPEND
payable..................................DUE
pay dirt..................................ORE
pay for another......................TREAT
pay homage in feudal law .ATTORN
payment, press for ...................DUN
pay out.................................SPEND
pea...............................LEGUME
peaceful.............IRENIC, SERENE
peace of mind.......................REST
peacock blue.......................PAON
peacock constellation............PAVO
peacock fish ...............WRASSE
peak ..................ALP, TOR; ACME,
.................APEX; PITON; ZENITH
peanut.....................MANI; GOOBER
pear, autumn...........................BOSC
pear cider.............................PERRY
pearl, imitation.....................OLIVET
pearlweeds.........................SAGINA
peat .......................................TURF

peat spade .........................SLADE c
pecan tree .........................NOGAL
pedal..................................TREADLE
peddle..........HAWK, SELL, VEND
pedestal for a bust ...............GAINE
pedestal part ..........DADO; PLINTH
peel ..................PARE, RIND, SKIN
peep-show .........................RAREE
peer.........................PEEP; EQUAL
Peer Gynt, mother of ...............ASE
peeve .........................IRK, VEX;
.....................ANNOY; BOTHER
peg, golf ..................................TEE
peg, wooden ..........NOG; TRENAIL
pellucid....................CLEAR; LIMPID
pelma....................................SOLE
pelota court .....................FRONTON
pelt ........................SKIN; STONE
pelvic bone, of the.................ILIAC
pelvic bones..............................ILIA
penalty...................................FINE
pendulum weight ......................BOB
penetrate .................GORE; ENTER
penitential season.....................LENT
penmanship.........................HAND
pen name, Della Ramee.......OUIDA
pen name, Dickens...................BOZ
pen name, Lamb ....................ELIA
pennant, ship's....................BURGEE
Pennsylvania sect.................AMISH
pen point....................NEB, NIB d
Penrod dog ..........................DUKE
Pentateuch .........................TORAH
people.............MEN; FOLK, ONES;
.............RACE; CROWD, DEMOS;
.................MASSES; POPULACE
pepper, climbing ...................BETEL
Pequod, captain of the ..........AHAB
perceive ...................SEE; SENSE;
.........................................DESCRY
perch........................SIT; ROOST
perch, climbing ................ANABAS
perchlike fish ...................DARTER
percolate ......OOZE, SEEP; LEACH
perfect........IDEAL, SHEER, TOTAL
perforate ..................BORE; DRILL,
.........................PUNCH; RIDDLE
perform ...........ACT; PLAY; STAGE
performer.................DOER; ACTOR
perfume..............AROMA; SMELL
perfume base.........................MUSK
perfumed pad ....................SACHET
Pericles, consort of ..........ASPASIA
period .............DOT, ERA; TIME
period, five-year..............LUSTRUM
periphery ......RIM; EDGE; MARGIN;
.................CIRCUIT, COMPASS
permission .........................LEAVE
permit .......LET; ALLOW; LICENSE
perplex ...........BAFFLE; CONFUSE

Persephone, husband of ....HADES, PLUTO
Persia today .............................IRAN
Persian, ancient....................MEDE
Per. coin, ancient..................DARIC
Per. fairy ...............................PERI
Per. governor......................SATRAP
Per. headdress ....................TIARA
Per. king............DARIUS, XERXES
Per. lord................................KHAN
Per. mystic ...........................SUFI
Per. poet................................OMAR
Per. potentate ......................SHAH
Per. priestly caste ..................MAGI
Per. province, ancient ...........ELAM
Per. ruler..............................SHAH
Per. sect ............................BABISM
person, annoying ........CUSS, PEST
person, contemptible ...........WORM
person, foolish ..........BOZO, JERK,
.............................TWIT, YOYO
person, impudent ..................SNOT
person, insipid ..........DRIP; LOSER
person, remarkable ...............DARB
person, smugly superior ........SNOB
person, troublesome .............PEST
person, uncouth .........CAD; BOOR;
.............................YAHOO; GALOOT
person, very skilled ................WHIZ
person, wealthy ..................NABOB

personification of folly ..............ATE
personnel..................CREW; STAFF
perspiration ..........SUDOR, SWEAT
perspire...............................EGEST
pert girl..........................CHIT, MINX
pertinent.........................APT, PAT
perturb................................UPSET;
.........................BOTHER, RUFFLE;
.........................FLUSTER; AGITATE
peruse .........................READ, SCAN
peruser ...........................CONNER
Peruvian relic .......GUACO, HUACO
pervade .....................FILL; IMBUE
peso, silver ..........................DURO
pester ..................ANNOY, TEASE
pestle vessel......................MORTAR
Peter and the Wolf bird .......SASHA
Peter and the Wolf duck .......SONIA
Peter Pan children.................JOHN;
.........................WENDY; MICHAEL
Peter Pan dog.......................NANA
Peter Pan family name.....DARLING
Peter Pan pirate .....................SMEE
petiole .................................STIPE
pet lamb ..............................CADE
Petrarch, love of....................LAURA
petrol ....................................GAS
petty officer, ship's ..............BO'S'N
peyote .............................MESCAL
phantom(s) .......EIDOLA; EIDOLON

Pharaoh ..................SETI; RAMSES
phase ..................FACET, STAGE
pheasant brood ......................NIDE
Phidias, statue by .............ATHENA
philippic ...............................TIRADE
Philippine Islands..See also islands.
P.I. ancestral spirit ................ANITO
P.I. dyewood tree ...........TUI; IPIL
P.I. food............................POI; SABA
P.I. Muslim ...........................MORO
P.I. peasant .........................TAO
P.I. skirt ..............................SAYA
P.I. tree ................................DITA
P.I. woody vine ......................IYO
Philippines archipelago ..........SULU
Philistine city ...................GATH,
.........................GAZA; EKRON
philosopher's stone...............ELIXIR
philosophy, of Zeno's .......ELEATIC
phloem .................................BAST
phoebe..................PEWEE, PEWIT;
.............................LAPWING
Phoebe, daughter of ...............LETO
Phoebe on dice .......................FIVE
Phoebus ....................SOL, SUN;
.............................APOLLO
Phoenician city .....................TYRE
Phoenician port....................SIDON
Phoenician princess...........EUROPA
phosphate of lime.............APATITE
photo-developing powder ....METOL
photographer's solution .........BATH,
.............................HYPO
Phrygian god...............MEN; ATTIS
physician ................GALEN, MEDIC
physician(s), for short....DOC, MDS;
.............................DOCS
physician's symbol .......CADUCEUS
physicist, noted.........RABI; BOYLE,
.........................CURIE; EINSTEIN
picket ...................................PALE
pickled bamboo ...................ACHAR
pickled meat .........................SOUSE
pickling fluid ........................BRINE
pickling herb .........................DILL
pick out ....................CULL; GLEAN
pickpocket ...............................DIP
Picnic playwright ..................INGE
picture, composite..........MONTAGE
picture, medical .....................X-RAY
picture border .........................MAT
picturesque .........................SCENIC
pie, meat ...............................PASTY
piebald pony .........................PINTO
piece, large .................HUNK, SLAB
"Pied Piper" town ............HAMELIN
pier ....................DOCK, QUAY
pierce ..........GORE, STAB; SPEAR
pier support .........................PILING
pig ....................HOG, SOW; SHOAT

a pig, wild.............................BOAR
pig, young........................GRICE
pigeon .............NUN; BARB; DOVE;
..............................POUTER
pigeon hawk .......................MERLIN
pigeon pea...............................TUR
piglike animal, S.A. ........PECCARY
pigment, blue-green.................BICE
pigment, brown.....................SEPIA;
...............................BISTRE
pigment, deep blue ..............SMALT
pigment, red.........................LAKE
pigment, without................ALBINO
pigmentation, lack of.....ACHROMIA
pigment test crystalline .........DOPA
pigs, litter of......................FARROW
pigs, red............................DUROC
pigtail..............................QUEUE
pike, walleyed.......................DORE
pilaster..................................ANTA
pilchard............................SARDINE
pilchardlike fish ..................SPRAT
pile.............NAP; HEAP; SPILE
pile driver .........................OLIVER
pile driver ram ........................TUP
pile of hay ...............RICK; STACK
pile wood............................ALDER
pilfer..................................STEAL
pilgrim..............................PALMER
pilgrimage city...................MECCA

b pilgrimage to Mecca.....HADJ, HAJJ
pillage.....................LOOT, SACK;
.................STEAL; PLUNDER
pillar, resembling a.............STELAR
pillar, tapering ..................OBELISK
pill for an animal, large.........BOLUS
pillow...............................BOLSTER
pilot...................GUIDE, STEER
pin ..................................BROOCH
pin, gunwale........................THOLE
pin, machine.......................COTTER
pin, metal...........................RIVET
pin, old-time firing ..................TIGE
pin, pivot..........................PINTLE
pin, Rom............................ACUS
pin, splicing ...........................FID
pin, very small ........................LILL
pin, wooden ...............NOG, PEG;
.................................DOWEL
pinafore...................................TIER
pincer claw .........................CHELA
pinch.......................................NIP
Pindar work ............................ODE
pine, Mex. ............OCOTE, PINON
pinion...................................WING
pinnacle.......................TOP; APEX
pinnacle, ice.......................SERAC
pinniped.................SEAL; WALRUS
Pinocchio, carver of ........GEPETTO
pint, half...................................CUP

c pin wrench .....................SPANNER
pioneered .................................LED
pious biblical Jew .................TOBIT
pipe...........................TUBE; RISER
pipe, Irish clay..................DUDEEN
pipe, tobacco.........................BRIER
pipelike..............................TUBATE
pique.................................PEEVE
pirate .................ROVER; CORSAIR
pirate in War of 1812 ..........LAFITTE
pismire.................ANT; EMMET
pistil part ............................CARPEL
pistol .............MAUSER; SIDEARM
pit ...............HOLE; ABYSS, STONE
pit, medical............................FOSSA
pit, small ...............FOVEA; LACUNA
pitch ...............................KEY, TAR;
......................TONE; THROW
pitcher ......................JUG; EWER
pitcher's false move .................BALK
pith ...........................NUB; GIST
pith helmet................TOPI; TOPEE
pithy ..................................TERSE
pithy plant ..............................SOLA
pitiful quality ......................PATHOS
pittance ................................TRIFLE
pitted ..............................FOVEATE
pit viper, Jap.......................HABU
pity ........................................RUTH
placard ..............................POSTER

d place ..........................SET; LIEU;
..........................SPOT; STEAD
placid......................CALM; SERENE
plagiarize .............................STEAL
plague .....................................PEST
plain, Arctic ......................TUNDRA
plain, Argentine .................PAMPAS
plain, Russ..........................STEPPE
plain, S.A. ...........................LLANO
plain, treeless ...............SAVANNAH
plait ....................................BRAID
plan ...............DESIGN, LAYOUT,
.................METHOD, SCHEME
plane, Fr. ...............................SPAD
plane, Ger. .........................STUKA
plane, Jap. ...........................ZERO
plane, Russ. ...........................MIG
plane part ...............FLAP, NOSE,
.............TAIL, WING; NACELLE
planetarium ......................ORRERY
planetary aspect........CUSP; TRINE
planets and satellites ........................
.................(in order from the sun)
.................................MERCURY,
.............VENUS, EARTH (LUNA),
.........MARS (DEIMOS, PHOROS),
............JUPITER (IO, EUROPA,
.........CALLISTO, GANYMEDE),
.........SATURN (RHEA, DIONE,
.........JANUS, MIMAS, PHOEBE,

89

a planets and satellites, *continued*......
......TETHYS, IAPETUS,
......HYPERION, ENCELADUS),
......URANUS (ARIEL, OBERON,
......MIRANDA, TITANIA,
......UMBRIEL), NEPTUNE
......(NEREID, TRITON), PLUTO
plank's curve on a ship .............SNY
plant......SOW; SEED
plant, any sea-bottom ........ENALID
plant, bayonet......DATIL
plant, broom ......SPART
plant, bulb ......CAMASS
plant, medicinal ......ALOE; SENNA;
......IPECAC
plant, mustard family......KALE;
......CRESS
plant, soap......AMOLE
plant disease......RUST, SMUT
plant growth ......LEAF
plant joined to another ......GRAFT
plant life......FLORA
plant louse......APHID
plant of the iris family ......IRID
plant pod......BOLL
plant stem......CAULIS
plant stem tissue......PITH
plant used as a medicine ......HERB
plasterer's float ......DARBY
plaster of Paris ......GESSO
b plate, battery ......GRID
plate, Eucharist......PATEN
plate, reptile's......SCUTE
plateau......MESA
plateau, Andes......PUNA
platform......DAIS; STAGE
platform, ancient church ......BEMA
platinum, of......OSMIC
play ......DRAMA
player......ACTOR
play on words ......PUN
play part......ACT; SCENE
plead ......BEG, SUE;
......ENTREAT
pleasant......NICE
please ......SUIT
pleat......FOLD
pledge......VOW; GAGE,
......OATH, PAWN; TROTH
plexus ......RETE; RETIA
pliant ......LITHE
plinth ......ORLO; SOCLE
plot ......LOT; PLAT; CABAL
plow, sole of a......SHARE
pluck ......PICK
plucky ......GAMY
plug......CORK; STOPPER
plug, barrel......SPILE
plum ......GAGE, SLOE
plummet......DROP; PLUNGE

c plunder......ROB; LOOT, SACK;
......BOOTY; PILFER, RAVAGE
plunge ......DIVE, DROP
plus ......AND; ALSO; ASSET
Pluto ......DIS; HADES, ORCUS
Pluto, mother-in-law of......DEMETER
pneumonia, kind of ......LOBAR
pocket billiards ......POOL
pod, cotton ......BOLL
poem......ODE; ELEGY, EPODE
poem, Biblical ......PSALM
poem, eight-line ......TRIOLET
poem, heroic......EPIC, EPOS
poem, love ......SONNET
poem, mournful ......ELEGY
poem, pastoral ......IDYL; IDYLL
poem division ......CANTO, VERSE
poet......BARD; ODIST
poet, famous Bengal......TAGORE
poet, Norse......SKALD
poet, old English ......SCOP
poetry syllable, Gr. ......ARSIS
point ......END, TIP; BARB;
......PUNTO; JUNCTURE
pointed ......SHARP; ACUATE
pointed arch......OGEE
pointed end ......CUSP
pointed missile ......DART; SPEAR
pointed remark ......BARB
pointed staff......PIKE
pointer......WAND
point of land ......SPIT
point of the crescent moon ....CUSP
point of view......ANGLE
point on a curve ......NODE
poison ......BANE; TAINT
poison, arrow ......UPAS; URALI;
......CURARE, OORALI
poison, hemlock ......CONINE
poisonous protein ......RICIN
poisonous snakes, of ......ELAPINE
poisonous weed......LOCO
poison tree ......UPAS
poi source ......TARO
poke ......JAB; PROD; NUDGE
poke fun at......KID; JOSH; TEASE
poker hand......PAIR; FLUSH
poker stake......ANTE
poker winnings......POT
pokeweed......POCAN, SCOKE
polar explorer......BYRD
pole, boat......MAST, SPAR; SPRIT
polecat, Cape ......ZORIL;
......ZORILLE
pole in Gaelic games ......CABER
pole to pole, from ......AXIAL
police line ......CORDON
policeman......COP
policeman, state ......TROOPER
polish......RUB, WAX; SHINE

a Polish assembly ......................SEJM
Polish rum cake ......................BABA
polished .................SHINY, SLEEK;
.....................URBANE; ELEGANT
polisher .................................EMERY
Polish general .........BOR; ANDERS
polishing material ...............RABAT,
.........................................ROUGE
polite ....................CIVIL; GENTEEL
political booty .....................GRAFT
political party .........DEM, GOP, IND
politition, veteran.......................POL
pollack fish ..........................SAITHE
pollen brush ........................SCOPA
Pollux, mother of....................LEDA
Pollux, twin of ...................CASTOR
polo stick ...........................MALLET
Polydorus, father of.............CREON
Polydorus, mother of.........HECUBA
Polynesian, N. Z. ................MAORI
Polynesian amulet ...................TIKI
Polynesian cloth ....................TAPA
Polynesian dance ...................SIVA
Polynesian drink...........AVA; KAVA
Polynesian god......AKUA, ATUA
Polynesian spirit ...................MANA
pome ...................................APPLE
"Pomp and Circumstances"
composer ...................................
.........................................ELGAR

b pompous ...........STUFFY, TURGID
poncho, Colombian .............RUANA
pond ...........................MERE, POOL
ponder....................MULL, MUSE;
..........................THINK; REFLECT
pontiff .....................................POPE
pony, student's .......................CRIB
pool ...........................POND, TARN;
.........................BAYOU; LAGOON
pool shot ...................BANK, KISS;
.............BREAK, CAROM, MASSE
pool stick ................................CUE
poor .....................................NEEDY
poorly .........................................ILL
poor-quality goods .................CRAP;
.....................................SCHLOCK
Pope......LEO; JOHN, PAUL, PIUS;
.........................LINUS, URBAN
Pope, Eng. ..........................ADRIAN
Pope's triple crown ................TIARA
Popeye, foe of .....................BLUTO
Popeye, girlfriend of ......OLIVE OYL
poplar ....................ALAMO, ASPEN
poplar, white ........................ABELE
poppy red ......GRANAT; PONCEAU
poppy seed..............................MAW
populace, Gr. .....................DEMOS
popular girl ...........................BELLE
porcelain...............CHINA; SEVRES;
.........................................LIMOGES

c porcelain, ancient Rom. .....MURRA
porcelain, Eng. ....................SPODE
porch .........ANTA; LANAI, STOOP;
.......................................VERANDA
porch, Gr. ...............................STOA
porch swing .......................GLIDER
porcupine anteater...........ECHIDNA
pore .....................................STOMA
porgy, brown-and-white .........SCUP
porgy, Eur. ..........................PARGO
porgy, Jap. ...............................TAI
porous volcanic rock....TUFA, TUFF
porpoise .........................DOLPHIN
porridge ...................POBS; BROSE
porridge, cornmeal .................SAMP
porridge, S.A. ......................ATOLE
port.............................LEFT, WINE;
.............CARRY, HAVEN; HARBOR
port, Black Sea...................ODESSA
port, leave .................................SAIL
port, Samoan ...........................APIA
port, Suez ................................SAID
portable chair ......................SEDAN
portal .........................DOOR, GATE
portend...................BODE; AUGUR;
.......................................PRESAGE
portent .......................OMEN, SIGN
porter, Oriental....................HAMAL
Portia, handmaid of .........NERISSA
portico ....................................STOA

d portion ....................PART; SHARE
portion out.....DOLE, METE; ALLOT
port of Rome .........................OSTIA
port opposite Gibraltar .........CEUTA
portray ....................................DRAW,
.............................PLAY; DEPICT
Portuguese coin .........................REI
Port. colony in India ................GOA
Port. explorer .........DIAS; DA GAMA
Port. folk tune .........................FADO
Port. lady .................................DONA
Port. man .................................DOM
Port. port...........................OPORTO
Port. Timor's capital....................DILI
pose ..............................SIT; SHAM;
.......................................STANCE
posed for a portrait....................SAT
Poseidon ........................NEPTUNE
Poseidon, son of.....................ARION,
.............................ORION; TRITON
position ...........PLACE; STATUS
positive terminal ..................ANODE
possessed...................HAD; HELD;
.........................................OWNED
possesses .................HAS; OWNS;
.........................................KEEPS
possum of the comics ...........POGO
post............................MAIL, SEND;
.........................................STAKE
postage stamp paper .........PELURE

## post-crucifixion depiction / Prefixes: (female)

a

| | |
|---|---|
| post-crucifixion depiction | PIETA |
| postpone | DEFER |
| postulate | POSIT; THEORY |
| posture | STANCE |
| pot, small | CRUSE |
| pot, Indian brass | LOTAH |
| potassium chloride | MURIATE |
| potassium nitrate | NITER |
| potation, small | DRAM |
| potato | SPUD |
| potato, sweet | YAM; BATATA |
| pother | ADO; FUSS |
| pot herb | WORT |
| potpourri | OLIO |
| pottage, beef | BREWIS |
| potter's blade | PALLET |
| pottery, of | CERAMIC |
| pottery, once | CLAY |
| pottery fragment | SHARD |
| pouch | SAC |
| poultry | HENS |
| poultry disease | PIP; ROUP |
| pounce | SWOOP |
| pound down | RAM; TAMP |
| pour | RAIN; TEEM |
| pour off gently | DECANT |
| pour out | LIBATE |
| poverty | NEED, WANT |
| powder, astringent | BORAL |
| powdered pumice | TALC |

b

| | |
|---|---|
| power | DINT; FORCE, MIGHT |
| practical joke | HOAX |
| practice | WONT; DRILL, HABIT, TRAIN; CUSTOM |
| practice exercise, musical | ETUDE |
| prairie copse | MOTTE |
| praise | LAUD; EXTOL; TRIBUTE |
| prance | CAPER |
| prank | DIDO |
| prate | GAB, YAP |
| pray: Yiddish | DAVEN |
| prayer | AVE; PLEA; ORISON |
| prayer, nine-day | NOVENA |
| prayer book | ORDO |
| prayer form | LITANY |
| prayer position, Hindu | ASANA |
| praying figure | ORANT |
| preacher, Gospel | EVANGEL |
| precept | LAW; EDICT; DICTUM |
| precipitous | STEEP |
| preclude | AVERT, DETER |
| predicament | FIX; SCRAPE |
| predicate | BASE; FOUND; AFFIRM |
| predict | AUGUR; FORECAST |
| predisposed | PRONE |
| preen | PLUME, PRINK |
| preface | PROEM |

c

PREFIXES:

| | |
|---|---|
| abnormal | DYS- |
| about | PERI- |
| above | HYPER- |
| acid | ACET-; ACETO- |
| across | DIA-; TRANS- |
| African | AFRO- |
| against | ANTI- |
| ahead | PRE- |
| air | AER-; AERI-, AERO- |
| angle | GONI-; GONIO- |
| animal | ZOO- |
| apart | DIS- |
| away | ABS-; CATA- |
| back | NOTO- |
| backward | RETRO- |
| bad | MAL-; CACO- |
| badly | MIS- |
| before | PRE-; ANTE- |
| benzene, derived from | PHEN- |
| bile | CHOL-; CHOLE- |
| billionth | NANO- |
| birds | AVI- |
| bitter | PICR-; PICRO- |
| blood | VAS-; HEMA-, HEMO-, VASO- |
| bone | OSSI- |
| both | AMBI- |
| bromine | BROM-; BROMO- |
| bull | TAUR-; TAURI-, TAURO- |
| carbon | CARB-; CARBO- |
| change | MET-; META- |
| child | PED-; PEDO- |
| Chinese | SINO- |
| cloud | NEPH-; NEPHO- |
| coil | SPIR-; SPIRO- |
| common | CEN-; CENO- |
| copper | CUPR-; CUPRI-, CUPRO- |
| correct | ORTH-; ORTHO- |
| current | RHEO- |
| custom | NOMO- |
| death | NECR-; NECRO- |
| deputy | VICE- |
| destroying | PHAG-; PHAGO- |
| disease | NOS-; NOSO- |
| distant | TELE-, TELO- |
| down | CATA- |
| dry | XER-; XERO- |
| dung | COPR-; COPRO- |
| ear | OTO- |
| earth | GEO- |
| egg | OVI-, OVO- |
| eight | OCT-; OCTA-, OCTO- |
| end | TELO- |
| equal | ISO-; PARI- |
| everywhere | OMNI- |
| eye | OCUL-; OCULO- |
| fat | LIP-; LIPO-, SEBI-, SEBO- |
| female | GYN-; GYNO- |

d

92

*a* PREFIXES: *continued*

| | |
|---|---|
| fermentation | ZYM-; ZYMO- |
| fever | FEBR-; FEBRI- |
| few | OLIG-; OLIGO- |
| fibrous | FIBR-; FIBRO- |
| fire | PYR-; IGNI-, PYRO- |
| fish | PISC-; PISCI- |
| fluorine | FLUO-; |
| | FLUOR-; FLUORO- |
| food | SITO- |
| foot | PED-; PEDI- |
| foreign | XEN-; XENO- |
| four | TETRA- |
| freeing | LYS-; LYSI- |
| freezing | CRYO- |
| fungus | FUNG-, MYCO-; FUNGI- |
| glass | HYAL-; HYALO- |
| grain | SITO- |
| ground | PED-; PEDO- |
| gyrating | GYR-; GYRO- |
| hair | PILI- |
| half | DEMI-, HEMI-, SEMI- |
| hand | CHIR-; CHIRO- |
| hatred | MISO- |
| hearing | ACOU-; ACOUO- |
| high | ALTI-; ALTO- |
| highest | ACRO- |
| horse | HIPP-; HIPPO- |
| hundred | HECT-; HECTO- |
| idea | IDEO- |

*b*

| | |
|---|---|
| ileum | ILE-; ILEO- |
| India | INDO- |
| iodine | IOD-; IODO- |
| kernel | KARY-; KARYO- |
| ketone | KET-; KETO- |
| kidney | REN-; RENI-, RENO- |
| large | MEG-; MEGA- |
| leftside | LEV-; LEVO- |
| life | BIO- |
| lip | CHIL-; CHILO- |
| main | ARCH- |
| many | POLY- |
| many times more than | |
| | MULT-; MULTI- |
| middle | MESO- |
| moon | LUNI- |
| mountain | ORO- |
| movie | CINE- |
| mucus | MYX-; MUCO-, MYXO- |
| naked | GYMN-, NUDI-; GYMNO- |
| negative | NON- |
| nerve | NEUR-; NEURO- |
| new | NEO- |
| night | NOCT-; NOCTI- |
| nitrogen, containing | AZO-; |
| | NITR-; NITRO- |
| nose | NAS-; NASO-, |
| | RHIN-; RHINO- |
| numerous | MYRI-; MYRIA- |
| oil | OLEO- |

*c*

| | |
|---|---|
| one | UNI- |
| one's own | IDIO- |
| outer | ECT-, ECTO- |
| outside | EXO- |
| over | EPI- |
| oxygen | OXA-, OXY- |
| pair | ZYG-; ZYGO- |
| partly | SEMI- |
| pelvis | PYEL-; PYELO- |
| people | ETHN-; ETHNO- |
| physician | MEDI-; MEDIO- |
| pointed | ACU-, OXY-; ACRO- |
| power | DYN-; DYNA- |
| pray | ORA- |
| pressure | BARO-, TONO- |
| quintillionth | ATTO- |
| rain | HYET-; HYETO- |
| reproductive | GON-; GONO- |
| root | RHIZ-; RHIZO- |
| sacred | HIER-; HIERO- |
| same | ISO-; EQUI-, HOMO- |
| scales | CTEN-; CTENO- |
| serum | SER-; SERO- |
| seven | HEPT-; HEPTA- |
| sex | SEX-; SEXI- |
| sexually united | GAM-; GAMO- |
| single | HAPL-, MONO-; HAPLO- |
| six | HEX-; HEXA- |
| sleep | NARC-; NARCO- |
| small | MINI- |
| snake | OPHI- |

*d*

| | |
|---|---|
| sound | PHON-; PHONO- |
| sound of a thump | KER- |
| spinal cord | MYEL-; MYELO- |
| spore | SPOR-; SPORO- |
| star | ASTR-; ASTRO- |
| starch | AMYL-; AMYLO- |
| stone | PETR-; PETRO- |
| sub- | SUS- |
| sulfur | THIO- |
| sunlight | HELI-; HELIO- |
| sword | XIPH- |
| ten | DEC-; DEK-; |
| | DECA-, DEKA- |
| tendon | TENO- |
| thin | LEPT-; LEPTO- |
| thousand | KILO- |
| three | TER-, TRI- |
| to or from a distance | TEL-; |
| | TELE- |
| trillion | TERA- |
| two | DUA-; DIPL-, DIPLO- |
| two, in | DICH-; DICHO- |
| under | SUB- |
| universe | COSM-; COSMO- |
| uterus | UTER-; UTERO- |
| variation | ALLO- |
| vein | VEN-; VENI-, VENO- |
| water | HYDR-; HYDRO- |
| wax | CER-; CERO- |

## Prefixes: (weakly colored) / progeny

*a* PREFIXES: *continued*
weakly colored ...LEUC-, LEUK-;
.....................LEUCO-, LEUKO-
wet .................HYGR-; HYGRO-
whole .................HOLO-, TOTI-
wide .....................................EURY-
wine ..................OENO-, VINI-
wing ..............PTER-; PTERO-
with ....................COM-, SYN-
within ..................END-, ENT-;
.....................ENDO-, ENTO-
womb..............METR-; METRO-
wood...............HYL-, XYL-;
.....................HYLO-, LIGN-,
.............XYLO-; LIGNI-; LIGNO-
wrong ....................................MIS-
prehistoric mound....................TERP
prejudice ..................................BIAS
prelate, high ....................PRIMATE
premium exchange ................AGIO
prepare....................FIX; READY
prepare for publication ...........EDIT
presage..............OMEN; AUGURY,
................HERALD; PORTENT
prescribed ....................THETIC
prescribed quantity ................DOSE
present .............NOW; GIFT, GIVE;
...............................DONATE
present, be.......................ATTEND
presently ..................ANON, SOON
*b* preserve............CAN; JAM; KEEP;
.....................SAVE; MAINTAIN
preserve in brine.........CORN, SALT
presidential nickname ............ABE,
.....................CAL, IKE
presidents, US.........See page 190.
press coverage .........................INK
press together.................SERRY
pressure.........COERCE, DURESS;
................STRESS; CONSTRAIN
pretend ....................ACT; FAKE,
.....................POSE; FEIGN;
.....................HAZARD; VENTURE
pretense................................SHAM
pretensions ............................AIRS
prevail ....................................WIN
prevail on................INDUCE
prevalent...................RIFE
prevent....................AVERT, DETER
prevent by law................ESTOP
prey.......................VICTIM
prey upon................RAVINE
Priam, son of........PARIS; HECTOR
Priam, wife of .................HECUBA
price ....................FEE, TAB;
.....................COST, RATE, TOLL
prickly plant .........BRIER; NETTLE
prickly seed coat ....................BURR
pride .................EGO; VANITY
pride member ....................LION

priest ....................FRA; ABBE, *c*
.....................CURE; PADRE
priest, Celtic............................DRUID
priest, Zoroastrian...............MAGUS
priestess, Rom. .................VESTAL
priest in the *Iliad*..............CALCHAS
priestly caste, Zoroastrian.......MAGI
prima donna............................DIVA
primeval ....................OLD; EARLY;
.....................PRIMAL; PRISTINE
prince, Arabian ..........EMIR; SAYID;
.....................SAYYID
prince, Indian....................RAJAH
prince, Oriental......................KHAN
prince, petty ................SATRAP
prince, Slavic.........................KNEZ
princely....................................ROYAL
Prince of Darkness.............SATAN
princess, Indian........RANI; RANEE
princess in Gr. myth...............IOLE
principal....................HEAD, MAIN;
.....................CHIEF, PRIME
principal commodity ..........STAPLE
principle, accepted ............AXIOM,
.....................PRANA, TENET
print.........................STAMP
printer's direction .........DELE, STET
printer's mistake ....................TYPO
printer's mistakes ...............ERRATA
printing press handle .......ROUNCE
printing roller ....................PLATEN *d*
prison ....................JUG; JAIL, STIR
prison: Brit. .............GAOL, QUOD
prison sentence..............RAP; LIFE
prison spy................MOUTON
privation .................................LOSS
prize ....................PRY; AWARD
pro............................................FOR
probe, medical ................STYLET
problem....................ISSUE, POSER
proboscis .............................SNOUT
proceed.............COME; ADVANCE
proceedings............................ACTA
procession ............TRAIN; PARADE
proclaim....................CRY; VOICE;
.....................HERALD; DECLARE
procreation ..............................SEX
procurer....................PIMP
prod ....................................URGE
produce ............BEGET, YIELD;
.....................CREATE; GENERATE
profane..............................VIOLATE
profession .............ART; CAREER,
.....................METIER; CALLING
professional, not.....................LAIC
profit ....................GAIN; AVAIL
profit, to yield ...........................NET
profound ..............................DEEP
progenitor...............SIRE; PARENT
progeny ....................ISSUE

94

a prohibit.................BAN, BAR; VETO;
..............................DEBAR, ESTOP
prohibition .....................EMBARGO
project.................JUT; IDEA, PLAN
projectile.................DART; MISSILE
projecting edge .........RIM; FLANGE
projecting piece ........ARM; TENON
projecting tooth .....................SNAG
projection .......EAR; BARB; PRONG
projection, fireplace .................HOB
promenade ...........................MALL
promise ..............................WORD
Promised Land ........................ZION
promise to pay ...............IOU; NOTE
promontory ................CAPE, NESS
promontory, rocky ....................TOR
promote ...................HYPE, TOUT;
.....................FOSTER; ADVANCE
prompt.........SPUR, STIR; TIMELY
prone .............................APT; FLAT
prong .........................TINE; TOOTH
pronghorn ..........................CABRET
___ pro nobis .........................ORA
pronoun .......HER, HIM, ONE, SHE,
..............YOU; THAT, THIS, THEM,
................THEY; THESE, THOSE
pronoun, possessive .......HER, HIS,
................ITS, OUR; HERS, MINE,
.......OURS, YOUR; THEIR, YOURS
pronoun, Quaker.....................THY;

b ..............THEE, THOU; THINE
pronounce indistinctly.............SLUR
pronouncement.................DICTUM
pronounce strongly ............STRESS
proof, corrected.................REVISE
proof, legal ...............................IDS
proofreader's mark ..............DELE,
..............................STET; CARET
prop .............HOLD, STAY; BRACE;
.....................BOLSTER, SUSTAIN
propeller ..................................OAR
proper..................DUE, FIT; RIGHT
property, hold on ......................LIEN
property, item of .................ASSET;
..................................CHATTEL
property, landed ................ESTATE
property, receiver of.........ALIENEE
prophesy .............AUGUR; DIVINE;
..................................FORETELL
prophet......................................SEER
prophetess ..........SIBYL; SEERESS
proportion................................RATIO
proportionally assess......PRORATE
proposition ......................THESIS;
..................................PREMISE
proposition, logic .................LEMMA
proposition, math ............THEOREM
prosecutor...............................SUER
proselyte to Judaism ................GER
prospect.....................VIEW; VISTA

c prospects .............ODDS; FUTURE;
..............................OUTLOOK
prosperity ...........................WEALTH
Prospero, servant of .............ARIEL
prostrate ...................FLAT; PRONE;
..................................FLATTEN
protagonist............................HERO
protected ...........................HOUSED
protection .............................AEGIS
prototype ........MASTER; ORIGINAL
protuberance......JAG, NUB; HUMP,
..................KNOB, NODE, WART
prove a claim by dueling..DERAIGN
proverb .....................SAW; ADAGE,
................AXIOM, MAXIM; SAYING
provide...................................GIVE;
..........................OFFER; SUPPLY;
.....................DELIVER, FURNISH
province, Rom. ........................DACIA
provisional clause ............PROVISO
provoke ....................RILE; ANGER
prow...........................BOW; STEM
Prussian spa site...................EMS
pry .............NOSE; LEVER, SNOOP
Psalm, 51st ..................MISERERE
Psalmist ...............................DAVID
Psalms, 113 to 118 .............HALLEL
Psalms ending......................SELAH
pseudonym .........................ALIAS
pseudonym of H.H. Munro.......SAKI
pseudonym of Viaud .............LOTI

d psyche.................................SOUL
psychiatrist, noted .................JUNG;
..............ADLER, FREUD; HORNEY
Ptah, embodiment of...............APIS
ptarmigan .............................RYPE
pub fare .....................ALE; BEER;
..................................LAGER, STOUT
public .........OPEN; CIVIL; PEOPLE
public, make.................................AIR
publication style .................FORMAT
public esteem .....................REPUTE
public gardens .......................PARK
public vehicle.........BUS, CAB; TAXI
publish ....................ISSUE, PRINT
publish illegally ....................PIRATE
Puccini heroine ......................MIMI
puck material.....................RUBBER
pudding ..................DUFF, SAGO;
..................TRIFLE; TAPIOCA
Pueblo Indian ........................HOPI,
................MOKI, TANO, ZUNI;
..................KERES, MOQUI
Pueblo sacred chamber...........KIVA
puffer fish ...........................TAMBOR
pull ...................TOW, TUG; DRAG
pull abruptly ...........JERK, YANK
pulley wheel......................SHEAVE
pulp, fruit..........................POMACE
pulpit.......................AMBO, BEMA

95

*a*

| | |
|---|---|
| pump handle | SWIPE |
| pumpkin seed | PEPO |
| punch | JAB; POKE, SOCK; VIGOR; PUMMEL |
| punch, engraver's | MATTOIR |
| Punch and Judy dog | TOBY |
| punctuation mark | DASH; COLON, COMMA; PERIOD |
| pungent | ACRID; BITING; MORDANT, PIQUANT |
| punish by fine | AMERCE |
| punishment, of | PENAL |
| punishment stick | FERULE |
| Punjab inhabitant | JAT |
| punk | AMADOU |
| punt | KICK |
| pupa | INSTAR |
| puppet | DOLL |
| purchase | BUY; GRIP |
| pure thought | NOESIS |
| purification, Rom. | LUSTRUM |

*c*

| | |
|---|---|
| purloin | STEAL |
| purple dye source | MUREX |
| purplish-brown | PUCE |
| purpose | AIM, END; GOAL; INTENT |
| purse net | SEINE |
| pursy | STOUT |
| push up | BOOST |
| put away | STORE |
| put back | REPLACE |
| put down | LAY; QUASH, WRITE |
| put off | DEFER |
| put out | OUST; EJECT |
| puzzle | POSER, REBUS; ENIGMA |
| Pygmalion's statue | GALATEA |
| Pylos, kin of | NESTOR |
| Pyramus, lover of | THISBE |
| pyromaniac | FIREBUG |
| Pythias, friend of | DAMON |
| python | BOA |

# Q

*b*

| | |
|---|---|
| QED, part of | ERAT, QUOD |
| quack | CHARLATAN |
| quack medicine | NOSTRUM |
| quadrant | ARC |
| quadrate | SQUARE |
| quaff | DRINK |
| quail | COLIN, COWER |
| quake | SHAKE; SHIVER, TREMOR; TREMBLE |
| Quaker | FRIEND |
| Quaker poet | WHITTIER |
| quaking | TREPID |
| qualify | MARK; ENABLE |
| qualified | FIT; ABLE |
| quality | CLASS, TRAIT, VALUE; CALIBER |
| ___ qua non | SINE |
| quantity, indeterminate | SOME |
| quantity, math | SCALAR, VECTOR |
| quarrel | ROW; FEUD, SPAT; CLASH, FIGHT |
| quarrel, trivial | MIFF, TIFF |
| quartz, green | PRASE |
| quartz, opaque reddish | JASPER |
| quaternion | TETRAD |
| quay | LEVEE, WHARF |
| Quebec, patron saint of | ANNE |
| Queen Boadicea's people | ICENI |
| queenly | REGAL, ROYAL; REGINAL |
| Queen of Italy | ELENA |
| Queen of Ithaca | PENELOPE |

*d*

| | |
|---|---|
| Queen of Scots | MARY |
| Queen of Spain, last | ENA |
| Queen of the fairies | MAB |
| queen of the gods, Eg. | SATI |
| queen of the gods, Rom. | JUNO |
| Queen of the Nile | CLEO |
| Queensland hemp plant | SIDA |
| quell | CRUSH, QUASH; QUENCH, SQUASH |
| quench | SLAKE |
| quench steel | AUSTEMPER |
| quern | MILL |
| query | ASK |
| queue | LINE |
| question | ASK; GRILL |
| question, hard | POSER |
| question starter | HOW, WHO, WHY; WHAT, WHEN, WHOM; WHERE, WHICH, WHOSE |
| quetzal | TROGON |
| quibble | CARP; CAVIL; BICKER |
| quick | FAST; AGILE, ALIVE, RAPID |
| quicken | HASTEN |
| quickly | APACE; PRESTO, PRONTO |
| quickly, move | SCAT, SCUD |
| quickly: music | TOSTO |
| quicksilver | MERCURY; HEAUTARIT |
| quid | CUD |
| quid ___ quo | PRO |
| quiescent | LATENT; DORMANT |

*a* quiet............................CALM; STILL;
..................HUSHED, LOW-KEY,
..................PLACID; TRANQUIL
quill ...........................PEN; SPINE
quill feather(s) ...................REMEX;
..............................REMIGES
quill for winding silk ................COP
quilt.....................COVER, EIDER
quince yellow ....................MELINE

quincunx...............................FIVE *c*
quinine .........................CINCHONA
quintessence ..............PITH; ELIXIR
quirt, cowboy's .....................ROMAL
quit .....................CEASE, LEAVE
quite .............JUST, WELL; FULLY;
..............................WHOLLY
*quod ___ demonstrandum* .....ERAT
quote...................................CITE

# R

Ra, consort of..........................MUT
Ra, son of ..............................SHU
rabbit, female ..........................DOE
rabbit, invisible ..................HARVEY
rabbit, small S.A. ................TAPETI
rabbit cage.........................HUTCH
rabbit community..............WARREN
rabbit fur ..............................CONY;
..................CONEY, LAPIN
rabble ...................................MOB
rabies...............................LYSSA
raccoon, briefly......................COON
raccoonlike mammal .............COATI
race, boat .........................REGATTA
race, segmented .................RELAY
*b* race, short........................SPRINT
racetrack circuit......................LAP
racetrack tipster.....................TOUT
Rachel, father of.................LABAN
Radames, love of...................AIDA
radar screen ......................SCOPE
radar signal ..........................BLIP
radiate............................EMANATE
radioactive ray ...................GAMMA
radio wire ............................LITZ
radium discoverer ...............CURIE
radium emanation ...............NITON,
..............................RADON
rag doll ............................MOPPET
rage................................FAD, IRE;
................FURY; CRAZE, FUROR,
..................MANIA, WRATH
ragout, game .......................SALMI
raid....................FORAY; INROAD
raiding soldier............COMMANDO
rail at ...............................REVILE
rail bird ......................SORA, WEKA;
..............................CRAKE
railing...............................PARAPET
railroad bridge.................TRESTLE
railroad tie.....................SLEEPER
railroad timber ........................TIE
railroad warning light ...........FLARE
railroad-yard signal ..........TRIMMER
railway station: Fr. ................GARE

rain from a clear sky ...........SEREIN
rainbow, of a .......................IRIDAL
rainbow goddess ....................IRIS
raincoat ...............MACK; PONCHO
rain forest .................SELVA, SILVA
rain gauge .....................UDOMETER
rain tree ............................SAMAN
rainy ..................................WET
raise ........................REAR; BREED;
..............................ELEVATE
raised...............................BRED
raising device ........................JACK
rake .................ROUE; LOTHARIO
rake with aerial gunfire.......STRAFE
rake with gunfire ............ENFILADE
ram ..............TUP; TAMP; ARIES *d*
Ramachandra, wife of.............SITA
ramble .....................GAD; ROVE
rampart .............AGGER; VALLUM
ran...................BLED; OPERATED
range ........AREA; GAMUT, SCOPE
Rangoon's state .....................PEGU
ran into ................................MET
rank ..........ROW; RATE; DEGREE
rankle ...............................FESTER
ransom ............................REDEEM
rapeseed ............................COLZA
rapidly ..............................APACE
rapids, river ............................SOO
rapier ...............................BILBO
rare-earth element ...........CERIUM,
..................ERBIUM; HOLMIUM,
..................TERBIUM, THORIUM,
..................YTTRIUM; SCANDIUM
rascal .......................IMP; ROGUE
rasp ........................FILE; GRATE
raspberry variety ...........BLACKCAP
rasse..................................CIVET
rat, Indian...................BANDICOOT
rate..........RANK; GRADE; ASSESS
rational ..............................SANE
rational integer ......................NORM
rational principle .................LOGOS
ratite bird ...............KIWI; OSTRICH;
..............................CASSOWARY

97

a rattan...................................CANE
rave.................RANT; HARANGUE
"Raven, The" poet.....................POE
"Raven, The" woman...........LENORE
ravine........................DALE, GLEN,
..........................WADI; GORGE
rawboned..............................LEAN
rawboned animal.................SCRAG
ray.............BEAM; SHAFT, SKATE
rayon...........ACETATE; CELANESE
rays, like...............................RADIAL
raze...................LEVEL; DESTROY
razor-billed auk.......................ALCA
reach..................RANGE, SCOPE;
.....................EXTENT; BREADTH
reach across...........................SPAN
react...............................RESPOND
read, inability to..................ALEXIA
reader, first.......................PRIMER
reading desk.......AMBO; LECTERN
read metrically.........................SCAN
read publicly....................PRELECT
reality...................................FACT
realm.......ARENA, ORBIT, SCOPE;
.....................DOMAIN; PURVIEW
real thing, the.....................MCCOY
rear.............BACK; ERECT, RAISE
rear, to the.................AFT; ABAFT;
..................................ASTERN
rearhorse............................MANTIS

b reasoning............................LOGIC
reasoning, deductive........A PRIORI
Rebecca, son of.......ESAU; JACOB
rebound..........CAROM; RICOCHET
rebuff..................SLAP, SNUB
rebuke.................CHIDE, SCOLD;
...............REPROVE, UPBRAID
recalcitrant.......UNRULY; DEFIANT
recant...............UNSAY; RETRACT
recede...................................EBB
recent...........................NEW; LATE
receptacle..............BIN, BOX, CUP;
..................................VESSEL
receptacle, shallow.................TRAY
reception, morning..............LEVEE
recess................APSE; BREAK,
.....................NICHE; ALCOVE
recipient...............................DONEE
reckless................................RASH
reckon..................COUNT, TALLY;
................FIGURE; COMPUTE
reclaim.............................REDEEM
recline.............LIE; LOLL; REPOSE
recluse..............HERMIT; ASCETIC
recoil............SHY; QUAIL, WINCE;
.....................FLINCH; REBOUND
recombinant letters..................DNA
recompense...................FEE, PAY;
..................................REWARD
reconnaissance..................PROBE

c reconnoiter.......SCOUT; EXPLORE
record.....LOG; DISC, NOTE, TAPE
recorded proceedings............ACTA
records............................ANNALS
recover strength..................RALLY
recovery of goods, legal....TROVER
rectifier, current.....................DIODE
rectify...............AMEND, EMEND;
....................CORRECT, RESOLVE
red...............CARMINE, CRIMSON,
..................SCARLET, MAGENTA
red, Venetian.........................SIENA
redact.....................................EDIT
redbreast...............................ROBIN
redcap.................................PORTER
red cedar..............................SAVIN
red deer, like a.............ELAPHINE
reddish-yellow color.............ALOMA,
..................................SUDAN
red dye root.............CHAY, CHOY;
..................CHAYA, CHOYA
redeem..........RANSOM; RECLAIM
redeye fish...........................RUDD
red hog...............................DUROC
red horse.......................BAY; ROAN
red ocher...............BOLE; RUDDLE
Red or White team.................SOX
red pigment..........................ROSET;
..................BRAZIL; ASTACIN
red pine.................................RIMU
red planet.............................MARS
red powder, Indian..................ABIR
red squirrel.................CHICKAREE
reduce...........................CUT; PARE;
..................................DEVALUE
reduce sails...........................REEF
reedbuck..............................NAGOR
reek.........................FUG; STENCH
reef.......................................SHOAL
reel, fishing............................PIRN
refer.................APPLY; MENTION,
..................PERTAIN; TRANSFER
refer to....................................VIDE
reflection................GLARE, IMAGE
refracting device.....................LENS
refractor, light.......................PRISM
refrain..............................ABSTAIN;
..................................FORBEAR
refrain, musical........FA-LA; TRA-LA
refrigerant..........................FREON
refuge................HAVEN; ASYLUM;
..................SHELTER; RECOURSE
refugee...........................ESCAPEE,
..................................RUNAWAY
refuse....................DENY; SPURN;
..................................REJECT
refuse.........SCUM; OFFAL, TRASH
refuse, piece of.....................SCRAP
refuse, metal........DROSS; SCORIA

a refuse, wool ...........................COT
refute .....................BELIE, REBUT;
.................DISPROVE; DISCREDIT
regale................................ENTERTAIN
regalia...............FINERY; SYMBOLS
regard ........CARE, HEED; HONOR;
......................ESTEEM; CONCERN
regarding ..................IN RE; ANENT
regenerate .........................RENEW
region .......................AREA; TRACT;
......................SECTOR; QUARTER
region, Fr.-Ger. ...................ALSACE
register .....................FILE; ENROLL
regret .....................RUE; REPENT;
.........................................DEPLORE
regurgitate.................PUKE; VOMIT
reign, of a ...........................REGNAL
reimbursed ..............................PAID
reindeer, Santa's............COMET,
...............CUPID, VIXEN; DANCER;
.......DASHER, DONNER; BLITZEN;
......................PRANCER, RUDOLPH
reiterate ..........REPEAT; RESTATE
reject..................SPURN; DECLINE
reject a lover ............................JILT
relate ......................TELL; RECITE;
.....................REPORT; NARRATE
related ..................AKIN, TOLD;
......................................COGNATE
related on father's side......AGNATE
b related on mother's side.......ENATE
relative.......................................KIN
relative, family..........BRO, SIB, SIS;
......................AUNT; NIECE, UNCLE
relative pronoun ..........WHO; THAT,
.............................................WHAT
relatives, favoring ..........NEPOTISM
relative speed......................TEMPO
relax ...........EASE, REST; LET UP
......................LOOSE; UNWIND
relaxing of state tensions DETENTE
relay of horses ................REMUDA
release.........EMIT, UNDO; LOOSE
relevant............................GERMANE
reliable ..................SURE; TRUSTY
relief ...................DOLE; WELFARE
relieve ....................EASE; ALLAY
religieuse ..................................NUN
religion...................................FAITH
religion, Jap. ......................SHINTO
religious festival ..............EASTER
religious law, Rom. .................FAS
religious laywoman ..........BEGUINE
religious sayings ...............LOGIA
relinquish ..............CEDE; FORGO,
............WAIVE, YIELD; ABANDON
reliquary ..................ARCA; CHEST
relish .........................ZEST; GUSTO
reluctant...............LOATH; AVERSE
rely ......................TRUST; DEPEND

remain ...............BIDE, STAY, WAIT; c
.................ABIDE, TARRY; LINGER
remainder ..................................REST
remaining ...................LEFT; OVER;
..............................................LEFTOVER
remark ..................NOTE; COMMENT
remark, witty ...........MOT; SALLY
remarks, defamatory......MUD; DIRT
remiss...............................................LAX
remit......................................SEND
remnant......................END; SHRED
remote .......FAR; ALOOF; DISTANT
remove ...................................DELETE
remove, legally ..................ELOIGN
remove (one's hat) ................DOFF
remove the interior ...................GUT
remunerate ................................PAY
rend .............RIP; TEAR; WREST
rendezvous...............................TRYST
renegade .........REBEL; APOSTATE
renounce ......................ABNEGATE
renown ......................FAME, NOTE;
.................EMINENCE, PRESTIGE
rent......................LET; HIRE,
.............................TORN; LEASE
renter ................LESSEE; TENANT
repair..................FIX; DARN, MEND
repartee ........COUNTER, RIPOSTE
repast ..........................................MEAL
repay ..............AVENGE; REQUITE
repay in kind ................RETALIATE d
repeat ................ECHO; ITERATE
repeat: music....................................BIS
repeatedly hit ...................POMMEL
repeated phrase ..............REPRISE
repeat performance ..........ENCORE
repeat sign: music...............SEGNO
repetition .......................................ROTE
replete .....FULL; SATED; GORGED
report .....................POP; ACCOUNT
repose ..................LIE; EASE, REST
representative.........................AGENT
reproach...............CHIDE; REBUKE
reptiles, of ........................SAURIAN
Republican ..............................G.O.P.
repulse ...............PARRY; DISGUST
reputation...........FAME; RENOWN,
......................REPUTE; PRESTIGE
request....................ASK; SOLICIT
rescind...............CANCEL, REPEAL
resentment .........PIQUE; RANCOR
reserve supply ......................STORE
residence ...........HOME; ABODE
residence, church................MANSE
residence, Irish chief's...........RATH
residence, rundown ...DUMP, SLUM
resign .........................QUIT; LEAVE
resin ................GUM, LAC; ANIME,
.................COPAL, ELEMI, JALAP;
............MYRRH; BALSAM, MASTIC

99

a resin, fossil.......AMBER; GLESSITE
resist................COMBAT, OPPOSE
resist authority......................REBEL
resistor, current............RHEOSTAT
resort...................HAUNT; REFUGE
resort, Fr. ......................PAU; NICE;
........................CANNES; RIVIERA
resort, health..........................SPA
resources ...........................FUND;
........................MEANS; ASSETS
respect ...............HONOR; ESTEEM
respiratory organ....................LUNG
respond................................REACT
rest .....................EASE; REPOSE;
................................REMAINDER
restaurant, small ................BISTRO
restive ....................EDGY; JUMPY;
................................FIDGETY
restore .................RENEW; REVIVE
restrain ....................CURB, REIN;
................................BRAKE, CHECK
restrict...................LIMIT; CONFINE
retail business ........SHOP; STORE
retain ..............KEEP, HIRE, HOLD
retaliate.........RETORT; COUNTER
retch ....................................KECK
retinue....................SUITE; TRAIN
retract...........ABJURE; WITHDRAW
retreat...............HAVEN; SHELTER
retreat, cozy .....DEN; NEST, NOOK
b retreat house, female ......CENACLE
retribution ........................REVENGE
retrograde...................BACKWARD
return ..............RECUR; PROFIT
return on investment..............YIELD
revelry, drunken.....................ORGY
revelry cry ............................EVOE
reverberate ..........................ECHO
revere ...............ADORE; WORSHIP
reverence ...........AWE; WORSHIP
reversion to type..............ATAVISM
revert (land) to state.........ESCHEAT
revise ....................EDIT; AMEND
revive wine ..........................STUM
revolve ....................SPIN, TURN
revolver .....GAT, GUN, ROD; COLT
reward....................MEED; BONUS
Rhine, city on the .................KOLN;
...............ESSEN, MAINZ, WORMS
Rhine tributary .......................AAR;
....................AARE, RUHR
rhinoceros, black ..............BORELE;
................................NASICORN
rhinoceros beetle ..................UANG
Rhone tributary ....................SAONE
rhythm .....................TIME; METER;
................................CADENCE
rhythmical accent....................BEAT
riata ..........ROPE; LASSO; LARIAT
rib..........................................COSTA

c ribbed fabric...............REP; CORDS;
................................CORDUROY
ribbon, badge ..................CORDON
ribs, having.....................COSTATE
rice bran ..........................DARAC
rice dish ..........PIAF; PILAU, PILAF
rice field ............................PADDY
rice in the husk ...................PALAY
riches .....................PELF; WEALTH
rich man ...............MIDAS, NABOB;
................................CROESUS
richness ...............................LUXE
rid .......................................FREE
riddle ...............................ENIGMA
ridge ...................................ARETE
ridge, glacial.......................ESKAR
ridge created by a glacier ......KAME
ridge on cloth .......................WALE
ridge on skin ........................WELT
ridicule ...................MOCK; DERIDE
ridicule personified .............MOMUS
riding academy .................MANEGE
riding outfit...........................HABIT
rifle ...............GARAND; CARBINE;
................................ENFIELD
rifle bullet, 19th-century.........MINIE
right, in law.........................DROIT
right, turn ...............................GEE
rightfully ..............................DULY
right-hand page ..................RECTO
d right to speak ........................SAY
Rigoletto, daughter of ...........GILDA
rigorous ...............HARSH, STERN;
........STRICT, SEVERE; AUSTERE
rim ...................LIP; EDGE; FLANGE
ring .................PEAL, TOLL; KNELL
ring, naut. ...................GROMMET
ring, rubber jar ......................LUTE
ring, seal .........................SIGNET
ring, stone of a .................CHATON
ring for reins.......................TERRET
ring inscription ......................POSY
ringlet .....................CURL; TRESS
ring of light.................AURA, HALO;
................NIMBUS; AUREOLE
ring-shaped game-piece .......QUOIT
ringworm................TINEA; TETTER
ripening agent ......................AGER
ripple............................LAP; WAVE
rise over.............................TOWER
risible...................COMIC, DROLL,
................FUNNY; HUMOROUS
risky ......................................IFFY
rites, religious ...................SACRA
river, Bremen's.....................WESER
river, Munich's .........................ISAR
river, Polish border .................ODER
river, St. Petersburg's.............NEVA
river, Southwest...................PECOS
___ Rivera, CA.......................PICO

riverbank, growing by a..RIPARIAN; ..........................................LITTORAL
river bed, dry Afr. .....................WADI
river crossed by Caesar...RUBICON
river in Essex ..............................CAM
river in "Kubla Khan"................ALPH
river into Tatar Strait..............AMUR
river into the Caspian Sea......KURA
river into the Firth of Clyde ....DOON
river into the Humber ...........OUSE; ..........................................TRENT
river into the Moselle ..............SAAR
river into the Rhone .............SAONE
river into the Yellow Sea..........LIAO
river islet ......................................AIT
river mouth ...........................DELTA
river nymph .................NAIS; NAIAD
river of Balmoral Castle ...........DEE
River of Woe .................ACHERON
river through Florence and Pisa...... ..........................................ARNO
river through Orleans .............LOIRE
river to the Sea of Azov............DON
rivulet............................................RILL
RNA element.....................CODON
road ...........VIA, WAY; ITER, PATH; ..........................AVENUE, STREET
roadhouse.....................................INN
roam ...........................GAD; ROVE; ..........................TRAVEL, WANDER
Roanoke Island message .............. ..........................................CROATOAN
roast ...........................BAKE, BURN; ..........................BROIL; SCORCH
roasted meat strip ...............KABOB
roasting rod.................................SPIT
rob......................DIVEST, HOLD UP
robber ......................THIEF; BANDIT
robe ......................CLOAK; MANTLE
*Roberta* composer .................KERN
robot, Klaatu's.........................GORT
robot in *Forbidden Planet*....ROBBY
robot of "The Jetsons" .........ROSEY
robot on "Captain Video" .....TOBOR
robot on "Get Smart"............HYMIE
robot play .....................................RUR
rock, basic igneous ................SIMA
rock, dark volcanic .............BASALT
rock, fine grained igneous ......TRAP
rock, flintlike.........................CHERT
rock, granitoid ....................DUNITE
rock, hard igneous.................WHIN
rock, jutting ................................TOR
rock, laminated....................SHALE; ..........................SLATE; GNEISS
rock, melted ...........................LAVA
rock, mica-bearing..............DOMITE
rock, rugged.............................CRAG
rock cavity .................VUGG, VUGH; ..........................................GEODE

rock elm ..............................WAHOO
rockfish ...........GOPHER, RASHER, ..........................TAMBOR; GROUPER
Rockies peak...........YALE; BROSS, ..............EOLUS, EVANS; ANTERO, ..........................CASTLE, ELBERT; ..........................LA PLATA, MAROON
Rockies range .........TETON, UINTA
rock oyster ..........................CHAMA
rockweed ............................FUCUS
rod ...........POLE, SPAR, WAND; ..........................BATON, STAFF
rod, pool ......................................CUE
rod, punishment .................FERULE
rodent.............................RAT; HARE
rodent, rabbitlike .......................PIKA
rodent, S. A. ............CAVY, DEGU, ..........................MARA, PACA; ..........................COYPU; AGOUTI
rogue .........IMP; SCAMP; RASCAL
roguish .........................SLY; ARCH
roister.....................RIOT; REVEL; ..........................FROLIC; CAROUSE
roll ..........BUN, YAW; LIST, TILT; ..........................PITCH; ROSTER
roll-call response ...................HERE
rolled meat........................ROULADE
roll of cloth ..............................BOLT
roll of paper........................SCROLL
roll up........................................FURL
romaine ......................................COS
Roman assembly .............COMITIA
Rom. author ................CATO, LIVY, ..........................PLINY; CICERO, ..........SENECA, SILIUS; SALLUST
Rom. box ..............................CAPSA
Rom. boxing glove.............CESTUS
Rom. bronze ...............................AES
Rom. brooch .........................FIBULA
romance, tale of ....................GESTE
Rom. cloak.................................TOGA
Rom. Curia court....................ROTA
Rom. date .................IDES; NONES
Rom. dictator ..........................SULLA
Rom. dish .............................PATERA
Rom. farce ..........................MIMUS
Rom. galley ......................TRIREME
Rom. gaming cube ...............TALUS
Rom. garment ..........................TOGA; ..........................STOLA, TUNIC
Rom. highway .................VIA; ITER
Rom. historian ...........LIVY; NEPOS
Rom. house.........................INSULA
Romanian money .........BAN; BANI
Rom. market(s) .......FORA; FORUM
Rom. numerals .........1-I, 5-V, 10-X, ............50-L, 100-C, 500-D, 1,00-M
Rom. official ......................AEDILE; ......................CONSUL; PRAETOR, ..........................................TRIBUNE

*a* Rom. patriot ...........................CATO
Rom. plate .............................LANX
Rom. poet ...............OVID; LUCAN;
...............................HORACE, VIRGIL
Rom. public games .................LUDI
Rom. public lands .................AGER
Rom. religious festivals .........VOTA
Rom. ruler....NERO, NUMA, OTHO;
.................GALBA, NERVA, TITUS
Rom. weapon .........................FALX
Rome, conqueror of .........ALARIC
Rome, founders of ............REMUS;
.......................................ROMULUS
Rome, fountain of .................TREVI
Rome, river of......................TIBER
Romulus, twin of .................REMUS
rood ......................................CROSS
rood screen ...........................JUBE
roof, rounded :......DOME; CUPOLA
roof, type of ............HIP: MANSARD
roof edge ..............................EAVES
roofing material ..........TAR; TILE;
..........................................SLATE
roofing slate..............................RAG
roofing timber.....................PURLIN
roof of the mouth ...............PALATE
room ................................CHAMBER
rooms, connecting .................SUITE
roomy ..............WIDE; SPACIOUS
roost ......................................PERCH
*b* rooster .................................COCK
root.......................BASE; SOURCE
root, edible ..............................TARO
root, fragrant ........................ORRIS
rope...........LASSO, RIATA; LARIAT
rope, naut. .........FOX, TYE; STAY,
...............VANG; HAWSER, RATLIN;
.......................LANYARD, RATLINE
rope, weave ..........................REEVE
rope, yardarm ...................SNOTTER
rope fiber ........COIR, HEMP, JUTE;
.................................ABACA, SISAL
rope for animals................TETHER
rope loop ...........BIGHT, NOOSE
rope-splicing tool ......................FID
ropes, unite .......................SPLICE
Rosalinda's maid ................ADELE
rosary bead................................AVE
Rosebud, e.g. .........................SLED
rose fruit...................................HIP
roselike plant.......................AVENS
rose oil..................................ATTAR
rose-shaped ornament....ROSETTE
roster ............................LIST, ROTA
rotate ...................TURN; GYRATE
rotating muscle ..............EVERTOR
rotating part.............CAM; ROTOR
rotation producer ...........TORQUE
rotten .................................PUTRID
rouge ..................................RUDDLE

rough ......RUDE, CRUDE; UNEVEN *c*
rough copy ...........................DRAFT
roulette bet .........RED; NOIR, TIER;
...............................BLACK, ROUGE
rounded projection.................LOBE
round room.....................ROTUNDA
Round Table knights................KAY,
.............TOR; BORS, MARK; FLOLL;
.......ACOLON, GARETH, GAWAIN,
......LIONEL, MODRED; GALAHAD;
.............LAMORACK, LANCELOT,
..............TRISTRAM; PALOMIDES,
...........................................PERCIVALE
round-up event...................RODEO
rouse ...................WAKE; WAKEN
Rousseau novel hero .........EMILE
route..........WAY; PATH; COURSE
row......................LINE; SPAT, TIER
rower .........................................OAR
rowing cadence caller .............COX
royal family, Fr. .................VALOIS
royal rod .........................SCEPTER
royal treasury ..........................FISC
rub .....................CHAFE; ABRADE,
.......................................SCRAPE
rubber ..................................LATEX
rubber, black ..................EBONITE
rubber, synthetic ....................BUNA
rubber, wild ..........................CEARA
rubber tree ..................ULE; HULE
rubbery .............................ELASTIC *d*
rubbish...................JUNK; TRASH
rubbish: Brit. ...........................RAFF
rubella .............................MEASLES
rub harshly ..........................GRATE
rub out ....................KILL; ERASE
rub to shine ........................POLISH
ruby red quartz.................RUBASSE
ruby spinel .............................BALAS
rudder ....................................GUIDE
rudderfish ...........................CHOPA
rudder pivot pin....................PINTLE
ruddle................................RED ORE
rudiment .....................BASE, ROOT
rue ........................................REGRET
ruff, female ...............................REE
ruffle .....................................CRIMP
ruffle, neck ............JABOT, RUCHE
rug ...............CARPET, RUNNER
ruin.....................BANE; DESTROY
rule ......................LAW; DOMINEER
"Rule Britannia" composer .....ARNE
ruler...........REGENT; MONARCH
ruler, Eastern .........................EMIR;
.............................NAWAB, SHEIK;
......................CALIPH, SULTAN
rules, dueling ...................DUELLO
rumen .......................................CUD
ruminant...................DEER, GOAT;
.........CAMEL, LLAMA; ANTELOPE

a ruminate ...............MULL; PONDER
rumor ......................BUZZ; GOSSIP
rumor personified ...................FAMA
rumple.....................................MUSS
run...........................RACE; OPERATE
run at top speed..................SPRINT
run before the wind ...............SCUD
run into ........................RAM; MEET
runner, distance ..................MILER
run of the mill ......PAR; AVERAGE
rupee, fraction of a ................ANNA
rupee, legal weight of a .........TOLA
rural .............RUSTIC; PASTORAL
rush ......................HASTE, SPEED
rush, marsh .........................SPART
Russell's viper ...................DABOIA
Russ. beer, weak ................KVASS
Russ. community farm..............MIR
Russ. co-op ..........................ARTEL
Russ. council, Czarist............DUMA

c Russ. despot..............CZAR, TSAR
Russ. distance measure .....VERST;
...................................................SAGENE
Russ. edict, Czarist.............UKASE
Russ. emperor .........IVAN; PETER
Russ. peninsula.....................KOLA
Russ. range ..............ALAI, URAL
Russ. sea, inland ........ARAL, AZOV
Russ. secret police ..................KGB;
........................................NKVD, OGPU
Russ. three-stringed viol .....GUDOK
Russ. urn........................SAMOVAR
rust ....................................UREDO
rustic .......................BOOR, RUBE;
...........................YOKEL; BUCOLIC
Ruth, husband of..................BOAZ
Ruth, mother-in-law of..........NAOMI
Ruth, son of ...........................OBED
rye disease .........................ERGOT
Ryukyu Islands viper..............HABU

# S

sable ..............................MARTEN
sack.......................LOOT; PILLAGE
sack fiber.................................JUTE
saclike cavity .......................BURSA
b sacred asp symbol ...........URAEUS
sacred bull of Eg. ..................APIS
sacred chalice ......................GRAIL
sacred city of India ..........BENARES
sacred fig, Indian ..................PIPAL
sacred image ..........................ICON
sacred lily ............................LOTUS
sacred lots, O.T. .URIM; THUMMIM
sacred place ......................SHRINE
sacrifice, place of................ALTAR
sad: music ..........................MESTO
sad comment ...........ALAS; ALACK
saddle, rear of a.................CANTLE
saddle horses, fresh ........REMUDA
saddle knob .....................POMMEL
safe.....................VAULT; SECURE
safe place .............................HAVEN
safety lamp...........................DAVY
saga.........................................TALE
saga, Icelandic .....................EDDA
sagacious ...............WISE; ASTUTE
sail, square ...............................LUG
sail, triangular ...........................JIB
sailboat ...........................YAWL;
.............................KETCH, SLOOP
sail fastener ...........................CLEW
sailing race .....................REGATTA
sail-line .............................EARING
sailor ..............................GOB, TAR;
..............................SALT; SEADOG

sailor, Indian .......................LASCAR
sails of the constellation Argo .VELA
saint, Brit. ............................ALBAN
saint, Buddhist .....................ARHAT
d St. Anthony's cross ...................TAU
St. Catherine, home of ..........SIENA
St. Francis, birthplace of.......ASSISI
St. John's bread ..................CAROB
St. Johnswort tree .................POON
"St. Louis Blues" composer .HANDY
St. Vitus dance .................CHOREA
salacious ..................GAMY, LEWD;
....................................................BAWDY
salad green ..................UDO; KALE;
.............................CRESS; ENDIVE;
.....................................................LETTUCE
salamander.....................EFT; NEWT
salary ...........PAY; WAGE; WAGES
salient angle ...........................CANT
salientia ...............................ANURA
salientian............................ANURAN
sally ....................RETORT; SORTIE
salmon, smoked.........................LOX
salmon, female .........................HEN
salmon, male .........................COCK
salmon, second year ...........SMOLT
salmon, silver .......................COHO
salmon, young ........PARR; GRILSE
salt, rock ...........................HALITE
salt factory .......................SALTERN
saltpeter .............................NITER
salt pond...............................SALINA
salt solution ............BRINE; SALINE
salt tax, Fr. ......................GABELLE

a salt tree, tamarisk....................ATLE
saltwort.....................KALI; BARILLA
salutation .......AVE; HAIL; SALUTE;
...................WELCOME; GREETING
Salvation Army founder.......BOOTH
salver......................................TRAY
sambar deer ..............MAHA, RUSA
same again.............................DITTO
Samuel, king killed by...........AGAG
Samuel, son of.......................ABIA
Samuel, teacher of ....................ELI
sanction......LET; ALLOW; PERMIT;
...................CONSENT, PENALTY
sanctuary.................FANE, NAOS;
...................CELLA; REFUGE
sand........................................GRIT
sand, mound of .........DENE, DUNE
sandals, Mex. ...............HUARACHES
sandalwood tree ...................MAIRE
sandarac powder .............POUNCE
sandarac tree wood ...........THYINE
sand bar ..................REEF; SHOAL
sandbox tree .........................HURA
sand-hill bird ......................CRANE
sand island ...............................BAR
sandpiper, Eur. ...................TEREK
sandpiper, red-backed..........STINT
sandstorm .......................HABOOB,
...................................SIMOOM
sandwich, type of .......CLUB, HERO

b Sandwich Islands, discoverer of ......
...................................COOK
Sanskrit dialect.........................PALI
Sao Salvador's state ............BAHIA
sap spout .............................SPILE
Saracen.....ARAB, MOOR; MUSLIM
Sarah, slave of ...................HAGAR
sarcasm .........IRONY; MORDANCY
sartor ...................................TAILOR
sash, kimono..........................OBI
sassafras tree ......................AGUE
Satan ....................DEVIL; LUCIFER
satellite....................................MOON
satellites, Earth .................TIROS;
...................SKYLAB; SPUTNIK,
...................PIONEER; VANGUARD
satellite's path .....................ORBIT
satiate ................CLOY, FILL, GLUT
satisfy....................SUIT; PLEASE
saturate .......SOAK; IMBUE, STEEP
Saturn, wife of .........................OPS
Saturnalia .............................ORGY
satyr.................LECHER, WANTON
sauce ...............GRAVY; RAGOUT
sauce, fish ..............................ALEC
sauce, Oriental ........................SOY
sauce, peppery ................TABASCO
sauce, tomato .................KETCHUP
sauce thickener .....................ROUX
saucy .....................................PERT

c Saul, father of .........................KISH
Saul, grandfather of......NER; ABIEL
Saul's army leader...............ABNER
Saul's successor ...................DAVID
sausage, spicy .....................SALAMI
savage .....................WILD; FERAL;
...................FIERCE; VICIOUS
savanna, S. Afr. .......VELD; VELDT
save .......................KEEP; RESCUE
savior ..........................REDEEMER
savory .................SAPID, TASTY
saw ...................ADAGE, AXIOM,
...................MAXIM; SAYING
sawbill duck ..........................SMEW
say ...................STATE, UTTER
say again ........................ITERATE
sayings, religious ..................LOGIA
scabbard, put into a .........SHEATHE
scale ....................SKIN; CLIMB
scalloped.........................CRENATE
scamp .................ROGUE; RASCAL
scandalous material.......MUD; DIRT
Scandinavian ..........DANE; SWEDE
Scand., old ..........................NORSE
Scand. chieftain, early .............JARL
Scand. legend ........................SAGA
Scand. people ........GEAT; GEATS
scanty ..................................SPARSE
scarce...............RARE; SPORADIC
scarf .............BOA; ASCOT, STOLE
Scarlett's home.........................TARA

d scatter ............STREW; DISPERSE
scene ...................VIEW; TABLEAU
scenic view .................PANORAMA
scent ..................ODOR; AROMA
schedule......................LIST, PLAN;
...................AGENDA, DOCKET,
...................LINE-UP, ROSTER
scheme ...................................PLOT
schism.....................................SPLIT
scholar.................PUPIL; PUNDIT,
...................SAVANT; STUDENT
scholars, Islamic ..................ULEMA
school, type of .......................PREP
school grounds ...................CAMPUS
school organization: Abbr. ......PTA
school residence ....................DORM
schooner, three-masted .........TERN
schuss ......................................SKI
science class...............................LAB
science fiction award............HUGO;
...................................NEBULA
scissors .............................SHEARS
scoff .........MOCK; TAUNT; DERIDE
scold ......................CHIDE; HARPY
scoop .......................................DIP
scope..........KEN; RANGE, REACH;
...................LEEWAY; PURVIEW
scorch ......................CHAR; SINGE
score ........GOAL: TALLY; TWENTY

104

| | |
|---|---|
| *a* scoria ......................SLAG; DROSS | |
| scoter ......................................COOT | |
| Scotland..............................SCOTIA | |
| Scot. alderman.....................BAILIE | |
| Scot. cake ...........................SCONE | |
| Scot. cut of beef.......................SEY | |
| Scot. garb ..............................KILT | |
| Scot. highlander ..................GAEL | |
| Scot. king............................BRUCE | |
| Scot. landholder..................THANE | |
| Scot. playwright ................BARRIE | |
| Scot. poet .........................BURNS | |
| Scot. proprietor..................LAIRD | |

SCOTTISH WORDS:
advise ...................................REDE
breeches.........................TREWS
broth ...................BREE, BROO
brow of a hill.......................SNAB
child ...................................BAIRN
church ..................................KIRK
devil ......................................DEIL
dusty ................................MOTTY
enough ..............................ENOW
family .....................................ILK
finely dressed..................BRAW
fox .......................................TOD
friends.................................KITH
from ...................................FRAE
give ......................................GIE
have ....................................HAE
*b* hillside ...............................BRAE
kiss.....................................PREE
lake ....................................LOCH
land under tenure ................FEU
locker ................................KIST
loyal ...................................LEAL
mountain ...........................BEN
no ......................................NAE
oatmeal ..........................BROSE
old ....................................AULD
out....................................OOT
own....................................AIN
pantry ..........................SPENCE
pipe ..............................CUTTY
quarter year ...................RAITH
river valley ..................STRATH
rowboat...........................COBLE
scone ............FARL; FARLE
scorn..................................GECK
self ......................................SEL
sheep walk......................SLAIT
since .................................SYNE
small ........................SMA, WEE
snow ..................................SNA
song............................STROUD
son of.................................MAC
stupid one........................CUIF
to..........................................TAE
turnip.................................NEEP
uncanny ..........................UNCO

uncle ..................................EME *c*
very ......................................VERA
young woman ..................BURD
Scott poem, Sir Walter....MARMION
scoundrel .............ROGUE; VARLET
scout unit .......DEN; PACK; TROOP
scow...................BARGE; LIGHTER
scrape ...................RASP; GRATE,
.............SCOUR, SCRUB; SCRIMP
scrape bottom ..................DREDGE
scraps, table........................ORTS
scratch ..........MAR; RASP; SCORE
scratching ground for food .............
......................................RASORIAL
screed ...............................TIRADE
screen .................SIFT; SHADE
screen, altar ...................REREDOS
screen, wind ................PARAVENT
script, upright .....................RONDE
scrutinize .............STUDY; PERUSE
scuffle ..................................MELEE
scum, metal........................DROSS
scup....................BREAM, PORGY
scuttle, coal .............................HOD
scythe handle .......SNATH, SNEAD;
.........................................SNATHE
Scythian people...................ALANS
sea anemone .......POLYP; OPELET
sea bass, Eur. .....................LOUP
sea bird .........ERNE, GULL, SKUA;
..........TERN; SCAUP; FULMAR, *d*
.........GANNET, PETREL, PUFFIN,
.........................................SCOTER
sea cow ........DUGONG; MANATEE
sea cucumber ..................TREPANG
sea duck..............EIDER; SCOTER
sea green ........................CELADON
sea gull, Pac. .........................MEW
seal.........................SIGIL; SIGNET
seal, eared........................OTARY
seal, fur............................URSAL
seal, group of .........................POD
seal, letter........................CACHET
seal, official ......................SIGNET
seal, papal ..........................BULLA
seal, young ............................PUP
sea lettuce.......ALGA, NORI, ULVA;
........................LAVER; AMANORI
seamark .............................BEACON
seamen: Brit. ..................RATINGS
seamlike ridge; anat. .........RAPHE
seams of a boat, fill .............CAULK
sea nymph ........................NEREID
search .................................GROPE
search for ..................HUNT, SEEK
search for food...................FORAGE
sea serpent ........................ELOPS
sea shell .............................TRITON
sea skeleton .......................CORAL
sea snail .............................WHELK

*a* sea snake............................KERRIL
season ................AGE; FALL, SALT
season, church.......LENT; ADVENT
seasoning herb ......................SAGE;
........................BASIL, THYME
seasons, goddesses of the .HORAE
seat, chancel .......................SEDILE
seat, long ................PEW; SETTEE
seat, Rom. ..........................SELLA
seaweed ..................AGAR, KELP;
........................LAVER, VAREC
seaweed, red ........DULCE, DULSE
secluded ...........HIDDEN, REMOTE
second.............AIDE, WINK; TRICE
secondary.............PETTY; LESSER
second brightest star .............BETA
second-growth crop...........ROWEN
Second Punic War's end, site of .....
........................................ZAMA
second team ......................SCRUB
secret ...............COVERT, HIDDEN;
........................SUB-ROSA
secret agent................SPY; MOLE;
........................SLEEPER
secreted ...................HID; HIDDEN
secret place ..........................MEW
secret police, Russ. ...........CHEKA
secrets ............................ARCANA
secrets, one learning ..........EPOPT
sect............................................CULT
*b* section of a journey.................LEG
secular.......................LAY; LAIC
secure ........................SAFE, SURE
secure firmly ...................ANCHOR
secure with rope ................BELAY
security .............PLEDGE, SHIELD
sedate ......GRAVE, SOBER, STAID
sediment.......................LEES, SILT;
........................DREGS; SILTAGE
see.............ESPY; LOOK; BEHOLD
see, church..................BISHOPRIC
seed..................................PIP, PIT;
........................GRAIN, SPORE
seed, edible.................PEA; BEAN;
........................POPPY; LENTIL;
........................PINOLE, SESAME
seed, immature ....................OVULE
seedcase, prickly ...................BUR
seed coat .........ARIL, HULL, HUSK;
........................TESTA; TEGMEN
seedless plant ........................FERN
seed plant, annual..................HERB
seeds, remove ..........................GIN
seek ...................ASPIRE, STRIVE
seem.......................LOOK; APPEAR
seeping...............................OOZY
seesaw...............................TEETER
segment, circle .......................ARC
segment, stinging ..............TELSON
seine ........................................NET

*c* seize .............NAB; GRAB; GRASP
Selene, lover of .....................METIS
self .........................................EGO
self-assurance...................APLOMB
self-reproach .................REMORSE
self-satisfied ........................SMUG
sell....................VEND; MARKET
seller ...........VENDER; MERCHANT
selling price equivocation .........OBO
semblance ............................GUISE
semester ...............................TERM
semicircular room ..................APSE
semi-diameter....................RADIUS
Seminole chief ...............OSCEOLA
semi-precious stone...ONYX, SARD
Semitic deity ...........................BAAL
sen, tenth of a .........................RIN
senate house of Rome....CURIA
send ...........................PASS, SHIP;
........................CONVEY; DISPATCH
send back.............REMIT; REMAND
send out.......................EMIT; ISSUE
senility ...............................DOTAGE
senior ...................................ELDER
senna, source of .................CASSIA
sense ......................................FEEL
senseless ................INANE, SILLY
sensitive..............SORE; TOUCHY
sentence, analyze a ...........PARSE
sentence part.....................CLAUSE,
........................PHRASE
*Sentimental Journey* author ..........
........................................STERNE
sentinel ...............GUARD; SENTRY
sentinel, mounted ...........VEDETTE
separate ....................PART, SORT;
........................APART, SPLIT; DIVIDE
separation .........................SCHISM
sequence, three-card.........TIERCE
sequester ........................ISOLATE
seraglio .............................HAREM
Serbo-Croatian folk dance .....KOLO
serene ..................CALM; PLACID
serf ........................................SLAVE
serf, A.-S. ...........................ESNE
serf, Spartan .......................HELOT
sergeant fish .........COBIA, SNOOK;
........................ROBALO
sergeant-major fish ..........PINTANO
series ...............SET; CHAIN, ROUND
series of tones .....................SCALE
serious............................GRAVE,
........................SOBER; SEDATE,
........................SEVERE, SOMBER
sermon ..............................HOMILY
serpent, Gr. .........................SEPS
serpent, large ..........BOA; PYTHON
serpentine.........................OPHITE
serpent monster .................ELOPS
serpent worship .................OPHISM

*d*

106

a servant ..................... MAID; HAMAL;
.......................................... MENIAL
servant, man's ...................... VALET
servant at Cambridge, male ..... GYP
server .................... TRAY; SALVER
serve soup ............................ LADLE
service, Rom. Cath. .............. MASS
service tree fruit ...................... SORB
servile ................................. MENIAL
serving boy ............................. PAGE
sesame .................... TIL; TEEL
session, held a ............... MET, SAT
session, hold a .............. SIT; MEET
set aside ............. DEFER, TABLE
setback ........................... REVERSE
Seth, brother of ........... ABEL, CAIN
Seth, parent of ............ EVE; ADAM
Seth, son of ........................... ENOS
set in type .............................. PRINT
set price ................................. RATE
setting ....... SITE; SCENE; LOCALE
settled ..................................... ALIT
seven, group of ............... HEPTAD,
................................ PLEIAD, SEPTET
Seven Deadly Sins ............. ENVY,
............... LUST; ANGER, PRIDE,
.................... SLOTH; GLUTTONY;
.................... COVETOUSNESS
Seven Dwarfs ........... DOC; DOPEY;
.......... HAPPY; GRUMPY, SLEEPY,
b ................ SNEEZY; BASHFUL
Seven Hills of Rome ..... CAELIAN;
................. VIMINAL; AVENTINE,
................. PALATINE, QUIRINAL;
.......... ESQUILINE; CAPITOLINE
Seven Pleiades .................. MAIA;
............ MEROPE; ALCYONE,
.................. CELAENO, ELECTRA,
.......... TAYGATE; ASTEROPE
sever ............ CUT; SPLIT; CLEAVE
severe ............ DOUR; GRAVE,
.......................................... HARSH
Severn tributary ...................... WYE
sexes, both ...................... COED
sexual assault ...................... RAPE
shabby ................................. WORN
shabby woman ................... DOWD
shackle .................... BOND, GYVE;
.................... FETTER; MANACLE
shaddock ......................... POMELO
shade ....... HUE; TINT; COLOR
shade of meaning ............. NUANCE
shadow ............... TAIL; GHOST
shadow, eclipse ................ UMBRA
shaft ............. BAR, RAY, ROD
shaft, wooden ................... ARROW
shafter ................................ HORSE
shaft of a column ................. FUST
shake .......... JAR; CHURN, QUAKE;
.................... TREMOR; AGITATE

c Shakespeare ............ See page 192.
Shakespeare, daughter of ... JUDITH;
.......................................... SUSANNA
Shakespeare, father of ........... JOHN
Shakespeare, mother of ........ MARY
Shakespeare, poem by ... LUCRECE
Shakespeare, river of ............ AVON
Shakespeare, son of ........ HAMNET
Shakespeare, wife of ............ ANNE
Shak. clown ..................... BOTTOM,
.......................................... LAVACHE
Shak. contraction ......... AS'T, E'EN,
.................... E'ER, IS'T, O'ER,
.................... ON'T, 'TIS; NE'ER,
.................... TA'EN, 'TWAS; 'TWERE
Shak. forest ......................... ARDEN
Shak. king ............................. LEAR
Shak. shepherdess ............ MOPSA
Shak. shrew .......................... KATE
Shak. sprite ........................... PUCK
Shak. villain ........................... IAGO
shaking table ..................... VANNER
sham ...................... FAKE; BOGUS;
.......................................... ERSATZ
Shang dynasty ........................ YIN
shank ........................... CRUS, SHIN
shanty .................................... HUT
shape ................... FORM, MOLD
shaping tool .......... LATHE, SWAGE
share ...................... LOT; RATION
shark, long-nosed ................ MAKO
shark, nurse ........................ GATA
shark, small ......................... TOPE
shark parasite fish ............ REMORA
sharp .................... ACERB, ACUTE
sharpen .................... HONE, WHET
sharpshooter ............ ACE; SNIPER
shear .................................... CLIP
shed, sheep ......................... COTE
shed feathers ......... MOLT; MOULT
sheen ................................. GLOSS
sheep ................................ MERINO
sheep, Afr. ..................... AOUDAD
sheep, Asian ..................... ARGALI,
.................... BHARAL, NAHOOR
sheep, black-faced ............... LONK
sheep, female ....................... EWE
sheep, male ........................... RAM
sheep, of ............................ OVINE
sheep, two-year old ................ TEG
sheep, young ........................ LAMB
sheep disease ....... COE, GID, ROT
sheep dog ......................... COLLIE
sheep's cry ................... BAA, MAA
sheep shelter ........................ FOLD
shelf ................................... LEDGE
shelf above an altar ......... RETABLE
shell, exploding .................... BOMB
shell, large ...................... CONCH
shell, marine ..................... TRITON

107

a shellfish, edible .................CRAB;
.....................MUSSEL, ABALONE,
.....................................SCALLOP
shell money.............KINA; COWRIE
shellac ..........................LAC; LAKH
shelter ..............LEE; COTE, SHED;
...........................HAVEN; SCREEN
shelter, hillside .........................ABRI
shelter, toward .......................ALEE
Shem, descendant of..........SEMITE
Shem, brother of....HAM; JAPHETH
Shem, son of ...............LUD; ARAM,
...............................................ELAM
Sheol ......................HELL; HADES
shepherd prophet .................AMOS
shepherd's song............MADRIGAL
sheriff's men ........................POSSE
sherry-wine coating ...............FLOR
shield..................BLOCK; DEFEND
shield, Athena's....................AEGIS
shield, medieval ........................ECU
shield, Rom. ......................SCUTUM
shield border ..........................ORLE
shield-shaped.................PELTATE,
.................SCUTATE; SCUTIFORM
shield strap ........................ENARME
shift ...........................TURN; STINT
shine ..........GLOW; GLEAM, GLINT
shingles....................................ZONA
Shinto deity's power ...............KAMI
b Shinto temple gate ...............TORII
ship ...........................BOAT; LINER;
.....................TANKER, VESSEL
ship, ironclad....................MONITOR
ship, lowest part of a .............BILGE
ship, oar-propelled .............GALLEY
ship, one-masted ................SLOOP
ship, part of a ..............DECK, KEEL
ship, to ...................................SEND
ship, two-masted ....................BRIG
ship employee.................BURSAR;
...................................STEWARD
ship frame ..............................HULL
ship plank ..........................STRAKE
ship's deck .............POOP; ORLOP
ship's drainage hole........SCUPPER
ship's front......BOW; FORE, PROW
ship-shaped clock .....................NEF
ship's kitchen ....................GALLEY
ship's mooring place .............DOCK;
...................................BERTH
ship's pole ..................MAST, SPAR
ship's rear ....................AFT; STERN
ship's wheel ............................HELM
ship timber's curve.....................SNY
shipworm ..........BORER; TEREDO
shirt, light long-sleeved ......CAMISE
shoal.......................................REEF
shoal water deposit ................CULM
shock..........JOLT, STUN; TRAUMA

c shoe....................MULE, PUMP;
..........BUSKIN, GAITER, LOAFER,
.........................OXFORD, WEDGIE
shoe, armored ...............SOLLERET
shoe, gym ......................SNEAKER
shoe, heavy ....BROGAN, BROGUE
shoe, open ...............ZORI, SANDAL
shoe, wooden...........GETA; SABOT
shoe, wooden-soled...............CLOG
shoe form .................................LAST
shoe front.................................VAMP
shoe gripper .........................CLEAT
shoemaker's saint .............CRISPIN
shoemaker's tool .......................AWL
shoes, Mercury's winged ..TALARIA
shoe's interior ....................INSOLE
shoot ......................FIRE; SPRIG
shoot, plant ........SOBOL; SOBOLE
shoot, sugar cane .............RATOON
shooter, hidden .................SNIPER
shooter marble...........TAW; AGGIE
shoot from cover ...................SNIPE
shooting match ...........................TIR
shoot wide .............................MISS
shop ....................STORE; MARKET
shopping center ....................MALL
shop's nameplate ...............FASCIA
shore ...................COAST; STRAND
short ...........CURT; BRIEF, TERSE;
.....................CONCISE, WANTING
d shortchange............................GYP
short comedy sketch ...............SKIT
shortcut.................................ATAJO
shorten ...............CUT, LOP; CROP
shortly ......................ANON, SOON
short-spoken ..........CURT; TERSE
short syllable indicator .........BREVE
Shoshonean .................UTE; KOSO
shoulder, road.......................BERM
shoulder blade.................SCAPULA
shoulder ornament..........EPAULET
shoulder wrap.....................SHAWL
shout..................CRY; CALL, YELL
shove .......................................PUSH
shovel ....................................SPADE
Showboat playwright .........FERBER
show off...............................FLAUNT
showroom model ...................DEMO
showy..................VIVID; SPLASHY
shrew ..................HARPY; VIRAGO
shrewd ..................CAGEY, CANNY
shrill..........................HIGH; TREBLE
shrimp, Brit. .....................PRAWN
shrink ...........SHY; QUAIL, WINCE;
.....................RECOIL; CONTRACT
shrub, Amer. ........................SALAL
shrub, Australian .................MULGA
shrub, berry-bearing.............ELDER
shrub, evergreen.....................YEW;
.......................HEATH; OLEANDER

a shrub, flowering.................AZALEA,
....................PRIVET, SPIREA;
..................................SYRINGA
shrub, Hawaiian...................OLONA
shrub, Med. ........................CAPER
shrub, poisonous.................SUMAC
shrub, spiny........................GORSE
shrub, strong-scented............BATIS
shrubbery .............................BUSH
shun .........................DUCK, SNUB;
.................AVOID, DODGE, ELUDE
shy .............COY; TIMID; WANTING
Siamese ...............................THAI
Siamese garment .............PANUNG
Siamese twin............ENG; CHANG
Siberian wild cat .................MANUL
Sicilian resort ......................ENNA
sickle, curved like a.........FALCATE
side .........................FACET, FLANK
side, pass to the ..............LATERAL
sidearm ......................GUN; PISTOL
side post..............................JAMB
sideshow performer ..............GEEK
sidetrack ..........................SHUNT
sidewalk's edge ...................CURB
sidewalk's edge: Brit. ...........KERB
sidewinder ...................CROTALUS
sidle ....................................EDGE
Siegfried, murderer of .........HAGEN
siesta ....................................NAP

b sieve .......................SIFT; ROLTER
sift........................SORT; WINNOW
sifter ..................................SIEVE
sigh ...................................SOUGH
sight, come into .....................LOOM
sight, gun...............................BEAD
sight, of ...........................OCULAR
sign ..........................MARK, OMEN;
.................TOKEN; SYMBOL
sign, music...........PRESA, SEGNO
sign a contract............................INK
signal, actor's ..........................CUE
signet .................................SIGIL
signify .................MEAN; DENOTE,
......................INTEND; CONNOTE
sign one's name .............ENDORSE
sign up ............................ENROLL
*Silas Marner* author .............ELIOT
silence.................................HUSH;
.........................QUIET, SHUSH
silence: music.....................TACET
silent...................DUMB, MUTE;
...........................QUIET, TACIT
silica .....................SAND; SILEX
silicate, complex.....................MICA
silk, Indian.............ROMAL, RUMAL
silk, old heavy ..................CAMACA
silk, raw ..............................GREGE
silk, unravel .....................SLEAVE
silk, watered ........................MOIRE

silk-cotton tree .......CEIBA, KAPOK, c
..........................................SIMAL
silk fabric...................GROS; PEKIN,
................................SATIN, TULLE
silk substitute .......NYLON, ORLON,
..........................RAYON; DACRON
silk thread ...........................FLOSS
silk tree ...............SIRIS; LEBBEK
silkworm disease ......................UJI
silly ...................MAD; ZANY; GIDDY
silver ingots...........................SYCEE
silver-iron ore ........................PACO
silvery ................................ARGENT
silvery-white metal ...........COBALT
Simenon's detective .......MAIGRET
simian ...................................APE
similar...........................LIKE; ALIKE
simpatico ..........NICE; CONGENIAL
simper ................................SMIRK
simple .........EASY; PLAIN; FACILE
simpleton ...............ASS, OAF; BOOB,
.....................DOLT, FOOL, GABY,
...............GAWK, SIMP; GOOSE
simulate .....................APE; SHAM;
........................FEIGN; PRETEND
sin .......................................ERR; EVIL
sin, petty ...................PECCADILLO
Sinai, Mount ......................HOREB
Sinbad's bird ..........................ROC
*sine ___ non*...........................QUA
sinew.................................TENDON d
sinewy ...................WIRY; BRAWNY
sing ....................CAROL, CHANT
singe wood ...................GENAPPE
singer, synagogue ............CANTOR
single .......................ONE; BILL,
..................LONE, SOLE; UNWED
single out ..........................CHOOSE
singleton ...............................ACE
sing softly..........................CROON
sing Swiss style ..................YODEL
sink a putt.............................HOLE
sinuous .............SNAKY; WINDING
sinus cavities ........................ANTRA
Sioux tribe ............................OTOE
siren, Rhine......................LORELEI
sister, religious .....................NUN
*Sistine Madonna* painter .RAPHAEL
sitting on ...........................ASTRIDE
Siva, consort of ....DEVI, KALI, SATI
six, group of .......................SESTET,
......................................SEXTET
six-line verse.....................SESTINA
sixth: music.............................SEXT
sixth sense.............................ESP
sixth sense, having a ...............FEY
skate ....................................RAY
skating surface ......................RINK
skeggar ...............................PARR
skein of yarn.........................HANK

109

*a* skeletal.................................BONY
skeletal element....................BONE
skeleton, marine ................CORAL;
.............................................SPONGE
skeptic .............................DOUBTER
sketch......................SKIT; DRAFT;
.............................................OUTLINE
sketched..................................DREW
ski...........................................SCHUSS
skiing maneuver ................WEDELN
skiing position .................VORLAGE
skilled person ......................ADEPT
skillful........ABLE, DEFT; ADEPT
skin..................................FLAY; DERMA
skin design .........................TATTOO
skin disease .......................MANGE,
.............................PSORA; TETTER
skin eruption................ACNE, RASH
skinflint...................................MISER
skin infection .......................LEPRA
skin layer ..............CUTIS, DERMA;
.................CORIUM; ENDERON
skink, Eg. ...............................ADDA
skip...........................................OMIT
skipjack ...............BONITO, ELATER
skirmish................CLASH, RUN-IN
skirt, ballet ...........................TUTU
ski run................................SLALOM
skittle.........................................PIN
ski wax ..............................KLISTER
*b* skulk..........LURK; CREEP; PROWL
skull, of the .................INIAC, INIAL
skullcap, Arabic................CHECHIA
skull protuberance(s) ....INIA; INION
sky, highest point in the ......ZENITH
sky-blue ...............................AZURE
slab, engraved ...................TABLET
slag.......................DROSS; SCORIA
slalom........................................SKI
slam..........BANG, WHAM; WHACK
slam in cards ..........................VOLE
slander ....................MUD; MALIGN;
...........................................CALUMNY
slang.......................................ARGOT
slant.......................BEVEL, SLOPE
slanted: naut. .....................ARAKE
slanting................................ASKEW
slantingly, hammer ..................TOE
slanting type.........................ITALIC
slap ..............CUFF, DRUB; SPANK
slash ...................CUT; FLAY, GASH
slate-trimming tool.....................ZAX
Slav in Saxony ..........SORB, WEND
slave ...................ESNE, SERF;
............................................THRALL
sled, type of............................LUGE
sleep .............................NAP, NOD;
...........................DOZE; SNOOZE
sleep, deep .........................SOPOR
sleeping .............ABED; DORMANT

*c* sleeping location ............BED, COT;
....................BUNK, CRIB; BERTH
sleeping sickness fly ..........TSETSE
sleep state: Abbr. .....................REM
sleep symbols........................ZEES
sleepy....................................DOZY
sleeve, large ....................DOLMAN
sleigh .....................................PUNG
sleight-of-hand ...................MAGIC
slender..........LEAN, THIN; GAUNT;
............................SPARE; MEAGER
slender woman ......................SYLPH
slice, thick ...............................SLAB
slice of bacon .....................RASHER
slick .....................SLY; GLIB, WILY;
................SHIFTY, SHREWD;
...........................................SLIPPERY
slide ...................SKID, SLIP; GLIDE
sliding piece ..............................CAM
sliding valve ........................PISTON
slight............SLIM, SNUB; GENTLE
slimy.......................................OOZY
slimy stuff ...........GOOK, GOOP,
.................GUCK, GUNK, SCUM
sling around................SLEW, SLUE
slip ............................ERR; BONER,
.................GLIDE, LAPSE, SLIDE
slip, plant............SCION; CUTTING
slip by.................................ELAPSE
slipknot.................................NOOSE
slipper .....................................MULE
slope ...................RAMP; GRADIENT
slope, steep ........SCARP; ESCARP
slope of land....................VERSANT
sloping edge ........................BEZEL
sloth, two-toed ......................UNAU
sloths, S.A.................................AIS
slow ........POKY; SLACK; RETARD
slow: music............LARGO, LENTO;
...........................ADAGIO; ANDANTE
slower: music.............................RIT.
slow loris ............................KOKAM
slugger's stat............................RBI
sluggish..................SLOW; TORPID
sluice ....................................CLOW
slump.......................DROP, SINK;
...................SLOUCH; RECESSION;
............................DEPRESSION
slur over.................................ELIDE
sly look...................................LEER
small ............................WEE; TINY;
............................PETIT, PETTY
small amount.............DRAM, DRIB,
............................LICK; MINIM
small bottle ...............................VIAL
small cluster .........................SPRIG
smallest .................................LEAST
small number ...........................FEW
smallpox .........................VARIOLA
small stream .....RUN; RILL; RILLET

*d*

a smaragd..........................EMERALD
smart.................CHIC, WISE; STING
smear on ................................DAUB
smell.........ODOR; AROMA, SCENT
smell, bad.................REEK; FETOR
smelting waste.........SLAG; DROSS
smile.......................................GRIN
smirch....................................SULLY
smock..................................CAMISE
smoke....................................FUME
smoke, wisp of........................FLOC
smoked beef..................PASTRAMI
smoking pipe...........BONG; BRIAR,
........................BRIER; HOOKAH
smoky ................................FUMOUS
smooth ....................EVEN; LEVEL
smooth feathers...................PREEN
smoothing tool......................PLANE
smooth-spoken .......................GLIB
smudge...................................BLUR
snail, large......................WHELK;
.........................................ABALONE
snail, marine ...................TRITON
snake..............ASP, BOA; ABOMA,
.............ADDER, COBRA, KRAIT,
.............MAMBA, RACER, URUTU,
.............VIPER; DABOIA, PYTHON;
.............RATTLER; ANACONDA
snakelike............................SINUOUS
snakeroot, white ..................STEVIA

b snare .................NET, WEB; TRAP
snarl .........MESH, MESS; JUMBLE
snatch ....................GRAB; SEIZE
sneer.................SCORN; SNICKER
sneezewood .......................ALANT
snoring ............................STERTOR
snow, watery .......................SLOP
snow field.................FIRN, NEVE
snow house .......................IGLOO
snow leopard......................OUNCE
snow mouse .........................VOLE
snug .................COZY, TIDY; TIGHT
snuggery...............................NEST
so.....................THUS, TRUE, VERY
so, about ...............................YAY
soak .........................SOP; DOUSE,
..............................SOUSE, STEEP;
..................DRENCH; SATURATE
soak flax....................................RET
soap, fine .........................CASTILE
soap-frame bar ......................SESS
soap plant.............................AMOLE
soapstone ...............................TALC
soap vine ..............................GOGO
so be it ! ...............................AMEN
sober.......................GRAVE, STAID
social affair..............................TEA
social climber.........................SNOB
social division .....................CASTE
social unit ................SEPT; CLIQUE

c society .....................CLUB; GUILD;
......................LEAGUE; COMPANY
society, entrance into ...........DEBUT
sod..........................................TURF
sodium carbonate ................TRONA
sodium chloride ...........NACL, SALT
sodium compound .................SODA
sodium nitrate.......................NITER
sofa .......................COUCH, DIVAN
soft .............................LAX; EASY;
.........................QUIET; GENTLE;
.....................LOW-KEY, TENDER
soften .....................CALM; PACIFY,
.......................................SUBDUE
soft palate ...........................VELUM
soft palate lobe...................UVULA
soil, organic part of .............HUMUS
soil, rich...............LOAM; LOESS
solar-lunar year differential ..EPACT
soldier, Indian .....................SEPOY
soldier, former ...........................VET
soldier from down under ......ANZAC
soldiers ....................................GIS
soldier's shelter...............FOXHOLE
solemn declaration ....VOW; OATH
sole of a plow ......................SLADE
sole of the foot.......................VOLA
solicit .....................ASK; REQUEST
solicitude..........................REGARD;
.......................................CONCERN

d solid, become..................GEL, SET;
................................HARDEN
solid shape ...CONE, CUBE; PRISM
solitary ...........LONE, ONLY, SOLE;
.....................SINGLE; SECLUDED
solo, opera ...............................ARIA
Solomon's temple, rebuilder of .........
...............................................HIRAM
solution ............................ANSWER
some......................ANY; SUNDRY;
.......................................SEVERAL
so much: music ....................TANTO
song .................LAY; TUNE; DITTY
song, Christmas ......NOEL; CAROL;
..............................................WASSAIL
song, mournful .....................DIRGE
song, nationalistic .............ANTHEM
song, religious .........HYMN; CHANT
song group .............................GLEE
song of praise ......................PAEAN
*Song of the South* uncle......REMUS
song thrush ..........................MAVIS
son-in-law..........................GENER
son of, in Arabic names ...........IBN
son of, in Gaelic names..MAC; FITZ
soon ......................................ANON
soot .......................................SMUT
soothe .........CALM; ALLAY, QUIET
soothsayer.............................SEER
sora .......................................RAIL

111

a sorb ................................WEND
sorceress ................CIRCE, LAMIA
sore ......................ACHY; PAINFUL
sorghum variety........................MILO
sorrel...............................DOCK
sorrow .........WOE; DOLOR, GRIEF
sorrowful......................SAD; BLUE
sort ..............KIND, TYPE; ASSORT
sortie ..................................SALLY
so-so ..................................OKAY
soul ......................ANIMA; SPIRIT
soul, Hindu .........................ATMAN
sound .......................FIT; HALE;
..................NOISE, SOLID;
.............COGENT; PRUDENT
sound, attention-getting ........AHEM
sound, buzzing .........WHIR, WHIZ;
..................WHIRR, WHIZZ
sound, dull.............................THUD
sound, explosive ...................BOOM
sound, gagging .....................YECH;
..................YUCH, YUCK
sound, monotonous ..............HUM;
.............................DRONE
sound, of ...........................SONANT
sound, puffing......................CHUG
sound, sibilant........................HISS
sound, throat-clearing...........AHEM
sound, vibratory .....................PURR
sound, whirring .......................BIRR

b sound loudly .......................BLARE
sound of a horn ...................BEEP;
..................HONK, TOOT
sound of pleasure or pain......MOAN
sound perception .....................EAR
sound reasoning .................LOGIC
sound system ..........HI-FI; STEREO
sound waves........................AUDIO
soup, thick...........PUREE; BISQUE,
.............................POTAGE
soup spoon .........................LADLE
soup vessel ......................TUREEN
sour ......GLUM, TART; ACRID
sour milk drink .......LEBAN, LEBEN;
.............................KOUMISS
soursop .............................ANNONA
South African ..........................BOER
S. Afr. assembly .....................RAAD
S. Afr. dialect.........................TAAL
S. Afr. hyrax...............DAS; DASSIE
S. Afr. savanna .........VELD; VELDT
S. Afr. town ...........................STAD
S. Afr. village.........................KRAAL
Southern Cross constellation.CRUX
Southern France......................MIDI
South Pacific hero ................EMILE
sovereign................................FREE
Soviet news agency................TASS
Soviet newspaper..............PRAVDA
sow .........PIG; GILT, SEED; PLANT

sower................................SEEDER c
soybean ...............................SOYA
spa, Bohemian .......................BILIN
spa, Eng. ...............................BATH
spa, Ger. .................EMS; BADEN
spade ......................LOY; SHOVEL
spade, peat ..........................SLANE
Sp. article ...............LAS, LOS, UNO
Sp. cellist ...........................CASALS
Sp. coin, old .....................PISTOLE
Sp. cooking pot......................OLLA
Sp. dance...............JOTA; BOLERO;
.............................FLAMENCO
Sp. hero................................EL CID
Sp. painter .................GOYA, MIRO,
..................SERT; PICASSO
Sp. peninsula .....................IBERIA
Sp. poet ..............................ENCINA
SPANISH WORDS:
abbey................................ABADIA
afternoon .......................TARDE
another ................................OTRO
aunt .......................................TIA
bay.......................................BAHIA
before ..............................ANTES
black ................................NEGRO
blue ....................................AZUL
boy.....................................NINO
bravo ....................................OLE
bull.......................................TORO
but................MAS; PERO, SINO d
canyon ...........................CAJON
chaperon ........................DUENA
church ..........................IGLESIA
city ...................................CIUDAD
day.........................................DIA
dove...............................PALOMA
evil..........................MAL; MALO
for..............................POR; PARA
friend................................AMIGO
girl .......................NINA; CHICA
God .....................................DIOS
gold.......................................ORO
good-bye .........................ADIOS
gulch ............................ARROYO
gypsy .............................GITANO
hall .......................................SALA
hamlet ............................ALDEA
here...................................AQUI
house ...................................CASA
Indian ................................INDIO
inn .................................POSADA
king.........................................REY
lady ..........DAMA; SENORA
lake ...................................LAGO
land, plowed..................ARADO
letter ................................CARTA
love ....................................AMOR
man .............VARON; HOMBRE
meadow ........................PRADO

*a* SPANISH WORDS: *continued*

| | |
|---|---|
| mine | MIA, MIO |
| mouth | BOCA |
| other | OTRO |
| pot | OLLA |
| priest | CURA; PADRE |
| queen | REINA |
| red | ROJO |
| river | RIO |
| road | CAMINO |
| room | SALA; CUARTO |
| saint | SAN; SANTO |
| saint, feminine | SANTA |
| she | ELLA |
| shortcut | ATAJO |
| silver | PLATA |
| six | SEIS |
| south | SUR |
| tall | ALTO |
| this | ESTA, ESTE |
| three | TRES |
| tomorrow | MANANA |
| uncle | TIO |
| very | MUY; MUCHO |
| water | AGUA |
| work | OBRA |
| spar | BOX; BOOM, MAST, POLE, YARD |
| spar, heavy | BARITE |
| spar, loading | STEEVE |

*b* spar, small ......SPRIT
spare ......LEAN; EXTRA, GAUNT
spar for colors......GAFF
sparkle ......GLITTER
sparrow, hedge ......DONEY
Sparta, queen of ......LEDA
Spartan magistrate ......EPHOR
spasm ......FIT, TIC; THROE
spawning ground ......REDD
speak ......SAY; TALK; ORATE, UTTER
speak, inability to ......ALALIA, ALOGIA, MUTISM
speaker ......ORATOR; LOCUTOR
speaking, keep from ......GAG
speak theatrically ......EMOTE
spear ......PIKE; LANCE; ASSEGAI, JAVELIN
spear, three-pronged ......TRIDENT
spear dance, Balinese......BARIS
spear-shaped ......HASTATE
spear-thrower, Austral. WOOMERA
species......ILK; KIND, SORT, TYPE; ORDER; VARIETY
specimen ......SAMPLE
speck ......DOT; MOTE; FLECK
speckle ......DAPPLE, MOTTLE, PEPPER; STIPPLE
spectacle ......PAGEANT
specter......BOGY; GHOST, SHADE

*c* speech ......LECTURE, ORATION
speech, art of ......RHETORIC
speech, local ......PATOIS
speech, long ......SPIEL
speech, loss of ......APHASIA
speech, violent......TIRADE
speech defect......LISP; STAMMER
speechless ......DUMB, MUTE
speech peculiarity......IDIOM
speed ......PACE; HASTE, HURRY, TEMPO; VELOCITY
speed-of-sound number ......MACH
spelling contest ......BEE
spelunker's mecca ......CAVE
Spenser heroine ......UNA
Spenser's name for Ireland...IRENA
sphere......ORB; SCOPE; PURVIEW
sphere of action ......ARENA
Sphinx site ......GIZA
spicy......RACY
spiders' nests......NIDI
spigot......TAP
spin ......REEL; TWIRL; ROTATE
spinal membrane ......DURA
spindle ......AXLE
spindle, yarn ......HASP
spine, slender ......SETA

*d* spine bones ......SACRA
spirit ......VIM; BRIO, ELAN, SOUL; GHOST, VERVE; ANIMUS
spirited......FIERY; LIVELY
spirit of air......ARIEL
spirit of evil......DEMON, DEVIL
spirits and water......GROG
spirits of the dead......MANES
spiritualist meeting ......SEANCE
splash......LAP; SLOSH; SPATTER
splash, large ......GOUT
splendid ......GRAND, REGAL; SUPERB
splendor......GLORY; MAJESTY
split ......RIFT; BREAK, SEVER
Splitsville......RENO
spoil......ROT; DECAY; MOLDER
spoil, as eggs......ADDLE
spoils of war ......LOOT
spoken......ORAL
spokes, having ......RADIAL
sponge, bath ......LUFFA; LOOFAH
sponge, young......ASCON
sponsor......PATRON
sponsorship......AEGIS
spool......REEL
spore ......SEED
spore cluster......SORUS

113

*a*

| | |
|---|---|
| spore sac(s) | ASCI; ASCUS |
| sport | GAME, PLAY, WEAR |
| sports arena | RINK; STADIUM |
| sports fig. | STAT |
| sports hall | GYM |
| spot on cards or dice | PIP |
| spotted | SAW; PIED; PINTO; DAPPLED; MACULOSE |
| spotted eagle ray | OBISPO |
| spouse | MATE, WIFE; HUSBAND |
| spray | ATOMIZE |
| spray, sea | LIPPER |
| spread, as gossip | BRUIT |
| spread (out) | FAN |
| spread to dry | TED |
| sprightly | PERT |
| spring | SPA; COIL; VAULT; VERNAL |
| spring, small | SEEP |
| spring back | RECOIL |
| spring rice, Indian | BORO |
| sprinkle | DUST; DAPPLE; SPECKLE |
| sprint | DART, DASH, RACE, RUSH; HASTEN, ROCKET |
| sprite | ELF; PIXIE |
| sprout | GROW; SCION |
| spruce | TRIG, TRIM; NATTY |
| spume | FOAM, SUDS; FROTH |

*b*

| | |
|---|---|
| spun wool | YARN |
| spur | GOAD; CALCAR |
| spur, mountain | ARETE |
| spur, wheel | ROWEL |
| spurt | JET; GUSH |
| squall | HOWL, WAIL, WAUL, WAWL |
| squama | ALULA; TEGULA |
| squander | WASTE; DISSIPATE |
| square dance | REEL |
| squash | CRUSH, GOURD; FLATTEN |
| squash bug | ANASA |
| squirrel skin | VAIR |
| squirrel's nest | DRAY, DREY |
| stab | TRY; PANG; PRICK |
| stabilize | STEADY |
| stable | FIRM; SOLID |
| stable compartment | STALL |
| stableman | OSTLER; HOSTLER |
| stables in London, royal | MEWS |
| stack of hay | RICK |
| staff | ROD; CANE; STICK; PERSONNEL |
| staff, bishop's | CROSIER |
| staff, royal | SCEPTER, SCEPTRE |
| staff-bearer | MACER |
| staff of office | MACE |
| stag | DEER, HART, MALE |
| stage | ENACT, PHASE |

*c*

| | |
|---|---|
| stage between molts | INSTAR |
| stage direction | EXUENT |
| stage equipment | PROPS |
| stage extra | SUPER |
| stage horn signal | SENNET |
| stage setting | SCENE |
| stage whisper | ASIDE |
| stagger | REEL |
| stagnation | TORPOR |
| stagnation, blood | STASIS |
| stain | DYE; SOIL, SPOT |
| stair part | RISER, TREAD |
| stair post | NEWEL |
| stake | ANTE; WAGER |
| stake, pointed | PALISADE |
| stale | FLAT; BANAL, TRITE |
| stalk | STEM; SHAFT |
| stalk, flower | SCAPE; PEDICEL; PEDUNCLE |
| stalk, frond | STIPE |
| stalk, plant | CAULIS |
| stalk, sugarcane | RATOON |
| stammer | HAW, HEM |
| stamp | MARK, SIGN; IMPRESS |
| stamping device | DIE |
| stamping machine | DATER |
| stamp-sheet segment | PANE |
| stanch | STEM |
| stand | BEAR, RISE; ABIDE; ENDURE; TOLERATE |
| stand, cuplike | ZARF |
| stand, small | TABORET |
| stand, three-legged | TRIPOD |
| standard | PAR; FLAG; NORM; ENSIGN |
| standing | STATUS |
| stannum | TIN |
| stanza, last | ENVOY |
| stanza, part of a | STAVE |
| star, blue | VEGA |
| star, day | SUN |
| star, evening | VENUS; HESPER; VESPER; HESPERUS |
| star, exploding | NOVA |
| starch | AMYL, ARUM, SAGO; FARINA; CASSAVA |
| starchy rootstock | TARO |
| star cluster | NEBULA |
| stare fixedly | GAZE |
| stare stupidly | GAWK |
| star facet | PANE |
| starfish | ASTEROID |
| starnose | MOLE |
| starred lizard | AGAMA; HARDIM |
| stars, location of | See page 207. |
| stars, look at | GAZE |
| star-shaped | STELLATE |
| start | JUMP; BEGIN, ONSET; OUTSET; GENESIS |

*d*

a  starting with .............................FROM
   startling shout...........................BOO
   Star Trek android....................DATA
   starwort ....................................ASTER
   state..........AIR, SAY; AVER, VENT;
   ..................UTTER, VOICE; NATION
   station ........POST; DEPOT; PLACE
   stationary ................FIXED; STATIC
   stationary motor part ........STATOR
   statistics...................................DATA
   statute ..............................ACT, LAW
   stave, barrel ..............................LAG
   stay ..............HOLD, WAIT; TARRY
   stay rope ....................................GUY
   stays...........................................CORSET
   steady look .............................GAZE
   steal ..............COP, ROB; GLOM;
   ............................SKULK; PILFER;
   ..........................SNITCH; PURLOIN
   steal cattle .............................RUSTLE
   steel: Ger. ............................STAHL
   steel: Russ. ..........................STALIN
   steel beam ........................GIRDER
   steep .....................SOAK; SHEER
   steep in lime........................BOWK
   steer......................GUIDE; CATTLE
   stellar........................................STARRY
   stem.......................CORM; STALK;
   ...........................................STAUNCH
   stem, hollow ............................CANE
b  stem, jointed grass................CULM
   stem, ship's..............................PROW
   stem of hops .........................BINE
   stem-to-stern planking .......STRAKE
   stench ..................ODOR; FETOR
   stentorian ...............................LOUD
   step ...........RUNG; PHASE; TREAD
   step, dance .............PAS; CHASSE
   step part ...............RISER, TREAD
   steppes storm.....................BURAN
   steps, outdoor...................PERRON
   steps over a fence.................STILE
   step up to the mark...................TOE
   sterilize (a female animal) ......SPAY
   stern .............................AFT; BACK,
   ...............................GRIM; HARSH
   stick ..............................BAR, ROD;
   ....................................CANE, WAND
   stick, conductor's .................BATON
   sticks, bundle of ..................FAGOT
   stick to .....................GLUE; PASTE;
   ...............................................ADHERE
   stick together ...................COHERE
   stick used in hurling ..........CAMAN;
   ...........................................CAMMOCK
   sticky stuff........GOO, GUM; PASTE
   stiffly nice ..................................PRIM
   stigma........................BLOT; TAINT
   still..................................BUT, YET;
   ..............................ALSO; QUIET

c  stimulant, coffee .............CAFFEINE
   stimulant, tea .....................THEINE
   stimulate...............STIR; PROVOKE
   sting.........................BITE; SMART
   stinging herb......................NETTLE
   stingy .........................MEAN; TIGHT
   stint............TASK; CHORE, SHIFT;
   ..................SKIMP, SPELL; SCRIMP
   stipend, church ...............PREBEND
   stipulation ............TERM; PROVISO
   stir ...........................................ADO, MIX;
   ...............................TO-DO; ROUSE
   stir up ......................RILE, ROIL
   stitch ...........................SEW; PUNTO
   stitchbird .........................................IHI
   stitched fold ............................TUCK
   stithy ......................................ANVIL
   stock ...................BREED, CARRY
   ...............................STORE; SUPPLY
   stock exchange membership..SEAT
   stock exchange, Paris......BOURSE
   stocking run: Brit. ..............LADDER
   stockings ................................HOSE
   stock market crash................PANIC
   stocky ...................DUMPY, SQUAT
   stolen goods..........................SWAG
   stomach......................MAW, CRAW
   stomach, first.......................RUMEN
   stomach, ruminant's ............TRIPE;
   ............................................OMASUM
d  stone .........AGATE, LAPIS, SLATE
   stone, aquamarine ...............BERYL
   stone, breastplate .............JASPER
   stone, fruit........................DRUPE
   stone, hollow .......................GEODE
   stone, monument................MENHIR
   stone, precious ..........GEM; JEWEL
   stone, red ................SARD; SPINEL
   stone, square-cut ............ASHLAR
   stone, woman turned to ........NIOBE
   stone, yellow........TOPAZ; CITRINE
   stone chest ..............................CIST
   stone chip ...............................SPALL
   stone-cutter's chisel .............DROVE
   stone hammer.......................MASH
   stone-hatchet, Austral. .........MOGO
   stone heap.............CAIRN, SCREE;
   .............................................RUBBLE
   stone implement ...................CELT;
   ....................EOLITH; NEOLITH
   stone pillar ...............................STELE
   stone to death .................LAPIDATE
   stone worker .......................MASON
   stool pigeon ...............RAT; NARK
   stop ........DAM, END; HALT, STEM,
   ................................WHOA; DESIST,
   ....................STATION, STAUNCH
   stop: naut. ................AVAST, BELAY
   stop an engine ......................STALL
   stoppage ....................JAM; TIEUP

115

a stopper ..........BUNG, CORK, PLUG
stop short ....................................BALK
storage battery plate ..............GRID
storage place .......BIN; BARN, SILO
store fodder ..........................ENSILE
storehouse ............................ETAPE
storehouse, army ................DEPOT
stork, type of ..................MARABOU
storm ..............FUME, FURY, RAGE
stout ..........................FAT; BURLY
stout, kind of ......................PORTER
stove ....................................RANGE
Stowe character ............EVA, TOM;
.............................................TOPSY
Stowe villain ......................LEGREE
straight ..................NEAT; FRANK;
...........................................DIRECT
straight-edge ......................RULER
strain....................TUNE; PAINS,
.........................TINGE; EFFORT,
........................STRESS; TRAVAIL
strained ..............................TENSE
strainer ................................SIEVE
strainer, wool cloth ...............TAMIS
straining for effect..................CUTE
strange....................ODD; ALIEN,
......................WEIRD; PECULIAR
strap, falcon's ..........JESS; JESSE
strass ..................................PASTE
stratagem.......PLOY, RUSE; TRICK

b stratum ................................LAYER
straw braid ..........................TAGAL
straw hat ..................BAKU, TOYO;
........................MILAN; PANAMA
stray ........................ERR; SWERVE,
...........................................WANDER
stray animal ........................DOGIE
stray child..............................WAIF
streak ..........................RUN; LINE,
.................................VEIN; STRIA
stream ......................RUN; FLOW,
.............................RILL; BROOK,
............................CREEK; RIVULET
street, narrow......................LANE
strength ................MIGHT, POWER
stress ................ACCENT, STRAIN
stretched out ..................PROLATE
stretcher..............................LITTER
stretching frame..................TENTER
strife ......................WAR; DISCORD
strike......................BOP, HIT, RAP;
..................CONK, SLUG, SOCK;
...............................SWAT; SMITE
stringed instrument, ancient .....DEL;
.............................................NABLA
string of mules ...................ATAJO
stringy ..................................ROPY
strip ......................BARE; DIVEST;
..................................UNDRESS
stripe ..........BAND, VEIN; VARIETY

stripling .............................BOY, LAD  c
strip off skin ...........................FLAY
strip of wood ..........................LATH
strive ..........TRY; WORK; TRAVAIL
strobile ..................................CONE
stroke, successful ..................COUP
stroll ...................................AMBLE
strong-arm man.....................GOON
strongbox ..............................SAFE
stronghold .........FORT; FORTRESS
strong man: Biblical ..........SAMSON
strong man, Gr. ....................ATLAS
strong point ...........................FORTE
strong-scented............OLID, RANK;
.............................................FETID
structure, tall ......................TOWER
struggle..................VIE; CONTEND
struggle helplessly.......FLOUNDER
stud ....................................BOSS
student in charge ............MONITOR
studio, art .........................ATELIER
study ................CON, DEN; READ
study group ....................SEMINAR
study of numbers, briefly........MATH
stuff ..........................PAD; CRAM
stuffing, soft ......................KAPOK
stum ....................................MUST
stunted trees......................SCRUB
stupefy ....................DAZE, STUN;
...........................................BENUMB
stupid..........SLOW; DENSE, THICK  d
stupid person ......ASS, OAF; CLOD,
......................DOLT, FOOL; IDIOT
stupor..............FOG; COMA, DAZE;
........................SOPOR; TRANCE
sturgeon, small ..................STERLET
style ..................MODE; FASHION
style of art...........................GENRE
stylet, surgical ..................TROCAR
stymie ..................FOIL; THWART
Styx ferryman ...................CHARON
subbase ..............................PLINTH
subdued shade ..................PASTEL
subject ................THEME, TOPIC
subject in grammar................NOUN
subject (to) ..........................LIABLE
subjoin ....................................ADD
sublime ..............GRAND, ROYAL;
........................AUGUST, SUPERB
submit.........BOW; YIELD; TURN IN
subordinate ..........MINOR; JUNIOR
subside .........EBB; WANE; ABATE,
..........................LET UP; RELENT
substantial ......BIG; REAL; LARGE,
..................COPIOUS; ABUNDANT
substantial amount................MUCH
substantiate ......................VERIFY
substantive word ..................NOUN
substitute.........SWITCH; STAND-IN
subtle....................FINE; DELICATE

*a* subtle variation...................NUANCE
subtract...................TAKE; DEDUCT
subway, London........................TUBE
subway, Paris.........................METRO
subway entrance.....................KIOSK
succinct ..................BRIEF, TERSE
succor.............AID; HELP; RELIEF
suckling, stop ..........................WEAN
Sudan lake............................CHAD
suet ...................................TALLOW
suffer ...........LET; ALLOW; MOURN
sufficiently............................DULY
SUFFIXES:
   action...................................-ANCE
   adherent..................................-IST
   adjective-forming..............-ARY,
   ..............-ENT, -IAL, -INE, -ISH,
   ...................-IST, -ITE, -ORY,
   ..................-OUS, -EOUS, -IBLE,
   ...........................-ICAL, -IOUS
   belonging to ........................-EAN
   blood disease.....................-EMIA
   carbohydrate........................-OSE
   cavity ..............-COEL, -COELE
   characterized by ................-IOUS
   comparative ..............-IER, -IOR
   condition .................-ATE, -ISE;
   ..............-ANCE, -OSIS, -SION,
   .....................-STER, -TION
   decomposition ....................-LYTE
*b*  diminutive.....-ULA, -ULE; -ETTE
   disease, urinary .................-URIA
   dissolve ...............-LYSE, -LYZE
   dividing...............................-TOMY
   doctrine ................................-ISM
   eye defect ...........................-OPIA
   females.............................-GYNY
   feminine.........-INA, -INE; -ELLA,
   ...................-ETTA, -TRIX
   follower........................-IST, -ITE
   foot.....................................-PEDE
   full of .................................-OSE
   having ..................................-FUL
   indicating, in a way ...........-ABLY
   inflammation .........................-ITIS
   inhabitant of ..........................-ITE
   instrument.........................-TRON
   killer...................................-CIDE
   like......................................-OID
   little ...................................-OCK
   lizard.................................-SAUR
   mineral ..................-ITE; -LITE
   noun-forming ..........-ACY, -ARY,
   ..........-ATE, -ENT, -ERY, -ESS,
   ..........-IER, -IST, -ORY; -ANCY,
   .............-ENCE, -ENCY, -ENSE,
   .......................-MENT, -STER,
   .....................-TION, -TUDE
   number .................-ETH; -TEEN
   occasion of many .............-FEST

*c* of the kind of......................-ATIC
one that eats .......-VORA, -VORE
one who is ............................-NIK
ordinal .................................-ETH
origin ................................-GENY
pain ....................-ALGY; -ALGIA
participle............................-ING
quality ..................-ANCE; -ILITY
recent .................................-CENE
ruler ....................................-ARCH
sayings ..................-ANA; -IANA
science of ............................-ICS
scientific name..............-ACEA,
.....................................-IDAE, -PODA
skin .....................................-DERM
small ....................................-CULE
stabilizing instrument........-STAT
stone ......................-LITE, -LITH
superlative ...........................-EST
supporter ..............................-CRAT
systematized knowledge -NOMY
teeth, animal ...................-ODUS
teeth, having...................-ODONT
that which acts..................-ATOR
times as many.................-FOLD
tumor ....................-OMA; -CELE
verb-forming ...........-ISE; -ESCE
vision.......................-OPY; -OPIA
Sufi disciple ......................MURID
sugar, crude ..........GUR; JAGGERY
*d* sugar, fruit .....................KETOSE
sugarcane byproduct ......BAGASSE
sugarcane disease................ILIAU
sugarcane shoot, new............LALO
sugar source ........................CANE
suggestion .........CUE; CLUE; HINT;
.............................TINGE, WHIFF
suitable ................APT; FIT; RIGHT
suitcase ..........BAG; GRIP; VALISE
suit of mail .........................ARMOR
suitor....................BEAU; SWAIN
sullen....................DOUR, GLUM;
.................GLOOMY; SATURNINE
sullen, act .........................MOPE
sullen, be ..............POUT, SULK
sully .....................SOIL; DIRTY
sultan, Turk. ....................SELIM
sultan's decree .....................IRADE
sultan's residence .................SERAI
sultry .......................HOT; HUMID
*summa ___ laude* ...................CUM
summary ..........BRIEF, RECAP
summit .......................TOP; PEAK
summon ..................CALL; EVOKE
sun.....................SOL; HELIOS
sun, halo around the ........CORONA
sun, of the .........................SOLAR
Sunday in Lent, fourth .....LAETARE
sunder.....................SPLIT; DIVIDE
sundial ............................GNOMON

117

*a*
sun disk .................................ATON
sun-dried brick ....................ADOBE
sunfish ................................BREAM
sunken fence ......................HA-HA
sun room .........................SOLARIUM
superfluous: Fr. .............DE TROP
superintendent ...............MANAGER
superior .............PRIME; BETTER,
.............................HIGHER, SENIOR
Superman, girlfriend of ...........LOIS
Superman, real name of ......KAL-EL
supplication ............PLEA; PRAYER
supply ...............STOCK; FURNISH
support .............PROP; BRACE
support structure ....................WALL
suppose ................GUESS, INFER
suppress ..............QUASH; STIFLE
surcoat .................................TUNIC
surety agreement..................BOND
surf, sound of ......................ROTE
surface ................TOP, FACE;
.............................................VISAGE
surface, smooth ...............VENEER
surfeit ..............CLOY, GLUT, SATE
surge .................GUSH; SWELL
surgeon's instrument .......TREPAN,
..................TROCAR; ABLATOR;
.............................................SCALPEL
surgical thread ....SETON; SUTURE
surly .......................GRUFF, TESTY

*b*
surmise ...............GUESS; THEORY
surpass...................TOP; BEST
surplus ............EXTRA; EXCESS
surrender ................CEDE; YIELD
surrender legally................REMISE
surround ..............HEM; GIRD;
.....................CIRCLE; ENCLOSE
surrounding area..................ZONE
survey .............EYE; LOOK;
.............................................WATCH
surveyor's assistant........RODMAN
surveyor's instrument .......ALIDADE
Susa inhabitant................ELAMITE
suspend ...............HANG; DELAY;
..................TABLE; SHELVE
suspenders.......................BRACES
suture .............................STITCH
svelte ......................SLIM, TRIM
swab ......................................MOP
swain.......................BEAU; LOVER
swallow.................GULP; MARTIN
swallow, sea......................TERN
swamp ...........BOG, FEN; MARSH;
.............................................MORASS
swamp gas........................MIASMA
swan, female ...........................PEN
swan, male .............................COB
swan, whistling....................OLOR
swap .....................................TRADE
sward ............................SOD; TURF

*c*
swarm ..........NEST, TEEM; HORDE
swarthy....................................DARK
swastika ............................FYLFOT
sway ...........................ROCK, ROLL
sway, hold .........RULE; DOMINATE
swear ................AVER; CURSE
swear words, use ....................CUSS
sweat .....................PERSPIRE
Swed. coin...............................ORE
Swed. county ..........................LAN
Swed. sculptor .................MILLES
sweep, scythe's...................SWATH
sweet .............................SUGARY
sweet flag .......................CALAMUS
sweetheart, Irish ...................AGRA
sweet liquid ........................NECTAR
sweetness, with: music........SOAVE
sweet potato ..........YAM; OCARINA
sweet red wine ...............ALICANTE
sweet-smelling.............REDOLENT
sweetsop ...............ATES; ANNONA
sweet spire................................ITEA
swell ............................WAX; GROW
swelling .......LUMP, NODE; EDEMA
swell of water.........................WAVE
swerve ...........SKEW, SLEW, SLUE
swift .........................FAST; FLEET
swift, common ......................CRAN
swiftly, run .............DART, SCUD
swimming...........................NATANT

*d*
swindle .............CON, GYP; DUPE;
.................GULL; CHEAT, COZEN;
.................FRAUD, MULCT, STING
swindler ...........................COZENER
swine.........HOG, PIG, SOW; BOAR
swing music ...........................JAZZ
swinish ...........................PORCINE
swirl ...........................................EDDY
Swiss card game....................JASS
Swiss state........................CANTON
switch ...................SHIFT, TRADE;
..................TOGGLE, WAGGLE
switch positions ............ONS; OFFS
swollen ................................TURGID
swoon ..................................FAINT
sword........EPEE; BLADE, SABER;
.............................................RAPIER
sword, King Arthur's ....EXCALIBUR
sword, matador's .............ESTOQUE
sword, medieval..................ESTOC
sword, put away a ...........SHEATHE
syllable, last ......................ULTIMA
syllable, short .......................MORA
symbol ................................TOKEN
symbol of authority ...............MACE
synagogue .............SHUL; TEMPLE
syncopated music..........RAGTIME
syncope .................FAINT, SWOON
syphilis ...........................POX; LUES
Syria, ancient.........................ARAM

a Syrian port, ancient..............SIDON
Syrian city...........................ALEPPO
system of rules .....................CODE

system of weights .................TROY c
system of worship ..................CULT
syzygy......................................PAIR

# T

tab.............................FLAP; LABEL
tableland.............MESA; PLATEAU
tablet .............................PAD; PILL;
.................................BLOCK, SLATE
tableware ...................CUP; BOWL,
.........DISH, FORK; GLASS, KNIFE,
............PLATE, SPOON; SAUCER,
................TUREEN; PLATTER
Tacoma's sound .................PUGET
tact.....................................FINESSE
tag............................................LABEL
tail, of a...........CAUDAL; CAUDATE
tail, rabbit's.............................SCUT
tail, thickly furred ...................BUSH
tail of a coin .........................VERSO
tailor ..................................SARTOR
Taj Mahal site .......................AGRA
take away by force..............REAVE
take back words .................RECANT
take off a hat .........................DOFF
take on cargo .............LADE, LOAD
b take out ...............DELE; EXPUNGE
take part......................................SIDE
take up again ....................RESUME
tale.............................YARN; STORY
tale, medieval .........GEST; GESTE
tale, medieval Fr. .......................LAI
tale, Norse ............................SAGA
talent ............GIFT; FLAIR, KNACK
*Tale of Two Cities, A* girl .......LUCIE
talipot palm ..............................BURI
talisman.................JUJU; CHARM;
.............................AMULET, FETISH
talisman, voodoo ................GRI-GRI
talk.....................GAB, YAK; CHAT;
.............................PRATE; PALAVER
talk, wildly .................RANT, RAVE;
..................................HARANGUE
talking horse .......................MR. ED
talk pompously....................ORATE
talk stupidly............YAUP, YAWP
tall group of Afr. people .......SERER
tall tale ...........................LIE; YARN;
..................................WHOPPER
tally .............TAB; COUNT, SCORE
Talmud commentary.........GEMARA
talon ...........................CLAW, NAIL
tamarack...............................LARCH
tamarisk....................ATLE; ATHEL
Tammany leader..............SACHEM
tan..............................BUFF; BEIGE

tanager, Asian .......................YENI
tanager, S.A. .......................LINDO
tanbark....................................ROSS
tangle ...................SNARL; SLEAVE
tangled mass...............MAT; SHAG
tanning, plant for .................ALDER
tanning gum ...........................KINO
tanning shrub ......................SUMAC
tanning solution ......................BATE
tan skins ..................................TAW
tantalize......................BAIT; TEASE;
.....................................TORMENT
Tantalus, daughter of...........NIOBE
tantrum..........................FIT; HUFF
tap............................PAT; COCK;
..........................SPIGOT, FAUCET
tape, sample .........................DEMO
tapering dagger .................ANLACE
tapering piece ........................SHIM
tapestry ...................ARRAS, TAPIS
tapeworm ...........................TAENIA
tapiocalike food ...................SALEP d
tapioca source.................CASSAVA
tapir, S.A. ............................DANTA
taradiddle .........................FIB, LIE
tarboosh ...................................FEZ
target ..........................AIM; GOAL
Tariff Act writer.................SMOOT;
.....................................HAWLEY
Tarkington character ...............SAM
tarnish ...................................SULLY
taro ......................GABI; DASHEEN
taro paste .................................POI
taro root ................................KALO
tarpon .................................SABALO
tarry .................BIDE, STAY, WAIT;
....................................LINGER
tarsus .....................................ANKLE
tart ..............ACID, SOUR; WENCH
tartan pattern ..........................SETT
tartar, crude ..........ARGAL, ARGOL
Tarzan's chimp ....................CHETA
task...............................JOB; DUTY;
..............................CHORE, STINT
task, punishment ...............PENSUM
taste .................SIP, SUP; SAPOR
tasteful .........SUBDUED; ARTISTIC
tasty.......................................SAPID
Tatar dynasty ...........................WEI
*Tatler* founder....................STEELE
tattle ...............................RAT; BLAB

a  taunt..........JEER, MOCK; HECTOR
   taut ...........................TENSE, TIGHT
   taut, pull .........................STRETCH
   tautomeric compound.............ENOL
   tavern .....................BAR, INN, PUB
   tax ..................CESS, GELD, LEVY;
   ............ASSESS, EXCISE, IMPOST
   tax, church ...........................TITHE
   tax, import .........................OCTROI
   tax group: Abbr. .......................IRS
   tea, black.........BOHEA, PEKOE
   tea, green ............................HYSON
   tea, herbal ...........................PTISAN
   tea, Indian ...........................ASSAM
   tea, marsh ...........................LEDUM
   tea, Oriental ...........CHA; OOLONG
   tea, Paraguay .........MATE; YERBA
   tea box ............CADDY; CANISTER
   tea cake .............................SCONE
   teacher ...........DOCENT, MENTOR
   teacher, Heb. .......................RABBI
   teacher, Islamic ........ALIM; MULLA
   teakettle: Fr. slang......SUKE, SUKY
   team, three-horse ..............RANDEM
   team of horses ......................SPAN
   tear.....................RIP; DROP, RENT
   tease ................HARRY; HARASS,
   ................PESTER; BEDEVIL
   tedious writer .......................PROSER
   teem ...........RAIN, POUR; SWARM

b  Telamon, son of .....................AJAX
   telegraph...............................WIRE
   telegraph, underwater .........CABLE
   telegraph inventor ...............MORSE
   telegraph key ......................TAPPER
   telegraph signal ............DOT; DASH
   telegraph speed unit .............BAUD
   telephone inventor..................BELL
   telescope part ......................LENS
   television ............................VIDEO
   television alien .......................ALF
   television award ...................EMMY
   television cable ..................COAXIAL
   television channel .......See channel.
   television station abbr. ....UHF, VHF
   tell ..................IMPART, RELATE;
   ....................NARRATE, RECOUNT
   telling blow ...........................COUP
   Tell legend site.........................URI
   temper ..................RAGE; ANNEAL
   *Tempest* servant ...................CALIBAN
   *Tempest* sprite ....................ARIEL
   temple ..................................FANE
   temple, Asian ....................PAGODA
   temple, inner part of a..........CELLA
   temple chamber, Gr. .............NAOS
   tempo: music ........................TAKT
   temporary decline ................SLUMP
   temporary fashion ....................FAD
   temporary relief..............REPRIEVE

c  tempt....................LURE; COURT;
   ...........ALLURE, ENTICE, SEDUCE
   tenant ...............................LESSEE
   tend..........................MIND; SERVE
   tennis, served perfectly in ......ACED
   tennis score .............LOVE; DEUCE
   tennis stroke ...................ACE, LOB;
   .........................SMASH; VOLLEY
   tennis term .............LET, NET, SET
   Tennyson character...............ENID;
   .............ARDEN, ENOCH; ELAINE
   tenon ......................................COG
   tense .........EDGY, TAUT; UNEASY
   tentacle ...............................FEELER
   tent flap.....................................FLY
   tenth part .............DECI; TITHE
   tentmaker, the .......................OMAR
   ten years ...........................DECADE
   tepid .......................MILD, WARM
   Tereus, son of ........................ITYS
   term.........................SPAN; WORD;
   ...........................................PERIOD
   termagant .............................SHREW
   term in office........................TENURE
   term of address .........................SIR;
   ...........................SIRE; MADAM
   terpene alcohol ......................NEROL
   terrapin ..............................EMYD;
   ........................POTTER, SLIDER
   terrible ......................DIRE; AWFUL
   terrier, kind of ............SKYE; CAIRN
   terrified...............AFRAID, SCARED
   ......................................PANICKED
   territory ....................LAND, SOIL
   territory, surrounded ........ENCLAVE
   terror............................FEAR; PANIC
   tessera....................................TILE
   test...........EXAM; ASSAY, TEMPT;
   ......................TRIAL; EXAMINE
   testament..................................WILL
   testifier .......................DEPONENT
   testify ...............................DEPONE
   tetrad ....................................FOUR
   Teucer, half-brother of ...........AJAX
   Teutonic barbarian................GOTH
   Texas shrine ......................ALAMO
   texture ......................PITH; FIBER;
   .....................................ESSENCE
   Thailand, once......................SIAM
   Thames estuary ....................NORE
   thankless person .............INGRATE
   thatcher's peg .......................SCOB
   thatching palm .......................NIPA
   thaw ......................................MELT
   theater .................ODEON, STAGE
   theater box seat ....................LOGE
   theater district .....................RIALTO
   theater floor ............................PIT
   theater sign .............................SRO
   Theban Bard.......................PINDAR

120

Thebes, king of ................CREON; OEDIPUS
theme ......................ESSAY, MOTIF
theme: music ...........................TEMA
theme-park thrill.........................RIDE
then: music ...............................POI
therefore ..................ERGO, THEN; THUS; HENCE
Theseus, father of ............AEGEUS
Theseus, killer of ................CREON
thesis, opposite of ...............ARSIS
thespian.................................ACTOR
Thessaly, king of ...............AEOLUS
Thessaly mountain ................OSSA
Thessaly valley ...................TEMPE
thicket .................COPSE; COVERT
thick-lipped.....................LABROSE
thickness .................................PLY
thief, Yidd. .........................GANEF
thigh, of the .....................FEMORAL
thigh bone ...........................FEMUR
thin...............LANK, LEAN; GAUNT, SHEER; DILUTE, PAPERY; SPARSE; TENUOUS
thin cake..............................WAFER
things added...................ADDENDA
things done ...........................ACTA
things to be done .............AGENDA
think.............DEEM, HOLD; OPINE; PONDER; COGITATE
think (over) .............MULL, MUSE
thin layer ,.............................FILM
*Thin Man, The*, dog in............ASTA
thin out........................ATTENUATE
thin-toned.............................REEDY
third day, every ...............TERTIAN
thirsty ...................DRY; PARCHED
thither ...................................THERE
thong ...................................STRAP
thong, braided .....................ROMAL
Thor, wife of...............................SIF
thorax, organ in the ...............LUNG
Thor in Ger. myth ...............DONAR
thorn ........................BRIER, SPINE
thorny plant ...........................BRIER
thoroughfare ..............WAY; ROAD; AVENUE, STREET
thoroughgoing ..................ARRANT
thought...................IDEA; NOTION
thoughts, form ....................IDEATE
thousand ...................................MIL
Thrace, ancient people of .....EDONI
thrall ...........................ESNE; SLAVE
thrash ..........BEAT, WHIP; POUND; BATTER, PUMMEL
thread, cotton ........................LISLE
thread, of a.........................FILAR
threaded fastener ....................NUT
threadlike .......................FIBROUS; NEMALINE

threadlike parts: anat. .............FILA
threads, cross ...................RETICLE
threads crossed by woof .......WARP
threads crossing warp...........WEFT, WOOF
threaten.................COW; MENACE
Three Fates..CLOTHO; ATROPOS; LACHESIS
threefold ..............TRINE; TREBLE; TERNARY, TERNATE
Three Furies .ALECTO; MEGAERA; TISIPHONE
Three Graces ......AGLAIA, THALIA; EUPHROSYNE
three-masted ship ..............XEBEC; FRIGATE
three-spot .............................TREY
Three Stooges .........MOE; CURLY, LARRY, SHEMP
threshhold................................SILL
thrifty................................FRUGAL
thrive..............................PROSPER
throat .............GORGE; GULLET
throat, of the .......................GULAR
throb......................BEAT; PULSE; PULSATE
throe ...................................PANG
throng.................MOB; HORDE
throw .............CAST, HURL, TOSS; FLING, PITCH
throw, underhand......................LOB
throw back.............................REPEL
thrush, song .......................MAVIS
thrust .............BUTT; PROD, PUSH; LUNGE, SHOVE
thunderfish ...........................RAAD
thunder sound.......................CLAP
thurible ..............................CENSER
Thuringian city .......................JENA
Thursday god .......................THOR
thus ......................................SIC
thus far ...................................YET
thwart.......................FOIL; DEFEAT, STYMIE; TRAVERSE
Tiber tributary .......................NERA
Tibetan priest ......................LAMA
Tibeto-Burmese people ..........KAW; AKHA
tibia ................................CNEMIS
tick ..................................ACARID
ticket, half a ...........................STUB
tickets, sell illegally ..............SCALP
tickle .............................TITILLATE
Ticonderoga, commander at GATES
tidal flood.................BORE; EAGRE
tide, largest change in ...........NEAP
tidings ....................NEWS, WORD
tidings, Biblical .................GOSPEL
tidy ..............................NEAT, TRIM; ORDERED

a tie....................BIND, BOND, LASH;
.............................TRUSS; CRAVAT
tie, kind of ..........................ASCOT
tie, railway ......................SLEEPER
tie-breaking game ............RUBBER
tie off ...............................LIGATE
tier ..........................ROW; LEVEL
tight ....................SNUG, TAUT
tighten: naut. .........................FRAP
tightly stretched ..................TENSE
tight spot...........FIX, JAM; SCRAPE
til ...................................SESAME
tiles, hexagonal ....................FAVI
tile, roofing ......................PANTILE
tilelike ...........................TEGULAR
tilled land ...........................ARADO
tiller ...................................HELM
till the earth................FARM, PLOW
tilt .....................TIP; CANT, LIST
tilting: naut. ..........................ALIST
timber, flooring ..................BATTEN
timber bend............................SNY
timber tree, Braz. ..............ARACA
timber tree, Indian ................DAR
timber wolf..........................LOBO
time .....................SPAN; CLOCK,
...........................SPELL, TEMPO;
..................PERIOD; DURATION
time being ..........................NONCE
time gone by ........................PAST
b *Time Machine, The* people .....ELOI;
...............................MORLOCKS
time off...............................LEAVE
time out ............................RECESS
time period ..................AGE, DAY,
.............EON, ERA; AEON, HOUR,
...............................WEEK, YEAR;
.........MONTH; DECADE, MINUTE,
....................SECOND; CENTURY
times, old ..................ELD; YORE
timid .......................SHY; BASHFUL
timorous .............................TIMID
timothy ...............................HAY
tin....................CAN; STANNUM
tin, containing ...............STANNOUS
tine ...................................PRONG
tine of an antler ..................SNAG
tinge ...................................TAINT
tinge deeply ....................IMBUE
tingle with feeling ..............THRILL
tip .....................END; CANT, LEAN;
......................ADVICE; GRATUITY
tipping....................ALIST, ATILT
tire ......................PALL; WEARY;
...................................FATIGUE
tire casing ...........................SHOE
tire face ............................TREAD
tire support ............................RIM
tire tread groove ..................SIPE
Titania, husband of ..........OBERON

c Titans, The Twelve ....RHEA, THEA;
...........................COIUS, CRIUS;
.......CRONUS, PHOEBE, TETHYS,
.....THEMIS; IAPETUS, OCEANUS;
.............HYPERION; MNEMOSYNE
Tithonus, brother of .............PRIAM
titlark ...................................PIPIT
title ...................................NAME
title, baronet's.........................SIR
title, Benedictine ..................DOM
title, Eth. ............................RAS
title, knight's ..........................SIR
title, lady's...MRS.; DAME; MADAM
title, man's........SIR; SIRE; MISTER
title, Turk. ..........................PASHA
title of property ....................DEED
titmouse ....................CHICKADEE
tittle ..................JOT; IOTA, WHIT
toad, tree .............................HYLA
toasting word........SALUD, SKOAL;
...................................PROSIT
tobacco, chewing .......CHAW, QUID
tobacco, coarse ...................SHAG;
...................................CAPORAL
tobacco, fine Cuban ...............CAPA
tobacco ash ......................DOTTEL
toe ...................................DIGIT
toe, bump one's ..................STUB
toe, fifth..........................MINIMUS
together..............................BOTH
togs ...................................DUDS
Tokyo, old name of .............YEDO;
...................................YEDDO
Tokyo Bay, city on .................CHIBI
tolerable..............................SO-SO
toll ..........................FEE; KNELL
Tolstoy heroine ....................ANNA
tomboy ............................HOYDEN
tomcat ...................................GIB
tone .......HUE; MOOD, NOTE;
...........................SHADE; TIMBRE
tone, lack of ........................ATONY
tone, of ...............................TONAL
tone down..........................SOFTEN
tone quality ......................TIMBRE
tones, series of.................OCTAVE
tongue, articulated with the .APICAL
tongue, of the ..................GLOSSAL
tongue-clicking sound ......TSK, TUT
tongue of a wagon.................NEAP
tonic ...........................ROBORANT
tonic herb..................ALOE; TANSY
too early ....................PREMATURE
took a chair .........................SAT
tool, abrasive ...............FILE, RASP
tool, boring......................AWL, BIT;
..........................AUGER; GIMLET
tool, cleaving ........................FROE
tool, cutting ....................ADZ, AXE,
...................................SAW; ADZE

122

a tool, engraver's ....................BURIN;
...........................................MATTOIR
tool, enlarging ....................REAMER
tool, grass-cutting ............SCYTHE,
...........................................SICKLE
tool, machine ......................LATHE
tool, machine cutting ................HOB
tool, molding ...........................DIE
tool, pointed............................AWL;
.........................BODKIN, BROACH
tool, post hole ...........................LOY
tool, splitting ............FROE, FROW
tool, stone ..............CELT; EOLITH;
...........................................NEOLITH
tool, threading ..................CHASER
too much ................................TROP
tooth..................COG; FANG, TINE;
............MOLAR; CANINE, CUSPID
tooth, long.............FANG, TUSK
tooth cover.................................CAP
toothed formation ..................SERRA
toothed wheel .........................GEAR
toothless ........................EDENTATE
toothlike ornament..............DENTIL
tooth pulp............................NERVE
top ....................................CAP, LID;
.................ACME, APEX; OUTDO
topaz hummingbird ...................AVA
toper...........................SOT; SOUSE
topic ..................................THEME

b topmast crossbar support..........FID
top-notch ...........................A-ONE
topsail, triangular.................RAFFE;
...........................................RAFFEE
torment ....................BAIT; ANNOY,
..................DEVIL, HARRY, TEASE
torn place ...............................RENT
torrid zone ........................TROPIC
tortoise, freshwater ...........EMYDID
*Tosca* villain ....................SCARPIA
toss .................CAST, FLIP, HURL;
...........................FLING, PITCH
tosspot ....................SOT; DRUNK
total....................ALL, SUM; TALLY
....................WHOLE; COMPLETE
totalitarian ruler..............DICTATOR
totem pole ...............................XAT
toucan, S.A. ..........................TOCO;
...........................................ARACARI
touch..........................ABUT, FEEL;
...........................................CONTACT
touch, of .............HAPTIC, TACTIC;
....................TACTILE, TACTUAL
touch, organ of......................PALP
touch lightly .................PAT, TAP
touchwood............................PUNK
tough ....................HARD; SEVERE,
...........................................STURDY
tour guide, museum ..........DOCENT
tourmaline, colorless......ACHROITE

tournament walkover ...............BYE c
tow ..............................DRAW, PULL
towel ...................................WIPER
towel fabric...........................TERRY
tower, Biblical .....................BABEL
tower, Indian ........................MINAR
tower, little ........................TURRET
tower, mosque .................MINARET
towering ....................HIGH; LOFTY
towhead.............................BLONDE
toxic protein from jequirity .....ABRIN
toy (with)...............................TRIFLE
trace ..................TINGE; VESTIGE
track ........................................RAIL
track, animal ................RUN; SLOT;
...........................................SPOOR
track, put off ....................DERAIL
track, put on another..........SHUNT;
...........................................SWITCH
track, ship's ...........................WAKE
track circuit ..............................LAP
tract............................LOT; PLOT,
.....................FIELD; PARCEL
trade.................SWAP; BARTER;
...................TRAFFIC; EXCHANGE
trader...............DEALER, MONGER
traduce .................SLUR; DEFAME
traffic .....................................TRADE
trail .........................TAIL; TRACK
train, stopping..................LOCAL
train of attendants ...........RETINUE d
trajectory.....................................ARC
tramp..................HOBO; VAGRANT
trample ................................TREAD
tranquil ...........................SERENE
transaction ..................DEAL, SALE
transfer ...............GRANT; CONFER
transform ........................CONVERT
transgress.......................ERR, SIN
___ *transit gloria mundi*..............SIC
transitional editing effect .........WIPE
transmit ...............................SEND
transom ..............................TRAVE
transparent as glass .........HYALINE
transpire ............................OCCUR;
...........................................HAPPEN
transverse pin ...................TOGGLE
trap ....................................SNARE
trappings.........................REGALIA
trapshooting ......................SKEET
travel .......................ROAM, TREK;
....................WANDER; JOURNEY
tray ...................SALVER, SERVER
tread softly .................PAD; SNEAK
treasure ...............................TROVE
treasurer, college .............BURSAR
treasury agents ...................T-MEN
treat .................DOCTOR, MORSEL
treatment.............CARE; THERAPY
treat with malice.....................SPITE

123

*a* tree.................ASH, BAY, ELM, FIG;
..................FIR, GUM, OAK, YEW;
.............LIME, PALM, PEAR, PINE;
.........PLUM, TEAK, UPAS; ALDER;
.............APPLE, ASPEN, BALSA;
.............BEECH, BIRCH, CACAO;
.............CEDAR, CLOVE, EBONY,
.............ELDER, GUAVA, HENNA,
.............HOLLY, LARCH, LEMON,
.............MANGO, MAPLE, OLIVE,
.............PAPAW, PEACH, PECAN,
.............PLANE, SENNA; ACACIA;
.....ALMOND, BALSAM, BANYAN;
........CASHEW, CASSIA, CHERRY,
.........CITRON, LAUREL, LINDEN,
.........LITCHI, LOCUST, MEDLAR;
......MIMOSA, NUTMEG, ORANGE,
.........PAPAYA, POPLAR, QUINCE,
........SPRUCE, WALNUT, WILLOW
tree, Afr. ....................AKEE, BAKU;
....................COLA, ROKA, SHEA;
...................BUMBO; MAFURA
tree, black gum ..................TUPELO
tree, body of a..................TRUNK
tree, Braz. gum .......ICICA; BALATA
tree, buckwheat ........................TITI
tree, chicle ......................SAPOTA;
.................................SAPODILLA
tree, Chin. ....................GINKGO
tree, flowering ..................CATALPA
*b* tree, Indian ...........................POON
tree, live oak ......................ENCINA
tree, N.A. ....................TAMARACK
tree, P.I. ...........................DITA
tree, pod ...........................CAROB
tree, trembling....................ASPEN
tree, W. Afr. ...........AFARA, LIMBA
tree cobra..........................MAMBA
tree knot ...............................BURL
treeless plain ....................PAMPAS,
.................TUNDRA, STEPPE
tree moss.........................USNEA
trees of a region ....................SILVA
tree stump ...........................BOLE
tremble.....ROCK; QUAKE, SHAKE;
...................TWITTER, VIBRATE
trend..............FAD; TEND; VOGUE
trespass ...............SIN; BREACH
trespass for game ..............POACH
trespass to recover goods.TROVER
triad .................................TRIO
trial ........................TEST; ORDEAL;
.................................ENDEAVOR
triangle ..........................TRIGON;
.................................SCALENE
triangle, ancient..................TRIGON
triangle side ..........................LEG
triangular insert....................GORE
tribal symbol ......................TOTEM
tribe .................CLAN, FOLK, RACE

tribulation ..............TRIAL; ORDEAL; *c*
....................................CRUCIBLE
tribunal .................................FORUM
tribute..................PRAISE, SALUTE
trick............FEAT; PRANK, STUNT;
....................SLEIGHT; ARTIFICE
tricks, game for no ..............NULLO
tricks, win all .........SLAM; CAPOT
trifle...........TOY; FLIRT; WHATNOT
trifling....................SMALL; SLIGHT
trig.............................NEAT, TRIM
trigonometry function .............SINE;
....................COSINE; SECANT
trim ........................NEAT, TRIG;
....................ADORN; DECORATE
trimming, dress........GIMP; RUCHE
trinket, worthless .........FICO, GAUD
triple ...................................TREBLE
tripod, six-footed ......................CAT
Tristram's beloved ..............ISOLDE
*Tristram Shandy* author.....STERNE
trite...........BANAL, STALE; CLICHE
triton....................................SNAIL
troche ..................PASTIL, ROTULA;
.................................PASTILLE
Trojan hero ..........PARIS; AENEAS,
....................AGENOR, DARDAN;
....................HECTOR; ACHILLES
trolley .................................TRAM
troops .................................MEN
troops, spread ..................DEPLOY *d*
trophy .................................CUP
tropical fever....DENGUE, NAGANA
trot ...........................JOG; AMBLE
trouble .............AIL; CARE; PAINS;
....................WORRY; TORMENT
troubles.................................ILLS
trough, inclined ..................CHUTE
trough, mining ....................SLUICE
trout, Brit. ...........SEWEN, SEWIN
trout, lake.............................CISCO
trout, red-belly .....................CHAR
trowel, plasterer's ................DARBY
Troy .................................ILIUM
Troy, founder of.......................ILUS
Troy, land of .......................TROAS
Troy, last king of ......PARIS, PRIAM
truancy ...............................HOOKY
truck, Brit. ..........................LORRY
trudge ...............PLOD, SLOG, TOIL
trumpet ...............HORN; CLARION
trumpet shell ........CONCH; TRITON
trunkfish .............................CHAPIN
trunk of a car: Brit. ...............BOOT
trunk of the body .................TORSO
truss up.................................TIE
trust ....................RELY; RELIANCE
truth: Chin. ............................TAO
truth drug...................PENTOTHAL
try ..........TEST; ESSAY; ATTEMPT

try to equal .............VIE; EMULATE
tsetse-fly disease ..............NAGANA
tub .......................................VAT; BATH
tub, brewer's............KEEVE, KIEVE
tub, broad...............................KEELER
tube...............................DUCT, PIPE
tube, glass ..............................PIPET
tuber, edible ..........YAM; TARO;
.............................................POTATO
tuber, orchid ............................SALEP
tuber, S.A. .............ANU, OCA, OKA
Tuesday god.................................TYR
tufted plant..................................MOSS
tulip tree...............................POPLAR
tumor, skin ...................................WEN
tumult ...........FRAY, RIOT; BRAWL;
....................MELEE; FRACAS
tune ...................AIR; ARIA, SONG;
....................................MELODY
tungstite ...................................OCHER
tuning fork......................DIAPASON
Tunis, ruler of .................BEY, DEY
tunnel, Alps train .................CENIS
tunny ...................TUNA; BLUEFIN
*Turandot* threesome .............PANG,
....................PING, PONG
turban, Oriental................MANDIL
turco ...............................TAPACOLO
turf.................................................SOD
turf, piece of .........................DIVOT
turkeys group of.................RAFTER
Turkish caliph .............................ALI
Turk. government ...............PORTE
Turk. inn ...............................IMARET
Turk. president, former .........INONU
Turk. sultan ........................SELIM
Turk. title ...................AGA; AGHA,
....................EMIR; PASHA
turmeric.................................MIMOSA
turmoil ...................CHAOS, SNARL
turn .........................BEND, MOVE;
.................CROOK, SPOIL, STINT,
....................WHIRL; DIVERT
turn aside ....SKEW, VEER; SHUNT
turn back (to) ....................REVERT
turning point .......................CRISIS
turn inside out ....................EVERT
turnip ......................NEEP; SWEDE;
....................RUTABAGA

turnover .......................................PIE
turpentine, crude ..............GALIPOT
turtle, Amazon .....................ARRAU
turtle, edible ...................TERRAPIN
Tuscany town .........................SIENA
tusk, elephant ......................IVORY
twelve and one half cents............BIT
twenty-fourth part................CARAT,
.............................................KARAT
twenty quires ........................REAM
twig, willow.............................WITHE
twilight ........................EVE; DUSK;
....................GLOAM; EVENTIDE
twin crystal ..........................MACLE
twine...............COIL, WIND; TWIST
twins .....................................GEMINI
twist...............COIL, TURN, WARP;
....................SPIRAL; CONTORT
twisted ....................WRY; AWRY;
....................ASKEW; WARPED
twitch ...........................................TIC
two ...................DUO; DUAD, PAIR;
....................COUPLE, DOUBLE
two, the ......................................BOTH
two elements, having..........BINARY
two feet, verse of.................DIPODY
twofold ..........DUAL, TWIN; BINAL
two-footed .........................BIPEDAL
two-horse chariot....................BIGA
two-hulled boat .........CATAMARAN
two-spot .................................DEUCE
*2001: A Space Odyssey* computer ..
.................................................HAL
two-wheeled vehicle ......GIG; CART
tycoon ....................................NABOB
Tyndareus, wife of .................LEDA
type, set of.............................FONT
type, conforming to ...........TYPICAL
type, five and one half point.AGATE
type, slanting........................ITALIC
type separation ....................KERN
type size .......PICA, AGATE, ELITE;
.............................................BREVIER
typewriter roller .................PLATEN
tyrant ..................................DESPOT
Tyre, king of....................HIRAM
Tyre, princess of .....................DIDO
Tyr in Ger. myth.........................TIU
tyro ....................NOVICE, ROOKIE

# U

ukase......................................EDICT
*Ulalume*, author of .....................POE
Ulysses .......................ODYSSEUS
*Ulysses* author ......................JOYCE
umbrella, large......................GAMP

umbrella part ...........................RIB
umbrella tree .....................WAHOO
umpire .............................REFEREE
unable to hear ......................DEAF
unaccented vowel sound ....SCHWA

*a* unadulterated.....................PURE
unaffected.........SIMPLE; ARTLESS
Unalaskan ............................ALEUT
unaspirate ...........................LENIS
unassuming ...........MEEK; LOWLY;
...................HUMBLE, MODEST
unattractive............................UGLY
unbeliever.......................HERETIC
unbleached shade ....ECRU; BEIGE
unburnt brick.......................ADOBE
uncanny................EERIE, WEIRD
Uncas, beloved of.................CORA
unceasing.....................ENDLESS,
.................NONSTOP, ETERNAL;
..................................PERPETUAL
uncivil..................................RUDE
unclean in Jewish law.............TREF
"Uncle Remus" author.........HARRIS
"Uncle Remus" rabbit ...........BR'ER
unclose .......................OPE; OPEN
uncommon ...........RARE; SCARCE
...............UNUSUAL; SINGULAR;
.................................INFREQUENT
unconcerned ......................ALOOF
unconscious state .................COMA
unction....................................BALM
unctuous ...........OILY; SMARMY
under............NEATH; NETHER
under: naut. .........................ALOW
underclothes........CYMAR; CAMISE;
*b* ....................................SKIVVIES
underground growth ..............BULB
underground reservoir.......CENOTE
underground space ...............CAVE
underhanded ......SHIFTY, SNEAKY
understand ................GET; GRASP
understanding............KEN; SENSE
under the weather..................SICK
underwear.....................BRA; SLIP
....................CORSET, GIRDLE;
.................SHORTS; PANTIES
underworld.............HADES, SHEOL
underworld god ...........DIS; PLUTO
underworld god, Eg. .........OSIRIS;
..................................SERAPIS
underwrite..........ENSURE, INSURE
undeveloped.....................LATENT
undraped.............................NUDE
undulating............................WAVY
undulation .................CURL, WAVE
unequal angles, having ...SCALENE
uneven ................ROUGH; JAGGED
unevenly edged ..................EROSE
unfair move.............................FOUL
unfasten .............UNTIE; LOOSEN
unfavorable......................BAD, ILL
unfeeling ............NUMB; CALLOUS
unfold.....................OPEN; EVOLVE
ungula .............CLAW, HOOF, NAIL
ungulate, S. A. .....................TAPIR

unhappy ......................SAD; BLUE; *c*
...................MOROSE, RUEFUL
unicorn fish....................NARWHAL
uniform .....................EVEN; ALIKE;
..................................REGULAR
uninteresting .........................DULL
union .............................MERGER
union, political ......................BLOC
unit ...........................ACE, ONE
unit, of a ........................MONADIC
unite..................WED; ALLY, JOIN,
...................KNIT, WELD; MERGE
units, measurement ..See page 246.
unity............................................ONE
universal .........GLOBAL; GENERAL
universe ...........WORLD; COSMOS
universe, of the ..................COSMIC
universities.................See page 200.
unkind .......................ILL; NASTY
unless.....................BUT; SAVE
unless, in law ........................NISI
unload.....................................DUMP
unlock ..................................OPEN
unmarried..........................SINGLE
unmatched ...............................ODD
unmixed ...................PURE; SHEER
unnecessary .................NEEDLESS
unrelenting.....................ADAMANT
unruffled .................CALM; SERENE
unsophisticated ...........NAIF; NAIVE
unspoken .............................TACIT *d*
unstable ............FLUID; VOLATILE
unsuitable ...............................INAPT
untamed ...................WILD; FERAL
untidy person ...........................SLOB
untrained................................RAW
unusual .....................ODD; RARE;
....................QUAINT; SINGULAR
unwavering ............SURE; STEADY
unwieldy object ......................HULK
unwilling...............LOATH; AVERSE
unwilling to listen ...................DEAF
unyielding......................FIRM;
.................FIXED; ADAMANT
unyielding: naut. ......................FAST
upbraid ..................CHIDE, SCOLD
upland plain .........................WOLD
upon ......................................ATOP
upright................ERECT; HONEST
upright column .....................STELE
upright piece ................JAMB, STUD
uprising ............................REVOLT
uproar.......................................DIN
uraeus.....................................ASP
urban center.............................CITY
urban office holder ..............MAYOR
urchin .........................IMP; GAMIN
Urfa, today ......................EDESSA
urge ...........................PROD; PRESS;
..................................EXHORT

126

urticaria .........................HIVES
usage .............WAY; FORM; HABIT;
.........................CUSTOM, PRAXIS
use, be of ................................AVAIL
used to be ................................WAS
used up ........................DEPLETED
useful ....................GOOD; HANDY;
.................HELPFUL; SALUTARY
useless ......................IDLE; FUTILE
u-shaped device .................CLEVIS

usual ..............NORMAL; REGULAR
utensil .......................................TOOL
uterus .....................................WOMB
utmost ..................TOP; SUPREME;
.........................................ULTIMATE
utter ..............SAY; SHEER, STARK
uttered ...........ORAL, SAID; SPOKE
utter loudly ...............VOCIFERATE
utterly ................ALL; JUST; QUITE;
.........................PURELY, WHOLLY

# V

vacant.....................BARE; CLEAR,
.....................EMPTY; HOLLOW,
.....................OTIOSE; VACUOUS
vacation spot ...............SPA; CAMP;
.........................................RESORT
vacuum.....................................VOID
vacuum, opposite of ..........PLENUM
vacuum tube ........................DIODE
vagabond....................BUM; HOBO;
.........................TRAMP; VAGRANT
vague ......................HAZY; LOOSE
vainglorious ........................PROUD
vair fur ................................MINIVER
valance, decorative............PELMET
vale ..........................................VALLEY
valiant ..........BRAVE; STALWART
valley..............DALE, DELL, GLEN,
.............................VALE; GLADE
valley, deep ........................COULEE
valley, Jordan .......................GHOR
value ........................RATE; PRIZE,
.....................WORTH; APPRAISE
valve ..........................................COCK
vampire, female...................LAMIA
vandal.........................................HUN
vanish ............FADE; EVAPORATE
vanity ........EGO; PRIDE; CONCEIT
vanity case ..............................ETUI
vantage, point of.................COIGN
vapid ...................INANE, STALE
vapor .............HAZE, MIST; STEAM
vaporous .................................FUMY
variable ..............................PROTEAN
variation, small....SHADE; NUANCE
variegated in color...PIED; CALICO
variety ...........................KIND, SORT
varnish, kind of ................SHELLAC
varnish ingredient..........LAC; KINO;
.................COPAL, ELEMI, RESIN
vase............................................URN
vat ..............................TUB; CISTERN
vat, brewer's ...........KEEVE, KIEVE
vat, large ...................................KIER
vault ............................JUMP, SAFE

vault, church .........................CRYPT
vaulted alcove .......................APSE
vaunt....................BRAG; BOAST
Vedic dialect...........................PALI
veer...........................TURN; SHIFT
veer off...................................SHEER
vegetable .........PEA; BEAN, BEET,
.................KALE, OKRA; CHARD;
.........CARROT, ENDIVE, TOMATO
vegetable fuel ........................PEAT
vehicle ...........CAR; CART; CYCLE
vehicle, exercise ....................BIKE
vehicle, four-wheeled ........LANDAU
vehicle, moon: Abbr. ...............LEM
vehicle, Native Amer. ......TRAVOIS
vehicle, rugged.......................JEEP
vehicle, Russ. ....................TROIKA
vehicle, war ............................TANK
vehicle compartment ..CAB; TRUNK
vein.........................................CAVA
vein, throat .....................JUGULAR
vein of ore ...........LODE; SCRIN
velum....................................PALATE
velvetlike cloth ...................PANNE
velvet grass......................HOLCUS
vend...................SELL; PEDDLE
vendetta ..................................FEUD
venerable ..................OLD; HOARY
"Venerable" monk...................BEDE
venerate.......HAIL; LAUD; ADORE;
..............EXALT, EXTOL, HONOR;
........PRAISE, REVERE; GLORIFY
veneration ..........AWE; WORSHIP
Venetian magistrate .............DOGE
Venetian red.........................SIENA
Venetian resort ......................LIDO
Venetian traveler....................POLO
Venezuelan copper center.....AROA
Venice bridge ......................RIALTO
Venice canals ...........................RII
venture ..................RISK; WAGER;
.....................CHANCE, GAMBLE,
.....................HAZARD; PROJECT
Venus, island of ...................MELOS

127

a Venus, son of......................CUPID
Venus, youth loved by........ADONIS
veranda, Hawaiian.................LANAI
verb, old-style...........DOST, DOTH,
.................HAST, HATH, SHEW,
.........SMIT, WAST, WERT; DIDST
verbal.....................................ORAL
verbally.................................ALOUD
verbal noun.......................GERUND
verbal rhythm......................METER
verb form............................ TENSE
Verdi heroine .........................AIDA
verily ......................YEA; AMEN
verity .....................................TRUTH
Verne's captain.....................NEMO
versatile ........PROTEAN, VARIOUS
verse.......................POEM; STICH
vertebral bones.................SACRA
vesicle, skin..................SAC; CYST;
.................................................BLISTER
vessel .............ARK; SHIP; CRAFT
vessel, anatomical.................VASA
vessel, cooking.....PAN, POT, WOK
vessel, drinking.........MUG; GOURD
vessel, liquor.......FLASK; FLAGON
vessel, shallow.....................BASIN
vessel for liquors .........DECANTER
vestal ..................................CHASTE
vestige ....................RELIC, TRACE
vestment.........ALB; COPE; AMICE;

b .............................EPHOD, STOLE
vesuvianite, brown .............EGERAN
vetch ......................................TARE
vetch, bitter ...............................ERS
vex......................IRK; FRET, GALL;
.............ANNOY, CHAFE, PEEVE;
.......BOTHER, NETTLE; IRRITATE
via ..........................................PER
viands ...................................FOOD
vibrate ...............SHAKE; TREMBLE
vibration: music ..............TREMOLO
vice..........................................SIN
vice presidents, US...See page 190.
Vichy premier.......................LAVAL
victim ......................................PREY
victorious, was........................WON
victor's crown ...................LAURELS
victuals...................................FOOD
vie ......................RIVAL; CONTEND
Viennese park ...................PRATER
view .......................SCENE, VISTA
vigilant ......WARY; ALERT, AWAKE
vigor ............PEP, VIM, ZIP; FORCE
Viking .........ERIC, OLAF; ROLLO
vilify .........SLUR; MALIGN, REVILE
village......DORP, TOWN; HAMLET
villain ..........HEAVY; SCOUNDREL
vindicate ..........AVENGE, EXCUSE
vine ...................................IVY; BINE
vine, woody..............ABUTA, LIANA

c vinegar, of ...........................ACETIC
vinegar of ale.....................ALEGAR
vinous ....................................WINY
viol, ancient..........................REBEC
violent .....................WILD; FIERCE
violin, famous.......................STRAD
violin maker, Italian ..............AMATI
viper ...........................ASP; ADDER
viper, horned.................CERASTES
Virgil's hero.......................AENEAS
Virginia willow .........................ITEA
visage ........................FACE, LOOK
viscous ...................SLIMY; VISCID
Vishnu, 7th incarnation of ......RAMA
Vishnu's bow .......................SARAN
Vishnu's serpent ...................NAGA
visible juncture .....................SEAM
Visigoths, king of the...........ALARIC
vision ......................DREAM, SIGHT
vision, of...............................OPTIC
visionary .............SEER; UTOPIAN
visit ..............................CALL, STAY;
...............................................SOJOURN
vison .....................................MINK
vital fluid................................SAP
vitalize ..............................ANIMATE
vital principle .........................SOUL
vitamin A source .........CAROTENE
vitamin B ...........BIOTIN, NIACIN;
...............................................CHOLINE
vitamin B1 .......................THIAMINE
vitamin B source ......LIVER, YEAST
vitamin B2...................RIBOFLAVIN
vitamin C deficiency .........SCURVY
vitamin D deficiency .........RICKETS
vitamin D source ..........MILK, YOLK
vitamin H ..............................BIOTIN
vitamin K source.....FISH; ALFALFA
vitiate......................SPOIL, TAINT;
..............................NULLIFY, POLLUTE
Viti Levu Island seaport...........SUVA
vituperate .............ABUSE; ASSAIL,
...............................................REVILE
vivacious..............PERT; CHIPPER
vivacity ............................VIM; BRIO,
....................DASH, ELAN; VERVE,
..............................VIGOR; SPIRIT
vocal flourish...................ROULADE
vocation ...........CAREER; CALLING
___ voce ..............................SOTTO
voice..............SAY; VOTE; UTTER;
........................SINGER; DECLARE
voice, singing .............ALTO, BASS;
........................TENOR; SOPRANO
voiced............................SONANT
voiced, not .......................ASONANT
void ............NULL; ABYSS, SPACE
void, make...........ANNUL; CANCEL
volcanic crater, Jap. .............ASO
volcanic cinder ...................SCORIA

*a* volcanic rock ............... TUFA, TUFF;
................... LATITE
volcanic scoria matter .LAVA, SLAG
volcano, Caribbean .............. PELEE
volcano, Mex. .................... COLIMA
volcano, P. I. ........................ APO
volcano, Sicilian ................... ETNA
volcano crater ...................... MAAR
volcano hole ...................... CRATER
Volga tributary ...................... KAMA
volition ................................. WILL
Voltaire ............................. AROUET
Voltaire play ......................... ZAIRE
volt-ampere .......................... WATT
voluble .................... GLIB; FACILE
volume .......... BOOK, BULK, MASS,
................ OPUS, SIZE, TOME
vomiting ............................ EMESIS

voodoo charm ........ MOJO; GRI-GRI  *c*
vote ................................... BALLOT
vote, negative ...................... NAY
vote, positive ............... AYE, YEA
vote, right to ............... FRANCHISE
vote, take a ........................ POLL
vote into office ................... ELECT
votes ........... AYES, NAYS, YEAS
voucher ...................... CHIT, NOTE
vouch for ...................... SPONSOR
vowel, line over a ............ MACRON
vowel suppression ........... ELISION
voyaging ............................ ASEA
V-shaped piece ................ WEDGE
Vulcan, wife of ................... MAIA
vulcanite .......................... EBONITE
vulgar ............ COARSE, COMMON
vulture ............... URUBU; CONDOR

# W

*W*, old English ........................ WEN
wade across .......................... FORD
wading bird ....... IBIS, RAIL; CRANE
................ EGRET, HERON, STILT;
................ AVOCET; FLAMINGO
wag .............. WIT; JOKER; SWITCH
*b* wages ..................... PAY; SALARY
Wagner, son-in-law of ........... LISZT
Wagner heroine ....... ELSA; SENTA;
................ ISOLDE
wagon ........... CART, DRAY, WAIN
wagon, Russ. .................... TELEGA
wagon-pin holder ................ CLEVIS
wagon shaft .......................... THILL
wagon tongue ............. NEAP, POLE
wahoo fish ............................ PETO
wail ........ BAWL, KEEN; LAMENT
waistcoat ..... VEST; GILET; JERKIN
wait ............ BIDE, STAY; PAUSE,
............ TARRY; LINGER, REMAIN
waive ...................... CEDE; YIELD
waken ................ ROUSE; AROUSE
wale ................................. WELT
Wales ............ CYMRU; CAMBRIA
walk ........... PACE, STEP; TREAD
walk, inability to .................. ABASIA
walk affectedly ................... MINCE
walk heavily ............ PLOD; SLOG
walking stick ........................ CANE
walk lamely ........................ LIMP
walk purposefully ............... STRIDE
walk through ...................... WADE
walkway, tree-lined ........ ALAMEDA
wall .................. FENCE; BARRIER,
................ ENCLOSE; PARTITION
wall, divided by a ............ SEPTATE

wall, fortification .............. RAMPART
wall, of a .......................... MURAL
walled city in Nigeria .............. KANO
wallop .................. SMASH; IMPACT
wallow ................................. LURCH;
................ FLOUNDER
wall paneling ................ WAINSCOT  *d*
wall section ............. DADO; PANEL
walnut tree .......................... NOGAL
wampum ............. PEAG; SEWAN;
................ SEAWAN
wan .............. ASHY, PALE; ASHEN
wand ...................... BATON, STICK
wander ....... ROAM, ROVE; STRAY
wanderer ........................... NOMAD
wane ........................ EBB; EASE;
................ ABATE; LET UP
want ............. LACK, NEED; DESIRE
wapiti ................................. ELK
war, religious ...... JIHAD; CRUSADE
war, Russ.-Eng. ............... CRIMEA
warble ........... SING; TRILL, YODEL
warclub, medieval ................ MACE
warden, fire ...................... RANGER
ward off ............... FEND; AVERT,
................ PARRY, REPEL, STAVE
warehouse .......................... DEPOT
warehouse area ..................... LOFT
war god ............ TYR, ARES, MARS
war goddess ........................ ENYO
war horse ...................... CHARGER
warm ...................... HEAT; TEPID
warn ................................. ALERT
warning signal ..................... SIREN
warning system, early ........... D.E.W.
warp yarn ............................. ABB

129

a warship ..........................CRUISER;
..................................DESTROYER
warship, sailing................FRIGATE
wary ....................CANNY; CHARY;
..................................PRUDENT
wash ............LAVE; BATHE, RINSE
wasp ................................HORNET
waste................LOSS; SQUANDER
waste allowance ....................TRET
waste away.....................ATROPHY
wasted ..................................LOST
waste growth...................RUDERAL
wasteland.............................MOOR
waste matter............SLAG; DROSS
waste silk.........................FRISON
waste time ...................IDLE, LOAF
watch ............SEE; GUARD, VIGIL
watch chain...........................FOB
watchful ................WARY; ALERT
watchful guardian ...............ARGUS
watchtower .....TURRET; MIRADOR
water ................................DILUTE;
..................IRRIGATE, SPRINKLE
water, body of ...............BAY, SEA;
.........COVE, GULF, LAKE, LOCH,
.........MERE, POND, POOL, TARN;
................BAYOU, BROOK, CANAL,
.................CREEK, INLET, LOUGH,
...............OCEAN, RIVER, SOUND;
.......HARBOR, LAGOON, STREAM

b water, covered by ...............AWASH
water, seek...........................DOUSE
water arum.........................CALLA
waterbuck ...................KOB; KOBA,
...........................POKU, PUKU
water chestnut, Chin. ..............LING
watercock.............................KORA
watercourse ........BROOK, CANAL,
..................................RIVER; STREAM
watered silk ..........................MOIRE
watering hole.......................OASIS
water lily.............................LOTUS
water passage....................CANAL;
.............................SOUND; SLUICE;
.......................STRAIT; CHANNEL
water pipe ...HOOKAH; NARGHILE;
...............................NARGILEH
waterproof canvas .................TARP
water reservoir, natural .....CENOTE
water sound............PLOP; SPLASH
water spirit ...........ARIEL; SPRITE
water spirit, Gaelic...............KELPIE
water sprite, female ...............NIXIE;
..................................UNDINE
water sprite, male.......................NIX
waterthrush .....................WAGTAIL
watertight, make................CAULK
water vessel, Indian .............LOTAH
water wheel ..........................NORIA
watery ...............................SEROUS

c wattle tree .............BOREE, MYALL
wave ....................FLAP; FLUTTER;
..................................BRANDISH
waver...................SWAY; TEETER;
..................................VACILLATE
wax, of................................CERE
wax, of..............................CERAL
wax, yellow or white .........CERESIN
wax for skis .......................KLISTER
wax ointment ....................CERATE
wax plant...............................HOYA
waxy chemical ......................CERIN
way...............MODE, PATH, ROAD;
.........USAGE; AVENUE, METHOD,
..................STREET; TECHNIQUE
way of walking .........................GAIT
way out...................EXIT; EGRESS
wayside.................................EDGE
weak..........PUNY; FRAIL; FEEBLE
weaken ............SAP; FLAG, WANE;
..................ENERVATE, ENFEEBLE
weakling ...............................WIMP
weakness...............................ATONY
weal .......WALE, WELT; BENEFIT
wealth...............MEANS; ASSETS,
..................................RICHES
weapon.......................GUN; BOMB;
..................KNIFE, LANCE, RIFLE,
..................................SPEAR, SWORD
weapon, gaucho's ...............BOLAS
weapon, Maori ......................PATU
weapon, P. I. .........................BOLO
weapons ...............................ARMS
wear...........................DON; SPORT
wear away ........ERODE; ABRADE
wear away slowly...........CORRODE
wear by friction .........................RUB
wearing down................ATTRITION
weary ........PALL; TIRED; FATIGUE
weasel ............ERMINE, FERRET
weasel, Eng. ......................STOAT
weather................LAST; PERSIST,
..................RIDE OUT, SURVIVE
weather, inclement ...................FOG;
..................GALE, HAIL, RAIN,
..................SMOG, SNOW; SLEET
weathercock ...........................VANE
weather indicator......BAROMETER
weaverbird .....BAYA, MAYA, TAHA;
..................WHYDAH; AVADAVAT
weaver's bobbin or shuttle.......PIRN
weaver's reed ........................SLEY
weaving frame ......................LOOM
weaving tool ....................EVENER
web...................MESH, TELA
wed...................MARRY, UNITE
wedge..................................SHIM
wedge, steel .........................FROE
wedgelike piece...................QUOIN
wedge-shaped ................CUNEATE

130

a Wednesday god ................WODEN
weed............BUR; TARE; DARNEL
weed, coarse ........DOCK; SORREL
week ..............................SENNIGHT
weekday, R.C. ......................FERIA
weep ........CRY, SOB; BOOHOO,
......................................LAMENT
weeping statue......................NIOBE
weft ....................................WOOF
weight ..............HEFT, ONUS;
..................................LEVERAGE
weight, ancient ........MINA; TALENT
weight, Asian............................TAEL
weight, balance ..................RIDER
weight, Eng. ..........................STONE
weight, heavy ............................TON
weight allowance........TARE, TRET
weights ..................See page 246.
weight system ........................TROY
weir ........................................DAM
weird ..................EERIE; SPOOKY
welcome ..............................GREET
welfare ..........DOLE, GOOD, SAKE
well-bred people ................GENTRY
Welsh ..........CYMRIC; CAMBRIAN
Welsh capital ....................CARDIFF
Welsh dog ............................CORGI
Welsh people ....................CYMRY
Welsh river ............................WYE
Welsh saint ............................DAVID

b Welsh symbol ........................LEEK
welt ....................WALE, WEAL
W. Australia capital ..............PERTH
Western shrub ......................SAGE
"Western Star" writer............BENET
W. Indies island................CUBA;
..........NEVIS; NASSAU, TOBAGO
W. Indies islands ..........BAHAMAS;
......................................ANTILLES
Westphalia, city in ..............HERNE
West Pointer..........CADET; PLEBE
West Point mascot ..................MULE
wet............................DAMP; MOIST
whale............ORC; BELUGA;
..................................GRAMPUS
whalebone ..........................BALEEN
whales, group of............GAM, POD
whale's tail ..........................FLUKES
wharf............................PIER, QUAY
whatever ................................SUCH
whatnot shelf..................ETAGERE
wheat............................DURUM,
..................................EMMER, SPELT
wheat, Indian ..............SUJI; SUJEE
wheat disease ......................BUNT
wheat middlings............SEMOLINA
wheedle ................COAX; CAJOLE
wheel ....................RING; PIVOT;
..................................GYRATE
wheel, furniture ..................CASTER

c wheel, grooved ................SHEAVE
wheel center ................HUB; NAVE
wheel horse ........................POLER
wheel part ......RIM; FELLY, SPOKE
wheel projection ......................CAM
wheels, of............................ROTAL
wheel shaft ............AXLE; ARBOR
wheel tread ............................TIRE
whetstone ................BUHR, HONE
whiff ....................SNIFF, TRACE
while ....................................WHEN
whimper ..................MEWL, PULE
whin............FURZE, GORSE
whine ..............PULE; GROUCH
whinny ................................NEIGH
whip ............BEAT, FLOG, LASH
whip, cowboy's................CHICOTE
whip, Russ...........................KNOUT
whip mark ......WALE, WEAL, WELT
whipsocket............................SNEAD
whirl............................REEL, SPIN
whirlpool ..........EDDY; VORTEX
whiskers..............BEARD; GOATEE
whiskey, Irish....................POTEEN
whistle ..................PIPE; SIREN
whist win..............................SLAM
whit ............BIT, JOT; ATOM, IOTA
white alkaline ........................SODA
white ermine .....LASSET; MINIVER
white-flecked..........................ROAN

d white matter of the brain ........ALBA
whiten ............................ETIOLATE
white oak............................ROBLE
white poplar........................ABELE
white with age ........................HOAR
whitish ..............................HOARY
whitlow grass ........................DRABA
Whittier heroine ....................MAUD
whiz............HUM; BUZZ; WHOOSH
whoa ..................STOP; HOLLA
whole amount......................GROSS
wholesome ..............HALE; SOUND;
..................................QUITE; UTTERLY
wholly ..................QUITE; UTTERLY
wicked..............BAD; EVIL; NASTY
wicker basket .....CESTA; PANNIER
wicker box........................HANAPER
wickerwork......................RATTAN
wicket, croquet ..........HOOP
wide-mouthed vessel ..........EWER,
..................................OLLA; PITCHER
wield ..........PLY; EXERT; HANDLE
wife's property ........................DOS
wig............................RUG; PERUKE
wigwam ..............................TEPEE
wild ..............FERAL; SAVAGE
wild ass ..............KIANG; ONAGER
wild buffalo ............................ARNA
wildcat............................LYNX
wildcat, Afr. ..................CHAUS
wildcat, Siberian ..................MANUL

131

*a*

| | |
|---|---|
| wild dog | DHOLE |
| wild dog, Australian | DINGO |
| *Wild Duck* playwright | IBSEN |
| wildebeest | GNU |
| wild garlic | MOLY |
| wild ginger | ASARUM |
| wild hog | BOAR |
| wildlife park | ZOO |
| wild lime | COLIMA |
| wild ox | ANOA, GAUR |
| wild ox, extinct | URUS |
| wild plum | SLOE |
| wild plum, California | ISLAY |
| wild sheep, Asian | ARGALI |
| wild sheep, horned | MUFLON; MOUFLON |
| wild sheep, Indian | URIAL; BHARAL, NAHOOR |
| wild sheep, N. Afr. | AOUDAD |
| wild vanilla | LIATRIS |
| will | DESIRE; VOLITION |
| will, one making a | DEVISOR |
| will addition | CODICIL |
| willingly | LIEF |
| willow | OSIER |
| willow twig | SALLOW |
| will power, loss of | ABULIA |
| Wilson's thrush | VEERY |
| wilt | SAG; FLAG; DROOP |
| wily | SLY; FOXY; |

*b*

| | |
|---|---|
| | CANNY, SLICK; CLEVER, SHIFTY; CUNNING |
| wimple | TWIST |
| win | GET; GAIN; VICTORY |
| winch | HOIST |
| wind | COIL, GALE, TURN |
| wind, cold Adriatic | BORA |
| wind, Andes | PUNA, PUNO |
| wind, Australian | BUSTER |
| wind, away from the | ALEE |
| wind, cold alpine | BISE |
| wind, cold Med. | MISTRAL |
| wind, east | EURUS |
| wind, god of the north | BOREAS |
| wind, hot dry | SIMOOM; SIROCCO |
| wind, hot Med. | SOLANO |
| wind, warm dry | FOEHN |
| wind-blown loam | LOESS |
| windborne | AEOLIAN |
| windflower | ANEMONE |
| wind indicator | SOCK, VANE |
| wind instrument, hole in a | LILL |
| windlass | CAPSTAN |
| windmill sail | AWE |
| window, bay | ORIEL |
| window lead | CAME |
| window ledge | SILL |
| window part | SASH |
| window setter | GLAZIER |
| windrow | SWATH |

*c*

| | |
|---|---|
| windstorm | GALE; CYCLONE, TORNADO |
| wine | HOCK, PORT, SACK, VINO; MEDOC, TOKAY; CLARET, MALAGA, MUSCAT, SHERRY; CHABLIS, MOSELLE |
| wine, Amer. | CATAWBA |
| wine, dry | SEC; SECCO |
| wine, golden | BUAL |
| wine, honey and | MULSE |
| wine, mulberry flavored | MORAT |
| wine, new | MUST |
| wine, revived | STUM |
| wine, very dry | BRUT |
| wine, white | SAUTERNE |
| wine-and-lemon drink | NEGUS |
| wine cask | TUN, BUTT |
| wine container, Gr. | OLPE |
| wine county, California | NAPA |
| wine cup | AMA; AMULA |
| wine merchant | VINTNER |
| wine region, It. | ASTI |
| wine stopper | CORK |
| wine vessel | AMULA; CHALICE |
| wing | ALA; PINION |
| wing, bastard | ALULA |
| wing, beetle | TEGUMEN |
| winged fruit | SAMARA |
| winged god | EROS; CUPID |
| winged victory | NIKE |

*d*

| | |
|---|---|
| wing-footed | ALIPED |
| wing-footed god | MERCURY |
| wingless | APTERAL; APTEROUS |
| winglike | ALAR |
| wing movement | FLAP |
| wings | ALAE |
| wings, having | ALATE |
| wink | BLINK, GLINT; INSTANT |
| wink eyes rapidly | BAT |
| *Winnie the Pooh* donkey | EEYORE |
| *Winnie the Pooh* owl | WOL |
| winnow | SIFT, SORT; SEPARATE |
| winter, of | BRUMAL; HIEMAL; HIBERNAL |
| wipe out | ERASE |
| wire measure | MIL |
| wire service | UPI; REUTERS |
| wisdom | LORE; SENSE; GNOSIS |
| wise | SAGE; SENSIBLE |
| wise advisor | MENTOR |
| wisecrack | JAB, DIG; QUIP; CRACK |
| wise man | SAGE; SOLON; NESTOR |
| Wise Men | MAGI; GASPAR; MELCHIOR; BALTHAZAR |

wish .............WANT, WILL; CRAVE, .............YEARN; DESIRE; HANKER
wish undone .............................RUE
wisp .......................................HINT
wit.................WAG; COMIC, SENSE
witch .........HAG; CRONE; HECATE; ...................................SORCERESS
witch, male ....................WARLOCK
witch city .........................SALEM
witchcraft, W. Indies ............OBEAH
witch doctor ......................SHAMAN
witch in *The Faerie Queene*.............. ....................................DUESSA
with ...................................HAVING
withdraw ..........RECALL, RECANT, .................REMOVE; RETREAT
wither ....................SEAR; WIZEN; .................MUMMIFY, SHRIVEL
withered ....................DRY; SERE
within ....................INTO; INSIDE
with joy .................................FAIN
witless chatter.........................GAB
witness..........SEE; MARK; ATTEST
witness, legal ...............DEPONENT
witty remark ....................MOT; QUIP
witty reply .....................REPARTEE
Wizard of Oz dog .................TOTO
Wizard of Oz witch ...........GLINDA
wobble .......REEL, SWAY; FALTER, .......................TEETER; STAGGER
Woden.................................ODIN
woe .......BANE; AGONY; MISERY
woe is me...............................ALAS
wolf, gray...............................LOBO
wolfish ...............................LUPINE
wolframite..............................CAL
woman, ill-tempered .........SHREW; .....................................VIRAGO
woman, loose .....BIM; DOXY, SLUT
woman: obs. .......................FEME
Wonderland girl .....................ALICE
wont ...................................HABIT
wood .................................FOREST
wood, black .......................EBONY
wood, flexible.......................EDDER
wood, fragrant ...................CEDAR
wood, light .............ANDA, CORK; .....................................BALSA
wood, long piece of...POLE; PLANK
wood, piece of ....................SLAT; .................SPRAG; BILLET
woodchuck .......................MARMOT
wooded grove .....................BOSK
wooden ...............................STOIC
wooden peg .......SKEG; DOWEL
wooden shoe .......SABOT; PATTEN
wood gum............................XYLAN
woodland deity.............PAN; FAUN; .....................................SATYR
woodpecker, green ........HICKWALL

woodpecker, small ............PICULET
woodpeckers, of .................PICINE
wood sorrel ....................OCA, OKA
woodwind.........OBOE; BASSOON, ....................................CLARINET
woodworm ...........................TERMITE
woody fiber .............................BAST
woody plant ..........................TREE
woof ....................................WEFT
wool.................ANGORA, MERINO
wool, reclaimed ..................MUNGO
wool cluster...............................NEP
woolen cloth, coarse.........KERSEY
woolen thread .......................YARN
wool fat .............................LANOLIN
woolly ...............LANATE, LANOSE
wool package, Australian.....FADGE
word, scrambled ............ANAGRAM
word blindness ....................ALEXIA
word by word ......................LITERAL
wording ...............................TEXT
word of God.........................LOGOS
word of mouth .....................GOSSIP
work .........TOIL; LABOR; TRAVAIL
work, musical .........OPUS; OPERA; .....................................SONATA
work, piece of ...............JOB; STINT
work, unit of.............................ERG
work aimlessly ...................POTTER
work at steadily ......................PLY
work basket, woman's...........CABA; .....................................CABAS
worker...........HAND; OPERATOR
work hard...........MOIL, TOIL; SLAVE
work unit.................................CREW
world holder ........................ATLAS
World War I battle site .........MONS; .....................................MARNE
worm, eye-infesting.................LOA
wormwood paste ..................MOXA
worn-out ..............................EFFETE
worn-out horse .............NAG; PLUG
worry ............CARE, CARK, FRET; .....................ANGST; POTHER
worship .............ADORE; REVERE; .....................VENERATE; .....................................REVERENCE
worship, form of..................RITUAL
worship, house of................BETHEL; .................CHURCH, TEMPLE; .....................................TABERNACLE
worship, object of .........GOD; IDOL
worship, place of .................ALTAR
worship of saints...................DULIA
worsted cloth....................ETAMINE
worthless ........................NO-GOOD; .....................................USELESS
worthless mineral waste ...GANGUE
worthless trifle ............FICO, GAUD
wound ....................HURT; INJURE

a wound crust............................SCAB
wound mark .........................SCAR
wrangle ...................BRAWL; FIGHT;
..............................BICKER; QUIBBLE
wrap..........SWATHE; SWADDLE
wrath ..............................IRE; ANGER
wrathful..................................IRATE
wreath...............RING; CIRCLET
wreathe .......COIL; TWINE; SPIRAL
wrest................WRING; WRENCH
wrestle...................................TUSSLE
wriggle.................................SQUIRM
wrinkle .......RUCK, RUGA; RIMPLE
wrinkled ...........RUGATE, RUGOSE
wrist.....................................CARPUS

wrist bone, of the ..............CARPAL    c
wrist guard ........................BRACER
writ, issue in a .........................MISE
write ..........................................PEN
write marginal comments ....POSTIL
write music..........................NOTATE
writer......................................SCRIBE
writing table ....DESK; ESCRITOIRE
writ of execution.................ELEGIT
writ to arrest.......................CAPIAS
wrong ........OFF, SIN; AWRY, EVIL;
...........AMISS, FALSE; SPECIOUS
wrong, legal...........................TORT
wrongdoing.......................SIN; EVIL
wry face.................................MOUE

# Y

yacht pennant ...................BURGEE
Yahi tribe survivor .....................ISHI
Yak's-tail fan .....................CHAMAR
Yale student...............................ELI
Yang, counterpart of .................YIN
Yangtze River's other name...
..............................................CHANG
Yangtze tributary .....................HAN
b yarn.......................TALE; FABLE;
..............STORY; WHOPPER
yarn count..............................TYPP
yarn lump...............................SLUB
yarn measure ...........................LEA
yarn measure, old .................HEER
yarn mop.................................SWAB
yarn quantity........................SKEIN
yataghan ...............................SABER
yaupon ..............................CASSENA
yawn.........................................GAPE
yearly .............ANNUAL; ETESIAN
yearly church payment........ANNAT
yearn...............ACHE, FEEL, PINE,
..........................PITY; CRAVE
yeast .................................LEAVEN
yeast, brewer's .....................BARM
yell....................CRY; BAWL; CALL;
........................SHOUT, WHOOP;
........................BELLOW, HOLLER
yellow ...........................AZO; BUFF,
................GOLD; AMBER, GREGE;
.........OCHER; GOLDEN, MELINE;
....................QUINCE; CITRINE;
.................SAFFRON; PRIMROSE
yellow, sickly ...................SALLOW;
..............................JAUNDICE
yellow ide....................ORF; ORFE
yellow ocher...........................SIL
yellow, pale ..........BEIGE, CREAM;
..............................FALLOW

yellow pigment..............GAMBOGE;
..............................ORPIMENT
yellow quartz.......................TOPAZ
Yellow Sea arm...................BO HAI
yellow wood .....................AVODIRE
yelp.................YAP, YIP; SQUEAL
Yemen capital.......................SA'NA
yet...................BUT; EVEN; STILL
yield.................BEAR; OUTPUT;
..............................CONCEDE    d
yin, counterpart of.................YANG
Yogi...................................SWAMI
Yogi's buddy ...................BOOBOO
yokel............OAF; HICK, RUBE
yolk of an egg..................VITELLUS
yolky ......................................EGGY
yon.......................................THERE
Yorkshire city.......................LEEDS
Yorkshire river .............ESK, URE;
..................NIDD, OUSE; DERWENT
young animal..........CUB, KID, PUP;
..............CALF, COLT; WHELP
young bull: Brit. .....................STOT
younger son .........................CADET
young female pig.......................GILT
young kangaroo.......................JOEY
youngster................KID, TAD, TOT;
..............................SHAVER
young weaned pig .............SHOAT,
..............................SHOTE
youth ........................................LAD
youth shelter ......................HOSTEL
Yucatan people ....................MAYA
yuccalike plant ....................SOTOL
Yugoslavian .............SERB; CROAT
Yugoslavian leader, former......TITO
Yum-yum's friend.................KOKO;
..............................NANKIPOO
___ Yutang ................................LIN

134

# Z

Z, Brit. ................................ZED
zeal .........ELAN; ARDOR; FERVOR
zealous ....................................AVID
Zebedee, son of ......JOHN; JAMES
zebra, S. Afr. ....................QUAGGA
zebra, young..........................COLT
zebra-ass hybrid..............ZEBRASS
zenith ....................ACME, APEX,
........................................PEAK; CREST;
..........................CLIMAX, SUMMIT
zenith, opposite of................NADIR
Zeno, follower of ...................STOIC
zeppelin..................................BLIMP
zeppelin, famous:....................GRAF
zero .....................ZILCH; CIPHER
zest.........................TANG; GUSTO
Zeus, daughter of ....................ATE;
..................HEBE; AEGLE, HELEN,
..............IRENE; AGLAIA, ATHENA,
.............................CLOTHO, THALIA
Zeus, epithet for ................AMMON
Zeus, maiden loved by .........LEDA;
............................................EUROPA

Zeus, mother of......................RHEA
Zeus, old Doric name of............ZAN
Zeus, sister of ........................HERA
Zeus, son of ...........ARES; ARCAS,
.............BELUS, MINOS; AEACUS,
.........................APOLLO, CASTOR,
........HERMES, POLLUX, ZETHUS
Zeus, wife of.............HERA; METIS
Zilpah, son of .............GAD; ASHER
zinc in slabs ...................SPELTER
zodiac sign .................LEO; ARIES,
.............LIBRA, VIRGO; CANCER,
........................GEMINI, PISCES,
.....................TAURUS; SCORPIO;
.............AQUARIUS; CAPRICORN;
.............................SAGITTARIUS
Zola novel ............................NANA
zone ......................................AREA
zoophyte, marine ................CORAL
Zoroastrian ..........PARSI; PARSEE
Zoroastrian scripture..........AVESTA
Zulu language ....................BANTU
Zulu warriors............................IMPI

---

# SPECIAL SECTIONS

---

You will find the following sections very helpful when solving crossword puzzles. Use these sections in conjunction with the Clues & Definitions Section. Most of the information in the Special Sections is found only there, so you should familiarize yourself with these sections.

Information is presented in easy-to-understand lists in many categories. The order of presentation is; people, places, and things. You will find most of the lists from the original edition of this dictionary and many new ones. Lists are an efficient way to present information, therefore, this part of the book has been greatly expanded.

When the information presented is not straightforward, a brief introduction is given at the beginning of the Special Section.

All three- and four-letter words are cross-referenced from the Word Finder.

# NAME FINDER

Many crossword puzzle clues involve the first and last names of famous people. When the clue tells you the last name, discovering the first name may be difficult but possible if you have a wide variety of reference sources available. For example, you can look up "Composer Khatchaturian" in an encyclopedia. However, many clues give you a first name and perhaps a profession. With the Name Finder either type of clue can be unravelled simply by looking up the first or last name. Thousands of names of famous people are cross-referenced here. If you have the clue, "Singer Bob," simply look up "Bob," listed alphabetically in the Name Finder, and you will see a listing of 32 people named Bob. Three of them, Dylan, Marley, and Seger are followed by the code letter "x." Code letters refer to the source of a person's fame. The chart below lists the meaning of each code letter. In this example, the code letter "x" indicates that the person is a singer.

Names are listed alphabetically, letter by letter, dictionary style. When there are instances of a name which is used as both a first and a last name, people with the first name are listed first followed by a separate list of people with the name used as a last name.

| | | | |
|---|---|---|---|
| a | ACTOR, | n | HOCKEY PLAYER |
| | DANCER, | o | JOURNALIST, |
| | MAGICIAN, | | TELEVISION REPORTER |
| | MODEL | p | MILITARY LEADER |
| b | ARCHITECT | q | MOVIE DIRECTOR, |
| c | ARTIST, | | PRODUCER, |
| | DESIGNER | | STAGE DIRECTOR |
| d | ASTRONAUT, | r | MUSICIAN, |
| | PILOT | | CONDUCTOR |
| e | BASEBALL PLAYER | s | OLYMPIC ATHLETE |
| f | BASKETBALL PLAYER | t | POET |
| g | BOXER | u | POLITICIAN, |
| h | BUSINESS LEADER, | | LAWYER, |
| | LABOR LEADER, | | JUDGE |
| | GANGSTER | v | RACE CAR DRIVER |
| i | CARTOONIST | w | SCIENTIST, |
| j | COMEDIAN | | PSYCHIATRIST, |
| k | COMPOSER, | | INVENTOR |
| | LYRICIST | x | SINGER |
| l | FOOTBALL PLAYER | y | TENNIS PLAYER |
| m | GOLFER | z | WRITER |

A.A. ...............MILNE(z)
A.E. .........HOUSMAN(t)
A.J. ................FOYT(v)
Aaron ..............BURR(u)
................COPLAND(k)
................SPELLING(q)
Aaron, ...........HANK(e)
Abbott, ................BUD(j)
................GEORGE(z)
Abby ..........DALTON(a)
Abdul, ..........PAULA(x)
Abdul-Jabbar,
................KAREEM(z)
Abe .........BURROWS(z)
...............FORTAS(u)
..................VIGODA(a
Abigail ....Van BUREN(o)
Abner .........................
.............DOUBLEDAY(p)
Abraham .....LINCOLN(u)
Abraham, .....................
.............F. MURRAY(a)
Abramovitz, .......MAX(b)
Abrams, .......................
.............CREIGHTON(p)
Abzug, .............BELLA(u)
Acheson, .........DEAN(u)
Acuff, .................ROY(r)
Ada ...............REHAN(a)
Adam ................ANT(x)
......SMITH(z), WEST(a)
Adams, ...........ALICE(z)
...............BROOKE(a)
.......BRYAN(x), DON(a)
................DOUGLAS(z)
...........EDIE(x), JOHN(u)
...........JOHN QUINCY(u)
....................MASON(a)
.....................MAUD(a)
....................SAMUEL(u)
Addams, ....CHARLES(i)
Adderley, .......JULIAN
..............."Cannonball"(r)
Ade, ...........GEORGE(z)
Adela................ROGERS
................ST. JOHN(z)
Adele...........ASTAIRE(a)
Adelina.............PATTI(x)
Adenauer, ..KONRAD(u)
Adjani, .....ISABELLE(a)
Adlai E. ......................
............STEVENSON(u)
Adler, .........ALFRED(w)
.......CYRUS(z), FELIX(z)
....................LARRY(r)
Adolf .........HITLER(u)
Adolph ..........GREEN(a)
.....OCHS(o), ZUKOR(q)
Adolphe.......MENJOU(a)
Adolphus........BUSCH(h)

Adoree, ........RENEE(a)
Adrian .....DANTLEY(f)
Adrienne...BARBEAU(a)
Agar, .............JOHN(a)
Agassi, .........ANDRE(y)
Agatha .......CHRISTIE(z)
Agee, ...........JAMES(z)
Ager, ..........MILTON(k)
Agnes.........De MILLE(a)
............MOOREHEAD(a)
Agnew, .........SPIRO(u)
Agutter, .......JENNY(a)
Aherne, .........BRIAN(a)
Ahmad .........RASHAD(l)
Aidan .........QUINN(a)
Aiello, .........DANNY(a)
Aiken, .........CONRAD(t)
Aikman, ...........TROY(l)
Ailey, .........ALVIN(a)
Aimee, .........ANOUK(a)
Ainge, ...........DANNY(f)
Akim.........TAMIROFF(a)
Akira ...KUROSAWA(q)
Al .............ALBERT(o)
.....CAPONE(h), CAPP(i)
................GEIBERGER(m)
.....GORE(u), GREEN(x)
.............HIRSCHFELD(i)
..............JARREAU(x)
..................JOLSON(a)
..................KALINE(e)
................MARTINO(x)
................MICHAELS(o)
........MOLINARO(a)
.................OERTER(s)
........PACINO(a), RITZ(j)
................STEWART(x)
....................UNSER(v)
Alain................DELON(a)
................Le SAGE(z)
....................PROST(v)
Alan..............ALDA(a)
.......ARKIN(a), BATES(a)
........CRANSTON(u)
.............HALE(a), KING(j)
..................KULWICKI(v)
......................LADD(a)
................MOWBRAY(a)
....................PATON(z)
..................RACHINS(a)
............SHEPARD, Jr.(d)
...................SILLITOE(z)
.....................THICKE(a)
Alastair................SIM(a)
Alban ..............BERG(k)
Albee, ........EDWARD(z)
Alben .........BARKLEY(u)
Alberghetti, ...............
.............ANNA MARIA(a)
Albert .........BROOKS(a)

.......................CAMUS(z)
.................EINSTEIN(w)
......................FINNEY(a)
.............MICHELSON(w)
Albert, ..AL(o), EDDIE(a)
.......MARV(o), STEVE(o)
Alberto .......................
.............GIACOMETTI(c)
....................MORAVIA(z)
Albert Pinkham ............
.......................RYDER(c)
Albertson, .........JACK(a)
Albrecht .........DURER(c)
Alcott, ...............AMY(m)
............LOUISA MAY(z)
Alda, ...............ALAN(a)
....................FRANCES(x)
......................ROBERT(a)
Aldiss, .......BRIAN W.(z)
Aldo.................RAY(a)
Aldous .........HUXLEY(z)
Aldrin, ...........EDWIN(d)
Alec .........BALDWIN(a)
....................GUINNESS(a)
Alejandro.............REY(a)
Aleksandr...BORODIN(k)
......................PUSHKIN(z)
.......................SCRIABIN(k)
.........SOLZHENITSYN(z)
Alessandro.................
.....................SCARLATTI(k)
Alex.................CORD(a)
.............DELVECCHIO(n)
.....................ENGLISH(f)
...........................HALEY(z)
......................RAYMOND(i)
.......................TREBEK(a)
Alexander .....................
.............ARCHIPENKO(c)
....................CALDER(c)
......................FLEMING(w)
..........................HAIG(p)
................HAMILTON(u)
.............................POPE(t)
..................WOOLLCOTT(z)
Alexander, GROVER(e)
.......JANE(a), JASON(a)
Alexander Graham .........
...........................BELL(w)
Alexandre ......DUMAS(z)
Alexis .............SMITH(a)
Alf................LANDON(u)
Alfonse .......D'AMATO(u)
Alfre.........WOODARD(a)
Alfred .........ADLER(w)
......................DRAKE(a)
......................DREYFUS(p)
.................HITCHCOCK(q)
............................KRUPP(h)
.......LUNT(a), NOBEL(w)

137

Alfred *continued*...........
..................NOYES(t)
.............TENNYSON(t)
Alfred A. ........KNOPF(h)
Alger .................HISS(u)
Alger, ........HORATIO(z)
Algernon
.............SWINBURNE(t)
Ali .............MacGRAW(a)
Ali, ........MUHAMMAD(g)
Alice .............ADAMS(z)
....COOPER(x), FAYE(a)
..............GHOSTLEY(a)
..................MARBLE(y)
..................WALKER(z)
Alighieri, ........DANTE(t)
Alison ..............LURIE(z)
Alistair..........COOKE(z)
Alla .........NAZIMOVA(z)
Allan .........SHERMAN(x)
Allen...............DRURY(z)
..............GINSBERG(t)
..................JENKINS(a)
Allen, ............DEBBIE(a)
.......ETHAN(p), FRED(j)
....GRACIE(j), KAREN(a)
.......MARCUS(l), MEL(o)
..................NANCY(a)
..................STEVE(a,j)
..................WOODY(a,q)
Alley, ..........KIRSTIE(a)
Allison, ..........DAVEY(v)
Allman, ..........DUANE(r)
..................GREGG(r)
Ally ............SHEEDY(a)
Allyce .........BEASLEY(a)
Allyson, ...........JUNE(a)
Alma ...........GLUCK(x)
Alomar, ...ROBERTO(e)
..................SANDY(e)
Alonso,
....MARIA CONCHITA(a)
Alonzo .....MOURNING(f)
Alou,.............FELIPE(e)
.....JESUS(e), MATTY(e)
Alpert, ...........HERB(r)
Althea ..........GIBSON(y)
Alther, ..............LISA(z)
Altman, ......ROBERT(q)
Alvin ...............AILEY(a)
Alworth, .........LANCE(l)
Amanda....PLUMMER(a)
Ambler, ...........ERIC(z)
Ambrose......BIERCE(z)
Ameche, ..........DON(a)
Amedeo
.............MODIGLIANI(c)
Amelia ......BLOOMER(u)
..................EARHART(d)
Ames, ..ED(x), LEON(a)

Amilcare.............
.........PONCHIELLI(k)
Amis, .......KINGSLEY(z)
Amos .................OZ(z)
Amos, ...........JOHN(a)
..................TORI(x)
Amsterdam, ...MOREY(j)
Amy .........ALCOTT(m)
....GRANT(x), IRVING(a)
..................LOWELL(t)
..................MADIGAN(a)
Anaïs ................NIN(z)
Anatole ......FRANCE(z)
Andersen,
.......HANS CHRISTIAN(z)
Anderson, .......HARRY(a)
.........IAN(r,x), JACK(o)
........JON(x), JUDITH(a)
..................LINDSAY(q)
..................LONI(a), LYNN(x)
..................MARIAN(a)
..................MAXWELL(z)
..................OTTIS(l)
.......RICHARD DEAN(a)
..................SHERWOOD(z)
Andersson, .......BIBI(a)
Andie ....MacDOWELL(a)
André ............AGASSI(y)
..................BRETON(z)
..................CHENIER(t)
...DAWSON(e), GIDE(z)
..................KOSTELANETZ(r)
..................MALRAUX(z)
..................NORTON(z)
...PREVIN(r), WATTS(r)
Andrea ............DORIA(u)
..................McARDLE(a)
..................MITCHELL(o)
Andrés ........SEGOVIA(r)
Andress, ......URSULA(a)
Andretti, ..........MARIO(v)
Andrew ....CARNEGIE(h)
..................JACKSON(u)
..................JOHNSON(u)
..................McCARTHY(a)
..................MELLON(h)
..................STEVENS(a)
..................WYETH(c)
..................YOUNG(u)
Andrew Lloyd...........
..................WEBBER(k)
Andrews, ..ANTHONY(a)
.........DANA(a), JULIE(a)
..................LA VERNE(x)
....MAXENE(x), PATTI(x)
Andric, ..............IVO(z)
Andy ............DEVINE(j)
.......GARCIA(a), GIBB(x)
..................GRIFFITH(a)
..................NORTH(m)

.............ROBUSTELLI(l)
..................ROONEY(o)
..............Van SLYKE(e)
..................WARHOL(c)
..................WILLIAMS(x)
Aneurin..........BEVAN(u)
Angela ............DAVIS(u)
..................LANSBURY(a)
Angelico, ............FRA(c)
Angelou,..........MAYA(t)
Angie ......DICKINSON(a)
Angus...........WILSON(z)
Anita ...............BAKER(x)
..................BROOKNER(z)
..................EKBERG(a)
..................GILLETTE(a)
.......LOOS(z), O'DAY(x)
..................POINTER(x)
Anjelica ........HUSTON(a)
Anka, ..............PAUL(x)
Ann ...............BEATTIE(z)
...BLYTH(a), JILLIAN(a)
..................LANDERS(o)
..................MILLER(a)
..................REINKING(a)
..................RICHARDS(u)
..................SHERIDAN(a)
..................SOTHERN(a)
..................WILSON(x)
Ann B. ...........DAVIS(a)
Anna ...........MAGNANI(a)
..................MOFFO(x)
..................NEAGLE(a)
..................PAVLOVA(a)
..................STEN(a)
Anna Maria ...........
..................ALBERGHETTI(a)
Anna May .....WONG(a)
Anne............ARCHER(a)
..................BANCROFT(a)
..................BAXTER(a)
..................BOLEYN(u)
..................BRONTE(z)
..................De SALVO(a)
..................FRANCIS(a)
..................JACKSON(a)
..................JEFFREYS(a)
..................MEARA(a)
..................MURRAY(a)
..................SEXTON(t)
..................TYLER(z)
Anne Morrow ...........
..................LINDBERGH(z)
Annenberg, ...........
..................WALTER(h)
Annette ........BENING(a)
..................FUNICELLO(a)
..................O'TOOLE(a)
Annie ...........LENNOX(x)
..................POTTS(a)

Annunzio...........................
..............MANTOVANI(r)
Anouk...............AIMEE(a)
Ansara,.......MICHAEL(a)
Anspach, .......SUSAN(a)
Ant, ...................ADAM(x)
Anthony....ANDREWS(a)
..................BURGESS(z)
......................EDEN(u)
................EDWARDS(a)
..................HOPKINS(a)
..................NEWLEY(x)
..................PERKINS(a)
......................QUINN(a)
.................TROLLOPE(z)
.................Van DYCK(c)
........................ZERBE(a)
Anthony, ....SUSAN B.(u)
Anthony M. ...................
.................KENNEDY(u)
Antoine ...LAVOISIER(w)
Anton......BRUCKNER(k)
................CHEKHOV(z)
Anton, .........SUSAN(a)
Antonin ........DVORAK(k)
........................SCALIA(u)
Antonio ......CANOVA(c)
....MORO(c), VIVALDI(k)
Anwar al-........SADAT(u)
Anya............SETON(z)
Aoki, ............ISAO(m)
Aparicio, ............LUIS(e)
Applegate, ...................
..............CHRISTINA(a)
Ara.......PARSEGHIAN(l)
Arafat,.........YASIR(u)
Aram .....................
......KHACHATURIAN(k)
Arbuckle, .......FATTY(j)
Archer, .............ANNE(a)
...................GEORGE(m)
Archibald ....MacLEISH(t)
Archibald, .........NATE(f)
Archie ...........MOORE(g)
Archipenko, ...................
.............ALEXANDER(c)
Arden, ....ELIZABETH(h)
.............................EVE(a)
Arens, ...........MOSHE(u)
Aretha .......FRANKLIN(x)
Ari.................MEYERS(a)
Arie.........LUYENDYK(v)
Ariel...........SHARON(u)
Aristotle ......ONASSIS(h)
Arkin, ...............ALAN(a)
Arledge, ........ROONE(h)
Arlen,.........SPECTER(u)
Arlen ........HAROLD(k)
Arlene ...............DAHL(a)
...................FRANCIS(a)

Arliss, ........GEORGE(a)
Arlo.............GUTHRIE(x)
Armand......ASSANTE(a)
...................HAMMER(h)
Armstrong, .......BESS(a)
....LOUIS "Satchmo"(r)
.......................NEIL(d)
Arnaz, ...............DESI(a)
......................LUCIE(a)
Arne, ......:..THOMAS(k)
Arness, ..........JAMES(a)
Arno...........PENZIAS(w)
Arno, ................PETER(i)
Arnold ........PALMER(m)
..............SCHOENBERG(k)
................SCHWARZEN-
.......................EGGER(a)
........................STANG(j)
Arnold, .....BENEDICT(p)
.........................EDDY(x)
...................MATTHEW(t)
............ROSEANNE(a,j)
..........................TOM(j)
Arquette, ..........CLIFF(j)
...............ROSANNA(a)
Arsenio ............HALL(j)
Arshile .........GORKY(c)
Art .................BLAKEY(r)
................BUCHWALD(o)
....................CARNEY(a)
..................DONOVAN(l)
............GARFUNKEL(x)
............LINKLETTER(j)
........MONK(l), TATUM(r)
Arte ............JOHNSON(j)
Arthur.................ASHE(y)
...................BALFOUR(u)
.....................FIEDLER(r)
...................GODFREY(j)
.........HAILEY(z), HILL(q)
.................HONEGGER(k)
...................KENNEDY(u)
......................MILLER(z)
................O'CONNELL(a)
..........................PENN(q)
...................RIMBAUD(t)
...............RUBINSTEIN(r)
...................TREACHER(a)
Arthur, .....BEATRICE(a)
....CHESTER ALAN(u)
.........................JEAN(a)
Arthur C. ......CLARKE(z)
Arthur Conan ...................
.......................DOYLE(z)
Arthur S. ...SULLIVAN(k)
Artie..................SHAW(r)
Artis .............GILMORE(f)
Arturo.......TOSCANINI(k)
Asa ..................GRAY(w)
...................CANDLER(h)

Asch, ..........SHOLEM(z)
Ashe, .........ARTHUR(y)
Asher............DURAND(c)
Ashford, .......EVELYN(s)
Ashley, ...ELIZABETH(a)
Asimov, ..........ISAAC(z)
Asner, ....................ED(a)
Aspin, ..................LES(u)
Assante, ....ARMAND(a)
Astaire, .........ADELE(a)
..........................FRED(a)
Astin, ...............JOHN(a)
Astor, ..JOHN JACOB(h)
..................GERTRUDE(a)
.........................MARY(a)
Astrud.......GILBERTO(x)
Atherton ......WILLIAM(a)
Athol ...........FUGARD(z)
Atkins,.............CHET(r)
Attenborough, ...................
..............................DAVID(w)
....................RICHARD(a,q)
Attlee, .......CLEMENT(u)
Atwill, .........LIONEL(a)
Atwood,...................
..................MARGARET(z)
Auberjonois, ....RENE(a)
Aubrey .....................
..................BEARDSLEY(c)
Auchincloss, ....LOUIS(z)
Auden, .............W.H.(t)
Audie ........MURPHY(a)
Audrey ......HEPBURN(a)
....................MEADOWS(a)
Audubon,...................
..........JOHN JAMES(c,w)
Auer, ........LEOPOLD(r)
Auerbach, ..........RED(f)
August ...................
............STRINDBERG(z)
.......................WILSON(z)
Auguste .........COMTE(z)
..........................RODIN(c)
Aumont, ...................
..................JEAN-PIERRE(a)
Austen, .........JANE(z)
Austin, ...........TRACY(y)
Autry, ...........GENE(a,h)
Ava ...........GARDNER(a)
Avalon, ........FRANKIE(x)
Avery, ..................TEX(i)
Axton, ............HOYT(x)
Aykroyd, ............DAN(a)
Ayn ................RAND(z)
Ayres, ..............LEW(a)
Ayrton...........SENNA(v)
Aznavour, ..CHARLES(x)

B(ernard) ........KLIBAN(i)
B.F. ...........SKINNER(w)

142

## Bushman / Cavendish

Bushman, .....................
...............FRANCIS X.(a)
Buster............CRABBE(a)
....................KEATON(a)
Butkus, ................DICK(l)
Butler, ............JERRY(x)
............SAMUEL(c,k,z)
Butterfly ....McQUEEN(s)
Button, ..............DICK(s)
Buttons, .............RED(a)
Buzzi, ................RUTH(j)
Byington, .....SPRING(a)
Byner, ........EARNEST(l)
Byrne, ...........DAVID(x)
Byron............NELSON(m)
.......................WHITE(u)

C.C. .................BECK(i)
C.S. ........FORESTER(z)
....................LEWIS(z)
C.Thomas ....HOWELL(a)
Caan, .............JAMES(a)
Cab .........CALLOWAY(r)
Cabot, ............BRUCE(a)
............SEBASTIAN(a)
Caesar, ................SID(j)
Cage, .................JOHN(k)
..................NICOLAS(a)
Cagney, .........JAMES(a)
Cain, .................BOB(o)
............JAMES M.(z)
Caine, .........MICHAEL(a)
Cal .............HUBBARD(l)
................RIPKEN, Jr.(e)
Calcavecchia, .................
......................MARK(m)
Calder, ...ALEXANDER(z)
Caldwell, ....ERSKINE(c)
.........SARAH(r), ZOE(a)
Cale .............................
.......YARBOROUGH(v)
Calhoun, .....JOHN C.(u)
...........................RORY(a)
Calisher, ........................
..............HORTENSE(z)
Callas, ..........MARIA(x)
Calloway, ...........CAB(r)
Calvé, .............EMMA(x)
Calvin ......COOLIDGE(u)
......KLEIN(h), PEETE(m)
........................TRILLIN(o)
Calvino, .........ITALO(z)
Camacho, ...HECTOR(g)
Cameron...MITCHELL(a)
Cameron, ..........KIRK(a)
Camille ....PISSARRO(c)
........SAINT-SAENS(k)
Camp, .....HAMILTON(a)
Campanella, .................
.......JOSEPH(a), ROY(e)

Campbell, ...............BEN
.........NIGHTHORSE(u)
...........EARL(l), GLEN(x)
Camus, ........ALBERT(z)
Canby, ......VINCENT(o)
Candice......BERGEN(a)
Candler, ...............ASA(h)
Candy, ...........JOHN(a)
Caniff, ..........MILTON(i)
Cannon, .........DYAN(a)
.....................FREDDY(x)
Canova, .....ANTONIO(c)
Canseco, ..........JOSE(e)
Cantor, ...........EDDIE(a)
Cantrell, ..........LANA(x)
Capek, .........KAREL(z)
Capone, ................AL(h)
Caponi, .......DONNA(m)
Capote, ....TRUMAN(z)
Capp, ...................AL(i)
Cappelletti, ........GINO(l)
Capra, ...........FRANK(q)
Capriati, ...JENNIFER(y)
Cara, ...............IRENE(x)
Cardozo, .BENJAMIN(u)
Carew, .............ROD(e)
Carey, .........................
...............MacDONALD(a)
......................MARIAH(x)
Cariou, ...............LEN(a)
Carl ...................ELLER(l)
....ICAHN(h), JUNG(w)
....LEWIS(s), REINER(a)
....................SAGAN(w)
................SANDBURG(t)
........YASTRZEMSKI(e)
Carlin, ........GEORGE(j)
Carlisle, .....BELINDA(x)
........................KITTY(a)
Carlo ...............PONTI(q)
Carlos........SANTANA(x)
Carlotta..........PATTI(x)
Carlton, ..........STEVE(e)
Carly ...............SIMON(x)
Carlyle, ......THOMAS(z)
Carmen ......MIRANDA(x)
Carmen, ............ERIC(x)
Carmichael, ..HOAGY(k)
.............................IAN(a)
Carne, .................JUDY(j)
Carnegie, ...ANDREW(h)
Carner, ......JOANNE(m)
Carnera, .........PRIMO(g)
Carnes, ...............KIM(x)
Carney, ..............ART(a)
Carol .........BURNETT(j)
................CHANNING(a)
.......................KANE(a)
.................LAWRENCE(a)
..........................REED(q)

Carole ...............KING(x)
.......................LANDIS(a)
....................LOMBARD(a)
Carolyn.............JONES(a)
Caron, ...........LESLIE(a)
Carpenter, .......JOHN(q)
..........................KAREN(x)
Carr, ................VIKKI(x)
Carradine, ......DAVID(a)
.........JOHN(a), KEITH(a)
Carrie ..........FISHER(a)
Carrie Chapman ...........
..............................CATT(u)
Carrier, ..........MARK(l)
Carrillo, .............LEO(a)
Carroll .............BAKER(a)
....................O'CONNOR(a)
Carroll, ......DIAHANN(a)
.....LEO G.(a), LEWIS(z)
..............................PAT(j)
Carson ...........................
...............McCULLERS(z)
Carson, ...........JACK(j)
..................JOHNNY(j)
Carter, .............JACK(j)
.....JIMMY(u), JOE(e)
.........JUNE(x), LYNDA(a)
...............................NELL(a)
....................ROSALIND(u)
Caruso, .......ENRICO(x)
Carvel, ..............TOM(h)
Carvey, .........DANA(j)
Cary .............ELWES(a)
.............................GRANT(a)
...............MIDDLECOFF(m)
Casals, ...........PABLO(r)
Casey ...........KASEM(a)
...................STENGEL(e)
Cash, .........JOHNNY(x)
....................ROSANNE(x)
Casper, .........BILLY(m)
Cass, ...........ELLIOT(x)
...................GILBERT(b)
Cass, ............PEGGY(j)
Cassatt, ..........MARY(c)
Cassavetes, .....JOHN(q)
Cassidy, ........DAVID(x)
........................SHAUN(x)
Castle, ............IRENE(a)
.......................VERNON(a)
Castro, ...........FIDEL(u)
Cat............STEVENS(x)
Cather, .........WILLA(z)
Catherine ..DENEUVE(a)
Cathy .......GUISEWITE(i)
.........................RIGBY(s)
Catlin, ........GEORGE(c)
Catt, ..........CARRIE
................CHAPMAN(u)
Cavendish, ...HENRY(w)

144

Clara............BARTON(h)
.........................BOW(a)
Clarence ....DARROW(u)
.................THOMAS(u)
Clark.............GABLE(a)
Clark, ...............DANE(a)
.........................DICK(a)
............GARY(l), JIM(v)
.......MARY HIGGINS(z)
.......PETULA(x), ROY(r)
.......SUSAN(a), WILL(e)
Clarke, ...ARTHUR C.(z)
Clary, .........ROBERT(a)
Claude.......DEBUSSY(k)
.....MONET(c), RAINS(a)
Claudette...COLBERT(a)
Clavell, ..........JAMES(z)
Clay, ...........HENRY(u)
Clayburgh, ........JILL(a)
Clayton .........MOORE(a)
Clayton, .........MARK(l)
Cleavon ..........LITTLE(a)
Cleese, ............JOHN(j)
Clemens ....ROGER(e)
Clement .......ATTLEE(u)
Clement C. ....MOORE(t)
Clemente, .............
.................ROBERTO(e)
Cleo.................LAINE(a)
Clete ..............BOYER(e)
Cleveland, ..GROVER(u)
Cliburn, ............VAN(r)
Cliff...........ARQUETTE(j)
...............DRYSDALE(y)
...................RICHARD(x)
............ROBERTSON(a)
Clifford...........ODETS(z)
Clift, .................
........MONTGOMERY(a)
Clifton ...........WEBB(a)
Cline, ..........PATSY(x)
Clint ...............BLACK(r)
...............EASTWOOD(a)
Clinton, .............BILL(u)
...................De WITT(u)
.....................HILLARY(u)
Clive.........BARKER(q, z)
.....................BARNES(o)
Clooney, .............
...............ROSEMARY(x)
Cloris ......LEACHMAN(a)
Close, ..........GLENN(a)
Clu..........GULAGHER(a)
Clyde ........DREXLER(f)
...........McPHATTER(x)
Cobb, ..........LEE J.(a)
.............................TY(e)
Coburn, ....CHARLES(a)
.....................JAMES(a)
Coca, .........IMOGENE(j)

Cocker, ............JOE(x)
Cocteau, .......JEAN(q,z)
Coe, ......SEBASTIAN(s)
Coen, ...........ETHAN(q)
Cohan, ..GEORGE M.(q)
Cohen, ..LEONARD(t,x)
...................MYRON(j)
............WILLIAM S.(u)
Cohn, ..........MARC(r,x)
Colbert, ..............JIM(m)
.............CLAUDETTE(a)
Cole, ..........PORTER(k)
Cole, ...............COZY(r)
...............NAT "King"(x)
...................NATALIE(x)
...................THOMAS(c)
Coleman .....HAWKINS(r)
Coleman, ..............CY(k)
...DABNEY(a), GARY(a)
...................ORNETTE(r)
Coleridge, .............
......SAMUEL TAYLOR(t)
Colette, ..........SIDONIE
...............GABRIELLE(z)
Colgate, .....WILLIAM(h)
Colin ...........POWELL(u)
Collins, .........JACKIE(z)
.......................JOAN(a)
.............JUDY(x), PHIL(x)
...................WILKIE(z)
Colm..........MEANEY(a)
Colman, ......RONALD(a)
Colter, ...........JESSI(x)
Coltrane, .......JOHN(r)
Columbo, .......RUSS(r)
Comaneci, ......NADIA(s)
Como, ..........PERRY(x)
Compton-Burnett ..........
.........................IVY(z)
Comte, .......AUGUSTE(z)
Conchata....FERRELL(a)
Condón, .......EDDIE(r)
Cone, ..........DAVID(e)
Connelly, ........MARC(z)
Conner, ...........BART(s)
Connery, .......SEAN(a)
Connick, Jr., ..HARRY(x)
Connie............CHUNG(o)
..................FRANCIS(x)
...................HAWKINS(f)
.......................MACK(a)
...............SELLECCA(a)
...................STEVENS(a)
Conniff, ...........RAY(r)
Connolly, .MAUREEN(y)
Connors, .......CHUCK(a)
........JIMMY(y), MIKE(a)
Conrad.............AIKEN(t)
.......BAIN(a), HILTON(h)
......NAGEL(a), VEIDT(a)

Conrad, .....JOSEPH(z)
...................ROBERT(a)
.....................WILLIAM(a)
Conried, ...........HANS(j)
Conroy, ...........PAT(z)
Constable, .......JOHN(c)
Constance .............
.........................BENNETT(a)
Constantin .............
.................BRANCUSI(c)
Conte, ......RICHARD(a)
Conti, ...............TOM(a)
Conway ........TWITTY(x)
Conway, ...........TIM(j)
Coogan, .......JACKIE(a)
Cook, .............JOHN(m)
.......................PETER(j)
...................THOMAS(h)
Cooke, ......ALISTAIR(z)
.........................SAM(x)
Coolidge, ......CALVIN(u)
.........................RITA(x)
Cooper, ..........ALICE(x)
......GARY(a), JACKIE(a)
...JAMES FENIMORE(z)
.......................PETER(h)
...............L. GORDON(d)
Copernicus, .............
...............NICHOLAS(w)
Copland, ........AARON(k)
Copley, .............
...JOHN SINGLETON(c)
Coppola, .............
.......FRANCIS FORD(q)
Corbett, ......JAMES J.(g)
Corbin .......BERNSEN(a)
Corby, ...........ELLEN(a)
Cord, ...............ALEX(a)
Cordell.............HULL(u)
Corea, .........CHICK(r)
Coretta Scott .....KING(u)
Corey ........FELDMAN(a)
.........................HAIM(a)
.........................PAVIN(m)
Corey, .....WENDELL(a)
Corman, ......ROGER(q)
Cornelius .............
.............VANDERBILT(h)
Cornell, ...........EZRA(h)
...............KATHARINE(a)
Cornwallis, .............
.....................CHARLES(p)
Corot, ..JEAN-BAPTISTE
.........................CAMILLE(c)
Cortés, ......HERNAN(p)
Cosby, ...........BILL(j)
Cosell, ......HOWARD(o)
Costas, ..............BOB(o)
Costello, ..........ELVIS(x)
.............................LOU(j)

147

Danza, ............TONY(a)
Daphne ..........................
............du MAURIER(z)
Darby, ................KIM(a)
Darin, .......BOBBY(x)
Darlene ............LOVE(x)
Damell, .......:.LINDA(a)
Darrell .........EVANS(e)
...........WALTRIP(v)
Darren .....McGAVIN(a)
Darrow, ..CLARENCE(u)
Darryl ......PONICSAN(z)
.........STRAWBERRY(e)
Darryl F. ......ZANUCK(q)
Darwin, ...CHARLES(w)
Daryl ................HALL(x)
................HANNAH(a)
Dashiell.....HAMMETT(z)
Dave ...............BARRY(o)
....BING(f), BRUBECK(r)
.................COWENS(f)
...DAVIES(r), HILL(m)
.................KINGMAN(e)
.......MARR(m), STIEB(e)
................STOCKTON(m)
.................WINFIELD(e)
Davey ..............ALLISON(v)
David ..............................
....ATTENBOROUGH(w)
.........BEN-GURION(u)
....................BIRNEY(a)
....................BOWIE(a,x)
...................BRENNER(j)
..................BRINKLEY(o)
....................BRODER(o)
.......................BYRNE(x)
................CARRADINE(a)
....................CASSIDY(x)
.......................CONE(e)
....................CROSBY(x)
....................DINKINS(u)
....DOYLE(a), DUKES(a)
.................FARRAGUT(p)
.....FROST(o), GATES(x)
...................GILMOUR(r)
....................GRAHAM(m)
........................GROH(a)
...........HALBERSTAM(z)
................HARTMAN(o)
.............HEMMINGS(a)
.................HOCKNEY(c)
........................HUME(z)
.................JANSSEN(a)
....KEITH(a), LEAN(q)
.................LEISURE(j)
.............LETTERMAN(j)
.....LEVINE(i), LYNCH(z)
.....................MAMET(z)
.................McCALLUM(a)
....................MERRICK(q)

........NIVEN(a), RABE(z)
.......................RUFFIN(x)
.................STEINBERG(j)
.........SMITH(c), SOUL(a)
.....................SOUTER(u)
.........................SPADE(j)
.......................STOREY(z)
.......................WAYNE(a)
David, ..........................
.....JACQUES-LOUIS(c)
David Lee ........ROTH(x)
David O. ...SELZNICK(q)
David Ogden.................
.......................STIERS(a)
Davidson, ,.......JOHN(a,x)
Davies, ............DAVE(r)
.......LAURA(m), RAY(x)
da Vinci, ......................
.................LEONARDO(c)
Davis............LOVE III(m)
Davis, .........ANGELA(u)
.........................ANN B.(a)
.....BETTE(a), GEENA(a)
................JEFFERSON(u)
.................JIM(i), JOAN(a)
.........JUDY(a), MAC(x)
........MILES(r), OSSIE(a)
.......................SKEETER(x)
Davis, Jr., .....SAMMY(x)
Davy ..............JONES(x)
Davy, .....HUMPHRY(w)
Dawber, ............PAM(a)
Dawn .........FRASER(s)
Dawson, .......ANDRE(e)
......LEN(l), RICHARD(a)
Day, ..........DORIS(a, x)
......................LARAINE(a)
Dayan, .........MOSHE(p)
Day-Lewis, ...DANIEL(a)
Dean.........ACHESON(u)
.....................CHANCE(a)
.......................JAGGER(a)
.........................JONES(a)
....................MARTIN(a, x)
............STOCKWELL(a)
Dean, .............DIZZY(e)
....................JAMES(a)
Deanna........DURBIN(a)
Dean R. ......KOONTZ(z)
DeBarge, ......ELDRA(x)
Debbie ...........ALLEN(a)
....................GIBSON(x)
.................REYNOLDS(a)
Debby .........BOONE(a)
DeBerg, .........STEVE(l)
Deborah .......HARRY(x)
.........................KERR(a)
Debra........WINGER(a)
Debs, .......EUGENE(u)
Debussy, .....CLAUDE(k)

De Camp, ......................
...............ROSEMARY(a)
DeCarlo, .....YVONNE(a)
Dee, ................JOEY(x)
..........KIKI(x), RUBY(a)
.........................SANDRA(a)
Dee Dee .......SHARP(x)
Defoe, ...........DANIEL(z)
Deford, .........FRANK(o)
Defore, .............DON(a)
DeForest....KELLEY(a)
De Forest, ........LEE(w)
Degas, ........EDGAR(c)
De Gaulle, ..................
...............CHARLES(p,u)
DeHaven, ...GLORIA(a)
De Havilland, .............
.......................OLIVIA(a)
Deidre..............HALL(a)
Deion .......SANDERS(e)
de Kooning, ...............
.....................WILLEM(c)
Del ............SHANNON(x)
Delacorte......................
................GEORGE T.(h)
Delacroix, ...EUGENE(c)
de la Mare, .WALTER(z)
Delany, ..........DANA(a)
..................SAMUEL R.(z)
Delbert ..........MANN(q)
Delibes, .............LEO(k)
Della .........REESE(a, x)
della Robbia, ....LUCA(c)
DeLoach, .........JOE(s)
Delon, .........ALAIN(a)
Del Rio, ....DOLORES(a)
Delta ...........BURKE(a)
DeLuise, ...........DOM(a)
Delvecchio, .....ALEX(n)
Demarest, ...WILLIAM(a)
Demaret, .....JIMMY(m)
Demi .............MOORE(a)
De Mille, ........AGNES(a)
...........................CECIL B.(q)
Demme, ..JONATHAN(q)
Demond ........WILSON(a)
De Mornay, ................
....................REBECCA(a)
Dempsey, ......JACK(g)
Deneuve, ....................
.............CATHERINE(a)
Denholm ....ELLIOTT(a)
De Niro, ......ROBERT(a)
Dennehy, .......BRIAN(a)
Dennis ........HOPPER(a)
.......................MILLER(j)
....................O'KEEFE(a)
.....................QUAID(a)
...................RODMAN(f)
...................WEAVER(a)

Dennis, .........SANDY(a)
Denny, ....REGINALD(a)
.....................SANDY(x)
Dent, ................JIM(m)
..............RICHARD(l)
Denver, .............BOB(a)
.....................JOHN(x)
Denzel ...............................
.......WASHINGTON(a)
DePalma, ......BRIAN(q)
Depardieu, ..GERARD(a)
Depp, .......JOHNNY(a)
Derek............JACOBI(a)
Derek, ................BO(a)
.....................JOHN(a)
Dern, ..........BRUCE(a)
.....................LAURA(a)
Des .........O'CONNOR(x)
De Salvo, ........ANNE(a)
Descartes, ......RENE(w)
DeShannon, ..JACKIE(x)
Desi...............ARNAZ(a)
De Sica, ....VITTORIO(q)
De Valera, ....EAMON(u)
Devane, .....WILLIAM(a)
Devers, ..........GAIL(s)
Devine, ..........ANDY(j)
DeVito, .........DANNY(a)
De Vries, .......PETER(z)
Dewey, ..THOMAS E.(u)
De Wilde, ...........................
...............BRANDON(a)
De Witt........CLINTON(u)
DeWitt, .........JOYCE(a)
De Wolfe, .......BILLY(a)
Dexter .........GORDON(r)
Dey, .............SUSAN(a)
Diahann....CARROLL(a)
Diamond, .........NEIL(x)
.....................SELMA(a)
Diamond Jim.....................
.....................BRADY(h)
Diana ..............DORS(a)
...............MULDAUR(a)
.........RIGG(a), ROSS(x)
Diane ..........KEATON(a)
.........LADD(a), LANE(a)
.....................SAWYER(o)
Dianne....FEINSTEIN(u)
.....................WIEST(a)
Dick............BUTKUS(l)
.....................BUTTON(s)
....CAVETT(j), CLARK(a)
..............FOSBURY(s)
..............FRANCIS(z)
............GREGORY(j,u)
.....................MARTIN(j)
.....................POWELL(a)
.............SMOTHERS(j)
.....................TIGER(g)

.....................TRICKLE(v)
...............Van DYKE(a)
Dick (Night Train)...............
.....................LANE(l)
Dickens, ....CHARLES(z)
Dickerson, ..........ERIC(l)
Dickey, ........JAMES(z)
Dickinson, ......ANGIE(a)
.....................EMILY(t)
Diddley, ................BO(r)
Didion, ............JOAN(z)
Didrikson, ......BABE(s)
Diego.............RIVERA(c)
..........VELAZQUEZ(c)
Diesel, .....RUDOLPH(w)
Dietrich, ....MARLENE(a)
Dik ..........BROWNE(i)
Diller, .........PHYLLIS(j)
Dillman, ..............................
.............BRADFORD(a)
Dillon, .............MATT(a)
DiMaggio, .........DOM(e)
.....................JOE(e)
Di Muci, ..........DION(x)
Dina ............MERRILL(a)
Dinah ...........SHORE(x)
.............WASHINGTON(x)
Dinesen, .........ISAK(z)
Dinkins, .........DAVID(u)
Dion ..........Di MUCI(x)
Dionne .....WARWICK(x)
Dionne, ......MARCEL(n)
Dior, .......CHRISTIAN(c)
Dirk............BENEDICT(a)
..............BOGARDE(a)
Dirksen, ....EVERETT(u)
Disch, ....THOMAS M.(z)
Disney, .........WALT(i,q)
Disraeli, ..BENJAMIN(u)
Ditka, ..............MIKE(l)
Dizzy ..............DEAN(e)
..............GILLESPIE(r)
Dmitri ...................................
......SHOSTAKOVICH(k)
Dobson, .........KEVIN(a)
Doc .....SEVERINSEN(r)
Doctorow, ...........E.L.(z)
Dodie .........STEVENS(x)
Dole, ................BOB(u)
..............ELIZABETH(u)
Dolly ............PARTON(x)
Dolores ........DEL RIO(a)
Dom, .......DeLUISE(a)
...............DiMAGGIO(e)
Domingo, ...PLACIDO(x)
Domino, ...............................
...........FATS(Antoine)(x)
Don.................ADAMS(a)
...............AMECHE(a)
.....................BUDGE(y)

.....................DEFORE(a)
...............DRYSDALE(e)
.....................EVERLY(x)
.......HENLEY(x), HO(x)
.............JANUARY(m)
...............JOHNSON(a)
.....................KNOTTS(a)
.....................LARSEN(e)
...............MARQUIS(i)
...............MATTINGLY(e)
...............MAYNARD(l)
...............McLEAN(x)
...............MURRAY(a)
.............NOVELLO(a)
.....................RICKLES(j)
.....................SHULA(l)
.............WILLIAMS(x)
Donahue, ...........PHIL(o)
.....................TROY(a)
Donald.............CRISP(a)
......FAGEN(x), MEEK(a)
...............O'CONNOR(a)
.............PLEASENCE(a)
...........SUTHERLAND(a)
.....................TRUMP(h)
Donaldson, ........SAM(o)
Donat, .........ROBERT(a)
Donegan, ......LONNIE(x)
Donizetti, ..GAETANO(k)
Donleavy, ...........J.P.(z)
Donlevy, ........BRIAN(a)
Donna.........CAPONI(m)
.....................FARGO(x)
.....................KELLEY(o)
.......MILLS(a), REED(a)
.....................SUMMER(x)
Donne, ..............JOHN(t)
Donny, ......OSMOND(x)
Donovan, ............ART(z)
Dooley, ......THOMAS(w)
Doppler, ...................................
.................CHRISTIAN(w)
Doria, .........ANDREA(u)
Dorian ...HAREWOOD(a)
Doris................DAY(a, x)
..............LESSING(z)
...............ROBERTS(a)
Dom, .......MICHAEL(a)
Dorothy .................................
.............DANDRIDGE(a)
....GISH(a), LAMOUR(a)
...............LOUDON(a)
...............MALONE(a)
...............McGUIRE(a)
...............PARKER(z)
Dorothy L. ...SAYERS(z)
Dors, ............DIANA(a)
Dorsett, .............TONY(l)
Dorsey, .............JIMMY(r)
.....................TOMMY(r)

Edison, ......THOMAS(w)
Edith...............EVANS(a)
.........................PIAF(x)
.................WHARTON(z)
Edmond .......O'BRIEN(a)
.................ROSTAND(z)
Edmund.........BURKE(z)
.....................GWENN(a)
.....................HALLEY(w)
........KEAN(a), LOWE(a)
.....................MUSKIE(u)
.................SPENSER(t)
.....................WHITE(z)
.....................WILSON(z)
Edna .........FERBER(z)
Edna St.Vincent
.....................MILLAY(t)
Edouard...........LALO(z)
.....................MANET(c)
Edvard .........GRIEG(k)
.....................MUNCH(c)
Edward...........ALBEE(z)
.................BROOKE(u)
.....................ELGAR(k)
........FOX(a), HEATH(u)
.................HERRMANN(a)
.................HOPPER(c)
.................JENNER(w)
.................KENNEDY(u)
.....................KOCH(u)
.................VILLELLA(a)
.................WOODWARD(a)
Edward Everett
.................HORTON(a)
Edward G. ......
.................ROBINSON(a)
Edward James
.................OLMOS(a)
Edward R. ......
.................MURROW(o)
Edwards, ..ANTHONY(a)
.....................BLAKE(q)
Edwin ......ALDRIN, Jr.(d)
.....................BOOTH(a)
.................HUBBLE(w)
.....LAND(w), MOSES(s)
Edwin Arlington
.................ROBINSON(t)
Eero ........SAARINEN(b)
Efrem ......
.....ZIMBALIST, Jr.(a)
Ehrlich, ...........PAUL(w)
Eichhorn, ..........LISA(a)
Eikenberry, .......JILL(a)
Eileen........BRENNAN(a)
.................HECKART(a)
Einstein, ......ALBERT(w)
Eisenhower, ......
.....DWIGHT DAVID(p, u)
.........................MAMIE(u)

Eisenstein, ...SERGEI(q)
Eisner, ......MICHAEL(h)
Ekberg, ...........ANITA(a)
Ekland, ...........BRITT(a)
Elaine.................MAY(j)
.................STRITCH(a)
Elam, .............JACK(a)
Elayne .......BOOSLER(j)
Eldra .........DEBARGE(x)
Eleanor ......PARKER(a)
.................POWELL(a)
.................ROOSEVELT(u)
Eleonora...........DUSE(a)
Elgar, .........EDWARD(k)
Elgin.............BAYLOR(f)
Eli.................WALLACH(a)
.................WHITNEY(w)
Elia .......KAZAN(g, z)
Elias.................HOWE(w)
Elie.................WIESEL(z)
Eliel .......SAARINEN(b)
Elihu.................ROOT(u)
Elio.................VITTORINI(z)
Eliot, .............T.S.(z)
Eliot (Marian Evans), .....
.....................GEORGE(z)
Elisha.................OTIS(w)
Elizabeth........ARDEN(h)
.....ASHLEY(a), DOLE(u)
.................MONTGOMERY(a)
.....................PERKINS(a)
.....................TAYLOR(a)
Elizabeth Barrett
.................BROWNING(t)
Elke .............SOMMER(a)
Elkington, ......STEVE(m)
Ella .......FITZGERALD(x)
.....................LOGAN(a)
Ellen.............BARKIN(a)
.................BURSTYN(a)
.....CORBY(a), DREW(a)
.................GLASGOW(t)
.....................TERRY(a)
Eller, .............CARL(l)
Elliman, ......YVONNE(x)
Ellington, ......DUKE(k, r)
Elliot, .............CASS(x)
Elliott.............GOULD(a)
Elliott, .............BILL(v)
.........BOB(j), CHRIS(j)
.................DENHOLM(a)
.........................SAM(a)
Ellison, ........HARLAN(z)
.....................RALPH(z)
Elman, ..........MISCHA(r)
Elmer .............RICE(z)
Elmo .........LINCOLN(a)
Elmore......LEONARD(z)
Elroy (Crazy Legs)..........
.....................HIRSCH(l)

Els, .................ERNIE(m)
Elsa....LANCHESTER(a)
.........SCHIAPARELLI(c)
Elton .................JOHN(x)
Elvis.........COSTELLO(x)
.....................PRESLEY(x)
Elway, .............JOHN(l)
Elwes, .............CARY(a)
Emerson, ......
.................RALPH WALDO(t)
Emil .......JANNINGS(a)
.....................ZATOPEK(s)
Emile .........GRIFFITH(g)
.........................ZOLA(z)
Emiliano .......ZAPATA(u)
Emilio.........ESTEVEZ(a)
Emily .........BRONTE(z)
.................DICKINSON(t)
.........................POST(z)
Emma .............CALVE(x)
.................LAZARUS(t)
.....................SAMMS(a)
.................THOMPSON(a)
Emmett.............KELLY(j)
Emmylou...HARRIS(x)
Engelbert ......
.................HUMPERDINCK(k)
.................HUMPERDINCK(x)
Engels, ......
.................FRIEDRICH(u)
English, .............ALEX(f)
Englund, ....ROBERT(a)
Enid .........BAGNOLD(z)
Eno, .................BRIAN(r)
Enos .....SLAUGHTER(e)
Enrico.........CARUSO(x)
.....................FERMI(w)
Ephron, .........NORA(z)
Eric .............AMBLER(z)
.....................BLORE(a)
.................CARMEN(x)
.................CLAPTON(x)
.................DICKERSON(l)
.....................FROMM(z)
.....HEIDEN(s), IDLE(j)
.................ROBERTS(a)
.................ROHMER(q)
.....................STOLTZ(a)
Erica .............JONG(z)
Erich ......LEINSDORF(r)
.........Von STROHEIM(a)
Erich Maria
.................REMARQUE(z)
Erik .........ESTRADA(a)
.....................SATIE(k)
Erin.................GRAY(a)
.....................MORAN(a)
Erle Stanley ......
.................GARDNER(z)
Erma.........BOMBECK(o)

Flack, ......ROBERTA(x)
Flannery......................
...............O'CONNOR(z)
Flaubert, ...GUSTAVE(z)
Fleetwood, ........MICK(r)
Fleming, ......................
.........ALEXANDER(w)
.........IAN(z), PEGGY(s)
..................RHONDA(a)
.....................VICTOR(q)
Fletcher, ......LOUISE(a)
Flip ..............WILSON(j)
Florence......................
........HENDERSON(a)
Florenz....ZIEGFELD(q)
Floyd ...PATTERSON(g)
Floyd, ....RAYMOND (m)
Flynn, ..........ERROL(x)
.........................JOE(a)
Foch, .................NINA(a)
Fogelberg, .........DAN(x)
Fogerty, ...........JOHN(x)
Fokine, ....MICHAEL(a)
Foley, .....THOMAS S.(u)
Follows, .......MEGAN(a)
Fonda, ......BRIDGET(a)
.....................HENRY(a)
......JANE(a), PETER(a)
Fontaine, ........JOAN(a)
Fonteyn, ...MARGOT(a)
Forbes, ...MALCOLM(h)
Ford, ............BETTY(u)
.........FORD MADOX(z)
..................GERALD(u)
...................GLENN(a)
.............HARRISON(a)
......HENRY(h), JOHN(q)
.............TENNESSEE
...ERNIE(x), WHITEY(e)
Ford Madox.....FORD(z)
Foreman, ...GEORGE(g)
Forester, ............C.S.(z)
Forget, ..............GUY(y)
Forman, .........MILOS(q)
Forrest.........TUCKER(a)
Forster, .............E.M.(z)
Forsythe, ........JOHN(a)
Fortas, ..............ABE(u)
Fosbury, ..........DICK(s)
Fosse, ................BOB(q)
Foster, ..........JODIE(a)
.................PRESTON(a)
.............STEPHEN(k)
Foucault, ........JEAN(w)
Fountain, ..........PETE(r)
Fouts, .................DAN(l)
Fowles, ..........JOHN(z)
Fox, ..........EDWARD(a)
...................JAMES(a)
.............MICHAEL J.(a)

Foxworth, ...ROBERT(a)
Foxx, ..............JIMMY(e)
.........................REDD(j)
Foy, ..............EDDIE(a)
Foyt, ....................A.J.(v)
Fra ..........ANGELICO(c)
Fra Filippo..........LIPPI(c)
Frampton, ......PETER(x)
Fran......TARKENTON(l)
France, ....ANATOLE(z)
Frances..............ALDA(x)
..................FARMER(a)
........STERNHAGEN(a)
Franchot...........TONE(a)
Franciosa, ......TONY(a)
Francis............BACON(c)
..................POULENC(k)
Francis, ..........ANNE(a)
......................ARLENE(a)
......CONNIE(x), DICK(z)
Francisco ....FRANCO(u)
Francis Ford ..............
..................COPPOLA(q)
Francis Scott....KEY(t)
Francis X. ...................
................BUSHMAN(a)
Franco............HARRIS(l)
............ZEFFIRELLI(q)
Franco, .......................
.........FRANCISCO(u)
François ..DUVALIER(u)
..................MAURIAC(z)
..............MITTERRAND(u)
..................RABELAIS(z)
.................TRUFFAUT(q)
.....................VILLON(t)
Frakes, ...JONATHAN(a)
Frank ......BORMAN(d)
................BORZAGE(q)
....................CAPRA(q)
..................CHANCE(e)
..................DEFORD(o)
..................GIFFORD(l)
..................GORSHIN(a)
..................HERBERT(z)
..................HOWARD(e)
................LANGELLA(a)
....................LLOYD(q)
..................LORENZO(h)
.....MUIR(z), PARKER(y)
.............ROBINSON(e)
.............SEDGMAN(y)
...................SESNO(o)
................SHORTER(s)
..................SINATRA(x)
..................TASHLIN(q)
..................ZAPPA(r)
Frankenheimer, .........
........................JOHN(q)
Frankfurter, ......FELIX(u)

Frankie.........AVALON(x)
.........................LAINE(x)
......LYMON(x), VALLI(x)
Franklin, ......ARETHA(x)
............BENJAMIN(u, w)
........BONNIE(a), JOE(o)
Franklin Delano ..........
............ROOSEVELT(u)
Frank Lloyd...................
.....................WRIGHT(b)
Frann, .............MARY(a)
Frans.................HALS(c)
Franz .............KAFKA(z)
.......KLINE(c), LEHAR(k)
.........LISZT(k), MARC(c)
..................SCHUBERT(k)
Franz Joseph ..............
......................HAYDN(k)
Fraser, ...........DAWN(s)
.......................NEALE(y)
Frawley, .....WILLIAM(a)
Frazier, ...............JOE(g)
Fred..................ALLEN(l)
.....................ASTAIRE(a)
.............BILETNIKOFF(l)
.................COUPLES(m)
....................DRYER(a,l)
....................GWYNNE(a)
.............MacMURRAY(a)
.................McGRIFF(e)
.......................PERRY(y)
.....................ROGERS(a)
.....................SAVAGE(a)
.....................STOLLE(y)
.......................WARD(a)
.............ZINNEMANN(q)
Freda...........PAYNE(x)
Freddie .....MERCURY(x)
.....................PRINZE(j)
Freddy.........CANNON(x)
.....................FENDER(x)
Frederic ........CHOPIN(k)
......................MISTRAL(t)
.................REMINGTON(c)
Frederick.....CHURCH(c)
.........................POHL(z)
Frederick L. ...............
...................OLMSTED(b)
Fredric ..........MARCH(a)
Freeman ......GOSDEN(j)
Freeman, ...MORGAN(a)
Freleng, ..........FRIZ(i)
French, ........................
....DANIEL CHESTER(c)
...................MARILYN(z)
Freud, ......SIGMUND(w)
Frey, ................GLEN(x)
Friedan, .........BETTY(z)
Friedkin, .....WILLIAM(q)

George Frederic .............
...................WATTS(c)
George Frideric.............
.............HANDEL(k)
George M. .....COHAN(q)
George Roy .........HILL(q)
George S. ......................
................KAUFMAN(z)
Georges .........BIZET(k)
...............BRAQUE(c)
................DANTON(u)
................ROUAULT(c)
................SEURAT(c)
George T. ......................
...........DELACORTE(h)
George Wesley ..............
............BELLOWS(c)
Georgia .....O'KEEFFE(c)
Gephardt, ..RICHARD(u)
Gerald .............FORD(u)
.............McRANEY(a)
Geraldine ......................
............FITZGERALD(a)
......................PAGE(a)
Geraldo .........RIVERA(o)
Gerard ...DEPARDIEU(a)
Gere, ........RICHARD(a)
Germond.............JACK(o)
Gerry........MULLIGAN(r)
................RAFFERTY(x)
Gershwin, ..GEORGE(k)
......................IRA(a)
Gertrude.........ASTOR(a)
......................BERG(j)
.............LAWRENCE(a)
......................STEIN(z)
Gerulaitis, ........VITAS(y)
Getty, .........ESTELLE(a)
............JEAN PAUL(h)
Getz, ................STAN(r)
Ghostley, .......ALICE(a)
Giacometti, ...................
................ALBERTO(c)
Giacomo .......................
............MEYERBEER(k)
................PUCCINI(k)
Gian-Carlo .....................
................MENOTTI(k)
Gianlorenzo ...................
................BERNINI(c)
Gibb, ...............ANDY(x)
.......................BARRY(x)
................MAURICE(x)
......................ROBIN(x)
Gibbs, .........MARLA(a)
Gibran, .........KAHLIL(t)
Gibson, ......ALTHEA(y)
....BOB(e), CHARLES(o)
....DEBBIE(x), HENRY(j)
.............HOOT(a), MEL(a)

Gide, .............ANDRE(z)
Gielgud, ..........JOHN(a)
Gifford, ...........FRANK(l)
Gig ................YOUNG(a)
Gigi .......FERNANDEZ(y)
Gil ..............HODGES(e)
Gilbert...........ROLAND(a)
.......................STUART(c)
Gilbert, ...........CASS(b)
......................JOHN(a)
....MELISSA(a),SARA(a)
Gilberto, .....ASTRUD(x)
Gilda ..........RADNER(a)
Gillespie, ..........DIZZY(r)
Gillette, .........ANITA(a)
Gilley, ..........MICKEY(x)
Gilliam, ..........TERRY(j)
Gilmore, .........ARTIS(f)
Gilmour, .........DAVID(r)
Gina ...........................
.........LOLLOBRIGIDA(a)
Ginger ........ROGERS(a)
Gingold, .HERMIONE(a)
Gingrich, ........NEWT(u)
Gino .....CAPPELLETTI(l)
Ginsberg, ........ALLEN(t)
Gioacchino...ROSSINI(k)
Giovanni........BELLINI(c)
................BOCCACCIO(t)
................CIMABUE(c)
................TIEPOLO(c)
Giraudoux, ........JEAN(z)
Gisele .....MacKENZIE(x)
Gish, ........DOROTHY(a)
......................LILLIAN(a)
Giuseppe ........VERDI(k)
Givens, ..........ROBIN(a)
Gladstone, ..WILLIAM(u)
Gladys ..........KNIGHT(x)
Glasgow, ........ELLEN(t)
Glass, .............PHILIP(k)
Glavine, ...........TOM(e)
Gleason, .........JACKIE(j)
Glen.........CAMPBELL(x)
......................FREY(x)
Glenda.......JACKSON(a)
Glenn ...........CLOSE(a)
......FORD(a), GOULD(k)
................MILLER(r)
........YARBOROUGH(x)
Glenn, .......JOHN(d, u)
......................SCOTT(a)
Gless, ........SHARON(a)
Gloria........DeHAVEN(a)
................ESTEFAN(a)
................GRAHAME(a)
................LORING(a, x)
................STEINEM(o)
................SWANSON(a)
.............VANDERBILT(h)

Glover, .........DANNY(a)
Gluck, .............ALMA(x)
................CHRISTOPH(k)
Glynis .............JOHNS(a)
Godard, .....JEAN-LUC(q)
Goddard, ......................
................PAULETTE(a)
Godden, ......RUMER(z)
Gödel, ...........KURT(w)
Godfrey, .....ARTHUR(j)
Godunov, ......BORIS(a)
Gogol, .........NIKOLAI(z)
Golda ...........MEIR(u)
Goldberg, .......RUBE(i)
................WHOOPI(a)
Goldblum, .......JEFF(a)
Goldie ..........HAWN(a)
Golding, .....WILLIAM(z)
Goldman, ......JAMES(z)
Goldsboro, ....BOBBY(x)
Goldsmith, ....OLIVER(z)
Goldwater, ....BARRY(u)
Goldwyn, ....SAMUEL(q)
Gomez, ........LEFTY(e)
Gonzales, ...PANCHO(y)
Gooden, ......DWIGHT(e)
Goodman, ......BENNY(r)
......................JOHN(a)
Goodyear, .....................
................CHARLES(w)
Goolagong ...................
................EVONNE(y)
Gorbachev, ..................
................MIKHAIL(u)
......................RAISA(u)
Gorcey, ............LEO(j)
Gordie .............HOWE(n)
Gordimer, .....NADINE(z)
Gordon ...JOHNCOCK(v)
......................JUMP(z)
................LIGHTFOOT(x)
................MacRAE(a, x)
................PINSENT(a)
Gordon, ........DEXTER(r)
........GALE(a), RUTH(a)
Gore ................VIDAL(z)
Gore, ................AL(u)
................LESLEY(x)
................TIPPER(u)
Gorky, .......ARSHILE(c)
................MAXIM(z)
Gorme, ........EYDIE(x)
Gorshin, ......FRANK(a)
Gosden, ....FREEMAN(j)
Gossett, Jr., .....LOUIS(a)
Gottlieb.......DAIMLER(h)
Gould, ........CHESTER(i)
................ELLIOTT(a)
................GLENN(k)
................SHANE(s)

## Goulet / Hamilton

Goulet, ........ROBERT(x)
Gounod, ...CHARLES(k)
Gowdy, ............CURT(o)
Gower .....CHAMPION(a)
Grable, ..........BETTY(a)
Grace..............JONES(x)
........KELLY(a), SLICK(x)
Gracie ............ALLEN(j)
....................FIELDS(a)
Graf, ............STEFFI(y)
Grafton, ............SUE(z)
Graham .....CHAPMAN(j)
..................GREENE(z)
..........HILL(v), NASH(x)
..................PARKER(x)
Graham, .........BOB(a)
..................DAVID(m)
.....MARTHA(a), OTTO(l)
..................VIRGINIA(a)
Grahame, .....GLORIA(a)
Graig .........NETTLES(e)
Gramm, ............LOU(x)
......................PHIL(u)
Grammer, ....KELSEY(a)
Grange, ............RED(l)
Granger, .....FARLEY(a)
..................STEWART(a)
Grant............TINKER(h)
..................WOOD(c)
Grant, ............AMY(a)
..........CARY(a), LEE(a)
..........ULYSSES S.(p,u)
Grass, ........GUNTER(z)
Grau, .SHIRLEY ANN(z)
Graves, .........PETER(a)
..................ROBERT(z)
Gray, ...............ASA(w)
.........ERIN(a), LINDA(a)
..................THOMAS(t)
Grayson, .KATHRYN(a)
Graziano, ......ROCKY(g)
Greeley, .....HORACE(o)
Green, ........ADOLPH(a)
........AL(x), HUBERT(m)
Greenberg, .....HANK(e)
Greene, ............BOB(o)
..................GRAHAM(a)
..................LORNE(a)
..................MICHELE(a)
..................SHECKY(j)
Greenfield, ......JEFF(o)
Greenstreet, ..................
..................SYDNEY(a)
Greer .........GARSON(a)
Greg ................LAKE(x)
..........LOUGANIS(s)
..................MORRIS(a)
..................NORMAN(m)
Gregg...........ALLMAN(r)
Gregor ........MENDEL(w)

Gregory ...HARRISON(a)
........HINES(a), PECK(a)
Gregory, ..........DICK(j,u)
Greta .............GARBO(a)
Gretzky, .......WAYNE(n)
Grey, ........JENNIFER(a)
..........JOEL(a), ZANE(z)
Grieg, ..........EDVARD(k)
Griese, ............BOB(l)
Griffin ..........DUNNE(a)
Griffin, ............MERV(x)
Griffith, ............ANDY(a)
..........D.W.(q), EMILE(g)
......................HUGH(a)
..................MELANIE(a)
Grimes, ......MARTHA(z)
..................TAMMY(a)
Grimm, ..........JAKOB(z)
..................WILHELM(z)
Gris, ...............JUAN(c)
Grisham, .........JOHN(z)
Grissom, .......VIRGIL(d)
Grizzard, ....GEORGE(a)
Grodin, .....CHARLES(a)
Groening, ........MATT(i)
Grofe, ..........FERDE(k)
Groh, .............DAVID(a)
Gropius, .....WALTER(b)
Grosbard, .......ULU(q)
Gross, ............MARY(a)
..................MICHAEL(a)
Groucho (Julius) .............
..................MARX(j)
Grove, .............LEFTY(e)
Grover ..ALEXANDER(e)
..................CLEVELAND(u)
Groza, ............LOU(a)
Guardino, ......HARRY(a)
Guest, ..........EDGAR(t)
Guevara, ........CHE(p,u)
Guglielmo ..................
..................MARCONI(w)
Guido ............RENI(c)
Guillaume, ..ROBERT(a)
Guillermo..........VILAS(y)
Guinness, ......ALEC(a)
Guion .......BLUFORD(d)
Guisewite, .....CATHY(i)
Guitry, ......SACHA(a, z)
Gulagher .........CLU(a)
Gumble, .....BRYANT(o)
Gummo (Milton) ..............
..................MARX(j)
Günter..........GRASS(z)
Gus ...............BELL(a)
Gustav ..........HOLST(k)
..................KLIMT(c)
..................MAHLER(k)
Gustave ....COURBET(c)
..................FLAUBERT(z)

Guthrie, ............ARLO(x)
..................WOODY(x)
Guttenberg, ...STEVE(a)
Gutzon......BORGLUM(c)
Guy.............FORGET(y)
..................KIBBEE(a)
..................LOMBARDO(r)
Guy, ............JASMINE(a)
Gwen......TORRENCE(a)
..................VERDON(a)
Gwenn, .......EDMUND(a)
Gwynn, ..........TONY(e)
Gwynne, .........FRED(a)
Gypsy Rose........LEE(a)

H.G. ............WELLS(z)
H.H. (Saki) ....MUNRO(z)
H.L. .........MENCKEN(z)
H.Ross.......PEROT(h, u)
H.Ryder....HAGGARD(z)
Hackett, .........BUDDY(j)
Hackman, .......GENE(a)
Hagar, .........SAMMY(x)
Hagen, .............UTA(a)
..................WALTER(m)
Haggard, ...H.RYDER(z)
..................MERLE(x)
Hagler, .........MARVIN(g)
Hagman, ........LARRY(a)
Hahn, ............OTTO(w)
Haid, ........CHARLES(a)
Haig, ....ALEXANDER(p)
..................DOUGLAS(p)
Haile..........SELASSIE(u)
Hailey, ........ARTHUR(z)
Haim, ............COREY(a)
Hal .........HOLBROOK(a)
..................LINDEN(a)
Halas, .........GEORGE(l)
Halberstam, ....DAVID(z)
Hale ..............IRWIN(m)
Hale, ..............ALAN(a)
..................BARBARA(a)
..................NATHAN(p)
Haley, ............ALEX(z)
..................BILL(r)
..................JACK(a)
Hall, .........ARSENIO(j)
..................DARYL(r)
..................DEIDRE(a)
..................HUNTZ(a)
..................MONTY(a)
..................TOM T.(x)
Halldór .......LAXNESS(z)
Halle............BERRY(a)
Halley, ........EDMUND(w)
Hals, .............FRANS(c)
Hamel, ...VERONICA(a)
Hamill, ............MARK(a)
Hamilton...........CAMP(a)

Jack continued............
....................CARSON(j)
....................CARTER(j)
...................DEMPSEY(g)
....................ELAM(a)
................GERMOND(o)
....................HALEY(a)
.................HAWKINS(a)
.......HOLT(a), JONES(x)
....................KEMP(a)
...................KEROUAC(z)
.................KLUGMAN(a)
...................KRAMER(y)
...................LEMMON(a)
...LONDON(z), LORD(a)
................NICHOLSON(a)
....................NICKLAUS(m)
.....OAKIE(a), PAAR(j)
...................PALANCE(a)
....SOO(j), WARDEN(b)
....................WEBB(a)
....................WESTON(a)
Jackie..........COLLINS(z)
...................COOGAN(a)
...................COOPER(a)
.............DeSHANNON(a)
.................GLEASON(j)
....................MASON(a)
.................ROBINSON(e)
...................STEWART(v)
....................WILSON(x)
Jacklin, ...........TONY(m)
Jackson ......BROWNE(x)
.................POLLOCK(c)
Jackson....ANDREW(u)
.........ANNE(a), BO(l)
...................GLENDA(a)
....................JANET(x)
...................JERMAINE(a)
.....JESSE(u), JOE(x)
....KATE(a), MAHALIA(x)
...................MICHAEL(x)
...................REGGIE(e)
....................THOMAS
.................(Stonewall)(p)
...................VICTORIA(j)
Jaclyn...............SMITH(a)
Jacob..................RIIS(o)
Jacobi, .........DEREK(a)
Jacopo ........BELLINI(c)
Jacqueline .....BISSET(a)
Jacques ............
.................COUSTEAU(w)
...................LIPCHITZ(c)
...........OFFENBACH(k)
Jacques-Louis ...........
.....................DAVID(c)
Jaffe, ...............SAM(a)
Jagger, ...........DEAN(a)
....................MICK(x)

Jake ...............GARN(d,u)
....................LAMOTTA(g)
Jakob .........GRIMM(z)
James................AGEE(z)
....................ARNESS(a)
....................BELUSHI(a)
...................BOSWELL(z)
.................BRODERICK(a)
....................BROLIN(a)
....................BROWN(x)
....................BUCHANAN(u)
....CAAN(a), CAGNEY(a)
....................CLAVELL(z)
................:.COBURN(a)
......DEAN(a), DICKEY(z)
.................FARENTINO(a)
.......FOX(a), GALWAY(r)
....................GARNER(a)
...................GOLDMAN(z)
....................HOBAN(b)
....................HOFFA(h)
....................INGRAM(x)
......IVORY(q), JONES(z)
.....JOYCE(z), LEVINE(r)
.........LOVELL, Jr.(d)
..................MADISON(u)
....................MASON(a)
...................MONROE(u)
....................POLK(b)
.....................RESTON(o)
....................SPADER(a)
....................STEWART(a)
....................TAYLOR(x)
...................THURBER(z)
....................WATT(w)
.................WHITMORE(a)
....................WOODS(a)
....................WORTHY(f)
James, ...........ETTA(x)
...................HARRY(r)
...................HENRY(z)
.............TOMMY(x)
...............WILLIAM(z)
James A. .......BAKER(u)
.................GARFIELD(u)
...................MICHENER(z)
James Abbott McNeill.....
.............WHISTLER(c)
James Clerk...........
.................MAXWELL(w)
James Earl .....JONES(a)
James Fenimore............
.................COOPER(z)
James J. ...CORBETT(g)
James L. ....BROOKS(q)
James M. .........CAIN(z)
....................IVES(c)
Jameson ......PARKER(a)
Jamie .............FARR(a)
Jamie Lee .....CURTIS(a)

Jan ..............HAMMER(r)
....................HOOKS(j)
....................NERUDA(t)
....................PEERCE(x)
....SMUTS(u), STEEN(c)
.........STEPHENSON(m)
....................VERMEER(c)
Jana .........NOVOTNA(y)
Jane......ALEXANDER(a)
....................AUSTEN(z)
....................BRODY(o)
....................CURTIN(a)
....................FONDA(a)
....................PAULEY(o)
....................POWELL(a)
....................RUSSELL(a)
...................SEYMOUR(a)
....................WITHERS(a)
....................WYATT(a)
....................WYMAN(a)
Jane Bryant ....QUINN(o)
Janet .............EVANS(s)
...................GAYNOR(a)
...................JACKSON(x)
....................LEIGH(a)
...............MARGOLIN(a)
Janis....................IAN(x)
.....JOPLIN(x), PAIGE(a)
Jan-Michael ...........
....................VINCENT(a)
Jann ...........WENNER(o)
Jannings, ...........EMIL(a)
Janssen, .........DAVID(a)
January, .........DON(m)
Jarreau, ..............AL(x)
Jarrett, .............KEITH(r)
Jascha......HEIFETZ(r)
Jasmine ............GUY(a)
Jason ...ALEXANDER(a)
...................BATEMAN(a)
.........ROBARDS, JR.(a)
Jasper ...........JOHNS(c)
Jawaharlal .....NEHRU(u)
Jay ..................LENO(j)
....................THOMAS(a)
Jay, ..................JOHN(u)
Jayne .......KENNEDY(a)
...............MANSFIELD(a)
...................MEADOWS(a)
Jayne Anne..............
....................PHILLIPS(z)
Jean ............ARTHUR(a)
.................COCTEAU(z)
.................FOUCAULT(w)
....................GENET(z)
................GIRAUDOUX(z)
....................HARLOW(a)
....................MARSH(a)
....................RACINE(z)
....................RENOIR(q)

| | | |
|---|---|---|
| Joffe, .........ROLAND(q) | .................HERSEY(z) | John C. .....CALHOUN(u) |
| Joffrey, ........ROBERT(a) | .................HILLERMAN(a) | Johncock, ..GORDON(v) |
| Johann.......STRAUSS(k) | .................HODIAK(a) | John Cougar |
| Johanna.........SPYRI(z) | .................HOUSEMAN(a) | .........MELLENCAMP(x) |
| Johann Christian | ....HURT(a), HUSTON(q) | John D. |
| .................BACH(k) | .....IRVING(z), JAY(u) | .................MacDONALD(z) |
| Johannes ....BRAHMS(k) | .....KANDER(k), KAY(x) | .................ROCKEFELLER(h) |
| .................KEPLER(w) | .................KEATS(t), KERR(a) | John F. ....KENNEDY(u) |
| Johann Sebastian | .................KNOWLES(z) | John Foster |
| .................BACH(k) | .................La FARGE(c) | .................DULLES(u) |
| Johansson, | .................LANDIS(q) | John Gregory |
| .................INGEMAR(g) | .................LARROQUETTE(a) | .................DUNNE(z) |
| John.............ADAMS(u) | .................Le CARRE(z) | John Jacob ....ASTOR(h) |
| .....AGAR(a), AMOS(a) | .................LEGUIZAMO(j) | John James |
| .................ASTIN(a) | .................LENNON(r) | .................AUDUBON(c,w) |
| .................BARRYMORE(a) | .................LITHGOW(a) | John Kenneth |
| .................BARTH(z) | .................LOCKE(z) | .................GALBRAITH(z) |
| .................BELUSHI(a,j) | .................MADDEN(l) | John L. .....SULLIVAN(g) |
| .................BERRYMAN(t) | .................MAJOR(u) | John M. .....SYNGE(t,z) |
| .................BETJEMAN(t) | .................MALKOVICH(a) | John Maynard |
| .................BRODIE(l,m) | .................MARIN(c) | .................KEYES(z) |
| .................BRUNNER(z) | .................MARSHALL(u) | Johnnie .............RAY(x) |
| .................BUCHAN(z) | .................MASEFIELD(t) | John Nance |
| .................BUNYAN(z) | .................McENROE(y) | .................GARNER(u) |
| .................BURGOYNE(p) | .................McGRAW(e) | Johnny .........BENCH(e) |
| .....CAGE(k), CANDY(a) | .....McVIE(r), MILLS(a) | .....CARSON(j), CASH(x) |
| .................CARPENTER(q) | .....MILTON(t), MUIR(w) | .....DEPP(a), HART(i) |
| .................CARRADINE(a) | .................NAPIER(w) | .................MATHIS(x) |
| .................CASSAVETES(q) | .................NEWCOMBE(y) | .................MILLER(m) |
| .................CHANCELLOR(o) | .................O'HARA(z) | .................PAYCHECK(x) |
| .................CHEEVER(z) | .................OLERUD(e) | .................RIVERS(x) |
| .................CIARDI(t) | .................OSBORNE(z) | .................RUTHERFORD(v) |
| .................CLEESE(j) | .................PERSHING(p) | .................TILLOTSON(x) |
| .................COLTRANE(r) | .................RAITT(x) | .................UNITAS(x) |
| .................CONSTABLE(c) | ....RATZENBERGER(a) | .....WEISSMULLER(a,s) |
| .................COOK(m) | .................RIGGINS(l) | John Paul .......JONES(p) |
| .................CUSACK(a) | .................RITTER(a) | .................STEVENS(u) |
| .................DALY(m) | .................SAXON(a) | John Peter...ZENGER(o) |
| .................DAVIDSON(x) | .................SAYLES(q) | John Philip .....SOUSA(k) |
| .................DENVER(x) | .................SCHLESINGER(z) | John Pierpont |
| ....DEREK(a), DONNE(t) | .................SEBASTIAN(x) | .................MORGAN(h) |
| ....DOS PASSOS(z) | .................SHEA(a) | John Quincy ..ADAMS(u) |
| .................DRYDEN(t) | .................SINGLETON(q) | Johns, .........GLYNIS(a) |
| .................DUNS SCOTUS(z) | .................SLOAN(c) | .................JASPER(c) |
| .....ELWAY(l), EVERS(e) | .................STAMOS(a) | John Singer |
| .................FOGERTY(x) | .................STEINBECK(z) | .................SARGENT(c) |
| .................FORD(q) | .................STOCKTON(f) | John Singleton |
| .................FORSYTHE(a) | .................SUNUNU(u) | .................COPLEY(c) |
| .................FOWLES(z) | .................TRAVOLTA(a) | Johnson, ....ANDREW(u) |
| ....FRANKENHEIMER(z) | .................TRUMBULL(c) | .................ARTE(j), DON(a) |
| .................GALSWORTHY(z) | ....TYLER(u), UPDIKE(z) | .................HOWARD(e) |
| .................GARFIELD(a) | .................VARLEY(z) | .................HOWARD(h) |
| .................GAY(k,t) | .................WAITE(x) | .................LYNDON(u) |
| .................GIELGUD(a) | .................WANAMAKER(h) | .......MAGIC(f), PHILIP(b) |
| .................GILBERT(a) | .................WATERS(q) | .................SAMUEL(z) |
| .................GLENN(d, u) | .................WAYNE(a) | .....VAN(a), WALTER(e) |
| .................GOODMAN(a) | .................WILLIAMS(k) | John Steuart...CURRY(c) |
| .................GRISHAM(z) | .................WOODEN(f) | Johnston, .........LYNN(i) |
| .................HANCOCK(u) | .................WYNDHAM(z) | John Stuart........MILL(z) |
| .................HAVLICEK(f) | John, .............ELTON(x) | John W..........YOUNG(d) |

| Lee, *continued*.............. | Leonard, .....ELMORE(z) | Lincoln, ....ABRAHAM(u) |
|---|---|---|
| ...............MICHELE(a) | ....RAY(g), SHELDON(j) | ...................ELMO(a) |
| ...................PEGGY(x) | Leonardo......da VINCI(c) | Lind, ...............JENNY(x) |
| ..............ROBERT E.(p) | Leoncavallo, ............ | Linda ...............BLAIR(a) |
| .........SPIKE(q), STAN(i) | ...............RUGGIERO(k) | ...............DARNELL(a) |
| Lee A. .......IACOCCA(h) | Leonhard .........EULER(w) | .....EVANS(a), GRAY(x) |
| Lee J. ................COBB(a) | Leor.id.....BREZHNEV(u) | ..................HAMILTON(a) |
| Lefty ..............GOMEZ(e) | Leontyne........PRICE(x) | .........HUNT(a), LAVIN(a) |
| .....................GROVE(e) | Leopold ...........AUER(r) | ................RONSTADT(x) |
| Le Gallienne, ......EVA(a) | ...............STOKOWSKI(r) | Lindbergh.................... |
| Léger, ......FERNAND(c) | Leroy "Satchel" ............ | .....ANNE MORROW(z) |
| Legrand, .......MICHEL(r) | ...................PAIGE(e) | ..................CHARLES(d) |
| LeGuin, ..URSULA K.(z) | LeRoy, .......MERVYN(a) | Linden, ................HAL(a) |
| Leguizamo, ....JOHN(j) | Les..............ASPIN(u) | Lindfors, ......VIVECA(a) |
| Lehár, ...........FRANZ(k) | ...................BROWN(r) | Lindsay ..ANDERSON(q) |
| Lehmann, ....LOTTE(x) | Le Sage, ......ALAIN(z) | ...................CROUSE(a) |
| Lehrer, ..............JIM(o) | Lesley ............GORE(x) | ...................WAGNER(a) |
| Leiber, ...........FRITZ(z) | ...................STAHL(o) | Lindsay, .......VACHEL(t) |
| Leibman, ..........RON(a) | Lesley Ann ......DOWN(a) | Linkletter, ........ART(j) |
| Leigh, ...........JANET(a) | ...................WARREN(a) | Linn-Baker, ....MARK(a) |
| .....JENNIFER JASON(a) | Leslie ...........CARON(a) | Linus ......PAULING(w) |
| ...................VIVIEN(a) | ...................HOWARD(a) | Lionel..........ATWILL(a) |
| Leinsdorf, .......ERICH(r) | ...................NIELSEN(a) | ..................BARRYMORE(a) |
| Leisure, ........DAVID(j) | ...................UGGAMS(x) | .................HAMPTON(r) |
| Lema, .............TONY(m) | Lessing, ........DORIS(z) | ....................RICHIE(x) |
| Le May, ......CURTIS(p) | Letterman, .......DAVID(j) | ..................STANDER(a) |
| Lemieux, ........MARIO(n) | Levant, .........OSCAR(a) | Liotta, ..............RAY(a) |
| Lemmon, ........JACK(a) | LeVar ...........BURTON(a) | Lipchitz, ...JACQUES(c) |
| Len ...........BERMAN(o) | Levin, .............IRA(z) | Lippi, ......FILIPPINO(c) |
| ...................CARIOU(a) | Levine, .........DAVID(l) | ..................FRA FILIPPO(c) |
| ...................DAWSON(l) | ...................IRVING R.(o) | Lippmann, ..WALTER(o) |
| ...................DYKSTRA(e) | ...................JAMES(r) | Lisa..........ALTHER(z) |
| Lena ...........HORNE(x) | Levinson, .......BARRY(q) | ...................BONET(a) |
| ...................OLIN(a) | Levon, ........HELM(a,x) | ...................EICHHORN(a) |
| Lendl, .............IVAN(y) | Lew ................AYRES(a) | ...................HARTMAN(a) |
| L'Enfant, ......PIERRE(b) | ...................WALLACE(z) | Lise ...........MEITNER(w) |
| Lenin, ............ | Lewis .........CARROLL(z) | Lisi, ...........VIRNA(a) |
| .....VLADIMIR ILYICH(u) | ...................MILESTONE(q) | Lister, .........JOSEPH(w) |
| Lennon, ........JULIAN(x) | ...................STONE(a) | Liston, .........SONNY(g) |
| ..............JOHN(r, x, z) | Lewis, ...........C.S.(z) | Liszt, ...........FRANZ(k) |
| Lennox, ........ANNIE(a) | ...................CARL(s) | Lithgow, ........JOHN(a) |
| Lenny ..............BRUCE(j) | ....HUEY(x), JERRY(j) | Little, ........CLEAVON(a) |
| Leno, ...............JAY(j) | ...................JERRY LEE(x) | ...............MALCOLM X(u) |
| Lenya, ...........LOTTE(x) | ...................JOE E.(a) | ....................RICH(x) |
| Leo ...........CARRILLO(a) | ...................RAMSEY(r) | Littler, ............GENE(m) |
| ...................DELIBES(k) | ...................RICHARD(j) | Liv ..........ULLMANN(a) |
| ...................GORCEY(j) | ...................SHARI(j) | Liz..........CLAIBORNE(h) |
| ...................SAYER(x) | .....SINCLAIR(z), TED(j) | ....................SMITH(o) |
| ...................TOLSTOY(z) | Liam .....O'FLAHERTY(z) | Liza ......MINNELLI(a,x) |
| Leo G. .......CARROLL(a) | Light, ..........JUDITH(a) | Lizabeth .......SCOTT(a) |
| Leon ...............AMES(a) | Lightfoot, ..GORDON(x) | Lloyd..........BENTSEN(u) |
| ...................ERROL(a) | Lilli ...........PALMER(a) | ...................BRIDGES(a) |
| ...................RUSSELL(x) | Lillian ..................GISH(a) | .....NOLAN(a), PRICE(x) |
| ...................SPINKS(g) | ...................HELLMAN(z) | ....................WANER(e) |
| ...TROTSKY(u), URIS(z) | ...................RUSSELL(x) | Lloyd, ............ |
| Leonard ...................... | Lillie ...........LANGTRY(a) | .........CHRISTOPHER(a) |
| ...............BERNSTEIN(k) | Lillie, ...........BEATRICE(j) | ...................FRANK(o) |
| ...................COHEN(t,x) | Lily...................PONS(x) | ...................HAROLD(j) |
| ...................MALTIN(o) | ...................TOMLIN(j) | Locke, ...............JOHN(z) |
| ...................NIMOY(a) | Lina ...WERTMULLER(q) | ...................SONDRA(a) |

## Magda / Martha

Magda ...........GABOR(a)
Maggie ...........SMITH(a)
Magic .........JOHNSON(f)
Magnani, ........ANNA(a)
Magritte, ........RENE(c)
Mahalia .....JACKSON(x)
Mahler, ........GUSTAV(k)
Mahre, ............PHIL(s)
Mailer, ........NORMAN(z)
Main, .........MARJORIE(a)
Major, ...........JOHN(u)
Majors, .............LEE(a)
Makeba, .........MIRIAM(x)
Malamud, ..BERNARD(z)
Malcolm ......FORBES(h)
............McDOWELL(a)
Malcolm-Jamal .............
.................WARNER(a)
Malcolm X......LITTLE(u)
Malden, ...........KARL(a)
Malkovich, ......JOHN(a)
Mallarmé, ....................
.................STEPHANE(t)
Malle, ............LOUIS(q)
Mallon, .............MEG(m)
Malone, ...DOROTHY(a)
.......KARL(f), MOSES(f)
Malory, .......THOMAS(z)
Malraux, .......ANDRE(z)
Maltin, .....LEONARD(o)
Mamet, .........DAVID(z)
Mamie .........................
..........EISENHOWER(u)
.............Van DOREN(a)
Man .................RAY(c)
Manchester, ...................
.................MELISSA(x)
Mancini, .....HENRY(k, r)
Mandel, .......HOWIE(j)
Mandela, ....NELSON(u)
Mandlikova, .....HANA(y)
Mandrel, ...BARBARA(x)
Mandy ......PATINKIN(a)
Manet, .....EDOUARD(c)
Mangione, .....CHUCK(r)
Manilow, .......BARRY(x)
Mankiewicz, ...................
.................JOSEPH L.(q)
Mann, .........BARRY(k)
................DELBERT(q)
..................HERBIE(r)
.................THOMAS(z)
Mansell, .......NIGEL(v)
Mansfield, .......JAYNE(a)
.............KATHERINE(z)
Mantle, .......MICKEY(e)
Mantovani, ...................
.............ANNUNZIO(r)
Mapplethorpe, ..............
.................ROBERT(c)

Marat, ....JEAN PAUL(u)
Maravich, .........PETE(f)
Marble, ..........ALICE(y)
Marc...........CHAGALL(c)
.................COHN(r,x)
............CONNELLY(z)
Marc, ............FRANZ(c)
Marceau, ....MARCEL(a)
Marcel ........DIONNE(n)
.................DUCHAMP(c)
.................MARCEAU(a)
.................PROUST(z)
Marcello ......................
..........MASTROIANNI(a)
March, .......FREDRIC(a)
Marchand, .....NANCY(a)
Marciano, ......ROCKY(g)
Marconi, ......................
.........GUGLIELMO(w)
Marcos, .......................
............FERDINAND(u)
.................IMELDA(u)
Marcus ...........ALLEN(l)
Margaret.....ATWOOD(z)
.................COURT(y)
................DRABBLE(z)
.................DUMONT(a)
.............HAMILTON(a)
.....................MEAD(z)
.................MITCHELL(z)
.................O'BRIEN(a)
..........RUTHERFORD(a)
..........SULLAVAN(a)
.............THATCHER(u)
Margaux. .....................
..........HEMINGWAY(a)
Marge.....CHAMPION(a)
Margolin, .......JANET(a)
Margot........FONTEYN(a)
..................KIDDER(a)
Maria.............BUENO(y)
.....................CALLAS(x)
...........MONTESSORI(w)
.........OUSPENSKAYA(a)
.................SCHELL(a)
..................SHRIVER(o)
Maria Conchita ..............
.................ALONSO(a)
Mariah .........CAREY(x)
Marian ....ANDERSON(x)
.................MERCER(a)
Marianne ...FAITHFUL(x)
Marichal, ........JUAN(e)
Marie .............CURIE(w)
.................DRESSLER(a)
.................OSMOND(x)
.....................WILSON(a)
Mariel ...HEMINGWAY(a)
Mariette......HARTLEY(a)
Marilu ........HENNER(a)

Marilyn.........FRENCH(z)
.................HORNE(x)
.................MONROE(a)
Marin, ........CHEECH(j)
.....................JOHN(c)
Marina............SIRTIS(a)
Marino, .............DAN(l)
Mario ........ANDRETTI(v)
....CUOMO(u), LANZA(x)
.................LEMIEUX(n)
.....................PUZO(z)
.........Van PEEBLES(a)
Marion ...........ROSS(a)
Maris, .........ROGER(e)
Marjorie ..........MAIN(a)
Mark.............................
.....CALCAVECCHIA(m)
.................CARRIER(l)
.................CLAYTON(l)
.....................DUPER(l)
.............GASTINEAU(l)
.................HAMILL(a)
.................HARMON(a)
.................KNOPFLER(r)
.............LINN-BAKER(a)
.................McGWIRE(e)
.................MESSIER(n)
.................O'MEARA(m)
.....................ROTHKO(c)
.................RUSSELL(a)
.....RYPIEN(l), SPITZ(s)
.....................TWAIN(z)
Markie.............POST(a)
Marla .............GIBBS(a)
Marlee ........MATLIN(a)
Marlene .....DIETRICH(a)
Marley, ...........BOB(x)
Marlo ........THOMAS(a)
Marlon.........BRANDO(a)
Marlowe, ......................
.............CHRISTOPHER(t)
Marquis, ...........DON(i)
Marr, .............DAVE(m)
Marriner, .....NEVILLE(r)
Marsalis, ......................
.................BRANFORD(r)
.................WYNTON(r)
Marsh, .........JEAN(a)
.................NGAIO(z)
Marsha .........MASON(a)
Marshall ....MCLUHAN(z)
Marshall, .......E.G.(a)
.............GEORGE C.(p)
.................HERBERT(a)
.......JOHN(u), PENNY(a)
.....................PETER(a)
.................THURGOOD(u)
Martha ........GRAHAM(a)
.................GRIMES(z)
.................REEVES(x)

168

Nadia.......COMANECI(s)
Nadine ....GORDIMER(z)
Nagel, ......CONRAD(a)
Nagurski, .....BRONKO(l)
Nagy, ................IMRE(u)
Naipaul, ..............V.S.(z)
Naish, ......J.CARROL(a)
Naldi, ................NITA(a)
Namath, ............JOE(l)
Nance, ..............JIM(l,o)
Nancy.............ALLEN(a)
............DUSSAULT(a)
......KULP(a), LOPEZ(m)
............MARCHAND(a)
................MITFORD(z)
..................REAGAN(u)
....................WALKER(a)
...................WILSON(x)
Nanette .......FABRAY(a)
Naomi .............JUDD(x)
Napier, ...........JOHN(w)
Napoleon................
............BONAPARTE(p)
Nash, ........GRAHAM(x)
..................OGDEN(t)
Nashe, .......THOMAS(z)
Nasser, .........GAMAL(u)
Nast, ..........THOMAS(l)
Nastase, ............ILIE(y)
Nastassia........KINSKI(x)
Nat "King" ......COLE(x)
Natalie ........COLE(x)
...................WOOD(a)
Nate .......ARCHIBALD(f)
..............THURMOND(f)
Nathan ..........HALE(z)
Nathanael........WEST(z)
Nathaniel........CURRIER(c)
..........HAWTHORNE(z)
Natwick, ....MILDRED(a)
Navratilova, .......
..............MARTINA(y)
Nazimova, ......ALLA(a)
Neagle, ..........ANNA(a)
Neal ..............HEFTI(r)
Neal, .........PATRICIA(a)
Neale .........FRASER(y)
Nealon, ...........KEVIN(j)
Ned..............BEATTY(a)
..................ROREM(o)
..................SPARKS(a)
Negri, .............POLA(a)
Nehemiah .............
..................PERSOFF(a)
Nehru, ....................
...........JAWAHARLAL(u)
Neil......ARMSTRONG(d)
..............DIAMOND(a)
..................SEDAKA(x)
....SIMON(z), YOUNG(x)

Neill, ................SAM(a)
Nell .............CARTER(a)
Nellie .............MELBA(x)
Nelligan, ...........KATE(a)
Nelson .............EDDY(x)
..................MANDELA(u)
..................PIQUET(v)
..................RIDDLE(r)
Nelson, .........BYRON(m)
.....ED(a), HARRIET(a)
...............HORATIO(p)
........JUDD(a), OZZIE(a)
.....RICKY(x), WILLIE(x)
Nelson A.
............ROCKEFELLER(u)
Neruda, ...............JAN(t)
..................PABLO(z)
Nesmith, .....MICHAEL(r)
Nettles, .........GRAIG(e)
Neuwirth, .......BEBE(a)
Nevers, .........ERNIE(l)
Neville..................
...........CHAMBERLAIN(u)
..................MARRINER(r)
Newcombe, ......JOHN(y)
Newhart, .............BOB(j)
Newley, ....ANTHONY(x)
Newman, .........PAUL(a)
...................RANDY(x)
Newt.........GINGRICH(u)
Newton, .........ISAAC(w)
......JUICE(x), WAYNE(x)
Newton-John, .......
..................OLIVIA(x)
Ney, ...........MICHEL(p)
Ngaio ............MARSH(z)
Niccolo .................
............MACHIAVELLI(z)
..................PAGANINI(r)
Nicholas .................
............COPERNICUS(w)
Nichols, ............MIKE(q)
..................RED(r)
Nicholson, .......JACK(a)
Nick .............FALDO(m)
......LOWE(x), NOLTE(a)
..................PRICE(a)
Nicklaus, ........JACK(m)
Nicks, ..........STEVIE(x)
Nicol.....WILLIAMSON(a)
Nicolai ...........RIMSKY-
..............KORSAKOV(k)
Nicolas .........CAGE(a)
..................ROEG(q)
Nicole .........KIDMAN(a)
Niekro, ............PHIL(e)
Niels ..............BOHR(w)
Nielsen, .......LESLIE(a)
Nietzsche, .............
..............FRIEDRICH(z)

Nigel ............BRUCE(a)
..................MANSELL(v)
Nijinsky, .......VASLAV(a)
Niki ................LAUDA(v)
Nikita...................
............KHRUSHCHEV(u)
Nikola ...........TESLA(w)
Nikolai ...........GOGOL(z)
Nilsson, ........BIRGIT(a)
..................HARRY(x)
Nimitz, ......CHESTER(p)
Nimoy, ......LEONARD(a)
Nin ................ANAIS(z)
Nina...................FOCH(a)
..................SIMONE(x)
Nino .......BENVENUTI(g)
Nipsey .......RUSSELL(j)
Nita ..............NALDI(a)
Nitschke, ............RAY(l)
Niven, ..........DAVID(a)
..................LARRY(z)
Nixon, .............OTIS(a)
.....PAT(u), RICHARD(u)
Noah .............BEERY(a)
Noah, .......YANNICK(y)
Noam........CHOMSKY(z)
Nobel ........ALFRED(w)
Noel ......HARRISON(x)
..................COWARD(k,z)
Noguchi, .........ISAMU(c)
Nolan ..............RYAN(e)
Nolan, ...........LLOYD(a)
Nolte, ..............NICK(a)
Noone, ..........PETER(x)
Nora ........EPHRON(z)
Norbert .......WIENER(w)
Norm ..........SNEAD(l)
...........Van BROCKLIN(l)
Norma.......SHEARER(a)
..................TALMADGE(a)
Norman ......COUSINS(z)
....FELL(a), JEWISON(q)
..................MAILER(z)
..................ROCKWELL(c)
........SCHWARZKOPF(p)
..................THOMAS(u)
Norman; ........GREG(m)
Normand, ......MABEL(a)
Norris, ..........CHUCK(a)
North, .........ANDY(m)
..................OLIVER(p)
..................SHEREE(a)
Norton, ........ANDRE(z)
..................KEN(g)
Norvo, ................RED(r)
Novak, ..............KIM(a)
..................ROBERT(o)
Novarro, ......RAMON(a)
Novello, ..........DON(j)
..................IVOR(a)

Peter *continued* ...............
...................NOONE(x)
...................O'TOOLE(a)
...................SCOLARI(a)
...................SELLERS(j)
...................SNELL(s)
...................STRAUSS(a)
...................THOMSON(m)
...................UEBERROTH(h)
...................USTINOV(a)
.........WEIR(q), WOLF(x)
...................YARROW(x)
Peter Ilyich ...................
.........TCHAIKOVSKY(k)
Peter Paul....RUBENS(c)
Peters, ...................
.........BERNADETTE(a)
...................ROBERTA(x)
Petit, ...........ROLAND(a)
Petty, ...................KYLE(v)
....LORI(a), RICHARD(v)
...................TOM(z)
Petula ...........CLARK(x)
Pfeiffer, ....MICHELLE(a)
Phil ...........COLLINS(x)
...................DONAHUE(o)
...................ESPOSITO(n)
...................EVERLY(x)
...GRAMM(u), HARRIS(j)
...................HARTMAN(a)
...................MAHRE(s)
...NIEKRO(e), OCHS(x)
...SILVERS(j), SIMMS(l)
...................SPECTOR(r)
Philip...............GLASS(k)
...................JOHNSON(b),
...................ROTH(z)
...................SHERIDAN(p)
...................WYLIE(z)
Philip José...FARMER(z)
Phillips, ...................
...................JAYNE ANNE(z)
...........LOU DIAMOND(a)
...................MacKENZIE(a)
...................MICHELLE(a)
Phoebe...........SNOW(x)
Phoenix, ...........RIVER(a)
Phylicia........RASHAD(a)
Phyllis ...........DILLER(j)
Pia ...............ZADORA(x)
Piaf, ...............EDITH(x)
Picasso, ...........PABLO(c)
Pickens, ...T. BOONE(h)
Pickett, ........WILSON(x)
Pickford, ...........MARY(a)
Pidgeon, .....WALTER(a)
Pie ...........TRAYNOR(e)
Pierce ......BROSNAN(a)
Pierce, ....FRANKLIN(u)
Pier Paolo..PASOLINI(q)

Pierre........BONNARD(c)
...................CURIE(w)
...................LAPLACE(w)
...................L'ENFANT(b)
Pierre Auguste...............
...................RENOIR(c)
Pierre Elliott ...................
...................TRUDEAU(u)
Pierre Paul ...................
...................PRUD'HON(c)
Piet......MONDRIAN(c)
Pieter........BRUEGEL(c)
Pietro......BELLUSCHI(b)
Pinchas...............
...................ZUCKERMAN(r)
Pinchot, ...BRONSON(a)
Pinsent, ......GORDON(a)
Pinter, ......HAROLD(q)
Pinza, ...............EZIO(x)
Piper...........LAURIE(a)
Pippen, .....SCOTTIE(f)
Piquet, ......NELSON(v)
Pirandello, ......LUIGI(z)
Piscopo, .........JOE(j)
Pissarro, ...CAMILLE(c)
Pitney, ...........GENE(x)
Pitt, ...........WILLIAM(u)
Pitts, ...............ZASU(a)
Placido ....DOMINGO(x)
Planck, ...........MAX(w)
Plant, ...........ROBERT(x)
Plath, ......SYLVIA(t,z)
Player, ...........GARY(m)
Pleasence, .DONALD(a)
Pleshette, ..SUZANNE(a)
Plowright, ...........JOAN(a)
Plumb, ...............EVE(a)
Plummer, ...AMANDA(a)
...................CHRISTOPHER(a)
Plunkett, ...........JIM(l)
Poe, ...................
.........EDGAR ALLAN(t,z)
Pohl, .....FREDERICK(z)
Poincaré, ......HENRI(w)
Pointer, ...........ANITA(x)
...................BONNIE(x)
.........JUNE(x), RUTH(x)
Poitier, ......SIDNEY(a)
Pola...........NEGRI(a)
Polanski, .....ROMAN(q)
Polk, ...........JAMES(u)
Pollack, .....SYDNEY(q)
Pollock, .....JACKSON(c)
Polly ...........BERGEN(a)
...................HOLLIDAY(a)
Ponchielli, ...................
...................AMILCARE(k)
Ponicsan, ...DARRYL(z)
Pons, ...............LILY(x)
Ponselle, ...........ROSA(x)

Ponti, ...........CARLO(q)
Pope, ....ALEXANDER(t)
Porter....WAGGONER(x)
Porter, ...........COLE(k)
...KATHERINE ANNE(z)
Post, ...............EMILY(z)
...................MARKIE(a)
.........MIKE(r), WILEY(d)
Poston, ...........TOM(j)
Potter, .....STEWART(a)
Potter, ........BEATRIX(z)
Potts, ...........ANNIE(a)
Poulenc, .....FRANCIS(k)
Pound, ...............EZRA(t)
Powell, ...........COLIN(p)
...DICK(a), ELEANOR(a)
...........JANE(a), WILLIAM(a)
Power, ......TYRONE(a)
Powers, ....STEFANIE(a)
Preminger, ......OTTO(q)
Prentiss, ........PAULA(a)
Presley, ...........ELVIS(x)
...................PRISCILLA(a)
Preston ...........FOSTER(a)
...................STURGES(q)
Preston, ...........BILLY(r)
...................ROBERT(a)
Previn, ...........ANDRE(r)
Price, ......LEONTYNE(x)
.........LLOYD(x), NICK(m)
...........RAY(x), VINCENT(a)
Pride, ......CHARLEY(x)
Prima, ...........LOUIS(r)
Primo ........CARNERA(g)
Principal, ..VICTORIA(a)
Prinze, ......FREDDIE(j)
Priscilla ......PRESLEY(a)
Prokofiev, .....SERGEI(k)
Prosky, .....ROBERT(a)
Prosper....MERIMEE(z)
Prost, ...........ALAIN(v)
Proust, ........MARCEL(z)
Prud'hon, ...................
...................PIERRE PAUL(c)
Pryce, .....JONATHAN(a)
Pryor, ...........RICHARD(j)
Puccini, ....GIACOMO(k)
Puckett, ...........KIRBY(e)
Pushkin, ...................
...................ALEKSANDR(t,z)
Puzo, ...........MARIO(z)
Pyle, ...........ERNIE(o)
Pynchon, ....THOMAS(z)

Qaddafi, ...................
...........MUAMMAR al-(u)
Quaid, ........DENNIS(a)
...................RANDY(a)
Quasimodo, ...................
...................SALVATORE(t)

175

Robert *continued*............
.......................WALDEN(a)
........................WALKER(a)
........................WALPOLE(a)
.....WISE(q), WRENN(m)
........................YOUNG(a)
Roberta..........FLACK(x)
........................PETERS(x)
Robert A.....HEINLEIN(z)
Robert E.............LEE(p)
........................SHERWOOD(z)
Robert F. ....KENNEDY(u)
Robert "Kool" .....BELL(x)
Robert Louis
........................STEVENSON(z)
Roberto........ALOMAR(e)
........................CLEMENTE(e)
........................DURAN(e)
........................ROSSELLINI(q)
Robert Penn
........................WARREN(t, z)
Roberts, ........DORIS(a)
........ERIC(a), JULIA(a)
........................PERNELL(a)
........................TONY(a)
Robertson, ....CLIFF(a)
....DALE(a), OSCAR(f)
........................ROBBIE(x)
Robeson, ........PAUL(a)
Robin ............GIBB(x)
........................GIVENS(a)
........................LEACH(o)
........................VENTURA(e)
........................WILLIAMS(a,j)
........................YOUNT(e)
........................ZANDER(x)
Robinson, ...BROOKS(e)
........EDWARD G.(a)
........................EDWIN
........................ARLINGTON(t)
........................FRANK(e), JACKIE(e)
........................SUGAR RAY(g)
........................SMOKEY(x)
Robustelli, ........ANDY(l)
Roby, ...........REGGIE(l)
Roche, ............TONY(y)
Rock ............HUDSON(a)
Rock, ............CHRIS(j)
Rockefeller,
........................JOHN D.(h)
........................NELSON A.(u)
Rockne............KNUTE(l)
Rockwell, ....NORMAN(c)
Rocky ...GRAZIANO(g)
........................MARCIANO(g)
Rod ...............CAREW(e)
........................LAVER(y)
........................STEIGER(a)
........................STEWART(x)
........................TAYLOR(a)

Roddy.....McDOWALL(a)
Rodgers, ........JIMMIE(x)
........................PAUL(x)
........................RICHARD(k)
Rodin, .......AUGUSTE(c)
Rodman, .......DENNIS(f)
Rodney .....CROWELL(x)
........DANGERFIELD(j)
Roeg, .......NICOLAS(q)
Roger .....BANNISTER(s)
........................CLEMENS(e)
........................CORMAN(q)
........................CRAIG(l)
........................DALTRY(x)
........................EBERT(o)
........................KINGDOM(s)
........................MARIS(e)
........................McGUINN(x)
........................MILLER(x)
........................MOORE(a)
........................MUDD(o)
........................PENROSE(w)
........................REES(a)
........................STAUBACH(l)
........................WATERS(r)
........................WILLIAMS(r)
Rogers.....HORNSBY(e)
Rogers, ...........FRED(a)
........................GINGER(a)
....KENNY(x), MIMI(a)
........ROY(a), WILL(j)
Rogers St. John,
........................ADELA(o)
Rohmer, ..........ERIC(q)
Roland ...........JOFFE(q)
........................PETIT(a)
Roland, .....GILBERT(a)
Rolle, .......ESTHER(a)
Rollie ..........FINGERS(e)
Rollins, .....HOWARD(a)
........................SONNY(r)
Roman......POLANSKI(q)
Roman, ..........RUTH(a)
Romero, ........CESAR(a)
Rommel, .......ERWIN(p)
Ron..............BROWN(u)
........................HOWARD(a,q)
........................LEIBMAN(a)
........................MOODY(a)
........................PERLMAN(a)
........SILVER(a), WOOD(r)
Ronald .......COLMAN(a)
........................REAGAN(u)
Ronnie................LOTT(l)
........................MILSAP(x)
........................SPECTOR(x)
Ronstadt, .......LINDA(x)
Roone .......ARLEDGE(h)
Rooney, ...........ANDY(o)
........................MICKEY(a)

Roosevelt,
........................ELEANOR(u)
........................FRANKLIN D.(u)
........................THEODORE(u)
Root, ...............ELIHU(u)
Rorem, .............NED(o)
Rory ..........CALHOUN(a)
Rosa........BONHEUR(c)
........................PONSELLE(x)
Rosalind .....CARTER(u)
........................RUSSELL(a)
Rosanna
........................ARQUETTE(a)
Rosanne ..........CASH(x)
Roscoe .......TANNER(y)
Roscoe Lee
........................BROWNE(a)
Rose, .......CHARLIE(o)
........................PETE(e)
Roseanne....ARNOLD(a)
Rosemary
........................CLOONEY(x)
........................De CAMP(a)
........................HARRIS(a)
Rosenbloom,
........................MAXEY(g)
Rosewall, .........KEN(y)
Ross............HUNTER(q)
........................MacDONALD(z)
........................MARTIN(a)
Ross, ...........DIANA(x)
........................KATHARINE(a)
........................MARION(a)
Rossano ......BRAZZI(a)
Rossellini,
........................ISABELLA(a)
........................ROBERTO(q)
Rossetti,
........DANTE GABRIEL(t)
Rossini,
........GIOACCHINO(k)
Rostand, ....EDMOND(z)
Rostenkowski, ...DAN(u)
Rote, ...............KYLE(l)
Roth, ......DAVID LEE(x)
........................PHILIP(z)
Rothko, ...........MARK(c)
Rouault, .....GEORGES(c)
Rourke, .....MICKEY(a)
Rousseau, .....HENRI(c)
........JEAN JACQUES(z)
Rowan, ............DAN(j)
Rowlands, ......GENA(a)
Roy................ACUFF(r)
........................CAMPANELLA(e)
........................CLARK(r)
........................DOTRICE(a)
........................ORBISON(x)
........................ROGERS(a)
........................SCHEIDER(a)

179

Sayers,
............DOROTHY L.(z)
............GALE(l)
Sayles, ............JOHN(q)
Scaggs, ............BOZ(x)
Scalia, ......ANTONIN(u)
Scarlatti,
............ALESSANDRO(k)
Scatman
............CROTHERS(a)
Schallert, ....WILLIAM(a)
Scheckter, ........JODY(v)
Scheider, ........ROY(a)
Schell, ............MARIA(a)
............MAXIMILIAN(a)
Schenkel, ........CHRIS(o)
Schiaparelli, ......ELSA(z)
Schirra, ......WALTER(d)
Schlesinger, ......JOHN(q)
Schmeling, ........MAX(g)
Schmidt, ........MIKE(e)
Schoenberg,
............ARNOLD(k)
Scholz, ............TOM(r)
Schroder, ........RICK(a)
Schubert, ......FRANZ(k)
Schulz, ......CHARLES(i)
Schumann, ..ROBERT(k)
Schwarzenegger,
............ARNOLD(a)
Schwarzkopf,
............NORMAN(p)
Scofield, ..........PAUL(a)
Scolari, ..........PETER(a)
Scorsese, ....MARTIN(q)
Scott ............BAIO(a)
...BAKULA(a), GLENN(x)
............HAMILTON(s)
............JOPLIN(k)
............SIMPSON(m)
Scott, ....GEORGE C.(a)
............LIZABETH(a)
............RANDOLPH(a)
............WALTER(z)
............ZACHARY(a)
Scottie ............PIPPEN(f)
Scotto, ........RENATA(x)
Scowcroft, ....BRENT(u)
Scriabin,
............ALEKSANDR(k)
Scully, ............VIN(o)
Seals, ....DAN(x), JIM(x)
Sean ........CONNERY(a)
............O'CASEY(z)
............O'GRADY(x)
............PENN(a)
Seau, ........JUNIOR(l)
Seaver, ............TOM(e)
Sebastian......CABOT(a)
............COE(s)

Sebastian, ......JOHN(x)
Seberg, ............JEAN(a)
Sedaka, ............NEIL(x)
Sedgman, ......FRANK(y)
Seeger, ............PETE(x)
Segal, ........GEORGE(a)
Seger, ............BOB(x)
Segovia, ......ANDRES(r)
Seidelman, ....SUSAN(q)
Seiji ............OZAWA(r)
Seinfeld, ........JERRY(j)
Selassie, ........HAILE(u)
Seles, ........MONICA(y)
Sellecca, ....CONNIE(a)
Selleck, ............TOM(a)
Sellers, ..........PETER(j)
Selma ........DIAMOND(a)
............LAGERLOF(z)
Selznick, ....DAVID O.(q)
Sendak, ....MAURICE(z)
Senna, ........AYRTON(v)
Sennett, ........MACK(q)
Serge
............KOUSSEVITZKY(r)
Sergei ...EISENSTEIN(q)
............PROKOFIEV(k)
............RACHMANINOFF(k)
Sergio ........MENDES(r)
Sesno, ............FRANK(o)
Seton, ............ANYA(z)
Seurat, ......GEORGES(c)
Seve
............BALLESTEROS(m)
Severinsen, ........DOC(r)
Sexton, ............ANNE(t)
Seymour, ........JANE(a)
Shackelford, ......TED(a)
Shaffer, ..........PAUL(r)
Shahn, ............BEN(c)
Shakespeare,
............WILLIAM(z)
Shamir, ......YITZHAK(u)
Shandling, ......GARRY(j)
Shane ........GOULD(y)
Shankar, ........RAVI(r)
Shannon, ........DEL(x)
Shaquille ........O'NEAL(f)
Shari ....BELAFONTE(a)
............LEWIS(j)
Sharif, ............OMAR(a)
Sharon............GLESS(a)
Sharon, ........ARIEL(u)
Sharp, ........DEE DEE(x)
Shatner, ....WILLIAM(a)
Shaun ........CASSIDY(x)
Shaw, ............ARTIE(r)
............BERNARD(a)
............GEORGE
............BERNARD(z)
............ROBERT(a)

Shea, ............JOHN(a)
Shearer, ........MOIRA(a)
............NORMA(a)
Shearing, ....GEORGE(r)
Shecky ........GREENE(j)
Sheedy, ............ALLY(a)
Sheehan, ......PATTY(m)
Sheen, ......CHARLIE(a)
............MARTIN(a)
Sheena ........EASTON(x)
Sheldon ......LEONARD(j)
Shelley ........BERMAN(j)
............DUVALL(a)
............FABARES(a)
............LONG(a)
............WINTERS(a)
Shelley, ..........MARY(z)
............PERCY BYSSHE(t)
Shemp............HOWARD(j)
Shepard,............SAM(z)
Shepard, Jr., ....ALAN(d)
Shepherd, ....CYBILL(a)
............JEAN(z)
Sheree ............NORTH(a)
Sheridan, ..........ANN(a)
............PHILIP(p)
............RICHARD(z)
Sherman ...HEMSLEY(a)
Sherman, ......ALLAN(x)
............BOBBY(x)
............WILLIAM T.(p)
Sherwood
............ANDERSON(z)
Sherwood,
............ROBERT E.(z)
Shields, ......BROOKE(a)
Shimon............PERES(u)
Shire, ............TALIA(a)
Shirley ........BASSEY(x)
....BOOTH(a), JONES(a)
............MacLAINE(a)
............TEMPLE(a)
Shirley Ann........GRAU(z)
Sholem............ASCH(z)
Shore, ........DINAH(x)
Short, ........BOBBY(r)
............MARTIN(j)
Shorter, ........FRANK(s)
Shostakovich,
............DMITRI(k)
Shriver, ........MARIA(o)
............PAM(y)
Shula, ............DON(l)
Sibelius, ........JEAN(k)
Sid ............CAESAR(j)
............LUCKMAN(l)
Sidney ............LUMET(q)
............POITIER(a)
............TOLER(a)
Sidney, ........SYLVIA(a)

Sidonie Gabrielle ...........
.................COLETTE(z)
Siegfried ....SASSOON(t)
Sierra, .........RUBEN(e)
Sigmund........FREUD(w)
Signe .............HASSO(a)
Signoret, ......SIMONE(a)
Sigourney ...WEAVER(a)
Sikorsky, .........IGOR(w)
Sillitoe, ..........ALAN(z)
Sills, .........BEVERLY(x)
Silver, ............RON(a)
Silverberg, ..ROBERT(z)
Silvers, .............PHIL(j)
Sim, .........ALASTAIR(a)
Simmons, ........JEAN(a)
Simms, ............PHIL(j)
Simon .......BOLIVAR(p)
................LEBON(x)
.................WARD(a)
Simon, .........CARLY(x)
..........NEIL(z), PAUL(u)
..................PAUL(x)
Simone ....SIGNORET(a)
Simone, ..........NINA(x)
Simpson, ..........O.J.(l)
..................SCOTT(m)
Sims, .............ZOOT(r)
Sinatra, ........FRANK(x)
Sinclair .......LEWIS(z)
Sinclair, .......UPTON(z)
Sinead.....O'CONNOR(x)
Singer, .................
......ISAAC BASHEVIS(z)
Singh, ...........VIJAY(m)
Singleton, ........JOHN(q)
Sirtis, ...........MARINA(a)
Siskel, .........GENE(o)
Sissy ........SPACEK(a)
Skeeter ............DAVIS(x)
Skelton, .............RED(j)
Skerritt, .........TOM(a)
Skinner, ........B.F.(w)
Skitch ...HENDERSON(r)
Slater, .........HELEN(a)
Slaughter, ....ENOS(e)
Sledge, .........PERCY(x)
Slick, .........GRACE(x)
Slim ..SUMMERVILLE(a)
Sloan, .........JOHN(c)
Sluman, .........JEFF(m)
Sly.........STONE(a)
Smetana, ...BEDRICH(k)
Smith, .........ADAM(z)
.................ALEXIS(a)
..................BESSIE(x)
......BRUCE(l), BUBBA(l)
.........BUFFALO BOB(a)
.................DAVID(c)
.....JACLYN(a), KATE(x)

.........KEELY(x), LIZ(o)
.................MAGGIE(a)
.................OZZIE(e)
........PATTI(x), STAN(y)
Smits, .........JIMMY(a)
Smokey ...ROBINSON(x)
Smothers, .........DICK(j)
................TOM(j)
Smuts, .........JAN(u)
Snead, .........J.C.(m)
........NORM(l), SAM(m)
Snell, .........PETER(s)
Sneva, .........TOM(v)
Snider, .........DUKE(e)
Snipes, .....WESLEY(a)
Snow, .........HANK(x)
.................PHOEBE(a)
Snyder, .........GARY(t)
..................TOM(o)
Solti, .........GEORG(r)
Solzhenitsyn, .........
..........ALEKSANDR(z)
Somers, ...SUZANNE(a)
Sommer, .........ELKE(a)
Sondheim, .........
.................STEPHEN(k)
Sondra .........LOCKE(a)
Sonia .........BRAGA(a)
Sonja .........HENIE(s)
Sonny.........BONO(x)
........JURGENSEN(l)
................LISTON(g)
................ROLLINS(r)
Sontag, .........SUSAN(z)
Soo, .........JACK(j)
Sophia .........LOREN(a)
Sophie .........TUCKER(x)
Soren .........
.........KIERKEGAARD(z)
Sorvino, .........PAUL(a)
Sothern, .........ANN(a)
Soul, .........DAVID(a)
Soupy.........SALES(j)
Sousa, ..JOHN PHILIP(k)
Souter, .........DAVID(u)
Spacek, .........SISSY(a)
Spade, .........DAVID(j)
Spader, .........JAMES(a)
Spahn, ......WARREN(e)
Spanky.........
.........McFARLAND(a)
Spano, .........JOE(a)
................VINCENT(a)
Spark, .........MURIEL(z)
Sparks, .........NED(a)
Sparky.........LYLE(e)
Speaker, .........TRIS(e)
Specter, .....ARLEN(u)
Spector, .........PHIL(r)
.................RONNIE(x)

Spelling, .........AARON(q)
Spencer.........TRACY(a)
Spender, ....STEPHEN(t)
Spenser, .....EDMUND(t)
Spielberg, ....STEVEN(q)
Spike .............JONES(r)
.................LEE(q)
Spillane, ......MICKEY(z)
Spiner, .........BRENT(a)
Spinks, .........LEON(g)
.................MICHAEL(g)
Spinoza, ......BARUCH(z)
Spiro .............AGNEW(u)
Spitz, .............MARK(s)
Spock, ....BENJAMIN(w)
Spring ...BYINGTON(a)
Springfield, ....DUSTY(x)
.................RICK(x)
Springsteen, .BRUCE(x)
Spyri, .........JOHANNA(z)
Stabler, .............KEN(l)
Stack, .........ROBERT(a)
Stacy, .........KEACH(a)
Stacy, .........HOLLIS(m)
Stadler, .........CRAIG(m)
Stafford, ....JIM(x), JO(x)
Stahl, .........LESLEY(o)
Stalin, .........JOSEPH(u)
Stallone, .........
.........SYLVESTER(a)
Stamos, .........JOHN(a)
Stamp, ......TERENCE(a)
Stan.................GETZ(r)
.................KENTON(r)
..........LAUREL(j), LEE(i)
.................MIKITA(n)
....MUSIAL(e), SMITH(y)
Stander, .........LIONEL(a)
Stanford .........WHITE(b)
Stang, .........ARNOLD(j)
Stanley......BALDWIN(u)
.................KRAMER(q)
.................KUBRICK(q)
Stanley, .........KIM(a)
Stanton, .........
.........HARRY DEAN(a)
Stanwyck, .........
.................BARBARA(a)
Stapledon, ........OLAF(z)
Stapleton, .........JEAN(a)
.................MAUREEN(a)
Stargell, .........WILLIE(e)
Starr, .........BART(l)
..........KAY(x), RINGO(r)
Staubach, ......ROGER(l)
Steele, ......RICHARD(o)
Steen, .........JAN(c)
Steenburgen, ..MARY(a)
Stefan.........EDBERG(y)
Stefanie ......POWERS(a)

Steffi .................GRAF(y)
Stegner, ...WALLACE(z)
Steiger, .........ROD(a)
Stein, .....GERTRUDE(z)
Steinbeck, ........JOHN(z)
Steinberg, ....DAVID(j)
Steinbrenner, ...............
..................GEORGE(h)
Steinem, ....GLORIA(o)
Stella .........STEVENS(a)
Sten................ANNA(a)
Stengel, ........CASEY(e)
Stenmark, ..INGEMAR(s)
Stéphane ...................
................MALLARME(t)
Stephen ......BECKER(z)
....................BISHOP(x)
......BOYD(a), CRANE(z)
......FOSTER(k), KING(z)
..........SONDHEIM(k)
..................SPENDER(t)
.....................STILLS(x)
Stephen A. ..................
................DOUGLAS(u)
Stephenson, ......JAN(m)
Stephen Vincent ............
..................BENET(t)
Stephen W. ..................
...............HAWKING(w)
Stepin.......FETCHIT(a)
Sterling...HOLLOWAY(a)
Stern, ........HOWARD(j)
......................ISAAC(r)
Sterne, ..LAURENCE(z)
Sternhagen, ................
...............FRANCES(a)
Steve .........ALBERT(o)
..................ALLEN(a,j)
.........BARTKOWSKI(l)
..............CARLTON(e)
....................DeBERG(l)
...................ELKINGTON(m)
..................GARVEY(e)
.........GUTTENBERG(a)
....HOWE(r), KANALY(a)
..............LAWRENCE(x)
....................MARTIN(a)
................McQUEEN(a)
....MILLER(r), OVETT(s)
.....PATE(m), PERRY(x)
................WINWOOD(a)
......................YOUNG(l)
Steven....SPIELBERG(q)
........................WRIGHT(j)
Stevens, ...ANDREW(a)
........CAT(x), CONNIE(a)
.......................DODIE(x)
..................GEORGE(q)
........................INGER(a)
..............JOHN PAUL(u)

........RAY(x), STELLA(a)
..................WALLACE(t)
Stevenson, .ADLAI E.(u)
........................McLEAN(a)
........................PARKER(a)
.........ROBERT LOUIS(z)
......................TEOFILO(g)
Stevie ..............NICKS(x)
......................WONDER(x)
Stewart.....GRANGER(a)
Stewart, .................AL(x)
....JACKIE(v), JAMES(a)
........................PATRICK(a)
........................PAYNE(m)
......POTTER(u), ROD(x)
Stieb, ................DAVE(e)
Stiers, .......................
..........DAVID OGDEN(a)
Stiller, ..............JERRY(j)
Stills, .........STEPHEN(x)
Stockard .....................
................CHANNING(a)
Stockton, ........DAVE(m)
..........................JOHN(f)
Stockwell, .......DEAN(a)
Stoker, .............BRAM(z)
Stokowski, ................
.................LEOPOLD(r)
Stolle, ................FRED(y)
Stoltz, ................ERIC(a)
Stone, .............LEWIS(a)
...................MILBURN(a)
.........OLIVER(q), SLY(r)
Stones, .......DWIGHT(s)
Stookey, ...........PAUL(x)
Stoppard, ..........TOM(z)
Storch, .............LARRY(j)
Storey, .........DAVID(z)
Storm, .............GALE(x)
Stottlemyre..........MEL(e)
Stout, ..................REX(z)
Stowe, .........HARRIET
................BEECHER(z)
Strachey, .......LYTTON(z)
Straight, ...BEATRICE(a)
Strait, ........GEORGE(x)
Strange, .......CURTIS(m)
Strasberg, .........LEE(a)
Strauss, ......JOHANN(k)
.......................PETER(a)
....................RICHARD(a)
Stravinsky, .......IGOR(k)
Strawberry, ..DARRYL(e)
Streep, ...........MERYL(a)
Streisand, ...BARBRA(x)
Strindberg, ..AUGUST(z)
Stritch, .........ELAINE(a)
Strom.....THURMOND(u)
Struthers, ......SALLY(a)
Stu...................ERWIN(a)

Stuart, ........GILBERT(c)
.............................J.E.B.(p)
Sturges, .......PRESTON(q)
Styne, ................JULE(k)
Styron, ......WILLIAM(z)
Sue ............GRAFTON(z)
..............................MILLER(z)
Sugar Ray.....................
........................ROBINSON(g)
Sukova, ......HELENA(y)
Sullavan, ...................
....................MARGARET(a)
Sullivan, .ARTHUR S.(k)
....BARRY(a), DANNY(v)
.......ED(o), JOHN. L.(g)
...............................LOUIS(b)
..............................SUSAN(a)
Sully, .........THOMAS(c)
Sumac, ..............YMA(x)
Summer, ........DONNA(x)
Summerville, ....SLIM(a)
Sun......................RA(r)
Sununu, ...........JOHN(u)
Susan.......ANSPACH(a)
.........................ANTON(a)
.................BLAKELY(a)
.......CLARK(a), DEY(a)
..................HAYWARD(a)
.............................LUCCI(a)
........................RUTTAN(a)
................ST. JAMES(a)
.............SARANDON(a)
.............SEIDELMAN(q)
...................SONTAG(z)
.................SULLIVAN(a)
Susan B. .....ANTHONY(u)
Susannah.........YORK(a)
Sutherland, ..KIEFER(a)
..........................DONALD(a)
..............................JOAN(x)
Suzanne .....................
...............PLESHETTE(a)
........................SOMERS(a)
Swann, ............LYNN(l)
Swanson, .....GLORIA(a)
Swayze, .....PATRICK(a)
Swift, .........JONATHAN(z)
Swinburne, ...................
...................ALGERNON(t)
Swit, ..........LORETTA(a)
Swoosie.........KURTZ(a)
Sybil ......THORNDIKE(a)
Sydney...........................
........GREENSTREET(a)
........................POLLACK(a)
Sylvester...................
.................STALLONE(a)
Sylvia ............PLATH(t,z)
.........................SIDNEY(a)
Synge, .....JOHN M.(t,z)

Syngman ..........RHEE(u)
Szell, ..........GEORGE(r)

T. Boone.....PICKENS(h)
T.E. .......LAWRENCE(p)
T.H. .................WHITE(z)
T.S. ..............ELIOT(z)
Tab .......HUNTER(a, x)
Taft, .......WILLIAM H.(u)
Tagore, ............................
......RABINDRANATH(z)
Tai ...........BABILONIA(s)
Talia .............SHIRE(a)
Tallulah...BANKHEAD(a)
Talmadge, ....NORMA(a)
Tamblyn, .........RUSS(a)
Tambor, .....JEFFREY(a)
Tamiroff, ..........AKIM(a)
Tammy .........GRIMES(a)
.................WYNETTE(x)
Tandy, ........JESSICA(a)
Tanguy, ...........YVES(c)
Tanner, ......ROSCOE(y)
Tanya ........TUCKER(x)
Tarbell, ................IDA(z)
Tarkenton, .......FRAN(l)
Tarkington, ....BOOTH(z)
Tashlin, ........FRANK(q)
Tasso, ....TORQUATO(t)
Tatum .............O'NEAL(a)
Tatum, ................ART(r)
Taylor, ...ELIZABETH(a)
.........................JAMES(x)
.............LAWRENCE(l)
.......RENEE(a), RIP(j)
......ROBERT(a), ROD(a)
...................ZACHARY(u)
Tchaikovsky, ................
.........PETER ILYICH(k)
Teasdale, ..........SARA(t)
Tebaldi, ......RENATA(x)
Ted...............DANSON(a)
...................HUGHES(a)
...................KENNEDY(u)
.........KEY(i), KNIGHT(j)
...................KOPPEL(o)
.......................LEWIS(j)
...................NUGENT(r)
........SHACKELFORD(a)
...................TURNER(h)
...................WILLIAMS(e)
Teddy..............................
.......PENDERGRASS(x)
Te Kanawa, .......KIRI(x)
Telly ..........SAVALAS(a)
Tempestt ...BLEDSOE(a)
Temple, ........SHIRLEY(a)
Tennant, ...VICTORIA(a)
Tennessee......................
...................WILLIAMS(z)

Tennessee Ernie ............
....................FORD(x)
Tennille, ............TONI(x)
Tennyson, ....ALFRED(t)
Teofilo ..STEVENSON(g)
Terence.........STAMP(a)
Teresa.......BREWER(a)
...................WRIGHT(a)
Teri...................GARR(a)
Terry .......BRADSHAW(l)
....GILLIAM(j), JONES(j)
Terry, .............ELLEN(a)
Tesla, ...........NIKOLA(w)
Tess .........HARPER(a)
Tevis, .........WALTER(z)
Tex .................AVERY(i)
...................RITTER(x)
Tex, .................JOE(s)
Thad ....MUMFORD(z)
Thant, ....................U(u)
Thatcher, .....................
.............MARGARET(u)
Thaves, .............BOB(i)
Theda ...........BARA(a)
Theismann, .........JOE(l)
Thelma ......RITTER(a)
Thelonious.......MONK(r)
Theodore........BIKEL(a)
...................DREISER(z)
.............ROOSEVELT(u)
Theresa.....RUSSELL(a)
Theroux, ..........PAUL(z)
Thicke, .........ALAN(a)
Thomas .........ARNE(k)
...................BERGER(z)
........COLE(c), COOK(h)
...................CARLYLE(z)
...................DOOLEY(w)
...................EAKINS(c)
...................EDISON(o)
....GAINSBOROUGH(c)
.......GRAY(t), HARDY(z)
...................HEARNS(g)
...................JEFFERSON(u)
...MALORY(z), MANN(z)
......MOORE(t), MORE(z)
.......NASHE(z), NAST(i)
...................PAINE(z)
...................PYNCHON(z)
.....SULLY(c), TRYON(z)
...................WILLIAMS(z)
Thomas, .............B.J.(x)
...................CLARENCE(u)
...................DANNY(j)
.........DYLAN(t), ISIAH(f)
.........JAY(a), KURT(s)
...................MARLO(a)
...................NORMAN(u)
...................RICHARD(a)
Thomas E. ....DEWEY(u)

Thomas Hart...................
...................BENTON(c)
Thomas M. .....DISCH(z)
Thomas S. .....FOLEY(u)
Thomas (Stonewall).......
...................JACKSON(p)
Thompson, ......DALEY(s)
...................EMMA(a)
....J.WALTER(h), JIM(z)
...........LEA(a), SADA(a)
Thomson, .....PETER(m)
Thor......HEYERDAHL(z)
Thoreau, .........................
...........HENRY DAVID(z)
Thorndike, ......SYBIL(a)
Thornton ......WILDER(z)
Thorpe, ...........JIM(s)
Thurber, .....JAMES(z)
Thurgood .......................
.................MARSHALL(u)
Thurman, .........UMA(a)
Thurmond, ......NATE(f)
...................STROM(u)
Tiant, ............LUIS(s)
Tiegs, .........CHERYL(a)
Tiepolo, ...GIOVANNI(c)
Tierney, ..........GENE(a)
Tiffany, ............................
....LOUIS COMFORT(c)
Tiger, .............DICK(s)
Tilden, ...............BILL(y)
Tillis, .............MEL(x)
Tillotson, ....JOHNNY(x)
Tilly, ...............MEG(a)
Tim ...........CONWAY(j)
......CURRY(a), HOLT(t)
...................MATHESON(a)
...................McCARVER(e)
.......RAINES(e), REID(a)
Timi ............YURO(x)
Timothy.....BOTTOMS(a)
...................BUSFIELD(a)
...................DALTON(a)
...................HUTTON(a)
Tina ...........LOUISE(a)
...................TURNER(x)
...................YOTHERS(a)
Tinker, ..........GRANT(h)
...................JOE(e)
Tipper .............GORE(u)
Tito, .....JOSIP BROZ(u)
Tittle, ..................Y.A.(l)
Tobe ..........HOOPER(q)
Tod.........BROWNING(q)
Todd ..CHRISTENSEN(f)
Todd, ..........MICHAEL(a)
...................RICHARD(q)
Toler, ...........SIDNEY(a)
Tolkien, ..............J.R.R.(z)
Tolstoy, ..............LEO(z)

Youngman, ....HENNY(j)
Yount, ............ROBIN(e)
Yukio..........MISHIMA(z)
Yul ............BRYNNER(a)
Yuri ...........GAGARIN(d)
Yuro, ...................TIMI(x)
Yves .............TANGUY(c)
Yvonne....DECARLO(a)
...................ELLIMAN(x)

Zachary.........SCOTT(a)
...............TAYLOR(u)
Zadora, ...............PIA(x)
Zander, .........ROBIN(x)
Zane ................GREY(z)

Zanuck, ............................
...............DARRYL F.(q)
Zapata, .....EMILIANO(u)
Zappa, ...........FRANK(r)
Zarley, ........KERMIT(m)
Zasu ................PITTS(a)
Zatopek, ...........EMIL(s)
Zeffirelli, ...FRANCO(q)
Zenger, ............................
...............JOHN PETER(o)
Zeppo ...............................
.........(Herbert) MARX (j)
Zerbe, .....ANTHONY(a)
Zero............MOSTEL(a)
Zevon, .......WARREN(x)

Ziegfeld, ....FLORENZ(q)
Zimbalist, Jr., .................
.....................EFREM(a)
Zinnemann, .....FRED(q)
Zoe...........CALDWELL(a)
Zoeller, .........FUZZY(m)
Zola .................BUDD(s)
Zola, ...............EMILE(z)
Zoltán..........KODALY(k)
Zoot ...................SIMS(r)
Zsa Zsa .........GABOR(a)
Zubin ...........MEHTA(r)
Zuckerman, ....................
.........................PINCHAS(r)
Zukor, .........ADOLPH(q)

# KENTUCKY DERBY WINNERS

| Year | Winner | Jockey |
|------|--------|--------|
| 1920 | Paul Jones | Rice |
| 1921 | Behave Yourself | Thompson |
| 1922 | Morvich | Johnson |
| 1923 | Zev | Sande |
| 1924 | Black Gold | Mooney |
| 1925 | Flying Ebony | Sande |
| 1926 | Bubbling Over | Johnson |
| 1927 | Whiskery | McAtee |
| 1928 | Reigh Count | Lang |
| 1929 | Clyde Van Dusen | McAtee |
| 1930 | * Gallant Fox | Sande |
| 1931 | Twenty Grand | Kurtsinger |
| 1932 | Burgoo King | James |
| 1933 | Brokers Tip | Meade |
| 1934 | Cavalcade | Garner |
| 1935 | * Omaha | Saunders |
| 1936 | Bold Venture | Hanford |
| 1937 | * War Admiral | Kurtsinger |
| 1938 | Lawrin | Arcaro |
| 1939 | Johnstown | Stout |
| 1940 | Gallahadion | Bierman |
| 1941 | * Whirlaway | Arcaro |
| 1942 | Shut Out | Wright |
| 1943 | * Count Fleet | Longden |
| 1944 | Pensive | McCreary |
| 1945 | Hoop, Jr. | Arcaro |
| 1946 | * Assault | Mehrtens |
| 1947 | Jet Pilot | Guerin |
| 1948 | * Citation | Arcaro |
| 1949 | Ponder | Brooks |
| 1950 | Middleground | Boland |
| 1951 | Count Turf | McCreary |
| 1952 | Hill Gail | Arcaro |
| 1953 | Dark Star | Moreno |
| 1954 | Determine | York |
| 1955 | Swaps | Shoemaker |
| 1956 | Needles | Erb |
| 1957 | Iron Liege | Hartack |
| 1958 | Tim Tam | Valenzuela |
| 1959 | Tomy Lee | Shoemaker |
| 1960 | Venetian Way | Hartack |
| 1961 | Carry Back | Sellers |
| 1962 | Decidedly | Hartack |
| 1963 | Chateaugay | Baeza |
| 1964 | Northern Dancer | Hartack |
| 1965 | Lucky Debonair | Shoemaker |
| 1966 | Kauai King | Brumfield |
| 1967 | Proud Clarion | Ussery |
| 1968 | Dancer's Image (or Forward Pass) | Ussery |
| 1969 | Majestic Prince | Hartack |
| 1970 | Dust Commander | Manganello |
| 1971 | Canonero II | Avila |
| 1972 | Riva Ridge | Turcotte |
| 1973 | * Secretariat | Turcotte |
| 1974 | Cannonade | Cordero |
| 1975 | Foolish Pleasure | Vasquez |
| 1976 | Bold Forbes | Cordero |
| 1977 | * Seattle Slew | Cruguet |
| 1978 | * Affirmed | Cauthen |
| 1979 | Spectacular Bid | Franklin |
| 1980 | Genuine Risk | Vasquez |
| 1981 | Pleasant Colony | Velasquez |
| 1982 | Gato del Sol | Delahoussaye |
| 1983 | Sunny's Halo | Delahoussaye |
| 1984 | Swale | Pincay |
| 1985 | Spend a Buck | Cordero |
| 1986 | Ferdinand | Shoemaker |
| 1987 | Alysheba | McCarron |
| 1988 | Winning Colors | Stevens |
| 1989 | Sunday Silence | Valenzuela |
| 1990 | Unbridled | Perret |
| 1991 | Strike the Gold | Antley |
| 1992 | Lil E. Tee | Day |

* Triple Crown Winner

# NATIVE AMERICAN PEOPLE

Tribes are separated into groups based on the language spoken by members of the tribe. The language family is indicated at the beginning of each group of tribes.

Algonquin

ABENAKI
ARAPAHO
BLACKFOOT
CHEYENNE
CHIPPEWA
CREE
DELAWARE
FOX
GROS VENTRE
KICKAPOO
LENAPE
MAHICAN (MOHICAN)
MENOMINI
MIAMI
MOHEGAN
OJIBWA
OTTAWA
PIEGAN
POTAWATAMI
SAUK
SHAWNEE
YUROK

Athabaskan

APACHE
DENE
HUPA
NAVAHO

Caddoan

ARIKARA
CADDO
KIOWA
PAWNEE
REE

Coos

COOS

Haidan

HAIDA

Hokan

KAROK
POMO
YUMA

Inupiaq or Inuktitut

ALEUT
ESKIMO
INUIT
YUPIK

Iroquoian

CAYUGA
CHEROKEE
ERIE
HURON
IROQUOIS
MOHAWK
ONEIDA
ONONDAGA
SENECA

Muskhogean

CHICKASAW
CHOCTAW
CREEK
SEMINOLE

Penutian

CHINOOK
MAIDU

Pueblo

KERES
TANO
TEWA
ZUNI

Sahaptin

NEZ PERCE
UMATILLA
YAKIMA

Salish

FLATHEAD
KUTENAI (KUTENAY)
SALISH

Shoshonean

COMANCHE
HOPI
MISSION
PAIUTE
SHOSHONE
UINTA
UTE

Siouan

ASSINIBOINE
BILOXI
CATAWBA
CROW
DAKOTA
IOWA
MANDAN
MISSOURI
OGLALA
OMAHA
OSAGE
OTOE
PONCA
TETON
WINNEBAGO

Tlingit

TLINGIT

Uto-Aztecan

PAPAGO
PIMA

Wakashan

KWAKIUTL
NOOTKA

# UNITED STATES PRESIDENTS

| President & First Lady | Party | V.P. | Born | Term |
|---|---|---|---|---|
| 1. WASHINGTON, George<br>Martha Dandridge Custis | Fed. | Adams | VA | 1789-1797 |
| 2. ADAMS, John<br>Abigal Smith | Fed. | Jefferson | MA | 1797-1801 |
| 3. JEFFERSON, Thomas<br>Martha Wayles Skelton | Dem.-Rep. | Burr,<br>Clinton | VA | 1801-1809 |
| 4. MADISON, James<br>Dorothea (Dolley) Payne Todd | Dem.-Rep. | Clinton,<br>Gerry | VA | 1809-1817 |
| 5. MONROE, James<br>Elizabeth Kortright | Dem.-Rep. | Tompkins | VA | 1817-1825 |
| 6. ADAMS, John Quincy<br>Louise Catherine Johnson | Dem.-Rep. | Calhoun | MA | 1825-1829 |
| 7. JACKSON, Andrew<br>Rachel Donelson Robards | Dem. | Calhoun,<br>Van Buren | SC | 1829-1837 |
| 8. VAN BUREN, Martin<br>Hannah Hoes | Dem. | Johnson | NY | 1837-1841 |
| 9. HARRISON, William Henry<br>Anna Symmes | Whig | Tyler | VA | 1841 |
| 10. TYLER, John<br>Letitia Christian and<br>Julia Gardiner | Dem. | | VA | 1841-1845 |
| 11. POLK, James Knox<br>Sarah Childress | Dem. | Dallas | NC | 1845-1849 |
| 12. TAYLOR, Zachary<br>Margaret Smith | Whig | Fillmore | VA | 1849-1850 |
| 13. FILLMORE, Millard<br>Abigail Powers and<br>Caroline Carmichael McIntosh | Whig | | NY | 1850-1853 |
| 14. PIERCE, Franklin<br>Jane Mears Appleton | Dem. | King | NH | 1853-1857 |
| 15. BUCHANAN, James<br>none | Dem. | Breckenridge | PA | 1857-1861 |
| 16. LINCOLN, Abraham<br>Mary Todd | Rep. | Hamlin,<br>Johnson | KY | 1861-1865 |
| 17. JOHNSON, Andrew<br>Eliza McCardle | Dem. | | NC | 1865-1869 |
| 18. GRANT, Ulysses Simpson<br>Julia Dent | Rep. | Colfax,<br>Wilson | OH | 1869-1877 |
| 19. HAYES, Rutherford Birchard<br>Lucy Ware Webb | Rep. | Wheeler | OH | 1877-1881 |
| 20. GARFIELD, James Abram<br>Lucretia Rudolph | Rep. | Arthur | OH | 1881 |
| 21. ARTHUR, Chester Alan<br>Ellen Lewis Herndon | Rep. | | VT | 1881-1885 |

| President & First Lady | Party | V.P. | Born | Term |
|---|---|---|---|---|
| 22. CLEVELAND,Stephen Grover Frances Folsom | Dem. | Hendricks | NJ | 1885-1889 |
| 23. HARRISON, Benjamin Caroline Lavinia Scott and Mary Scott Lord Dimmick | Rep. | Morton | OH | 1889-1893 |
| 24. CLEVELAND,Stephen Grover Frances Folsom | Dem. | Stevenson | NJ | 1893-1897 |
| 25. MCKINLEY, William Ida Saxton | Rep. | Hobart, Roosevelt | OH | 1897-1901 |
| 26. ROOSEVELT, Theodore Alice Hathaway Lee and Edith Kermit Carow | Rep. | Fairbanks | NY | 1901-1909 |
| 27. TAFT, William Howard Helen Herron | Rep. | Sherman | OH | 1909-1913 |
| 28. WILSON, Thomas Woodrow Ellen Louise Axson and Edith Bolling Galt | Dem. | Marshall | VA | 1913-1921 |
| 29. HARDING, Warren Gamaliel Florence Kling De Wolfe | Rep. | Coolidge | OH | 1921-1923 |
| 30. COOLIDGE, John Calvin Grace Anna Goodhue | Rep. | Dawes | VT | 1923-1929 |
| 31. HOOVER, Herbert Clark Lou Henry | Rep. | Curtis | IA | 1929-1933 |
| 32. ROOSEVELT, Franklin Delano Anna Eleanor Roosevelt | Dem. | Garner, Wallace, Truman | NY | 1933-1945 |
| 33. TRUMAN, Harry S Elizabeth (Bess) Wallace | Dem. | Barkley | MO | 1945-1953 |
| 34. EISENHOWER, Dwight David Mamie Geneva Doud | Rep. | Nixon | TX | 1953-1961 |
| 35. KENNEDY, John Fitzgerald Jacqueline Lee Bouvier | Dem. | Johnson | MA | 1961-1963 |
| 36. JOHNSON, Lyndon Baines Claudia (Lady Bird) Alta Taylor | Dem. | Humphrey | TX | 1963-1968 |
| 37. NIXON, Richard Milhous Thelma Catherine Patricia Ryan | Rep. | Agnew, Ford | CA | 1968-1974 |
| 38. FORD, Gerald Rudolph ne, Leslie Lynch King, Jr. Elizabeth Bloomer Warren | Rep. | Rockefeller | NE | 1974-1977 |
| 39. CARTER, James Earl, Jr. Rosalynn Smith | Dem. | Mondale | GA | 1977-1981 |
| 40. REAGAN, Ronald Wilson Anne Frances Robbins Davis | Rep. | Bush | IL | 1981-1989 |
| 41. BUSH, George Herbert Walker Barbara Pierce | Rep. | Quayle | MA | 1989-1993 |
| 42. CLINTON, William Jefferson Hillary Rodham | Dem. | Gore | AR | 1993- |

# SHAKESPEARE

**1.** *The First Part of King Henry the Sixth*
Sir William LUCY; King HENRY the Sixth; BASSET, Lord TALBOT, John TAL-BOT, VERNON; Duke of ALENÇON, Duke of BEDFORD, CHARLES, Duke of GLOSTER, Earl of SUFFOLK, Earl of WARWICK; Countess of AUVERGNE, Thomas, Henry, and John BEAUFORT, Duke of BURGUNDY, Sir John FAS-TOLFE, Sir Thomas GARGRAVE, MARGARET, Edmund MORTIMER, REIGNIER; Sir William GLANSDALE, Earl of SALISBURY, WOODVILLE; Richard PLANTAGENET; JOAN LA PUCELLE (Joan of Arc)

**2.** *The Second Part of King Henry the Sixth*
Lord SAY; Jack CADE, DICK the butcher, John HUME, Alexander IDEN, VAUX; George BEVIS, Matthew GOUGH, King HENRY the Sixth, PETER, SMITH the weaver; EDWARD, Thomas HORNER, Lord SCALES; ELEANOR, John HOLLAND, MICHAEL, MARGERY Jourdain, RICHARD, Saunder SIMP-COX, Sir John STANLEY, Duke of SUFFOLK, Earl of WARWICK; Cardinal BEAUFORT, Lord CLIFFORD and his son young CLIFFORD, HUMPHREY, MARGARET, Duke of SOMERSET, Sir Humphrey and William STAFFORD; Earl of SALISBURY, John SOUTHWELL; Duke of BUCKINGHAM; Roger BOLING-BROKE, Richard PLANTAGENET

**3.** *The Third Part of King Henry the Sixth*
BONA, Lady GRAY; King HENRY the Sixth; EDMUND, EDWARD, Duke of EXETER, GEORGE, Earl of OXFORD, Lord RIVERS; LOUIS XI, Duke of NOR-FOLK, RICHARD, Sir William STANLEY, Earl of WARWICK; Lord CLIFFORD, Lord HASTINGS, Queen MARGARET, Marquess of MONTAGUE, Sir John and Sir Hugh MORTIMER, Earl of PEMBROKE, Duke of SOMERSET, Lord STAFFORD; Sir John MONTGOMERY, Sir John SOMERVILLE; Richard PLAN-TAGENET; Earl of WESTMORELAND; Earl of NORTHUMBERLAND

**4.** *King Richard the Third*
Lady ANNE, Lord GREY, Duchess of YORK; HENRY, Lord LOVEL; Sir James BLOUNT, Marquess of DORSET, King EDWARD the Fourth, GEORGE, John MORTON, Earl of OXFORD, Earl RIVERS, Earl of SURREY, Sir James TYRREL; Sir William CATESBY, Sir Walter HERBERT, Duke of NORFOLK, King RICHARD the Third, Lord STANLEY, TRESSEL, Christopher URSWICK, Sir Thomas VAUGHAN; BERKELEY, Lord HASTINGS, MARGARET, Sir Richard RATCLIFF; Cardinal BOURCHIER, ELIZABETH, Thomas ROTHERHAM; Duke of BUCKINGHAM, Sir Robert BRAKENBURY

**5.** *Titus Andronicus*
AARON, CAIUS; CHIRON, LUCIUS, MUTIUS, TAMORA; ALARBUS, LAVINIA, MARTIUS, PUBLIUS, QUINTUS; AEMILIUS; BASSIANUS, DEMETRIUS, VALENTINE; SATURNINUS, SEMPRONIUS; TITUS ANDRONICUS; MARCUS ANDRONICUS

**6.** *The Comedy of Errors*
LUCE; PINCH; AEGEON, ANGELO, DROMIO (of Ephesus and of Syracuse, twin attendants); AEMILIA, ADRIANA, LUCIANA, SOLINUS; BALTHAZAR; ANTIPHOLUS (of Ephesus and of Syracuse, twins)

**7.** *The Two Gentlemen of Verona*
JULIA, SPEED; LAUNCE, SILVIA, THURIO; ANTONIO, LUCETTA, PROTEUS; EGLAMOUR, PANTHINO; VALENTINE

**8. *Love's Labour's Lost***
DULL, MOTH; BOYET, MARIA; Don Adriano de ARMADO, BEROWNE, COSTARD, DUMAINE, MERCADE; PRINCESS of France, ROSALINE; FERDINAND, KATHERINE, Sir NATHANIEL; HOLOFERNES, JAQUENETTA, LONGAVILLE

**9. *Romeo and Juliet***
Friar JOHN; PARIS, PETER, ROMEO; JULIET, TYBALT; ABRAHAM, CAPULET, ESCALUS, GREGORY, SAMPSON; BENVOLIO, Friar LAURENCE, MERCUTIO, MONTAGUE; BALTHASAR

**10. *A Midsummer Night's Dream***
LION, MOTH, PUCK, SNUG, WALL; EGEUS, FLUTE, SNOUT; BOTTOM, COBWEB, HELENA, HERMIA, OBERON, QUINCE, THISBE; PYRAMUS, THESEUS, TITANIA; LYSANDER; DEMETRIUS, HIPPOLYTA, MOONSHINE; STARVELING; MUSTARD-SEED, PHILOSTRATE, PEAS-BLOSSOM

**11. *King John***
King JOHN; Robert BIGOT, Prince HENRY, LOUIS, MELUN, PETER of Pomfret; ARTHUR, BLANCH, ELINOR, James GURNEY, King PHILIP of France; Hubert DE BURGH; Cardinal PANDULPH; CONSTANCE, CHATILLON, Geffrey FITZPETER, William LONGSWORD, William MARESHALL; Robert, Philip, and Lady FAULCONBRIDGE

**12. *The Taming of the Shrew***
BIANCA, CURTIS, GREMIO, GRUMIO, PEDANT, TRANIO; BAPTISTA, LUCENTIO; BIONDELLO, HORTENSIO, KATHARINA, PETRUCHIO, VINCENTIO; CHRISTOPHER SLY

**13. *King Richard the Second***
Lord ROSS, Duchess of YORK; BAGOT, BUSHY, GREEN, HENRY Bolingbroke, Henry PERCY; EDMUND of Langley, Sir PIERCE of Exton, Sir Stephen SCROOP, Duke of SURREY; Duke of AUMERLE, Lord BERKLEY, Duchess of GLOSTER, Thomas MOWBRAY, King RICHARD the Second; Lord FITZWATER, Earl of SALISBURY; Lord WILLOUGHBY; JOHN OF GAUNT; Earl of NORTHUMBERLAND

**14. *The Merchant of Venice***
Launcelot GOBBO and his father, TUBAL; PORTIA; ANTONIO, Prince of ARRAGON, JESSICA, LORENZO, Prince of MOROCCO, NERISSA, SOLANIO, SHYLOCK; BASSANIO, GRATIANO, LEONARDO, SALARINO, STEPHANO; BALTHAZAR

**15. *The First Part of King Henry the Fourth***
Prince JOHN, PETO; Sir Walter BLUNT, King HENRY the Fourth, Henry, and Lady PERCY; POINTZ, SCROOP, Sir Richard VERNON; HOTSPUR, Sir MICHAEL, Mistress QUICKLY; BARDOLPH, Sir John FALSTAFF, GADSHILL, Edmund and Lady MORTIMER; ARCHIBALD, Owen GLENDOWER; Earl of WESTMORELAND

**16. *The Second Part of King Henry Fourth***
DAVY, FANG, Prince JOHN, PAGE, PETO, WART; BLUNT, GOWER, King HENRY the Fourth, SNARE; FEEBLE, MORTON, MOULDY, PISTOL, POINTZ, RUMOUR, SHADOW, SURREY, THOMAS of Clarence; MOWBRAY, Hostess QUICKLY, SHALLOW, SILENCE, TRAVERS, WARWICK; Lord BARDOLPH, BULLCALF, COLEVILE, FALSTAFF, HARCOURT, HASTINGS, HUMPHREY; WESTMORELAND; DOLL TEARSHEET; NORTHUMBERLAND

### Shakespeare

17. *King Henry the Fifth*
NYM; Sir Thomas GREY, JAMY, Duke of YORK; ALICE, John BATES, Alexander COURT, GOWER, King HENRY the Fifth, LOUIS; Duke of EXETER, ISABEL, PISTOL, Lord SCROOP; Duke of BEDFORD, Duke of BOURBON, CHARLES the Sixth of France, Duke of GLOSTER, MONTJOY, Duke of ORLEANS, Mistress QUICKLY, Earl of WARWICK; BARDOLPH, Duke of BURGUNDY, FLUELLEN, GRANDPRE, RAMBURES, Michael WILLIAMS; Earl of CAMBRIDGE, Sir Thomas ERPINGHAM, KATHARINE, MACMORRIS, Earl of SALISBURY; Earl of WESTMORELAND

18. *Much Ado about Nothing*
HERO; URSULA, VERGES; ANTONIO, CLAUDIO, CONRADE, DON JOHN, Friar FRANCIS, LEONATO; BEATRICE, BENEDICK, BORACHIO, DOGBERRY, DON PEDRO, MARGARET; BALTHAZAR

19. *The Merry Wives of Windsor*
NYM; ANNE Page, FORD, PAGE; Doctor CAIUS, Sir Hugh EVANS, ROBIN, RUGBY; FENTON, PISTOL, SIMPLE; Mistress QUICKLY, SHALLOW, SLENDER, WILLIAM Page; BARDOLPH, Sir John FALSTAFF.

20. *Julius Caesar*
Young CATO; CASCA, CINNA, VARRO; CICERO, CLITUS, LUCIUS, PORTIA, STRATO; CASSIUS, FLAVIUS, MESSALA, PUBLIUS; CLAUDIUS, LIGARIUS, LUCILIUS, MARULLUS, PINDARUS, TITINIUS; DARDANIUS, TREBONIUS, VOLUMNIUS; CALPHURNIA; ARTEMIDORUS; DECIUS BRUTUS, JULIUS CAESAR, MARCUS BRUTUS, POPILIUS LENA; MARCUS ANTONIUS, METELLUS CIMBER, OCTAVIUS CAESAR; M. AEMILIUS LEPIDUS,

21. *As You Like It*
ADAM, DUKE; CELIA, CORIN, DENIS, HYMEN, PHEBE; AMIENS, AUDREY, JAQUES, LE BEAU, OLIVER; CHARLES, Sir Oliver MARTEXT, ORLANDO, SILVIUS, WILLIAM; ROSALIND; FREDERICK; TOUCHSTONE

22. *Twelfth Night; or, What You Will*
CLOWN, CURIO, MARIA, VIOLA; FABIAN, OLIVIA, ORSINO; ANTONIO; MALVOLIO; Andrew AGUECHEEK, SEBASTIAN, TOBY BELCH, VALENTINE

23. *Hamlet, Prince of Denmark*
OSRIC; HAMLET; HORATIO, LAERTES, OPHELIA; BERNARDO, CLAUDIUS, GERTRUDE, POLONIUS, REYNALDO; CORNELIUS, FRANCISCO, MARCELLUS, VOLTIMAND; FORTINBRAS; ROSENCRANTZ; GUILDENSTERN

24. *Troilus and Cressida*
AJAX; HELEN, PARIS, PRIAM; AENEAS, HECTOR, NESTOR; ANTENOR, CALCHAS, HELENUS, TROILUS, ULYSSES; ACHILLES, CRESSIDA, DIOMEDES, MENELAUS, PANDARUS; AGAMEMNON, ALEXANDER, CASSANDRA, DEIPHOBUS, PATROCLUS, THERSITES; ANDROMACHE, MARGARELON

25. *All's Well That Ends Well*
DIANA, LAFEU; HELENA; BERTRAM, LAVACHE, MARIANA, STEWARD; PAROLLES, VIOLENTA; Countess of ROUSILLON

26. *Measure for Measure*
ELBOW, FROTH, LUCIO, Friar PETER; ANGELO, JULIET, POMPEY, Friar THOMAS; CLAUDIO, ESCALUS, MARIANA, PROVOST, VARRIUS; ABHORSON, ISABELLA, OVERDONE; FRANCISCA, VINCENTIO; BARNARDINE

27. *Othello, the Moor of Venice*
IAGO; CLOWN; BIANCA, CASSIO, EMILIA; MONTANO, OTHELLO; GRA-
TIANO, LODOVICO, RODERIGO; BRABANTIO, DESDEMONA

28. *Macbeth*
ROSS; ANGUS; BANQUO, DUNCAN, HECATE, LENNOX, SEYTON, SIWARD;
FLEANCE, MACBETH, MACDUFF, MALCOLM; MENTEITH; CAITHNESS,
DONALBAIN; LADY MACBETH, LADY MACDUFF

29. *King Lear*
Earl of KENT, LEAR; CURAN, EDGAR, REGAN; Duke of ALBANY, EDMUND,
OSWALD; Earl of GLOSTER, GONERIL; CORDELIA, Duke of BURGUNDY,
Duke of CORNWALL

30. *Antony and Cleopatra*
EROS, IRAS; MENAS, PHILO; ALEXAS, GALLUS, SCARUS, SILIUS, TAURUS;
AGRIPPA, MARDIAN, OCTAVIA, THYREUS, VARRIUS; CANIDIUS, CHARMI-
AN, DERCETAS, DIOMEDES, MAECENAS, SELEUCUS; CLEOPATRA,
DEMETRIUS, DOLABELLA, VENTIDIUS; EUPHRONIUS, MARK ANTONY,
MENECRATES, PROCULEIUS; OCTAVIUS CAESAR, SEXTUS POMPEIUS; M.
AEMILIUS LEPIDUS; DOMITIUS ENOBARBUS

31. *Coriolanus*
VALERIA; COMINIUS, VIRGILIA, VOLUMNIA; CAIUS MARCIUS (Coriolanus),
JUNIUS BRUTUS, TITUS LARTIUS; TULLUS AUFIDIUS; MENENIUS AGRIP-
PA, SICINIUS VELUTUS

32. *Timon of Athens*
CUPID, TIMON, TITUS; CAPHIS, LUCIUS; FLAVIUS, PHRYNIA; LUCILIUS,
LUCULLUS, PHILOTUS, TIMANDRA; APEMANTUS, FLAMINIUS, SERVILIUS,
VENTIDIUS; ALCIBIADES, HORTENSIUS, SEMPRONIUS

33. *Pericles*
BOULT, CLEON, DIANA, GOWER; MARINA, THAISA; CERIMON, DIONYZA,
ESCANES, LEONINE; PERICLES, PHILEMON, THALIARD; ANTIOCHUS,
HELICANUS, LYCHORIDA, SIMONIDES; LYSIMACHUS

34. *Cymbeline*
HELEN, QUEEN; CLOTEN, IMOGEN; IACHIMO, PISANIO; BELARIUS, PHI-
LARIO; ARVIRAGUS, CORNELIUS, CYMBELINE, GUIDERIUS; CAIUS
LUCIUS; POSTHUMUS LEONATUS

35. *The Winter's Tale*
DION; CLOWN, MOPSA; DORCAS, EMILIA; CAMILLO, LEONTES, PAULINA,
PERDITA; FLORIZEL, HERMIONE; ANTIGONUS, AUTOLYCUS, CLEOMENES,
MAMILLIUS, POLIXENES; ARCHIDAMUS

36. *The Tempest*
IRIS, JUNO; ARIEL, CERES; ADRIAN, King ALONSO; ANTONIO, CALIBAN;
GONZALO, MIRANDA; PROSPERO, STEPHANO, TRINCULO; FERDINAND,
FRANCISCO, SEBASTIAN

37. *King Henry the Eighth*
Sir Nicholas VAUX; Doctor BUTTS, Sir Anthony DENNY, King HENRY the
Eighth, Lord SANDS; Sir Thomas LOVELL, Earl of SURREY, Cardinal WOLSEY;
BRANDON, CRANMER, Duke of NORFOLK, Duke of SUFFOLK; Cardinal
CAMPEIUS, CAPUCIUS, CROMWELL, GARDINER, GRIFFITH, PATIENCE; Sir
Henry GUILDFORD, KATHARINE; ANNE BULLEN, Duke of BUCKINGHAM;
Lord ABERGAVENNY

# BIBLE CHARACTERS

## OLD TESTAMENT
(Names used in the Douay Bible, when different from the King James Version, are in parentheses)

1. GENESIS
2. EXODUS
3. LEVITICUS
4. NUMBERS
5. DEUTERONOMY
6. JOSHUA
7. JUDGES
8. RUTH
9. I SAMUEL (I KINGS)
10. II SAMUEL (II KINGS)
11. I KINGS (III KINGS)
12. II KINGS (IV KINGS)
13. I CHRONICLES
    (I PARALIPOMENON)
14. II CHRONICLES
    (II PARALIPOMENON)
15. EZRA (I ESDRAS)
16. NEHEMIAH (II ESDRAS)
17. ESTHER
18. JOB
19. PSALMS
20. PROVERBS
21. ECCLESIASTES
22. SONG OF SOLOMON
    (CANTICLE OF CANTICLES)
23. ISAIAH (ISAIAS)
24. JEREMIAH (JEREMIAS)
25. LAMENTATIONS
26. EZEKIEL (EZECHIEL)
27. DANIEL
28. HOSEA (OSEE)
29. JOEL
30. AMOS
31. OBADIAH (ABDIAS)
32. JONAH (JONAS)
33. MICAH (MICHEAS)
34. NAHUM
35. HABAKKUK (HABACUC)
36. ZEPHANIAH
    (SOPHONIAS)
37. HAGGAI (AGGEUS)
38. ZECHARIAH (ZACHARIAS)
39. MALACHI (MALACHIAS)

## BOOKS OF THE APOCRYPHA

I Esdras (III Esdras)
II Esdras (IV Esdras)
Tobit (Tobias)
Judith
Additions to Esther
Wisdom of Solomon
Ecclesiasticus
Baruch
Letter of Jeremiah
Additions to Daniel:
    Song of the Three Holy Children,
    Susanna, and
    Bel and the Dragon
Prayer of Manasses
I Maccabees (I Machabees)
II Maccabees (II Machabees)

## NEW TESTAMENT

1. MATTHEW
2. MARK
3. LUKE
4. JOHN
5. THE ACTS
6. ROMANS
7. I CORINTHIANS
8. II CORINTHIANS
9. GALATIANS
10. EPHESIANS
11. PHILIPPIANS
12. COLOSSIANS
13. I THESSALONIANS
14. II THESSALONIANS
15. I TIMOTHY
16. II TIMOTHY
17. TITUS
18. PHILEMON
19. HEBREWS
20. JAMES
21. I PETER
22. II PETER
23. I JOHN
24. II JOHN
25. III JOHN
26. JUDE
27. REVELATION (APOCALYPSE)

<u>Prophets</u>

AMOS
EZRA
JOEL
HOSEA
JONAH
MICAH
MOSES
NAHUM
DANIEL
ELISHA
HAGGAI
ISAIAH
EZEKIEL
JEREMIAH

<u>Men of the Bible</u>

ARA
ASA
DAN
ELI
GOG
HAM
IRA
LOT
NUN
URI
ABEL
ADAM
AGAG
AHAB
AHAZ
AMOS
BOAZ
CAIN
CUSH
DOEG
ENOS
ESAU
HETH
IRAD
JADA
JEHU
JOAB
KISH
LEVI
MASH
MOAB
NOAH
OBAL

OBED
OMAR
OMRI
OREB
OZEM
SAUL
SETH
SHEM
SODI
ULAM
UNNI
URIA
AARON
ABIAH
ABIEL
AHIRA
AMASA
ANNAS
CALEB
CHUZA
CYRUS
DAVID
ENOCH
HAMAN
HARAN
HEROD
HIRAM
HOHAM
IBZAN
ISAAC
JACOB
JAMES
JARED
JORAM
LABAN
MASSA
MOREH
NABAL
NADAB
NAHBI
NAHOR
OPHIR
PELEG
REZON
SACAR
SERUG
TERAH
URIAH
ZAHAM
GIDEON
JOSHUA
LAMECH

REUBEN
SAMSON
ABRAHAM
ANANIAS
GOLIATH
ISHMAEL
JAPHETH
MESHACH
SOLOMON
ABEDNEGO
JEPHTHAH
JONATHAN
SHADRACH

<u>Women of the Bible</u>

EVE
ADAH
JAEL
LEAH
MARY
RUTH
DINAH
EGLAH
HAGAR
JULIA
JUNIA
LYDIA
MERAB
NAOMI
PHEBE
RAHAB
SARAH
TAMAR
BILHAH
DORCAS
ESTHER
HANNAH
HOGLAH
MAACAH
MAHLAH
MICHAL
MILCAH
MIRIAM
RACHEL
RIZPAH
SALOME
VASHTI
ZILLAH
ZILPAH
ABIGAIL
HAMUTAL

197

# GODS & GODDESSES

## GREEK MYTHOLOGY

chief god ....................................ZEUS
demigod ....................SATYR; TRITON
goddess of agriculture .......DEMETER
goddess of criminal folly ..............ATE
goddess of dawn ...........................EOS
goddess of discord......................ERIS
goddess of earth .......................GAEA
goddess of fate ......................MOIRA
goddess of love ...............APHRODITE
goddess of magic ................HECATE
goddess of mischief .....................ATE
goddess of peace....................IRENE
goddess of revenge ............NEMESIS
goddess of the moon ...........HECATE,
...............................SELENE; ARTEMIS
goddess of the night .....................NYX
goddess of victory.....................NIKE
goddess of wisdom...............ATHENA
goddess of youth ......................HEBE
god of fields, flocks, forests .........PAN
god of love .............................EROS
god of mirth...........................COMUS
god of revelry...................DIONYSUS
god of ridicule ......................MOMUS
god of the harvest...............CRONUS
god of the north wind...........BOREAS
god of the sea.......NEREUS, TRITON;
.........................................POSEIDON
god of the southeast wind........EURUS
god of the underworld .......................
....................................HADES, PLUTO
god of war................................ARES
god of wealth..........................PLUTUS
god of wind ...........................AEOLUS
god of youth ..........................APOLLO
herald of the gods.................HERMES
mother of the gods ....................RHEA
queen of the gods .....................HERA
Zeus, consort of............HERA, LEDA,
.............LETO, MAIA; DANAE, METIS;
.............AEGINA, CALYCE, EUROPA,
.............SEMELE, SELENE, THEMIS;
......................ALCMENE, ANTIOPE
Zeus, offspring of.............ATE; ARES,
........HEBE; AEGLE, ARCAS, BELUS,
...................HELEN, MINOS; AEACUS,
.............AGLAIA, APOLLO, ATHENE,
...........CLOTHO, HERMES, POLLUX,
.................................THALIA, ZETHUS

## EGYPTIAN MYTHOLOGY

chief deity ..............................AMON
goddess of the heavens................NUT
god of evil................BES, SET; SETH
god of fertility ...........................AMON
god of magic ...........................THOTH
god of Memphis ...........................PTAH
god of pleasure ............................BES
god of the lower world .........SERAPIS
god of the sun ...................AMON-RE
god of the underworld .............OSIRIS
god of wisdom...........................THOTH
hawk-headed god..................HORUS
Nile as a god...............................HAPI
Queen of the gods.......................SATI
serpent goddess........................BUTO

## NORSE MYTHOLOGY

chief god....................................ODIN
earlier race of gods ..................VANIR
fates .......................................NORNS
goddess of beauty & love.........FREYA
goddess of the earth .................ERDA
goddess of the underworld...........HEL
god of discord & mischief............LOKI
god of fertility .............................FREY
god of light ............................BALDER
god of poetry .........................BRAGI
god of the sea .........................AEGIR
god of the sky............................TYR
god of thunder.........................THOR
home of the gods ..................ASGARD
Norse pantheon.........................AESIR

## ROMAN MYTHOLOGY

chief god ..................................JOVE
goddess of agriculture .............CERES
goddess of crops ................ANNONA
goddess of dawn..................AURORA
goddess of faith ........................FIDES
goddess of grain ......................CERES
goddess of hope........................SPES
goddess of horses ...................EPONA
goddess of love.........................VENUS
goddess of prosperity .............SALUS
goddess of the earth ...............TERRA
goddess of the harvest ..............OPS
goddess of the hearth...............VESTA
goddess of the moon .......DIAN, LUNA
god of death .............................MORS
god of fields and herds ..............FAUN
god of fire...............................VULCAN
god of love.................AMOR, CUPID
god of mirth and joy ...............COMUS
god of music ..........................APOLLO
god of revelry.....................BACCHUS
god of the north wind.............BOREAS

god of the sea .....................NEPTUNE
god of the sun...............SOL; APOLLO
god of war.........................MARS
gods of the underworld.................DIS;
.................................................ORCUS
queen of the gods........................JUNO

OTHER MYTHOLOGIES

Assyrian god of war.................ASHUR

Babylonian goddess of love....ISHTAR
Babylonian god of earth ..........DAGAN
Celtic chief god.........................DAGDA
Celtic god of the sea ....................LER
Celtic queen of the gods ...........DANU
Hindu goddess of evil..................KALI
Hindu god of love .......................KAMA
Phoenician goddess of fertility ............
.................................................ASTARTE
Welsh gods ..................GWYN, LLEW

# ACADEMY AWARD WINNERS

| | |
|---|---|
| 1992........Al Pacino, Emma Thompson | 1960..............................Burt Lancaster, |
| 1991 ....Anthony Hopkins, Jodie Foster | ........................................Elizabeth Taylor |
| 1990 ...........Jeremy Irons, Kathy Bates | 1959 ...........................Charlton Heston, |
| 1989 ........................Daniel Day-Lewis, | ........................................Simone Signoret |
| ...............................................Jessica Tandy | 1958 ....David Niven, Susan Hayward |
| 1988.......Dustin Hoffman, Jodie Foster | 1957 ..............................Alec Guinness, |
| 1987................Michael Douglas, Cher | ......................................Joanne Woodward |
| 1986.......Paul Newman, Marlee Matlin | 1956.......Yul Brynner, Ingrid Bergman |
| 1985.......William Hurt, Geraldine Page | 1955 ...........................Ernest Borgnine, |
| 1984 .....................F. Murray Abraham, | .........................................Anna Magnani |
| .....................................................Sally Field | 1954 .........Marlon Brando, Grace Kelly |
| 1983 ...........................Robert Duvall, | 1953 ............................William Holden, |
| ............................Shirley MacLaine | ........................................Audrey Hepburn |
| 1982...........Ben Kingsley, Meryl Streep | 1952 .........Gary Cooper, Shirley Booth |
| 1981 .............................Henry Fonda, | 1951 ...Humphrey Bogart, Vivien Leigh |
| ..............................Katharine Hepburn | 1950 ...........Jose Ferrer, Judy Holliday |
| 1980.......Robert DeNiro, Sissy Spacek | 1949 .....................Broderick Crawford, |
| 1979 .........Dustin Hoffman, Sally Field | ....................................Olivia de Havilland |
| 1978 .............Jon Voight, Jane Fonda | 1948 ....Laurence Olivier, Jane Wyman |
| 1977.........................Richard Dreyfuss, | 1947....Ronald Colman, Loretta Young |
| ...........................................Diane Keaton | 1946 .............................Fredric March, |
| 1976........Peter Finch, Faye Dunaway | ....................................Olivia de Havilland |
| 1975 ..............................Jack Nicholson, | 1945 .........Ray Milland, Joan Crawford |
| ...........................................Louise Fletcher | 1944 .......Bing Crosby, Ingrid Bergman |
| 1974............Art Carney, Ellen Burstyn | 1943 ..........Paul Lukas, Jennifer Jones |
| 1973 ...Jack Lemmon, Glenda Jackson | 1942 .....James Cagney, Greer Garson |
| 1972........Marlon Brando, Liza Minnelli | 1941........Gary Cooper, Joan Fontaine |
| 1971 ......Gene Hackman, Jane Fonda | 1940 .....James Stewart, Ginger Rogers |
| 1970 ............................George C. Scott, | 1939 .......Robert Donat, Vivien Leigh |
| ..........................................Glenda Jackson | 1938 .........Spencer Tracy, Bette Davis |
| 1969 .........John Wayne, Maggie Smith | 1937........Spencer Tracy, Luise Rainer |
| 1968 ................................Cliff Robertson, | 1936 ..........Paul Muni, Luise Rainer |
| .............................Katharine Hepburn & | 1935 .......Victor McLaglen, Bette Davis |
| .......................................Barbra Streisand | 1934 ....Clark Gable, Claudette Colbert |
| 1967 .................................Rod Steiger, | 1933.........................Charles Laughton, |
| ...............................Katharine Hepburn | ......................................Katharine Hepburn |
| 1966 ....Paul Scofield, Elizabeth Taylor | 1932..............................Fredric March & |
| 1965..........Lee Marvin, Julie Christie | ..............Wallace Beery, Helen Hayes |
| 1964........Rex Harrison, Julie Andrews | 1931 ..........................Lionel Barrymore, |
| 1963.........Sidney Poitier, Patricia Neal | .........................................Marie Dressler |
| 1962 ...Gregory Peck, Anne Bancroft | 1930.....George Arliss, Norma Shearer |
| 1961 ........................Maximilian Schell, | 1929 ......Warner Baxter, Mary Pickford |
| ...........................................Sophia Loren | 1928 .......Emil Jannings, Janet Gaynor |

# COLLEGES & UNIVERSITIES

The nickname of the sports teams of each college or university is indicated in parentheses. The location of the school follows the team nickname. The location is not given when the city and state are a part of the name of the school.

Adelphi U. (Panthers)
　Garden City, NY
Akron, U. of (Zips) Akron, OH
Alabama A&M U.(Bulldogs)
　Normal, AL
Alabama-Birmingham, U. of (Blazers)
Alabama-Huntsville, U. of (Chargers)
Alabama State U. (Hornets)
　Montgomery, AL
Alabama-Tuscaloosa, U. of
　(Crimson Tide)
Alaska-Anchorage, U. of (Seawolves)
Alaska-Fairbanks, U. of (Nanooks)
Alcorn State U. (Scalping Braves)
　Lorman, MS
Alfred U. (Saxons) Alfred, NY
Amherst Coll. (Lord Jeffs)
　Amherst, MA
Arizona, U. of (Wildcats) Tucson, AZ
Arizona State U. (Sun Devils)
　Tempe, AZ
Arkansas-Fayetteville, U. of
　(Razorbacks)
Arkansas-Little Rock, U. of (Trojans)
Arkansas-Monticello, U. of (Weevils)
Arkansas-Pine Bluff, U. of
　(Golden Lions)
Arkansas State U. (Indians)
　State University, AR
Auburn U. (Tigers) Auburn, AL
Augusta Coll. (Jaguars) Augusta, GA
Austin Peay State U. (Governors)
　Clarksville, TN

Babson Coll. (Beavers)
　Babson Park, MA
Ball State U. (Cardinals) Muncie, IN
Bard Coll. (Blazers)
　Annandale-on-Hudson, NY
Bates Coll. (Bobcats) Lewiston, ME
Baylor U. (Bears) Waco, TX
Belmont U. (Rebels) Nashville, TN
Beloit Coll. (Buccaneers) Beloit, WI
Bethune-Cookman Coll. (Wildcats)
　Daytona Beach, FL
Boise State U. (Broncos) Boise, ID
Boston Coll. (Eagles) Boston, MA
Boston U. (Terriers) Boston, MA
Bowdoin Coll. (Polar Bears)
　Brunswick, ME
Bowie State U. (Bulldogs) Bowie, MD

Bowling Green State U. (Falcons)
　Bowling Green, OH
Bradley U. (Braves) Peoria, IL
Brandeis U. (Judges) Waltham, MA
Brigham Young U. (Cougars)
　Provo, UT
Brown U. (Bears) Providence, RI
Bryant Coll. (Indians) Smithfield, RI
Bryn Mawr Coll. (Mawrters)
　Bryn Mawr, PA
Bucknell U. (Bison) Lewisburg, PA
Butler U. (Bulldogs) Indianapolis, IN

California-Berkeley, U. of
　(Golden Bears)
California-Davis, U. of (Aggies)
California-Irvine, U. of (Anteaters)
California-Los Angeles, U. of (Bruins)
California-Riverside, U. of
　(Highlanders)
California-San Diego, U. of (Tritons)
California-Santa Barbara, U. of
　(Gauchos)
California-Santa Cruz, U. of
　(Banana Slugs)
California State U. at Bakersfield
　(Roadrunners)
California State U. at Chico (Wildcats)
California State U. at Dominguez Hills
　(Toros)
California State U. at Fresno
　(Bulldogs)
California State U. at Fullerton
　(Titans)
California State U. at Hayward
　(Pioneers)
California State U. at Long Beach
　(49'ers)
California State U. at Los Angeles
　(Golden Eagles)
California State U. at Northridge
　(Matadors)
California State U. at Sacramento
　(Hornets)
California State U. at San Bernardino
　(Coyotes)
Campbell U. (Fighting Camels)
　Buies Creek, NC
Canisius Coll. (Griffs) Buffalo, NY
Carnegie Mellon U. (Tartans)
　Pittsburgh, PA

200

Case Western Reserve U. (Spartans)
Cleveland, OH
Catholic U. of America (Cardinals)
Washington, DC
Chicago, U. of (Maroons) Chicago, IL
Chicago State U. (Cougars)
Chicago, IL
Christian Brothers U. (Buccaneers)
Memphis, TN
Cincinnati, U. of (Bearcats)
Cincinnati, OH
Citadel, The (Bulldogs)
Charleston, SC
City College of New York (Beavers)
New York, NY
Clarkson, U. (Golden Knights)
Potsdam, NY
Clemson U. (Tigers) Clemson, SC
Cleveland State U. (Vikings)
Cleveland, OH
Coe Coll. (Kohawks)
Cedar Rapids, IA
Colby Coll. (White Mules)
Waterville, ME
Colgate U. (Red Raiders)
Hamilton, NY
Colorado-Boulder, U. of (Buffaloes)
Colorado-Colorado Springs, U. of
(Gold)
Colorado State U. (Rams)
Fort Collins, CO
Columbia U. (Lions) New York, NY
Concord Coll. (Mountain Lions)
Athens, WV
Concordia Coll. (Cobbers)
Moorhead, MN
Connecticut-Avery Point, U. of
(Pointers) Groton, CT
Connecticut Coll. (Camels)
New London, CT
Connecticut-Storrs, U. of (Huskies)
Cornell U. (Big Red) Ithaca, NY
Creighton U. (Bluejays) Omaha, NE

Dallas, U. of (Crusaders) Irving, TX
Dartmouth Coll. (The Big Green)
Hanover, NH
Davidson Coll. (Wildcats)
Davidson, NC
Delaware, U. of (Fightin' Blue Hens)
Newark, DE
Delaware State Coll. (Hornets)
Dover, DE
Denison U. (Big Red) Granville, OH
Denver, U. of (Pioneers) Denver, CO
DePaul U. (Blue Demons) Chicago, IL
DePauw U. (Tigers) Greencastle, IN
Detroit, U. of (Titans) Detroit, MI
Dickinson Coll. (Red Devils)
Carlisle, PA

Dillard U. (Blue Devils)
New Orleans, LA
Drake U. (Bulldogs) Des Moines, IA
Drew U. (Rangers) Madison, NJ
Drexel U. (Dragons) Philadelphia, PA
Dubuque, U. of (Spartans)
Dubuque, IA
Duke U. (Blue Devils) Durham, NC
Duquesne U. (Dukes) Pittsburgh, PA

Eckerd Coll. (Tritons)
St. Petersburg, FL
Elmira Coll. (Soaring Eagles)
Elmira, NY
Elon Coll. (Fighting Christians)
Elon, NC
Emerson Coll. (Lions) Boston, MA
Emory U. (Eagles) Atlanta, GA

Fairfield U. (Stags) Fairfield, CT
Fairleigh Dickinson U. (Knights)
Teaneck, NJ
Florida, U. of (Gators) Gainesville, FL
Florida A&M U. (Rattlers)
Tallahassee, FL
Florida State U. (Seminoles)
Tallahassee, FL
Fordham U. (Rams) Bronx, NY
Franklin & Marshall Coll. (Diplomats)
Lancaster, PA
Friends U. (Falcons) Wichita, KS
Furman U. (Paladins) Greenville, SC

Gallaudet U. (Bison) Washington, DC
Gannon U. (Golden Knights) Erie, PA
George Mason U. (Patriots)
Fairfax, VA
Georgetown U. (Hoyas)
Washington, DC
George Washington U. (Colonials)
Washington, DC
Georgia, U. of (Bulldogs) Athens, GA
Georgia Institute of Technology
(Yellow Jackets) Atlanta, GA
Georgia State U. (Panthers)
Atlanta, GA
Gonzaga U. (Bulldogs) Spokane, WA
Grambling State U. (Tigers)
Grambling, LA

Hampton U. (Pirates) Hampton, VA
Harding U. (Bison) Searcy, AR
Hartwick Coll. (Warriors) Oneonta, NY
Harvard U. (Crimson) Cambridge, MA
Haverford Coll. (The Red Wave)
Fords, PA
Hawaii, U. of (Rainbows) Honolulu, HI
Hawaii-Pacific U. (Sea Warriors)
Honolulu, HI
Hobart Coll. (Statesmen) Geneva, NY

Hofstra U. (Flying Dutchmen)
  Hempstead, NY
Houston, U. of (Cougars) Houston, TX
Howard U. (Bison) Washington, DC

Idaho, U. of (Vandals) Moscow, ID
Idaho State U. (Bengals) Pocatello, ID
Illinois-Champaign, U. of
  (Fighting Illini)
Illinois-Chicago, U. of (Flames)
Illinois State U. (Redbirds) Normal, IL
Illinois Wesleyan U. (Titans)
  Bloomington, IL
Indiana State U. (Sycamores)
  Terre Haute, IN
Indiana U. (Hoosiers) Bloomington, IN
Indiana U. at Kokomo (Knights)
Iona Coll. (Gaels) New Rochelle, NY
Iowa, U. of (Hawkeyes) Iowa City, IA
Iowa State U. (Cyclones) Ames, IA
Ithaca Coll. (Bombers) Ithaca, NY

Jackson State U. (Tigers)
  Jackson, MS
Jacksonville State U. (Gamecocks)
  Jacksonville, FL
Jacksonville U. (Dolphins)
  Jacksonville, FL
James Madison U. (Dukes)
  Harrisonburg, VA
John Brown U. (Golden Eagles)
  Siloam Springs, AR
John Jay Coll. (Bloodhounds)
  New York, NY
Johns Hopkins U. (Bluejays)
  Baltimore, MD
Johnson & Wales U. (Griffins)
  Providence, RI

Kalamazoo Coll. (Hornets)
  Kalamazoo, MI
Kansas, U. of (Jayhawks)
  Lawrence, KS
Kansas State U. (Wildcats)
  Manhattan, KS
Kent State U. (Golden Flashes)
  Kent, OH
Kentucky, U. of (Wildcats)
  Lexington, KY
Kentucky State U. (Thorobreds)
  Frankfort, KY
Kenyon Coll. (Lords) Gambier, OH
King's Coll. (Monarchs)
  Wilkes-Barre, PA

Lafayette Coll. (Leopards) Easton, PA
LaSalle U. (Explorers)
  Philadelphia, PA
Lawrence U. (Vikings) Appleton, WI
Lehigh U. (Engineers) Bethlehem, PA

LeMoyne Coll. (Dolphins)
  Syracuse, NY
Liberty U. (Flames) Lynchburg, VA
Lincoln U. (Blue Tigers)
  Jefferson City, MO
Long Island U, CW Post Campus
  (Pioneers) Brookville, NY
Long Island U. (Blackbirds)
  Brooklyn, NY
Long Island U. (Colonials)
  Southampton, NY
Louisiana State U. (Tigers)
  Baton Rouge, LA
Louisiana State U. (Pilots)
  Shreveport, LA
Louisville, U. of (Cardinals)
  Louisville, KY
Loyola, U (Ramblers) Chicago, IL

Maine-Farmington, U. of (Beavers)
Maine-Fort Kent, U. of (Bengals)
Maine-Machias, U. of (Clippers)
Maine-Orono, U. of (Black Bears)
Maine-Presque Isle, U. of (Owls)
Manhattan Coll. (Jaspers) Bronx, NY
Marist Coll. (Red Foxes)
  Poughkeepsie, NY
Marquette U. (Warriors)
  Milwaukee, WI
Marshall U. (Thundering Herd)
  Huntington, WV
Maryland-Baltimore, U. of (Retrievers)
Maryland-College Park, U. of
  (Terrapins)
Maryland-Eastern Shore, U. of
  (Hawks) Princess Anne, MD
Marywood Coll. (Pacers)
  Scranton, PA
Massachusetts-Amherst, U. of
  (Minutemen)
Massachusetts-Boston, U. of
  (Beacons)
Massachusetts-Dartmouth, U. of
  (Corsairs)
Massachusetts-Lowell, U. of (Chiefs)
Mass. Inst. of Tech. (Engineers)
  Cambridge, MA
Memphis State U. (Tigers)
  Memphis, TN
Mercer U. (Bears) Macon, GA
Mercy Coll. (Flyers) Dobbs Ferry, NY
Miami, U. of (Hurricanes)
  Coral Gables, FL
Miami U. (Redskins) Oxford, OH
Michigan-Ann Arbor, U. of
  (Wolverines)
Michigan-Dearborn, U. of (Wolves)
Michigan State U. (Spartans)
  East Lansing, MI
Minnesota-Duluth, U. of (Bulldogs)

Minnesota-Minneapolis, U. of
(Golden Gophers)
Minnesota-Morris, U. of (Cougars)
Mississippi, U. of (Rebels)
University, MS
Mississippi State U. (Bulldogs)
Mississippi State, MS
Missouri-Columbia, U. of (Tigers)
Missouri-Kansas City, U. of
(Kangaroos)
Missouri-Rolla, U of (Miners)
Missouri-St. Louis, U. of (Rivermen)
Molloy Coll. (Lions)
Rockville Centre, NY
Monmouth Coll. (Hawks)
West Long Branch, NJ
Montana, U. of (Grizzlies)
Missoula, MT
Montana State U. (Bobcats)
Bozeman, MT
Moorhead State U. (Dragons)
Moorhead, MN
Moravian Coll. (Greyhounds)
Bethlehem, PA
Morehead State U. (Eagles)
Morehead, KY
Morehouse Coll. (Tigers) Atlanta, GA
Morgan State U. (Grizzly Bears)
Baltimore, MD
Mount Holyoke Coll. (Lyons)
South Hadley, MA
Murray State U. (Racers) Murray, KY

Nebraska-Kearney, U. of (Antelopes)
Nebraska-Lincoln, U. of(Cornhuskers)
Nebraska-Omaha, U. of (Mavericks)
Nevada-Las Vegas, U. of (Rebels)
Nevada-Reno, U. of (Wolf Pack)
New Hampshire, U. of (Wildcats)
Durham, NH
New Mexico, U. of (Lobos)
Albuquerque, NM
New Mexico State U. (Aggies)
Las Cruces, NM
New Orleans, U. of (Privateers)
New Orleans, LA
New York, State U. of, College at
Binghamton (Colonials)
New York, State U. of, College at
Brockport (Golden Eagles)
New York, State U. of, College at
Cortland (Red Dragons)
New York, State U. of, College at
Farmingdale (Rams)
New York, State U. of, College at
Fredonia (Blue Devils)
New York, State U. of, College at
Geneseo (Blue Knights)
New York, State U. of, College at
New Paltz (Hawks)

New York, State U. of, College at
Oneonta (Red Dragons)
New York, State U. of, College at
Plattsburgh (Cardinals)
New York, State U. of, College at
Purchase (Panthers)
New York-Albany, State U. of
(Great Danes)
New York-Buffalo, State U. of (Bulls)
New York City U. of Lehman College
(Lancers) New York, NY
New York-Potsdam, State U. of
(Bears)
New York-Stony Brook, State U. of
(Patriots)
New York U. (Violets) New York, NY
Niagara U. (Purple Eagles)
Niagara, NY
Nicholls State U. (Colonels)
Thibodaux, LA
Norfolk State U. (Spartans)
Norfolk, VA
North Carolina-Ashville, U. of
(Bulldogs)
North Carolina-Chapel Hill, U. of
(Tar Heels)
North Carolina-Charlotte, U. of
(49'ers)
North Carolina-Greensboro, U. of
(Spartans)
North Carolina State U. (Wolfpack)
Raleigh, NC
North Carolina-Wilmington, U. of
(Seahawks)
North Dakota, U. of (Fighting Sioux)
Grand Forks, ND
North Dakota State U. (Bison)
Fargo, ND
Northeastern U. (Huskies)
Boston, MA
Northwestern U. (Wildcats)
Evanston, IL
Notre Dame. U. of (Fighting Irish)
Notre Dame, IN
Nova U. (Knights) Ft. Lauderdale, FL

Oberlin Coll. (Yeomen) Oberlin, OH
Ohio State U. (Buckeyes)
Columbus, OH
Ohio U. (Bobcats) Athens, OH
Oklahoma, U. of (Sooners)
Norman, OK
Oklahoma State U. (Cowboys)
Stillwater, OK
Old Dominion U. (Monarchs)
Norfolk, VA
Oral Roberts U. (Titans) Tulsa, OK
Oregon, U. of (Ducks) Eugene, OR
Oregon State U. (Beavers)
Corvallis, OR

Pace U. (Setters) Pleasantville, NY
Pennsylvania, U. of
(Quakers / Red & Blue)
Philadelphia, PA
Pennsylvania State U. (Nittany Lions)
University Park, PA
Pepperdine U. (Waves) Malibu, CA
Pittsburgh, U. of (Panthers)
Pittsburgh, PA
Portland, U. of (Pilots) Portland, OR
Portland State U. (Vikings)
Portland, OR
Pratt Institute (Cannoneers)
Brooklyn, NY
Princeton U. (Tigers) Princeton, NJ
Providence Coll. (Friars)
Providence, RI
Purdue U. (Boilermakers)
West Lafayette, IN

Queens Coll. (Knights) Flushing, NY

Radford U. (Highlanders) Radford, VA
Randolph-Macon Coll.
(Yellow Jackets) Ashland, VA
Reed Coll. (Griffins) Portland, OR
Regis Coll. (Beacons) Weston, MA
Rensselaer Inst. of Technology
(Engineers) Troy, NY
Rhode Island, U. of (Rams)
Kingston, RI
Rice U. (Owls) Houston, TX
Richmond, U. of (Spiders)
Richmond, VA
Rider Coll. (Broncs)
Lawrenceville, NJ
River Coll. (Raiders) Nashua, NH
Roanoke Coll. (Maroons) Salem, VA
Robert Morris Coll. (Colonials)
Coraopolis, PA
Rochester, U. of (Yellow Jackets)
Rochester, NY
Rochester Inst. of Technology
(Tigers) Rochester, NY
Rockhurst Coll. (Hawks)
Kansas City, MO
Roger Williams Coll. (Hawks)
Bristol, RI
Rollins Coll. (Tars) Winter Park, FL
Roosevelt U. (Lakers) Chicago, IL
Russell Sage Coll. (Gators) Troy, NY
Rutgers U. (Scarlet Knights)
New Brunswick, NJ

Sacred Heart U. (Pioneers)
Fairfield, CT
St. Cloud State U. (Huskies)
St. Cloud, MN
St. John's U. (Redmen) Jamaica, NY
St. Lawrence U. (Saints) Canton, NY

Samford U. (Bulldogs)
Birmingham, AL
Sam Houston State U. (Bearkats)
Huntsville, TX
San Diego, U. of (Toreros)
San Diego, CA
San Diego State U. (Aztecs)
San Diego, CA
San Francisco, U. of (Dons)
San Francisco, CA
San Francisco State U. (Gators)
San Francisco, CA
San Jose State U. (Spartans)
San Jose, CA
Santa Clara U. (Broncos)
Santa Clara, CA
Scranton, U. of (Royals) Scranton, PA
Seattle U. (Chieftains) Seattle, WA
Seton Hall U. (Pirates)
South Orange, NJ
Shaw U. (Bears) Raleigh, NC
Skidmore Coll. (Thoroughbreds)
Saratoga Springs, NY
Slippery Rock U. (The Rockets)
Slippery Rock, PA
Smith Coll. (Pioneers)
Northampton, MA
South Carolina, U. of
(Fighting Gamecocks)
Columbia, SC
South Carolina State U. (Bulldogs)
Orangeburg, SC
South Dakota, U of (Coyotes)
Vermillion, SD
South Dakota State U. (Jackrabbits)
Brookings, SD
Southern California, U. of (Trojans)
Los Angeles, CA
Southern Methodist U. (Mustangs)
Dallas, TX
South Florida, U. of (Bulls) Tampa, FL
Stanford U. (Cardinal) Stanford, CA
Stetson U. (Hatters) Deland, FL
Susquehanna U. (Crusaders)
Selinsgrove, PA
Swarthmore Coll. (Little Quakers)
Swarthmore, PA
Syracuse U. (Orangemen)
Syracuse, NY

Tampa, U. of (Spartans) Tampa, FL
Temple U. (Owls) Philadelphia, PA
Tennessee, U. of (Volunteers)
Knoxville, TN
Tennessee State U. (Tigers)
Nashville, TN
Texas A&M U. (Aggies)
College Station, TX
Texas-Arlington, U. of (Mavericks)
Texas-Austin, U. of (Longhorns)

Texas Christian U. (Horned Frogs)
  Fort Worth, TX
Texas-El Paso, U. of (Miners)
Texas-San Antonio, U. of
  (Roadrunners)
Texas-Tyler, U. of (Patriots)
Toledo, U. of (Rockets) Toledo, OH
Towson State U. (Tigers) Towson, MD
Transylvania U. (Pioneers)
  Lexington, KY
Trenton State Coll. (Lions)
  Trenton, NJ
Trinity Coll. (Bantams) Hartford, CT
Tufts U. (Jumbos) Medford, MA
Tulane U. (Green Wave)
  New Orleans, LA
Tulsa, U. of (Golden Hurricane)
  Tulsa, OK
Tuskegee U. (Golden Tigers)
  Tuskegee, AL

Union Coll. (Dutchmen)
  Schenectady, NY
US Air Force Academy (Falcons)
  Colorado Springs, CO
US International U. (Soaring Gulls)
  San Diego, CA
US Military Academy (Black Knights)
  West Point, NY
US Naval Academy (Midshipmen)
  Annapolis, MD
Ursinus Coll. (Grizzly Bears)
  Collegeville, PA
Utah, U. of (Utes) Salt Lake City, UT
Utah State U. (Aggies) Logan, UT

Vanderbilt U. (Commodores)
  Nashville, TN
Vassar Coll. (Brewers)
  Poughkeepsie, NY
Vermont, U. of (Catamounts)
  Burlington, VT
Villanova U. (Wildcats) Villanova, PA
Virginia, U. of (Cavaliers)
  Charlottesville, VA
Virginia Military Inst. (Keydets)
  Lexington, VA

Virginia State U. (Trojans)
  Pertersburg, VA

Wake Forest U. (Demon Deacons)
  Winston-Salem, NC
Washington, U. of (Huskies)
  Seattle, WA
Washington & Jefferson Coll.
  (Presidents) Washington, PA
Washington & Lee U. (Generals)
  Lexington, VA
Washington State U. (Cougars)
  Pullman, WA
Wayne State U. (Tartars) Detroit, MI
Webster U. (Gorloks) St. Louis, MO
Wesleyan U. (Cardinals)
  Middletown, CT
West Virginia U. (Mountaineers)
  Morgantown, WV
Wheaton Coll. (Lyons) Norton, MA
Williams Coll. (Ephs)
  Williamstown, MA
Wisconsin-Eau Claire, U. of (Blugolds)
Wisconsin-Green Bay, U. of (Phoenix)
Wisconsin-Lacrosse, U. of (Eagles)
Wisconsin-Madison, U. of (Badgers)
Wisconsin-Milwaukee, U. of
  (Panthers)
Wisconsin-Oshkosh, U. of (Titans)
Wisconsin-Parkside, U. of (Rangers)
Wisconsin-Platteville, U. of (Pioneers)
Wisconsin-River Falls, U. of (Falcons)
Wisconsin-Stevens Point, U. of
  (Pointers)
Wisconsin-Stout, U. of (Blue Devils)
Wisconsin-Superior, U. of
  (Yellow Jackets)
Wisconsin-Whitewater, U. of
  (Warhawks)
Wyoming, U. of (Cowboys)
  Laramie, WY

Xavier U. (Musketeers) Cincinnati, OH

Yale U. (Bulldogs) New Haven, CT
Yeshiva U. (Maccabees)
  New York, NY

# SPORTS TEAMS

| LOCATION | BASEBALL | BASKETBALL | FOOTBALL | HOCKEY |
|---|---|---|---|---|
| ATLANTA | BRAVES | HAWKS | FALCONS | |
| BALTIMORE | ORIOLES | | | |
| BOSTON | RED SOX | CELTICS | | BRUINS |
| BUFFALO | | | BILLS | SABRES |
| CALGARY | | | | FLAMES |
| CALIFORNIA | ANGELS | | | |
| CAROLINA | | | PANTHERS | |
| CHARLOTTE | | HORNETS | | |
| CHICAGO | WHITE SOX | BULLS | BEARS | BLACKHAWKS |
| CHICAGO | CUBS | | | |
| CINCINNATI | REDS | | BENGALS | |
| CLEVELAND | INDIANS | CAVALIERS | BROWNS | |
| COLORADO | ROCKIES | | | |
| DALLAS | | MAVERICKS | COWBOYS | |
| DENVER | | NUGGETS | BRONCOS | |
| DETROIT | TIGERS | PISTONS | LIONS | REDWINGS |
| EDMONTON | | | | OILERS |
| FLORIDA | MARLINS | | | |
| GOLDEN STATE | | WARRIORS | | |
| GREEN BAY | | | PACKERS | |
| HARTFORD | | | | WHALERS |
| HOUSTON | ASTROS | ROCKETS | OILERS | |
| INDIANA | | PACERS | | |
| INDIANAPOLIS | | | COLTS | |
| JACKSONVILLE | | | JAGUARS | |
| KANSAS CITY | ROYALS | | CHIEFS | |
| LOS ANGELES | DODGERS | LAKERS | RAMS | KINGS |
| LOS ANGELES | | CLIPPERS | RAIDERS | |
| MIAMI | | HEAT | DOLPHINS | |
| MILWAUKEE | BREWERS | BUCKS | | |
| MINNESOTA | TWINS | TIMBERWOLVES | VIKINGS | NORTH STARS |
| MONTREAL | EXPOS | | | CANADIENS |
| NEW ENGLAND | | | PATRIOTS | |
| NEW JERSEY | | NETS | | DEVILS |
| NEW ORLEANS | | | SAINTS | |
| NEW YORK | YANKEES | KNICKS | GIANTS | RANGERS |
| NEW YORK | METS | | JETS | ISLANDERS |
| OAKLAND | ATHLETICS | | | |
| ORLANDO | | MAGIC | | |
| OTTAWA | | | | SENATORS |
| PHILADELPHIA | PHILLIES | 76ERS | EAGLES | FLYERS |
| PHOENIX | | SUNS | CARDINALS | |
| PITTSBURGH | PIRATES | | STEELERS | PENGUINS |
| PORTLAND | | TRAIL BLAZERS | | |
| QUEBEC | | | | NORDIQUES |
| SACRAMENTO | | KINGS | | |
| ST. LOUIS | CARDINALS | | | BLUES |
| SAN ANTONIO | | SPURS | | |
| SAN DIEGO | PADRES | | CHARGERS | |
| SAN FRANCISCO | GIANTS | | 49ERS | |
| SAN JOSE | | | | SHARKS |
| SEATTLE | MARINERS | SUPERSONICS | SEAHAWKS | |
| TAMPA BAY | | | BUCCANEERS | LIGHTNING |
| TEXAS | RANGERS | | | |
| TORONTO | BLUE JAYS | | | MAPLE LEAFS |
| UTAH | | JAZZ | | |
| VANCOUVER | | | | CANUCKS |
| WASHINGTON | | BULLETS | REDSKINS | CAPITALS |
| WINNIPEG | | | | JETS |

# CONSTELLATIONS & STARS

Andromeda..............................ROSS;
.............................ALMACH, MIRACH;
....................................ALPHERATZ
Antlia (Air Pump) .....................................
Apus (Bird of Paradise) ......................
Aquarius (Water Bearer) ........LUYTEN
Aquila (Eagle) ......................ALTAIR
Ara (Altar) .............................................
Aries (Ram) ..........................HAMAL;
...................................................SHERATAN
Auriga (Charioteer)..............CAPELLA
Boötes (Herdsman)..............NEKKAR;
.....................................ARCTURUS
Caelum (Chisel).....................................
Camelopardalis (Giraffe) ...................
Cancer (Crab).........................................
Canes Venatici (Hunting Dogs) ...........
....................................LALANDE
Canis Major (Greater Dog) ..................
...............................WEZEN; ADHARA,
...............................MURZIM, SIRIUS
Canis Minor (Lesser Dog)....................
.........................................PROCYON
Capricornus (Horned Goat) ......DABIH,
...........................DENEB, GAEDI
Carina (Keel)...........................ARGUS;
.....................CANOPUS, VELORUM
Cassiopeia.............................CAPH;
.....................RUCHBAH, SCHEDAR
Centaurus (Centaur) ..............HADAR;
........................................MENKENT;
.............................ALPHA CENTAURI
Cepheus ...............................ER RAI;
............................ALFIRK, KRUGER
Cetus (Whale) ............MIRA; DIPHDA;
............................LUYTEN, MENKAR
Chamaeleon ............................................
Circinus (Dividers) ...............................
Columba (Noah's Dove) ......................
Coma Berenices (Berenice's Hair) .......
Corona Australis (Southern Crown).......
Corona Borealis (Northern Crown).........
.....................GEMMA; ALPHECCA
Corvus (Crow)......................GEINAH;
...................AL CHIBA, AL GORAH
Crater (Cup)............................................
Crux (Southern Cross) ...........ACRUX;
............ALNAIR, GACRUX, MIMOSA
Cygnus (Swan) ......................SADR;
.................CYGNI, DENEB; ALBIREO
Delphinus (Dolphin)...........ROTANEV;
.....................................SUALOCIN
Dorado (Swordfish)...............................
Draco (Dragon) ...................THUBAN;
.................ELTANIN; RASTABAN
Equuleus (Colt)......................................

Eridanus (River) ....................CURSA;
.....................ACAMAR; ERIDANI;
....................................ACHERNAR
Fornax (Furnace)..................................
Gemini (Twins) .....................ALHENA,
.....................CASTOR, POLLUX,
.............PROPUS; MEBSUTA,
.........................................MEKBUDA
Grus (Crane) ..........................................
Hercules ................................................
Horologium (Clock) ...............................
Hydra (Female Water Snake)................
.........................................ALPHARD
Hydrus (Male Water Snake) .......ROSS
Indus (Indian).........................................
Lacerta (Lizard).....................................
Leo (Lion) ...................WOLF; ZOSMA;
.....................CHERTAN, REGULUS;
.................RASSELAS; DENEBOLA
Leo Minor (Lesser Lion)........................
Lepus (Hare)................ARNEB, NIHAL
Libra (Balance) ......................................
.......................ZUBEN EL GENUBI;
...............................ZUBENESCHAMALI
Lupus (Wolf) ...........................................
Lynx ........................................................
Lyra (Lyre) .................................VEGA
Mensa (Table) .........................................
Microscopium (Microscope)..................
.........................................LACAILLE
Monoceros (Unicorn) ............................
Musca (Fly).............................................
Norma (Ruler)..........................................
Octans (Octant) .....................................
Ophiuchus (Serpent Bearer) .........YED;
.........................................SABIK;
.............................BARNARD'S STAR
Orion (Hunter)..........................RIGEL,
.............................SAIPH; MINTAKA;
...................ALNILAM, ALNITAK
.........................................BELLATRIX;
.....................................BETELGEUSE
Pavo (Peacock) ......................................
Pegasus (Winged Horse) ...........ENIF;
.................BIHAM, HOMAM, MATAR;
.....................MARKAB, SCHEAT
Perseus....................ALGOL; MIRFAK
Phoenix ..................................ANKAA
Pictor (Painter)....................KAPTEYN
Pisces (Fish) ..............VAN MAANEN
Piscis Austrinus (Southern Fish) .........
.................LACAILLE; FOMALHAUT
Pleiades ....................MAIA; MEROPE,
.....................ALCYONE, CELAENO,
.........................ELECTRA, PLEIONE,
.....................TAYGETA; ASTEROPE

207

## Constellations & Stars / Olympic Games Sites

Puppis (Deck) ..............................
Pyxis (Mariner's Compass) ..................
Reticulum (Net) .............................
Sagitta (Arrow) .............................
Sagittarius (Bowman) ............... KAUS,
.......................... ROSS; NUNKI;
..................... AL NASL; ASCELLA
Scorpio (Scorpion) ............... LESATH,
.................. SHAULA; ANTARES;
............. GRAFFIAS; DSCHUBBA
Scutum (Shield) ..............................
Serpens (Serpent) ...........................
Sextans (Sextant) ...........................
Taurus (Bull) ........ EL NATH, HYADES;
........................... ALDEBARAN
Telescopium (Telescope) ....................
Triangulum (Triangle) ............... AVIOR

Triangulum Australe ........................
.......................... (Southern Triangle)
Tucana (Toucan) ............................
Ursa Major (Greater Bear) ..................
........................ ALCOR, DUBHE,
............... MERAK, MIZAR; ALIOTH,
............. ALKAID, MEGREZ, PHECDA;
.................. MUSCIDA, TALITHA;
........................ GROOMBRIDGE
Ursa Minor (Lesser Bear) ..................
............................ KOCHAB;
.................. PHERKAD, POLARIS
Vela (Sails) ..................... SUHAIL
Virgo (Virgin) ...................... SPICA;
.............. PORRIMA; ZAVIJAVA
Volans (Flying Fish) ........................
Vulpecula (Little Fox) ......................

# OLYMPIC GAMES SITES

## SUMMER GAMES

| 1896 | Athens, Greece |
| 1900 | Paris, France |
| 1904 | St. Louis, MO, USA |
| 1908 | London, England |
| 1912 | Stockholm, Sweden |
| 1916 | not held |
| 1920 | Antwerp, Belgium |
| 1924 | Paris, France |
| 1928 | Amsterdam, Netherlands |
| 1932 | Los Angeles, CA, USA |
| 1936 | Berlin, Germany |
| 1940 | not held |
| 1944 | not held |
| 1948 | London, England |
| 1952 | Helsinki, Finland |
| 1956 | Melbourne, Australia |
| 1960 | Rome, Italy |
| 1964 | Tokyo, Japan |
| 1968 | Mexico City, Mexico |
| 1972 | Munich, West Germany |
| 1976 | Montreal, Canada |
| 1980 | Moscow, USSR |
| 1984 | Los Angeles, CA, USA |
| 1988 | Seoul, South Korea |
| 1992 | Barcelona, Spain |
| 1996 | Atlanta, GA, USA |
| 2000 | Sydney, Australia |

## WINTER GAMES

| 1924 | Chamonix, France |
| 1928 | St. Moritz, Switzerland |
| 1932 | Lake Placid, NY, USA |
| 1936 | Garmisch-Partenkirchen, Germany |
| 1940 | not held |
| 1944 | not held |
| 1948 | St. Moritz, Switzerland |
| 1952 | Oslo, Norway |
| 1956 | Cortina d'Ampezzo, Italy |
| 1960 | Squaw Valley, CA, USA |
| 1964 | Innsbruck, Austria |
| 1968 | Grenoble, France |
| 1972 | Sapporo, Japan |
| 1976 | Innsbruck, Austria |
| 1980 | Lake Placid, NY, USA |
| 1984 | Sarajevo, Yugoslavia |
| 1988 | Calgary, Alberta, Canada |
| 1992 | Albertville, France |
| 1994 | Lillehammer, Norway |

# UNITED STATES INFORMATION

* Indicates one of the Thirteen Original States

**ALABAMA**: AL, Ala.; capital, MONTGOMERY; nicknames, COTTON, HEART OF DIXIE, YELLOWHAMMER; state flower, CAMELLIA; state bird, YELLOWHAMMER; motto, WE DARE DEFEND OUR RIGHTS.

**ALASKA**: AK, Alas.; capital, JUNEAU; nickname, THE LAST FRONTIER; state flower, FORGET-ME-NOT; state bird, WILLOW PTARMIGAN; motto, NORTH TO THE FUTURE.

**ARIZONA**: AZ, Ariz.; capital, PHOENIX; nickname GRAND CANYON; state flower, SAGUARO; state bird, SAGUARO CACTUS BLOSSOM; motto, *DITAT DEUS* (God enriches).

**ARKANSAS**: AR, Ark; capital, LITTLE ROCK; nickname, LAND OF OPPORTUNITY; state flower, APPLE BLOSSOM; state bird, MOCKINGBIRD; motto, *REGNAT POPULUS* (The people rule).

**CALIFORNIA**: CA, Cal., Calif.; capital, SACRAMENTO; nicknames, GOLDEN, EL DORADO; state flower, GOLDEN POPPY; state bird, CALIFORNIA VALLEY QUAIL; motto, EUREKA (I have found it).

**COLORADO**: CO, Colo.; capital, DENVER; nicknames CENTENNIAL, SILVER; state flower, COLUMBINE; state bird, LARK BUNTING; motto, *NIL SINE NUMINE* (Nothing without providence).

**\*CONNECTICUT**: CT, Conn.; capital, HARTFORD; nicknames, CONSTITUTION, NUTMEG; state flower, MOUNTAIN LAUREL; state bird, ROBIN; motto, *QUI TRANSTULIT SUSTINET* (He who transplanted still sustains).

**\*DELAWARE**: DE, Del., Dela.; capital, DOVER; nicknames FIRST, DIAMOND, BLUE HEN; state flower, PEACH BLOSSOM, AMERICAN BEAUTY ROSE; state bird, BLUE HEN CHICKEN; motto, LIBERTY AND INDEPENDENCE.

**FLORIDA**: FL, Fla.; capital, TALLAHASSEE; nickname, SUNSHINE; state flower, ORANGE BLOSSOM; state bird, MOCKINGBIRD; motto, IN GOD WE TRUST.

**\*GEORGIA**: GA, Ga.; capital, ATLANTA; nicknames, PEACH, EMPIRE STATE OF THE SOUTH; state flower, CHEROKEE ROSE; state bird, BROWN THRASHER; motto, WISDOM, JUSTICE, AND MODERATION.

**HAWAII**: HI, Haw.; capital, HONOLULU; nicknames, ALOHA, PARADISE OF THE PACIFIC; state flower, HIBISCUS; state bird, NENE; motto, THE LIFE OF THE LAND IS PERPETUATED IN RIGHTEOUSNESS.

**IDAHO**: ID, Ida.; capital, BOISE; nickname, GEM; state flower, SYRINGA; state bird, MOUNTAIN BLUEBIRD; motto, *ESTO PERPETUA* (It is perpetual).

**ILLINOIS**: IL, Ill.; capital SPRINGFIELD; nicknames, PRAIRIE, SUCKER, THE INLAND EMPIRE; state flower, VIOLET; state bird, CARDINAL; motto, STATE SOVEREIGNTY—NATIONAL UNION.

**INDIANA**: IN, Ind.; capital, INDIANAPOLIS; nickname, HOOSIER; state flower, PEONY; state bird,CARDINAL; motto, CROSSROADS OF AMERICA.

**IOWA**: IA, Ia.; capital, DES MOINES; nickname, HAWKEYE; state flower, WILD ROSE; state bird, EASTERN GOLDFINCH; motto, OUR LIBERTIES WE PRIZE AND OUR RIGHTS WE WILL MAINTAIN.

**KANSAS**: KS, Kan., Kans.; capital, TOPEKA; nicknames, SUNFLOWER, JAY-HAWKER; state flower, SUNFLOWER; state bird, WESTERN MEADOWLARK; motto, *AD ASTRA PER ASPERA* (To the stars through difficulties).

**KENTUCKY**: KY, Ky.; capital, FRANKFORT; nickname, BLUEGRASS; state flower, GOLDENROD; state bird, CARDINAL; motto, UNITED WE STAND, DIVIDED WE FALL.

**LOUISIANA**: LA, La.; capital, BATON ROUGE; nicknames, PELICAN, CREOLE; state flower, MAGNOLIA; state bird, EASTERN BROWN PELICAN; motto, UNION, JUSTICE, AND CONFIDENCE.

**MAINE**: ME, Me.; capital, AUGUSTA; nicknames, PINE TREE, LUMBER; state flower, PINE CONE AND TASSEL; state bird, CHICKADEE; motto, *DIRIGO* (I direct).

**\*MARYLAND**: MD, Md.; capital, ANNAPOLIS; nicknames, OLD LINE, FREE, COCKADE; state flower, BLACK-EYED SUSAN; state bird, BALTIMORE ORIOLE; motto, *FATTI MASCHII, PAROLE FEMINE* (Manly deeds, womanly words).

**\*MASSACHUSETTS**: MA, Mass.; capital, BOSTON; nicknames, BAY, OLD COLONY; state flower, MAYFLOWER; state bird, CHICKADEE; motto, *ENSE PETIT PLACIDAM SUB LIBERTATE QUIETEM* (By the sword we seek peace, but peace only under liberty).

**MICHIGAN**: MI, Mich.; capital, LANSING; nicknames, WOLVERINE, GREAT LAKE; state flower, APPLE BLOSSOM; state bird, ROBIN; motto, *SI QUAERIS PENINSULAM AMOENAM CIRCUMSPICE* (If you seek a pleasant peninsula, look about you).

**MINNESOTA**: MN, Minn.; capital, ST. PAUL; nicknames, NORTH STAR, GOPHER; state flower, LADY'S-SLIPPER; state bird, COMMON LOON; motto, *L'ETOILE DU NORD* (The star of the north).

**MISSISSIPPI**: MS, Miss.; capital, JACKSON; nicknames, MAGNOLIA, BAYOU; state flower, MAGNOLIA; state bird, MOCKINGBIRD; motto, *VIRTUTE ET ARMIS* (By valor and arms).

**MISSOURI**: MO, Mo.; capital, JEFFERSON CITY; nicknames, SHOW ME, BULLION; state flower, HAWTHORN; state bird, BLUEBIRD; motto, *SALUS POPULI SUPREMA LEX ESTO* (Will of the people shall be the supreme law).

**MONTANA**: MT, Mont.; capital, HELENA; nicknames, TREASURE, MOUNTAIN; state flower, BITTERROOT; state bird, WESTERN MEADOWLARK; motto, *ORO Y PLATA* (Gold and silver).

**NEBRASKA**: NE, Nebr.; capital, LINCOLN; nicknames, CORNHUSKER, BLACKWATER; state flower, GOLDENROD; state bird, WESTERN MEADOWLARK; motto, EQUALITY BEFORE THE LAW.

**NEVADA**: NV, Nev.; capital, CARSON CITY; nicknames, SAGE BRUSH, SILVER; state flower, SAGEBRUSH; state bird, MOUNTAIN BLUEBIRD; motto, ALL FOR OUR COUNTRY.

**\*NEW HAMPSHIRE**: NH, N.H.; capital, CONCORD; nickname, GRANITE; state flower, PURPLE LILAC; state bird, PURPLE FINCH; motto, LIVE FREE OR DIE.

**\*NEW JERSEY**: NJ, N.J.; capital, TRENTON; nickname, GARDEN; state flower, VIOLET; state bird, EASTERN GOLDFINCH; motto, LIBERTY AND PROSPERITY.

**NEW MEXICO**: NM, N.M.; capital, SANTA FE; nicknames, LAND OF ENCHANTMENT, SUNSHINE; state flower, YUCCA; state bird, ROADRUNNER; motto, *CRESCIT EUNDO* (It grows as it goes).

**\*NEW YORK**: NY, N.Y.; capital, ALBANY; nickname, EMPIRE; state flower, ROSE; state bird, BLUEBIRD; motto, EXCELSIOR (Ever upward).

**\*NORTH CAROLINA**: NC, N.C.; capital, RALEIGH; nicknames, TAR HEEL, OLD NORTH; state flower, DOGWOOD; state bird, CARDINAL; motto, *ESSE QUAM VIDERI* (To be rather than to seem).

**NORTH DAKOTA**: ND, N.D.; capital, BISMARCK; nicknames, PEACE GARDEN, SIOUX, FLICKERTAIL; state flower, WILD PRAIRIE ROSE; state bird, WESTERN MEADOWLARK; motto, LIBERTY AND UNION, NOW AND FOREVER, ONE AND INSEPARABLE.

**OHIO**: OH, O.; capital, COLUMBUS; nickname, BUCKEYE; state flower, SCARLET CARNATION; state bird, CARDINAL; motto, WITH GOD, ALL THINGS ARE POSSIBLE.

**OKLAHOMA**: OK, Okla.; capital, OKLAHOMA CITY; nickname, SOONER; state flower, MISTLETOE; state bird, SCISSOR-TAILED FLYCATCHER; motto, *LABOR OMNIA VINCIT* (Labor conquers all).

**OREGON**: OR, Ore.; capital, SALEM; nicknames, BEAVER, SUNSET, VALENTINE, WEBFOOT; state flower, OREGON GRAPE; state bird, WESTERN MEADOWLARK; motto, SHE FLIES WITH HER OWN WINGS.

**\*PENNSYLVANIA**: PA, Penn., Penna.; capital, HARRISBURG; nickname, KEYSTONE; state flower, MOUNTAIN LAUREL; state bird, RUFFED GROUSE; motto, VIRTUE, LIBERTY, AND INDEPENDENCE.

**\*RHODE ISLAND**: RI, R.I.; capital, PROVIDENCE; nicknames, LITTLE RHODY, OCEAN; state flower, VIOLET; state bird, RHODE ISLAND RED; motto, HOPE.

**\*SOUTH CAROLINA**: SC, S.C.; capital, COLUMBIA; nickname, PALMETTO; state flower, YELLOW JESSAMINE; state bird, CAROLINA WREN; motto, *DUM SPIRO SPERO* (While I breathe, I hope).

**SOUTH DAKOTA**: SD, S.D.; capital, PIERRE; nicknames, COYOTE, SUNSHINE; state flower, PASQUE FLOWER; state bird, RINGNECKED PHEASANT; motto, UNDER GOD, THE PEOPLE RULE.

**TENNESSEE**: TN, Tenn.; capital, NASHVILLE; nickname, VOLUNTEER; state flower, IRIS; state bird, MOCKINGBIRD; motto, AGRICULTURE AND COMMERCE..

**TEXAS**: TX, Tex.; capital, AUSTIN; nickname, LONE STAR; state flower, BLUEBONNET; state bird, MOCKINGBIRD; motto, FRIENDSHIP.

**UTAH**: UT, Ut.; capital, SALT LAKE CITY; nicknames, BEEHIVE, MORMON; state flower, SEGO LILY; state bird, SEAGULL; motto, INDUSTRY.

**VERMONT**: VT, Vt.; capital, MONTPELIER; nickname, GREEN MOUNTAIN; state flower, RED CLOVER; state bird, HERMIT THRUSH; motto, FREEDOM AND UNITY.

**\*VIRGINIA**: VA, Va.; capital, RICHMOND; nicknames, OLD DOMINION, MOTHER OF PRESIDENTS; state flower, DOGWOOD; state bird, CARDINAL; motto, *SIC SEMPER TYRANNIS* (Thus always to tyrants).

**WASHINGTON**: WA, Wash.; capital, OLYMPIA; nicknames, EVERGREEN, CHINOOK; state flower, WESTERN RHODODENDRON; state bird, WILLOW GOLDFINCH; motto, ALKI (By and by).

**WEST VIRGINIA**: WV, W.Va.; capital, CHARLESTON; nickname, MOUNTAIN; state flower, BIG RHODODENDRON; state bird, CARDINAL; motto, *MONTANI SEMPER LIBERI* (Mountaineers are always free).

**WISCONSIN**: WI, Wis., Wisc.; capital, MADISON; nickname, BADGER; state flower, WOOD VIOLET; state bird, ROBIN; motto, FORWARD.

**WYOMING**: WY, Wyo.; capital, CHEYENNE; nickname, EQUALITY; state flower, INDIAN PAINTBRUSH; state bird, MEADOWLARK; motto, EQUAL RIGHTS.

# NATIONS INFORMATION

* Indicates official language.

**AFGHANISTAN**: capital, KABUL; ethnic groups, TAJIK, UZBEK, HAZARA, PUSHTUN; languages, UZBEK, PUSHTU, DARI PERSIAN; money, AFGHANI / PUL.

**ALBANIA**: capital, TIRANE; other cities, LEZHA, VLORA, DURRES; ethnic groups, GEG (GHEG), TOSK; languages, GREEK, ALBANIAN; money, LEK / QINTAR.

**ALGERIA**: capital, ALGIERS(El Djazair); other cities, ORAN, WAHRAN, QACENTINA; ethnic groups, ARAB, BERBER; languages, *ARABIC, BERBER; money, DINAR / CENTIME.

**ANDORRA**: capital, ANDORRA LA VELLA; ethnic groups, CATALAN, SPANISH, ANDORRAN, FRENCH; languages, *CATALAN, SPANISH, FRENCH; money, FRENCH FRANC and SPANISH PESETA.

**ANGOLA**: capital, LUANDA; ethnic groups, BAKONGO, KIMBUNDU, OVIMBUNDU; languages, PORTUGUESE, BANTU; money, KWANZA / LWEI.

**ANTIGUA AND BARBUDA**: capital, ST. JOHN'S; ethnic groups, AFRICANS; language, ENGLISH; money, DOLLAR / CENT.

**ARGENTINA**: capital, BUENOS AIRES; other cities, CORDOBA, MENDOZA, ROSARIO; ethnic groups, EUROPEANS, MESTIZOS, INDIANS; language, SPANISH; money, AUSTRAL / CENTAVO.

**ARMENIA**: capital, YEREVAN; ethnic groups, ARMENIAN, AZERBAIJAN; language, ARMENIAN; money, RUBLE / KOPECK.

**AUSTRALIA**: capital, CANBERRA; other cities, PERTH, SYDNEY, ADELAIDE, BRISBANE, MELBOURNE; states, VICTORIA, TASMANIA, QUEENSLAND, NEW SOUTH WALES; ethnic groups, EUROPEAN, ASIANS, ABORIGINES; language, ENGLISH; money, DOLLAR / CENT.

**AUSTRIA**: capital, VIENNA; other cities, INNSBRUCK, BREGENZ, LECH, GRAZ, LINZ, SALZBURG; ethnic groups, GERMAN, SLOVENE, CROATIAN; language, GERMAN; money, SCHILLING / GROSCHEN.

**AZERBAIJAN**: capital, BAKU; ethnic groups, AZERBAIJAN, RUSSIAN; languages, AZERI, TURKISH, RUSSIAN; money, RUBLE / KOPECK.

**BAHAMAS, THE**: capital, NASSAU; other cities, FREEPORT, NEW PROVIDENCE; ethnic groups, AFRICAN, CAUCASIAN; language, ENGLISH; money, DOLLAR / CENT.

**BAHRAIN**: capital, MANAMA; ethnic groups, BAHRAINI, ARAB, IRANIAN, ASIANS; language; ARABIC, FARSI, URDU; money, DINAR / FILS.

**BANGLADESH**: capital, DHAKA; other cities, KHULNA, CHITTAGONG; ethnic groups, BIHARI, BENGALI; languages, *BENGALI, MAGH, CHAKMA; money, TAKA / PAISA.

**BARBADOS**: capital, BRIDGETOWN; ethnic groups, AFRICAN, CAUCASIAN; language, ENGLISH; money, DOLLAR / CENT.

**BELARUS**: capital, MINSK; ethnic groups, BELARUS, POLES; language, BELORUSSIAN; money, RUBLE / KOPECK.

**BELGIUM**: capital, BRUSSELS; other cities, GHENT, LIEGE, ANTWERP; ethnic groups, FLEMING, WALLOON; languages, FRENCH, FLEMISH; money, FRANC / CENTIME.

**BELIZE**: capital, BELMOPAN; ethnic groups, MAYA, CREOLE, MESTIZO; languages, *ENGLISH, SPANISH, and CREOLE DIALECTS; money, DOLLAR / CENT.

**BENIN**: capital, PORTO-NOVO; other city, COTONOU; ethnic groups, FON, ADJA, BARIBA, YORUBA; languages, *FRENCH, FON, SOMBA, YORUBA; money, FRANC / CENTIME.

**BHUTAN**: capital, THIMPHU; other city, PARO DZONG; ethnic groups, BHOTE, NEPALESE; languages, *DZONGKHA, GURUNG, ASSAMESE; money, NGULTRUM / CHETRUM.

**BOLIVIA**: capitals, LA PAZ, SUCRE; other cities, SANTA CRUZ; ethnic groups, AYMARA, QUECHUA; languages, *AYMARA, *QUECHUA, *SPANISH; money, BOLIVIANO / PESO; river, BENI.

**BOSNIA AND HERZEGOVINA**: capital, SARAJEVO; other city, MOSTAR; ethnic groups, SERBIAN, MUSLIM-SLAV, CROATIAN; languages, SERBO-CROATIAN; money, DINAR / PARA.

**BOTSWANA**: capital, GABORONE; ethnic groups, TSWANA, KALANGA; languages, *ENGLISH, SHONA, TSWANA; money, PULA / THEBE.

**BRAZIL**: capital, BRASILIA; other cities, BELEM, RECIFE, SALVADOR, SAO PAULO, PORTO ALEGRE, RIO DE JANEIRO; states (selected), ACRE, PARA, AMAPA, BAHIA, CEARA, GOIAS, PIAUI, PARANA, ALAGOAS, GUAPORE, PARAIBA, SERGIPE, AMAZONAS; ethnic groups, PORTUGUESE, AFRICAN, MULATTO, AND OTHERS; language, PORTUGUESE; money, CRUZADO / CENTAVO.

**BRUNEI DARUSSALAM**: capital, BANDAR SERI BEGAWAN; ethnic groups, MALAY, CHINESE; languages, *MALAY, *ENGLISH, CHINESE; money, DOLLAR / CENT.

**BULGARIA**: capital, SOFIA; other cities, VARNA, PLOVDIV; ethnic groups, BULGARIAN, TURKS; languages, *BULGARIAN, TURKISH; money, LEV / STOTINKA.

**BURKINA FASO**: capital, OUAGADOUGOU; ethnic groups, BOBO, MANDE, MOSSI; languages, *FRENCH, VARIOUS TRIBAL LANGUAGES; money, FRANC / CENTIME.

**BURMA** (See **MYANMAR**).

**BURUNDI**: capital, BUJUMBURA; ethnic groups, TWA, HUTU, TUTSI; languages, *RUNDI, *FRENCH; money, FRANC / CENTIME.

**CAMBODIA**: capital, PHNOM PENH; ethnic groups, CAMBODIAN, VIETNAMESE, CHINESE; languages, *KHMER, FRENCH; money, RIEL / SEN.

**CAMEROON**: capital, YAOUNDE; other city, DOUALA; ethnic groups, FULANI, BAMILEKE; languages, *ENGLISH, *FRENCH; money, FRANC / CENTIME.

**CANADA**: capital, OTTAWA; other cities, QUEBEC, CALGARY, TORONTO, EDMONTON, MONTREAL, WINNIPEG, VANCOUVER; provinces, QUEBEC, ALBERTA, ONTARIO, MANITOBA, NOVA SCOTIA, NEW BRUNSWICK, NEW-FOUNDLAND, SASKATCHEWAN, BRITISH COLUMBIA, PRINCE EDWARD ISLAND; ethnic groups, BRITISH, FRENCH, EUROPEAN; language, *ENGLISH, *FRENCH; money, DOLLAR / CENT.

**CAPE VERDE**: capital, PRAIA; ethnic groups, CREOLE, SERER, AFRICAN; languages, *PORTUGUESE, CRIOULO; money, ESCUDO / CENTAVO.

**CENTRAL AFRICAN REPUBLIC**: capital, BANGUI; ethnic groups, BAYA, SARA, BANDA, MANDJA; language, FRENCH; money, FRANC / CENTIME.

**CHAD**: capital, N'DJAMENA; ethnic groups, VARIOUS TRIBAL; languages, *FRENCH, *ARABIC; money, FRANC / CENTIME.

**CHILE**: capital, SANTIAGO; ethnic groups, MESTIZOS, SPANISH, INDIAN; languages, SPANISH; money, PESO / CENTESIMO.

**CHINA**: capital, BEIJING; other cities, WUHAN, CANTON, TIANJIN, SHANGHAI; ethnic groups, HAN, LOLO, NOSU, MANCHU, MONGOL, KOREAN; languages, GAN, HUI, MIN, YUE, HAKKA, XIANG, ZHUANG, MANDARIN; Chinese provinces, ANHUI, GANSU, HEBEI, HENAN, HUBEI, HUNAN, JILIN, FUJIAN; money, YUAN / FEN.

**COLOMBIA**: capital, BOGOTA; other cities, CALI, MEDELLIN; ethnic groups, MESTIZOS, CAUCASIANS, MULATTO; language, SPANISH; money, PESO / CENTAVO.

**COMOROS**: capital, MORONI; ethnic groups, ARABS, AFRICANS, EAST INDIANS; languages, *ARABIC, *FRENCH; money, FRANC / CENTIME.

**CONGO**: capital, BRAZZAVILLE; other cities, LOUBOMO, POINT-NOIRE; ethnic groups, BATEKE, BAKONGO; languages, *FRENCH, TEKE, KONGO; money, FRANC / CENTIME.

**COSTA RICA**: capital, SAN JOSE; ethnic groups, SPANISH, MESTIZOS, language, SPANISH; money, COLON / CENTIMO.

**COTE D'IVOIRE**: capital, ABIDJAN; ethnic groups, BETF, BAULE, SENUFO, MALINKE; languages, *FRENCH, KRU, AKAN, MALINKE, VOLTAIC; money, FRANC / CENTIME.

**CROATIA**: capital, ZAGREB; other cities, CAMAGUEY; ethnic groups, CROATS, SERBIANS; languages, SERBO-CROATIAN; money, DINAR / PARA.

**CUBA**: capital, HAVANA; other city, GUANTANAMO; ethnic groups, SPANISH, AFRICAN; language, SPANISH; money, PESO / CENTAVO.

**CYPRUS**: capital, NICOSIA; ethnic groups, GREEKS, TURKS, ARMENIANS, MARONITES; languages, *GREEK, *TURKISH, ENGLISH; money, POUND / CENT.

**CZECH REPUBLIC**: capital, PRAGUE; other cities, BRNO, OSTRAVA, BRATISLAVA; ethnic group, CZECHS; language, CZECH; money, KORUNA / HALER.

**DENMARK**: capital, COPENHAGEN; ethnic group, SCANDINAVIAN; languages, DANISH; money, KRONE / ORE.

**DJIBOUTI**: capital, DJIBOUTI; ethnic groups, ISSA, AFAR, EUROPEAN; languages, *FRENCH, *ARABIC, AFAR, ISSA; money, FRANC / CENTIME.

**DOMINICA**: capital, ROSEAU; ethnic groups, AFRICAN, CARIB; languages, *ENGLISH, FRENCH CREOLE; money, DOLLAR / CENT.

**DOMINICAN REPUBLIC**: capital, SANTO DOMINGO; ethnic groups, CAUCASIAN, AFRICAN; languages, SPANISH; money, PESO / CENTAVO.

**ECUADOR**: capital, QUITO; other city, GUAYAQUIL; ethnic groups, MESTIZOS, AFRICAN, INDIANS, SPANISH; languages, *SPANISH, QUECHUAN, JIVAROAN; money, SUCRE / CENTAVO.

**EGYPT**: capital, CAIRO; other cities, GAZA, AL-JIZAH, ALEXANDRIA; ethnic groups, NUBIAN, BEDOUIN, HAMITIC; language, ARABIC; money, POUND / PIASTER; river, NILE.

**EL SALVADOR**: capital, SAN SALVADOR; ethnic groups, MESTIZO, INDIAN; language, SPANISH; money, COLON / CENTAVO.

**EQUATORIAL GUINEA**: capital, MALABO; ethnic groups, BUBI, FANG; languages, *SPANISH, BUBI, FANG; money, FRANC / CENTIME.

**ESTONIA**: capital, TALLINN; ethnic groups, ESTONIAN, RUSSIAN; languages, *ESTONIAN, RUSSIAN; money, RUBLE / KOPECK.

**ETHIOPIA**: capital, ADDIS ABABA; other cities, ASMERA, HARER, DESE, GONDER; ethnic groups, TIGRE, OROMO, AMHARA, SIDAMA, KAFA, SAHO, GALLA, KAFFA; languages, *AMHARIC, GALLA, TIGRE; money, BIRR / CENT; river, JUBA.

**FIJI**: capital, SUVA; ethnic groups, INDIAN, FIJIAN; languages, *ENGLISH, FIJIAN, HINDI; money, DOLLAR / CENT.

**FINLAND**: capital, HELSINKI; other cities, TURKU, TAMPERE; ethnic groups, FINNS, LAPPS, SWEDES; languages, *FINNISH, *SWEDISH; money, MARKKA / PENNI.

**FRANCE**: capital, PARIS; other cities, PAU, LYON, METZ, NICE, BREST, TOURS, NANCY, ROUEN, RENNES, TOULON; ethnic group, FRENCH; languages, *FRENCH, BASQUE, BRETON, CATALAN; money, FRANC / CENTIME; rivers, SEINE, SAONE, LOIRE.

**GABON**: capital, LIBREVILLE; ethnic groups, FANG, BAPOUNON; language, *FRENCH, BANTU; money, FRANC / CENTIME.

**GAMBIA, THE**: capital, BANJUL; ethnic groups, FULA, WOLOF, MANDINKA; languages, *ENGLISH, WOLOF, MALINKE; money, DALASI / BUTUT.

**GEORGIA**: capital, TBILISI; other cities, SUCHUMI, BATUMI; ethnic groups, GEORGIAN, RUSSIAN; languages, GEORGIAN, RUSSIAN; money, RUBLE / KOPECK.

**GERMANY**: capital, BERLIN; other cities, ULM, BONN, KOLN, ESSEN, BREMEN, ERFURT; ethnic group, GERMAN; language, GERMAN; money, DEUTSCHE MARK / PFENNIG; rivers, ISAR, RHINE, WESER, ELBE.

**GHANA**: capital, ACCRA; ethnic groups, AKAN, AKRA, MOSHI-DAGOMBA, EWE, GA; languages, *ENGLISH, MOSHI, EWE, AKAN; money, CEDI / PESEWA.

**GREECE**: capital, ATHENS; other cities, LARISA, PATRAS, CORINTH, PIRAEUS, THESSALONIKI; ethnic groups, GREEK; languages, GREEK; money, DRACHMA / LEPTON.

**GRENADA**: capital, ST. GEORGE'S; ethnic group, AFRICAN; language, *ENGLISH, FRENCH; money, DOLLAR / CENT.

**GUATEMALA**: capital, GUATEMALA CITY; other cities, ANTIGUA, QUEZALTENANGO; ethnic groups, MAYA, MESTIZOS; languages, *SPANISH, MAYAN; money, QUETZAL / CENTAVO.

**GUINEA**: capital, CONAKRY; other cities, LABE, KANKAN; ethnic groups, FOULAH, MALINKE, SOUSSOUS; languages, *FRENCH, PEUL, MANDE; money, FRANC / CENTIME.

**GUINEA-BISSAU**: capital, BISSAU; ethnic groups, BALANTA, FULA, MANDINKA, MANJACA; languages, *PORTUGUESE, CRIOULD; money, PESO / CENTAVO.

**GUYANA**: capital, GEORGETOWN; ethnic groups, EAST INDIAN, AFRICAN; language, ENGLISH; money, DOLLAR / CENT.

**HAITI**: capital, PORT-AU-PRINCE; ethnic group, AFRICAN; languages, *FRENCH, *CREOLE; money, GOURDE / CENTIME.

**HONDURAS**: capital, TEGUCIGALPA; ethnic groups, MESTIZO, INDIAN; languages, SPANISH; money, LEMPIRA / CENTAVO.

**HUNGARY**: capital, BUDAPEST; other cities, GYOR, PECS, MISKOLC, SZEGED, DEBRECEN; ethnic groups, MAGYAR, GERMAN, GYPSY; languages, HUNGARIAN; money, FORINT / FILLER.

**ICELAND**: capital, REYKJAVIK; ethnic groups, NORWEGIAN, CELT; languages, ISLENSKA (ICELANDIC); money, KRONA / EYRIR.

**INDIA**: capital, NEW DELHI; other cities, MADRAS, CALCUTTA, BOMBAY, AGRA, BENARES, AMRITSAR, PATNA, LUCKNOW, JAIPUR; states (selected) ASSAM, BIHAR, DELHI, BOMBAY, KERALA, MYSORE, ORISSA, PUNJAB; ethnic groups, INDO-ARYAN, DRAVIDIAN, MONGOLOID; languages, *HINDI; money, RUPEE / PAISA.

**INDONESIA**: capital, JAKARTA; other cities, DILI, SURABAYA, BANDUNG, MEDAN; ethnic groups, MAYAY, CHINESE, IRIANESE, DYAK; languages, *BAHASA, DAYAK (DYAK); money, RUPIAH / SEN.

**IRAN**: capital, TEHRAN; other cities, SHIRAZ, YAZD, ESFAHAN, MASHHAD, TABRIZ; ethnic groups, PERSIAN, AZERBAIJANI, KURD; languages, *FARSI, ARABIC, KURDISH, TURKISH; money, RIAL / DINAR.

**IRAQ**: capital, BAGHDAD; other cities, BASRA, MOSUL, IRBIL, KIRKUK; ethnic groups, ARAB, KURD, TURK; languages, *ARABIC, KURDISH; money, DINAR / FILS.

**IRELAND, REPUBLIC OF**: capital, DUBLIN; other cities, LIMERICK, CORK, GALWAY, WEXFORD; ethnic group, CELTIC; language, ENGLISH, IRISH-GAELIC; money, POUND / PENNY.

**ISRAEL**: capital, JERUSALEM; other cities, ACRE, TEL AVIV, HAIFA; ethnic groups, JEWISH, ARAB; languages, *HEBREW, *ARABIC; money, SHEKEL / AGORA.

217

## Nations (Italy / Libya)

**ITALY**: capital, ROME (ROMA); other cities, MILAN (MILANO), FLORENCE (FIRENZE), VENICE (VENEZIA), PADUA (PADOVA), UDINE, TURIN (TORINO), GENOA (GENOVA), NAPLES (NAPOLI), BOLOGNA, LIVORNO, ANCONA, BRINDISI, TARANTO, BARI, SALERNO, PARMA, VERONA, TRIESTE, RIMINI, PALERMO (SICILY); ethnic groups, ITALIAN; languages, ITALIAN; money, LIRA / CENTESIMO.

**JAMAICA**: capital, KINGSTON; ethnic groups, various AFRICAN, CAUCASIAN, CHINESE; languages, *ENGLISH, JAMAICAN CREOLE; money, DOLLAR / CENT.

**JAPAN**: capital, TOKYO; other cities, OSAKA, HIROSHIMA, NAGASAKI, KOBE, KYOTO, YOKOHAMA, NAGOYA, SAPPORO, KAWASAKI, FUKUOKA; ethnic groups, JAPANESE; languages, JAPANESE; money, YEN / SEN.

**JORDAN**: capital, AMMAN; other cities, IRBID, AZ-ZARQA; ethnic groups, ARAB; languages, ARABIC; money, DINAR / FILS.

**KAZAKHSTAN**: capital, ALMA-ATA; ethnic groups, KAZAKH, RUSSIAN, GERMAN, UKRAINIAN; languages, KAZAKH, RUSSIAN; money, RUBLE / KOPECK.

**KENYA**: capital, NAIROBI; other city, MOMBASA; ethnic groups, KIKUYU, LUHYA, KELENJIN, LUO, KAMBA; languages, *SWAHILI, MERU, KIKUYU, LUHYA, LUO; money, SHILLING / CENT.

**KIRIBATI**: capital, TARAWA; ethnic groups, MICRONESIAN, POLYNESIAN; languages, *ENGLISH, GILBERTESE; money, DOLLAR / CENT(Australian).

**KOREA, NORTH**: capital, PYONGYANG; ethnic group, KOREAN; language, KOREAN; money, WON / JEON or JUN.

**KOREA, SOUTH**: capital, SEOUL; other cities, TAEGU, PUSAN, KWANGJU, INCHON; ethnic group, KOREAN; language, KOREAN; money, WON.

**KUWAIT**: capital, KUWAIT; other city, HAWALLI; ethnic groups, KUWAITI, ARAB, IRANIAN, INDIAN, PAKISTANI; languages, ARABIC; money, DINAR / FILS.

**KYRGYZSTAN**: capital, BISHKEK; ethnic groups, KYRGHIZ, RUSSIAN, UZBEK; languages, KYRGHIZ, RUSSIAN; money, RUBLE / KOPECK

**LAOS**: capital, VIENTIANE; ethnic groups, LAO, MON-KHMER, THAI, MEO, YAO; languages, *LAO, TAI, PALAUNG-WA; money, KIP / AT.

**LATVIA**: capital, RIGA; ethnic groups, LATVIAN, RUSSIAN; languages, LATVIAN; money, RUBLE / KOPECK.

**LEBANON**: capital, BEIRUT; other cities, TRIPOLI, TYRE; ethnic groups, ARAB, PALESTINIAN, ARMENIAN; languages, *ARABIC, FRENCH; money, POUND / PIASTER.

**LESOTHO**: capital, MASERU; other cities, ; ethnic groups, SOTHO; languages, *ENGLISH, *SOTHO; money, LOTI / LISENTE.

**LIBERIA**: capital, MONROVIA; ethnic groups, KRU, VAI, VEI, GOLA, AMERICO-LIBERIAN; languages, ENGLISH; money, DOLLAR / CENT.

**LIBYA**: capital, TRIPOLI; other cities, BANGHAZI, TUBRUQ; ethnic groups, ARAB-BERBER; languages, ARABIC; money, DINAR / DIRHAM.

**LIECHTENSTEIN**: capital, VADUZ; other city, SCHAAN; ethnic groups, ALE-MANNIC, ITALIAN; languages, *GERMAN, ALEMANNIC; money, FRANC / CENTIME(Swiss).

**LITHUANIA**: capital, VILNIUS; other city, KAUNAS; ethnic groups, LITHUANIAN, RUSSIAN, POLISH; languages, LITHUANIAN, RUSSIAN; money, RUBLE / KOPECK.

**LUXEMBOURG**: capital, LUXEMBOURG; ethnic groups, FRENCH, GERMAN; languages, *FRENCH, *GERMAN, LUXEMBOURGISH; money, FRANC / CEN-TIME.

**MADAGASCAR**: capital, ANTANANARIVO; ethnic groups, HOVA, MERINA, MALAY, INDONESIAN, ARAB; languages, *MALAGASY, *FRENCH; money, FRANC / CENTIME.

**MALAWI**: capital, LILONGWE; other city, BLANTYRE; ethnic groups, CHEWA, NYANJA, LOMWE, BANTU; languages, *CHEWA, *ENGLISH, YAO, LOMWE; money, KWACHA / TAMBALA.

**MALAYSIA**: capital, KUALA LUMPUR; other cities, PINANG, KUCHING; ethnic groups, MALAY, CHINESE, INDIAN, DAYAK (DYAK); languages, *MALAY, ENGLISH, CHINESE; money, RINGGIT / SEN.

**MALDIVES**: capital, MALE; ethnic groups, SINHALESE, DRAVIDIAN, ARAB; languages, DIVEHI; money, RUFIYAA / LARI.

**MALI**: capital, BAMAKO; ethnic groups, MANDE, BAMBARA, MALINKE, SARAKOLE, PEUL, VOLTAIC, SONGHAI, TUAREG, MOOR; languages, *FRENCH, BAMBARA, SENUFO; money, FRANC / CENTIME.

**MALTA**: capital, VALLETTA; other cities, QORMI, BIRKIRKARA; ethnic groups, ITALIAN, ARAB, FRENCH; languages, *MALTESE, *ENGLISH; money, LIRA / CENT.

**MARSHALL ISLANDS**: capital, MAJURO; ethnic group, MARSHALLESE; languages, *ENGLISH, MARSHALLESE; money, DOLLAR / CENT (US).

**MAURITANIA**: capital, NOUAKCHOTT; other cities, NOUADHIBOU, KAEDI; ethnic groups, ARAB-BERBER, NEGROS; languages, ARABIC, FRENCH, HAS-SANYA; money, OUGUIYA / KHOUMS.

**MAURITIUS**: capital, PORT LOUIS; ethnic groups, INDO-MAURITIAN, CREOLE; languages, *ENGLISH, CREOLE, BHOJPURI; money, RUPEE / CENT.

**MEXICO**: capital, MEXICO CITY; other cities, GUADALAJARA, MONTERREY, TIJUANA, MEXICALI, JUAREZ, VERACRUZ, ACAPULCO, TAMPICO, DURAN-GO, MAZATLAN, CANCUN, PUEBLA, MATAMOROS; states (selected), COLI-MA, DURANGO, HIDALGO, JALISCO, MORELOS, NAYARIT, OAXACA, PUEBLA, SONORA; ethnic groups, MESTIZO, NATIVE AMERICAN, CAU-CASIAN; language, SPANISH ; money, PESO / CENTAVO.

**MICRONESIA**: capital, POHNPEI; ethnic groups, TRUKESE, POHNPEIAN; language, ENGLISH; money, DOLLAR / CENT (US).

**MOLDOVA**: capital, KISHINEV; ethnic groups, MOLDOVIAN, UKRAINIAN, RUSSIAN; languages, ROMANIAN, UKRAINIAN; money, RUBLE / KOPECK.

**MONACO**: capital, MONACO; ethnic groups, FRENCH, ITALIAN, MONE-GASQUE; language, FRENCH; money, FRANC / CENTIME(French).

**MONGOLIA**: capital, ULAANBAATAR; other city, DARHAN; ethnic group, MONGOL; language, MONGOLIAN; money, TUGRIK / MONGO.

**MOROCCO**: capital, RABAT; other cities, TANGER, FES, CASABLANCA, MARRAKECH, IFNI, AGADIR, MEKNES, SAFI; ethnic groups, ARAB-BERBER; languages, *ARABIC, BERBER; money, DIRHAM / CENTIME.

**MOZAMBIQUE**: capital, MAPUTO; other city, BEIRA; ethnic group, BANTU; languages, *PORTUGUESE, MAKUA, MALAWI, SHONA, TSONGA; money, METICAL / CENTAVO.

**MYANMAR**: capital, YANGON; other cities, KARBE, MANDALAY, MOULMEIN; ethnic groups, BURMANS, SHAN, LAI, KAREN, RAKHINE; languages, *BURMESE, KAREN, SHAN; money, KYAT / PYA.

**NAMIBIA**: capital, WINDHOEK; ethnic groups, OVAMBO, KAVANGO, HERERO, DAMARA; languages, *ENGLISH, AFRIKAANS; money, RAND / CENT (South African).

**NAURU**: capital, YAREN; ethnic groups, NAURUANS, PACIFIC ISLANDERS, CHINESE, EUROPEANS; language, NAURUAN; money, DOLLAR / CENT(Australian).

**NEPAL**: capital, KATMANDU; other cities, POKHARA, BIRGANI; ethnic groups, KIRANTI, INDIANS, TIBETANS; l anguage, NEPALI; money, RUPEE / PICE.

**NETHERLANDS**: capital, AMSTERDAM; other cities, ROTTERDAM, THE HAGUE, HAARLEM, BREDA, ARNHEM; ethnic group, DUTCH; language, DUTCH; money, GUILDER / CENT.

**NEW ZEALAND**: capital, WELLINGTON; other cities, AUCKLAND, MANUKAU, DUNEDIN, TIMARU; ethnic groups, EUROPEAN, POLYNESIAN, MAORI; languages, *ENGLISH, *MAORI; money, DOLLAR / CENT.

**NICARAGUA**: capital, MANAGUA; ethnic groups, MESTIZO, CAUCASIAN; languages, SPANISH; money, CORDOBA / CENTAVO.

**NIGER**: capital, NIAMEY; other cities, MARADI, ZINDER; ethnic groups, HAUSA, DJERMA, FULANI, TUAREG; languages, *FRENCH, HAUSA, FULANI; money, FRANC / CENTIME.

**NIGERIA**: capital, ABUJA; other cities, LAGOS, IBADAN; ethnic groups, HAUSA, FULANI, IBO, EDO, IGBO, EFIK, YORUBA; languages, *ENGLISH, HAUSA, IBO, YORUBA; money, NAIRA / KOBO.

**NORWAY**: capital, OSLO; other city, BERGEN; ethnic groups, GERMANIC, LAPPS; language, NORWEGIAN; money, KRONE / ORE.

**OMAN**: capital, MUSCAT; ethnic groups, OMANI ARAB, PAKISTANI; languages, ARABIC; money, RIAL / BAIZA.

**PAKISTAN**: capital, ISLAMABAD; other cities, LAHORE, KARACHI, HYDERABAD, RAWALPINDI; ethnic groups, PUNJABI, SINDHI, PUSHTUN, URDU, BALUCHI; languages, *URDU, PUNJABI, SINDHI, PUSHTU, BALUCHI, BRAHVI; money, RUPEE / PAISA.

**PANAMA**: capital, PANAMA; other cities, COLON, DAVID; ethnic groups, MESTIZO, CAUCASIAN, WEST INDIAN; languages, *SPANISH, ENGLISH; money, BALBOA / CENT.

**PAPUA NEW GUINEA**: capital, PORT MORESBY; other city, LAE; ethnic groups, PAPUAN, MELANESIAN, POLYNESIAN; languages, *ENGLISH, MELANESIAN; money, KINA / TOEA; river, SEPIK.

**PARAGUAY**: capital, ASUNCION; ethnic group, MESTIZOS; languages, *SPANISH, GUARANI; money, GUARANI / CENTIMO.

**PERU**: capital, LIMA; other cities, CALLAO, IQUITOS; ethnic groups, INDIANS, MESTIZOS, CAUCASIANS; languages, *SPANISH, *QUECHUA, AYMARA; money, INTI / SOL.

**PHILIPPINES**: capital, QUEZON CITY; other cities, CEBU, MANILA; ethnic groups, MALAYS, CHINESE, SPANISH; languages, *PILIPINO, *ENGLISH, TAGALOG, CEBUANO, BICOL, ILOCANO, PAMPANGO; money, PESO / CENTAVO.

**POLAND**: capital, WARSAW; other cities, LODZ, KRACOW, LUBLIN, POSNAN, WROCLAW; ethnic group, POLES; languages, POLISH; money, ZLOTY / GROSZ.

**PORTUGAL**: capital, LISBON; other cities, BRAGA, PORTO, COIMBRA, SETUBAL; ethnic group, PORTUGUESE; language, PORTUGUESE; money, ESCUDO / CENTAVO.

**QATAR**: capital, DOHA; ethnic groups, ARAB, IRANIAN, PAKISTANI, INDIAN; languages, ARABIC; money, RIYAL / DIRHAM.

**ROMANIA**: capital, BUCHAREST; other cities, ARAD, CLUJ, DEVA, IASI, BRASOV, GALATI, ORADEA, CONSTANTA ; ethnic groups, ROMANIANS, HUNGARIANS; languages, ROMANIAN; money, LEU / BAN; river, DANUBE.

**RUSSIAN FEDERATION**: capital, MOSCOW; other cities, ST. PETERSBURG, SAMARA; ethnic groups, RUSSIANS, TATARS; language, RUSSIAN; money, RUBLE / KOPECK.

**RWANDA**: capital, KIGALI; ethnic groups, HUTU, TUTSI, TWA; languages, *RWANDA, *FRENCH; money, FRANC / CENTIME.

**ST. KITTS AND NEVIS**: capital, BASSETERRE; ethnic groups, AFRICAN; languages, ENGLISH; money, E. CARIBBEAN DOLLAR.

**SAINT LUCIA**: capital, CASTRIES; ethnic groups, AFRICAN; languages, ENGLISH; money, DOLLAR / CENT.

**SAINT VINCENT AND THE GRENADINES**: capital, KINGSTOWN; ethnic groups, AFRICAN; languages, ENGLISH; money, DOLLAR / CENT.

**SAN MARINO**: capital, SAN MARINO; ethnic groups, SANMARINESE, ITALIANS; languages, ITALIAN; money, LIRA / CENTESIMO(Italian).

**SAO TOME AND PRINCIPE**: capital, SAO TOME; ethnic groups, PORTUGUESE, VARIOUS AFRICAN; languages, PORTUGUESE; money, DOBRA / CENTAVO.

**SAUDI ARABIA**: capital, RIYADH; other cities, JIDDA, MECCA; ethnic group, ARAB; language, ARABIC; money, RIYAL / HALALA.

**SENEGAL**: capital, DAKAR; other city, THIES; ethnic groups, WOLOF, SERER, FULANI, DIOLA, MANDINGO; languages, *FRENCH, WOLOF, SERER, PEUL, TUKULOR; money, FRANC / CENTIME.

**SEYCHELLES**: capital, VICTORIA; ethnic group, CREOLES; languages, *ENGLISH, *FRENCH; money, RUPEE / CENT.

**SIERRA LEONE**: capital, FREETOWN; other cities, KENEMA, MAKENI, BO; ethnic groups, TEMNE, MENDE; languages, *ENGLISH; money, LEONE / CENT.

**SINGAPORE**: capital, SINGAPORE; ethnic groups, CHINESE, MALAYS, INDIANS; languages, *CHINESE, *TAMIL, *ENGLISH, *MALAY; money, DOLLAR / CENT.

**SLOVENIA**: capital, LJUBLJANA; ethnic group, SLOVENES; languages, SLOVENIAN, YUGOSLAVIAN; money, DINAR / PARA.

**SOLOMON ISLANDS**: capital, HONIARA; ethnic groups, MELANESIAN, POLYNESIAN; languages, *ENGLISH, MELANESIAN, PAPUAN; money, DOLLAR / CENT.

**SOMALIA**: capital, MOGADISHU; ethnic group, HAMITIC; languages, *SOMALI, *ARABIC; money, SHILLING / CENT.

**SOUTH AFRICA**: capitals, CAPE TOWN (legislative), PRETORIA (administrative), and BLOEMFONTEIN (judicial); other cities, JOHANNESBURG, DURBAN; ethnic groups, EUROPEANS, BANTU, ZULU, SWAZI, SOTHO; languages, *AFRIKAANS, *ENGLISH, NGUNI, SOTHO; money, RAND / CENT; river, ORANGE.

**SOVIET UNION** (See under individual republics).

**SPAIN**: capital, MADRID; other cities, LEON, BILBAO, MALAGA, CORDOBA, GRANADA, VALENCIA, BARCELONA; ethnic groups, CASTILIAN, VALENCIAN, ANDALUSIAN, ASTURIAN; languages, *SPANISH, CATALAN, BASQUE, GALICIAN; money, PESETA / CENTIMO; river, EBRO.

**SRI LANKA**: capital, COLOMBO; other cities, GALLE, JAFFNA, KANDY; ethnic groups, SINHALESE, TAMILS, VEDDA, MOORS; languages, *SINHALESE, TAMIL; money, RUPEE / CENT.

**SUDAN**: capital, KHARTOUM; other cities, PORT SUDAN, OMDURMAN; ethnic groups, ARAB, BEJA, NUBIAN; languages, *ARABIC, DINKA, NUBIAN, NUER, BEJA; money, POUND / PIASTER; river, NILE.

**SURINAM**: capital, PARAMARIBO; ethnic groups, HINDUSTANIS, CREOLE; languages, DUTCH, ENGLISH, SRANANTONGA; money, GUILDER / CENT.

**SWAZILAND**: capital, MBABANE; other city, MANZINI; ethnic groups, SWAZI, ZULU, EUROPEAN; languages, *SWAZI, *ENGLISH; money, LILANGENI / CENT.

**SWEDEN**: capital, STOCKHOLM; other cities, MALMO, GOTEBORG; ethnic groups, SWEDISH, FINNISH, LAPP; languages, SWEDISH; money, KRONA / ORE.

**SWITZERLAND**: capital, BERN; other cities, BASEL, GENEVA, ZURICH; ethnic groups, MIXED EUROPEANS; languages, *FRENCH, *GERMAN, *ITALIAN; money, FRANC / CENTIME.

**SYRIA**: capital, DAMASCUS; other cities, HAMA, HOMS, ALEPPO; ethnic groups, ARAB, KURDS, ARMENIAN; languages, *ARABIC, KURDISH, ARMENIAN; money, POUND / PIASTER.

**TAIWAN**: capital, TAIPEI; other city, TAINAN; ethnic groups, TAIWANESE, CHINESE; languages, *MANDARIN, TAIWANESE, HAKKA; money, DOLLAR / CENT.

**TAJIKSTAN**: capital, DUSHANBE; ethnic groups, TAJIK, UZBEK, RUSSIAN; languages, TADZHIK, RUSSIAN; money, RUBLE / KOPECK.

**TANZANIA**: capital, DAR-ES-SALAAM; ethnic groups, VARIOUS; languages, *SWAHILI, *ENGLISH; money, SHILLING / CENT.

**THAILAND**: capital, BANGKOK; other cities, HAT YAI, KHON KAEN; ethnic groups, THAI, CHINESE; languages, *THAI, CHINESE, MALAY; money, BAHT / SATANG; river, CHAO PHRAYA.

**TOGO**: capital, LOME; ethnic groups, EWE, MINA, KABYE; languages, *FRENCH, GUR, KWA; money, FRANC / CENTIME.

**TONGA**: capital, NUKU'ALOFA; ethnic group, TONGAN; languages, TONGAN, ENGLISH; money, PA'ANGA / SENITI.

**TRINIDAD AND TOBAGO**: capital, PORT-OF-SPAIN; ethnic groups, AFRICANS, EAST INDIAN; languages, ENGLISH; money, DOLLAR / CENT.

**TUNISIA**: capital, TUNIS; other city, SFAX; ethnic group, ARAB; languages, *ARABIC, FRENCH; money, DINAR / MILLIME.

**TURKEY**: capital, ANKARA; other cities, ADANA, BURSA, IZMIR; ethnic groups, TURKS, KURDS; languages, *TURKISH, ARABIC, KURDISH; money, LIRA / KURUS.

**TURKMENISTAN**: capital, ASHKHABAD; ethnic groups, TURKMEN, UZBEK, RUSSIAN; languages, TURKMEN, RUSSIAN; money, RUBLE / KOPECK.

**TUVALU**: capital, FUNAFULI; ethnic group, POLYNESIAN; languages, TUVALUAN; money, DOLLAR / CENT(Australian).

**UGANDA**: capital, KAMPALA; other city, MASAKA; ethnic groups, BANTU, NILO-HAMITIC, NILOTIC; languages, *ENGLISH, SWAHILI, LUGANDA; money, SHILLING / CENT.

**UKRAINE**: capital, KIEV; other cities, LVOV, ODESSA, KHARKIV; ethnic groups, UKRAINIAN, RUSSIAN; languages, UKRAINIAN; money, RUBLE / KOPECK.

**UNITED ARAB EMIRATES**: capital, ABU DHABI; other city, DUBAVY; ethnic groups, ARAB, IRANIAN, PAKISTANI, INDIAN; languages, ARABIC; money, DIRHAM / FILS.

**UNITED KINGDOM OF GREAT BRITAIN AND NORTHERN IRELAND**: capital, LONDON; other cities, BELFAST, CARDIFF, EDINBURGH; ethnic groups, ENGLISH, SCOTTISH, IRISH, WELSH; languages, *ENGLISH, WELSH; money, POUND / PENCE; rivers, AIN, DEE, ESK, EXE, TAW, OUSE, TYNE, CLYDE, FORTH, TAMAR, TRENT, HUMBER, SEVERN, THAMES; possessions, BERMUDA, GIBRALTAR, HONG KONG, CHANNEL ISLANDS, ISLE OF MAN, PITCAIRN ISLAND, ASCENSION, TRISTAN DA CUNHA, ST. HELENA, FALKLAND ISLANDS, MONTSERRAT, BRITISH VIRGIN ISLANDS, CAYMAN ISLANDS, TURKS AND CAICOS ISLANDS.

**UNITED STATES OF AMERICA**: capital, WASHINGTON DC; languages, ENGLISH; money, DOLLAR / CENT.

**UPPER VOLTA** (See Burkina Faso).

**URUGUAY:** capital, MONTEVIDEO; ethnic groups, SPANISH, ITALIANS, MESTIZO; language, SPANISH; money, PESO / CENTESIMO; river, URUGUAY.

**UZBEKISTAN:** capital, TASHKENT; ethnic groups, UZBEK, RUSSIAN; language, UZBEK; money, RUBLE / KOPECK.

**VANUATU:** capital, PORT-VILA; other city, VILA; ethnic group, MELANESIAN; languages, BISLAMA, FRENCH, ENGLISH; money, VATU.

**VATICAN CITY:** ethnic groups, ITALIANS, SWISS; languages, LATIN, ITALIAN; money, LIRA / CENTESIMO(Italian).

**VENEZUELA:** capital, CARACAS; other city, MARACAIBO, VALENCIA; ethnic groups, MESTIZO, SPANISH; language, SPANISH; money, BOLIVAR / CENTIMO; river, ORINOCO.

**VIETNAM:** capital, HANOI; other city, HO CHI MINH CITY; ethnic groups, VIETNAMESE, MUONG, MEO, KHMER, MAN, CHAM; language, VIETNAMESE; money, DONG; rivers, RED, MEKONG.

**WESTERN SAMOA:** capital, APIA; ethnic group, SAMOAN; languages, *SAMOAN, *ENGLISH; money, TALA / SENE; islands, SAVAI'I, UPOLU, MANONO, APOLIMA.

**YEMEN:** capital, SANAA; other city, ADEN; ethnic groups, ARAB, INDIAN; language, ARABIC; money, DINAR/FILS, RIYAL / FILS.

**YUGOSLAVIA** (See also SLOVENIA, CROATIA, BOSNIA-HERZEGOVINA).

**YUGOSLAVIA (SERBIA-MONTENEGRO):** capital, BELGRADE; other cities, NIS, SKOPJE; ethnic group, SERBIANS; language, SERBO-CROATIAN, money, DINAR / PARA.

**ZAIRE:** capital, KINSHASA; other city, LUBUMBASHI; ethnic group, BANTU; languages, *FRENCH, KONGO, LUBA, MONGO, RWANDA; money, ZAIRE / LIKUTA; river, CONGO.

**ZAMBIA:** capital, LUSAKA; other cities, KITWE, NDOLA; ethnic group, BANTU; languages, *ENGLISH, BANTU; money, KWACHA / NGWEE; river, ZAMBESI.

**ZIMBABWE:** capital, HARARE; other city, BULAWAYO; ethnic groups, SHONA, NDEBELE; languages, *ENGLISH, SHONA, SINDE BELE; money, DOLLAR / CENT.

# ANIMALS

## AMPHIBIANS

BULLFROG
CAECILIAN
EEL, CONGO
EFT
FROG
FROG, GRASS
FROG, GREEN
FROG, LEOPARD
FROG, PICKEREL
FROG, SPRING
FROG, TREE
FROG, WOOD
HELLBENDER
MUD PUPPY
NEWT
SALAMANDER
SIREN
TOAD
TOAD, MIDWIFE
TOAD, SURINAM
WATER DOG

## BIRDS

ADJUTANT BIRD
ALBATROSS
ARGALA
AUK
AVOCET
BALDPATE
BARBET
BIRD OF PARADISE
BITTERN
BLACKBIRD
BLACKCAP
BLUEBILL
BLUEBIRD
BLUE JAY
BOBOLINK
BOBWHITE
BOOBY
BRANT
BUDGERIGAR
BULLFINCH
BUNTING
BUNTING, INDIGO
BUNTING, SNOW
BUSTARD
BUTCHER BIRD
BUZZARD
CANARY
CAPERCAILLIE
CARACARA
CARDINAL

CASSOWARY
CATBIRD
CEDARBIRD
CEDAR WAXWING
CHAFFINCH
CHAT
CHEWINK
CHICKADEE
COCKATIEL
COCKATOO
CONDOR
COOT
CORMORANT
COWBIRD
CRAKE
CRANE
CREEPER
CROSSBILL
CROW
CUCKOO
CURLEW
CURLEW, STONE
CUSHAT
DABCHICK
DARTER
DIPPER
DODO
DOVE
DOVE, MOURNING
DOVE, ROCK
DUCK
DUCK, CANVASBACK
DUCK, FOOL
DUCK, RUDDY
DUCK, SCAUP
DUCK, SEA
DUCK, TEAL
DUCK, WILD
DUCK, WOOD
DUNLIN
EAGLE
EAGLE, BALD
EAGLE, GOLDEN
EAGLE, HARPY
EAGLE, SEA
EGRET
EGRET, CATTLE
EIDER DUCK
EMU
ERNE
FALCON
FALCON, PEREGRINE
FINCH
FINCH, HOUSE
FINCH, ZEBRA
FLAMINGO

FLICKER
FLYCATCHER
FRIGATE BIRD
FULMAR
GALLINULE
GANNET
GARGANEY
GOATSUCKER
GODWIT
GOLDENEYE
GOLDFINCH
GOOSE
GOOSE, BARNACLE
GOOSE, CANADA
GOOSE, SNOW
GOOSE, SOLAN
GOOSE, SWAN
GOSHAWK
GRACKLE
GREBE
GROSBEAK
GROUSE
GROUSE, BLACK
GROUSE, RED
GROUSE, RUFFED
GROUSE, SAGE
GUILLEMOT
GUINEA FOWL
GULL
GULL, SEA
GYRFALCON
HANGBIRD
HARRIER
HAWK
HAWK, CHICKEN
HAWK, FISH
HAWK, PIGEON
HAWK, SPARROW
HEN, MOOR
HEN, MUD
HEN, SAGE
HERON
HOBBY
HONKER
HOOPOE
HORNED SCREAMER
HUMMINGBIRD
IBIS
JACKDAW
JAY
JUNCO
JUNGLE FOWL
KEA
KESTREL
KILLDEER
KINGBIRD

## Animals (birds / cetaceans)

KINGFISHER
KINGLET
KITE
KITTIWAKE
KIWI
KOOKABURRA
LAMMERGEIER
LAPWING
LARK
LARK, MEADOW
LINNET
LOON
LOVEBIRD
LYREBIRD
MACAW
MAGPIE
MALLARD
MAN-O'-WAR BIRD
MARTIN
MARTIN, HOUSE
MARTIN, PURPLE
MARTIN, SAND
MAVIS
MERGANSER
MERL
MEW
MOA
MOCKINGBIRD
MURRE
MYNA BIRD
NIGHTHAWK
NIGHT-HERON
NIGHTINGALE
NIGHTJAR
NUTCRACKER
NUTHATCH
ORIOLE
ORTOLAN
OSPREY
OSTRICH
OUZEL
OUZEL, RING
OWL
OWL, BARN
OWL, HAWK
OWL, HOOT
OWL, HORNED
OWL, SCREECH
OWL, WOOD
OYSTER CATCHER
PARAKEET
PARROT
PARTRIDGE
PEAFOWL
PEEWEE
PELICAN
PENGUIN
PETREL
PETREL, STORMY
PEWIT

PHALAROPE
PHEASANT
PHEASANT, RING-
  NECKED
PHOEBE
PIGEON
PIGEON, PASSENGER
PIGEON, WOOD
PINTAIL
PIPIT
PLOVER
POCHARD
PTARMIGAN
PUFFIN
QUETZAL
RAIL
RAVEN
RAZORBILL
REDBIRD
REDHEAD
REDPOLL
REDSHANK
REDSTART
REDWING
REEDBIRD
RHEA
RICEBIRD
RINGDOVE
ROADRUNNER
ROBIN
ROOK
SANDPIPER
SAPSUCKER
SECRETARY BIRD
SHELDRAKE
SHOEBILL
SHOVELER
SHRIKE
SISKIN
SNIPE
SNOWBIRD
SONGBIRD
SPARROW
SPARROW, CHIPPING
SPARROW, ENGLISH
SPARROW, SONG
SPARROW, VESPER
SPOONBILL
SPRIG
STARLING
STILT
STILT PLOVER
STORK
STORK, MARABOU
SWALLOW
SWALLOW, BANK
SWALLOW, BARN
SWALLOW, CLIFF
SWALLOW, SEA
SWALLOW, TREE

SWAN
SWAN, MUTE
SWIFT
SWIFT, CHIMNEY
TANAGER
TANAGER, SCARLET
TEAL
TERN
THRASHER
THRASHER, BROWN
THRUSH
THRUSH, HERMIT
THRUSH, MISTLE
THRUSH, SONG
TIT
TITLARK
TITMOUSE
TOUCAN
TOWHEE
TRAGOPAN
TRUMPETER
TURKEY
TURKEY, BRUSH
TURKEY BUZZARD
TURKEY VULTURE
TURNSTONE
TURTLEDOVE
VEERY
VIREO
VULTURE
WARBLER
WARBLER, AUDUBON
WAXWING
WEAVERBIRD
WHEATEAR
WHIPPOORWILL
WHISTLER
WIDGEON
WILLET
WOODCOCK
WOODPECKER
WOODPECKER,
  RED-HEADED
WREN
WREN, BUSH
WREN-TIT
WRYNECK
YELLOWBIRD
YELLOWHAMMER
YELLOWLEGS
YELLOWTHROAT

## CETACEANS

BELUGA
CACHALOT
DOLPHIN
FINBACK
GRAMPUS
NARWHAL

226

PORPOISE
RORQUAL
WHALE, BALEEN
WHALE, BLUE
WHALE, HUMPBACK
WHALE, KILLER
WHALE, RIGHT
WHALE, SPERM

## DINOSAURS

ALLOSAUR(US)
AMMONITE
ARCHELON
AUROCHS
BRONTOPS
BRONTOSAUR(US)
CREODONT
DIPNOAN
EOHIPPUS
ERYOPSID
IGUANODON
MAMMOTH
MAMMOTH, WOOLLY
MASTODON
MEGATHERE
MERODUS
MIACIS
PTERODACTYL
SAUROPOD
SLOTH, GIANT
SMILODON
STEGOSAUR(US)
TIGER,
    SABER-TOOTHED
TYRANNOSAUR(US)
TYRANNOSAURUS
    REX
URUS

## DOGS

AFFENPINSCHER
AFGHAN HOUND
AIREDALE TERRIER
ALSATIAN
BADGER DOG
BASENJI
BASSET HOUND
BEAGLE
BLOODHOUND
BOARHOUND
BORZOI
BOSTON BULL
BOUVIER
    DES FLANDRES
BOXER
BRIARD
BULLDOG
BULLDOG, ENGLISH

BULLDOG, FRENCH
BULL MASTIFF
CHIHUAHUA
CHOW
COCKER SPANIEL
COCKER SPANIEL,
    ENGLISH
COLLIE
COLLIE, BORDER
COLLIE, WELSH
COONHOUND
CORGI, WELSH
DACHSHUND
DALMATIAN,
    aka COACH DOG
DEERHOUND
DEERHOUND,
    SCOTTISH
DOBERMAN
    PINSCHER
ELKHOUND
ELKHOUND,
    NORWEGIAN
FOXHOUND
FOXHOUND,
    AMERICAN
FOXHOUND, ENGLISH
GERMAN SHEPHERD
GREAT DANE
GREAT PYRENEES
GREYHOUND
GREYHOUND, ITALIAN
HAIRLESS, MEXICAN
HARRIER
HOUND
HOUND, GAZELLE
HUSKY
HUSKY, SIBERIAN
KEESHOND
KOMONDOR
KUVASZ
LHASA APSO
MALAMUTE
MALAMUTE, ALASKAN
MALTESE
MASTIFF
NEWFOUNDLAND
OTTER HOUND
PAPILLON
PEKINGESE
PINSCHER,
    MINIATURE
POINTER
POINTER, GERMAN
    SHORT-HAIRED
POINTER, GERMAN
    WIRE-HAIRED
POMERANIAN
POODLE
POODLE, MINIATURE

POODLE, TOY
PUG
PULI
RETRIEVER
RETRIEVER,
    CHESAPEAKE BAY
RETRIEVER,
    FLAT-COATED
RETRIEVER, GOLDEN
RETRIEVER,
    LABRADOR
RIDGEBACK,
    RHODESIAN
ROTTWEILER
SAINT BERNARD
SALUKI
SAMOYED
SCHIPPERKE
SCHNAUZER
SCHNAUZER, GIANT
SCHNAUZER,
    MINIATURE
SETTER
SETTER, ENGLISH
SETTER, GORDON
SETTER, IRISH
SHEEP DOG, BELGIAN
SHEEP DOG,
    OLD ENGLISH
SHEEP DOG,
    SHETLAND
SHIH TZU
SPANIEL
SPANIEL, BLENHEIM
SPANIEL, BRITTANY
SPANIEL, CLUMBER
SPANIEL, ENGLISH
    SPRINGER
SPANIEL,
    ENGLISH TOY
SPANIEL,
    IRISH WATER
SPANIEL, JAPANESE
SPANIEL,
    KING CHARLES
SPANIEL, NORFOLK
SPANIEL, SPRINGER
SPANIEL, SUSSEX
SPANIEL, TOY
SPANIEL, WATER
SPANIEL, WELSH
    SPRINGER
SPITZ
STAGHOUND
TERRIER
TERRIER,
    AUSTRALIAN
TERRIER,
    BEDLINGTON
TERRIER, BORDER

### Animals (dogs / fish)

TERRIER, BULL
TERRIER, CAIRN
TERRIER,
  CLYDESDALE
TERRIER, FOX
TERRIER, IRISH
TERRIER,
  KERRY BLUE
TERRIER, LAKELAND
TERRIER,
  MANCHESTER
TERRIER, NORWICH
TERRIER, RAT
TERRIER, SCOTTISH
TERRIER, SEALYHAM
TERRIER, SILKY
TERRIER, SKYE
TERRIER, TOY
TERRIER, WELSH
TERRIER, WEST
  HIGHLAND WHITE
TERRIER,
  WIRE-HAIRED
TERRIER, YORKSHIRE
TURNSPIT
VIZSLA
WATER SPANIEL,
  AMERICAN
WEIMARANER
WHIPPET
WOLFHOUND
WOLFHOUND, IRISH
WOLFHOUND,
  RUSSIAN

### FISH

ALBACORE
ALEWIFE
AMBER JACK
ANCHOVY
ANGEL FISH
ARCHERFISH
BARBEL
BARRACUDA
BASS
BASS, BLACK
BASS, CHANNEL
BASS, SEA
BASS, STRIPED
BLACKFISH
BLEAK
BLIND FISH
BLOWFISH
BLUE FISH
BLUEGILL
BONEFISH
BONITO
BOWFIN
BREAM

BREAM, SEA
BUFFALO FISH
BULLHEAD
BURBOT
BUTTERFISH
CANDLEFISH
CAPELIN
CARP
CATFISH
CHAR
CHIMAERA
CHUB
CICHLID
CISCO
COBIA
COD
COELACANTH
CONGER EEL
CRAPPIE
CROAKER
CUTLASS FISH
DACE
DARTER
DEVILFISH
DOCTOR FISH
DOGFISH
DORADO
DRAGON FISH
DRUM
EEL
EEL, ELECTRIC
EEL, MORAY
EELPOUT
FILEFISH
FLATFISH
FLOUNDER
FLUKE
FLYING FISH
FLYING GURNARD
GAR
GLOBEFISH
GOATFISH
GOBY
GOLDFISH
GOURAMI
GRAYLING
GROUPER
GRUNION
GRUNT
GUDGEON
GUITARFISH
GUNNEL
GUPPY
HADDOCK
HAKE
HALIBUT
HERRING
HOGFISH
JEWFISH
KINGFISH

LAMPREY
LANTERN FISH
LING
LOACH
LUNG FISH
MACKEREL
MACKEREL, HORSE
MANTA
MARLIN
MENHADEN
MILLER'S-THUMB
MINNOW
MUDFISH
MUSKELLUNGE
PADDLEFISH
PERCH
PERCH, SEA
PICKEREL
PIKE
PIKE, WALLEYE
PILCHARD
PILOT FISH
PIRANHA
PLAICE
POMPANO
PORGY
PUFFER
RAY
RAY, ELECTRIC
RAY, STING
RAY, THORNBACK
REDFIN
REDFISH
ROACH
SAILFISH
SALMON
SALMON, CHINOOK
SALMON, SILVER
SARDINE
SAWFISH
SCUP
SEA HORSE
SERGEANT MAJOR
  FISH
SHARK
SHARK, BASKING
SHARK, BLUE
SHARK,
  HAMMERHEAD
SHARK, MAKO
SHARK, PORBEAGLE
SHARK, SHOVELHEAD
SHARK, THRESHER
SHINER
SKATE
SKATE, BARN DOOR
SMELT
SNAPPER
SNOOK
SOLE

228

SPRAT
STICKLEBACK
STURGEON
SUCKER
SUNFISH
SWORDFISH
TARPON
TAUTOG
TENCH
TETRA
TOADFISH
TOPE
TORPEDO FISH
TRIGGERFISH
TROUT
TROUT, BROOK
TROUT, BROWN
TROUT, CUTTHROAT
TROUT,
    DOLLY VARDEN
TROUT, GOLDEN
TROUT, LAKE
TROUT, RAINBOW
TROUT, SALMON
TROUT, SEA
TROUT, SPECKLED
TROUT, STEELHEAD
TUNA
TURBOT
WAHOO
WEAKFISH
WHITEFISH
WHITING
YELLOWTAIL

## INSECTS

ANT
ANT LION
APHID
ASSASSIN BUG
BEDBUG
BEE
BEETLE
BEETLE, BUPRESTID
BEETLE, COLORADO
BEETLE,
    CUCUMBER FLEA
BEETLE, DUNG
BEETLE, ELM LEAF
BEETLE, FLEA
BEETLE, GRAIN
BEETLE, JAPANESE
BEETLE, ROSE
BEETLE, SCARAB
BEETLE, SNOUT
BEETLE, STAG
BILLBUG
BLOWFLY
BLUEBOTTLE

BOLL WEEVIL
BORER
BOTFLY
BRISTLETAIL
BUFFALO BUG
BUTTERFLY
CHAFER
CHIGOE
CHIGGER
CHINCH BUG
CICADA
COCKCHAFER
COCKROACH
CORN-NOSE
CRICKET
CRICKET, MOLE
CROTON BUG
CURCULIO
DAMSELFLY
DOBSONFLY
DRAGONFLY
DROSOPHILA
EARWIG
EPHEMERID
FIREBRAT
FIREFLY
FLEA
FLY
FLY, BEE
FLY, CADDIS
FLY, CRANE
FLY, DEER
FLY, FRUIT
FLY, HORN
FLY, LANTERN
FLY, ROBBER
FLY, SCORPION
FLY, SHAD
FLY, ST. MARK'S
FLY, STONE
FLY, SYRPHUS
FLY, TSETSE
GADFLY
GALLFLY
GLOWWORM
GNAT
GRASSHOPPER
HARLEQUIN
    CABBAGE BUG
HAWK, MOSQUITO
HAWK MOTH
HORNET
HORNTAIL
HORSEFLY
HOUSEFLY
JIGGER FLEA
JUNE BUG or BEETLE
KATYDID
KISSING BUG
LACEWING

LADYBUG
LEAFHOPPER
LOCUST
LOUSE
MANTIS
MANTIS, PRAYING
MAYFLY
MEALWORM
MEALYBUG
MIDGE
MILLER
MOSQUITO
MOTH
MOTH, CECROPIA
MOTH, CODLING
MOTH, FLOUR
MOTH, TIGER
PILL BUG
POTATO BUG
PUNKIE
ROACH
SAWFLY
SILVERFISH
SOW BUG
SPRINGTAIL
SQUASH BUG
STINK BUG
TERMITE
THRIPS
TICK, WOOD
TUMBLEBUG
WALKING STICK
WASP
WASP, WOOD
WATER BUG
WEEVIL
YELLOW JACKET

## MAMMALS

AARDVARK
AARDWOLF
ADDAX
AGOUTI
ALPACA
ANOA
ANT BEAR
ANTEATER
ANTELOPE
ANTELOPE, GOAT
ANTELOPE,
    HARNESSED
ANTELOPE, SABLE
AOUDAD
ARGALI
ARMADILLO
ASS
ASS, WILD
AUROCHS
BADGER

## Animals (mammals)

BANDICOOT
BANDICOOT, RABBIT
BARBIRUSA
BARONDUKI
BASSARISK
BAT
BEAR
BEAR, BLACK
BEAR, BROWN
BEAR, CINNAMON
BEAR, GRIZZLY
BEAR, ICE
BEAR, KODIAK
BEAR, POLAR
BEAR, SKUNK
BEAR, SYRIAN
BEAVER
BINTURONG
BISON
BOAR
BOAR, WILD
BOBCAT
BUCK, BLACK
BUFFALO
BUFFALO, CAPE
BUFFALO, INDIAN
BURRO
BUSH BABY
CACHALOT
CAMEL
CAMEL, BACTRIAN
CAMELOPARD
CAPYBARA
CARABAO
CARACAL
CARCAJOU
CARIBOU
CAT
CATAMOUNT
CATTALO
CAVY
CHAMOIS
CHEETAH
CHEVROTAIN
CHICKADEE
CHINCHILLA
CHIPMUNK
CIVET CAT'
COATI
COUGAR
COW
COYOTE
COYPU
DEER
DEER, BRUSH
DEER, BURRO
DEER, FALLOW
DEER, MOUSE
DEER, MULE
DEER, MUSK

DEER, RED
DEER, VIRGINIA
DEER, WHITE-TAILED
DINGO
DOG
DOG, PRAIRIE
DONKEY
DORMOUSE
DROMEDARY
ECHIDNA
ELAND
ELEPHANT
ELK
ERMINE
FERRET
FITCH
FOX
FOX, ARCTIC
FOX, BLACK
FOX, BLUE
FOX, FLYING
FOX, GRAY
FOX, KIT
FOX, POLAR
FOX, PRAIRIE
FOX, RED
FOX, SILVER
FOX, WHITE
GAUR
GAZELLE
GEMSBOK
GENET
GERBIL
GIRAFFE
GNU
GOAT
GOAT, ANGORA
GOAT, CASHMERE
GOAT, GNU
GOAT, MOUNTAIN
GOAT,
   ROCKY MOUNTAIN
GOAT, WILD
GOPHER
GOPHER, POCKET
GROUNDHOG
GUANACO
GUINEA PIG
HAMSTER
HARE
HARE, ARCTIC
HARE, BELGIAN
HARTEBEEST
HEDGEHOG
HIPPOPOTAMUS
HOG
HOG, HERRING
HOG, MUSK
HORSE
HYENA

HYRAX
IBEX
JACKAL
JACKASS
JACKRABBIT
JAGUAR
JAGUARUNDI
JERBOA
KAAMA
KANGAROO
KANGAROO, JERBOA
KARAKUL
KIANG
KINKAJOU
KOALA
KUDU
LEMMING
LEMUR, FLYING
LEOPARD
LION
LION, MOUNTAIN
LLAMA
LORIS
LYNX
MARA
MARGAY
MARMOT
MARMOT, FLYING
MARTEN
MEERKAT
MINK
MOLE
MOLE, SHREW
MONGOOSE
MOOSE
MOUFLON
MOUSE
MOUSE, COTTON
MOUSE, DEER
MOUSE, FIELD
MOUSE,
   GRASSHOPPER
MOUSE, HARVEST
MOUSE, JUMPING
MOUSE, KANGAROO
MOUSE, MEADOW
MOUSE, PINE
MOUSE, POCKET
MOUSE, WOOD
MULE
MUNTJAC
MUSK-OX
MUSKRAT
NILGAI
NUTRIA
OCELOT
OKAPI
ONAGER
OONT
OPOSSUM

ORYX
OTTER
OUNCE
PANDA
PANGOLIN
PANTHER
PECCARY
PHALANGER
PHALANGER, FLYING
PIG
PIKA
PLATYPUS
POLECAT
PORCUPINE
POTTO
PRONGHORN
PUMA
RABBIT
RABBIT, COTTONTAIL
RABBIT, SNOWSHOE
RABBIT, SWAMP
RACCOON
RAT
RAT, COTTON
RAT, KANGAROO
RAT, PACK
RAT, POCKET
RAT, POUCHED
RAT, WHARF
RAT, WOOD
REINDEER
RHINOCEROS
ROEBUCK
SABLE
SAIGA
SAMBAR
SERVAL
SHEEP
SHEEP, BIGHORN
SHEEP, BLACK
SHEEP, MOUNTAIN
SHEEP, WILD
SHREW
SHREW, TREE
SIKA
SKUNK
SLOTH
SLOTH,
    GIANT GROUND
SPRINGBOK
SQUIRREL
SQUIRREL, FLYING
SQUIRREL, GROUND
SQUIRREL, RED
SQUIRREL, ROCK
STEENBOK
STOAT
SUSLIK
SWINE
TAKIN

TAMANDUA
TAMARIN
TAPIR
TATOUAY
TIGER
URUS
VOLE
WALLABY
WAPITI
WARTHOG
WATERBUCK
WATER BUFFALO
WEASEL
WILDCAT
WILDEBEEST
WOLF
WOLF, BRUSH
WOLF, BUFFALO
WOLF, GRAY
WOLF, PRAIRIE
WOLF, TIMBER
WOLF, WHITE
WOLVERINE
WOMBAT
WOODCHUCK
YAK
ZEBRA
ZEBU
ZORIL

**MARINE ANIMALS**

CRUSTACEANS
DUGONG
MANATEE
MOLLUSKS
OCTOPUS
SEA CALF
SEA COW
SEA DOG
SEA ELEPHANT
SEAL
SEAL, ELEPHANT
SEAL, FUR
SEAL, HARBOR
SEA LION
SEA URCHIN
SHELLFISH
SQUID
WALRUS

**PRIMATES**

ANGWANTIBO
APE
APE, ANTHROPOID
APE, BARBARY
AYE-AYE
BABOON
CAPUCHIN

CHACMA
CHIMPANZEE
COLOBUS
DRILL
ENTELLUS
GIBBON
GORILLA
GORILLA, MOUNTAIN
GRIVET
GUENON
HANUMAN
LANGUR
LEMUR
MACAQUE
MAN
MANDRILL
MARMOSET
ORANGUTAN,
    aka ORANG
PROBOSCIS MONKEY
RHESUS
SAKI
SIAMANG
SPIDER MONKEY

**REPTILES**

AGAMA
ALLIGATOR
ANOLE
BASILISK
BLINDWORM
CAYMAN
CHAMELEON
CROCODILE
GAVIAL
GECKO
GILA MONSTER
IGUANA
LEATHERBACK
LIZARD
LIZARD, ALLIGATOR
LIZARD, BEADED
LIZARD, BEARDED
LIZARD,
    GIRDLE-TAILED
LIZARD, SAND
LIZARD,
    STUMP-TAILED
MONITOR
SKINK
SLOW-WORM
SNAKE, GLASS
TERRAPIN
TOAD, HORNED
TORTOISE
TORTOISE, SEA
TUATARA
TURTLE
TURTLE, BOX

TURTLE, GREEN
TURTLE, HAWKSBILL
TURTLE,
   LOGGERHEAD
TURTLE, SEA
TURTLE, SNAPPING
TURTLE,
  SOFT-SHELLED

**SNAKES**

ADDER
ANACONDA
ASP
BLACK SNAKE
BLIND SNAKE
BOA
BOA CONSTRICTOR
BULL SNAKE
BUSHMASTER

COBRA
COBRA, KING
COBRA, SPECKLED
CONSTRICTOR
COPPERHEAD
CORAL SNAKE
COTTONMOUTH
DABOIA
FER-DE-LANCE
GARTER SNAKE
GOPHER SNAKE
HAMADRYAD
HARLEQUIN SNAKE
HOG-NOSE SNAKE
KING SNAKE
KRAIT
MAMBA
MILK SNAKE
MOCCASIN
PINE SNAKE

PUFF ADDER
PYTHON
RACER
RAT SNAKE
RATTLESNAKE,
  aka RATTLER
RATTLESNAKE,
  DIAMONDBACK
RATTLESNAKE,
  HORNED
SHOVEL-NOSE SNAKE
SIDEWINDER
THUNDER SNAKE
URUTU
VIPER
VIPER, HORNED
VIPER, RUSSELL'S
WATER MOCCASIN
WATER SNAKE
WORM SNAKE

# GROUPS OF ANIMALS

| | |
|---|---|
| ants | COLONY |
| badgers | CETE |
| bears | SLEUTH |
| bees | GRIST, SWARM |
| birds | FLIGHT, VOLERY |
| boars | SOUNDER |
| cats | CLOWDER, CLUTTER |
| cattle | DROVE |
| chicks | BROOD, CLUTCH |
| clams | BED |
| cranes | SIEGE |
| crows | MURDER |
| ducks | TEAM |
| elephants | HERD |
| elk | GANG |
| fish | SHOAL, SCHOOL |
| foxes | LEASH, SKULK |
| geese | FLOCK, SKEIN; GAGGLE |
| gnats | CLOUD, HORDE |
| goats | TRIP; TRIBE |
| goldfinches | CHARM |
| gorillas | BAND |
| greyhounds | LEASH |
| hares | DOWN, HUSK |
| hawks | CAST |
| horses | TEAM |
| hounds | CRY; MUTE, PACK |
| kangaroos | MOB; TROOP |
| kittens | KINDLE |
| larks | EXALTATION |
| leopards | LEAP |
| lions | PRIDE |
| monkeys | TROOP |
| mules | SPAN |
| nightingales | WATCH |
| oxen | YOKE |
| oysters | BED |
| partridge | COVEY |
| peacocks | MUSTER |
| pheasants | NEST, NIDE |
| pigs | LITTER |
| pilchards | SHOAL |
| plovers | WING; CONGREGATION |
| quail | BEVY; COVEY |
| rhinoceros | CRASH |
| seals | POD |
| sheep | DROVE; FLOCK |
| swans | BEVY |
| swine | DRIFT; SOUNDER |
| teals | SPRING |
| toads | KNOT |
| turtles | BALE |
| vipers | NEST |
| whales | GAM, POD |
| wolves | PACK |

# MUSIC TERMINOLOGY

andante, slightly faster then..................
.........................................ANDANTINO
animatedly .........................CON MOTO
animation, with .....................ANIMATO
beats, pattern of .....................METER
brilliant flourish ....................CADENZA
chant with Biblical lyrics ......CANTICLE
composition, improvisational ...............
........................FANTASIA, RHAPSODY
composition, long dramatic..................
.........................................ORATORIO
composition, musical..............FUGUE,
..............PIECE; SONATA; CANTATA;
..................CONCERTO, SYMPHONY
composition, playful ............SCHERZO
composition, section of a.....PASSAGE
composition, simple pastoral ...............
..........................................IDYL; IDYLL
composition, slow, sad.............DIRGE,
..................................................ELEGY
composition especially for evening.......
..................NOCTURNE, SERENADE
composition for students ..........ETUDE
concluding series of notes
    or chords........................CADENCE
conductor.........................MAESTRO
conductor's stick......................BATON
contrapuntal song .............MADRIGAL
dance, Bohemian.....................POLKA
dance, lively .....................RIGADOON
dance, lively round .................GALOP
dance, lively Spanish............BOLERO;
........................................FANDANGO
dance, minuetlike but faster..................
..................................GAVOT; GAVOTTE
dance, Polish folk....MAZURKA
dance, Scottish ...............REEL; FLING
dance, slow and solemn ......................
.........................................CHACONNE
dance, slow and stately ........MINUET;
..............................................SARABAND
dance, slow Cuban ..........HABANERA
dance, South American ..........TANGO
dance, southern Italian ......................
.........................................TARANTELLA

dance, stately court .........................
.............................PAVAN; PAVANE
dance, stately Polish........POLONAISE
dance in duple time, Brazilian.............
..................................................SAMBA
effect, pulsating.....................VIBRATO
effect, sliding...................GLISSANDO
effect, tremulous .................TREMOLO
end ...............................................FINE
enthusiasm or devotion, with ...............
........................................CON AMORE
fast ......................PRESTO; ALLEGRO
fast, moderately ............ALLEGRETTO
fast and with excitement .......AGITATO
fast as possible, as ......PRESTISSIMO
from the beginning................DA CAPO
gracefully .......................LEGGIERO
gradually ....................POCO A POCO
half .............................................MEZZO
half note: Brit. ...........................MINIM
harmonize.................................CHORD
harmony, swelling burst of...................
...........................................DIAPASON
hymn, funeral .............DIRGE, ELEGY
improvise a musical interlude .....VAMP
in the style of...............................ALLA
keyboard ...............................CLAVIER
less .............................................MENO
little by little ................POCO A POCO
lively............................GAI; VIVO
lively and spirited....................VIVACE
loud.............................................FORTE
loud, very.......................FORTISSIMO
loudness, gradual decrease in.............
......................................DIMINUENDO;
.....................................DECRESCENDO
loudness, gradual increase in...............
.......................................CRESCENDO
lullaby................................BERCEUSE
measure, division of a ................BEAT
measured movement ..........CADENCE
medley of familiar tunes......FANTASIA
moderate in tempo ..............ANDANTE
moderately ..............................MEZZO
modulation .........................CADENCE

233

## Music Terminology

more ................................................PIU
much ..........................................MOLTO
muffling device.........MUTE; SORDINO
notes, with no breaks between .............
...............................................LEGATO
operatic solo.................................ARIA
part song.............................MADRIGAL
part song for 3 male voices.........GLEE
passage, concluding............................
.......................................CODA; FINALE
passage, concluding
   (with increasing speed)...STRETTO
passage, elaborate solo ......CADENZA
passage, slow and stately........LARGO
pause....................................FERMATA
pitch, half-step higher in ..........SHARP
pitch, half-step lower in ...............FLAT
pitch, standard of ...............DIAPASON
pitch, vary the ..................MODULATE
pitch symbol ...............................CLEF
plucked ..............................PIZZICATO
prolong, a tone or a rest .............HOLD
range.................................DIAPASON
repeat the passage...............DA CAPO
sign (esp. for end of a repeat) .............
...............................................SEGNO
silence, measured interval of ......REST
singer, female professional..................
.......................................CANTATRICE
singing style, pure ............BEL CANTO
sixteenth note ...............SEMIQUAVER
slow and stately ........................LARGO
slow...........................LENTO, TARDO
slower, becoming gradually .................
.....................................RITARDANDO
slower with more power,
   gradually............ALLARGANDO
slowing down by degrees ....................
...............................................LENTANDO
slowly............................LENTAMENTE
slowly and leisurely.................ADAGIO
smooth ....................................LEGATO
softly.......................................PIANO
softly, very ......................PIANISSIMO
solo, opera .....................................ARIA

solo, short............................ARIETTA;
.............................................CAVATINA
sonata, last movement of a .....RONDO
song...................................CHANSON
song, contrapuntal .............MADRIGAL
song, German...............................LIED
songlike ..........................CANTABILE
song of praise ........................ANTHEM
speed......................................TEMPO
spiritedly.............................CON BRIO
sung approximating speech.................
...........................................PARLANDO
sweet.......................................DOLCE
symbol on the staff ..........CLEF, FLAT,
..........................NOTE, REST; SHARP
tempo (in increasing order).....LARGO,
.......................LARGHETTO, ADAGIO,
....................ANDANTE, ANDANTINO,
.................ALLEGRETTO, ALLEGRO,
....................PRESTO, PRESTISSIMO
tempo, with moderation in ...................
...........................................MODERATO
tempo determined by performer .........
.......................................A CAPRICCIO
tenderly...........................CON AMORE
text of a musical work .........LIBRETTO
theme............................................TEMA
time signature indication ..........METER
tone used as a standard ............PITCH
tones, 3 or more
   sounded together ...............CHORD
tones, with distinct
   breaks between...........STACCATO
too much....................................TANTO
tuning fork .........................DIAPASON
vertical line dividing staff ...............BAR
very ........................................MOLTO
vocal style ...................ARIA; ARIOSO;
...........................................RECITATIVE
voice ............................................VOCE
voice part .................................CANTO
waltz.........................................VALSE
without instrumental
   accompaniment .........A CAPPELLA
without varying .....................SEMPRE

234

# ABBREVIATIONS & ACRONYMS

AAA...............Amer. Automobile Assn.
AAM ...............................air-to-air missile
AARP ................................Amer. Assn.
........................................of Retired Persons
ABBR. .............................abbreviation
ABA.................Amateur Boxing Assn.,
..............................Amer. Bar Assn.,
..................Amer. Basketball Assn.
ABC ................Amer. Broadcasting Co.
ABD. .................abdomen, abdominal
ABM .......................antiballistic missile
ABP. ..................................archbishop
ABR. .................abridged, abridgment
ABS...................able-bodied seaman,
................absent, absolute, abstract
ABT...................Amer. Ballet Theatre
ACAD. ....................................academy
ACC.................Atl. Coast Conference
ACCT. .................account, accountant
AC/DC ....................alternating current/
......................................direct current
ACLU.........Amer. Civil Liberties Union
ACP .........Amer. Coll. of Physicians
ACS ...............Amer. Cancer Society
ACTH ......adrenocorticotropic hormone
ADA ...................Amer. Dental Assn.
ADC..........Aid to Dependent Children,
.................................aide-de-camp
ADJ. .................adjacent, adjective
ADM. .....................................admiral
ADMIM. ..........................administration
ADP ............automatic data processing
ADV. ...........................................adverb
AEC .........Atomic Energy Commission
AEF ..........Amer. Expeditionary Forces
AERO. ....aeronautical, aeronautics
AFB................................air force base
AFC .........Amer. Football Conference,
....................automatic flight control,
.................automatic frequency control
AFDC...................Aid to Families with
...........................Dependent Children
AFG., AFGHAN. ...............Afghanistan
AFL...........Amer. Federation of Labor,
.....................Amer. Football League
AFL-CIO....................Amer. Federation
.....................of Labor and Congress of
.......................Industrial Organizations
AFR. ..............................Africa, African
AFTRA................Amer. Federation of
................Television and Radio Artists
AGCY. ...........................................agency
AGI .................adjusted gross income
AGRI. .............agriculture, agricultural
AGT. .........................agent, agreement
AHST .............Alaska Hawaii Std. Time

AIDS.......................acquired immune
......................deficiency syndrome
AIM ...............Amer. Indian Movement
AKA....................................also known as
AKC.......................Amer. Kennel Club
ALA. ..........................................Alabama
ALAS. ..........................................Alaska
ALB. ......................Albania, Albanian
ALG. ........algebra, Algeria, Algerian
ALS .........amyotrophic lateral sclerosis
ALTA. ...........................................Alberta
ALUM. ......................................aluminum
AMA....................Amer. Medical Assn.
AMB. ....................................ambassador
AMER. ......................................American
AMESLAN.........Amer. Sign Language
AMEX...............Amer. Stock Exchange
AMP. ................amperage, ampere
AMPH. ..........amphibian, amphibious
AMT. ............................................amount
ANAG. ........................................anagram
ANAT. ..........................................anatomy
ANC. .............................................ancient
ANG. ...........................................Angola
ANGL. ........................................Anglican
ANON. .....................................anonymous
ANSI........Amer. Natl. Standards Inst.
ANTH. ........................................anthology
ANZAC ....................Austral. and N. Z.
................................................Army Corps
APB...........................all points bulletin
APO ............................Army post office
APOC. ...........Apocalypse, Apocrypha
APOS. ......................................apostrophe
APR.......annual percentage rate, April
ARAB. ..........................Arabian, Arabic
ARC ............................Amer. Red Cross
ARCH. ...........archaic, archipelago,
.........................architect, architecture
ARG. ........................................Argentina
ARIZ. ...........................................Arizona
ARK. .........................................Arkansas
ARR. ....................arrangement, arrival
ARVN ......Army of the Rep. of Vietnam
ASAP .................as soon as possible
ASAT...............................anti-satellite
ASB. ..........................................asbestos
ASCAP.......................Amer. Society of
.......Composers, Authors, & Publishers
ASCII ................Amer. Standard Code
.................for Information Interchange
ASE...................Amer. Stock Exchange
ASI.....................air-speed indicator
ASN ...................Army service number
ASPCA................Amer. Society for the
..........Prevention of Cruelty to Animals

| | |
|---|---|
| ASSN. .................................association | BRO. .......................................brother |
| ASST. .....................................assistant | BROS. ...................................brothers |
| AST .................Atlantic standard time | BSA.................Boy Scouts of America |
| ASV .................Amer. Standard Version | B.SC. ...................Bachelor of Science |
| ATC...............................air traffic control | BTU.....................British thermal unit |
| ATF .......................Bureau of Alcohol, | BUL., BULG. .........Bulgaria, Bulgarian |
| .................Tobacco, and Firearms | BUR. .........................................bureau |
| ATL. ......................................Atlantic | BUS. ......................................business |
| ATM....................................atmosphere, | B.V.I. .....................Brit. Virgin Islands |
| ..............automated teller machine | B.V.M. .............Blessed Virgin Mary |
| AT.NO. .........................atomic number | BYOB ...................bring your own bottle |
| ATP...............................Assn. of Tennis | |
| ....................................Professionals | CAB.................Civil Aeronautics Board |
| ATTN. .......................................attention | CAD ............computer assisted design |
| ATTY. .......................................attorney | CAM...............................computer-aided |
| ATV ...........................all-terrain vehicle | ..................................manufacturing |
| AT. WT. ...........................atomic weight | CAN. , CANAD. .....Canada, Canadian |
| AUG. .........................................August | CANC. ...................................canceled |
| AUS ...........Army of the United States, | CAPT. .......................................captain |
| ...........................Austria, Austrian | CARE ..............Cooperative for Amer. |
| AUSTRAL. ..............................Australia | ...................Relief to Everywhere |
| AUTH. .....authentic, author, authority | CATH. ..................cathedral, Catholic |
| AUX. ........................................auxiliary | CAV. ..........................................cavalry |
| AVDP. ................................avoirdupois | CBC..............Can. Broadcasting Corp. |
| AVE. ..........................................avenue | CBT ...............Chicago Board of Trade |
| AVG. .........................................average | CCA .................circuit court of appeals |
| AWACS...................airborne warning | CCC ........Civilian Conservation Corps |
| ..............and control system | CCW...............................counterclockwise |
| AWOL ............absent without leave | CDC .........Centers for Disease Control |
| | CDT ......................central daylight time |
| BAPT. .........................................Baptist | CEA .............Council of Econ. Advisors |
| BART. .........................................baronet | CEL. ...........................................Celsius |
| BASIC...........Beginner's All-purpose | CENT. .......central, center, centigrade, |
| ...........Symbolic Instruction Code | ....................................centime, century |
| BAV. ......................Bavaria, Bavarian | CEO ..................chief executive officer |
| BBB.............Better Business Bureau | CERN...................................Eur. Center |
| BBC ..............Brit. Broadcasting Corp. | ......................for Nuclear Research |
| BELG. .....................Belgian, Belgium | CERT. ............certificate, certification, |
| BEV. .......................................beverage | ...................................certified, certify |
| BFA ....................Bachelor of Fine Arts | CETA................................Comprehensive |
| B.GEN. ....................brigadier general | .............Employment and Training Act |
| BIA ...............Bureau of Indian Affairs | CETI.....................communication with |
| BIBL. .................................bibliography | ................extraterrestrial intelligence |
| BIO. ...........................................biography | CFL ....................Can. Football League |
| BIOL. .......biological, biologist, biology | CFM ....................cubic feet per minute |
| BLDG. ........................................building | CFS ....................cubic feet per second |
| B.LIT.......................Bachelor of Letters | CGI .......................computer generated |
| BLS.............Bureau of Labor Statistics | ..........................................imagery |
| BLT.............bacon, lettuce, and tomato | CHEM. ...chemical, chemist, chemistry |
| BLVD. ....................................boulevard | CHIN. .........................................Chinese |
| BMI......................Broadcast Music Inc. | CHM. ...........chairman, checkmate |
| BMOC ...............big man on campus | CHOL. ..................................cholesterol |
| BMX .........................bicycle motocross | CHRON. ..........................Chronicles |
| BOL. ......................Bolivia, Bolivian | CIA...............Central Intelligence Agcy. |
| BOR. ........................................borough | .................Culinary Institute of Amer. |
| BOT. .........botanical, botanist, botany | CID .....................Criminal Investigative |
| BPOE...........................Benevolent and | .........................Dept. (Scotland Yard) |
| ..................Protective Order of Elks | C.I.F. .........cost, insurance, and freight |
| BRAZ. .......................Brazil, Brazilian | C IN C.....................Commander in Chief |
| BRIT. ...............................Britain, British | CIO ...........Congress of Industrial Org. |

CIR., CIRC. ...........circa, circle, circuit,
...............................circular, circulation,
....................................circumference
CIT. ...............................citation, citizen
CIV. ....................................civil, civilian
CKW .......................................clockwise
CLAR. ......................................clarinet
CLI.........................cost of living index
CMDR. .....................................commander
CNO..............chief of naval operations
CNS..................central nervous system
COBOL..................Common Business
...........................Oriented Language
C.O.D. .........................cash on delivery
COEF. ...........................coefficient
COLA............cost-of-living adjustment
COLL. ...................college, collegiate
COLO. ...............................Colorado
COMM. .........command, commandant,
.................commander, commanding,
....................commentary, commerce,
.....................commercial, commission,
.................commissioned, committee,
.........................common, commoner,
.................commonwealth, commune,
.................communication, communist
COMP. .............companion, company,
..........comparative, compare, compass,
..........compensation, compilation,
..........compiled, compiler, complement,
.......complete, composer, composition,
..............compound, comprehensive
COMR. ...........................commissioner
CONC. ......concentrate, concentrated,
....................concentration, concentric,
.............concerning, concrete, council
COND. ............condensed, condenser,
..............condition, conduct, conductor
CONF. ...........................confederation,
........................conference, confidential
CONG. ..........congregation, congress,
..........................................congressional
CONJ. ...............................conjugation,
.........................conjunction, conjunctive
CONN. ...............................Connecticut
CONT. ...........containing, contemporary,
........contents, continental, continued,
............................................contract, control
COR. ...................................Corinthians
CORE.......Congress of Racial Equality
CORP. ...............corporate, corporation
COS ......................chief of staff, cosine
CPA ....................Certified Public Acct.
CPB .......Corp. for Public Broadcasting
CPI .......................consumer price index
CPL. .........................................corporal
CPO...........................chief petty officer
CPR ........................cardiopulmonary
.................................................resuscitation
CPU .................central processing unit

CRC ...............Civil Rights Commission
CREEP...........................Committee to
...............................Re-elect the President
CRIM. ...................................criminal
CRIT. ...........................critical, criticism
CROC. ....................................crocodile
CRT ..........................cathode-ray tube
C.S.A. .................Confederate States
...........................................of America
CSC ............Civil Service Commission
C-Span .........................Cable Satellite
...........................Public Affairs Network
CST ...............central standard time
CTO ...........................................concerto
CTS. ..............................................cents
CVA....................Columbia Valley Auth.
CWO ...............chief warrant officer
CYO ...........................Cath. Youth Org.

DAR .......Daughters of the Amer. Rev.
DAT ...........................digital audio tape
DAV ......................Disabled Amer. Vet.
DBL. ...............................................double
DDC....................Dewey Decimal
....................................Classification
DDS .............Doctor of Dental Surgery
DDT ....dichlorodiphenyltrichloroethane
DEA..........Drug Enforcement Admin.
DEC. ...............................December
DECD. ...............................deceased,
..........................declared, decreased
DEF. ...............defense, definition
DEG. ...............................degree
DEL. ..........Delaware, delegate, delete
DEM. ...............Democrat, Democratic
DEN. ...............................Denmark
DEPT. ...................department, deputy
DESC. ...............................descendant
DEUT. ...........................Deuteronomy
DEW .....................distant early warning
DFC............Distinguished Flying Cross
DIAG. .....................diagonal, diagram
DIAM. ...............................diameter
DICT. ...............................dictionary
DIF. ...............................difference
DIR. ...............................director
DISC. ...........discharged, discontinue,
........................discount, discovered
DIST. ...........................distance, district
DIV. ..........dividend, division, divorced
DIY.......................................do-it-yourself
D.L.O. ...................dead letter office
DMV ...............Dept. of Motor Vehicles
DMZ...................demilitarized zone
DNA...................deoxyribonucleic acid
DNC ...............Dem. Natl. Committee
D.O.A. ...........................dead on arrival
DOC. ...............doctor, document
DOD...........................Dept. of Defense
DOE...............................Dept. of Energy

DOL. ................................................dollar
DOM. .....................domestic, dominion
DOS .....................disk operating system
DOT .................Dept. of Transportation
DOZ ...................................................dozen
D.PH. ....................Doctor of Philosophy
DPT ........diphtheria, pertussis, tetanus
DPW ...........Department of Public Works
DSC .........Distinguished Service Cross
DST ......................daylight saving time
D.TH. ......................Doctor of Theology
DTS...............................delirium tremens
DUI .............driving under the influence
DUP.................................duplex, duplicate
D.V.M. ...Doctor of Veterinary Medicine
DWI................driving while intoxicated

ECCL. ........ecclesiastic, ecclesiastical
ECCLES. ..........................Ecclesiastes
ECG. .......................electrocardiogram
ECOL. ....................ecological, ecology
ECON. ..............economic, economics,
........................................economist, economy
E-COM ....................electronic computer-
..........................................originated mail
ECUA. .................................................Ecuador
EDP .........electronic data processing
EDT ......................eastern daylight time
EDUC. ................educated, education,
...............................................educational
EEC...........Eur. Economic Community
EEG ..................electroencephalogram
EEOC .....................Equal Employment
......................Opportunity Commission
EFT .................electronic funds transfer
EKG ........................electrocardiogram
ELEC. ...electric, electrical, electrician,
.............................electricity, electrified
ELEM. ................element, elementary
ELEV. ...................................elevation
ELIZ. .....................................Elizabeth
EMB. ..................embargo, embassy
EMI .........electromagnetic interference
EMP. ....emperor, empire, employment
ENC., ENCL. .......enclosed, enclosure
ENCY. ............................encyclopedia
ENG. ....................England, English
ENGR. ................engineer, engraving
ENL. ....................enlarged, enlisted
ENS.................................................ensign
EOE.........equal opportunity employer
EPA .............................Environmental
......................................Protection Agency
EPCOT............Experimental Prototype
..................Community of Tomorrow
EPH. ..................................Ephesians
EPIS. ...................................Episcopal
EPIT. .........................................epitaph
EPROM ..........erasable programmable
...............................read-only memory

ERA......................earned run average
......................Equal Rights Amendment
ESL.......English as a second language
ESP..............extrasensory perception
ESQ. ....................................esquire
EST....................eastern standard time
......................establishment, estimate
ESTH.....................................Esther
ETA ...............estimated time of arrival
ET AL. ......................and elsewhere
ETC. ....................................et cetera
ETH. ...................Ethiopia, Ethiopian
ETI..............extraterrestrial intelligence
ETO......Eur. theater of operations
ETV.................educational television
EUR...................Europe, European
EVA.....................extravehicular activity
EXCH. .............exchange, exchequer
EXCL. .............exclamation, exclude,
....................................excluding, exclusive
EXEC. ...............executed, execution,
.................................executive, executor
EXP ..............expense, experimental
................exponent, export, express
EXOD. .....................................Exodus
EXT. .....................extension, exterior
EZEK. .....................................Ezekiel

FAA .............Federal Aviation Admin.
FAHR. .................................Fahrenheit
FAM. .........................................family
FBI .............................Federal Bureau
..........................................of Investigation
FCC ............Federal Communications
.......................................Commission
FDA..................Food and Drug Admin.
FDIC ......Fed. Deposit Insurance Corp.
FEB. ..........................................February
FED. .....................federal, federation
FEM. ..................female, feminine
FEPA.....................Fair Employment
...........................................Practices Act
FEPC.....................Fair Employment
..........................Practices Commission
FET ....................Federal Excise Tax
FFF ...................as loud as possible
FHA...............Federal Housing Admin.
FICA ......................Federal Insurance
.............................Contributions Act
FIG. .............................figurative, figure
FINN.............................................Finnish
FLA. ...............................................Florida
FLEM.............................................Flemish
FNMA.....Federal Natl. Mortgage Assn.
FOE.............Fraternal Order of Eagles
F.O.I.A.........Freedom of Info. Act
FORTRAN.............formula translation
FRB .................Federal Reserve Board
FREQ. ...................frequency, frequent
FRI. ...................................................Friday

238

FSLIC ..................Federal Savings and ..................................Loan Corporation
FTC ..........Federal Trade Commission
FUBAR ................fouled up beyond all ..................................recognition
FWD...........................four-wheel drive
FYI ..........................for your information

GAL. ..........................Galatians, gallon
GAO...........General Accounting Office
GARP ...................Global Atmospheric ..............................Research Program
GATT.................General Agreement of ...........................Tariffs and Trade
GED ........general equivalency diploma
GEN. ..................................Genesis
GENL. ....................................general
GEOG. ..........geographic, geography
GEOL. ...................geological, geology
GEOM. ............geometrical, geometry
GER. .........German, Germany, gerund
GHQ ................general headquarters
GIGO .............garbage in, garbage out
GLOS. ..................................glossary
GMT.................Greenwich mean time
GNP ....................gross natl. product
GOES...........geostationary operational ....................environmental satellite
GOP...........................Grand Old Party
GOVT. ............................government
GPA.....................grade-point average
GPO ...................general post office, ................Government Printing Office
GRAD. .................gradient, graduate
GRE .....Graduate Record Examination
GRO. ......................................gross
G.R.U. ...........Soviet Army Intelligence
GSA .................Girl Scouts of America
GSR .................galvanic skin response
GUAT. ..............................Guatemala
GUTS ..........grand unification theories

HAB. ..................................Habakkuk
HAG. ....................................Haggai
HBO...........................Home Box Office
HCAP. ....................................handicap
HCL...................high cost of living
HCP. ....................................handicap
HDBK. ..................................handbook
HDS .....Human Development Services
HDTV.............high definition television
HEB. ......................Hebrew, Hebrews
HEW ................Department of Health, ................Education, and Welfare
HGT. ......................................height
HIST. .........historian, historical, history
HMO ......................health maintenance ..................................organization
HMS ..........His (Her) Majesty's Service ......................His (Her) Majesty's Ship

HNS .......................Holy Name Society
HON. ........honor, honorable, honorary
HOND. ..................................Honduras
HOPE ................Health Opportunity for ..................................People Everywhere
HOR. ......................horizon, horizontal
HORT. ..................................horticulture
HOS. ......................................Hosea
HOSP. ....................................hospital
HOV .............high-occupancy vehicle
HRA ...........Health Resources Admin.
HRH ............His (Her) Royal Highness
HRIP ....................here rests in peace
HRS. ......................................hours
HST................Hawaiian standard time
HTS. ......................................heights
HUAC......................House Un-Amer. ..........................Activities Committee
HUD ...............Department of Housing ..................and Urban Development
HUNG. ..................Hungarian, Hungary
HWY. ......................................highway

IAS...........................indicated air speed
IBID. ........................in the same place
ICBM ..........................Intercontinental ..................................ballistic missile
ICC....................Interstate Commerce ..................................Commission
ICE. ........................................Iceland
ICEL. ....................................Icelandic
ICU ......................intensive care unit
IGN. ......................ignition, unknown
IGY ....................Intl. Geophysical Year
IHS ..........................................Jesus
ILA.............Intl. Longshoreman's Assn.
ILGWU................................Intl. Ladies' ..................Garment Workers' Union
ILL. ......................................Illinois
ILO.............................Intl. Labor Org.
IMF ....................Intl. Monetary Fund
IMIT. ......................................imitation
IMP. ..................imperative, imperfect, ..........................import, in the first place
INC. ................................incorporated
INCL. ......included, including, inclusive
IND. ..................independent, Indian ..................................Indiana, industry
INFO. ..................................information
INIT. ......................................initial
INRI ....................Jesus of Nazareth, ..............................King of the Jews
INS...........................Immigration and ..........................Naturalization Service
INSP. ....................................inspector
INST. .................installment, institute, ..........institution, instruction, instructor, ..........................instrument, instrumental
INT. ..................intelligence, interest
INTL. ..................................international

239

IOC ................Intl. Olympic Committee
I.O.M. ...................................Isle of Man
IOOF...................Independent Order of
............................................Odd Fellows
IOU ...........................................I owe you
I.O.W. ...............................Isle of Wight
IPA.................Intl. Phonetic Alphabet
IRA.................individual retirement acct.
I.R.A. ...................Irish Republican Army
IRC.............................Intl. Red Cross
IRE. ..............................................Ireland
IRR. .............................................irregular
IRS ...........Internal Revenue Service
ISA. ...............................................Isaiah
ISBN.........Intl. Standard Book Number
ISL. .................................................island
ISR. .................................................Israel
ITAL. ..............................italic, italicized
ITC ...................investment tax credit
ITO ...........................Intl. Trade Org.
IUD ...........................intrauterine device
IWW...................Industrial Workers of
.............................................the World

JAM. ...........................................Jamaica
JAN. .............................................January
JAP. ....................Japan, Japanese
JATO ....................jet-assisted takeoff
JBS ...........................John Birch Society
JCS ....................Joint Chiefs of Staff
JCT. ............................................junction
JDL ...........Jewish Defense League
JER. ..........................................Jeremiah
J.H.S. .....................junior high school
JOBS .............Job Opportunities in the
.................................Business Sector
JUL. .................................................July
JUN. ...............................................June

KAN., KANS. ...........................Kansas
KGB....................Soviet State Security
......................................Committee
KIA ..............................killed in action
KJV....................King James Version
KPH ...................kilometers per hour
KWH...............................kilowatt-hour

LAB. ...............laboratory, Labrador
LAM. .................................Lamentations
LANG. .........................................language
LASER.................Light Amplification
..................................by Stimulated
......................Emission of Radiation
LAT. ......latent, lateral, Latvia, latitude
LAV. .............................................lavatory
LBS. .............................................pounds
LCD ..........least common denominator,
.......................liquid crystal display
LCM ............least common multiple
LDS .....................Ladder-day Saints

LEB. ...................Lebanese, Lebanon
LED .................light-emitting diode
LEM .................lunar excursion module
LEV. .............................................Leviticus
LGE. ...............................................large
LGTH. ............................................length
LIB. .....................liberal, liberation
LIEUT. ....................................lieutenant
LITH. ...............Lithuania, Lithuanian
LOC. .........in this place, local, location
LOG. .........................................logarithm
LON. .........................................longitude
LOQ. ...............................he/she speaks
LORAN..............long-range navigation
LOST ................Law of the Sea Treaty
LPGA................Ladies Pro. Golf Assn.
LPN..............Licensed Practical Nurse
LSD...............................lysergic acid;
...................pounds, shillings, pence
LTD. .............................................limited
LUTH. ........................................Lutheran
LUX. ....................................Luxembourg
LWV.............League of Women Voters

MAG. ...................magazine, magnet
MAJ. ...............................................major
MAL. ............................................Malachi
MAR. ...............................................March
MASC. ....................................masculine
MASH ........mobile army surgical hosp.
MASS. ...............................Massachusetts
MATT. ..........................................Matthew
MAX. .........................................maximum
M.B.A. .............Master of Bus. Admin.
MCP....................male chauvinist pig
MDT.................mountain daylight time
MED. .....................medical, medicine,
....................Mediterranean, medium
MET. .......................................metropolitan
METH. .......................................Methodist
MEX. ....................Mexican, Mexico
MFD. ....................................manufactured
MFG. ...................................manufacturing
MFR. .........manufacture, manufacturer
MIA...........................missing in action
MIC. ...............................................Micah
MICH. ......................................Michigan
MIL. ............................military, million
MIN. ...............mineral, minor, minute
MINN. .......................................Minnesota
MIRV...............multiple independently
...............targeted reentry vehicle
MISC. .........miscellaneous, miscellany
MISS. ......................................Mississippi
MIXT. ............................................mixture
MLLE. ...................................mademoiselle
MME. ........................................Madame
MOD. .............................................modern
MON. ............................................Monday
MONT. .........................................Montana

MPG .............................miles per gallon
MPH..............................miles per hour
MRS. ...................................mistress
MSGR. .......messenger, monseigneur,
.........................................monsignor
M.SGT. ......................master sergeant
MSS. ...............................manuscripts
MST ............mountain standard time
MTS. ...................................mountains
MUS. ..........................museum, music
MVP ...................most valuable player

NAACP.................................Natl. Assn.
........................for the Advancement of
................................Colored People
NADA .......................Natl. Automobile
.................................Dealers Assn.
NAH. ....................................Nahum
NAS .................Natl. Acad. of Sciences,
.............................naval air station
NASA ......................Natl. Aeronautics
.............................and Space Admin.
NASCAR ..............................Natl. Assn.
.................of Stock Car Auto Racing
NASDAQ .......Natl. Assn. of Securities
...........Dealers Automated Quotations
NASL.......North Amer. Soccer League
NATL. ......................................national
NATO ................North Atl. Treaty Org.
NAUT. ......................................nautical
NAV. ........naval, navigable, navigate,
................navigation, navigator, navy
NBA ....................Natl. Basketball Assn.
NBC.................Natl. Broadcasting Co.
NBS ...........Natl. Bureau of Standards
NCAA ............Natl. Coll. Athletic Assn.
NCO..............noncommissioned officer
NDA .......................Natl. Dental Assn.
N. DAK. ........................North Dakota
NEA...............Natl. Educational Assn.,
................Natl. Endowment for the Arts
NEB., NEBR. ......................Nebraska
NEG. ...................................negative
NEH. ...................................Nehemiah
NETH. ............................Netherlands
NEUT. ........................neuter, neutral
NEV. ......................................Nevada
NFL....................Natl. Football League
N.H.I. ..............Natl. Health Insurance
NHL .....................Natl. Hockey League
NHRA.......Natl. Hot Rod Assn.
NHS ...................Natl. Health Service
NIRA.......Natl. Industrial Recovery Act
NIT .................................Natl. Invitational
........................................Tournament
NLRB.......Natl. Labor Relations Board
N. Mex. ..........................New Mexico
NMI ......................no middle initial
NOAA.....................Natl. Oceanic and
.............................Atmospheric Admin.

NOR. ...................Norway, Norwegian
NORAD.....................North Amer. Air
.............................Defense Command
NOS. ...................................numbers
NOV. ....................................November
NOW...................Natl. Org. for Women
NPR ....................Natl. Public Radio
NRA ................Natl. Recovery Admin.,
.............................Natl. Rifle Assn.
NRC ...........Natl. Research Council,
.........Nuclear Regulatory Commission
NSA...................Natl. Security Agency
NSC...................Natl. Security Council
NSF .............Natl. Science Foundation
N.S.W. ..................New South Wales
NTSB ...........Natl. Transportation
.............................Safety Board
NT. WT. ...............................net weight
NUM. ...................................Numbers
NWT ....................Northwest Territories
NYC ..........................New York City
NYSE .........New York Stock Exchange

OAS ...................Org. of Amer. States
OAU ....................Org. of African Unity
OBAD. ....................................Obadiah
O.B.E. ................Officer of the Order
.............................of the British Empire
OB-GYN.............obstetrics-gynecology
OBIT. ....................................obituary
OBJ. .........object, objection, objective
OBO .................................or best offer
OBS. ...............observation, obsolete
OCA...........Office of Consumer Affairs
OCS...........Officer Candidate School
OCT. ...................................October
OED .............Oxford English Dictionary
OEO ................Office of Econ. Opp.
OFF. ...offensive, office, officer, official
OKLA. ...................................Oklahoma
ONI ...........Office of Naval Intelligence
ONO ...........................or nearest offer
ONT. ....................................Ontario
OOB ...........................off-off-Broadway
OP. CIT...................in the work cited
OPEC ...............Org. of Petroleum
.............................Exporting Countries
OPP. ...............opportunities, opposite
ORCH. ...................................orchestra
ORE., OREG. ......................Oregon
ORG. ...............................organization
ORIG. .................................origin, original
ORK. ....................................Orkney
OSHA .........Occupational Safety and
.............................Health Admin.
OSS............Office of Strategic Services
OTB............................off-track betting
OTC...........................over-the-counter
OXFAM...................Oxford Committee
.............................for Famine Relief

OZS. .............................................ounces

PAC.................................................Pacific,
.........................political action committee
PAK. ............................................Pakistan
PAL ....................Police Athletic League
PAN. ...........................................Panama
PAR. ..........................................Paraguay
PAT ....................point after touchdown
PBA...............Police Benevolent Assn.
.................Professional Bowlers Assn.
PBK .................................Phi Beta Kappa
PBS........Public Broadcasting Service
PCT. ......................percent, percentage
PDT...........................Pacific daylight time
P.E.I. ..................Prince Edward Island
PENN. ............................Pennsylvania
PER. ..............................Persia, Persian
PERS. .....person, personal, personnel
PFC................................private first class
PGA........................Pro. Golfers' Assn.
PHAR. .......pharmaceutical, pharmacy
PH.D................Doctor of Philosophy
PHIL. ...................................Philippians
PIC. ................................................picture
PIN .............pers. identification number
PIX. .................................................pictures
PLO................Palestine Liberation Org.
PMS ...............premenstrual syndrome
POL. ...............................Poland, Polish
POP.........................................population
PORT. ................Portugal, Portuguese
POW ..............................prisoner of war
PPD. .........................postpaid, prepaid
P.P.S. .................additional postscript
PRES. ........................................president
PRO. ......................................professional
PROF. .........................................professor
PROM.................................programmable
.................................read-only memory
PROT. ........................................Protestant
PROV.............................................Proverbs
PSA...................................................Psalms
PST ....................Pacific standard time
PTA ....................parent-teacher Assn.
PTO .........Patent & Trademark Office
PVT. ...............................................private

Q.E.D. .........................which was to be
..................................................demonstrated
Q.E.F..................which was to be done

RAAF ..........Royal Australian Air Force
RAC ..................Royal Automobile Club
RAF..................................Royal Air Force
RAM ...............random access memory
RATO..................rocket-assisted takeoff
RBI.............................................runs batted in
RCA.................Rodeo Cowboys Assn.
RCAF...........Royal Canadian Air Force

RCMP .........................Royal Canadian
.........................................Mounted Police
RCN ..................Royal Canadian Navy
RCT. ..............................receipt, recruit
RDA.......................recommended daily
.........................................................allowance
REA ...........Rural Electrification Admin.
REF. .................................................referee
REG. ...........................regent, register,
....................................regular, regulation
REM ......................rapid eye movement
REP. .............representative, republic,
....................................................Republican
REQ. ...............request, requisition
RET. .................................................retired
REV. ....................Revelation, reverend
RFD ...........................rural free delivery
RFE ......................Radio Free Europe
RHIP ...............rank has its privileges
RIP ...............may he/she rest in peace
RIT. .............................................ritardando
RMS. ................................................rooms
RNA ...........................ribonucleic acid
RNC ...............Rep. Natl. Committee
R.O.C. ......................Republic of China
R.O.K. ......................Republic of Korea
ROM.........read-only memory, Roman,
.............Romania, Romanian, Romans
ROTC.......................Reserve Officers'
....................................Training Corps
RPM .................revolutions per minute
RSA...............Republic of South Africa
RSV ...........Revised Standard Version
R.S.V.P. ..........répondez s'il vous plait
RTE. .................................................route
RUSS. ........................Russia, Russian
RWY. .............................................railway

SAC ................Strategic Air Command
SAE ..................self-addressed envelope
S.AFR. .......South Africa, South African
SAG...................Screen Actors Guild
SALT ...............................Strategic Arms
....................................Limitation Talks
SAM....................surface-to-air missile
SAR ............Sons of the Amer. Rev.
SASK. ...........................Saskatchewan
SAT ................Scholastic Aptitude Test
SBA .......................Small Bus. Admin.
SCAND. ....Scandinavia, Scandinavian
SCH. .................................................school
SCI. .................................................science
SCI.-FI. ................................science fiction
SCOT. ...................Scotland, Scottish
SCUBA........self-contained underwater
..............................breathing apparatus
S.DAK. ........................South Dakota
SDI.............Strategic Defense Initiative
SDS .........Students for a Dem. Society
SEATO ......Southeast Asia Treaty Org.

242

SEC .............Securities and Exchange
...............................................Commission
SECY. .....................................secretary
SEN. ......................senate, senator
SEP., SEPT. .....................September
SEQQ. ..............in the following places
SER. ................serial, sermon, service
SESS. .......................................session
SGD. ............................................signed
SGT. ..........................................sergeant
SHAK. .......................Shakespearean
SKT. ...........................................Sanskrit
S.L.C. .............................Salt Lake City
SLR..............................single lens reflex
SNAFU .......................situation normal,
...............................................all fouled up
SNO.................Scottish Natl. Orchestra
SOC. ...........................socialist, society
SOP.......standard operating procedure
SOPH. ...................................sophomore
SOS...............................(distress signal)
SOV. .............................................soviet
S.P.C.A........Society for the Prevention
..............................of Cruelty to Animals
SPEC. ...................special, specialist,
.............species, specific, specification
SPQR..........................the senate and
..........................the people of Rome
S.P.Q.R.......small profits, quick returns
SRA. ............................................señora
SRO .................single room occupancy,
...............................standing room only
SRTA. .........................................señorita
SSA ...............Social Security Admin.
S.SGT. .............................staff sergeant
SSN .................Social Security number
SSR...............Soviet Socialist Republic
SSS.................Selective Service System
SST .......................supersonic transport
START ..........................Strategic Arms
...............................Reduction Talks
STAT. ............immediately, statistic
STD ............................................standard
STE. .........................saint (female Fr.)
STOL............short takeoff and landing
STR. ...............................strait, stringed
SUBJ. ...................subject, subjective,
.............................subjectively, subjunctive
SUN. ............................................Sunday
SUPT. ............superintendent, support
SURG. ........surgeon, surgery, surgical
SWAK.....................sealed with a kiss
SWAPO .................South-West African
..........................People's Organization
SWAT .......Special Weapons & Tactics
SWC.................Southwest Conference
SWED. .................Sweden, Swedish
SYL., SYLL. ...........................syllable
SYM. .................symbol, symmetrical,
...............................................symphony

SYR. ................................Syria, Syrian
SYS. .........................................system

TAC..................Tactical Air Command
TASM. ...................................Tasmania
TAT...........thematic apperception test
TBA...........................to be announced
TBS.......................................tablespoon,
................Turner Broadcasting System
TEL. ...................telegram, telephone
TEMP. ........temperance, temperature,
............template, temporal, temporary
TENN. ...............................Tennessee
TER. ...........................terrace, territory
TEX. ...............................................Texas
TGIF ...................thank God it's Friday
THU., THUR., THURS. .........Thursday
TIROS ..............television and infrared
.................................observation satellite
TIX...............................................tickets
TKO.....................technical knockout
TLC.......................tender loving care
TNT.................................trinitrotoluene
TOPO. .......topographic, topographical
TRIG. ...............................trigonometry
TRIN. ...........................................Trinidad
TUE., TUES. ........................Tuesday
TURK. ..........................Turkey, Turkish
TVA...........Tennessee Valley Authority
TWIMC ...........to whom it may concern
TWP. .........................................township

UAE ....................United Arab Emirates
UAR ....................United Arab Republic
UFO.............unidentified flying object
UFT......United Federation of Teachers
UFW..................United Farm Workers
UHF.........................ultrahigh frequency
UMW...................United Mine Workers
UNCF .......United Negro College Fund
UNESCO..................United Nations
....................Educational, Scientific, and
...............................Cultural Organization
UNICEF..................United Nations Intl.
.................Children's Emergency Fund
UPC ...................Universal Product Code
UPI ............................United Press Intl.
UPS....................United Parcel Service
URU. ...........................................Uruguay
USA .......................United States Army
USAF...............United States Air Force
USCG ........United States Coast Guard
USDA ..........United States Department
......................................of Agriculture
USIA..............United States Info. Agcy.
USMA...........United States Mil. Acad.
USMC .....United States Marines Corps
USN .......................United States Navy
USNA ...........United States Nav. Acad.
USNG ..........United States Natl. Guard

USNR .....United States Naval Reserve
USO ......United Service Organizations
USOC................United States Olympic
.............................................Committee
USPO ........United States Patent Office
USPS .....United States Postal Service
USS.........................United States ship
USSR ...........................Union of Soviet
...........................Socialist Republics
USTA.........United States Tennis Assn.
UXB...........................unexploded bomb

VAT .............................value-added tax
VCR................videocassette recorder
VDT...................video display terminal
VEN. ....................................Venezuela
VER. ..............................verse, version
VERT. ........................................vertical
VET.....................veteran, veterinarian
VFW.............Veterans of Foreign Wars
VIP .....................very important person
VISC. ........................................viscount
VISTA ................Volunteers in Service
.................................................to America
VOA...........................Voice of America
VOL. .......................volume, volunteer
VTOL .........vertical takeoff and landing

WAAC........Women's Army Aux. Corps
WAAF ...........Women's Aux. Air Force
WAC .................Women's Army Corps
WAF................Women in the Air Force
WASP............White Anglo-Saxon Prot.
WATS...................................Wide-area
.................Telecommunications Service

WBA ......................World Boxing Assn.
WBC...................World Boxing Council
WCT .......World Championship Tennis
WCTU....................Women's Christian
................................Temperance Union
WHA....................World Hockey Assn.
WHO..........World Health Organization
WIS., WISC. ........................Wisconsin
WKLY. ..........................................weekly
WPA...............Works Progress Admin.
WPM .........................words per minute
WRAF .........Women's Royal Air Force
W.VA. ...............................West Virginia
WYO. ...................................Wyoming

X DIV. ...................................ex dividend
XING .........................................crossing

YDS. .............................................yards
YHWH....................................Yahweh
YMCA .............................Young Men's
.................................Christian Assn.
YMHA.......Young Men's Hebrew Assn.
YRS. ..............................................years
YWCA .......................Young Women's
...............................Christian Assn.
YWHA .......................Young Women's
.........................................Hebrew Assn.

ZECH. ...............................Zechariah
ZEPH. ...............................Zephaniah
ZIP..................zone improvement plan
ZOOL. ...............zoological, zoologist,
..................................................zoology
ZPG..................zero population growth

# ELEMENTS

Elements are grouped according to length. Each element's two-letter abbreviation is given along with its atomic number.

gas. = gaseous
non. = nonmetallic
semi. = semimetallic
syn. = synthetic
all others are natural metallic elements

## 3 Letters
TIN-Sn-50

## 4 Letters
GOLD-Au-79
IRON-Fe-26
LEAD-Pb-82
NEON-Ne-10 (gas.)
ZINC-Zn-30

## 5 Letters
ARGON-Ar-18 (gas.)
BORON-B-5 (non.)
RADON-Rn-86 (gas.)
XENON-Xe-54 (gas.)

## 6 Letters
BARIUM-Ba-56
CARBON-C-6 (non.)
CERIUM-Ce-58
CESIUM-Cs-55
COBALT-Co-27
COPPER-Cu-29
CURIUM-Cm-96 (syn.)
ERBIUM-Er-68
HELIUM-He-2 (gas.)
INDIUM-In-49
IODINE-I-53 (non.)
NICKEL-Ni-28
OSMIUM-Os-76
OXYGEN-O-8 (gas.)
RADIUM-Ra-88
SILVER-Ag-47
SODIUM-Na-11
SULFUR-S-16 (non.)

## 7 Letters
ARSENIC-As-33
  (semi.)
BISMUTH-Bi-83
BROMINE-Br-35 (non.)
CADMIUM-Cd-48
CALCIUM-Ca-20
FERMIUM-Fm-100
  (syn.)

GALLIUM-Ga-31
HAFNIUM-Hf-72
HOLMIUM-Ho-67
IRIDIUM-Ir-77
KRYPTON-Kr-36 (gas.)
LITHIUM-Li-3
MERCURY-Hg-80
NIOBIUM-Nb-41
RHENIUM-Re-75
RHODIUM-Rh-45
SILICON-Si-14 (non.)
TERBIUM-Tb-65
THORIUM-Th-90
THULIUM-Tm-69
URANIUM-U-92
YTTRIUM-Y-39

## 8 Letters
ACTINIUM-Ac-89
ALUMINUM-Al-13
ANTIMONY-Sb-51
ASTATINE-At-85
  (semi.)
CHLORINE-Cl-17 (gas.)
CHROMIUM-Cr-24
EUROPIUM-Eu-63
FLUORINE-F-9 (gas.)
FRANCIUM-Fr-87
HYDROGEN-H-1 (gas.)
LUTETIUM-Lu-71
NITROGEN-N-7 (gas.)
NOBELIUM-No-102
  (syn.)
PLATINUM-Pt-78
POLONIUM-Po-84
RUBIDIUM-Rb-37
SAMARIUM-Sm-62
SCANDIUM-Sc-21
SELENIUM-Se-34
  (non.)
TANTALUM-Ta-73
THALLIUM-Tl-81
TITANIUM-Ti-22
TUNGSTEN-W-74
VANADIUM-V-23

## 9 Letters
AMERICIUM-Am-95
  (syn.)
BERKELIUM-Bk-97
  (syn.)
BERYLLIUM-Be-4
GERMANIUM-Ge-32
LANTHANUM-La-57
MAGNESIUM-Mg-12
MANGANESE-Mn-25
NEODYMIUM-Nd-60
NEPTUNIUM-Np-93
  (syn.)
PALLADIUM-Pd-46
PLUTONIUM-Pu-94
POTASSIUM-K-19
RUTHENIUM-Ru-44
STRONTIUM-Sr-38
TELLURIUM-Te-52
  (non.)
YTTERBIUM-Yb-70
ZIRCONIUM-Zr-40

## 10 Letters
DYSPROSIUM-Dy-66
GADOLINIUM-Gd-64
LAWRENCIUM-Lr-103
  (syn.)
MOLYBDENUM-Mo-42
PHOSPHORUS-P-15
  (non.)
PROMETHIUM-Pm-61
TECHNETIUM-Tc-43

## 11 Letters
CALIFORNIUM-Cf-98
  (syn.)
EINSTEINIUM-Es-99
  (syn.)
MENDELEVIUM-Md-101
  (syn.)

## 12 Letters
PRASEODYMIUM-Pr-59
PROTACTINIUM-Pa-91

# WEIGHTS & MEASURES

## AREA

Intl. .................ARE; ACRE; DECARE

China ...............................MOU; CHUO
Jap. ..............................................CHO
Thailand .......................................RAI

## DISTANCE

Intl. ...............ROD; METER; MICRON

Belgium .......................................AUNE
China .............................CH'IH, TSUN
Czech Republic .......................LATRO
Denmark ........................................FOD
Egypt .............................PIK; DIRAA
France ........................................TOISE
Greece .......................................PICKI
India .............................................KOSS
Iran .......................GUZ, ZER; GUEZA
Japan .............................KEN, SUN
Netherlands ...............................DUIM
Russ. ...............FUT; FOUTE, VERST
Sweden .........................................FOT
Thailand .............KUP, NIN, NIU, SEN
UK ...............ELL; POLE; PERCH
US ........................MIL; FOOT, HAND,
............................INCH, MILE, YARD;
.................................................FURLONG

## VOLUME

Intl. ...................................DRAM, KILO

China ............................................TOU
Cyprus ...........................................OKE
Denmark ........................................POT
Egypt ...........................................KELA
Germany .....................................EIMER
Israel .................CAB, COR, HIN, LOG;
.......................................BATH; EPHAH
Japan ..................SHO; KOKU, KWAN
Netherlands ......................KAN, MUD,
..........................................VAT, ZAK
Scottish ........................................FOU
S. Afr. ...........................................AUM
Switzerland .......................ELLE, IMMI
UK ......................................PIN, TUN;
...........................BUTT, GILL; MINIM
US .............GILL, PECK, PINT; MINIM

## WEIGHT

Intl. ..............KIP, TON; GRAM, KILO;
......................................CARAT, GRAIN

Bulgaria ........................................OKE
China .............................................TAN
Egypt .............................................OKA
Germany .........................................LOT
Greece .........................MNA; OBOLE
Japan ...............................KIN, RIO
Korea .............................................KON
Malaysia .........................GIN; CHEE;
.................................HOON, KATI;
.............................CATTY, TAHIL
Netherlands .................................ONS
Portugal .......................ONCA; LIBRA
Russia .........................................POOD
Thailand ...............BAT; BAHT; TICAL
Turkey ...........................................OCK
UK ...........TOD, WEY; PACK; STONE
US ..........................OUNCE, POUND

## OTHER

unit, power ratio ............................BEL
unit of capacity .......................FARAD
unit of conductance .....................MHO
unit of electrical intensity ......AMPERE
unit of electrical reluctance ...........REL
unit of electricity .............OHM; WATT;
.................................FARAD, WEBER
unit of electromotive force ..........VOLT
unit of energy ...............................ERG
unit of fluidity ...............................RHE
unit of force ................................DYNE
unit of heat ...........................CALORIE
unit of illumination .....................PHOT
unit of light....................LUX; LUMEN;
.................................................HEFNER
unit of loudness .........................SONE
unit of luminance.........................NIT
unit of power...............................OHM;
.................................DYNE, WATT;
.............................FARAD, WEBER
unit of pressure.........................TORR
unit of radiation .................RAD, REM
unit of resistance .......................OHM
unit of viscosity .......................POISE
unit of work ................................ERG

246

# WORD FINDER

When solving a crossword puzzle, you may reach the point where there remain a few three- or four-letter words you are unable to fill in. You may have tried unsuccessfully to find the clue for a word, and its crossing words, in the other sections of this book. The Word Finder gives you another option to resolve this dilemma.

When you know only the first and last letters, or any two adjoining letters, of a three- or four-letter word, you can use the Word Finder to find a list of all the words which have the two letters you know in the correct letter positions. Two-letter words have not been included in this book because their use in contemporary puzzles is frowned upon.

In the left column of each page are letter-position guides. They are listed alphabetically by the first known letter. If, for example, you are looking for a four-letter word with the second letter "J" and third letter "A," you should scan the letter-position guide until you find the combination "_ J A _". You will see an alphabetical listing of all four-letter words with "J" and "A" in those positions in boldface capital letters.

When two or more words are spelled the same, they are listed separately. They are listed in the following order: proper nouns, abbreviations of proper nouns, common nouns, suffixes, prefixes, and all other abbreviations.

The numbers in parentheses following each word are page numbers for cross-reference to all of the other sections in this book. Many words have several cross-references. They are listed in numerical order. Cross-references to pages in the Special Sections consist of page numbers only. Cross-references to the Clues & Definitions section also include a lower case "a," "b," "c," or "d." These letters refer to the four quadrants of each Clues & Definitions page. They are indicated by those same letters on the Clues & Definitions pages.

Some listed words are not followed by cross-reference page numbers. These words are plurals and various verb cases for the most part. In the case of plurals, you will find cross-references with listings of the singular forms of words. Clues for verbs are most often in the present tense. If, for example, you find no cross-references listed for a word which is a verb in the past tense, try looking up the present tense of the verb.

# THREE-LETTER WORDS

**A A _**    **AAA** (235), **aal** (79d), **AAM** (235), **Aar** (18c, 100b)

**A _ A**    **AAA** (235), **ABA** (235), **aba** (13d, 23c, 52d), **ADA** (235), **Ada** (83c, 137), **aga** (84d, 125b), **a-ha** (42c), **aka** (81c, 235), **Ala.** (209, 235), **ala** (16c, 132c), **a la** (9c), **AMA** (235), **ama** (23d, 25d, 27b, 29b, 32b, 132c), **ana** (12c, 29a, 72c), **-ana** (117c), **Apa** (12b), **apa** (21c), **Ara** (12a, 139, 197, 207), **ara** (73b), **Asa** (9a, 56a, 66b, 67d, 139, 197), **Ata** (73d), **Ava** (22d, 139), **ava** (61c, 91a, 123a)

**_ A A**    **AAA** (235), **baa** (107d), **FAA** (238), **Kaa** (67a), **maa** (107d)

**A B _**    **ABA** (235), **aba** (13d, 23c, 52d), **abb** (129d), **ABC** (26a, 235), **abd.** (235), **Abe** (94b, 137), **Abi** (59d), **ABM** (235), **abp.** (235), **abr.** (235), **ABS** (235), **abs-** (92c), **ABT** (33b, 235), **abu** (44d)

**A _ B**    **abb** (129d), **AFB** (235), **Alb.** (235), **alb** (52d, 128a), **amb.** (235), **APB** (235), **asb.** (235)

**_ A B**    **Bab** (16a), **CAB** (236), **Cab** (144), **cab** (95d, 127d, 246), **dab** (38b, 46d, 47d), **gab** (26b, 92b, 119b, 133a), **Hab.** (239), **jab** (60b, 90d, 96a, 132d), **Lab.** (240), **lab** (104d), **Mab** (44a, 96c), **nab** (14c, 24a, 24d, 106c), **Rab** (37b), **rab** (18a, 66c, 78d), **Tab** (183), **tab** (47b, 94b, 119b)

**A C _**    **ACC** (235), **ace** (24a, 46c, 60c, 84a, 107d, 109d, 120c, 126c), **ach** (11a, 42c, 53d), **ACP** (235), **ACS** (235), **act** (34b, 45a, 87d, 90b, 94b, 115a), **acu-** (93c), **-acy** (117b)

**A _ C**    **ABC** (26a, 235), **ACC** (235), **ADC** (15b, 235), **AEC** (235), **AFC** (235), **AKC** (235), **AMC** (26a), **anc.** (235), **ARC** (235), **arc** (27b, 32d, 96b, 106b, 123d), **ATC** (236)

**_ A C**    **bac** (27b), **lac** (43c, 99d, 108a, 127b), **Mac** (167), **mac** (45b, 74c, 105b, 111d), **Pac.** (242), **pac** (57b, 73c), **RAC** (242), **SAC** (242), **sac** (92a, 128a), **TAC** (243), **WAC** (244)

**A D _**    **ADA** (83c, 137), **ADC** (15b, 235), **add** (12d, 13c, 116d), **Ade** (43b, 137), **ade** (38a), **adj.** (235), **Adm.** (235), **ado** (21b, 22d, 29b, 52c, 92a, 115c), **ADP** (235), **ads** (27d), **adv.** (235), **adz** (33c, 122d)

**A _ D**    **abd.** (235), **add** (12d, 13c, 116d), **aid** (15a, 57d, 59b, 117a), **and** (30a, 90c)

**_ A D**    **bad** (42b, 44d, 126b, 131d), **CAD** (236), **cad** (21b, 59b, 88a), **dad** (11d, 44b, 44d), **fad** (31d, 97b, 120b, 124b), **Gad** (64d, 135c), **gad** (47c, 77a, 83a, 97d, 101a), **had** (61a, 91d), **lad** (21c, 45b, 74c, 116c, 134d), **mad** (12d, 63b, 109c), **pad** (32d, 47d, 48b, 116c, 119a, 123d), **rad** (40d, 246), **sad** (11d, 20a, 26b, 35a, 36c, 37c, 73c, 75d, 79b, 112a, 126c), **tad** (134d), **wad** (55a, 73c, 75b, 85b)

**A E _**   AEC (235), AEF (235), aer (25d), aer- (92c), aes (22a, 69c, 78a, 101d), aet (69c)

**A _ E**   Abe (94b, 137), ace (24a, 46c, 60c, 84a, 107d, 109d, 120c, 126c), Ade (43b, 137), ade (38a), age (41b, 41c, 41d, 53b, 71d, 75b, 106a, 122b), ale (18a, 72b, 95d), ame (51a), ane (50b), ape (30d, 62a, 77b, 78b, 109c, 231), are (68d, 76b, 84a, 246), ASE (235), Ase (61b, 87c), Ate (88b, 135a, 198), ate, -ate (117a, 117b), Ave. (236), ave (44b, 56c, 57b, 92b, 102b, 104a), awe (63d, 76d, 100b, 127d, 132b), axe (27a, 33c, 36c, 122d), aye (10b, 44d, 129c)

**_ A E**   hae (105a), kae (65b), Lae (221), Mae (167), nae (105b), Rae (176), sae (242), tae (105b), UAE (243)

**A F _**   AFB (235), AFC (235), Afg. (235), AFL (235), Afr. (235), aft (15b, 18b, 98a, 108b, 115b)

**A _ F**   AEF (235), Alf (120b, 137), ATF (236)

**_ A F**   kaf (11d, 12a), oaf (21a, 37b, 38c, 109c, 116d, 134d), qaf (11d), RAF (242), WAF (244)

**A G _**   aga (84d, 125b), age (41b, 41c, 41d, 53b, 71d, 75b, 106a, 122b), AGI (235), ago (23a, 55b, 87a), agt. (235)

**A _ G**   Afg. (235), Alg. (235), alg. (31b), Ang. (235), Arg. (235), Aug. (78c, 236), avg. (236)

**_ A G**   bag (24a, 117d), cag (63c), Dag (147), fag (27b), gag (26d, 66c, 113b), Hag. (239), hag (133a), jag (95c), lag (34c, 115a), mag (57c), mag. (240), nag (21b, 58a, 61a, 133d), rag (28b, 81c, 102a), SAG (242), sag (38a, 132a), tag (52b, 68b), wag (66d, 79c, 133a)

**A H _**   a-ha (42c), ahs (42c), ahu (53b)

**A _ H**   ach (11a, 42c, 53d), ash (40c, 58a, 124a)

**_ A H**   bah (42c), dah (68a), hah (42c), Nah. (241), pah (42c), rah (26b), yah (34c)

**A I _**   aid (15a, 57d, 59b, 117a), ail (124d), AIM (235), aim (54d, 83a, 96c, 119d), Ain (223), ain (105b), air (14b, 22a, 34d, 36c, 43a, 45a, 74c, 75d, 76d, 95d, 115a, 125a), ais (110d), ait (64b, 101a)

**A _ I**   Abi (59d), AGI (235), Ali (23b, 44d, 72b, 77c, 80c, 125b, 138), ami (50b), ani (19b, 19d, 32c), Ari (139), ASI (235), avi- (92c)

**_ A I**   gal (50c, 233), Kai (163), Lai (69a, 220), lai (119b), mai (49d), rai (246), sai (78b), Tai (62d, 183, 218), tai (65d, 91c), Vai (218), Yai (223)

**A _ J**   adj. (235)

**_ A J**   Maj. (240), raj (41a), Taj (74b)

**A K _**   aka (81c, 235), AKC (235), aku (46d)

**A _ K**   Ark. (209, 235), ark (20b, 128a), ask (31d, 64a, 96d, 99d, 111c), auk (19a, 225)

**_ A K**   oak (58a, 124a), Pak. (242), yak (85d, 119b, 231), zak (246)

**A L _**   Ala. (209, 235), ala (16c, 132c), a la (9c), Alb. (235), alb (52d, 128a), ale (18a, 72b, 95d), Alf (120b, 137), Alg. (235), alg. (31b), Ali (23b, 44d, 72b, 77c, 80c, 125b, 138), all (10d, 29c, 123b, 127c), alp (79b, 87b), ALS (235), als (54a), alt (54a)

**A _ L**   aal (79d), AFL (235), ail (124d), all (10d, 29c, 123b, 127c), Atl. (236), awl (108c, 122d, 123a)

**_ A L**   aal (79d), bal (50a), Cal (94b, 144), Cal. (209), cal (46c, 133b), dal (11d), Gal. (239), gal (45b, 54c), Hal (125d, 156), -ial (117a), kal (46c), Mal. (240), mal (42b, 50b, 112d), mal- (92c), PAL (242), pal (29b, 32a, 45b), Sal (52b, 179), sal (39b), Val (184)

**A M _**   AMA (235), ama (23d, 25d, 27b, 29b, 32b, 132c), amb. (235), AMC (26a), ame (51a), ami (50b), amo (69d), amp. (40a, 235), amt (31b), amt. (235), Amu (33d), Amy (11a, 73c, 138)

**A _ M**   AAM (235), ABM (235), Adm. (235), AIM (235), aim (54d, 83a, 96c, 119d), arm (13c, 21c, 49a, 72a, 95a), ATM (236), aum (246)

**_ A M**   AAM (235), CAM (236), cam (39c, 73d, 101a, 102b, 110c, 131c), dam (40b, 115d, 131a), fam. (238), Gam (154), gam (131b, 232), gam- (93c), Ham (81d, 108a, 197), ham (9d, 75c), Jam. (240), jam (35d, 85b, 94b, 115d, 122a), Lam. (240), lam (11d, 47c), Pam (173), pam (68a), RAM (242), ram (17c, 32c, 85b, 92a, 103a, 107d), SAM (242), Sam (24c, 119d, 179), tam (58b, 58c), yam (39c, 92a, 118c, 125a)

**A N _**   ana (12c, 29a, 72c), -ana (117c), anc. (235), and (30a, 90c), ane (50b), Ang. (235), ani (19b, 19d, 32c), Ann (138), Ant (139), ant (40c, 49a, 63b, 89c, 229), anu (59c, 125a), any (111d)

**A _ N**   Ain (223), ain (105b), Ann (138), arn (11b), ASN (235), awn (14b, 17d), Ayn (139), ayn (11d)

**_ A N**   ban (63c, 95a, 101d, 221), Can. (236), can (9a, 22c, 30b, 36c, 94b, 122b), Dan (64d, 147, 197), -ean (117a), fan (35c, 114a), Gan (215), Han (26d, 134a, 215), Ian (66c, 159), Jan (160), Jan. (78c, 240), Kan. (210, 240), kan (246), lan (31b, 118c), Man (64b, 168, 224), man (49a, 52c, 74c, 231), Nan (20c, Pan (45d, 55a, 59c, 133b, 198), Pan. (242), pan (18d, 79c, 128a), ran (19d, 29c, 84b), san (113a), tan (22b, 70d, 246), Van (184), van (48d), wan (57b, 86a), Zan (135c)

**A _ O**   ado (21b, 22d, 29b, 52c, 92a, 115c), ago (23a, 55b, 87a), amo (69d), APO (235), Apo (129a), Aro (84d), Aso (65d, 128d), azo (38d, 134b), azo- (93b)

**_ A O**    **dao** (68a), **GAO** (239), **iao** (60d), **Lao** (62d, 69a, 218), **Mao** (26d), **tao** (88c, 124d), **Yao** (218, 219)

**A P _**    **Apa** (12b), **apa** (21c), **APB** (235), **ape** (30d, 62a, 77b, 78b, 109c, 231), **APO** (235), **Apo** (129a), **APR** (235), **Apr.** (78c), **apt** (13d, 22a, 28a, 36c, 47b, 62c, 71d, 88b, 95a, 117d)

**A _ P**    **abp.** (235), **ACP** (235), **ADP** (235), **alp** (79b, 87b), **amp.** (40a, 235), **Arp** (33a), **asp** (10a, 28a, 111a, 126d, 128c, 232), **ATP** (236)

**_ A P**    **cap** (19b, 32b, 35b, 55c, 58c, 123a), **dap** (35d, 47a), **gap** (13b, 21d, 59d, 84b), **hap** (18b, 25d), **Jap.** (240), **lap** (26c, 27b, 31b, 97b, 100d, 113d, 123c), **map** (24c, 26b), **nap** (89a, 109a, 110b), **pap** (48b), **rap** (70d, 83d, 94d, 116b), **sap** (37d, 42d, 56d, 66d, 128c, 130c), **tap** (44d, 113c, 123b), **yap** (17b, 26b, 92b, 134c)

**A R _**    **Ara** (12a, 139, 197, 207), **ara** (73b), **ARC** (235), **arc** (27b, 32d, 96b, 106b, 123d), **are** (68d, 76b, 84a, 246), **Arg.** (235), **Ari** (139), **Ark.** (209, 235), **ark** (20b, 128a), **arm** (13c, 21c, 49a, 72a, 95a), **arn** (11b), **Aro** (84d), **Arp** (33a), **arr.** (235), **ars** (69c), **Art** (139), **art** (31d, 46a, 94d), **-ary** (117a, 117b)

**A _ R**    **Aar** (18c, 100b), **abr.** (235), **aer** (25d), **aer-** (92c), **Afr.** (235), **air** (14b, 22a, 34d, 36c, 43a, 45a, 74c, 75d, 76d, 95d, 115a, 125a), **APR** (235), **Apr.** (78c), **arr.** (235)

**_ A R**    **Aar** (18c, 100b), **bar** (20a, 31b, 32b, 42c, 60a, 62b, 71a, 95a, 104a, 107b, 115b, 120a, 234), **car** (72d, 127c), **DAR** (237), **dar** (53a, 122a), **ear** (15d, 25c, 51d, 57d, 95a, 112b), **far** (36d, 99c), **gar** (46c, 46d, 81b, 228), **jar** (27d, 30b, 56a, 107b), **lar** (54b, 74b), **Mar.** (78c, 240), **mar** (36b, 62a, 63a, 105c), **oar** (95b, 102c), **Pär** (173), **Par.** (242), **par** (16a, 41b, 41d, 55b, 82a, 103a, 114d), **SAR** (242), **tar** (55a, 89c, 102a, 103b), **UAR** (243), **war** (116b)

**A S _**    **Asa** (9a, 56a, 66b, 67d, 139, 197), **asb.** (235), **ASE** (235), **Ase** (61b, 87c), **ash** (40c, 58a, 124a), **ASI** (235), **ask** (31d, 64a, 96d, 99d, 111c), **ASN** (235), **Aso** (65d, 128d), **asp** (10a, 28a, 111a, 126d, 128c, 232), **ass** (17d, 20a, 37b, 37c, 41b, 48b, 84a, 85b, 109c, 116d, 229), **AST** (236), **as't** (107c), **ASV** (236)

**A _ S**    **ABS** (235), **abs-** (92c), **ACS** (235), **ads** (27d), **aes** (22a, 69c, 78a, 101d), **ahs** (42c), **ais** (110d), **ALS** (235), **als** (54a), **ars** (69c), **ass** (17d, 20a, 37b, 37c, 41b, 48b, 84a, 85b, 109c, 116d, 229), **AUS** (236), **aus** (54a)

**_ A S**    **bas** (50c), **das** (53c, 54a, 60b, 112b), **fas** (69c, 70a, 99b), **gas** (12c, 52a, 88b), **has** (91d), **ha's** (70b), **IAS** (239), **Jas.** (74d), **las** (50a, 112c), **mas** (112d), **NAS** (241), **nas-** (93b), **OAS** (241), **pas** (33b, 115b), **ras** (41d, 62d, 122c), **vas** (38c, 70a), **vas-** (92c), **was** (57a, 127a)

**A T _**    **Ata** (73d), **ATC** (236), **Ate** (88b, 135a, 198), **ate, -ate** (117a, 117b), **ATF** (236), **Atl.** (236), **ATM** (236), **ATP** (236), **ATV** (236)

**A _ T**   **ABT** (33b, 235), **act** (34b, 45a, 87d, 90b, 94b, 115a), **aet** (69c), **aft** (15b, 18b, 98a, 108b, 115b), **agt.** (235), **ait** (64b, 101a), **alt** (54a), **amt** (31b), **amt.** (235), **Ant** (139), **ant** (40c, 49a, 63b, 89c, 229), **apt** (13d, 22a, 28a, 36c, 47b, 62c, 71d, 88b, 95a, 117d), **Art** (139), **art** (31d, 46a, 94d), **AST** (236), **as't** (107c), **aut** (70a)

**_ A T**   **bat** (17b, 82a, 132d, 230, 246), **Cat** (144), **cat** (45a, 56c, 60b, 124c, 230), **DAT** (237), **eat** (31a), **fat** (31a, 83d, 116a), **gat** (57c, 100b), **Hat** (223), **hat** (58c), **Jat** (96a), **Lat.** (240), **lat** (29a), **mat** (47d, 88d, 119c), **Nat** (172), **oat** (16a, 25c, 55c), **PAT** (242), **Pat** (174), **pat** (88b, 119c, 123b), **rat** (16d, 35b, 101c, 115d, 119d, 231), **SAT** (242), **sat** (60a, 91d, 107a, 122d), **TAT** (243), **tat** (39c, 68c), **VAT** (244), **vat** (27b, 30b, 125a, 246), **Wat** (186), **xat** (123b)

**A U _**   **Aug.** (78c, 236), **auk** (19a, 225), **aum** (246), **AUS** (236), **aus** (54a), **aut** (70a), **aux.** (236)

**A _ U**   **abu** (44d), **acu-** (93c), **ahu** (53b), **aku** (46d), **Amu** (33d), **anu** (59c, 125a)

**_ A U**   **eau** (51b), **gau** (53c), **OAU** (241), **Pau** (39c, 59b, 100a, 216), **tau** (11d, 103d)

**A V _**   **Ava** (22d, 139), **ava** (61c, 91a, 123a), **Ave.** (236), **ave** (44b, 56c, 57b, 92b, 102b, 104a), **avg.** (236), **avi-** (92c)

**A _ V**   **adv.** (235), **ASV** (236), **ATV** (236)

**_ A V**   **Bav.** (236), **cav.** (236), **DAV** (237), **lav.** (240), **nav.** (241), **tav** (12a), **vav** (12a)

**A W _**   **awe** (63d, 76d, 100b, 127d, 132b), **awl** (108c, 122d, 123a), **awn** (14b, 17d)

**_ A W**   **caw** (19b), **daw** (55c), **Haw.** (209), **haw** (29b, 71a, 114c), **jaw** (75b), **Kaw** (121d), **law** (23d, 28d, 33a, 39c, 67c, 71a, 84c, 92b, 102d, 115a), **maw** (31d, 32a, 56d, 84b, 91b, 115c), **paw** (48b, 57d), **raw** (32b, 81a, 126d), **saw** (9d, 13b, 33c, 75b, 95c, 114a, 122d), **Taw** (223), **taw** (70d, 74d, 108c, 119c), **waw** (11d), **yaw** (101c)

**A X _**   **axe** (27a, 33c, 36c, 122d)

**A _ X**   **aux.** (236)

**_ A X**   **fax** (30d), **lax** (39b, 73a, 81b, 99c, 111c), **Max** (169), **Max.** (240), **max** (78d), **pax** (70a), **sax** (80a), **tax** (15a, 62b, 71c), **wax** (15d, 56d, 90d, 118c), **zax** (110b)

**A Y _**   **aye** (10b, 44d, 129c), **Ayn** (139), **ayn** (11d)

**A _ Y**   **-acy** (117b), **Amy** (11a, 73c, 138), **any** (111d), **-ary** (117a, 117b)

**_ A Y**   **bay** (12d, 17b, 58a, 61a, 61c, 63a, 70b, 98c, 124a, 130a), **cay** (64b), **Day** (148), **day** (33d, 122b), **Fay** (152), **fay** (44a), **Gay** (154), **gay**

252

(18b), **hay** (122b), **Jay** (160), **jay** (19b, 71c, 225), **Kay** (14d, 102c, 164), **lay** (16c, 75c, 82a, 96c, 106b, 111d), **May** (24a, 169), **may** (58c, 76d), **nay** (22d, 34d, 81b, 129c), **pay** (29c, 36a, 98b, 99c, 103d, 129b), **Ray** (176), **ray** (17d, 46d, 107b, 109d, 228), **Say** (192), **say** (100d, 113b, 115a, 127c, 128d), **Tay** (82b), **way** (31b, 74c, 76b, 101a, 102c, 121b, 127a), **yay** (9b, 111b), **zay** (11d)

A Z _     **azo** (38d, 134b), **azo-** (93b)

A _ Z     **adz** (33c, 122d)

_ A Z     **laz** (25a), **Paz** (174)

B A _     **baa** (107d), **Bab** (16a), **bac** (27b), **bad** (42b, 44d, 126b, 131d), **bag** (24a, 117d), **bah** (42c), **bal** (50a), **ban** (63c, 95a, 101d, 221), **bar** (20a, 31b, 32b, 42c, 60a, 62b, 71a, 95a, 104a, 107b, 115b, 120a, 234), **bas** (50c), **bat** (17b, 82a, 132d, 230, 246), **Bav.** (236), **bay** (12d, 17b, 58a, 61a, 61c, 63a, 70b, 98c, 124a, 130a)

B _ A     **baa** (107d), **Bea** (140), **BFA** (236), **BIA** (236), **boa** (30b, 45a, 81b, 96c, 104c, 106d, 111a, 232), **bra** (18d, 126b), **BSA** (236)

_ B A     **ABA** (235), **aba** (13d, 23c, 52d), **MBA** (240), **NBA** (241), **PBA** (242), **SBA** (242), **tba** (243), **WBA** (244)

B B _     **BBB** (236), **BBC** (26a, 236)

B _ B     **Bab** (16a), **BBB** (236), **bib** (28b), **Bob** (142), **bob** (47a, 79c, 87c), **bub** (45a, 74c)

_ B B     **abb** (129d), **BBB** (236), **ebb** (9a, 34b, 35d, 79c, 98b, 116d, 129d)

B _ C     **bac** (27b), **BBC** (26a, 236), **B.Sc.** (236)

_ B C     **ABC** (26a, 235), **BBC** (26a, 236), **CBC** (26a, 236), **NBC** (26a, 241), **WBC** (244)

B _ D     **bad** (42b, 44d, 126b, 131d), **bed** (21b, 52d, 110c, 232), **bid** (21d, 64a, 83c, 84c), **Bud** (143), **bud** (45a, 47d)

_ B D     **abd.** (235)

B E _     **Bea** (140), **bed** (21b, 52d, 110c, 232), **bee** (38a, 63b, 113c, 229), **beg** (31d, 90b), **bel** (34a, 246), **Ben** (141), **ben** (105b), **Bes** (39d, 198), **bet** (52b), **bev.** (236), **bey** (55c, 125a)

B _ E     **bee** (38a, 63b, 113c, 229), **bye** (32a, 123c)

_ B E     **Abe** (94b, 137), **NbE** (29c), **OBE** (241), **obe** (68b), **SbE** (29c)

B F _     **BFA** (236)

B _ G     **bag** (24a, 117d), **beg** (31d, 90b), **big** (69b, 74a, 116d), **bog** (39a, 75a, 118b), **bug** (21b, 53c, 63b)

B _ H     **bah** (42c)

B I _     **BIA** (236), **bib** (28b), **bid** (21d, 64a, 83c, 84c), **big** (69b, 74a, 116d), **Bil** (141), **bim** (133b), **bin** (21b, 98b, 116a), **bio** (71d), **bio-** (93b), **bio.** (31b, 236), **bis** (10c, 50b, 70b, 78c, 99d), **bit** (23d, 37d, 67b, 78d, 86d, 122d, 125c, 131c), **Bix** (141)

B _ I     **BMI** (236), **B.V.I.** (236)

_ B I     **Abi** (59d), **FBI** (238), **obi** (45c, 54c, 65d, 104b), **RBI** (110d, 242), **ubi** (70b)

_ B J     **obj.** (241)

_ B K     **PBK** (242)

B L _     **BLS** (236), **blt** (236), **Bly** (142)

B _ L     **bal** (50a), **bel** (34a, 246), **Bil** (141), **Bol.** (236), **Bul.** (236)

_ B L     **dbl.** (237)

B M _     **BMI** (236), **BMX** (236)

B _ M     **bim** (133b), **bum** (38a, 127a), **BVM** (236)

_ B M     **ABM** (235)

B _ N     **ban** (63c, 95a, 101d, 221), **Ben** (141), **ben** (105b), **bin** (21b, 98b, 116a), **bon** (45a, 50b, 65d, 67b), **bun** (57b, 101c)

_ B N     **EbN** (29c), **ibn** (111d), **WbN** (29c)

B O _     **boa** (30b, 45a, 81b, 96c, 104c, 106d, 111a, 232), **Bob** (142), **bob** (47a, 79c, 87c), **bog** (39a, 75a, 118b), **Bol.** (236), **bon** (45a, 50b, 65d, 67b), **boo** (36a, 115a), **bop** (60b, 66b, 116b), **Bor** (91a), **bor.** (236), **bot** (69b), **bot.** (236), **Bow** (142), **bow** (20c, 32d, 48d, 68c, 82a, 83a, 95c, 108b, 116d), **box** (30b, 98b, 113a), **boy** (74c, 116c), **Boz** (35c, 87c, 142)

B _ O     **bio** (71d), **bio-** (93b), **bio.** (31b, 236), **boo** (36a, 115a), **bro.** (99b, 236)

_ B O     **HBO** (26a, 239), **Ibo** (68c, 220), **obo** (106c, 241)

B _ P     **bop** (60b, 66b, 116b)

_ B P     **abp.** (235)

B R _     **bra** (18d, 126b), **bro.** (99b, 236)

B _ R     **bar** (20a, 31b, 32b, 42c, 60a, 62b, 71a, 95a, 104a, 107b, 115b, 120a, 234), **Bor** (91a), **bor.** (236), **bur** (106b, 131a), **bur.** (236)

254

_ B R    **abr.** (235)

B S _    **BSA** (236), **B.Sc.** (236)

B _ S    **bas** (50c), **Bes** (39d, 198), **bis** (10c, 50b, 70b, 78c, 99d), **BLS** (236), **bus** (95d), **bus.** (236)

_ B S    **ABS** (235), **abs-** (92c), **CBS** (26a), **EbS** (29c), **GBS** (43a), **JBS** (240), **lbs.** (240), **NBS** (241), **obs.** (241), **PBS** (26a, 242), **TBS** (26a), **tbs.** (243), **WbS** (29c)

B T _    **BTU** (10d, 236)

B _ T    **bat** (17b, 82a, 132d, 230, 246), **bet** (52b), **bit** (23d, 37d, 67b, 78d, 86d, 122d, 125c, 131c), **blt** (236), **bot** (69b), **bot.** (236), **but** (11d, 30a, 42b, 115b, 126c, 134c)

_ B T    **ABT** (33b, 235), **CBT** (236)

B U _    **bub** (45a, 74c), **Bud** (143), **bud** (45a, 47d), **bug** (21b, 53c, 63b), **Bul.** (236), **bum** (38a, 127a), **bun** (57b, 101c), **bur** (106b, 131a), **bur.** (236), **bus** (95d), **bus.** (236), **but** (11d, 30a, 42b, 115b, 126c, 134c), **buy** (17b, 96a)

B _ U    **BTU** (10d, 236)

_ B U    **abu** (44d)

B V _    **B.V.I.** (236), **BVM** (236)

B _ V    **Bav.** (236), **bev.** (236)

B _ W    **Bow** (142), **bow** (20c, 32d, 48d, 68c, 82a, 83a, 95c, 108b, 116d)

_ B W    **NbW** (29c), **SbW** (29c)

B _ X    **Bix** (141), **BMX** (236), **box** (30b, 98b, 113a)

B Y _    **bye** (32a, 123c)

B _ Y    **bay** (12d, 17b, 58a, 61a, 61c, 63a, 70b, 98c, 124a, 130a), **bey** (55c, 125a), **Bly** (142), **boy** (74c, 116c), **buy** (17b, 96a)

B _ Z    **Boz** (35c, 87c, 142)

C A _    **CAB** (236), **Cab** (144), **cab** (95d, 127d, 246), **CAD** (236), **cad** (21b, 59b, 88a), **cag** (63c), **Cal** (94b, 144), **Cal.** (209), **cal** (46c, 133b), **CAM** (236), **cam** (39c, 73d, 101a, 102b, 110c, 131c), **Can.** (236), **can** (9a, 22c, 30b, 36c, 94b, 122b), **cap** (19b, 32b, 35b, 55c, 58c, 123a), **car** (72d, 127c), **Cat** (144), **cat** (45a, 56c, 60b, 124c, 230), **cav.** (236), **caw** (19b), **cay** (64b)

C _ A    **CCA** (236), **CEA** (236), **cha** (120a), **CIA** (236), **CPA** (237), **CSA** (237), **CVA** (237)

255

| | |
|---|---|
| _ C A | **CCA** (236), **lca** (12b), **OCA** (241), **oca** (39c, 125a, 133c), **RCA** (242), **uca** (45d) |
| C B _ | **CBC** (26a, 236), **CBS** (26a), **CBT** (236) |
| C _ B | **CAB** (236), **Cab** (144), **cab** (95d, 127d, 246), **cob** (25c, 61a, 74c, 118b), **CPB** (237), **cub** (72b, 134d) |
| C C _ | **CCA** (236), **CCC** (236), **ccw** (236) |
| C _ C | **CBC** (26a, 236), **CCC** (236), **CDC** (236), **CRC** (237), **CSC** (237) |
| _ C C | **ACC** (235), **CCC** (236), **FCC** (238), **ICC** (239) |
| C D _ | **CDC** (236), **CDT** (236) |
| C _ D | **CAD** (236), **cad** (21b, 59b, 88a), **CID** (236), **COD** (237), **Cod** (24a), **cod** (46d, 228), **cud** (96d, 102d), **Cyd** (147) |
| _ C D | **LCD** (240) |
| C E _ | **CEA** (236), **cee** (55c, 71c), **Cel.** (236), **cen-** (92d), **CEO** (236), **cer-** (93d), **ces** (49d) |
| C _ E | **cee** (55c, 71c), **Che** (145), **cie** (49c), **Coe** (146, 201), **coe** (107d), **cue** (9d, 24d, 91b, 101c, 109b, 117d) |
| _ C E | **ace** (24a, 46c, 60c, 84a, 107d, 109d, 120c, 126c), **Ice.** (239), **ice** (30c, 51c) |
| C F _ | **CFL** (236), **cfm** (236), **cfs** (236) |
| C _ F | **CIF** (236) |
| C G _ | **CGI** (236) |
| C _ G | **cag** (63c), **cog** (53b, 120c, 123a) |
| _ C G | **ECG** (238) |
| C H _ | **cha** (120a), **Che** (145), **chi** (11d), **chm.** (236), **cho** (246) |
| _ C H | **ach** (11a, 42c, 53d), **ich** (53d), **och** (11a, 42c), **sch.** (242), **tch** (42c) |
| C I _ | **CIA** (236), **CID** (236), **Cie.** (49c), **CIF** (236), **CIO** (236), **cir.** (237), **cit.** (237), **civ.** (237) |
| C _ I | **CGI** (236), **chi** (11d), **CLI** (237), **CPI** (237) |
| _ C I | **ici** (50c), **sci.** (31b, 242) |
| C K _ | **ckw** (237) |
| _ C K | **ock** (246), **-ock** (117b) |

C L _    CLI (237), Clu (146)

C _ L    Cal (94b, 144), Cal. (209), cal (46c, 133b), Cel. (236), CFL (236), col (79b, 87a), Cpl. (237)

_ C L    HCL (239)

C _ M    CAM (236), cam (39c, 73d, 101a, 102b, 110c, 131c), cfm (236), chm. (236), com- (94a), cum (117d), cwm (79b)

_ C M    LCM (240)

C N _    CNN (26a), CNO (237), CNS (237)

C _ N    Can. (236), can (9a, 22c, 30b, 36c, 94b, 122b), cen- (92d), CNN (26a), con (10c, 26b, 65c, 116c, 118d)

_ C N    RCN (242)

C O _    cob (25c, 61a, 74c, 118b), COD (237), Cod (24a), cod (46d, 228), Coe (146, 201), coe (107d), cog (53b, 120c, 123a), col (79b, 87a), com- (94a), con (10c, 26b, 65c, 116c, 118d), coo (19b), cop (90d, 97a, 115a), coq (50a), Cor. (237), cor (246), cos (71c, 101d), cos. (237), cot (18a, 99a, 110c), cow (21b, 63d, 121c, 230), Cox (147), cox (102c), coy (17c, 109a)

C _ O    CEO (236), cho (246), CIO (236), CNO (237), coo (19b), CPO (237), cto. (237), CWO (237), CYO (237)

_ C O    NCO (241)

C P _    CPA (237), CPB (237), CPI (237), Cpl. (237), CPO (237), CPR (237), CPU (237)

C _ P    cap (19b, 32b, 35b, 55c, 58c, 123a), cop (90d, 97a, 115a), cup (38a, 55b, 89b, 98b, 119a, 124d)

_ C P    ACP (235), hcp. (239), MCP (240)

C _ Q    coq (50a)

C R _    CRC (237), CRT (237), cru (50d), cry (23b, 94d, 108d, 131a, 134b, 232)

C _ R    car (72d, 127c), cer- (93d), cir. (237), Cor. (237), cor (246), CPR (237), cur (78a)

_ C R    VCR (244)

C S _    CSA (237), CSC (237), CST (237)

C _ S    CBS (26a), ces (49d), cfs (236), CNS (237), cos (71c, 101d), cos. (237), cts. (237)

_ C S    **ACS** (235), **-ics** (117c), **JCS** (240), **OCS** (241)

C T _    **cto.** (237), **cts.** (237)

C _ T    **Cat** (144), **cat** (45a, 56c, 60b, 124c, 230), **CBT** (236), **CDT** (236), **cit.** (237), **cot** (18a, 99a, 110c), **CRT** (237), **CST** (237), **cut** (27a, 28a, 79c, 98d, 107b, 108d, 110b)

_ C T    **act** (34b, 45a, 87d, 90b, 94b, 115a), **ect-** (93c), **jct.** (240), **Oct.** (78c, 241), **oct-** (92d), **pct.** (242), **rct.** (242), **WCT** (244)

C U _    **cub** (72b, 134d), **cud** (96d, 102d), **cue** (9d, 24d, 91b, 101c, 109b, 117d), **cum** (117d), **cup** (38a, 55b, 89b, 98b, 119a, 124d), **cur** (78a), **cut** (27a, 28a, 79c, 98d, 107b, 108d, 110b)

C _ U    **Clu** (146), **CPU** (237), **cru** (50d)

_ C U    **acu-** (93c), **ecu** (47b, 108a), **ICU** (239)

C V _    **CVA** (237)

C _ V    **cav.** (236), **civ.** (237)

C W _    **cwm** (79b), **CWO** (237)

C _ W    **caw** (19b), **ccw** (236), **ckw** (237), **cow** (21b, 63d, 121c, 230)

_ C W    **ccw** (236)

C _ X    **Cox** (147), **cox** (102c)

C Y _    **Cyd** (147), **CYO** (237)

C _ Y    **cay** (64b), **coy** (17c, 109a), **cry** (23b, 94d, 108d, 131a, 134b, 232)

_ C Y    **-acy** (117b), **icy** (19c, 53b)

D A _    **dab** (38b, 46d, 47d), **dad** (11d, 44b, 44d), **Dag** (147), **dah** (68a), **dal** (11d), **dam** (40b, 115d, 131a), **Dan** (64d, 147, 197), **dao** (68a), **dap** (35d, 47a), **DAR** (237), **dar** (53a, 122a), **das** (53c, 54a, 60b, 112b), **DAT** (237), **DAV** (237), **daw** (55c), **Day** (148), **day** (33d, 122b)

D _ A    **DEA** (237), **dea** (69d), **dia** (112d), **dia-** (92c), **DNA** (53b, 98b, 237), **DOA** (237), **dua-** (93d)

_ D A    **ADA** (235), **Ada** (83c, 137), **FDA** (238), **Ida** (79b, 159), **Ida.** (209), **NDA** (241), **oda** (58a), **RDA** (242)

D B _    **dbl.** (237)

D _ B    **dab** (38b, 46d, 47d), **deb** (31a), **dib** (47a), **dub** (23b, 80b)

D _ C    **DDC** (237), **Dec.** (78c, 237), **dec-** (93d), **DFC** (237), **DNC** (237), **Doc** (88d, 107a, 149), **doc.** (237), **DSC** (238), **duc** (50b)

_ D C     **ADC** (15b, 235), **CDC** (236), **DDC** (237)

D D _     **DDC** (237), **DDS** (237), **DDT** (45c, 237)

D _ D     **dad** (11d, 44b, 44d), **did** (9c), **DOD** (237), **dod** (27d), **dud** (44a)

_ D D     **add** (12d, 13c, 116d), **odd** (116a, 126c, 126d)

D E _     **DEA** (237), **dea** (69d), **deb** (31a), **dec-** (93d), **Dec.** (78c, 237), **Dee** (82b, 101a, 148, 223), **def.** (237), **deg.** (237), **dek-** (93d), **Del** (148), **Del.** (209, 237), **del** (116b), **Dem.** (91a, 237), **Den.** (237), **den** (31c, 36d, 100a, 105c, 116c), **der** (53c, 54a), **Des** (149), **des** (51a), **DEW** (129d, 237), **dew** (77c), **Dey** (149), **dey** (11b, 86d, 125a)

D _ E     **Dee** (82b, 101a, 148, 223), **die** (24d, 34d, 43d, 54a, 87a, 114c, 123a), **DOE** (237), **doe** (34b, 97a), **due** (65c, 87b, 95b), **dye** (29a, 114c)

_ D E     **Ade** (43b, 137), **ade** (38a), **Ede** (29b, 38d, 53b), **ide** (46d), **ode** (61d, 89b, 90c)

D F _     **DFC** (237)

D _ F     **def.** (237), **dif.** (237)

D _ G     **Dag** (147), **deg.** (237), **dig** (42b, 132d), **dog** (12c, 23d, 32d, 48b, 230), **dug** (42b)

D H _     **Dhu** (68b)

D _ H     **dah** (68a), **D.Ph.** (238), **D.Th.** (238)

_ D H     **edh** (12c)

D I _     **dia** (112d), **dia-** (92c), **dib** (47a), **did** (9c), **die** (24d, 34d, 43d, 54a, 87a, 114c, 123a), **dif.** (237), **dig** (42b, 132d), **Dik** (149), **din** (27d, 61c, 126d), **dip** (23d, 62a, 88d, 104d), **dir.** (237), **Dis** (57a, 90c, 126b, 199), **dis-** (92c), **div.** (237), **Dix** (49a), **DIY** (237)

D _ I     **DUI** (38b, 238), **DWI** (38b, 238)

_ D I     **SDI** (242), **Udi** (82b)

_ D J     **adj.** (235)

D _ K     **dek-** (93d), **Dik** (149)

D L _     **DLO** (237)

D _ L     **dal** (11d), **dbl.** (237), **Del** (148), **Del.** (209, 237), **del** (116b), **dol.** (238)

_ D L     **JDL** (240)

259

**D M _**  DMV (237), DMZ (237)

**D _ M**  dam (40b, 115d, 131a), Dem. (91a, 237), dim (33d, 38d, 43d, 73d, 83a), Dom (79a, 149), dom (91d, 122c), dom. (238), DVM (238)

**_ D M**  Adm. (235)

**D N _**  DNA (53b, 98b, 237), DNC (237)

**D _ N**  Dan (64d, 147, 197), Den. (237), den (31c, 36d, 100a, 105c, 116c), din (27d, 61c, 126d), Don (101a, 149), don (50b, 130d), dun (18d, 38c, 56a, 87b), dyn- (93c)

**D O _**  DOA (237), Doc (88d, 107a, 149), doc. (237), DOD (237), dod (27d), DOE (237), doe (34b, 97a), dog (12c, 23d, 32d, 48b, 230), dol. (238), Dom (79a, 149), dom (91d, 122c), dom. (238), Don (101a, 149), don (50b, 130d), dop (32d), dor (18b, 38a, 38d, 63b, 67a), DOS (238), dos (50a, 131d), DOT (238), dot (59d, 80c, 87d, 113b, 120b), Dow (66d, 150), doz. (238)

**D _ O**  dao (68a), DLO (237), duo (85d, 125c)

**_ D O**  ado (21b, 22d, 29b, 52c, 92a, 115c), Edo (220), ido (14d, 41c), udo (26d, 65d, 66a, 103d)

**D P _**  D.Ph. (238), DPT (238), DPW (238)

**D _ P**  dap (35d, 47a), dip (23d, 62a, 88d, 104d), dop (32d), dup. (238)

**_ D P**  ADP (235), EDP (238)

**D R _**  Dru (150), dry (38c, 121b, 133a)

**D _ R**  DAR (237), dar (53a, 122a), der (53c, 54a), dir. (237), dor (18b, 38a, 38d, 63b, 67a), dur (74b)

**D S _**  DSC (238), DST (238)

**D _ S**  das (53c, 54a, 60b, 112b), DDS (237), Des (149), des (51a), Dis (57a, 90c, 126b, 199), dis- (92c), DOS (238), dos (50a, 131d), DTs (238), dys- (92c)

**_ D S**  ads (27d), DDS (237), HDS (239), IDs (95b), ids (51b), LDS (240), MDs (88d), SDS (242), yds. (244)

**D T _**  D.Th. (238), DTs (238)

**D _ T**  DAT (237), DDT (45c, 237), DOT (238), dot (59d, 80c, 87d, 113b, 120b), DPT (238), DST (238)

**_ D T**  CDT (236), DDT (45c, 237), EDT (238), MDT (240), PDT (242), VDT (244)

**D U _**  dua- (93d), dub (23b, 80b), duc (50b), dud (44a), due (65c, 87b,

95b), **dug** (42b), **DUI** (38b, 238), **dun** (18d, 38c, 56a, 87b), **duo** (85d, 125c), **dup.** (238), **dur** (74b), **dux** (52a, 70c)

**D _ U**    **Dhu** (68b), **Dru** (150)

**D V _**    **DVM** (238)

**D _ V**    **DAV** (237), **div.** (237), **DMV** (237)

**_ D V**    **adv.** (235)

**D W _**    **DWI** (38b, 238)

**D _ W**    **daw** (55c), **DEW** (129d, 237), **dew** (77c), **Dow** (66d, 150), **DPW** (238)

**_ D W**    **Edw.** (74d)

**D _ X**    **Dix** (49a), **dux** (52a, 70c)

**D Y _**    **dye** (29a, 114c), **dyn-** (93c), **dys-** (92c)

**D _ Y**    **Day** (148), **day** (33d, 122b), **Dey** (149), **dey** (11b, 86d, 125a), **DIY** (237), **dry** (38c, 121b, 133a)

**D _ Z**    **DMZ** (237), **doz.** (238)

**_ D Z**    **adz** (33c, 122d)

**E A _**    **-ean** (117a), **ear** (15d, 25c, 51d, 57d, 95a, 112b), **eat** (31a), **eau** (51b)

**E _ A**    **ela** (56d, 82c), **Ena** (11b, 96c), **EPA** (238), **ERA** (238), **era** (10d, 41b, 87d, 122b), **ETA** (238), **eta** (11d), **EVA** (238), **Eva** (116a, 152)

**_ E A**    **Bea** (140), **CEA** (236), **DEA** (237), **dea** (69d), **Kea** (64c), **kea** (19a, 86d, 225), **Lea** (21c, 165), **lea** (45d, 75b, 87a, 134b), **NEA** (241), **pea** (28c, 71b, 106b, 127c), **REA** (242), **Rea** (176), **sea** (42d, 47c, 130a), **tea** (61d, 111b), **yea** (10b, 128a, 129c)

**E B _**    **ebb** (9a, 34b, 35d, 79c, 98b, 116d, 129d), **EbN** (29c), **EbS** (29c)

**E _ B**    **ebb** (9a, 34b, 35d, 79c, 98b, 116d, 129d), **emb.** (238)

**_ E B**    **deb** (31a), **Feb.** (78c, 238), **Heb.** (239), **J.E.B.** (159), **Leb.** (240), **Neb.** (241), **neb** (17d, 18d, 19b, 87d), **reb** (30a), **W.E.B.** (185), **web** (41a, 75d, 76a, 81c, 111b)

**E C _**    **ECG** (238), **ect-** (93c), **ecu** (47b, 108a)

**E _ C**    **EEC** (238), **enc.** (238), **etc.** (72b, 238)

**_ E C**    **AEC** (235), **Dec.** (78c, 237), **dec-** (93d), **EEC** (238), **SEC** (242), **sec** (38b, 132c), **tec** (35b)

**E D _**  Ede (29b, 38d, 53b), **edh** (12c), **Edo** (220), **EDP** (238), **EDT** (238), Edw. (74d)

**E _ D**  eld (12c, 73a, 83d, 122b), **end** (10d, 32c, 54d, 90c, 96c, 99c, 115d, 122b), **end-** (94a)

**_ E D**  bed (21b, 52d, 110c, 232), **Fed.** (238), **fed** (82c), **GED** (239), **he'd** (30c), **LED** (240), **led** (46c, 89c), **Med.** (240), **Ned** (172), **OED** (241), **ped-** (92d, 93a), **QED** (242), **Red** (176, 224), **red** (32a, 48a, 102c), **sed** (69c), **Ted** (183), **ted** (58c, 114a), **wed** (66c, 75a, 126c), **we'd** (30c), **Yed** (207), **zed** (135a)

**E E _**  EEC (238), **EEG** (238), **eek** (79b), **eel** (30a, 46d, 68d, 78c, 228), **e'en** (30b, 107c), **e'er** (12a, 107c)

**E _ E**  Ede (29b, 38d, 53b), **eke** (54b), **eme** (105c), **ENE** (29c), **EOE** (238), 'ere (18b, 30b), **ESE** (29c), **ete** (51a), **Eve** (9a, 107a, 152, 197), **eve** (38d, 125c), **Ewe** (216, 223), **ewe** (107d), **Exe** (35c, 223), **eye** (73a, 118b)

**_ E E**  bee (38a, 63b, 113c, 229), **cee** (55c, 71c), **Dee** (82b, 101a, 148, 223), **fee** (26a, 47b, 94b, 98b, 122d), **gee** (29b, 71c, 100c), **Lee** (27c, 165), **lee** (108a), **nee** (19b, 21a, 74b), **Ree** (14b, 23a, 189), **ree** (102d), **see** (19c, 36a, 41c, 43c, 55d, 73a, 83b, 86b, 87d, 130a, 133a), **tee** (55a, 55b, 87c), **Vee** (185), **vee** (47b, 81a), **wee** (77b, 105b, 110d), **zee** (63a)

**E F _**  EFT (238), **eft** (72c, 81c, 103d, 225)

**E _ F**  elf (44a, 114a)

**_ E F**  AEF (235), **def.** (237), **kef** (13d, 58b), **nef** (28b, 108b), **QEF** (242), **ref.** (242)

**E G _**  egg (28c, 85c), **ego** (94b, 106c, 127b)

**E _ G**  ECG (238), **EEG** (238), **egg** (28c, 85c), **EKG** (238), **Eng** (109a), **Eng.** (238), **erg** (40d, 133c, 246)

**_ E G**  beg (31d, 90b), **deg.** (237), **EEG** (238), **Geg** (213), **keg** (24c), **leg** (31b, 72a, 106b, 124b), **Meg** (11a, 170), **meg-** (93b), **neg.** (241), **peg** (32a, 38a, 44c, 89b), **reg.** (242), **teg** (107d)

**E _ H**  edh (12c), **Eph.** (238), **Eth.** (238), **eth** (12c), **-eth** (117b, 117c)

**_ E H**  Neh. (241), **reh** (11b, 62d)

**E I _**  ein (53c, 53d, 54a), **eis** (53d)

**E _ I**  Eli (104a, 134a, 151, 197), **EMI** (238), **epi-** (93c), **ETI** (238)

**_ E I**  fei (16d), **lei** (52d, 58c), **P.E.I.** (242), **Pei** (174), **rei** (91d), **sei** (65c), **Vei** (218), **Wei** (119d)

**E K _**      eke (54b), EKG (238)

**E _ K**      eek (79b), elk (21c, 70d, 129d, 230), Esk (134d, 223)

**_ E K**      dek- (93d), eek (79b), lek (31c, 36c, 213)

**E L _**      ela (56d, 82c), eld (12c, 73a, 83d, 122b), elf (44a, 114a), Eli (104a, 134a, 151, 197), elk (21c, 70d, 129d, 230), ell (12d, 22c, 28b, 246), elm (124a), Els (151), els (73a), Ely (25a)

**E _ L**      eel (30a, 46d, 68d, 78c, 228), ell (12d, 22c, 28b, 246), enl. (238), ESL (238)

**_ E L**      bel (34a, 246), Cel. (236), Del (148), Del. (209, 237), del (116b), eel (30a, 46d, 68d, 78c, 228), gel (28c, 58a, 111d), Hel (72d, 198), Mel (170), mel (60d), rel (40a, 246), sel (51a, 105b), Tel (16a), Tel. (243), tel- (93d)

**E M _**      emb. (238), eme (105c), EMI (238), emp. (238), Ems (95c, 112c), emu (19b, 85a, 225)

**E _ M**      elm (124a)

**_ E M**      Dem. (91a, 237), fem. (238), Gem (209), gem (115d), hem (39c, 40d, 114c, 118b), LEM (78c, 127c, 240), mem (12a), REM (110c, 242), rem (246)

**E N _**      Ena (11b, 96c), enc. (238), end (10d, 32c, 54d, 90c, 96c, 99c, 115d, 122b), end- (94a), ENE (29c), Eng (109a), Eng. (238), enl. (238), Eno (151), cns (18b), ens. (238), -ent (117a, 117b), ent- (94a)

**E _ N**      -ean (117a), EbN (29c), e'en (30b, 107c), ein (53c, 53d, 54a), eon (10d, 41d, 122b), ern (39a)

**_ E N**      Ben (141), ben (105b), cen- (92d), Den. (237), den (31c, 36d, 100a, 105c, 116c), e'en (30b, 107c), fen (20c, 75a, 78c, 118b, 215), Gen. (239), gen (27d), hen (18d, 49b, 86d, 103d), Ken (17a, 164), ken (65d, 104d, 126b, 246), Len (166), Men (88d), men (87d, 124c), pen (30a, 40d, 62d, 97a, 118b, 134c), ren- (93b), Sen. (243), sen (214, 217, 218, 219, 246), ten (18d, 34a, 34d), Ven. (244), ven- (93d), wen (33c, 83d, 125a, 129a), xen- (93a), yen (35b, 58a, 73a, 218), Zen (22b)

**E O _**      EOE (238), eon (10d, 41d, 122b), Eos (15d, 33d, 198), eos (86d)

**E _ O**      Edo (220), ego (94b, 106c, 127b), Eno (151), ETO (238), exo- (93c)

**_ E O**      CEO (236), Geo. (74d), geo- (92d), Leo (76c, 91b, 135c, 166, 207), leo (72b), Meo (218, 224), neo (77c), neo- (93b), OEO (241), Reo (24a)

**E P _**      EPA (238), Eph. (238), epi- (93c)

**E _ P**      EDP (238), emp. (238), ESP (109d, 238), exp. (238)

**_ E P**    **hep** (23a, 60b), **nep** (28c, 45d, 68c, 133c), **Pep** (174), **pep** (40d, 128b), **Rep.** (242), **rep** (10d, 43b, 100c), **Sep.** (78c, 243), **yep** (10b)

**E _ Q**    **Esq.** (238)

**_ E Q**    **req.** (242)

**E R _**    **ERA** (238), **era** (10d, 41b, 87d, 122b), **'ere** (18b, 30b), **erg** (40d, 133c, 246), **ern** (39a), **err** (20b, 35c, 109c, 110c, 116c, 123d), **ers** (19c, 59d, 128b), **-ery** (117b)

**E _ R**    **ear** (15d, 25c, 51d, 57d, 95a, 112b), **e'er** (12a, 107c), **err** (20b, 35c, 109c, 110c, 116c, 123d), **Eur.** (238)

**_ E R**    **aer** (25d), **aer-** (92c), **cer-** (93d), **der** (53c, 54a), **e'er** (12a, 107c), **Ger.** (239), **ger** (30c, 95b), **her** (70c, 95a), **-ier** (40d, 117a, 117b), **Jer.** (240), **ker-** (93d), **Ler** (22b, 199), **mer** (51a), **Ner** (104c), **o'er** (30b, 107c), **Per.** (242), **per** (128b), **ser-** (93c), **ser.** (243), **ter-** (93d), **ter.** (243), **ver.** (244), **xer-** (92d), **zer** (246)

**E S _**    **ESE** (29c), **Esk** (134d, 223), **ESL** (238), **ESP** (109d, 238), **Esq.** (238), **ess** (32d, 71c), **-ess** (117b), **EST** (238), **est** (50b, 50c), **-est** (40d, 117c)

**E _ S**    **EbS** (29c), **eis** (53d), **Els** (151), **els** (73a), **Ems** (95c, 112c), **ens** (18b), **ens.** (238), **Eos** (15d, 33d, 198), **eos** (86d), **ers** (19c, 59d, 128b), **ess** (32d, 71c), **-ess** (117b)

**_ E S**    **aes** (22a, 69c, 78a, 101d), **Bes** (39d, 198), **ces** (49d), **Des** (149), **des** (51a), **Fes** (220), **he's** (30c), **Les** (166), **les** (50a), **mes** (49d), **pes** (48c), **res** (70a, 71a), **ses** (50c), **Wes** (186), **yes** (10b, 44d)

**E T _**    **ETA** (238), **eta** (11d), **etc.** (72b, 238), **ete** (51a), **Eth.** (238), **eth** (12c), **-eth** (117b, 117c), **ETI** (238), **ETO** (238), **ETV** (238)

**E _ T**    **eat** (31a), **ect-** (93c), **EDT** (238), **EFT** (238), **eft** (72c, 81c, 103d, 225), **-ent** (117a, 117b), **ent-** (94a), **EST** (238), **est** (50b, 50c), **-est** (40d, 117c), **ext.** (238)

**_ E T**    **aet** (69c), **bet** (52b), **FET** (238), **get** (9d, 29b, 52a, 83b, 126b, 132b), **het** (12a), **jet** (11a, 19d, 114b), **ket-** (93b), **let** (11c, 60b, 87d, 99c, 104a, 117a, 120c), **Met.** (240), **met** (40d, 97d, 107a), **met-** (92d), **net** (24a, 27d, 41a, 43b, 76a, 94d, 106b, 111b, 120c), **pet** (24b, 31a, 44d, 48b), **ret** (47c, 73b, 111b), **ret.** (242), **Set** (42b, 198), **set** (10a, 14c, 15c, 28a, 31a, 47b, 58a, 81b, 85a, 89d, 106d, 111d, 120c), **vet** (111c), **vet.** (244), **wet** (33b, 33c, 37d, 77c, 97c), **yet** (18c, 22d, 60b, 82c, 115b, 121d)

**E U _**    **Eur.** (238)

**E _ U**    **eau** (51b), **ecu** (47b, 108a), **emu** (19b, 85a, 225)

**_ E U**    **feu** (45c, 50b, 105b), **heu** (11a), **jeu** (50b), **leu** (221), **neu** (54a), **peu** (50c)

E V _     EVA (238), Eva (116a, 152), Eve (9a, 107a, 152, 197), eve (38d, 125c)

E _ V     ETV (238)

_ E V     bev. (236), Lev. (240), lev (214), lev- (93b), Nev. (211, 241), Rev. (242), rev (41a, 79a)

E W _     Ewe (216, 223), ewe (107d)

E _ W     Edw. (74d)

_ E W     DEW (129d, 237), dew (77c), few (110d), HEW (239), hew (27a, 33a), Jew (59a), Lew (166), mew (19a, 25a, 45a, 56d, 58c, 105d, 106a, 226), new (13a, 43c, 51b, 84d, 98b), pew (18c, 27a, 47a, 106a), sew (75d, 115c), yew (30a, 42a, 108d, 124a)

E X _     Exe (35c, 223), exo- (93c), exp. (238), ext. (238)

_ E X     hex (66c), hex- (93c), lex (70b), Mex. (240), Rex (176), rex (67c), sex (53b, 94d), sex- (93c), Tex (31c, 183), Tex. (212, 243), vex (12d, 21b, 36d, 64b, 87c)

E Y _     eye (73a, 118b)

E _ Y     Ely (25a), -ery (117b)

_ E Y     bey (55c, 125a), Dey (149), dey (11b, 86d, 125a), fey (109d), hey (42c), Key (164), key (25c, 28d, 64b, 68d, 89c), Ney (49d, 80d, 172), Rey (176), rey (112d), sey (105a), wey (246)

_ E Z     fez (58b, 58d, 119d), nez (50d)

F A _     FAA (238), fad (31d, 97b, 120b, 124b), fag (27b), fam. (238), fan (35c, 114a), far (36d, 99c), fas (69c, 70a, 99b), fat (31a, 83d, 116a), fax (30d), Fay (152), fay (44a)

F _ A     FAA (238), FDA (238), FHA (238), Fla. (209, 238), Fra (153), fra (22a, 51c, 78a, 94c)

_ F A     BFA (236), ufa (42c)

F B _     FBI (238)

F _ B     Feb. (78c, 238), fib (71c, 119d), fob (48a, 130a), FRB (238)

_ F B     AFB (235)

F C _     FCC (238)

F _ C     FCC (238), FTC (239)

_ F C     AFC (235), DFC (237), pfc (242)

265

**F D _**    **FDA** (238)

**F _ D**    **fad** (31d, 97b, 120b, 124b), **Fed.** (238), **fed** (82c), **fid** (17a, 44c, 89b, 102b, 123b), **fod** (246), **fwd** (239)

**_ F D**    **Mfd.** (240), **RFD** (242)

**F E _**    **Feb.** (78c, 238), **Fed.** (238), **fed** (82c), **fee** (26a, 47b, 94b, 98b, 122d), **fei** (16d), **fem.** (238), **fen** (20c, 75a, 78c, 118b, 215), **Fes** (220), **FET** (238), **feu** (45c, 50b, 105b), **few** (110d), **fey** (109d), **fez** (58b, 58d, 119d)

**F _ E**    **fee** (26a, 47b, 94b, 98b, 122d), **fie** (42c, 49a), **FOE** (238), **foe** (84c)

**_ F E**    **ife** (59b), **RFE** (242)

**F F _**    **fff** (238)

**F _ F**    **fff** (238)

**_ F F**    **fff** (238), **off** (9b, 59b, 79d, 134c), **off.** (241)

**F _ G**    **fag** (27b), **fig** (51d, 124a), **fig.** (238), **fog** (28b, 116d, 130d), **fug** (98d)

**_ F G**    **Afg.** (235), **Mfg.** (240)

**F H _**    **FHA** (238)

**F I _**    **fib** (71c, 119d), **fid** (17a, 44c, 89b, 102b, 123b), **fie** (42c, 49a), **fig** (51d, 124a), **fig.** (238), **fin** (11a, 47b, 67a), **fir** (16d, 30a, 42a, 124a), **fit** (9c, 10a, 13d, 41b, 75b, 86c, 95b, 96b, 112a, 113b, 117d, 119c), **fix** (10a, 12c, 14c, 15c, 31a, 35d, 55c, 60c, 75d, 81b, 92b, 94a, 99c, 122a)

**F _ I**    **FBI** (238), **fei** (16d), **Fri.** (238), **fyi** (239)

**F L _**    **Fla.** (209, 238), **Flo** (12c), **flu** (62a), **fly** (47c, 63b, 120c, 229)

**F _ L**    **-ful** (117b)

**_ F L**    **AFL** (235), **CFL** (236), **NFL** (241)

**F _ M**    **fam.** (238), **fem.** (238)

**_ F M**    **cfm** (236)

**F _ N**    **fan** (35c, 114a), **fen** (20c, 75a, 78c, 118b, 215), **fin** (11a, 47b, 67a), **Fon** (214), **fun** (52b, 66b)

**F O _**    **fob** (48a, 130a), **fod** (246), **FOE** (238), **foe** (84c), **fog** (28b, 116d, 130d), **Fon** (214), **fop** (31c, 33c, 38c, 44b), **for** (94d), **fot** (246), **fou** (246), **Fox** (153, 189), **fox** (23a, 23d, 54c, 102b, 230), **Foy** (153)

F _ O    **Flo** (12c), **fro** (16b)

_ F O    **UFO** (48a, 243)

F _ P    **fop** (31c, 33c, 38c, 44b)

F R _    **Fra** (153), **fra** (22a, 51c, 78a, 94c), **FRB** (238), **Fri.** (238), **fro** (16b), **fry** (30c, 47a)

F _ R    **far** (36d, 99c), **fir** (16d, 30a, 42a, 124a), **for** (94d), **fur** (28c, 57b)

_ F R    **Afr.** (235), **Mfr.** (240)

F _ S    **fas** (69c, 70a, 99b), **Fes** (220)

_ F S    **cfs** (236), **ifs** (30b)

F T _    **FTC** (239)

F _ T    **fat** (31a, 83d, 116a), **FET** (238), **fit** (9c, 10a, 13d, 41b, 75b, 86c, 95b, 96b, 112a, 113b, 117d, 119c), **fot** (246), **fut** (246)

_ F T    **aft** (15b, 18b, 98a, 108b, 115b), **EFT** (238), **eft** (72c, 81c, 103d, 225), **oft'** (30b), **UFT** (243)

F U _    **fug** (98d), **-ful** (117b), **fun** (52b, 66b), **fur** (28c, 57b), **fut** (246)

F _ U    **feu** (45c, 50b, 105b), **flu** (62a), **fou** (246)

F W _    **fwd** (239)

F _ W    **few** (110d)

_ F W    **UFW** (243), **VFW** (244)

F _ X    **fax** (30d), **fix** (10a, 12c, 14c, 15c, 31a, 35d, 55c, 60c, 75d, 81b, 92b, 94a, 99c, 122a), **Fox** (153, 189), **fox** (23a, 23d, 54c, 102b, 230)

F Y _    **fyi** (239)

F _ Y    **Fay** (152), **fay** (44a), **fey** (109d), **fly** (47c, 63b, 120c, 229), **Foy** (153), **fry** (30c, 47a)

F _ Z    **fez** (58b, 58d, 119d)

G A _    **gab** (26b, 92b, 119b, 133a), **Gad** (64d, 135c), **gad** (47c, 77a, 83a, 97d, 101a), **gag** (26d, 66c, 113b), **gai** (50c, 233), **Gal.** (239), **gal** (45b, 54c), **Gam** (154), **gam** (131b, 232), **gam-** (93c), **Gan** (215), **GAO** (239), **gap** (13b, 21d, 59d, 84b), **gar** (46c, 46d, 81b, 228), **gas** (12c, 52a, 88b), **gat** (57c, 100b), **gau** (53c), **Gay** (154), **gay** (18b)

G _ A    **Goa** (91d), **goa** (53b), **GPA** (239), **GSA** (239)

_ G A    **aga** (84d, 125b), **PGA** (242)

G B _     **GBS** (43a)

G _ B     **gab** (26b, 92b, 119b, 133a), **gib** (17d, 24d, 51c, 74c, 122d), **gob** (75b, 103b)

_ G B     **KGB** (103c, 240)

G _ D     **Gad** (64d, 135c), **gad** (47c, 77a, 83a, 97d, 101a), **GED** (239), **gid** (107d), **God** (66b), **god** (34c, 133d)

_ G D     **sgd.** (243)

G E _     **GED** (239), **gee** (29b, 71c, 100c), **Geg** (213), **gel** (28c, 58a, 111d), **Gem** (209), **gem** (115d), **Gen.** (239), **gen** (27d), **Geo.** (74d), **geo-** (92d), **Ger.** (239), **ger** (30c, 95b), **get** (9d, 29b, 52a, 83b, 126b, 132b)

G _ E     **gee** (29b, 71c, 100c), **gie** (105a), **GRE** (239)

_ G E     **age** (41b, 41c, 41d, 53b, 71d, 75b, 106a, 122b), **lge.** (240)

G_ G     **gag** (26d, 66c, 113b), **Geg** (213), **Gig** (155), **gig** (24a, 24c, 25d, 46d, 80d, 125d), **Gog** (74a, 197)

_ G G     **egg** (28c, 85c)

G H _     **GHQ** (239)

_ G H     **ugh** (42c)

G I _     **gib** (17d, 24d, 51c, 74c, 122d), **gid** (107d), **gie** (105a), **Gig** (155), **gig** (24a, 24c, 25d, 46d, 80d, 125d), **Gil** (155), **gin** (11a, 24a, 31b, 72b, 106b, 246), **GIs** (111c)

G _ I     **gai** (50c, 233)

_ G I     **AGI** (235), **CGI** (236)

G _ L     **Gal.** (239), **gal** (45b, 54c), **gel** (28c, 58a, 111d), **Gil** (155)

G M _     **GMT** (239)

G _ M     **Gam** (154), **gam** (131b, 232), **gam-** (93c), **Gem** (209), **gem** (115d), **gum** (10a, 43c, 62c, 78d, 99d, 115b, 124a), **gym** (114a)

G N _     **GNP** (239), **gnu** (13a, 132a, 230)

G _ N     **Gan** (215), **gen** (27d), **Gen.** (239), **gin** (11a, 24a, 31b, 72b, 106b, 246), **gon-** (93c), **gun** (46b, 100b, 109a, 130c), **gyn-** (92d)

_ G N     **ign.** (239)

G O _     **Goa** (91d), **goa** (53b), **gob** (75b, 103b), **God** (66b), **god** (34c, 133d), **Gog** (74a, 197), **gon-** (93c), **goo** (79c, 115b), **GOP** (91a, 99d, 239), **got** (23b, 83b), **goy** (82a)

268

**G _ O**   GAO (239), Geo. (74d), geo- (92d), goo (79c, 115b), GPO (239), gro. (239)

**_ G O**   ago (23a, 55b, 87a), ego (94b, 106c, 127b)

**G P _**   GPA (239), GPO (239)

**G _ P**   gap (13b, 21d, 59d, 84b), GNP (239), GOP (91a, 99d, 239), gyp (107a, 108d, 118d)

**G _ Q**   GHQ (239)

**G R _**   GRE (239), gro. (239), GRU (239)

**G _ R**   gar (46c, 46d, 81b, 228), Ger. (239), ger (30c, 95b), Gur (223), gur (117c), gyr- (93a)

**G S _**   GSA (239)

**G _ S**   gas (12c, 52a, 88b), GBS (43a), Gis (111c), Gus (156)

**G _ T**   gat (57c, 100b), get (9d, 29b, 52a, 83b, 126b, 132b), GMT (239), got (23b, 83b), gut (99c)

**_ G T**   agt. (235), hgt. (239), Sgt. (243)

**G U _**   gum (10a, 43c, 62c, 78d, 99d, 115b, 124a), gun (46b, 100b, 109a, 130c), Gur (223), gur (117c), Gus (156), gut (99c), Guy (156), guy (45a, 74c, 115a), guz (246)

**G _ U**   gau (53c), gnu (13a, 132a, 230), GRU (239)

**G Y _**   gym (114a), gyn- (92d), gyp (107a, 108d, 118d), gyr- (93a)

**G _ Y**   Gay (154), gay (18b), goy (82a), Guy (156), guy (45a, 74c, 115a)

**_ G Y**   IGY (239)

**G _ Z**   guz (246)

**H A _**   Hab. (239), had (61a, 91d), hae (105a), Hag. (239), hag (133a), hah (42c), Hal (125d, 156), Ham (81d, 108a, 197), ham (9d, 75c), Han (26d, 134a, 215), hap (18b, 25d), has (91d), ha's (70b), Hat (223), hat (58c), Haw. (209), haw (29b, 71a, 114c), hay (122b)

**H _ A**   HRA (239)

**_ H A**   a-ha (42c), cha (120a), FHA (238), Kha (69a), kha (11d), tha (11d), WHA (244)

**H B _**   HBO (26a, 239)

**H _ B**   Hab. (239), Heb. (239), hob (33c, 46b, 95a, 123a), hub (25c, 131c)

**H C _**   HCL (239), hcp. (239)

269

| | |
|---|---|
| **H _ C** | **hic** (70a), **hoc** (70a) |
| **H D _** | **HDS** (239) |
| **H _ D** | **had** (61a, 91d), **he'd** (30c), **hid** (31c, 106a), **hod** (21d, 28c, 78d, 105c), **HUD** (239) |
| **_ H D** | **Ph.D.** (242) |
| **H E _** | **Heb.** (239), **he'd** (30c), **Hel** (72d, 198), **hem** (39c, 40d, 114c, 118b), **hen** (18d, 49b, 86d, 103d), **hep** (23a, 60b), **her** (70c, 95a), **he's** (30c), **het** (12a), **heu** (11a), **HEW** (239), **hew** (27a, 33a), **hex** (66c), **hex-** (93c), **hey** (42c) |
| **H _ E** | **hae** (105a), **hie** (61d), **hoe** (32c, 52d), **hue** (29a, 107b, 122d) |
| **_ H E** | **Che** (145), **rhe** (47d, 246), **She** (57b), **she** (95a), **the** (14d) |
| **_ H F** | **UHF** (120b, 243), **VHF** (120b) |
| **H G _** | **hgt.** (239) |
| **H _ G** | **Hag.** (239), **hag** (133a), **hog** (88d, 118d, 230), **hug** (40c) |
| **H _ H** | **hah** (42c), **HRH** (239), **huh** (42c) |
| **H I _** | **hic** (70a), **hid** (31c, 106a), **hie** (61d), **him** (70c, 95a), **hin** (246), **hip** (44a, 66c, 102a, 102b), **his** (95a), **hit** (15a, 15c, 18c, 28b, 116b) |
| **H _ I** | **hoi** (42c), **Hui** (215), **hui** (15a) |
| **_ H I** | **chi** (11d), **ihi** (46d, 115c), **NHI** (241), **phi** (11d) |
| **H _ L** | **Hal** (125d, 156), **HCL** (239), **Hel** (72d, 198), **hyl-** (94a) |
| **_ H L** | **NHL** (241) |
| **H M _** | **HMO** (239), **HMS** (239) |
| **H _ M** | **Ham** (81d, 108a, 197), **ham** (9d, 75c), **hem** (39c, 40d, 114c, 118b), **him** (70c, 95a), **hum** (38a, 112a, 131d) |
| **_ H M** | **chm.** (236), **ohm** (40a, 53d, 246) |
| **H N _** | **HNS** (239) |
| **H _ N** | **Han** (26d, 134a, 215), **hen** (18d, 49b, 86d, 103d), **hin** (246), **Hon.** (239), **hon** (40d), **Hun** (127b) |
| **H O _** | **hob** (33c, 46b, 95a, 123a), **hoc** (70a), **hod** (21d, 28c, 78d, 105c), **hoe** (32c, 52d), **hog** (88d, 118d, 230), **hoi** (42c), **Hon.** (239), **hon** (40d), **hop** (33b, 67a), **hor.** (239), **Hos.** (239), **ho's** (70b), **hot** (12d, 117d), **HOV** (239), **how** (74c, 76b, 96d), **Hoy** (64d), **hoy** (17b, 20b) |
| **H _ O** | **HBO** (26a, 239), **HMO** (239) |

| | |
|---|---|
| _ H O | **cho** (246), **mho** (40a, 246), **o-ho** (42c), **rho** (11d), **sho** (246), **WHO** (244), **who** (96d, 99b) |
| H _ P | **hap** (18b, 25d), **hcp.** (239), **hep** (23a, 60b), **hip** (44a, 66c, 102a, 102b), **hop** (33b, 67a), **hup** (23a, 29b) |
| _ H Q | **GHQ** (239) |
| H R _ | **HRA** (239), **HRH** (239), **hrs.** (239) |
| H _ R | **her** (70c, 95a), **hor.** (239) |
| _ H R | **ihr** (54b) |
| H S _ | **HST** (239) |
| H _ S | **has** (91d), **ha's** (70b), **HDS** (239), **he's** (30c), **his** (95a), **HMS** (239), **HNS** (239), **Hos.** (239), **ho's** (70b), **hrs.** (239), **hts.** (239) |
| _ H S | **ahs** (42c), **IHS** (239), **JHS** (240), **NHS** (241), **ohs** (42c) |
| H T _ | **hts.** (239) |
| H _ T | **Hat** (223), **hat** (58c), **het** (12a), **hgt.** (239), **hit** (15a, 15c, 18c, 28b, 116b), **hot** (12d, 117d), **HST** (239), **hut** (107c) |
| H U _ | **hub** (25c, 131c), **HUD** (239), **hue** (29a, 107b, 122d), **hug** (40c), **huh** (42c), **Hui** (215), **hui** (15a), **hum** (38a, 112a, 131d), **Hun** (127b), **hup** (23a, 29b), **hut** (107c) |
| H _ U | **heu** (11a) |
| _ H U | **ahu** (53b), **Dhu** (68b), **Shu** (97a), **Thu.** (243) |
| H _ V | **HOV** (239) |
| H W _ | **hwy.** (239) |
| H _ W | **Haw.** (209), **haw** (29b, 71a, 114c), **HEW** (239), **hew** (27a, 33a), **how** (74c, 76b, 96d) |
| H _ X | **hex** (66c), **hex-** (93c) |
| H Y _ | **hyl-** (94a) |
| H _ Y | **hay** (122b), **hey** (42c), **Hoy** (64d), **hoy** (17b, 20b), **hwy.** (239) |
| _ H Y | **shy** (17c, 31c, 77c, 98b, 108d, 122b), **thy** (95a), **why** (96d) |
| I A _ | **-ial** (117a), **Ian** (66c, 159), **iao** (60d), **IAS** (239) |
| I _ A | **Ica** (12b), **Ida** (79b, 159), **Ida.** (209), **ILA** (239), **Ila** (17a), **Ina** (159), **-ina** (117b), **ioa** (51c), **IPA** (240), **IRA** (64a, 240), **Ira** (159, 197), **Isa.** (240), **ita** (70a), **iva** (75a), **iwa** (51c) |

271

| _ I A | **BIA** (236), **CIA** (236), **dia** (112d), **dia-** (92c), **KIA** (240), **MIA** (240), **Mia** (170), **mia** (113a), **Pia** (175), **pia** (14d, 39b), **ria** (41d, 63a), **tia** (112c), **via** (65c, 101a, 101d) |
|---|---|
| I B _ | **ibn** (111d), **Ibo** (68c, 220) |
| _ I B | **bib** (28d), **dib** (47a), **fib** (71c,119d), **gib** (17d, 24d, 51c, 74c, 122d), **jib** (103b), **Lib.** (240), **lib** (49b), **mib** (11c, 74d), **nib** (17d, 19b, 87d), **rib** (31a, 33a, 70d, 75c, 125d), **sib** (99b) |
| I C _ | **Ica** (12b), **ICC** (239), **Ice.** (239), **ice** (30c, 51c), **ich** (53d), **ici** (50c), **-ics** (117c), **ICU** (239), **icy** (19c, 53b) |
| I _ C | **ICC** (239), **Inc.** (239), **IOC** (240), **IRC** (240), **ITC** (240) |
| _ I C | **hic** (70a), **Mic.** (240), **pic.** (242), **Ric** (177), **sic** (70a, 121d, 123d), **tic** (79d, 113b, 125c), **Vic** (32d, 185) |
| I D _ | **Ida** (79b, 159), **Ida.** (209), **ide** (46d), **ido** (14d,41c), **IDs** (95b), **ids** (51b) |
| I _ D | **Ind.** (91a, 210, 239), **iod-** (93b), **IUD** (240) |
| _ I D | **aid** (15a, 57d, 59b, 117a), **bid** (21d, 64a, 83c, 84c), **CID** (236), **did** (9c), **fid** (17a, 44c, 89b, 102b, 123b), **gid** (107d), **hid** (31c, 106a), **kid** (26c, 54d, 70d, 90d, 134d), **lid** (123a), **mid** (12b, 25c, 57c), **-oid** (117b), **rid** (27d, 36b, 40b, 49b), **Sid** (180) |
| I E _ | **-ier** (40d, 117a, 117b) |
| I _ E | **Ice.** (239), **ice** (30c, 51c), **ide** (46d), **ife** (59b), **Ike** (94b, 159), **ile** (50c), **ile-** (93b), **Ine** (12c), **-ine** (117a, 117b), **Ire.** (240), **ire** (12c, 26d, 52c, 97b, 134a), **Ise** (60d), **-ise** (117a, 117c), **-ite** (117a, 117b), **I've** (30c) |
| _ I E | **cie** (49c), **die** (24d, 34d, 43d, 54a, 87a, 114c, 123a), **fie** (42c, 49a), **gie** (105a), **hie** (61d), **lie** (44a, 55a, 98b, 99d, 119b, 119d), **nie** (54a), **Pie** (175), **pie** (35b, 125c), **sie** (54b), **tie** (12c, 20d, 31b, 37d, 41b, 42a, 69b, 72b, 97b, 124d), **vie** (30b, 116c, 125a) |
| I F _ | **ife** (59b), **ifs** (30b) |
| I _ F | **IMF** (239) |
| _ I F | **CIF** (236), **dif.** (237), **Sif** (121b), **vif** (50c) |
| I G _ | **ign.** (239), **IGY** (239) |
| I _ G | **Ing** (12c), **ing** (73c, 87a), **-ing** (86d, 117c) |
| _ I G | **big** (69b, 74a, 116d), **dig** (42b, 132d), **fig** (51d, 124a), **fig.** (238), **Gig** (155), **gig** (24a, 24c, 25d, 46d, 80d, 125d), **jig** (33b), **mig** (11c, 74d, 89d), **nig** (28d), **pig** (112b, 118d, 231), **rig** (41b, 53b, 85b), **wig** (57b) |

272

I H _     **ihi** (46d, 115c), **ihr** (54b), **IHS** (239)

I _ H     **ich** (53d), **-ish** (117a), **Ith** (25c)

I _ I     **ici** (50c), **ihi** (46d, 115c)

_ I I     **rii** (127d)

I K _     **Ike** (94b, 159)

I _ K     **ilk** (27d, 67c, 105a, 113b), **ink** (33c, 94b, 109b), **irk** (12d, 87c, 128b)

_ I K     **Dik** (149), **-nik** (117c), **pik** (246)

I L _     **ILA** (239), **lla** (17a), **ile** (50c), **ile-** (93b), **ilk** (27d, 67c, 105a, 113b), **Ill.** (210, 239), **I'll** (30c), **ill** (91b, 126b, 126c), **ILO** (239), **ils** (49d, 51a)

I _ L     **-ial** (117a), **Ill.** (210, 239), **I'll** (30c), **ill** (91b, 126b, 126c), **isl.** (240)

_ I L     **ail** (124d), **Bil** (141), **Gil** (155), **kil** (64a), **Li'l** (9a), **mil** (62c, 121b, 132d, 246), **mil.** (240), **nil** (82c), **oil** (13a, 52a, 56a), **sil** (26d, 134b), **til** (107a), **'til** (30b), **Wil** (186)

I M _     **IMF** (239), **imp** (34d, 97d, 101c, 126d), **imp.** (239)

I _ M     **I.O.M.** (240), **-ism** (117b)

_ I M     **AIM** (235), **aim** (54d, 83a, 96c, 119d), **bim** (133b), **dim** (33d, 38d, 43d, 73d, 83a), **him** (70c, 95a), **Jim** (161), **jim** (11d), **Kim** (67d, 164), **mim** (11d), **rim** (21a, 39c, 74d, 87d, 95a, 122b, 131c), **Sim** (181), **Tim** (35c, 183), **vim** (40d, 48c, 113d, 128b, 128d), **Wim** (187)

I N _     **Ina** (159), **-ina** (117b), **Inc.** (239), **Ind.** (91a, 210, 239), **Ine** (12c), **-ine** (117a, 117b), **Ing** (12c), **ing** (73c, 87a), **-ing** (86d, 117c), **ink** (33c, 94b, 109b), **Inn** (33c), **inn** (56d, 61c, 101a, 120a), **Ino** (15b, 23a), **INS** (239), **ins** (83c), **int.** (239)

I _ N     **Ian** (66c, 159), **ibn** (111d), **ign.** (239), **Inn** (33c), **inn** (56d, 61c, 101a, 120a), **Ion** (13b, 26a, 40a, 86d)

_ I N     **Ain** (223), **ain** (105b), **bin** (21b, 98b, 116a), **din** (27d, 61c, 126d), **ein** (53c, 53d, 54a), **fin** (11a, 47b, 67a), **gin** (11a, 24a, 31b, 72b, 106b, 246), **hin** (246), **kin** (26d, 63c, 68c, 99b, 246), **Lin** (134d), **Min** (215), **min.** (240), **Nin** (172), **nin** (246), **PIN** (242), **pin** (37c, 44c, 110a, 246), **rin** (106c), **sin** (11d, 12a, 83c, 123d, 124b, 128c, 134c), **tin** (30b, 74c, 76a, 114d, 245), **Vin** (185), **vin** (51b), **win** (9d, 52a, 94b), **Yin** (26d), **yin** (107c, 134a)

I O _     **ioa** (51c), **IOC** (240), **iod-** (93b), **I.O.M.** (240), **Ion** (13b, 26a, 40a, 86d), **-ior** (40d, 117a), **IOU** (95a, 240), **I.O.W.** (240)

I _ O     **iao** (60d), **Ibo** (68c, 220), **ido** (14d, 41c), **ILO** (239), **Ino** (15b, 23a), **iso-** (92d, 93c), **ITO** (240), **Ito** (65b), **Ivo** (159), **iyo** (10b, 88c)

273

**_ I O**    **bio** (71d), **bio-** (93b), **bio.** (31b, 236), **CIO** (236), **mio** (113a), **rio** (113a, 246), **tio** (113a)

**I P _**    **IPA** (240)

**I _ P**    **imp** (34d, 97d, 101c, 126d), **imp.** (239)

**_ I P**    **dip** (23d, 62a, 88d, 104d), **hip** (44a, 66c, 102a, 102b), **kip** (18a, 57c, 59d, 218, 246), **lip** (39c, 47b, 62c, 100d), **lip-** (92d), **nip** (19c, 38a, 62a, 89b), **Pip** (35c), **pip** (13c, 92a, 106b, 114a), **RIP** (242), **Rip** (177), **rip** (68b, 99c, 120a), **sip** (37d, 38a, 119d), **tip** (40d, 56a, 60b, 60d, 90c, 122a), **VIP** (35d, 244), **yip** (17b, 37b, 134c), **zip** (40d, 128b, 244)

**I R _**    **IRA** (64a, 240), **Ira** (159, 197), **IRC** (240), **Ire.** (240), **ire** (12c, 26d, 52c, 97b, 134a), **irk** (12d, 87c, 128b), **irr.** (240), **IRS** (120a, 240)

**I _ R**    **-ier** (40d, 117a, 117b), **ihr** (54b), **-ior** (40d, 117a), **irr.** (240), **Isr.** (240)

**_ I R**    **air** (14b, 22a, 34d, 36c, 43a, 45a, 74c, 75d, 76d, 95d, 115a, 125a), **cir.** (237), **dir.** (237), **fir** (16d, 30a, 42a, 124a), **mir** (103a), **pir** (80c), **sir** (68a, 120c, 122c), **tir** (51a, 108c), **vir** (69d)

**I S _**    **Isa.** (240), **Ise** (60d), **-ise** (117a, 117c), **-ish** (117a), **isl.** (240), **-ism** (117b), **iso-** (92d, 93c), **Isr.** (240), **-ist** (117a, 117b), **is't** (107c)

**I _ S**    **IAS** (239), **-ics** (117c), **IDs** (95b), **ids** (51b), **ifs** (30b), **IHS** (239), **ils** (49d, 51a), **INS** (239), **ins** (83c), **IRS** (120a, 240), **its** (95a), **it's** (30c), **ius** (70a)

**_ I S**    **ais** (110d), **bis** (10c, 50b, 70b, 78c, 99d), **Dis** (57a, 90c, 126b, 199), **dis-** (92c), **eis** (53d), **Gis** (111c), **his** (95a), **lis** (49a, 50c), **mis-** (92c, 94a), **Nis** (30b), **sis** (44b, 54c, 99b), **'tis** (30b, 107c), **vis** (69d, 70a), **Wis.** (212, 244)

**I T _**    **-ite** (117a, 117b), **ita** (70a), **ITC** (240), **Ith** (25c), **ITO** (240), **Ito** (65b), **its** (95a), **it's** (30c), **Itt** (10a)

**I _ T**    **int.** (239), **is't** (107c), **-ist** (117a, 117b), **Itt** (10a)

**_ I T**    **ait** (64b, 101a), **bit** (23d, 37d, 67b, 78d, 86d, 122d, 125c, 131c), **cit.** (237), **fit** (9c, 10a, 13d, 41b, 75b, 86c, 95b, 96b, 112a, 113b, 117d, 119c), **hit** (15a, 15c, 18c, 28b, 116b), **kit** (85b), **lit** (62a, 68d), **lit.** (31b), **mit** (54a), **NIT** (241), **nit** (39d, 246), **pit** (42b, 106b, 120d), **rit.** (110d, 242), **sit** (75d, 87d, 91d, 107a), **tit** (19a, 226), **wit** (36a, 61c, 66d, 129a)

**I U _**    **IUD** (240), **ius** (70a)

**I _ U**    **ICU** (239), **IOU** (95a, 240)

**_ I U**    **niu** (246), **piu** (234), **Tiu** (53c, 125d)

**I V _**    **iva** (75a), **I've** (30c), **Ivo** (159), **Ivy** (159), **ivy** (28a, 31d, 128b)

| | |
|---|---|
| _ I V | **civ.** (237), **div.** (237), **Liv** (166) |
| I W _ | **iwa** (51c), **IWW** (240) |
| I _ W | **I.O.W.** (240), **IWW** (240) |
| _ I X | **Bix** (141), **Dix** (49a), **fix** (10a, 12c, 14c, 15c, 31a, 35d, 55c, 60c, 75d, 81b, 92b, 94a, 99c, 122a), **Mix** (171), **mix** (11c, 76a, 115c), **nix** (82c, 130b), **pix** (242), **six** (57c), **tix** (243), **vix** (70a) |
| I Y _ | **iyo** (10b, 88c) |
| I _ Y | **icy** (19c, 53b), **IGY** (239), **Ivy** (159), **ivy** (28a, 31d, 128b) |
| _ I Y | **DIY** (237) |
| _ I Z | **Liz** (166), **viz** (80d), **wiz** (74a) |
| J A _ | **jab** (60b, 90d, 96a, 132d), **jag** (95c), **Jam.** (240), **jam** (35d, 85b, 94b, 115d, 122a), **Jan** (160), **Jan.** (78c, 240), **Jap.** (240), **jar** (27d, 30b, 56a, 107b), **Jas.** (74d), **Jat** (96a), **jaw** (75b), **Jay** (160), **jay** (19b, 71c, 225) |
| J B _ | **JBS** (240) |
| J _ B | **jab** (60b, 90d, 96a, 132d), **J.E.B.** (159), **jib** (103b), **Job** (196), **job** (27a, 119d, 133c) |
| J C _ | **JCS** (240), **jct.** (240) |
| J D _ | **JDL** (240) |
| J E _ | **J.E.B.** (159), **Jer.** (240), **jet** (11a, 19d, 114b), **jeu** (50b), **Jew** (59a) |
| J _ E | **Joe** (161), **joe** (45a) |
| J _ G | **jag** (95c), **jig** (33b), **jog** (66d, 82d, 124d), **jug** (89c, 94d) |
| J H _ | **JHS** (240) |
| J I _ | **jib** (103b), **jig** (33b), **Jim** (161), **jim** (11d) |
| _ J I | **uji** (109c) |
| J _ L | **JDL** (240), **Jul.** (78c, 240) |
| J M _ | **J.M.W.** (159) |
| J _ M | **Jam.** (240), **jam** (35d, 85b, 94b, 115d, 122a), **Jim** (161), **jim** (11d) |
| J _ N | **Jan** (160), **Jan.** (78c, 240), **Jon** (163), **Jun.** (78c, 240), **jun** (218) |
| J O _ | **Job** (196), **job** (27a, 119d, 133c), **Joe** (161), **joe** (45a), **jog** (66d, 82d, 124d), **Jon** (163), **Jos.** (74d), **jot** (64a, 86d, 122c, 131c), **joy** (34c) |

| | |
|---|---|
| J _ P | **Jap.** (240) |
| J R _ | **J.R.R.** (159) |
| J _ R | **jar** (27d, 30b, 56a, 107b), **Jer.** (240), **J.R.R.** (159) |
| J _ S | **Jas.** (74d), **JBS** (240), **JCS** (240), **JHS** (240), **Jos.** (74d), **jus** (50c, 70b) |
| J _ T | **Jat** (96a), **jct.** (240), **jet** (11a, 19d, 114b), **jot** (64a, 86d, 122c, 131c), **jut** (95a) |
| J U _ | **jug** (89c, 94d), **Jul.** (78c, 240), **Jun.** (78c, 240), **jun** (218), **jus** (50c, 70b), **jut** (95a) |
| J _ U | **jeu** (50b) |
| _ J V | **KJV** (240) |
| J _ W | **jaw** (75b), **Jew** (59a), **J.M.W.** (159) |
| J _ Y | **Jay** (160), **jay** (19b, 71c, 225), **joy** (34c) |
| K A _ | **Kaa** (67a), **kae** (65b), **kaf** (11d, 12a), **Kai** (163), **kal** (46c), **Kan.** (210, 240), **kan** (246), **Kaw** (121d), **Kay** (14d, 102c, 164) |
| K _ A | **Kaa** (67a), **Kea** (64c), **kea** (19a, 86d, 225), **Kha** (69a), **kha** (11d), **KIA** (240), **kra** (73b), **Kwa** (69a, 223) |
| _ K A | **aka** (81c, 235), **oka** (125a, 133c, 246), **ska** (65b) |
| K _ B | **KGB** (103c, 240), **kob** (13a, 130b) |
| _ K C | **AKC** (235) |
| K _ D | **kid** (26c, 54d, 70d, 90d, 134d) |
| _ K D | **ok'd** (13d) |
| K E _ | **Kea** (64c), **kea** (19a, 86d, 225), **kef** (13d, 58b), **keg** (24c), **Ken** (17a, 164), **ken** (65d, 104d, 126b, 246), **ker-** (93d), **ket-** (93b), **Key** (164), **key** (25c, 28d, 64b, 68d, 89c) |
| K _ E | **kae** (65b) |
| _ K E | **eke** (54b), **Ike** (94b, 159), **oke** (246) |
| K _ F | **kaf** (11d, 12a), **kef** (13d, 58b) |
| K G _ | **KGB** (103c, 240) |
| K _ G | **keg** (24c) |
| _ K G | **EKG** (238) |

276

K H _     **Kha** (69a), **kha** (11d)

K _ H     **kph** (240), **kwh** (240)

K I _     **KIA** (240), **kid** (26c, 54d, 70d, 90d, 134d), **kil** (64a), **Kim** (67d, 164), **kin** (26d, 63c, 68c, 99b, 246), **kip** (18a, 57c, 59d, 218, 246), **kit** (85b)

K _ I     **Kai** (163), **koi** (24b, 46d), **Kui** (67b)

_ K I     **ski** (104d, 110b)

K J _     **KJV** (240)

K _ L     **kal** (46c), **kil** (64a), **Kol** (18c)

K _ M     **Kim** (67d, 164)

K _ N     **Kan.** (210, 240), **kan** (246), **Ken** (17a, 164), **ken** (65d, 104d, 126b, 246), **kin** (26d, 63c, 68c, 99b, 246), **kon** (246)

K O _     **kob** (13a, 130b), **koi** (24b, 46d), **Kol** (18c), **kon** (246), **kop** (59d), **Kor** (60d), **Kos** (60b, 64c)

_ K O     **TKO** (21b, 243)

K P _     **kph** (240)

K _ P     **kip** (18a, 57c, 59d, 218, 246), **kop** (59d), **kup** (246)

K R _     **kra** (73b), **Kru** (215, 218)

_ K R     **ker-** (93d), **Kor** (60d)

K _ S     **Kos** (60b, 64c)

_ K S     **ok's** (13d)

K _ T     **ket-** (93b), **kit** (85b)

_ K T     **Skt.** (243)

K U _     **Kui** (67b), **kup** (246)

K _ U     **Kru** (215, 218)

_ K U     **aku** (46d)

K _ V     **KJV** (240)

K W _     **Kwa** (69a, 223), **kwh** (240)

K _ W     **Kaw** (121d)

_ K W     **ckw** (237)

**K _ Y**   **Kay** (14d, 102c, 164), **Key** (164), **key** (25c, 28d, 64b, 68d, 89c)

**_ K Y**   **sky** (46c)

**L A _**   **Lab.** (240), **lab** (104d), **lac** (43c, 99d, 108a, 127b), **lad** (21c, 45b, 74c, 116c, 134d), **Lae** (221), **lag** (34c, 115a), **Lai** (69a, 220), **lai** (119b), **Lam.** (240), **lam** (11d, 47c), **lan** (31b, 118c), **Lao** (62d, 69a, 218), **lap** (26c, 27b, 31b, 97b, 100d, 113d, 123c), **lar** (54b, 74b), **las** (50a, 112c), **Lat.** (240), **lat** (29a), **lav.** (240), **law** (23d, 28d, 33a, 39c, 67c, 71a, 84c, 92b, 102d, 115a), **lax** (39b, 73a, 81b, 99c, 111c), **lay** (16c, 75c, 82a, 96c, 106b, 111d), **laz** (25a)

**L _ A**   **Lea** (21c, 165), **lea** (45d, 75b, 87a, 134b), **Loa** (57b), **loa** (10c, 43c, 133d)

**_ L A**   **Ala.** (209, 235), **ala** (16c, 132c), **a la** (9c), **ela** (56d, 82c), **Fla.** (209, 238), **ILA** (239), **lla** (17a), **-ula** (117b)

**L B _**   **lbs.** (240)

**L _ B**   **Lab.** (240), **lab** (104d), **Leb.** (240), **Lib.** (240), **lib** (49b), **lob** (77a, 120c, 121d)

**_ L B**   **Alb.** (235), **alb** (52d, 128a)

**L C _**   **LCD** (240), **LCM** (240)

**L _ C**   **lac** (43c, 99d, 108a, 127b), **loc.** (240)

**_ L C**   **SLC** (243), **TLC** (243)

**L D _**   **LDS** (240)

**L _ D**   **lad** (21c, 45b, 74c, 116c, 134d), **LCD** (240), **LED** (240), **led** (46c, 89c), **lid** (123a), **LSD** (240), **LTD** (240), **Lud** (108a)

**_ L D**   **eld** (12c, 73a, 83d, 122b), **old** (10d, 12c, 60c, 94c, 127d)

**L E _**   **Lea** (21c, 165), **lea** (45d, 75b, 87a, 134b), **Leb.** (240), **LED** (240), **led** (46c, 89c), **Lee** (27c, 165), **lee** (108a), **leg** (31b, 72a, 106b, 124b), **lei** (52d, 58c), **lek** (31c, 36c, 213), **LEM** (78c, 127c, 240), **Len** (166), **Leo** (76c, 91b, 135c, 166, 207), **leo** (72b), **Ler** (22b, 199), **Les** (166), **les** (50a), **let** (11c, 60b, 87d, 99c, 104a, 117a, 120c), **leu** (221), **Lev.** (240), **lev** (214), **lev-** (93b), **Lew** (166), **lex** (70b)

**L _ E**   **Lae** (221), **Lee** (27c, 165), **lee** (108a), **lge.** (240), **lie** (44a, 55a, 98b, 99d, 119b, 119d), **lye** (11b)

**_ L E**   **ale** (18a, 72b, 95d), **ile** (50c), **ile-** (93b), **Ole** (173), **ole** (22c, 26b, 112c), **ule** (21c, 25a, 102c), **-ule** (117b)

**_ L F**   **Alf** (120b, 137), **elf** (44a, 114a)

**L G _**   **lge.** (240)

278

| | |
|---|---|
| L _ G | **lag** (34c, 115a), **leg** (31b, 72a, 106b, 124b), **log** (52a, 98c, 246), **log.** (240), **lug** (24c, 37c, 39a, 57d, 103b) |
| _ L G | **Alg.** (235), **alg.** (31b) |
| L I _ | **Lib.** (240), **lib** (49b), **lid** (123a), **lie** (44a, 55a, 98b, 99d, 119b, 119d), **Li'l** (9a), **Lin** (134d), **lip** (39c, 47b, 62c, 100d), **lip-** (92d), **lis** (49a, 50c), **lit** (62a, 68d), **lit.** (31b), **Liv** (166), **Liz** (166) |
| L _ I | **Lai** (69a, 220), **lai** (119b), **lei** (52d, 58c), **loi** (50c) |
| _ L I | **Ali** (23b, 44d, 72b, 77c, 80c, 125b, 138), **CLI** (237), **Eli** (104a, 134a, 151, 197) |
| L _ K | **lek** (31c, 36c, 213) |
| _ L K | **elk** (21c, 70d, 129d, 230), **ilk** (27d, 67c, 105a, 113b) |
| L _ L | **Li'l** (9a) |
| _ L L | **all** (10d, 29c, 123b, 127c), **ell** (12c, 22c, 28b, 246), **I'll** (30c), **Ill.** (210, 239), **ill** (91b, 126b, 126c) |
| L _ M | **Lam.** (240), **lam** (11d, 47c), **LCM** (240), **LEM** (78c, 127c, 240), **Lom** (167) |
| _ L M | **elm** (124a), **Ulm** (33c, 216) |
| L _ N | **lan** (31b, 118c), **Len** (166), **Lin** (134d), **Lon** (167), **lon.** (240), **LPN** (240) |
| L O _ | **Loa** (57b), **loa** (10c, 43c, 133d), **lob** (77a, 120c, 121d), **loc.** (240), **log** (52a, 98c, 246), **log.** (240), **loi** (50c), **Lom** (167), **Lon** (167), **lon.** (240), **loo** (24a), **lop** (27a, 33a, 108d), **loq** (70a), **loq.** (240), **los** (112c), **Lot** (9b, 58a, 197), **lot** (11c, 14c, 25d, 44d, 86c, 90b, 107c, 123c, 246), **Lou** (167), **low** (12d, 17b, 35a, 54c, 62a), **lox** (52a, 103d), **Loy** (167), **loy** (112c, 123a) |
| L _ O | **Lao** (62d, 69a, 218), **Leo** (76c, 91b, 135c, 166, 207), **leo** (72b), **loo** (24a), **Luo** (218) |
| _ L O | **DLO** (237), **Flo** (12c), **ILO** (239), **PLO** (242) |
| L P _ | **LPN** (240) |
| L _ P | **lap** (26c, 27b, 31b, 97b, 100d, 113d, 123c), **lip** (39c, 47b, 62c, 100d), **lip-** (92d), **lop** (27a, 33a, 108d) |
| _ L P | **alp** (79b, 87b) |
| L _ Q | **loq** (70a), **loq.** (240) |
| L _ R | **lar** (54b, 74b), **Ler** (22b, 199) |
| _ L R | **SLR** (243) |

279

**L S _**     **LSD** (240)

**L _ S**     **las** (50a, 112c), **lbs.** (240), **LDS** (240), **Les** (166), **les** (50a), **lis** (49a, 50c), **los** (112c), **lys** (71d), **lys-** (93a)

**_ L S**     **ALS** (235), **als** (54a), **BLS** (236), **Els** (151), **els** (73a), **ils** (49d, 51a)

**L T _**     **Ltd.** (240)

**L _ T**     **Lat.** (240), **lat** (29a), **let** (11c, 60b, 87d, 99c, 104a, 117a, 120c), **lit** (62a, 68d), **lit.** (31b), **Lot** (9b, 58a, 197), **lot** (11c, 14c, 25d, 44d, 86c, 90b, 107c, 123c, 246), **Lut** (35a)

**_ L T**     **alt** (54a), **blt** (236), **Olt** (33c)

**L U _**     **Lud** (108a), **lug** (24c, 37c, 39a, 57d, 103b), **Luo** (218), **Lut** (35a), **Lux** (240), **lux** (62a, 246)

**L _ U**     **leu** (221), **Lou** (167)

**_ L U**     **Clu** (146), **flu** (62a), **Ulu** (184), **ulu** (63d, 68a)

**L _ V**     **lav.** (240), **Lev.** (240), **lev** (214), **lev-** (93b), **Liv** (166), **LWV** (240)

**L W _**     **LWV** (240)

**L _ W**     **law** (23d, 28d, 33a, 39c, 67c, 71a, 84c, 92b, 102d, 115a), **Lew** (166), **low** (12d, 17b, 35a, 54c, 62a)

**L _ X**     **lax** (39b, 73a, 81b, 99c, 111c), **lex** (70b), **lox** (52a, 103d), **Lux** (240), **lux** (62a, 246)

**L Y _**     **lye** (11b), **lys** (71d), **lys-** (93a)

**L _ Y**     **lay** (16c, 75c, 82a, 96c, 106b, 111d), **Loy** (167), **loy** (112c, 123a)

**_ L Y**     **Bly** (142), **Ely** (25a), **fly** (47c, 63b, 120c, 229), **ply** (48a, 70c, 121a, 131d, 133c), **Sly** (181), **sly** (14d, 31d, 32c, 52c, 63b, 101c, 110c, 132a)

**L _ Z**     **laz** (25a), **Liz** (166)

**M A _**     **maa** (107d), **Mab** (44a, 96c), **Mac** (167), **mac** (45b, 74c, 105b, 111d), **mad** (12d, 63b, 109c), **Mae** (167), **mag** (57c), **mag.** (240), **mai** (49d), **Maj.** (240), **Mal.** (240), **mal** (42b, 50b, 112d), **mal-** (92c), **Man** (64b, 168, 224), **man** (49a, 52c, 74c, 231), **Mao** (26d), **map** (24c, 26b), **Mar.** (78c, 240), **mar** (36b, 62a, 63a, 105c), **mas** (112c), **mat** (47d, 88d, 119c), **maw** (31d, 32a, 56d, 84b, 91b, 115c), **Max** (169), **Max.** (240), **max** (78d), **May** (24a, 169), **may** (58c, 76d)

**M _ A**     **maa** (107d), **MBA** (240), **MIA** (240), **Mia** (170), **mia** (113a), **mna** (246), **moa** (19b, 226)

**_ M A**     **AMA** (235), **ama** (23d, 25d, 27b, 29b, 32b, 132c), **-oma** (117c), **sma** (105b), **Uma** (184), **Yma** (187)

**M B _**     **MBA** (240)

**M _ B**     **Mab** (44a, 96c), **mib** (11c, 74d), **mob** (97a, 121c, 232)

**_ M B**     **amb.** (235), **emb.** (238)

**M C _**     **MCP** (240)

**M _ C**     **Mac** (167), **mac** (45b, 74c, 105b, 111d), **Mic.** (240)

**_ M C**     **AMC** (26a)

**M D _**     **MDs** (88d), **MDT** (240)

**M _ D**     **mad** (12d, 63b, 109c), **Med.** (240), **Mfd.** (240), **mid** (12b, 25c, 57c), **mod** (30b), **mod.** (240), **mud** (39a, 99c, 104c, 110b, 246)

**M E _**     **Med.** (240), **Meg** (11a, 170), **meg-** (93b), **Mel** (170), **mel** (60d), **mem** (12a), **Men** (88d), **men** (87d, 124c), **Meo** (218, 224), **mer** (51a), **mes** (49d), **Met.** (240), **met** (40d, 97d, 107a), **met-** (92d), **mew** (19a, 25a, 45a, 56d, 58c, 105d, 106a, 226), **Mex.** (240)

**M _ E**     **Mae** (167), **Mme.** (240), **Moe** (121c, 171)

**_ M E**     **ame** (51a), **eme** (105c), **Mme.** (240), **ume** (13d, 65b)

**M F _**     **Mfd.** (240), **Mfg.** (240), **Mfr.** (240)

**_ M F**     **IMF** (239)

**M _ G**     **mag** (57c), **mag.** (240), **Meg** (11a, 170), **meg-** (93b), **Mfg.** (240), **mig** (11c, 74d, 89d), **mpg** (241), **mug** (38a, 52c, 128a)

**M H _**     **mho** (40a, 246)

**M _ H**     **mph** (241)

**M I _**     **MIA** (240), **Mia** (170), **mia** (113a), **mib** (11c, 74d), **Mic.** (240), **mid** (12b, 25c, 57c), **mig** (11c, 74d, 89d), **mil** (62c, 121b, 132d, 246), **mil.** (240), **mim** (11d), **Min** (215), **min.** (240), **mio** (113a), **mir** (103a), **mis-** (92c, 94a), **mit** (54a), **Mix** (171), **mix** (11c, 76a, 115c)

**M _ I**     **mai** (49d), **moi** (50d)

**_ M I**     **ami** (50b), **BMI** (236), **EMI** (238), **NMI** (241)

**M _ J**     **Maj.** (240)

**M _ L**     **Mal.** (240), **mal** (42b, 50b, 112d), **mal-** (92c), **Mel** (170), **mel** (60d), **mil** (62c, 121b, 132d, 246), **mil.** (240)

| M M _ | **Mme.** (240) |
|---|---|
| M _ M | **mem** (12a), **mim** (11d), **mom** (44b), **mum** (27a, 74a) |
| M N _ | **mna** (246) |
| M _ N | **Man** (64b, 168, 224), **man** (49a, 52c, 74c, 231), **Men** (88d), **men** (87d, 124c), **Min** (215), **min.** (240), **Mon.** (240), **mon** (16b) |
| M O _ | **moa** (19b, 226), **mob** (97a, 121c, 232), **mod** (30b), **mod.** (240), **Moe** (121c, 171), **moi** (50d), **mom** (44b), **Mon.** (240), **mon** (16b), **moo** (12d, 73c), **mop** (118b), **mot** (99c, 133a), **mou** (246), **mow** (28a, 33a) |
| M _ O | **Mao** (26d), **Meo** (218, 224), **mho** (40a, 246), **mio** (113a), **moo** (12d, 73c) |
| _ M O | **amo** (69d), **HMO** (239) |
| M P _ | **mpg** (241), **mph** (241) |
| M _ P | **map** (24c, 26b), **MCP** (240), **mop** (118b), **MVP** (241) |
| _ M P | **amp.** (40a, 235), **emp.** (238), **imp** (34d, 97d, 101c, 126d), **imp.** (239) |
| M R _ | **Mrs.** (122c, 241), **Mru** (69a) |
| M _ R | **Mar.** (78c, 240), **mar** (36b, 62a, 63a, 105c), **mer** (51a), **Mfr.** (240), **mir** (103a), **mur** (51b) |
| M S _ | **mss.** (241), **MST** (241) |
| M _ S | **mas** (112d), **MDs** (88d), **mes** (49d), **mis-** (92c, 94a), **Mrs.** (122c, 241), **mss.** (241), **Mts.** (241), **mus.** (241) |
| _ M S | **Ems** (95c, 112c), **HMS** (239), **PMS** (242), **rms.** (242) |
| M T _ | **Mts.** (241), **MTV** (26a) |
| M _ T | **mat** (47d, 88d, 119c), **MDT** (240), **Met.** (240), **met** (40d, 97d, 107a), **met-** (92d), **mit** (54a), **mot** (99c, 133a), **MST** (241), **Mut** (12b, 97a) |
| _ M T | **amt** (31b), **amt.** (235), **GMT** (239) |
| M U _ | **mud** (39a, 99c, 104c, 110b, 246), **mug** (38a, 52c, 128a), **mum** (27a, 74a), **mur** (51b), **mus.** (241), **Mut** (12b, 97a), **muy** (113a) |
| M _ U | **mou** (246), **Mru** (69a) |
| _ M U | **Amu** (33d), **emu** (19b, 85a, 225), **SMU** (33a) |
| M V _ | **MVP** (241) |
| M _ V | **MTV** (26a) |

| _ M V | DMV (237) |
|---|---|

**M _ W**  maw (31d, 32a, 56d, 84b, 91b, 115c), **mew** (19a, 25a, 45a, 56d, 58c, 105d, 106a, 226), **mow** (28a, 33a)

**_ M W**  J.M.W. (159), UMW (243)

**M _ X**  Max (169), Max. (240), max (78d), Mex. (240), Mix (171), mix (11c, 76a, 115c), **myx-** (93b)

**_ M X**  BMX (236)

**M Y _**  myx- (93b)

**M _ Y**  May (24a, 169), may (58c, 76d), muy (113a)

**_ M Y**  Amy (11a, 73c, 138)

**_ M Z**  DMZ (237)

**N A _**  nab (14c, 24a, 24d, 106c), nae (105b), nag (21b, 58a, 61a, 133d), Nah. (241), Nan (20c), nap (89a, 109a, 110b), NAS (241), nas- (93b), Nat (172), nav. (241), nay (22d, 34d, 81b, 129c)

**N _ A**  NBA (241), NDA (241), NEA (241), NRA (20b, 241), NSA (241)

**_ N A**  ana (12c, 29a, 72c), -ana (117c), DNA (53b, 98b, 237), Ena (11b, 96c), Ina (159), -ina (117b), mna (246), RNA (53b, 242), sna (105b), Una (43d, 113c, 184)

**N B _**  NBA (241), NBC (26a, 241), NbE (29c), NBS (241), NbW (29c)

**N _ B**  nab (14c, 24a, 24d, 106c), Neb. (241), neb (17d, 18d, 19b, 87d), nib (17d, 19b, 87d), nob (32a, 58c, 65b), nub (54c, 73c, 74b, 89c, 95c)

**N C _**  NCO (241)

**N _ C**  NBC (26a, 241), NRC (241), NSC (241), NYC (18d, 241)

**_ N C**  anc. (235), DNC (237), enc. (238), Inc. (239), RNC (242)

**N D _**  NDA (241)

**N _ D**  Ned (172), Nod (23a, 39b), nod (38b, 110b)

**_ N D**  and (30a, 90c), end (10d, 32c, 54d, 90c, 96c, 99c, 115d, 122b), end- (94a), Ind. (91a, 210, 239), und (53c)

**N E _**  NEA (241), Neb. (241), neb (17d, 18d, 19b, 87d), Ned (172), nee (19b, 21a, 74b), nef (28b, 108b), neg. (241), Neh. (241), neo (77c), neo- (93b), nep (28c, 45d, 68c, 133c), Ner (104c), net (24a, 27d, 41a, 43b, 76a, 94d, 106b, 111b, 120c), neu (54a), Nev. (211, 241), new (13a, 43c, 51b, 84d, 98b), Ney (49d, 80d, 172), nez (50d)

283

| N _ E | **nae** (105b), **NbE** (29c), **nee** (19b, 21a, 74b), **nie** (54a), **NNE** (29c), **nue** (50a) |
|---|---|
| _ N E | **ane** (50b), **ENE** (29c), **Ine** (12c), **-ine** (117a, 117b), **NNE** (29c), **one** (61d, 62d, 95a, 109d, 126c), **une** (49d, 50a, 50d) |
| N F _ | **NFL** (241) |
| N _ F | **nef** (28b, 108b), **NSF** (241) |
| N _ G | **nag** (21b, 58a, 61a, 133d), **neg.** (241), **nig** (28d), **nog** (11b, 20a, 37d, 39d, 77a, 87c, 89b) |
| _ N G | **Ang.** (235), **Eng** (109a), **Eng.** (238), **Ing** (12c), **ing** (73c, 87a), **-ing** (86d, 117c) |
| N H _ | **NHI** (241), **NHL** (241), **NHS** (241) |
| N _ H | **Nah.** (241), **Neh.** (241), **nth** (34c) |
| N I _ | **nib** (17d, 19b, 87d), **nie** (54a), **nig** (28d), **-nik** (117c), **nil** (82c), **Nin** (172), **nin** (246), **nip** (19c, 38a, 62a, 89b), **Nis** (30b), **NIT** (241), **nit** (39d, 246), **niu** (246), **nix** (82c, 130b) |
| N _ I | **NHI** (241), **NMI** (241) |
| _ N I | **ani** (19b, 19d, 32c), **ONI** (241), **uni-** (93c) |
| N _ K | **-nik** (117c) |
| _ N K | **ink** (33c, 94b, 109b) |
| N _ L | **NFL** (241), **NHL** (241), **nil** (82c) |
| _ N L | **enl.** (238) |
| N M _ | **NMI** (241) |
| N _ M | **nom** (50d), **Num.** (241), **Nym** (44a, 194) |
| N N _ | **NNE** (29c), **NNW** (29c) |
| N _ N | **Nan** (20c), **Nin** (172), **nin** (246), **non** (50d, 70a), **non-** (93b), **Nun** (197), **nun** (11d, 12a, 22c, 89a, 99b, 109d) |
| _ N N | **Ann** (138), **CNN** (26a), **Inn** (33c), **inn** (56d, 61c, 101a, 120a) |
| N O _ | **nob** (32a, 58c, 65b), **Nod** (23a, 39b), **nod** (38b, 110b), **nog** (11b, 20a, 37d, 39d, 77a, 87c, 89b), **nom** (50d), **non** (50d, 70a), **non-** (93b), **Nor.** (241), **nor** (12c, 30a, 31a), **nos** (70b), **nos-** (92d), **nos.** (241), **not** (81b), **Nov.** (78c, 241), **NOW** (241), **now** (49a, 62a, 94a) |
| N _ O | **NCO** (241), **neo** (77c), **neo-** (93b) |

**_ N O**      CNO (237), Eno (151), Ino (15b, 23a), Ono (173), ono (241), SNO (243), uno (65c, 112c)

**N P _**      NPR (241)

**N _ P**      nap (89a, 109a, 110b), nep (28c, 45d, 68c, 133c), nip (19c, 38a, 62a, 89b)

**_ N P**      GNP (239)

**N R _**      NRA (20b, 241), NRC (241)

**N _ R**      Ner (104c), Nor. (241), nor (12c, 30a, 31a), NPR (241)

**N S _**      NSA (241), NSC (241), NSF (241), NSW (241)

**N _ S**      NAS (241), nas- (93b), NBS (241), NHS (241), Nis (30b), nos (70b), nos- (92d), nos. (241)

**_ N S**      CNS (237), ens (18b), ens. (238), HNS (239), INS (239), ins (83c), ons (32a, 118d, 246), uns (54a)

**N T _**      nth (34c)

**N _ T**      Nat (172), net (24a, 27d, 41a, 43b, 76a, 94d, 106b, 111b, 120c), NIT (241), nit (39d, 246), not (81b), Nut (198), nut (22c, 28c, 31d, 44c, 51d, 67b, 121b), NWT (241)

**_ N T**      Ant (139), ant (40c, 49a, 63b, 89c, 229), ent- (94a), -ent (117a, 117b), int. (239), Ont. (241), on't (107c), TNT (26a, 43a, 243)

**N U _**      nub (54c, 73c, 74b, 89c, 95c), nue (50a), Num. (241), Nun (197), nun (11d, 12a, 22c, 89a, 99b, 109d), Nut (198), nut (22c, 28c, 31d, 44c, 51d, 67b, 121b)

**N _ U**      neu (54a), niu (246)

**_ N U**      anu (59c, 125a), gnu (13a, 132a, 230)

**N _ V**      nav. (241), Nev. (211, 241), Nov. (78c, 241)

**N W _**      NWT (241)

**N _ W**      NbW (29c), new (13a, 43c, 51b, 84d, 98b), NNW (29c), NOW (241), now (49a, 62a, 94a), NSW (241)

**_ N W**      NNW (29c), WNW (29c)

**N _ X**      nix (82c, 130b), Nyx (56b, 198)

**N Y _**      NYC (18d, 241), Nym (44a, 194), Nyx (56b, 198)

**N _ Y**      nay (22d, 34d, 81b, 129c), Ney (49d, 80d, 172)

**_ N Y**      any (111d), sny (18c, 32d, 90a, 108b, 122a)

285

**N _ Z**    nez (50d)

**O A _**    oaf (21a, 37b, 38c, 109c, 116d, 134d), oak (58a, 124a), oar (95b, 102c), OAS (241), oat (16a, 25c, 55c), OAU (241)

**O _ A**    OCA (241), oca (39c, 125a, 133c), oda (58a), oka (125a, 133c, 246), -oma (117c), ora (65c, 78a, 95a), ora- (93c), ova (39d), oxa- (93c)

**_ O A**    boa (30b, 45a, 81b, 96c, 104c, 106d, 111a, 232), DOA (237), Goa (91d), goa (53b), ioa (51c), Loa (57b), loa (10c, 43c, 133d), moa (19b, 226), poa (20b, 55d), toa (18a), VOA (244), zoa (39d)

**O B _**    OBE (241), obe (68b), obi (45c, 54c, 65d, 104b), obj. (241), obo (106c, 241), obs. (241)

**O _ B**    OOB (241), orb (43c, 54d, 113c), OTB (52b, 241)

**_ O B**    Bob (142), bob (47a, 79c, 87c), cob (25c, 61a, 74c, 118b), fob (48a, 130a), gob (75b, 103b), hob (33c, 46b, 95a, 123a), Job (196), job (27a, 119d, 133c), kob (13a, 130b), lob (77a, 120c, 121d), mob (97a, 121c, 232), nob (32a, 58c, 65b), OOB (241), Rob (177), rob (36c, 37a, 90c, 115a), sob (32b, 131a), tob (10c)

**O C _**    OCA (241),oca (39c, 125a, 133c), och (11a, 42c), ock (246), -ock (117b), OCS (241), Oct. (78c, 241), oct- (92d)

**O _ C**    orc (25d, 55d, 131b), OTC (241)

**_ O C**    Doc (88d, 107a, 149), doc. (237), hoc (70a), IOC (240), loc. (240), ROC (242), Roc (19b, 109c), soc (67c), soc. (243)

**O D _**    oda (58a), odd (116a, 126c, 126d), ode (61d, 89b, 90c)

**O _ D**    odd (116a, 126c, 126d), OED (241), -oid (117b), ok'd (13d), old (10d, 12c, 60c, 94c, 127d), Ord (23b, 49a), oud (80b)

**_ O D**    COD (237), Cod (24a), cod (46d, 228), DOD (237), dod (27d), fod (246), God (66b), god (34c, 133d), hod (21d, 28c, 78d, 105c), iod- (93b), mod (30b), mod. (240), Nod (23a, 39b), nod (38b, 110b), pod (61c, 71b, 105d, 131b, 232), Rod (178), rod (17a, 57c, 68d, 100b, 107b, 114b, 115b, 246), sod (118b, 125a), Tod (183), tod (22d, 105a, 246), Vod (16d), yod (12a)

**O E _**    OED (241), OEO (241), o'er (30b, 107c)

**O _ E**    OBE (241), obe (68b), ode (61d, 89b, 90c), oke (246), Ole (173), ole (22c, 26b, 112c), one (61d, 62d, 95a, 109d, 126c), ope (126a), Ore. (211, 241), ore (32b, 35a, 76b, 77a, 82b, 87b, 118c, 215, 220, 222), -ose (117a, 117b), owe (34a)

**_ O E**    Coe (146, 201), coe (107d), DOE (237), doe (34b, 97a), EOE (238), FOE (238), foe (84c), hoe (32c, 52d), Joe (161), joe (45a), Moe

(121c, 171), **Poe** (98a, 125b, 175), **poe** (86d), **roe** (25b, 34b, 34c, 39d, 47a, 60a), **toe** (55b, 110b, 115b), **voe** (63a), **woe** (23a, 56c, 112a), **Zoe** (188)

O F _    **off** (9b, 59b, 79d, 134c), **off.** (241), **oft'** (30b)

O _ F    **oaf** (21a, 37b, 38c, 109c, 116d, 134d), **off** (9b, 59b, 79d, 134c), **off.** (241), **orf** (134b)

O _ G    **org.** (241)

_ O G    **bog** (39a, 75a, 118b), **cog** (53b, 120c, 123a), **dog** (12c, 23d, 32d, 48b, 230), **fog** (28b, 116b, 130d), **Gog** (74a, 197), **hog** (88d, 118d, 230), **jog** (66d, 82d, 124d), **log** (52a, 98c, 246), **log.** (240), **nog** (11b, 20a, 37d, 39d, 77a, 87c, 89b), **tog** (28b)

O H _    **ohm** (40a, 53d, 246), **o-ho** (42c), **ohs** (42c)

O _ H    **och** (11a, 42c)

O I _    **-oid** (117b), **oil** (13a, 52a, 56a)

O _ I    **obi** (45c, 54c, 65d, 104b), **ONI** (241), **oui** (51b), **ovi-** (92d)

_ O I    **hoi** (42c), **koi** (24b, 46d), **loi** (50c), **moi** (50d), **poi** (36b, 58b, 88c, 119d, 121a), **roi** (50c), **toi** (49d, 51b)

O _ J    **obj.** (241)

O K _    **oka** (125a, 133c, 246), **ok'd** (13d), **oke** (246), **ok's** (13d)

O _ K    **oak** (58a, 124a), **ock** (246), **-ock** (117b), **Ork.** (241)

_ O K    **ROK** (68c, 242), **wok** (86a, 128a)

O L _    **old** (10d, 12c, 60c, 94c, 127d), **Ole** (173), **ole** (22c, 26b, 112c), **Olt** (33c)

O _ L    **oil** (13a, 52a, 56a), **owl** (19a, 226)

_ O L    **Bol.** (236), **col** (79b, 87a), **dol.** (238), **Kol** (18c), **Pol.** (242), **pol** (91a), **Sol** (88c, 199), **sol** (117d, 221), **vol.** (244), **wol** (132d)

O M _    **-oma** (117c)

O _ M    **ohm** (40a, 53d, 246)

_ O M    **com-** (94a), **Dom** (79a, 149), **dom** (91d, 122c), **dom.** (238), **I.O.M.** (240), **Lom** (167), **mom** (44b), **nom** (50d), **ROM** (29c, 242), **Rom** (57c), **Tom** (116a, 184), **tom** (74c), **yom** (33d, 67d)

O N _    **one** (61d, 62d, 95a, 109d, 126c), **ONI** (241), **Ono** (173), **ono** (241), **ons** (32a, 118d, 246), **Ont.** (241), **on't** (107c)

O _ N    **own** (9d, 29d)

287

**_ O N**     **bon** (45a, 50b, 65d, 67b), **con** (10c, 26b, 65c, 116c, 118d), **Don** (101a, 149), **don** (50b, 130d), **eon** (10d, 41d, 122b), **Fon** (214), **gon-** (93c), **Hon.** (239), **hon** (40d), **Ion** (13b, 26a, 40a, 86d), **Jon** (163), **kon** (246), **Lon** (167), **lon.** (240), **Mon.** (240), **mon** (16b), **non** (50d, 70a), **non-** (93b), **Ron** (67d, 178), **son** (59a, 74c), **ton** (131a, 246), **von** (53d), **won** (46c, 128b, 218), **yon** (36d, 85c)

**O O _**     **OOB** (241), **oot** (105b)

**O _ O**     **obo** (106c, 241), **OEO** (241), **o-ho** (42c), **Ono** (173), **ono** (241), **oro** (112d), **oro-** (93b), **oto-** (92c), **ovo-** (92d)

**_ O O**     **boo** (36a, 115a), **coo** (19c), **goo** (79c, 115b), **loo** (24a), **moo** (12d, 73c), **Soo** (181), **soo** (97d), **too** (12c, 18c, 62c, 78c), **woo** (31b), **zoo** (132a), **zoo-** (92c)

**O P _**     **ope** (126a), **opp.** (241), **Ops** (25c, 58b, 104b, 198), **opt** (27a), **-opy** (117c)

**O _ P**     **opp.** (241)

**_ O P**     **bop** (60b, 66b, 116b), **cop** (90d, 97a, 115a), **dop** (32d), **fop** (31c, 33c, 38c, 44b), **GOP** (91a, 99d, 239), **hop** (33b, 67a), **kop** (59d), **lop** (27a, 33a, 108d), **mop** (118b), **pop** (38a, 42d, 44b, 44d, 99d), **pop.** (242), **SOP** (243), **sop** (9b, 21d, 29d, 111b), **top** (31d, 42b, 59d, 85c, 89b, 117d, 118a, 118b, 127c)

**_ O Q**     **coq** (50a), **loq** (70a), **loq.** (240)

**O R _**     **ora** (65c, 78a, 95a), **ora-** (93c), **orb** (43c, 54d, 113c), **orc** (25d, 55d, 131b), **Ord** (23b, 49a), **Ore.** (211, 241), **ore** (32b, 35a, 76b, 77a, 82b, 87b, 118c, 215, 220, 222), **orf** (134b), **org.** (241), **Ork.** (241), **oro** (112d), **oro-** (93b), **Orr** (173), **ors** (12a), **ort** (48b, 71a), **-ory** (117a, 117b)

**O _ R**     **oar** (95b, 102c), **o'er** (30b, 107c), **Orr** (173), **our** (95a)

**_ O R**     **Bor** (91a), **bor.** (236), **Cor.** (237), **cor** (246), **dor** (18b, 38a, 38d, 63b, 67a), **for** (94d), **hor.** (239), **-ior** (40d, 117a), **Kor** (60d), **Nor.** (241), **nor** (12c, 30a, 31a), **por** (112d), **Tor** (102c), **tor** (31d, 67c, 87b, 95a, 101b)

**O S _**     **-ose** (117a, 117b), **OSS** (241)

**O _ S**     **OAS** (241), **obs.** (241), **OCS** (241), **ohs** (42c), **ok's** (13d), **ons** (32a, 118d, 246), **Ops** (25c, 58b, 104b, 198), **ors** (12a), **OSS** (241), **-ous** (117a), **ozs.** (242)

**_ O S**     **cos** (71c, 101d), **cos.** (237), **DOS** (238), **dos** (50a, 131d), **Eos** (15d, 33d, 198), **eos** (86d), **Hos.** (239), **ho's** (70b), **Jos.** (74d), **Kos** (60b, 64c), **los** (112c), **nos** (70b), **nos-** (92d), **nos.** (241), **SOS** (36d, 243)

**O T _**     **OTB** (52b, 241), **OTC** (241), **oto-** (92d), **Ott** (173)

**O _ T**  oat (16a, 25c, 55c), Oct. (78c, 241), oct- (92d), oft' (30b), Olt (33c), Ont. (241), on't (107c), oot (105b), opt (27a), ort (48b, 71a), Ott (173), out (9b, 49a, 55b, 82c)

**_ O T**  bot (69b), bot. (236), cot (18a, 99a, 110c), DOT (238), dot (59d, 80c, 87d, 113b, 120b), fot (246), got (23b, 83b), hot (12d, 117d), jot (64a, 86d, 122c, 131c), Lot (9b, 58a, 197), lot (11c, 14c, 25d, 44d, 86c, 90b, 107c, 123c, 246), mot (99c, 133a), not (81b), oot (105b), pot (90d, 128a, 246), rot (21a, 34a, 45c, 107d, 113d), sot (38b, 123a, 123b), tot (26c, 134d)

**O U _**  oud (80b), oui (51b), our (95a), -ous (117a), out (9b, 49a, 55b, 82c)

**O _ U**  OAU (241)

**_ O U**  fou (246), IOU (95a, 240), Lou (167), mou (246), sou (49c), tou (246), you (95a)

**O V _**  ova (39d), ovi- (92d), ovo- (92d)

**_ O V**  HOV (239), Nov. (78c, 241), Sov. (243)

**O W _**  owe (34a), owl (19a, 226), own (9d, 29d)

**_ O W**  Bow (142), bow (20c, 32d, 48d, 68c, 82a, 83a, 95c, 108b, 116d), cow (21b, 63d, 121c, 230), Dow (66d, 150), how (74c, 76b, 96c), I.O.W. (240), low (12d, 17b, 35a, 54c, 62a), mow (28a, 33a), NOW (241), now (49a, 62a, 94a), POW (242), row (14b, 46a, 72a, 83a, 96b, 97d, 122a), sow (88d, 90a, 118d), tow (37c, 59b, 95d), vow (90b, 111c), wow (42c), yow (42c)

**O X _**  oxa- (93c), oxy- (93c)

**_ O X**  box (30b, 98b, 113a), Cox (147), cox (102c), Fox (153, 189), fox (23a, 23d, 54c, 102b, 230), lox (52a, 103d), pox (36a, 118d), sox (17c, 98c), vox (70b)

**O _ Y**  -opy (117c), -ory (117a, 117b), oxy- (93c)

**_ O Y**  boy (74c, 116c), coy (17c, 109a), Foy (153), goy (82a), Hoy (64d), hoy (17b, 20b), joy (34c), Loy (167), loy (112c, 123a), Roy (178), soy (17d, 104b), toy (82c, 124c)

**O Z _**  ozs. (242)

**_ O Z**  Boz (35c, 87c, 142), doz. (238), Roz (179)

**P A _**  Pac. (242), pac (57b, 73c), pad (32d, 47d, 48b, 116c, 119a, 123d), pah (42c), Pak. (242), PAL (242), pal (29b, 32a, 45b), Pam (173), pam (68a), Pan (45d, 55a, 59c, 133b, 198), Pan. (242), pan (18d, 79c, 128a), pap (48b), Pär (173), Par. (242) par (16a, 41b, 41d, 55b, 82a, 103a, 114d), pas (33b, 115b), PAT (242), Pat (174), pat (88b, 119c, 123b), Pau (39c, 59b, 100a, 216), paw (48b, 57d), pax (70a), pay (29c, 36a, 98b, 99c, 103d, 129b), Paz (174)

**P _ A**  **PBA** (242), **pea** (28c, 71b, 106b, 127c), **PGA** (242), **Pia** (175), **pia** (14d, 39b), **poa** (20b, 55d), **Psa.** (242), **PTA** (104d, 242), **pua** (59b), **pya** (220)

**_ P A**  **Apa** (12b), **apa** (21c), **CPA** (237), **EPA** (238), **GPA** (239), **IPA** (240), **spa** (58d, 77a, 100a, 114a, 127a), **WPA** (244)

**P B _**  **PBA** (242), **PBK** (242), **PBS** (26a, 242)

**P _ B**  **pub** (120a)

**_ P B**  **APB** (235), **CPB** (237)

**P C _**  **pct.** (242)

**P _ C**  **Pac.** (242), **pac** (57b, 73c), **pfc** (242), **pic.** (242)

**_ P C**  **UPC** (243)

**P D _**  **PDT** (242)

**P _ D**  **pad** (32d, 47d, 48b, 116c, 119a, 123d), **ped-** (92d, 93a), **Ph.D.** (242), **pod** (61c, 71b, 105d, 131b, 232), **ppd.** (242), **pud** (57d, 87b)

**_ P D**  **ppd.** (242)

**P E _**  **pea** (28c, 71b, 106b, 127c), **ped-** (92d, 93a), **peg** (32a, 38a, 44c, 89b), **P.E.I.** (242), **Pei** (174), **pen** (30a, 40d, 62d, 97a, 118b, 134c), **Pep** (174), **pep** (40d, 128b), **Per.** (242), **per** (128b), **pes** (48c), **pet** (24b, 31a, 44d, 48b), **peu** (50c), **pew** (18c, 27a, 47a, 106a)

**P _ E**  **Pie** (175), **pie** (35b, 125c), **Poe** (98a, 125b, 175), **poe** (86d), **pre** (18b), **pre-** (92c)

**_ P E**  **ape** (30d, 62a, 77b, 78b, 109c, 231), **ope** (126a)

**P F _**  **pfc** (242)

**P G _**  **PGA** (242)

**P _ G**  **peg** (32a, 38a, 44c, 89b), **pig** (112b, 118d, 231), **pug** (37a, 77d, 227)

**_ P G**  **mpg** (241), **ZPG** (244)

**P H _**  **Ph.D.** (242), **phi** (11d)

**P _ H**  **pah** (42c)

**_ P H**  **D.Ph.** (238), **Eph.** (238), **kph** (240), **mph** (241)

**P I _**  **Pia** (175), **pia** (14d, 39b), **pic.** (242), **Pie** (175), **pie** (35b, 125c), **pig** (112b, 118d, 231), **pik** (246), **PIN** (242), **pin** (37c, 44c, 110a, 246), **Pip** (35c), **pip** (13c, 92a, 106b, 114a), **pir** (80c), **pit** (42b, 106b, 120d), **piu** (234), **pix** (242)

P _ I     **P.E.I.** (242), **Pei** (174), **phi** (11d), **poi** (36b, 58b, 88c, 119d, 121a), **psi** (11d)

_ P I     **CPI** (237), **epi-** (93c), **UPI** (81c, 132d, 243)

P _ K     **Pak.** (242), **PBK** (242), **pik** (246)

P L _     **PLO** (242), **ply** (48a, 70c, 121a, 131d, 133c)

P _ L     **PAL** (242), **pal** (29b, 32a, 45b), **Pol.** (242), **pol** (91a), **pul** (213)

_ P L     **Cpl.** (237)

P M _     **PMS** (242)

P _ M     **Pam** (173), **pam** (68a)

_ P M     **rpm** (242), **wpm** (244)

P _ N     **Pan** (45d, 55a, 59c, 133b, 198), **Pan.** (242), **pan** (18d, 79c, 128a), **pen** (30a, 40d, 62d, 97a, 118b, 134c), **PIN** (242), **pin** (37c, 44c, 110a, 246), **pun** (90b)

_ P N     **LPN** (240)

P O _     **poa** (20b, 55d), **pod** (61c, 71b, 105d, 131b, 232), **Poe** (98a, 125b, 175), **poe** (86d), **poi** (36b, 58b, 88c, 119d, 121a), **Pol.** (242), **pol** (91a), **pop** (38a, 42d, 44b, 44d, 99d), **pop.** (242), **por** (112d), **pot** (90d, 128a, 246), **POW** (242), **pox** (36a, 118d)

P _ O     **PLO** (242), **pro** (48c, 96d), **pro.** (242), **PTO** (242), **Pwo** (69a)

_ P O     **APO** (235), **Apo** (129a), **CPO** (237), **GPO** (239)

P P _     **ppd.** (242), **PPS** (242)

P _ P     **pap** (48b), **Pep** (174), **pep** (40d, 128b), **Pip** (35c), **pip** (13c, 92a, 106b, 114a), **pop** (38a, 42d, 44b, 44d, 99d), **pop.** (242), **pup** (105d, 134d)

_ P P     **opp.** (241)

P R _     **pre** (18b), **pre-** (92c), **pro** (48c, 96d), **pro.** (242), **pry** (71c, 94d)

P _ R     **Pär** (173), **Par.** (242), **par** (16a, 41b, 41d, 55b, 82a, 103a, 114d), **Per.** (242), **per** (128b), **pir** (80c), **por** (112d), **pyr-** (93a)

_ P R     **APR** (235), **Apr.** (78c), **CPR** (237), **NPR** (241)

P S _     **Psa.** (242), **psi** (11d), **PST** (242)

P _ S     **pas** (33b, 115b), **PBS** (26a, 242), **pes** (48c), **PMS** (242), **PPS** (242), **pus** (63a, 78b)

_ P S     **Ops** (25c, 58b, 104b, 198), **PPS** (242), **UPS** (243), **ups** (21a)

**P T _**    **PTA** (104d, 242), **PTO** (242)

**P _ T**    **PAT** (242), **Pat** (174), **pat** (88b, 119c, 123b), **pct.** (242), **PDT** (242), **pet** (24b, 31a, 44d, 48b), **pit** (42b, 106b, 120d), **pot** (90d, 128a, 246), **PST** (242), **put** (70c), **Pvt.** (242)

**_ P T**    **apt** (13d, 22a, 28a, 36c, 47b, 62c, 71d, 88b, 95a, 117d), **DPT** (238), **opt** (27a)

**P U _**    **pua** (59b), **pub** (120a), **pud** (57d, 87b), **pug** (37a, 77d, 227), **pul** (213), **pun** (90b), **pup** (105d, 134d), **pus** (63a, 78b), **put** (70c)

**P _ U**    **Pau** (39c, 59b, 100a, 216), **peu** (50c), **piu** (234)

**_ P U**    **CPU** (237)

**P V _**    **Pvt.** (242)

**P W _**    **Pwo** (69a)

**P _ W**    **paw** (48b, 57d), **pew** (18c, 27a, 47a, 106a), **POW** (242)

**_ P W**    **DPW** (238)

**P _ X**    **pax** (70a), **pix** (242), **pox** (36a, 118d), **pyx** (27b, 42a)

**P Y _**    **pya** (220), **pyr-** (93a), **pyx** (27b, 42a)

**P _ Y**    **pay** (29c, 36a, 98b, 99c, 103d, 129b), **ply** (48a, 70c, 121a, 131d, 133c), **pry** (71c, 94d)

**_ P Y**    **-opy** (117c), **spy** (36a, 41c, 106a)

**P _ Z**    **Paz** (174)

**Q A _**    **qaf** (11d)

**Q _ A**    **qua** (69c, 109c)

**Q _ D**    **QED** (242)

**Q E _**    **QED** (242), **QEF** (242)

**Q _ F**    **qaf** (11d), **QEF** (242)

**Q U _**    **qua** (69c, 109c)

**R A _**    **Rab** (37b), **rab** (18a, 66c, 78d), **RAC** (242), **rad** (40d, 246), **Rae** (176), **RAF** (242), **rag** (28b, 81c, 102a), **rah** (26b), **rai** (246), **raj** (41a), **RAM** (242), **ram** (17c, 32c, 85b, 92a, 103a, 107d), **ran** (19d, 29c, 84b), **rap** (70d, 83d, 94d, 116b), **ras** (41d, 62d, 122c), **rat** (16d, 35b, 101c, 115d, 119d, 231), **raw** (32b, 81a, 126d), **Ray** (176), **ray** (17d, 46d, 107b, 109d, 228)

**R _ A**    **RCA** (242), **RDA** (242), **REA** (242), **Rea** (176), **ria** (41d, 63a), **RNA** (53b, 242), **RSA** (242)

_ R A    **Ara** (12a, 139, 197, 207), **ara** (73b), **bra** (18d, 126b), **ERA** (238), **era** (10d, 41b, 87d, 122b), **Fra** (153), **fra** (22a, 51c, 78a, 94c), **HRA** (239), **IRA** (64a, 240), **Ira** (159, 197), **kra** (73b), **NRA** (20b, 241), **ora** (65c, 78a, 95a), **ora-** (93c), **Sra.** (243)

R B _    **RBI** (110d, 242)

R _ B    **Rab** (37b), **rab** (18a, 66c, 78d), **reb** (30a), **rib** (31a, 33a, 70b, 75c, 125d), **Rob** (177), **rob** (36c, 37a, 90c, 115a), **rub** (9b, 22d, 25d, 35d, 90d, 130d)

_ R B    **FRB** (238), **orb** (43c, 54d, 113c)

R C _    **RCA** (242), **RCN** (242), **rct.** (242)

R _ C    **RAC** (242), **Ric** (177), **RNC** (242), **ROC** (242), **Roc** (19b, 109c)

_ R C    **ARC** (235), **arc** (27b, 32d, 96b, 106b, 123d), **CRC** (237), **IRC** (240), **NRC** (241), **orc** (25d, 55d, 131b)

R D _    **RDA** (242)

R _ D    **rad** (40d, 246), **Red** (176, 224), **red** (32a, 48a, 102c), **RFD** (242), **rid** (27d, 36b, 40b, 49b), **Rod** (178), **rod** (17a, 57c, 68d, 100b, 107b, 114b, 115b, 246)

_ R D    **Ord** (23b, 49a), **urd** (17d)

R E _    **REA** (242), **Rea** (176), **reb** (30a), **Red** (176, 224), **red** (32a, 48a, 102c), **Ree** (14b, 23a, 189), **ree** (102d), **ref.** (242), **reg.** (242), **reh** (11b, 62d), **rei** (91d), **rel** (40a, 246), **REM** (110c, 242), **rem** (246), **ren-** (93b), **Reo** (24a), **Rep.** (242), **rep** (10d, 43b, 100c), **req.** (242), **res** (70a, 71a), **ret** (47c, 73b, 111b), **ret.** (242), **Rev.** (242), **rev** (41a, 79a), **Rex** (176), **rex** (67c), **Rey** (176), **rey** (112d)

R _ E    **Rae** (176), **Ree** (14b, 23a, 189), **ree** (102d), **RFE** (242), **rhe** (47d, 246), **roe** (25b, 34b, 34c, 39d, 47a, 60a), **rte.** (242), **Rue** (179), **rue** (35a, 59b, 59c, 99a, 133a), **rye** (11a, 25c, 55c, 72b)

_ R E    **are** (68d, 76b, 84a, 246), **'ere** (18b, 30b), **GRE** (239), **Ire.** (240), **ire** (12c, 26d, 52c, 97b, 134a), **Ore.** (211, 241), **ore** (32b, 35a, 76b, 77a, 82b, 87b, 118c, 215, 220, 222), **pre** (18b), **pre-** (92c), **tre** (65c), **Ure** (134d)

R F _    **RFD** (242), **RFE** (242)

R _ F    **RAF** (242), **ref.** (242)

_ R F    **orf** (134b)

R _ G    **rag** (28b, 81c, 102a), **reg.** (242), **rig** (41b, 53b, 85b), **rug** (47d, 57b, 131d)

_ R G    **Arg.** (235), **erg** (40d, 133c, 246), **org.** (241)

| | |
|---|---|
| R H _ | **rhe** (47d, 246), **rho** (11d) |
| R _ H | **rah** (26b), **reh** (11b, 62d) |
| _ R H | **HRH** (239) |
| R I _ | **ria** (41d, 63a), **rib** (31a, 33a, 70d, 75c, 125d), **Ric** (177), **rid** (27d, 36b, 40b, 49b), **rig** (41b, 53b, 85b), **rii** (127d), **rim** (21a, 39c, 74d, 87d, 95a, 122b, 131c), **rin** (106c), **rio** (113a, 246), **RIP** (242), **Rip** (177), **rip** (68b, 99c, 120a), **rit.** (110d, 242) |
| R _ I | **rai** (246), **RBI** (110d, 242), **rei** (91d), **rii** (127d), **roi** (50c) |
| _ R I | **Ari** (139), **Fri.** (238), **sri** (60b), **tri-** (93d), **Uri** (120b, 197) |
| R _ J | **raj** (41a) |
| R _ K | **ROK** (68c, 242) |
| _ R K | **Ark.** (209, 235), **ark** (20b, 128a), **irk** (12d, 87c, 128b), **Ork.** (241) |
| R _ L | **rel** (40a, 246) |
| R M _ | **rms.** (242) |
| R _ M | **RAM** (242), **ram** (17c, 32c, 85b, 92a, 103a, 107d), **REM** (110c, 242), **rem** (246), **rim** (21a, 39c, 74d, 87d, 95a, 122b, 131c), **ROM** (29c, 242), **Rom** (57c), **rpm** (242), **rum** (11a, 72b) |
| _ R M | **arm** (13c, 21c, 49a, 72a, 95a) |
| R N _ | **RNA** (53b, 242), **RNC** (242) |
| R _ N | **ran** (19d, 29c, 84b), **RCN** (242), **ren-** (93b), **rin** (106c), **Ron** (67d, 178), **run** (12d, 20d, 38a, 47c, 47d, 54d, 84b, 110d, 116b, 123c) |
| _ R N | **arn** (11b), **ern** (39a), **urn** (30b, 127b) |
| R O _ | **Rob** (177), **rob** (36c, 37a, 90c, 115a), **ROC** (242), **Roc** (19b, 109c), **Rod** (178), **rod** (17a, 57c, 68d, 100b, 107b, 114b, 115b, 246), **roe** (25b, 34b, 34c, 39d, 47a, 60a), **roi** (50c), **ROK** (68c, 242), **ROM** (29c, 242), **Rom** (57c), **Ron** (67d, 178), **rot** (21a, 34a, 45c, 107d, 113d), **row** (14b, 46a, 72a, 83a, 96b, 97d, 122a), **Roy** (178), **Roz** (179) |
| R _ O | **Reo** (24a), **rho** (11d), **rio** (113a, 246) |
| _ R O | **Aro** (84d), **bro.** (99b, 236), **fro** (16b), **gro.** (239), **oro** (112d), **oro-** (93b), **pro** (48c, 96d), **pro.** (242), **SRO** (120d, 243) |
| R P _ | **rpm** (242) |
| R _ P | **rap** (70d, 83d, 94d, 116b), **Rep.** (242), **rep** (10d, 43b, 100c), **RIP** (242), **Rip** (177), **rip** (68b, 99c, 120a) |

294

_ R P    **Arp** (33a)

R _ Q    **req.** (242)

R _ R    **RUR** (101b)

_ R R    **arr.** (235), **err** (20b, 35c, 109c, 110c, 116b, 123d), **irr.** (240), **J.R.R.** (159), **Orr** (173)

R S _    **RSA** (242), **RSV** (242)

R _ S    **ras** (41d, 62d, 122c), **res** (70a, 71a), **rms.** (242), **rus** (69c)

_ R S    **ars** (69c), **ers** (19c, 59d, 128b), **hrs.** (239), **IRS** (120a, 240), **Mrs.** (122c, 241), **ors** (12a), **yrs.** (244)

R T _    **rte.** (242)

R _ T    **rat** (16d, 35b, 101c, 115d, 119d, 231), **rct.** (242), **ret** (47c, 73b, 111b), **ret.** (242), **rit.** (110d, 242), **rot** (21a, 34a, 45c, 107d, 113d), **rut** (56c, 57a)

_ R T    **Art** (139), **art** (31d, 46a, 94c), **CRT** (237), **ort** (48b, 71a)

R U _    **rub** (9b, 22d, 25d, 35d, 90d, 130d), **Rue** (179), **rue** (35a, 59b, 59c, 99a, 133a), **rug** (47d, 57b, 131d), **rum** (11a, 72b), **run** (12d, 20d, 38a, 47c, 47d, 54d, 84b, 110d, 116b, 123c), **RUR** (101b), **rus** (69c), **rut** (56c, 57a)

_ R U    **Dru** (150), **GRU** (239), **Kru** (215, 218), **Mru** (69a), **Uru.** (243)

R _ V    **Rev.** (242), **rev** (41a, 79a), **RSV** (242)

R W _    **rwy.** (242)

R _ W    **raw** (32b, 81a, 126d), **row** (14b, 46a, 72a, 83a, 96b, 97d, 122a)

R _ X    **Rex** (176), **rex** (67c)

R Y _    **rye** (11a, 25c, 55c, 72b)

R _ Y    **Ray** (176), **ray** (17d, 46d, 107b, 109d, 228), **Rey** (176), **rey** (112d), **Roy** (178), **rwy.** (242)

_ R Y    **-ary** (117a, 117b), **cry** (23b, 94d, 108d, 131a, 134b, 232), **dry** (38c, 121b, 133a), **-ery** (117b), **fry** (30c, 47a), **-ory** (117a, 117b), **pry** (71c, 94d), **try** (12d, 15c, 40d, 41d, 114b, 116c), **wry** (64b, 125c)

R _ Z    **Roz** (179)

S A _    **SAC** (242), **sac** (92a, 128a), **sad** (11d, 20a, 26b, 35a, 36c, 37c, 73c, 75d, 79b, 112a, 126c), **sae** (242), **SAG** (242), **sag** (38a, 132a), **sai** (78b), **Sal** (52b, 179), **sal** (39b), **SAM** (242), **Sam** (24c, 119d, 179),

295

**san** (113a), **sap** (37d, 42d, 56d, 66d, 128c, 130c), **SAR** (242), **SAT** (242), **sat** (60a, 91d, 107a, 122d), **saw** (9d, 13b, 33c, 75b, 95c, 114a, 122d), **sax** (80a), **Say** (192), **say** (100d, 113b, 115a, 127c, 128d)

S _ A    **SBA** (242), **sea** (42d, 47c, 130a), **ska** (65b), **sma** (105b), **sna** (105b), **spa** (58d, 77a, 100a, 114a, 127a), **Sra.** (243), **SSA** (243), **sta** (80a)

_ S A    **Asa** (9a, 56a, 66b, 67d, 139, 197), **BSA** (236), **CSA** (237), **GSA** (239), **Isa.** (240), **NSA** (241), **Psa.** (242), **RSA** (242), **SSA** (243), **USA** (26a, 243)

S B _    **SBA** (242), **SbE** (29c), **SbW** (29c)

S _ B    **sib** (99b), **sob** (32b, 131a), **sub** (70b), **sub-** (93d)

_ S B    **asb.** (235)

S C _    **sch.** (242), **sci.** (31b, 242)

S _ C    **SAC** (242), **sac** (92a, 128a), **SEC** (242), **sec** (38b, 132c), **sic** (70a, 121d, 123d), **SLC** (243), **soc** (67c), **soc.** (243), **SWC** (243)

_ S C    **B.Sc.** (236), **CSC** (237), **DSC** (238), **NSC** (241)

S D _    **SDI** (242), **SDS** (242)

S _ D    **sad** (11d, 20a, 26b, 35a, 36c, 37c, 73c, 75d, 79b, 112a, 126c), **sed** (69c), **sgd.** (243), **Sid** (180), **sod** (118b, 125a), **std.** (243)

_ S D    **LSD** (240)

S E _    **sea** (42d, 47c, 130a), **SEC** (242), **sec** (38b, 132c), **sed** (69c), **see** (19c, 36a, 41c, 43c, 55d, 73a, 83b, 86b, 87d, 130a, 133a), **sei** (65c), **sel** (51a, 105b), **Sen.** (243), **sen** (214, 217, 218, 219, 246), **Sep.** (78c, 243), **ser-** (93c), **ser.** (243), **ses** (50c), **Set** (42b, 198), **set** (10a, 14c, 15c, 28a, 31a, 47b, 58a, 81b, 85a, 89d, 106d, 111d, 120c), **sew** (75d, 115c), **sex** (53b, 94d), **sex-** (93c), **sey** (105a)

S _ E    **sae** (242), **SbE** (29c), **see** (19c, 36a, 41c, 43c, 55d, 73a, 83b, 86b, 87d, 130a, 133a), **She** (57b), **she** (95a), **sie** (54b), **SSE** (29c), **Ste.** (243), **Sue** (182), **sue** (49c, 90b)

_ S E    **ASE** (235), **Ase** (61b, 87c), **ESE** (29c), **Ise** (60d), **-ise** (117a, 117c), **-ose** (117a, 117b), **SSE** (29c), **use** (38d, 40c, 43a, 52a)

S _ F    **Sif** (121b)

_ S F    **NSF** (241)

S G _    **sgd.** (243), **Sgt.** (243)

S _ G    **SAG** (242), **sag** (38a, 132a)

**S H _**     **She** (57b), **she** (95a), **sho** (246), **Shu** (97a), **shy** (17c, 31c, 77c, 98b, 108d, 122b)

**S _ H**     **sch.** (242)

**_ S H**     **ash** (40c, 58a, 124a), **-ish** (117a)

**S I _**     **sib** (99b), **sic** (70a, 121d, 123d), **Sid** (180), **sie** (54b), **Sif** (121b), **sil** (26d, 134b), **Sim** (181), **sin** (11d, 12a, 83c, 123d, 124b, 128b, 134c), **sip** (37d, 38a, 119d), **sir** (68a, 120c, 122c), **sis** (44b, 54c, 99b), **sit** (75d, 87d, 91d, 107a), **six** (57c)

**S _ I**     **sai** (78b), **sci.** (31b, 242), **SDI** (242), **sei** (65c), **ski** (104d, 110b), **sri** (60b), **Sui** (26d)

**_ S I**     **ASI** (235), **psi** (11d)

**S K _**     **ska** (65b), **ski** (104d, 110b), **Skt.** (243), **sky** (46c)

**_ S K**     **ask** (31d, 64a, 96d, 99d, 111c), **Esk** (134d, 223), **tsk** (42c, 122d)

**S L _**     **SLC** (243), **SLR** (243), **Sly** (181), **sly** (14d, 31d, 32c, 52c, 63b, 101c, 110c, 132a)

**S _ L**     **Sai** (52b, 179), **sal** (39b), **sel** (51a, 105b), **sil** (26d, 134b), **Sol** (88c, 199), **sol** (117d, 221), **syl.** (243)

**_ S L**     **ESL** (238), **isl.** (240)

**S M _**     **sma** (105b), **SMU** (33a)

**S _ M**     **SAM** (242), **Sam** (24c, 119d, 179), **Sim** (181), **sum** (10d, 123b), **sym.** (243)

**_ S M**     **-ism** (117b)

**S N _**     **sna** (105b), **SNO** (243), **sny** (18c, 32d, 90a, 108b, 122a)

**S _ N**     **san** (113a), **Sen.** (243), **sen** (214, 217, 218, 219, 246), **sin** (11d, 12a, 83c, 123d, 124b, 128b, 134c), **son** (59a, 74c), **SSN** (243), **Sun** (182), **Sun.** (243), **sun** (59a, 88c, 114d, 246), **syn-** (94a)

**_ S N**     **ASN** (235), **SSN** (243), **USN** (243)

**S O _**     **sob** (32b, 131a), **soc** (67c), **soc.** (243), **sod** (118b, 125a), **Sol** (88c, 199), **sol** (117d, 221), **son** (59a, 74c), **Soo** (181), **soo** (97d), **SOP** (243), **sop** (9b, 21d, 29d, 111b), **SOS** (36d, 243), **sot** (38b, 123a, 123b), **sou** (49c), **Sov.** (243), **sow** (88d, 90a, 118d), **sox** (17c, 98c), **soy** (17d, 104b)

**S _ O**     **sho** (246), **SNO** (243), **Soo** (181), **soo** (97d), **SRO** (120d, 243)

**_ S O**     **Aso** (65d, 128d), **iso-** (92d, 93c), **USO** (244)

**S P _**     **spa** (58d, 77a, 100a, 114a, 127a), **spy** (36a, 41c, 106a)

S _ P   **sap** (37d, 42d, 56d, 66d, 128c, 130c), **Sep.** (78c, 243), **sip** (37d, 38a, 119d), **SOP** (243), **sop** (9b, 21d, 29d, 111b), **sup** (39b, 119d)

_ S P   **asp** (10a, 28a, 111a, 126d, 128c, 232), **ESP** (109d, 238)

S _ Q   **suq** (74d)

_ S Q   **Esq.** (238)

S R _   **Sra.** (243), **sri** (60b), **SRO** (120d, 243)

S _ R   **SAR** (242), **ser-** (93c), **ser.** (243), **sir** (68a, 120c, 122c), **SLR** (243), **SSR** (243), **str.** (243), **sur** (50d, 51b, 79d, 113a), **Syr.** (243)

_ S R   **Isr.** (240), **SSR** (243)

S S _   **SSA** (243), **SSE** (29c), **SSN** (243), **SSR** (243), **SSS** (243), **SST** (66b, 243), **SSW** (29c)

S _ S   **SDS** (242), **ses** (50c), **sis** (44b, 54c, 99b), **SOS** (36d, 243), **SSS** (243), **sus-** (93d), **sys.** (243)

_ S S   **ass** (17d, 20a, 37b, 37c, 41b, 48b, 84a, 85b, 109c, 116d, 229), **ess** (32d, 71c), **-ess** (117b), **mss.** (241), **OSS** (241), **SSS** (243), **USS** (244)

S T _   **sta** (80a), **std.** (243), **Ste.** (243), **str.** (243), **Stu** (182), **sty** (43c)

S _ T   **SAT** (242), **sat** (60a, 91d, 107a, 122d), **Set** (42b, 198), **set** (10a, 14c, 15c, 28a, 31a, 47b, 58a, 81b, 85a, 89d, 106d, 111d, 120c), **Sgt.** (243), **sit** (75d, 87d, 91d, 107a), **Skt.** (243), **sot** (38b, 123a, 123b), **SST** (66b, 243)

_ S T   **AST** (236), **as't** (107c), **CST** (237), **DST** (238), **EST** (238), **est** (50b, 50c), **-est** (40d, 117c), **HST** (239), **is't** (107c), **-ist** (117a, 117b), **MST** (241), **PST** (242), **SST** (66b, 243)

S U _   **sub** (70b), **sub-** (93d), **Sue** (182), **sue** (49c, 90b), **Sui** (26d), **sum** (10d, 123b), **Sun** (182), **Sun.** (243), **sun** (59a, 88c, 114d, 246), **sup** (39b, 119d), **suq** (74d), **sur** (50d, 51b, 79d, 113a), **sus-** (93d)

S _ U   **Shu** (97a), **SMU** (33a), **sou** (49c), **Stu** (182)

S _ V   **Sov.** (243)

_ S V   **ASV** (236), **RSV** (242)

S W _   **SWC** (243)

S _ W   **saw** (9d, 13b, 33c, 75b, 95c, 114a, 122d), **SbW** (29c), **sew** (75d, 115c), **sow** (88d, 90a, 118d), **SSW** (29c)

_ S W   **NSW** (241), **SSW** (29c), **WSW** (29c)

S _ X   **sax** (80a), **sex** (53b, 94d), **sex-** (93c), **six** (57c), **sox** (17c, 98c)

**S Y _**    **syl.** (243), **sym.** (243), **syn-** (94a), **Syr.** (243), **sys.** (243)

**S _ Y**    **Say** (192), **say** (100d, 113b, 115a, 127c, 128d), **sey** (105a), **shy** (17c, 31c, 77c, 98b, 108d, 122b), **sky** (46c), **Sly** (181), **sly** (14d, 31c, 32c, 52c, 63b, 101c, 110c, 132a), **sny** (18c, 32d, 90a, 108b, 122a), **soy** (17d, 104b), **spy** (36a, 41c, 106a), **sty** (43c)

**T A _**    **Tab** (183), **tab** (47b, 94b, 119b), **TAC** (243), **tad** (134d), **tae** (105b), **tag** (52b, 68b), **Tai** (62d, 183, 218), **tai** (65d, 91c), **Taj** (74b), **tam** (58b, 58c), **tan** (22b, 70d, 246), **tao** (88c, 124d), **tap** (44d, 113c, 123b), **tar** (55a, 89c, 102a, 103b), **TAT** (243), **tat** (39c, 68c), **tau** (11d, 103d), **tav** (12a), **Taw** (223), **taw** (70d, 74d, 108c, 119c), **tax** (15a, 62b, 71c), **Tay** (82b)

**T _ A**    **tba** (243), **tea** (61d, 111b), **tha** (11d), **tia** (112c), **toa** (18a), **TVA** (243), **Twa** (214, 221)

**_ T A**    **Ata** (73d), **ETA** (238), **eta** (11d), **ita** (70a), **PTA** (104d, 242), **sta** (80a), **Uta** (184), **uta** (72c)

**T B _**    **tba** (243), **TBS** (26a), **tbs.** (243)

**T _ B**    **Tab** (183), **tab** (47b, 94b, 119b), **tob** (10c), **tub** (20b, 24c, 30b, 127b)

**_ T B**    **OTB** (52b, 241)

**T C _**    **tch** (42c)

**T _ C**    **TAC** (243), **tec** (35b), **tic** (79d, 113b, 125c), **TLC** (243)

**_ T C**    **ATC** (236), **etc.** (72b, 238), **FTC** (239), **ITC** (240), **OTC** (241)

**T _ D**    **tad** (134d), **Ted** (183), **ted** (58c, 114a), **Tod** (183), **tod** (22d, 105a, 246)

**_ T D**    **Ltd.** (240), **std.** (243)

**T E _**    **tea** (61d, 111b), **tec** (35b), **Ted** (183), **ted** (58c, 114a), **tee** (55a, 55b, 87c), **teg** (107d), **Tel** (16a), **Tel.** (243), **tel-** (93d), **ten** (18d, 34a, 34d), **ter-** (93d), **ter.** (243), **Tex** (31c, 183), **Tex.** (212, 243)

**T _ E**    **tae** (105b), **tee** (55a, 55b, 87c), **the** (14d), **tie** (12c, 20d, 31d, 37d, 41b, 42a, 69b, 72b, 97b, 124d), **toe** (55b, 110b, 115b), **tre** (65c), **Tue.** (243), **tye** (25d, 102b)

**_ T E**    **Ate** (88b, 135a, 198), **ate**, **-ate** (117a, 117b), **ete** (51a), **-ite** (117a, 117b), **rte.** (242), **Ste.** (243), **Ute** (108d, 189)

**_ T F**    **ATF** (236)

**T _ G**    **tag** (52b, 68b), **teg** (107d), **tog** (28b), **Tug** (184), **tug** (20b, 28d, 37c, 95d)

**T H _**    **tha** (11d), **the** (14d), **Thu.** (243), **thy** (95a)

T _ H     **tch** (42c)

_ T H     **D.Th.** (238), **Eth.** (238), **eth** (12c), **-eth** (117b, 117c), **lth** (25c), **nth** (34c)

T I _     **tia** (112c), **tic** (79d, 113b, 125c), **tie** (12c, 20d, 31d, 37d, 41b, 42a, 69b, 72b, 97b, 124d), **til** (107a), **'til** (30b), **Tim** (35c, 183), **tin** (30b, 74c, 76a, 114d, 245), **tio** (113a), **tip** (40d, 56a, 60b, 60d, 90c, 122a), **tir** (51a, 108c), **'tis** (30b, 107c), **tit** (19a, 226), **Tiu** (53c, 125d), **tix** (243)

T _ I     **Tai** (62d, 183, 218), **tai** (65d, 91c), **toi** (49d, 51b), **tri-** (93d), **tui** (38d, 81c, 86d, 88c), **Twi** (216)

_ T I     **ETI** (238)

T _ J     **Taj** (74b)

T K _     **TKO** (21b, 243)

T _ K     **tsk** (42c, 122d)

T L _     **TLC** (243)

T _ L     **Tel** (16a), **Tel.** (243), **tel-** (93d), **til** (107a), **'til** (30b)

_ T L     **Atl.** (236)

T _ M     **tam** (58b, 58c), **Tim** (35c, 183), **Tom** (116a, 184), **tom** (74c), **tum** (24b)

_ T M     **ATM** (236)

T N _     **TNT** (26a, 43a, 243)

T _ N     **tan** (22b, 70d, 246), **ten** (18d, 34a, 34d), **tin** (30b, 74c, 76a, 114d, 245), **ton** (131a, 246), **tun** (21d, 24c, 75b, 132c, 246)

T O _     **toa** (18a), **tob** (10c), **Tod** (183), **tod** (22d, 105a, 246), **toe** (55b, 110b, 115b), **tog** (28b), **toi** (49d, 51b), **Tom** (116a, 184), **tom** (74c), **ton** (131a, 246), **too** (12c, 18c, 62c, 78c), **top** (31d, 42b, 59d, 85c, 89b, 117d, 118a, 118b, 127c), **Tor** (102c), **tor** (31d, 67c, 87b, 95a, 101b), **tot** (26c, 134d), **tou** (246), **tow** (37c, 59b, 95d), **toy** (82c, 124c)

T _ O     **tao** (88c, 124d), **tio** (113a), **TKO** (21b, 243), **too** (12c, 18c, 62c, 78c), **two** (21c, 31b, 72c)

_ T O     **cto.** (237), **ETO** (238), **ITO** (240), **Ito** (65b), **oto-** (92d), **PTO** (242)

T _ P     **tap** (44d, 113c, 123b), **tip** (40d, 56a, 60b, 60d, 90c, 122a), **top** (31d, 42b, 59d, 85c, 89b, 117d, 118a, 118b, 127c), **tup** (32c, 87b, 89a, 97d), **twp.** (243)

_ T P     **ATP** (236)

300

**T R _**     tre (65c), tri- (93d), try (12d, 15c, 40d, 41d, 114b, 116c)

**T _ R**     tar (55a, 89c, 102a, 103b), ter- (93d), ter. (243), tir (51a, 108c), Tor (102c), tor (31d, 67c, 87b, 95a, 101b), tur (25a, 89a), Tyr (10b, 83b, 125a, 129d, 198)

**_ T R**     str. (243)

**T S _**     tsk (42c, 122d)

**T _ S**     TBS (26a), tbs. (243), 'tis (30b, 107c)

**_ T S**     cts. (237), DTs (238), hts. (239), its (95a), it's (30c), Mts. (241)

**T _ T**     TAT (243), tat (39c, 68c), tit (19a, 226), TNT (26a, 43a, 243), tot (26c, 134d), Tut (21c, 40a), tut (42c, 122d)

**_ T T**     ltt (10a), Ott (173)

**T U _**     tub (20b, 24c, 30b, 127b), Tue. (243), Tug (184), tug (20b, 28d, 37c, 95d), tui (38d, 81c, 86d, 88c), tum (24b), tun (21d, 24c, 75b, 132c, 246), tup (32c, 87b, 89a, 97d), tur (25a, 89a), Tut (21c, 40a), tut (42c, 122d), tux (35d)

**T _ U**     tau (11d, 103d), Thu. (243), Tiu (53c, 125d), tou (246)

**_ T U**     BTU (10d, 236), cru (50d), Stu (182)

**T V _**     TVA (243)

**T _ V**     tav (12a)

**_ T V**     ATV (236), ETV (238), MTV (26a)

**T W _**     Twa (214, 221), Twi (216), two (21c, 31b, 72c), twp. (243)

**T _ W**     Taw (223), taw (70d, 74d, 108c, 119c), tow (37c, 59b, 95d)

**T _ X**     tax (15a, 62b, 71c), Tex (31c, 183), Tex. (212, 243), tix (243), tux (35d)

**T Y _**     tye (25d, 102b), Tyr (10b, 83b, 125a, 129d, 198)

**T _ Y**     Tay (82b), thy (95a), toy (82c, 124c), try (12d, 15c, 40d, 41d, 114b, 116c)

**_ T Y**     sty (43c)

**U A _**     UAE (243), UAR (243)

**U _ A**     uca (45d), ufa (42c), -ula (117b), Uma (184), Una (43d, 113c, 184), USA (26a, 243), Uta (184), uta (72c), uva (51d, 55d)

**_ U A**     dua- (93d), pua (59b), qua (69c, 109c)

**U B _**     ubi (70b)

U _ B      **uxb** (244)

_ U B      **bub** (45a, 74c), **cub** (72b, 134d), **dub** (23b, 80b), **hub** (25c, 131c), **nub** (54c, 73c, 74b, 89c, 95c), **pub** (120a), **rub** (9b, 22d, 25d, 35d, 90d, 130d), **sub** (70b), **sub-** (93d), **tub** (20b, 24c, 30b, 127b)

U C _      **uca** (45d)

U _ C      **UPC** (243)

_ U C      **duc** (50b)

U D _      **Udi** (82b), **udo** (26d, 65d, 66a, 103d)

U _ D      **und** (53c), **urd** (17d)

_ U D      **Bud** (143), **bud** (45a, 47d), **cud** (96d, 102d), **dud** (44a), **HUD** (239), **IUD** (240), **Lud** (108a), **mud** (39a, 99c, 104c, 110b, 246), **oud** (80b), **pud** (57d, 87b)

U _ E      **UAE** (243), **ule** (21c, 25a, 102c), **-ule** (117b), **ume** (13d, 65b), **une** (49d, 50a, 50d), **Ure** (134d), **use** (38d, 40c, 43a, 52a), **Ute** (108d, 189)

_ U E      **cue** (9d, 24d, 91b, 101c, 109b, 117d), **due** (65c, 87b, 95b), **hue** (29a, 107b, 122d), **nue** (50a), **Rue** (179), **rue** (35a, 59b, 59c, 99a, 133a), **Sue** (182), **sue** (49c, 90b), **Tue.** (243), **Yue** (215)

U F _      **ufa** (42c), **UFO** (48a, 243), **UFT** (243), **UFW** (243)

U _ F      **UHF** (120b, 243)

U G _      **ugh** (42c)

_ U G      **Aug.** (78c, 236), **bug** (21b, 53c, 63b), **dug** (42b), **fug** (98d), **hug** (40c), **jug** (89c, 94d), **lug** (24c, 37c, 39a, 57d, 103b), **mug** (38a, 52c, 128a), **pug** (37a, 77d, 227), **rug** (47d, 57b, 131d), **Tug** (184), **tug** (20b, 28d, 37c, 95d), **vug** (25b, 53c)

U H _      **UHF** (120b, 243)

U _ H      **ugh** (42c)

_ U H      **huh** (42c)

U _ I      **ubi** (70b), **Udi** (82b), **uji** (109c), **uni-** (93c), **UPI** (81c, 132d, 243), **Uri** (120b, 197)

_ U I      **DUI** (38b, 238), **Hui** (215), **hui** (15a), **Kui** (67b), **oui** (51b), **Sui** (26d), **tui** (38d, 81c, 86d, 88c)

U J _      **uji** (109c)

_ U K      **auk** (19a, 225), **yuk** (70b)

**U L _**  -ula (117b), **ule** (21c, 25a, 102c), **-ule** (117b), **Ulm** (33c, 216), **Ulu** (184), **ulu** (63d, 68a)

**_ U L**  **Bul.** (236), **-ful** (117b), **Jul.** (78c, 240), **pul** (213), **Yul** (188)

**U M _**  **Uma** (184), **ume** (13d, 65b), **UMW** (243)

**U _ M**  **Ulm** (33c, 216)

**_ U M**  **aum** (246), **bum** (38a, 127a), **cum** (117d), **gum** (10a, 43c, 62c, 78d, 99d, 115b, 124a), **hum** (38a, 112a, 131d), **mum** (27a, 74a), **Num.** (241), **rum** (11a, 72b), **sum** (10d, 123b), **tum** (24b)

**U N _**  **Una** (43d, 113c, 184), **und** (53c), **une** (49d, 50a, 50d), **uni-** (93c), **uno** (65c, 112c), **uns** (54a)

**U _ N**  **urn** (30b, 127b), **USN** (243)

**_ U N**  **bun** (57b, 101c), **dun** (18d, 38c, 56a, 87b), **fun** (52b, 66b), **gun** (46b, 100b, 109a, 130c), **Hun** (127b), **Jun.** (78c, 240), **jun** (218), **Nun** (197), **nun** (11d, 12a, 22c, 89a, 99b, 109d), **pun** (90b), **run** (12d, 20d, 38a, 47c, 47d, 54d, 84b, 110d, 116b, 123c), **Sun** (182), **Sun.** (243), **sun** (59a, 88c, 114d, 246), **tun** (21d, 24c, 75b, 132c, 246), **Yun** (69a)

**U _ O**  **udo** (26d, 65d, 66a, 103d), **UFO** (48a, 243), **uno** (65c, 112c), **USO** (244)

**_ U O**  **duo** (85d, 125c), **Luo** (218)

**U P _**  **UPC** (243), **UPI** (81c, 132d, 243), **UPS** (243), **ups** (21a)

**_ U P**  **cup** (38a, 55b, 89b, 98b, 119a, 124d), **dup.** (238), **hup** (23a, 29b), **kup** (246), **pup** (105d, 134d), **sup** (39b, 119d), **tup** (32c, 87b, 89a, 97d)

**_ U Q**  **suq** (74d)

**U R _**  **urd** (17d), **Ure** (134d), **Uri** (120b, 197), **urn** (30b, 127b), **Uru.** (243)

**U _ R**  **UAR** (243)

**_ U R**  **bur** (106b, 131a), **bur.** (236), **cur** (78a), **dur** (74b), **Eur.** (238), **fur** (28c, 57b), **Gur** (223), **gur** (117c), **mur** (51b), **our** (95a), **RUR** (101b), **sur** (50d, 51b, 79d, 113a), **tur** (25a, 89a)

**U S _**  **USA** (26a, 243), **use** (38d, 40c, 43a, 52a), **USN** (243), **USO** (244), **USS** (244)

**U _ S**  **uns** (54a), **UPS** (243), **ups** (21a), **USS** (244)

**_ U S**  **AUS** (236), **aus** (54a), **bus** (95d), **bus.** (236), **Gus** (156), **ius** (70a), **jus** (50c, 70b), **mus.** (241), **-ous** (117a), **pus** (63a, 78b), **rus** (69c), **sus-** (93d)

**U T _**  **Uta** (184), **uta** (72c), **Ute** (108d, 189)

U _ T  **UFT** (243)

_ U T  **aut** (70a), **but** (11d, 30a, 42b, 115b, 126c, 134c), **cut** (27a, 28a, 79c, 98d, 107b, 108d, 110b), **fut** (246), **gut** (99c), **hut** (107c), **jut** (95a), **Lut** (35a), **Mut** (12b, 97a), **Nut** (198), **nut** (22c, 28c, 31d, 44c, 51d, 67b, 121b), **out** (9b, 49a, 55b, 82c), **put** (70c), **rut** (56c, 57a), **Tut** (21c, 40a), **tut** (42c, 122d

U _ U  **Ulu** (184), **ulu** (63d, 68a), **Uru.** (243)

U V _  **uva** (51d, 55d)

U _ W  **UFW** (243), **UMW** (243)

U X _  **uxb** (244)

_ U X  **aux.** (236), **dux** (52a, 70c), **Lux** (240), **lux** (62a, 246), **tux** (35d)

_ U Y  **buy** (17b, 96a), **Guy** (156), **guy** (45a, 74c, 115a), **muy** (113a)

_ U Z  **guz** (246)

V A _  **Vai** (218), **Val** (184), **Van** (184), **van** (48d), **vas** (38c, 70a), **vas-** (92c), **VAT** (244), **vat** (27b, 30b, 125a, 246), **vav** (12a)

V _ A  **via** (65c, 101a, 101d), **VOA** (244)

_ V A  **Ava** (22d, 139), **ava** (61c, 91a, 123a), **CVA** (237), **EVA** (238), **Eva** (116a, 152), **iva** (75a), **ova** (39d), **TVA** (243), **uva** (51d, 55d), **W.Va.** (212, 244)

V C _  **VCR** (244)

V _ C  **Vic** (32d, 185)

V D _  **VDT** (244)

V _ D  **Vod** (16d)

V E _  **Vee** (185), **vee** (47b, 81a), **Vei** (218), **ven-** (93d), **Ven.** (244), **ver.** (244), **vet** (111c), **vet.** (244), **vex** (12d, 21b, 36d, 64b, 87c)

V _ E  **Vee** (185), **vee** (47b, 81a), **vie** (30b, 116c, 125a), **voe** (63a)

_ V E  **Ave.** (236), **ave** (44b, 56c, 57b, 92b, 102b, 104a), **Eve** (9a, 107a, 152, 197), **eve** (38d, 125c), **I've** (30c)

V F _  **VFW** (244)

V _ F  **VHF** (120b), **vif** (50c)

V _ G  **vug** (25b, 53c)

_ V G  **avg.** (236)

V H _  **VHF** (120b)

**V I _**    via (65c, 101a, 101d), **Vic** (32d, 185), **vie** (30b, 116c, 125a), **vif** (50c), **vim** (40d, 48c, 113d, 128b, 128d), **Vin** (185), **vin** (51b), **VIP** (35d, 244), **vir** (69d), **vis** (69d, 70a), **vix** (70a), **viz** (80d)

**V _ I**    Vai (218), Vei (218)

**_ V I**    avi- (92c), B.V.I. (236), ovi- (92d)

**V _ L**    Val (184), vol. (244)

**V _ M**    vim (40d, 48c, 113d, 128b, 128d)

**_ V M**    BVM (236), DVM (238)

**V _ N**    Van (184), van (48d), **Ven.** (244), **ven-** (93d), **Vin** (185), **vin** (51b), **von** (53d)

**V O _**    VOA (244), Vod (16d), voe (63a), vol. (244), von (53d), vow (90b, 111c), vox (70b)

**_ V O**    Ivo (159), ovo- (92d)

**V _ P**    VIP (35d, 244)

**_ V P**    MVP (241)

**V _ R**    VCR (244), ver. (244), vir (69d)

**V _ S**    vas (38c, 70a), vas- (92c), vis (69d, 70a)

**V _ T**    VAT (244), vat (27b, 30b, 125a, 246), VDT (244), vet (111c), vet. (244)

**_ V T**    Pvt. (242)

**V U _**    vug (25b, 53c)

**V _ V**    vav (12a)

**V _ W**    VFW (244), vow (90b, 111c)

**V _ X**    vex (12d, 21b, 36d, 64b, 87c), vix (70a), vox (70b)

**_ V Y**    Ivy (159), ivy (28a, 31d, 128b)

**V _ Z**    viz (80d)

**W A _**    WAC (244), wad (55a, 73c, 75b, 85b), WAF (244), wag (66d, 79c, 133a), wan (57b, 86a), war (116b), was (57a, 127a), Wat (186), waw (11d), wax (15d, 56d, 90d, 118c), way (31b, 74c, 76b, 101a, 102c, 121b, 127a)

**W _ A**    WBA (244), WHA (244), WPA (244), W.Va. (212, 244)

**_ W A**    iwa (51c), Kwa (69a, 223), Twa (214, 221)

W B _     **WBA** (244), **WBC** (244), **WbN** (29c), **WbS** (29c)

W _ B     **W.E.B.** (185), **web** (41a, 75d, 76a, 81c, 111b)

W C _     **WCT** (244)

W _ C     **WAC** (244), **WBC** (244)

_ W C     **SWC** (243)

W _ D     **wad** (55a, 73c, 75b, 85b), **wed** (66c, 75a, 126c), **we'd** (30c)

_ W D     **fwd** (239)

W E _     **W.E.B.** (185), **web** (41a, 75d, 76a, 81c, 111b), **wed** (66c, 75a, 126c), **we'd** (30c), **wee** (77b, 105b, 110d), **Wei** (119d), **wen** (33c, 83d, 125a, 129a), **Wes** (186), **wet** (33b, 33c, 37d, 77c, 97c), **wey** (246)

W _ E     **wee** (77b, 105b, 110d), **woe** (23a, 56c, 112a), **Wye** (107b, 131a), **wye** (71c)

_ W E     **awe** (63d, 76d, 100b, 127d, 132b), **Ewe** (216, 223), **ewe** (107d), **owe** (34a)

W _ F     **WAF** (244)

W _ G     **wag** (66d, 79c, 133a), **wig** (57b)

W H _     **WHA** (244), **WHO** (244), **who** (96d, 99b), **why** (96d)

_ W H     **kwh** (240)

W I _     **wig** (57b), **Wil** (186), **Wim** (187), **win** (9d, 52a, 94b), **Wis.** (212, 244), **wit** (36a, 61c, 66d, 129a), **wiz** (74a)

W _ I     **Wei** (119d)

_ W I     **DWI** (38b, 238), **Twi** (216)

W _ K     **wok** (86a, 128a)

W _ L     **Wil** (186), **wol** (132d)

_ W L     **awl** (108c, 122d, 123a), **owl** (19a, 226)

W _ M     **Wim** (187), **wpm** (244)

_ W M     **cwm** (79b)

W N _     **WNW** (29c)

W _ N     **wan** (57b, 86a), **WbN** (29c), **wen** (33c, 83d, 125a, 129a), **win** (9d, 52a, 94b), **won** (46c, 128b, 218)

_ W N     **awn** (14b, 17d), **own** (9d, 29d)

**W O _**   woe (23a, 56c, 112a), wok (86a, 128a), wol (132d), won (46c, 128b, 218), woo (31b), wow (42c)

**W _ O**   WHO (244), who (96d, 99b), woo (31b), Wyo. (212, 244)

**_ W O**   CWO (237), Pwo (69a), two (21c, 31b, 72c)

**W P _**   WPA (244), wpm (244)

**_ W P**   twp. (243)

**W R _**   wry (64b, 125c)

**W _ R**   war (116b)

**W S _**   WSW (29c)

**W _ S**   was (57a, 127a), WbS (29c), Wes (186), Wis. (212, 244)

**W _ T**   Wat (186), WCT (244), wet (33b, 33c, 37d, 77c, 97c), wit (36a, 61c, 66d, 129a)

**_ W T**   NWT (241)

**W V _**   W.Va. (212, 244)

**_ W V**   LWV (240)

**W _ W**   waw (11d), WNW (29c), wow (42c), WSW (29c)

**_ W W**   IWW (240)

**W _ X**   wax (15d, 56d, 90d, 118c)

**W Y _**   Wye (107b, 131a), wye (71c), Wyo. (212, 244)

**W _ Y**   way (31b, 74c, 76b, 101a, 102c, 121b, 127a), wey (246), why (96d), wry (64b, 125c)

**_ W Y**   hwy. (239), rwy. (242)

**W _ Z**   wiz (74a)

**X A _**   xat (123b)

**_ X A**   oxa- (93c)

**_ X B**   uxb (244)

**X E _**   xen- (93a), xer- (92d)

**_ X E**   axe (27a, 33c, 36c, 122d), Exe (35c, 223)

**X _ L**   xyl- (94a)

**X _ N**   xen- (93a)

| _ X O | exo- (93c) |
|---|---|
| _ X P | exp. (238) |
| X _ R | xer- (92d) |
| X _ T | xat (123b) |
| _ X T | ext. (238) |
| X Y _ | xyl- (94a) |
| _ X Y | oxy- (93c) |
| Y A _ | yah (34c), Yai (223), yak (85d, 119b, 231), yam (39c, 92a, 118c, 125a), Yao (218, 219), yap (17b, 26b, 92b, 134c), yaw (101c), yay (9b, 111b) |
| Y _ A | yea (10b, 128a, 129c), Yma (187) |
| _ Y A | pya (220) |
| _ Y C | NYC (18d, 241) |
| Y D _ | yds. (244) |
| Y _ D | Yed (207), yod (12a) |
| _ Y D | Cyd (147) |
| Y E _ | yea (10b, 128a, 129c), Yed (207), yen (35b, 58a, 73a, 218), yep (10b), yes (10b, 44d), yet (18c, 22d, 60b, 82c, 115b, 121d), yew (30a, 42a, 108d, 124a) |
| Y _ E | Yue (215) |
| _ Y E | aye (10b, 44d, 129c), bye (32a, 123c), dye (29a, 114c), eye (73a, 118b), lye (11b), rye (11a, 25c, 55c, 72b), tye (25d, 102b), Wye (107b, 131a), wye (71c) |
| Y _ G | zyg- (93c) |
| Y _ H | yah (34c) |
| Y I _ | Yin (26d), yin (107c, 134a), yip (17b, 37b, 134c) |
| Y _ I | Yai (223) |
| _ Y I | fyi (239) |
| Y _ K | yak (85d, 119b, 231), yuk (70b) |
| Y _ L | Yul (188) |
| _ Y L | hyl- (94a), syl. (243), xyl- (94a) |

308

Y M _     Yma (187)

Y _ M     yam (39c, 92a, 118c, 125a), yom (33d, 67d)

_ Y M     gym (114a), Nym (44a, 194), sym. (243), zym- (93a)

Y _ N     yen (35b, 58a, 73a, 218), Yin (26d), yin (107c, 134a), yon (36d, 85c), Yun (69a)

_ Y N     Ayn (139), ayn (11d), dyn- (93c), gyn- (92d), syn- (94a)

Y O _     yod (12a), yom (33d, 67d), yon (36d, 85c), you (95a), yow (42c)

Y _ O     Yao (218, 219)

_ Y O     CYO (237), iyo (10b, 88c), Wyo. (212, 244)

Y _ P     yap (17b, 26b, 92b, 134c), yep (10b), yip (17b, 37b, 134c)

_ Y P     gyp (107a, 108d, 118d)

Y R _     yrs. (244)

_ Y R     gyr- (93a), pyr- (93a), Syr. (243), Tyr (10b, 83b, 125a, 129d, 198)

Y _ S     yds. (244), yes (10b, 44d), yrs. (244)

_ Y S     dys- (92c), lys (71d), lys- (93a), sys. (243)

Y _ T     yet (18c, 22d, 60b, 82c, 115b, 121d)

Y U _     Yue (215), yuk (70b), Yul (188), Yun (69a)

Y _ U     you (95a)

Y _ W     yaw (101c), yew (30a, 42a, 108d, 124a), yow (42c)

_ Y X     myx- (93b), Nyx (56b, 198), pyx (27b, 42a)

Y _ Y     yay (9b, 111b)

Z A _     zak (246), Zan (135c), zax (110b), zay (11d)

Z _ A     zoa (39d)

Z _ D     zed (135a)

Z E _     zed (135a), zee (63a), Zen (22b), zer (246)

Z _ E     zee (63a), Zoe (188)

Z _ G     ZPG (244), zyg- (93c)

Z I _     zip (40d, 128b, 244)

Z _ K     zak (246)

Z _ M     **zym-** (93a)

Z _ N     **Zan** (135c), **Zen** (22b)

Z O _     **zoa** (39d), **Zoe** (188), **zoo** (132a), **zoo-** (92c)

Z _ O     **zoo** (132a), **zoo-** (92c)

_ Z O     **azo** (38d, 134b), **azo-** (93b)

Z P _     **ZPG** (244)

Z _ P     **zip** (40d, 128b, 244)

Z _ R     **zer** (246)

_ Z S     **ozs.** (242)

Z _ X     **zax** (110b)

Z Y _     **zyg-** (93c), **zym-** (93a)

Z _ Y     **zay** (11d)

# FOUR-LETTER WORDS

A A _ _     **Aare** (18c, 100b), **AARP** (235)

_ A A _     **Baal** (106c), **baas**, **caam** (73a), **Caan** (144), **haab** (75b), **Kaat** (163), **laap** (41d), **ma'am** (74a), **maar** (129a), **Paar** (173), **raad** (15a, 40a, 112b, 121d), **RAAF** (242), **saal** (53d), **Saar** (49c, 78d, 101a), **Taal** (10c, 69a, 112b), **WAAC** (244), **WAAF** (244)

_ _ A A     **NCAA** (241), **NOAA** (241)

A _ _ A     **abba** (19c, 44d), **Abia** (104a), **-acea** (117c), **acta** (34b, 94d, 98c, 121a), **adda** (110a), **Adja** (214), **agha** (125b), **Agra** (24c, 119a), **agra** (64a, 118c), **agua** (113a), **Aïda** (84b, 97b, 128a), **Akha** (121d), **Akra** (216), **akua** (91a), **alba** (73c, 75c, 131d), **alca** (15d, 98a), **Alda** (137), **Alea** (15b), **alga** (105d), **Alla** (138), **alla** (233), **Alma** (138), **alma** (32a, 33b), **Alta.** (235), **Alva** (39c), **amia** (21b, 79c), **amla** (39b), **amma** (9a), **amra** (60c), **anba** (28a), **anda** (21c, 133b), **Anka** (138), **Anna** (84a, 122d, 138), **anna** (103a), **anoa** (48d, 85d, 132a, 229), **ansa** (57d), **anta** (89a, 91c), **Anya** (139), **Apia** (91c, 224), **aqua** (20b, 70b), **arca** (11d, 21b, 99b), **area** (36d, 37b, 45d, 72d, 97d, 99a, 135c), **aria** (75d, 111d, 125a, 234), **arna** (22b, 131d), **Aroa** (127d), **arpa** (65a), **Arta** (56d), **asea** (32b, 129c), **Asia** (39b), **Asta** (37b, 81d, 121b), **atta** (70c), **atua** (91a), **aula** (53d), **aura** (10d, 36d, 39d, 40b, 57c, 100d)

A B _ _     **a bas** (50b), **abba** (19c, 44d), **abbe** (28a, 49d, 94c), **abbr.** (235), **Abby** (137), **abcs** (46c), **abed** (110b), **Abel** (10a, 23a, 107a, 197), **Abes**, **abet** (10d, 48b, 59b), **Abia** (104a), **abib** (59a, 81d), **Abie** (81c), **abir** (98d), **able** (10a, 29c, 96b, 110a), **-ably** (117b), **abou** (44d), **abri** (51a, 108a), **abut** (21a, 75d, 123b)

310

**_ A B _**    baba (82d, 91a), Babe (140), babe (26c, 40d), Babi (16a), Babs, babu (60a), baby (26c, 40d, 83c), caba (133d), cabs, dabs, fabe (55b), gabi (119d), gabs, gaby (109c), habu (89c, 103c), jabs, Labe (217), labs, mabi (47d, 80b), nabs, PABA (86b), Rabe (176), Rabi (15c, 88d), rabi (78b), saba (45d, 88c), Sabe (67b), tabs, tabu (48c)

**_ _ A B**    Ahab (24a, 66c, 67d, 87d, 197), Arab (104b, 213, 217, 218, 219, 221, 222, 223, 224), Arab. (235), blab (119d), crab (32b, 108a), drab (22b, 26b, 29a, 38c, 43d, 47b), grab (80b, 106c, 111b), haab (75b), Joab (33d, 197), Moab (66b, 73b, 197), scab (134a), slab (88d, 110c), snab (22b, 105a), stab (15c, 68a, 88d), swab (57c, 78c, 134b)

**A _ _ B**    abib (59a, 81d), Agib (13d), Ahab (24a, 66c, 67d, 87d, 197), Arab (104b, 213, 217, 218, 219, 221, 222, 223, 224), Arab. (235)

**A C _ _**    acad. (235), acct. (235), AC/DC (235), -acea (117c), aced (120c), acer (74d), aces, acet- (92c), ache (73a, 85d, 134b), acht (53d), achy (112a), acid (119d), Acis (52b), acle (64b), ACLU (235), acme (32c, 87b, 123a, 135a), acne (110a), acou- (93a), Acre (214), acre (45d, 68d, 246), acro- (93a, 93c), acta (34b, 94d, 98c, 121a), ACTH (235), acts, acus (70a, 89b)

**_ A C _**    Bach (140), back (14c, 59b, 60a, 98a, 115b), caco- (92c), dace (46c, 228), each (13b), face (15a, 30a, 73a, 79d, 118a, 128c), fact (9d, 35b, 98a), hack (24c, 33a, 60b), jaca (65b), Jack (159), jack (17a, 24a, 68a, 78a, 97c), lace (47b), lack (34c, 129d), lacy (34c), mace (40c, 82d, 114b, 118d, 129d), mach (113c), Mack (167), mack (97c), Macy (167), NaCL (111c), paca (25b, 101c), Pace (204), pace (52a, 113c, 129b), pack (16d, 22c, 105c, 232, 246), paco (11d, 109c), pact (10d, 11c, 17b, 20d), race (87d, 103a, 114a, 124b), rack (10b, 28b), racy (20a, 113c), sack (30b, 36a, 89b, 90c, 132c), sacs, tack (13d, 15c, 31b, 44c, 80b), tact (35d), Waco (21d), WACs

**_ _ A C**    HUAC (239), WAAC (244)

**A _ _ C**    AC/DC (235), AFDC (235), Alec (137), alec (12c, 47a, 104b), Apoc. (235), -atic (117c), avec (51b)

**A D _ _**    adad (42c), Adah (41c, 197), Adak (64b), Adam (23d, 84d, 107a, 137, 194, 197), Adar (66d, 78c), Adas, adat (74b), adda (110a), adds, Aden (13d, 224), adit (41b, 77a), Adja (214), admi (53b), adze (122d)

**_ A D _**    bade, Cade (192), cade (59d, 67c, 88b), cadi (13d, 80c), cads, Dada (14d, 49c), dado (34b, 84d, 87c, 129d), dads, Eads (21d), fade (35c, 36a, 127b), fado (91d), fads, gads, hade (53c), hadj (89b), Jada (197), jade (53b, 56c), kadi (13d, 80d), Ladd (165), lade (24b, 35d, 72d, 76d, 119a), lads, lady (45b, 81d), made (31d), NADA (241), pads, qadi (13d, 80d), rads, Sada (179), sado (24c, 66a), Sadr (207), tads, Wade (185), wade (129b), wadi (38b, 83a, 98a, 101a), wads

**_ _ A D**   acad. (235), adad (42c), Arad (221), arad (65b), bead (17d, 109b), Brad (142), brad (44c, 54d, 80b), Chad (117a, 145, 215), clad (37d), dead (69b), duad (85d, 125c), dyad (85d), egad (83a), Fuad (44c), glad (66d), goad (62c, 114b), grad (25c), grad. (239), head (21a, 25d, 26c, 51c, 78a, 94c), Irad (197), Joad (55d), lead (29d, 35d, 56d, 58c, 245), load (10b, 22d, 24b, 119a), Mead (61a, 170), mead (18a, 37d, 60d), Obad. (241), quad (29a), raad (15a, 40a, 112b, 121d), read (63c, 88b, 116c), road (31b, 38a, 121b, 130c), scad (24d, 27b, 61b, 65b), shad (25b, 46d), spad (80b, 89d), stad (112b), Thad (183), toad (17c, 225), woad (20a, 38d)

**A _ _ D**   abed (110b), acad. (235), aced (120c), acid (119d), adad (42c), aged (12c, 83c, 83d), amid (12b), aped, apod (48c), Arad (221), arad (65b), arid (38b), Arnd (53d), auld (105b), avid (39a, 41b, 56b, 67b, 135a), awed, axed

**A E _ _**   aeon (122b), aeri- (92c), aero- (92c), aero. (235), aery (39a)

**_ A E _**   Baer (140), Baez (140), Caen (17c), Gaea (39b, 198), Gael (25c, 105a), haec (70a), Jael (197), Kael (163), Kaen (223), laet (49b), Maes, Raes, tael (71c, 131a), ta'en (107c)

**_ _ A E**   alae (132d), brae (60a, 105b), frae (105a), -idae (117c), irae (35c), koae (58b), prae (69c)

**A _ _ E**   Aare (18c, 100b), abbe (28a, 49d, 94c), Abie (81c), able (10a, 29c, 96b, 110a), ache (73a, 85d, 134b), acle (64b), acme (32c, 87b, 123a, 135a), acne (110a), Acre (214), acre (45d, 68d, 246), adze (122d), Agee (137), ague (26c, 45c, 74b, 104b), aide (10a, 15b, 59b, 106a), aine (51a), aire (64a), akee (51d, 124a), alae (132d), alee (59a, 108a, 132b), aloe (10c, 19c, 59b, 59c, 71d, 75c, 90a, 122d), alte (69d), amie (50b), -ance (117a, 117c), Anne (96b, 107c, 138, 192, 194), anse (50c), ante (68a, 69c, 90d, 114c), ante- (92c), a-one (42b, 46c, 123c), apse (12a, 27a, 98b, 106c, 127c), Arie (139), Arne (102d, 139), Arte (139), Ashe (139), asse (49b), atle (104a, 119b), aube (11a), auge (71b), aune (246), axle (113c, 131c)

**A F _ _**   Afar (41d, 216), afar (36d), AFDC (235), affy (18d), Afro (57b), Afro- (92c)

**_ A F _**   baff (55b), baft (43b), cafe (19c), daft (48b), gaff (46d, 47a, 113b), haft (60a), Kafa (32d, 216), oafs, raff (102d), Raft (176), raft (47c), S.Afr. (242), safe (106b, 116c, 127b), Safi (220), Taft (183, 191), waft (47c)

**_ _ A F**   deaf (125d, 126d), Graf (135a, 156), graf (53d, 81d), leaf (85b, 90a), loaf (61d, 73b, 130a), neaf (47b), Olaf (82b, 128b, 173), Piaf (49d, 100c, 175), RAAF (242), RCAF (242), USAF (243), WAAF (244), WRAF (244)

**A _ _ F**   alif (11d), atef (32b, 39d)

**A G _ _**   Agag (67c, 104a, 197), agal (18a, 30d), Agao (57c), Agar (137),

312

**agar** (32c, 106a), **agas**, **Agau** (57c), **agcy.** (235), **aged** (12c, 83c, 83d), **Agee** (137), **Ager** (137), **ager** (69d, 100d, 102a), **ages**, **agha** (125b), **Agib** (13d), **agio** (42c, 48d, 78a, 94a), **Agis** (67d), **Agni** (68c), **agog** (39a, 42c, 67b), **agon** (30b, 45c, 56b), **Agra** (24c, 119a), **agra** (64a, 118c), **agri.** (235), **agua** (113a), **ague** (26c, 45c, 74b, 104b)

_ A G _   **bago** (15a), **bags**, **Cage** (144), **cage** (30a, 40d), **cagy** (31d), **gaga** (24c, 76a), **gage** (90b), **gags**, **hagi** (65d), **hags**, **Iago** (44a, 85a, 107c, 195), **jags**, **kago** (86a), **lago** (65a, 112d), **lags**, **mage** (74a), **Magh** (213), **magh** (78b), **magi** (88a, 94c, 132d), **Naga** (15a, 69a, 128c), **naga** (23c, 28c, 60a), **nags**, **Nagy** (61c, 172), **Page** (173, 193, 194), **page** (12d, 41c, 48b, 70d, 107a), **raga** (80a), **rage** (26d, 74c, 116a, 120b), **ragi** (25c), **rags**, **saga** (71b, 104c, 119b), **sage** (14c, 70d, 77b, 106a, 131b, 132d), **sago** (44b, 86a, 95d, 114d), **sags**, **tags**, **vagi** (31d), **wage** (103d), **wags**

_ _ A G   **Agag** (67c, 104a, 197), **anag.** (235), **brag** (20b, 24a, 32b, 127c), **crag** (101b), **diag.** (237), **drag** (30d, 95d), **flag** (17a, 38a, 41a, 69a, 87b, 114d, 130c, 132a), **peag** (129d), **phag-** (92d), **quag** (20c), **shag** (57b, 119c, 122c), **slag** (28c, 38b, 76b, 105a, 111a, 129a, 130a), **snag** (13a, 24d, 60a, 68c, 95a, 122b), **stag** (34c, 52b, 76a), **swag** (115c)

A _ _ G   **Agag** (67c, 104a, 197), **agog** (39a, 42c, 67b), **anag.** (235)

A H _ _   **Ahab** (24a, 66c, 67d, 87d, 197), **Ahaz** (67d, 197), **ahem** (15c, 112a), **ahey** (42c), **ahir** (24d), **Ahom** (69a), **ahoy** (57b, 81a), **AHST** (235)

_ A H _   **Bahr** (140), **baht** (223, 246), **Dahl** (147), **Fahr.** (238), **ha-ha** (45b, 118a), **Hahn** (156), **hahs** (42c), **Kahn** (163), **kahu** (15d), **Lahr** (165), **maha** (25d, 69a, 104a), **Oahe** (33b), **Oahu** (64c), **paha** (60a), **rahs**, **Sahl** (179), **Saho** (32d, 57c, 216), **taha** (130d), **tahr** (55a)

_ _ A H   **Adah** (41c, 197), **amah** (74b, 82d, 84d), **ayah** (62d, 82d), **blah** (82a, 71d), **Elah** (67d), **Etah** (56c, 63d), **Leah** (65b, 68b, 197), **Noah** (68d, 76b, 172, 197), **opah** (22a, 46d), **Ptah** (75d, 198), **shah** (16c, 88a), **Utah** (212), **yeah** (10b)

A _ _ H   **ACTH** (235), **Adah** (41c, 197), **Alph** (101a), **amah** (74b, 82d, 84d), **amph.** (235), **ankh** (32a), **anth.** (235), **arch** (28a, 41b, 101c), **-arch** (117c), **arch-** (93b), **arch.** (235), **Asch** (139), **auth.** (236), **ayah** (62d, 82d)

A I _ _   **Aïda** (84b, 97b, 128a), **aide** (10a, 15b, 59b, 106a), **AIDS** (235), **aids**, **ails**, **aims**, **aine** (51a), **ains**, **ain't**, **aire** (64a), **airs** (94b), **airy** (41d, 66a, 71d)

_ A I _   **bail** (20d, 68b), **Bain** (140), **bain** (50a), **Baio** (140), **bait** (16b, 41b, 73d, 119c, 123b), **Cain** (9a, 10a, 41a, 68d, 79d, 107a, 144, 197), **dail** (40a, 64a), **dais** (41d, 90b), **fail** (35c, 44a, 48a), **Fain** (152), **fain** (35b, 54c, 133a), **fair** (10a, 17d, 41b, 45c, 62b, 67c), **fait** (9c, 50b), **Gaia** (39b), **Gail** (154), **gain** (9d, 44d, 83b, 94d, 132b), **gait**

(130c), **Haid** (156), **Haig** (156), **haik** (52d), **hail** (9c, 16a, 56c, 60d, 104a, 127d, 130d), **Haim** (156), **hair** (46a), **jail** (62b), **jain** (60b), **kail** (23a), **kain** (74c), **laic** (28a, 70c, 82a, 94d, 106b), **laid, lain, lair** (34d, 60c), **lait** (50d), **Maia** (59c, 107b, 129c, 198, 207), **maid** (37b, 54c, 107a), **mail** (14c, 76b, 91d), **maim** (80d), **Main** (168), **main** (26c, 29d, 67b, 94c), **mais** (50a), **naid** (51b), **naif** (126c), **nail** (27d, 44c, 119b, 126b), **Nair** (37d), **nair** (85a), **nais** (51b, 101a), **paid** (99a), **pail** (30b), **pain** (10b, 61d), **pair** (21c, 31b, 90d, 119c, 125c), **raid** (48c, 62d), **rail** (9c, 19a, 30d, 75a, 111d, 123c, 129a, 226), **rain** (92a, 120a, 130d), **rais** (24a), **saic** (71c), **Said** (91c), **said** (127c), **sail** (91c), **sain** (19d, 32b), **Sais** (39d), **sais** (56c), **tail** (13c, 25a, 40d, 48b, 89d, 107b, 123c), **tait** (15d, 60d), **vain** (40c, 63a), **vair** (52c, 114b), **waif** (116b), **wail** (32b, 61c, 68d, 114b), **wain** (129b), **wait** (24b, 72a, 99c, 115a, 119d)

_ _ A I    **Alai** (103c), **dhai** (76c), **Thai** (109a, 218, 223)

A _ _ I    **abri** (51a, 108a), **admi** (53b), **aeri-** (92c), **Agni** (68c), **agri.** (235), **Alai** (103c), **alti-** (93a), **ambi-** (92c), **a moi** (50d), **Andi** (25a), **ANSI** (235), **anti** (10c, 84c), **anti-** (92c), **Aoki** (139), **aqui** (112d), **arui** (13b), **asci** (114a), **assi** (60c), **Asti** (65a, 132c), **Atli** (15c, 56d, 61c)

A J _ _    **ajar** (84b), **Ajax** (56b, 120b, 120d, 194)

_ A J _    **Baja** (23b, 76c), **baju** (65b), **haje** (28c, 39d), **haji** (75c), **hajj** (75c, 89b), **Jaja** (79a), **maja** (31d), **raja** (60a)

A K _ _    **Akan** (69a, 215, 216), **akee** (51d, 124a), **Akha** (121d), **Akim** (137), **akin** (67c, 99a), **Akra** (216), **akua** (91a)

_ A K _    **bake** (30c, 101b), **Baku** (24b, 213), **baku** (116b, 124a), **cake** (35b), **fake** (45a, 62a, 94b, 107c), **hake** (46d, 228), **Jake** (160), **jako** (56a), **kaka** (81c), **kaki** (65d, 81c), **Lake** (165), **lake** (89a, 130a), **lakh** (84a, 108a), **laky** (84a, 108a), **make** (13c, 29c, 30c, 40d, 43d, 44c), **maki** (71b), **mako** (20b, 107d), **oaks, rake** (34a, 52d), **raki** (11a), **sake** (10b, 65d, 131a), **Saki** (95c), **saki** (78b, 231), **Saks** (179), **taka** (213), **take** (117a), **takt** (80a, 120b), **waka** (23d), **wake** (102c, 123c), **yaks**

_ _ A K    **Adak** (64b), **anak** (54b), **beak** (18d, 77d), **dhak** (39b), **Dyak** (217, 219), **flak** (13a), **Isak** (159), **leak** (72b, 84b), **N.Dak.** (241), **peak** (11d, 31d, 32c, 59a, 59d, 117d, 135a), **S.Dak.** (242), **Shak.** (243), **soak** (9b, 37d, 104b, 115a), **SWAK** (243), **teak** (39b, 124a), **weak** (45a, 62c, 63a)

A _ _ K    **Adak** (64b), **amok** (18c, 51b), **anak** (54b)

A L _ _    **alae** (132d), **Alai** (103c), **Alan** (137), **alar** (16c, 132d), **Alas.** (209, 235), **alas** (42c, 103b, 133b), **alba** (73c, 75c, 131d), **albs, alca** (15d, 98a), **Alda** (137), **Aldo** (137), **Alea** (15b), **Alec** (137), **alec** (12c, 47a, 104b), **alee** (59a, 108a, 132b), **ales, Alex** (137), **Alfs, alga** (105d), **-algy** (117c), **alif** (11d), **alim** (120a), **alit** (36c, 68d, 107a), **Alla** (138), **alla** (233), **allo-** (93d), **Ally** (138), **ally** (11b, 15b, 29d, 30a, 126c), **Alma** (138), **alma** (32a, 33b), **alms** (26a), **aloe**

314

(10c, 19c, 59b, 59c, 71d, 75c, 90a, 122d), **alop** (38a), **Alou** (138), **alow** (18c, 126a), **Alph** (101a), **Alps** (79b), **also** (12c, 18c, 62c, 78c, 90c, 115b), **Alta.** (235), **alte** (69d), **alti-** (93a), **alto** (113a, 128d), **alto-** (93a), **alum** (37c, 77a), **alum.** (235), **Alva** (39c)

**_ A L _**   **Bala** (53c), **bald** (17b), **bale** (22c, 232), **Bali** (64c), **balk** (16b, 89c, 116a), **Ball** (140), **ball** (17b), **balm** (83d, 126a), **Cale** (144), **calf** (134d), **Cali** (215), **calk** (61b), **call** (12d, 15a, 85b, 108d, 117d, 128c, 134b), **calm** (11c, 13c, 15b, 82a, 85b, 89d, 97a, 106d, 111c, 111d, 126c), **calx** (59a, 85d), **Dale** (26d, 147), **dale** (35d, 98a, 127b), **Dali** (147), **Daly** (147), **Fala** (44d), **fa-la** (98d), **Falk** (152), **fall** (38b, 57b, 106a), **falx** (102a), **gala** (45c), **Gale** (154), **gale** (130d, 132b, 132c), **gall** (18d, 25d, 64b, 128b), **gals**, **Hale** (12b, 156), **hale** (112a, 131d), **half** (77c), **Hall** (156), **hall** (31a, 87a), **halo** (27b, 71d, 81d, 100d), **Hals** (38d, 156), **halt** (14c, 25b, 32a, 59d, 87b, 115d), **kale** (23a, 78a, 90a, 103d, 127c), **Kali** (109d, 199), **kali** (104a), **kalo** (119d), **Lalo** (165), **lalo** (117d), **Male** (37d, 219), **male** (53b, 70b, 114b), **Mali** (219), **mall** (74c, 95a, 108c), **malm** (27d, 72a), **malo** (21d, 58c, 72d, 112d), **malt** (18a), **pale** (19d, 86a, 88d, 129d), **Pali** (22b, 104b, 127c), **pall** (28b, 122b, 130d), **palm** (124a), **palp** (13a, 45a, 123b), **pals**, **rale** (21d, 26c, 34a), **sala** (112d, 113a), **sale** (15c, 17b, 50b, 51a, 123d), **Salk** (179), **salp** (83b), **SALT** (242), **salt** (29d, 80b, 94b, 103b, 106a, 111c), **tala** (17c), **talc** (25d, 49c, 77a, 92a, 111b), **tale** (43a, 71b, 103b, 134a), **talk** (29d, 36a, 113b), **tall** (72d), **Vale** (184), **vale** (44b, 127b), **Vali** (83b), **wale** (55c, 100c, 130c, 131b, 131c), **walk** (85b), **Wall** (193), **wall** (118a), **Walt** (185), **Yale** (79b, 101c, 205)

**_ _ A L**   **agal** (18a, 30d), **anal** (51c), **Aral** (103c), **Baal** (106c), **bual** (132c), **coal** (13a, 40c, 52a), **deal** (17b, 36a, 36d, 123d), **dhal** (11d), **dial** (43d), **dual** (37c, 125c), **egal** (50b), **et al.** (69c, 238), **foal** (61b), **goal** (10d, 17c, 40d, 83a, 96c, 104d, 119d), **heal** (32d), **hyal-** (93a), **-ical** (117a), **ital.** (240), **leal** (73c, 105b), **meal** (56c, 99c), **Neal** (172), **Obal** (197), **opal** (19c, 53b, 54c, 64a), **oral** (79b, 113d, 127c, 128a), **oval** (39d, 40b), **peal** (100d), **real** (9d, 116c), **rial** (220), **ryal** (83c), **saal** (53d), **seal** (28b, 44c, 89b, 231), **sial** (85b), **Taal** (10c, 69a, 112b), **teal** (19a, 20b, 38c, 226), **udal** (59c), **Ural** (103c), **veal** (23b, 75c), **vial** (110d), **weal** (131b, 131c), **zeal** (14b, 45c)

**A _ _ L**   **Abel** (10a, 23a, 107a, 197), **agal** (18a, 30d), **amyl** (114d), **amyl-** (93d), **anal** (51c), **Angl.** (235), **anil** (38d, 62d), **Aral** (103c), **aril** (106b), **aryl** (14b), **AWOL** (236), **axil** (12c), **azul** (112c)

**A M _ _**   **amah** (74b, 82d, 84d), **amas** (69d), **amat** (69d), **ambi-** (92c), **ambo** (95d, 98a), **amen** (111b, 128a), **Amer.** (235), **amer** (50a), **Ames** (138), **AMEX** (235), **amia** (21b, 79c), **amid** (12b), **amie** (50b), **amir** (10b, 13d), **Amis** (138), **amis** (50b), **amla** (39b), **amma** (9a), **ammo** (12b), **a moi** (50d), **amok** (18c, 51b), **Amon** (67d, 198), **Amor** (32d, 198), **amor** (112d), **Amos** (108a, 138, 196, 197), **Amoy** (69a), **amph.** (235), **amps**, **amra** (60c), **Amur** (101a), **amyl** (114d), **amyl-** (93d), **Amys**

**_ A M _**   **came** (132b), **Camp** (144), **camp** (19c, 39d, 127a), **cams**, **dama** (65a, 112d), **dame** (45b, 54c, 68c, 81d, 122c), **damp** (33c, 77c,

315

131b), **dams, Fama** (103a), **fame** (99c, 99d), **gamb** (12d), **game** (114a), **gamo-** (93c), **Gamp** (35c), **gamp** (125b), **gams** (71b), **gamy** (90b, 103d), **Hama** (222), **hame** (61b), **hams, iamb** (48c), **jamb** (37c, 109a, 126d), **jams, Jamy** (194), **Kama** (199), **kama** (60a, 129a), **kame** (60a, 100c), **kami** (65d, 108a), **lama** (22b, 121d), **Lamb** (40b, 165), **lamb** (107d), **lame** (32a, 57c), **lamp** (71d, 73c), **lams, mama** (44b), **mamo** (58b), **Nama** (61c), **name** (10d, 13c, 28d, 38b, 82a, 122c), **Pams, Rama** (128c), **rami** (21c), **ramp** (52c, 62c, 110d), **Rams** (206), **rams, sama** (80d), **same** (36d, 61d), **samp** (55c, 60d, 91c), **Sams, tame** (37a, 37b, 53c), **tamp** (76d, 85b, 92a, 97d), **tams, vamp** (62c, 108c, 233), **yams, Zama** (106a)

_ _ **A M**   **Adam** (23d, 84d, 107a, 137, 194, 197), **Aram** (108a, 118d, 139), **beam** (98a), **Bram** (142), **caam** (73a), **Cham** (224), **clam** (19c, 77d), **cram** (116c), **diam.** (237), **dram** (38a, 38b, 84a, 92a, 110d, 246), **Edam** (26b, 38d), **Elam** (88a, 108a, 151), **Enam** (66d), **exam** (120d), **flam** (38b), **foam** (51c, 114a), **gram** (76b, 246), **Guam** (64c), **imam** (23b, 80c), **Liam** (166), **loam** (39a, 111c), **ma'am** (74a), **Noam** (172), **ogam** (64b), **pram** (16a, 24c), **ream** (18d, 31b, 41a, 86b, 125c), **roam** (123d, 129d), **seam** (66c, 67a, 128c), **sham** (9d, 34a, 45a, 49b, 77b, 91d, 94b, 109c), **Siam** (120d), **slam** (124c, 131c), **Spam** (73c), **swam, team** (32a, 48c, 56c, 85d, 232), **tram** (124c), **Ulam** (197), **wham** (110b)

**A _ _ M**   **Adam** (23d, 84d, 107a, 137, 194, 197), **ahem** (15c, 112a), **Ahom** (69a), **Akim** (137), **alim** (120a), **alum** (37c, 77a), **alum.** (235), **Aram** (108a, 118d, 139), **arum** (32c, 71d, 114d), **atom** (77d, 131c)

**A N _ _**   **anag.** (235), **anak** (54b), **anal** (51c), **anas, anat.** (235), **anba** (28a), **-ance** (117a, 117c), **-ancy** (117b), **anda** (21c, 133b), **Andi** (25a), **Andy** (138), **anew** (10b, 10c), **Angl.** (235), **anil** (38d, 62d), **anis, Anka** (138), **ankh** (32a), **Anna** (84a, 122d, 138), **anna** (103a), **Anne** (96b, 107c, 138, 192, 194), **anno** (70b), **Anns, anoa** (48d, 85d, 132a, 229), **anon** (10c, 15d, 62a, 94a, 108d, 111d), **anon.** (235), **ansa** (57d), **anse** (50c), **ANSI** (235), **ansu** (13d, 68c), **anta** (89a, 91c), **ante** (68a, 69c, 90d, 114c), **ante-** (92c), **anth.** (235), **anti** (10c, 84c), **anti-** (92c), **ants, Anya** (139)

_ **A N _**   **banc** (66d), **band** (56c, 116b, 232), **bane** (58a, 81b, 90d, 102d, 133b), **bang** (110b), **bani** (101d), **bank** (19a, 47c, 91b), **bans, Cana** (46c, 52b), **canc.** (236), **cane** (98a, 114b, 115a, 115b, 117d, 129b), **cans, cant** (62c, 63b, 66a, 70d, 103d, 122a, 122b), **Dana** (147), **Dane** (67c, 82b, 104c, 147), **dang** (42a), **dank** (33b, 77c), **Dans, dans** (50c), **Danu** (199), **fane** (104a, 120b), **Fang** (193, 216), **fang** (123a), **fans, gang** (16d, 32a, 232), **Hana** (157), **hand** (10d, 15a, 59b, 87c, 133d, 246), **hang** (118b), **Hank** (157), **hank** (57b, 109d), **Hans** (17b, 53d, 67a, 157), **-iana** (117c), **Ians, Jana** (80d, 160), **Jane** (160), **Jann** (160), **Jans, kana** (66a), **Kane** (163), **Kano** (129c), **Kans.** (210, 240), **Kant** (53d, 163), **Lana** (165), **lana** (70b), **Land** (165), **land** (9d, 36b, 120d), **Lane** (165), **lane** (11c, 21b, 116b), **Lang** (165), **lang.** (240), **lank** (121a), **lanx** (102a), **mana** (91a), **mand** (25c), **mane** (57b), **mani** (87b), **Mann** (168), **mano** (65a), **Manx** (25c), **manx** (24d), **many** (82d), **Nana** (88b, 135c),

316

**nano-** (92c), **Nans, pane** (114c, 114d), **Pang** (125a), **pang** (85d, 114b, 121c), **pans, pant** (18a, 21d), **rana** (51c, 60a), **Rand** (176), **rand** (220, 222), **rang, rani** (60a, 94c), **rank** (27d, 46a, 55c, 72a, 73d, 97d, 116c), **rant** (34b, 58a, 98a, 119b), **Sa'na** (134c), **Sand** (179), **sand** (78d, 109b), **sane** (97d), **sang, sank, sans** (51b), **Tana** (68b), **T'ang** (26d), **tang** (22a, 47b, 135a), **tank** (127d), **Tano** (95d, 189), **tans, uang** (100b), **vane** (130d, 132b), **vang** (57c, 102b), **vans, wand** (90d, 101c, 115b), **wane** (9a, 34b, 69a, 116d), **want** (34a, 35b, 68b, 81b, 92a, 133a), **yang** (134d), **Yank** (12b), **yank** (95d), **Zana** (58a), **Zane** (188), **zany** (28b, 38a, 48b, 109c)

_ _ A N    **Akan** (69a, 215, 216), **Alan** (137), **Aran** (52b, 64c), **azan** (80c), **Bean** (140), **bean** (58c, 60b, 71b, 106b, 127c), **bran** (22a, 22b, 55d, 61d), **Caan** (144), **clan** (124b), **cran** (118c), **Dean** (148), **dean** (83c), **Dian** (198), **duan** (52a), **Dyan** (150), **elan** (33d, 41b, 113d, 128d, 135a), **flan** (32d, 87a), **Fran** (153), **G-man** (45a), **guan** (19b), **Iban** (33d), **Iran** (88a, 217), **Ivan** (66c, 103c, 159), **Jean** (160), **Joan** (161), **Juan** (163), **Kean** (164), **Khan** (164), **khan** (10b, 63a, 88a, 94c), **kwan** (246), **Lean** (165), **lean** (24b, 29b, 98a, 110c, 113b, 121a, 122b), **loan** (17a, 78a), **mean** (9a, 16a, 17b, 34d, 76c, 109b, 115c), **moan** (32b, 112b), **Oman** (220), **Onan** (66d), **Oran** (213), **plan** (13d, 15c, 35b, 76b, 95a, 104d), **roan** (61a, 98c, 131c), **Ryan** (179), **scan** (47c, 73a, 88b, 98a), **Sean** (66c, 180), **Shan** (62d, 69a, 220), **span** (21d, 32a, 38d, 49a, 81d, 85d, 98a, 120a, 120c, 122a, 232), **Stan** (181), **Svan** (25a), **swan** (19a, 28c, 226), **than** (29b), **T-man** (45a), **tuan** (74c), **uran** (78a), **wean** (117a), **yean** (68d), **Yüan** (26d, 78a), **yuan** (215)

A _ _ N    **Aden** (13d, 224), **aeon** (122b), **agon** (30b, 45c, 56b), **Akan** (69a, 215, 216), **akin** (67c, 99a), **Alan** (137), **amen** (111b, 128a), **Amon** (67d, 198), **anon** (10c, 15d, 62a, 94a, 108d, 111d), **anon.** (235), **Aran** (52b, 64c), **ARVN** (235), **asin** (78b), **assn.** (236), **aton** (118a), **attn.** (236), **Avon** (107c), **axon** (81b), **ayin** (12a), **azan** (80c), **azon** (10b)

A O _ _    **Aoki** (139), **a-one** (42b, 46c, 123b), **aout** (49d)

_ A O _    **faon** (44d), **gaol** (94d), **gaon** (66c), **Laos** (218), **naos** (25b, 104a, 120b), **paon** (87b), **Taos** (81c)

_ _ A O    **Agao** (57c), **ciao** (65a), **Isao** (159), **Liao** (101a)

A _ _ O    **acro-** (93a, 93c), **aero-** (92c, **aero.** (235), **Afro** (57b), **Afro-** (92c), **Agao** (57c), **agio** (42c, 48d, 78a, 94a), **Aldo** (137), **allo-** (93d), **also** (12c, 18c, 62c, 78c, 90c, 115b), **alto** (113a, 128d), **alto-** (93a), **ambo** (95d, 98a), **ammo** (12b), **anno** (70b), **Argo** (14b, 66a), **Arlo** (139), **Arno** (101a, 139), **at. no.** (236), **atto-** (93c), **auto** (24a)

A P _ _    **apar** (14b), **aped, aper** (28b, 77a), **apes, apex** (32c, 59a, 59d, 87b, 89b, 123a, 135a), **Apia** (91c, 224), **Apis** (22c, 40a, 95d, 103b), **Apoc.** (235), **apod** (48c), **apos.** (235), **apse** (12a, 27a, 98b, 106c, 127c), **Apus** (207)

_ A P _    **Bapt.** (236), **capa** (122c), **cape** (37c, 58d, 74d, 95a), **Caph** (207),

**Capp** (144), **caps**, **Capt.** (236), **daps**, **gape** (134b), **gaps**, **Hapi** (198), **hapi** (53b), **hapl-** (93c), **jape** (66c), **Lapp** (82b, 222), **laps**, **mapo** (55a), **maps**, **Napa** (23b, 132c), **napa** (54d, 70d), **nape** (16b, 82d), **naps**, **papa** (12a, 44b), **Papp** (173), **paps**, **rape** (107b), **raps**, **rapt** (9b, 41a), **sapa** (55d), **saps**, **tapa** (17b, 28b, 43b, 45c, 79d, 86b, 91a), **tape** (19a, 98c), **taps**, **yapp** (20d), **yaps**

_ _ A P     **asap** (62a, 235), **atap** (86a), **chap** (45b, 74c), **clap** (13c, 121d), **crap** (82a, 91b), **flap** (48a, 79c, 89d, 119a, 130c, 132d), **frap** (37d, 122a), **hcap.** (239), **heap** (17a, 75b, 79a, 89a), **knap** (60a), **laap** (41d), **leap** (24a, 67a, 232), **neap** (121d, 122d, 129b), **reap** (9d, 33a, 58b), **slap** (22c, 98b), **snap** (17b, 21d, 31d, 39b, 44c, 66c), **soap** (17c), **swap** (123c), **trap** (24c, 24d, 41a, 54b, 55b, 101b, 111b), **whap** (60b), **wrap** (19a, 28a, 41b)

A _ _ P     **AARP** (235), **alop** (38a), **asap** (62a, 235), **atap** (86a), **atop** (85c, 126d), **avdp.** (236)

A Q _ _     **aqua** (20b, 70b), **aqui** (112d)

_ _ A Q     **Iraq** (217)

A R _ _     **Arab** (104b, 213, 217, 218, 219, 221, 222, 223, 224), **Arab.** (235), **Arad** (221), **arad** (65b), **Aral** (103c), **Aram** (108a, 118d, 139), **Aran** (52b, 64c), **Aras**, **arca** (11d, 21b, 99b), **arch** (28a, 41b, 101c), **-arch** (117c), **arch-** (93b), **arch.** (235), **arcs**, **area** (36d, 37b, 45d, 72d, 97d, 99a, 135c), **Ares** (13b, 41c, 59b, 75a, 129d, 135c, 198), **Argo** (14b, 66a), **aria** (75d, 111d, 125a, 234), **arid** (38b), **Arie** (139), **aril** (106b), **Ariz.** (209, 235), **arks**, **Arlo** (139), **arms** (130d), **army** (61c), **arna** (22b, 131d), **Arnd** (53d), **Arne** (102d, 139), **Arno** (101a, 139), **arns**, **Aroa** (127d), **arpa** (65a), **Arta** (56d), **Arte** (139), **arts**, **arty**, **arui** (13b), **arum** (32c, 71d, 114d), **ARVN** (235), **aryl** (14b)

_ A R _     **Aare** (18c, 100b), **AARP** (235), **Bara** (140), **barb** (47a, 89a, 90c, 95a), **Bard** (200), **bard** (14c, 16b, 90c), **bare** (36a, 40c, 43a, 76a, 116b, 127a), **Bari** (10a, 218), **bark** (12d, 37b), **barm** (134b), **barn** (116a), **baro-** (93c), **bars**, **Bart** (140), **Bart.** (236), **Cara** (144), **cara** (65a), **carb-** (92d), **card** (29a, 66d, 87a), **CARE** (236), **care** (13a, 25b, 29d, 59a, 77a, 99a, 123d, 124d, 133d), **cark** (24b, 133d), **Carl** (144), **caro** (65a), **carp** (25b, 32a, 46a, 46c, 96d, 228), **Carr** (144), **cars**, **cart** (125d, 127c, 129b), **Cary** (144), **darb** (88a), **dare** (25d, 34c), **dark** (38d, 54d, 118c), **darn** (42a, 75d, 83a, 99c), **dart** (14c, 33d, 68d, 77b, 90c, 95a, 114a, 118c), **Earl** (150), **earl** (82a), **earn** (35b, 52a, 76a), **ears**, **fare** (35c, 48b), **farl** (105b), **farm** (21d, 32a, 55d, 122a), **faro** (24b), **Farr** (152), **garb** (28b, 37d), **gare** (50d, 97b), **Garn** (154), **Garo** (69a, 154), **GARP** (239), **Garr** (154), **gars**, **Gary** (154), **hard** (123b), **hare** (101c, 230), **hark** (72b), **harl** (46a, 48a, 59b), **harm** (33b, 61d, 62a, 63a), **harp** (80b), **Hart** (157), **hart** (34c, 114b), **Harz** (79b), **jarl** (104c), **jars**, **kari** (15d), **Karl** (163), **kary-** (93b), **Lara** (23c), **lard** (44c, 50a, 56a, 83d), **lari** (219), **lark** (19a, 51c, 226), **mara** (101c, 230), **Marc** (168), **marc** (55d), **mare** (61a, 82c), **Mari** (16d), **mari** (50c), **Mark** (42a, 102c, 168, 196), **mark** (10d, 15c, 55c, 96b, 109b, 114c, 133a), **marl** (27d, 35a, 45c), **Marr** (168), **Mars** (89d, 98d, 129d, 199), **mars** (49d), **mart** (40c,

318

74d), **maru** (65d), **Marv** (169), **Marx** (169), **Mary** (96c, 107c, 169, 197), **narc-** (93c), **nard** (75b, 83d), **Nare** (72d), **nark** (63a, 115d), **nary** (82c), **oars**, **Para** (18b, 214), **para** (112d, 214, 215, 222, 224), **pard** (24d), **pare** (87c, 98d), **pari-** (92d), **park** (53b, 95d), **parr** (103d, 109d), **pars**, **part** (11c, 43d, 49b, 57b, 91d, 106d), **rare** (83b, 104c, 126a, 126d), **Sara** (179, 215), **sard** (24b, 25d, 53b, 84c, 106c, 115d), **sari** (52d, 60a), **Sark** (26a, 64b), **Sart** (64a), **Tara** (104d), **tara** (45b, 64a), **tare** (128b, 131a), **tarn** (68b, 79b, 91b, 130a), **taro** (14d, 39c, 52a, 90d, 102b, 114d, 125a), **tarp** (23d, 130b), **tars**, **tart** (87a, 112b), **vara** (72a), **vari** (71b), **vary** (26a, 35c, 77c), **Ward** (186), **ward** (27c, 35a, 67b), **ware** (76a), **warm** (10b, 58d, 120c), **warn** (11b, 25b), **warp** (30b, 121c, 125c), **wars**, **Wart** (193), **wart** (95c), **wary** (25b, 128b, 130a), **Yard** (187), **yard** (40d, 69a, 113a, 246), **yarn** (43a, 114b, 119b, 133c), **zarf** (28d, 32d, 114d)

_ _ A R     **Adar** (66d, 78c), **Afar** (41d, 216), **afar** (36d), **Agar** (137), **agar** (32c, 106a), **ajar** (84b), **alar** (16c, 132d), **apar** (14b), **Avar** (25a, 82b), **Bear** (79b), **bear** (40d, 114c, 134c, 230), **boar** (60c, 89a, 118d, 132a, 230), **char** (104d, 124d, 228), **clar.** (237), **czar** (103c), **dear** (40d), **fear** (11a, 51c, 86b, 120d), **gear** (13c, 28b, 41b, 85b, 123a), **gnar** (56d), **guar** (38b, 48c), **hear** (59a, 72b), **hoar** (51c, 131d), **Isar** (33d, 79d, 100d, 216), **iyar** (78c), **izar** (52d), **knar** (68c), **Lear** (30d, 107c, 195), **liar** (75d), **maar** (129a), **near** (13d, 28b, 81d), **Omar** (41c, 78d, 88a, 120c, 173, 197), **Paar** (173), **pear** (51d, 124a), **Phar.** (242), **rear** (10c, 21d, 40d, 41c, 60a, 97c), **roar** (12d, 13c), **Saar** (49c, 78d, 101a), **scar** (27b, 134a), **sear** (25b, 133a), **soar** (48a), **spar** (21b, 22c, 52a, 77a, 90d, 101c, 108b), **star** (15b, 73c), **tear** (68b, 99c), **Thar** (35a), **thar** (55a), **tsar** (103c), **usar** (11b, 17b, 62d), **wear** (114a), **year** (122b)

A _ _ R     **abbr.** (235), **abir** (98d), **acer** (74d), **Adar** (66d, 78c), **Afar** (41d, 216), **afar** (36d), **Agar** (137), **agar** (32c, 106a), **Ager** (137), **ager** (69d, 100d, 102a), **ahir** (24d), **ajar** (84b), **alar** (16c, 132d), **Amer.** (235), **amer** (50a), **amir** (10b, 13d), **Amor** (32d, 198), **amor** (112d), **Amur** (101a), **apar** (14b), **aper** (28b, 77a), **asor** (59a), **astr-** (93d), **-ator** (117c), **Auer** (61c, 139), **Avar** (25a, 82b), **aver** (10b, 15a, 16c, 34b, 74b, 115a, 118c), **azur** (50a)

A S _ _     **asap** (62a, 235), **Asas**, **ASAT** (235), **Asch** (139), **asci** (114a), **asea** (32b, 129c), **Ashe** (139), **ashy** (86a, 129d), **Asia** (39b), **asin** (78b), **asks**, **asor** (59a), **asps**, **asse** (49b), **assi** (60c), **assn.** (236), **asst.** (236), **Asta** (37b, 81d, 121b), **Asti** (65a, 132c), **astr-** (93d)

_ A S _     **base** (9a, 41d, 49a, 62a, 73c, 92b, 102b, 102d), **bash** (60b, 86d), **bask** (46d, 73d, 80b, 128d, 228), **bast** (17b, 45d, 88c, 133c), **casa** (112d), **case** (14b, 30b, 63b, 71a, 82c), **Cash** (144), **eash** (15a, 78a), **cask** (30b), **Caso** (64c), **Cass** (144), **cast** (15a, 73a, 121c, 123b, 232), **dash** (20a, 96a, 114a, 120b, 128d), **ease** (10b, 11c, 15b, 29b, 42d, 71b, 77b, 99b, 99d, 100a, 129d), **east** (84d), **easy** (43d, 53c, 55c, 77c, 109c, 111c), **fast** (46b, 47c, 96d, 118c, 126d), **gash** (33a, 110b), **gasp** (21d, 86b), **hash** (21b), **hasp** (44c, 113c), **hast** (128a), **lasi** (221), **jass** (118d), **lash** (42d, 47c, 122a, 131c), **lass** (45b, 74b), **last** (30b, 40d, 108c, 130d), **masa** (30d), **masc.** (240), **MASH** (240), **Mash** (197), **mash** (32b, 115d), **mask** (29d,

319

36b, 37c), **Mass.** (210, 240), **mass** (9c, 10d, 17a, 22c, 53a, 58d, 107a, 129a), **mast** (18a, 90d, 108b, 113a), **NASA** (241), **Nash** (172), **nasi** (87a), **NASL** (241), **naso-** (93b), **Nast** (172), **oast** (16b, 67b, 85c), **pass** (13d, 21d, 84a, 85c, 106c), **past** (55b, 60b, 122a), **rase** (34d), **rash** (98b, 110a), **rasp** (46a, 56a, 105c, 122d), **sash** (18c, 37c, 54c, 132b), **Sask.** (242), **sass** (16b, 62c), **task** (115c), **Tasm.** (243), **TASS** (81c, 112b), **vasa** (38c, 128a), **vase** (30b, 47d), **vaso-** (92c), **vast** (61c, 62a), **Wash.** (82b), **Wash.** (212), **wash** (14d), **WASP** (244), **wasp** (63b, 229), **wast** (128a), **Zasu** (188)

_ _ A S    **a bas** (50b), **Adas**, **agas**, **Alas.** (209, 235), **alas** (42c, 103b, 133b), **amas** (69d), **anas**, **Aras**, **Asas**, **Avas**, **baas**, **Beas**, **bias** (12c, 35c, 94a), **boas**, **bras** (49d), **Chas.** (74d), **Dias** (91d), **eras**, **Evas**, **eyas** (19b, 58c), **fras**, **goas**, **Idas** (24d), **Iras** (28a, 195), **keas**, **leas**, **Lias** (53c), **moas**, **okas**, **peas**, **seas**, **spas**, **teas**, **'twas** (30b, 107c), **Unas**, **upas** (66a, 90d, 124a), **utas** (40a), **Xmas** (27a), **yeas** (129c)

A _ _ S    **a bas** (50b), **abcs** (46c), **Abes**, **aces**, **Acis** (52b), **acts**, **acus** (70a, 89b), **Adas**, **adds**, **agas**, **ages**, **Agis** (67d), **AIDS** (235), **aids**, **ails**, **aims**, **ains**, **airs** (94b), **Alas.** (209, 235), **alas** (42c, 103b, 133b), **albs**, **ales**, **Alfs**, **alms** (26a), **Alps** (79b), **amas** (69d), **Ames** (138), **Amis** (138), **amis** (50b), **Amos** (108a, 138, 196, 197), **amps**, **Amys**, **anas**, **anis**, **Anns**, **ants**, **apes**, **Apis** (22c, 40a, 95d, 103b), **apos.** (235), **Apus** (207), **Aras**, **arcs**, **Ares** (13b, 41c, 59b, 75a, 129d, 135c, 198), **arks**, **arms** (130d), **arns**, **arts**, **Asas**, **asks**, **asps**, **ates** (118c), **atis** (60a), **auks**, **Avas**, **aves**, **avis** (69c), **avus** (69d), **awes**, **awls**, **awns**, **axes**, **axis** (25c, 34c, 60c), **ayes** (129c)

A T _ _    **atap** (86a), **atef** (32b, 39d), **ates** (118c), **-atic** (117c), **atis** (60a), **atle** (104a, 119b), **Atli** (15c, 56d, 61c), **at. no.** (236), **atom** (77d, 131c), **aton** (118a), **atop** (85c, 126d), **-ator** (117c), **atta** (70c), **attn.** (236), **atto-** (93c), **Attu** (64b), **atty.** (236), **atua** (91a), **at. wt.** (236)

_ A T _    **bate** (119c), **Bath** (41a, 112c), **bath** (35d, 88d, 125a, 246), **bats**, **batt** (16d), **cata-** (92c, 92d), **Cath.** (236), **Cato** (101d, 102a, 194), **cats**, **Catt** (144), **data** (29c, 63a, 115a), **date** (33d, 51d), **eats** (48b), **fate** (35b, 68a, 73b), **Fats** (152), **gata** (107d), **gate** (15c, 41b, 91c), **Gath** (88c), **gats**, **GATT** (239), **hate** (35b, 72d), **hath** (128a), **hats**, **JATO** (240), **Kate** (107c, 163), **kati** (246), **Kato** (56c), **late** (33d, 98b), **lath** (116c), **mate** (15b, 18d, 26c, 29b, 34c, 85d, 114a, 120a), **math** (116c), **Mats** (169), **Matt** (169, 240), **maty** (62d), **Nate** (172), **Natl.** (241), **NATO** (11c, 241), **Nats**, **oath** (90b, 111c), **oats**, **Pate** (174), **pate** (32b, 58c), **path** (101a, 102c, 130c), **pats**, **patu** (130d), **rata** (46a), **rate** (13d, 27d, 30b, 41d, 42a, 55c, 66d, 94b, 97d, 107a, 127b), **rath** (99d), **RATO** (242), **rats**, **sate** (28b, 54d, 56a, 118a), **Sati** (96d, 109d, 198), **SATs** (29a), **ta-ta** (44b), **tats**, **tatu** (14b), **vats**, **vatu** (224), **WATS** (244), **Watt** (63d, 186), **watt** (129a, 246), **yate** (41d)

_ _ A T    **adat** (74b), **amat** (69d), **anat.** (235), **ASAT** (235), **beat** (17c, 30a, 47c, 100b, 121b, 121c, 131c, 233), **bhat** (62d), **blat** (20b), **boat** (81b, 108b), **brat** (26c), **chat** (19a, 29d, 119b, 225), **coat** (52d), **-crat** (117c), **drat** (42a, 83a), **erat** (96a, 97c), **etat** (51a), **feat** (9d, 43a, 124c), **fiat** (34b, 84c), **flat** (42a, 63b, 95a, 95c, 114c, 234), **frat**

320

(29a), **Geat** (104c), **ghat** (28c, 79b), **gnat** (48a, 63b, 76c, 229), **goat** (81a, 102d, 230), **Guat.** (239), **Heat** (206), **heat** (129d), **Kaat** (163), **khat** (58b), **kyat** (220), **meat** (48b), **moat** (36d), **neat** (10a, 116a, 121d, 124c), **peat** (52a, 127c), **plat** (74d, 90b), **prat** (23a), **scat** (54b, 96d), **seat** (25d, 63b, 115c), **skat** (24b), **slat** (69b, 133b), **spat** (14b, 85d, 96b, 102c), **stat** (15c, 114a), **-stat** (117c), **stat.** (243), **SWAT** (243), **swat** (20a, 28b, 116b), **teat** (81d), **that** (34d, 95a, 99b), **what** (96d, 99b)

A _ _ T     **abet** (10d, 48b, 59b), **abut** (21a, 75d, 123b), **acct.** (235), **acet-** (92c), **acht** (53d), **adat** (74b), **adit** (41b, 77a), **AHST** (235), **ain't**, **alit** (36c, 68d, 107a), **amat** (69d), **anat.** (235), **aout** (49d), **ASAT** (235), **asst.** (236), **at. wt.** (236), **aunt** (44b, 99b)

A U _ _     **aube** (11a), **Auer** (61c, 139), **auge** (71b), **auks**, **aula** (53d), **auld** (105b), **aune** (246), **aunt** (44b, 99b), **aura** (10d, 36d, 39d, 40b, 57c, 100d), **auth.** (236), **auto** (24a)

_ A U _     **baud** (120b), **Baum** (85d, 140), **caul** (45c, 84a), **daub** (111a), **dauw** (22d), **eaux** (51b), **Faun** (45d, 133b, 198), **gaud** (124c, 133d), **Gaul** (49b), **gaur** (25a, 62d, 132a, 230), **haud** (70a), **haul** (37c), **Kaus** (208), **laud** (57b, 92b, 127d), **Maud** (131d, 169), **maud** (43b, 56a), **Maui** (64c), **maul** (17c, 57d, 74c), **naut.** (241), **Paul** (18a, 91b, 174), **Raul** (176), **Sauk** (49b, 56c, 189), **Saul** (67d, 87a, 179, 197), **-saur** (117b), **taur-** (92c), **taus, taut** (120c, 122a), **Vaux** (192, 195), **vaux** (49c), **waul** (114b), **yaup** (119b)

_ _ A U     **Agau** (57c), **Beau** (140), **beau** (117d, 118b), **Esau** (64b, 65b, 98b, 197), **frau** (54a), **Grau** (156), **luau** (58b), **Seau** (180), **unau** (110d)

A _ _ U     **abou** (44d), **ACLU** (235), **acou-** (93a), **Agau** (57c), **Alou** (138), **ansu** (13d, 68c), **Attu** (64b)

A V _ _     **Avar** (25a, 82b), **Avas**, **avdp.** (236), **avec** (51b), **aver** (10b, 15a, 16c, 34b, 74b, 115a, 118c), **aves**, **avid** (39a, 41b, 56b, 67b, 135a), **avis** (69c), **Avon** (107c), **avow** (9d, 15a, 16c, 29d, 30a, 34b, 85c), **avus** (69d)

_ A V _     **cava** (127d), **cave** (113c, 126b), **cavy** (56d, 101c, 230), **Dave** (148), **Davy** (148, 193), **davy** (103b), **favi** (122a), **gave, have** (20b), **Java** (64c), **java** (28d), **kava** (18d, 91a), **kavi** (66a), **lava** (77d, 101b, 129a), **lave** (130a), **nave** (27a, 131c), **navy** (20a, 47c), **pave** (66b), **Pavo** (87b, 207), **rave** (34b, 58a, 119b), **Ravi** (176), **save** (42b, 67b, 84b, 94b, 126c), **wave** (48a, 83b, 100d, 118c, 126b), **wavy** (126b)

_ _ A V     **Muav** (53c), **Slav** (14d)

A _ _ V     **Azov** (19d, 103c)

A W _ _     **away** (9b, 55b, 59b, 83c), **awed, awes, awls, awns, awny, AWOL** (236), **awry** (15a, 32a, 125c, 134c)

**_ A W _** bawd (22a), bawl (18c, 129b, 134b), caws, Dawn (148), dawn (14b, 15d, 33d), fawn (32a, 34c), gawk (109c, 114d), hawk (19a, 87c, 225), Hawn (157), haws, jaws, kawi (66a), lawn (31a, 43b, 69a, 72a), laws, maws, pawl (73d), pawn (26c, 60c, 90b), paws, sawn, saws, tawa (81c), taws, wawl (114b), yawl (20b, 103b), yawn (21a), yawp (12d, 119b), yaws

**_ _ A W** braw (105a), chaw (122c), claw (26b, 80b, 119b, 126b), craw (32a, 56d, 115c), draw (11d, 43c, 91d, 123c), flaw (19d, 34c), gnaw (19c, 26c), Shaw (41a, 43a, 180, 204), skaw (67c), slaw (28d), thaw (72b)

**A _ _ W** alow (18c, 126a), anew (10b, 10c), avow (9d, 15a, 16c, 29d, 30a, 34b, 85c)

**A X _ _** axed, axes, axil (12c), axis (25c, 34c, 60c), axle (113c, 131c), axon (81b)

**_ A X _** taxi (95d), waxy

**_ _ A X** Ajax (56b, 120b, 120d, 194), coax (131b), flax (72a, 72b), hoax (34a, 92b), olax (42b), Sfax (223)

**A _ _ X** Ajax (56b, 120b, 120d, 194), Alex (137), AMEX (235), apex (32c, 59a, 59d, 87b, 89b, 123a, 135a)

**A Y _ _** ayah (62d, 82d), ayes (129c), ayin (12a)

**_ A Y _** Baya (215), baya (130d), bays, cays, days, Faye (152), Fays, Gaya (18d), Gaye (154), gays (60d), Hays (157), jays, Kaye (164), kayo (68c), Kays, lays, Maya (134d, 169, 214, 217), maya (60a, 130d), Mayo (169), Mays (169), nays (129c), pays, raya (85a), rays, saya (88c), says, ways

**_ _ A Y** away (9b, 55b, 59b, 83c), bray (12d, 37c), chay (39b, 98c), Clay (146), clay (39a, 92a), D-Day (67a, 82a), dray (24c, 114b, 129b), flay (110a, 110b, 116c), fray (45d, 49b, 125a), Gray (21a, 41a, 156, 192), gray (60c), O'Day (173), okay (10b, 13d, 86d, 112a), play (51c, 52b, 87d, 91d, 114a), pray (18c, 41b), quay (68d, 88d, 131b), shay (84a), slay (36c, 79d), spay (115b), stay (34c, 57c, 95b, 99c, 102b, 119d, 128c, 129b), sway (29b, 37b, 63a, 67c, 76d, 79c, 85a, 130c, 133a), tray (98b, 104a, 107a), Tway (184), Wray (187), x-ray (12a, 75c, 88d)

**A _ _ Y** Abby (137), -ably (117b), achy (112a), aery (39a), affy (18d), agcy. (235), ahey (42c), ahoy (57b, 81a), airy (41d, 66a, 71d), -algy (117c), Ally (138), ally (11b, 15b, 29d, 30a, 126c), Amoy (69a), -ancy (117b), Andy (138), army (61c), arty, ashy (86a, 129d), atty. (236), away (9b, 55b, 59b, 83c), awny, awry (15a, 32a, 125c, 134c)

**A Z _ _** azan (80c), azon (10b), Azov (19d, 103c), azul (112c), azur (50a)

**_ A Z _**   daze (48a, 116c, 116d), faze (36a), Gaza (88c, 216), gaze (114d
115a), haze (28b, 48a, 77b, 127b), hazy (127a), Jazz (206), jazz
(61d, 118d), laze (61d), maze (68b), mazy, nazi (81a)
raze (34d, 35b, 36c, 71c), razz (59a), Yazd (217)

**_ _ A Z**   Ahaz (67d, 197), Boaz (103c, 197), Braz. (236), Diaz (76c), Graz
(213)

**A _ _ Z**   Ahaz (67d, 197), Ariz. (209, 235)

**B A _ _**   Baal (106c), baas, baba (82d, 91a), Babe (140), babe (26c, 40d),
Babi (16a), Babs, babu (60a), baby (26c, 40d, 83c), Bach (140),
back (14c, 59b, 60a, 98a, 115b), bade, Baer (140), Baez (140),
baff (55b), baft (43b), bago (15a), bags, Bahr (140), baht (223,
246), bail (20d, 68b), Bain (140), bain (50a), Baio (140), bait (16b,
41b, 73d, 119c, 123b), Baja (23b, 76c), baju (65b), bake (30c,
101b), Baku (24b, 213), baku (116b, 124a), Bala (53c), bald (17b),
bale (22c, 232), Bali (64c), balk (16b, 89c, 116a), Ball (140), ball
(17b), balm (83d, 126a), banc (66d), band (56c, 116b, 232), bane
(58a, 81b, 90d, 102d, 133b), bang (110b), bani (101d), bank (19a,
47c, 91b), bans, Bapt. (236), Bara (140), barb (47a, 89a, 90c,
95a), Bard (200), bard (14c, 16b, 90c), bare (36a, 40c, 43a, 76a,
116b, 127a), Bari (10a, 218), bark (12d, 37b), barm (134b), barn
(116a), baro- (93c), bars, Bart (140), Bart. (236), base (9a, 41d,
49a, 62a, 73c, 92b, 102b, 102d), bash (60b, 86d), bask (46d, 73d,
80b, 128d, 228), bast (17b, 45d, 88c, 133c), bate (119c), Bath
(41a, 112c), bath (35d, 88d, 125a, 246), bats, batt (16d), baud
(120b), Baum (85d, 140), bawd (22a), bawl (18c, 129b, 134b),
Baya (215), baya (130d), bays

**_ B A _**   a bas (50b), Iban (33d), Obad. (241), Obal (197)

**_ _ B A**   abba (19c, 44d), alba (73c, 75c, 131d), anba (28a), baba (82d,
91a), caba (133d), Cuba (64c, 131b, 215), Elba (64c, 80d), Juba
(216), koba (13a, 130b), Kuba (24b), Luba (224), PABA (86b),
peba (14b), Reba (67c, 176), saba (45d, 88c), tuba (80a, 86a)

**B _ _ A**   baba (82d, 91a), Baja (23b, 76c), Bala (53c), Bara (140), Baya
(215), baya (130d), Beja (82a, 222), Bela (18c, 39c, 140), bema
(90b, 95d), beta (11d, 106a), biga (125c), bina (60b), biwa (65b),
boca (113a), bola (53a), boma (10c), Bona (79b, 192), bona (69d,
70a), bora (132b), bosa (13d), boza (13d), brea (77a), buna (102c)

**_ B B _**   abba (19c, 44d), abbe (28a, 49d, 94c), abbr. (235), Abby (137),
ebbs

**_ _ B B**   bibb (75b), Cobb (146), Gibb (155), lobb (77a), Robb (177), Webb
(186)

**B _ _ B**   barb (47a, 89a, 90c, 95a), bibb (75b), blab (119d), bleb (20a, 22b,
54c), blob (29a, 75b), bomb (107d, 130c), boob (109c), bulb (30d,
126b), BYOB (236)

**_ B C _**   abcs (46c)

323

**B _ _ C**   banc (66d), bloc (126c), BMOC (236), bosc (87b)

**B _ _ D**   bald (17b), band (56c, 116b, 232), Bard (200), bard (14c, 16b, 90c), baud (120b), bawd (22a), bead (17d, 109b), bend (12c, 32d, 125b), bind (122a), Bird (141), bird (16a), bled (97d), Blvd. (236), bold (33d), Bond (142), bond (10a, 28d, 71d, 72b, 78a, 107b, 118a, 122a), bord (77a), Boyd (142), Brad (142), brad (44c, 54d, 80b), bred (97c), Budd (143), bund (40b), burd (105c), Byrd (90d)

**B E _ _**   bead (17d, 109b), beak (18d, 77d), beam (98a), Bean (140), bean (58c, 60b, 71b, 106b, 127c), Bear (79b), bear (40d, 114c, 134c, 230), Beas, beat (17c, 30a, 47c, 100b, 121b, 121c, 131c, 233), Beau (140), beau (117d, 118b), Bebe (140), bebe (50a), Beck (140), beck (82c), Bede (78a, 127d), beds, beef (29c, 75c), been, beep (112b), beer (18d, 95d), bees, beet (127c), begs, Beja (82a, 222), Bela (18c, 39c, 140), Belg. (236), Bell (140), bell (22c, 120b), bels, belt (16d, 27b), bema (90b, 95d), bend (12c, 32d, 125b), bene (65c, 70b), Beni (214), beno (86a), Bens, bent (13d, 32a, 55d, 62c), Berg (141), berg (61b), berm (23c, 71a, 108d), Bern (9a, 222), Bert (20c, 141), Bess (141), best (26d, 30a, 34c, 42b, 85c, 118b), beta (11d, 106a), Bete (215), bete (50a), Beth (11a, 141), beth (12a), bets, Bevs, bevy (16d, 31c, 47c, 232), beys

**_ B E _**   abed (110b), Abel (10a, 23a, 107a, 197), Abes, abet (10d, 48b, 59b), ibex (54d, 230), Obed (103c, 197), obex (21c), obey (29c, 59a, 67b, 10a)

**_ _ B E**   abbe (28a, 49d, 94c), aube (11a), Babe (140), babe (26c, 40d), Bebe (140), bebe (50a), cube (53c, 111d), Elbe (82b, 216), fabe (55b), gibe (10d, 35a), Hebe (32d, 59c, 135a, 198), imbe (30d, 45c), jibe (28d, 29d, 31a), jube (102a), kibe (26c), Kobe (60d, 218), Labe (217), lobe (70d, 102c), Rabe (176), robe (52d), Rube (179), rube (31b, 103c, 134d), Sabe (67b), Tobe (183), tobe (10c), tube (33c, 89c, 117a)

**B _ _ E**   Babe (140), babe (26c, 40d), bade, bake (30c, 101b), bale (22c, 232), bane (58a, 81b, 90d, 102d, 133b), bare (36a, 40c, 43a, 76a, 116b, 127a), base (9a, 41d, 49a, 62a, 73c, 92b, 102b, 102d), bate (119c), Bebe (140), bebe (50a), Bede (78a, 127d), bene (65c, 70b), Bete (215), bete (50a), bice (20b, 56c, 89a), bide (38d, 99c, 119d, 129b), bike (67a, 127c), bile (26d), bine (115b, 128b), bise (132b), bite (26c, 115c), Blue (142), blue (75d, 112a, 126c), boce (22a, 46d), bode (48d, 91c), bole (27d, 98c, 124b), bone (46a, 110a), bore (23b, 37d, 87d, 121d), Bowe (142), BPOE (236), brae (60a, 105b), bree (105a), brie (26b), Bute (64d), byre (31c)

**B _ _ F**   baff (55b), beef (29c, 75c), biff (60b), buff (119b, 134b)

**B G _ _**   B. Gen. (236)

**B _ _ G**   bang (110b), Belg. (236), Berg (141), berg (61b), Bing (141), bldg. (236), bong (111a), Borg (142), brag (20b, 24a, 32b, 127c), brig (81a, 108b), Bulg. (236), bung (116a), burg (21a, 57c)

**B H _ _**    bhat (62d), bhut (54b)

**_ _ B H**    Cobh (30d)

**B _ _ H**    Bach (140), bash (60b, 86d), Bath (41a, 112c), bath (35d, 88d, 125a, 246), Beth (11a, 141), beth (12a), blah (82a, 71d), bosh (82a), both (122c, 125c), bruh (73b), Bush (143, 191), bush (109a, 119a)

**B I _ _**    bias (12c, 35c, 94a), bibb (75b), Bibi (141), bibi (62d), bibl. (236), bibs, bice (20b, 56c, 89a), bide (38d, 99c, 119d, 129b), bids, bien (51b), bier (28d, 53d), biff (60b), biga (125c), bike (67a, 127c), bile (26d), bilk (26b, 34a, 34c), Bill (141), bill (17d, 109d), bina (60b), bind (122a), bine (115b, 128b), Bing (141), bino (86a), bins, biol. (236), Bion (56b), Bird (141), bird (16a), birl (72d), birn (27d), birr (112a, 216), bise (132b), bite (26c, 115c), bito (10c, 35b, 47a), bits (19a), bitt (44c), biwa (65d)

**_ B I _**    Abia (104a), abib (59a, 81d), Abie (81c), abir (98d), ibid. (70a, 239), ibis (19a, 39d, 40a, 129a, 225), obia (45c), obis, obit. (34a, 52c, 241)

**_ _ B I**    ambi- (92c), Babi (16a), Bibi (141), bibi (62d), Bubi (216), gabi (119d), Gobi (35a), mabi (47d, 80b), Rabi (15c, 88d), rabi (78b)

**B _ _ I**    Babi (16a), Bali (64c), bani (101d), Bari (10a, 218), Beni (214), Bibi (141), bibi (62d), Bubi (216), buri (119b)

**_ _ B J**    subj. (243)

**_ _ B K**    hdbk. (239)

**B _ _ K**    back (14c, 59b, 60a, 98a, 115b), balk (16b, 89c, 116a), bank (19a, 47c, 91b), bark (12d, 37b), bask (46d, 73d, 80b, 128d, 228), beak (18d, 77d), Beck (140), beck (82a), bilk (26b, 34a, 34c), Bock (142), bock (18a, 70d), book (71c, 129a), bosk (133b), bowk (115a), Buck (23b, 31c, 143), buck (34c, 84a), bulk (20c, 75b, 129a), bunk (82a, 110c), busk (20c, 31a, 45c)

**B L _ _**    blab (119d), blah (82a, 71d), blat (20b), bldg. (236), bleb (20a, 22b, 54c), bled (97d), blet (51d), bleu (26b, 50a), blew, blip (97b), B. Lit. (236), blob (29a, 75b), bloc (126c), blot (115b), blow (42d), Blue (142), blue (75d, 112a, 126c), blur (62d, 111a), blut (53d), Blvd. (236)

**_ B L _**    able (10a, 29c, 96b, 110a), -ably (117b), -ible (117a)

**_ _ B L**    bibl. (236)

**B _ _ L**    Baal (106c), bail (20d, 68b), Ball (140), ball (17b), bawl (18c, 129b, 134b), Bell (140), bell (22c, 120b), bibl. (236), Bill (141), bill (17d, 109d), biol. (236), birl (72d), boil (30c), Böll (142), boll (90a, 90c), bowl (78d, 119a), bual (132c), buhl (63a), bull (21b, 86b), Burl (143), burl (68c, 124b)

325

**B M _ _**    **BMOC** (236)

**_ _ B M**    **ICBM** (239)

**B _ _ M**    **balm** (83d, 126a), **barm** (134b), **Baum** (85d, 140), **beam** (98a), **berm** (23c, 71a, 108d), **boom** (43a, 112a, 113a), **Bram** (142), **brim** (21a), **brom-** (92c)

**_ _ B N**    **ISBN** (240)

**B _ _ N**    **Bain** (140), **bain** (50a), **barn** (116a), **Bean** (140), **bean** (58c, 60b, 71b, 106b, 127c), **been**, **Bern** (9a, 222), **B. Gen.** (236), **bien** (51b), **Bion** (56b), **birn** (27d), **Bonn** (18b, 216), **boon** (18c, 20a), **Born** (142), **born** (71d, 81a, 81b), **bo's'n** (20c, 88b), **bran** (22a, 22b, 55d, 61d), **bren** (73d), **burn** (62c, 101b)

**B O _ _**    **boar** (60c, 89a, 118d, 132a, 230), **boas**, **boat** (81b, 108b), **Boaz** (103c, 197), **Bobo** (214), **boca** (113a), **boce** (22a, 46d), **Bock** (142), **bock** (18a, 70d), **bode** (48d, 91c), **Bodo** (69a), **body** (56c), **Boer** (10c, 112b), **bogs**, **bogy** (13c, 113b), **Bohr** (15c, 33c, 142), **boil** (30c), **bois** (51b), **bola** (53a), **bold** (33d), **bole** (27d, 98c, 124b), **Böll** (142), **boll** (90a, 90c), **bolo** (68a, 130d), **Bolt** (142), **bolt** (44c, 47c, 67a, 101c), **boma** (10c), **bomb** (107d, 130c), **Bona** (79b, 192), **bona** (69d, 70a), **Bond** (142), **bond** (10a, 28d, 71d, 72b, 78a, 107b, 118a, 122a), **bone** (46a, 110a), **bong** (111a), **Bonn** (18b, 216), **Bono** (142), **bony** (110a), **boob** (109c), **book** (71c, 129a), **boom** (43a, 112a, 113a), **boon** (18c, 20a), **boor** (17a, 38c, 88a, 103c), **boos**, **boot** (29c, 67b, 124d), **bops**, **bora** (132b), **bord** (77a), **bore** (23b, 37d, 87d, 121d), **Borg** (142), **Born** (142), **born** (71d, 81a, 81b), **boro** (114a), **Bors** (102c), **bort** (35c), **Boru** (142), **bosa** (13d), **bosc** (87b), **bosh** (82a), **bosk** (133b), **bo's'n** (20c, 88b), **boss** (40c, 116c), **both** (122c, 125c), **bots**, **bott** (27d), **bout** (30b), **Bowe** (142), **bowk** (115a), **bowl** (78d, 119a), **bows**, **Boyd** (142), **boys**, **boza** (13d), **bozo** (38d, 88a)

**_ B O _**    **abou** (44d), **ebon** (19d), **oboe** (58b, 80a, 80c, 133c), **obol** (26b, 83d)

**_ _ B O**    **ambo** (95d, 98a), **Bobo** (214), **bubo** (85c), **Gobo** (16d), **gobo** (66a), **hobo** (123c, 127a), **Igbo** (68c, 220), **jobo** (60c), **kobo** (220), **lobo** (122a, 133b), **Nebo** (78d, 79a), **sebo-** (92d), **umbo** (21a)

**B _ _ O**    **bago** (15a), **Baio** (140), **baro-** (93c), **beno** (86a), **bino** (86a), **bito** (10c, 35b, 47a), **Bobo** (214), **Bodo** (69a), **bolo** (68a, 130d), **Bono** (142), **boro** (114a), **bozo** (38d, 88a), **brio** (33d, 113d, 128d), **Brno** (215), **broo** (105a), **bubo** (85c), **Buto** (198), **buyo** (18d)

**B P _ _**    **BPOE** (236)

**B _ _ P**    **beep** (112b), **blip** (97b), **bump** (66a, 66d), **burp** (18b)

**B R _ _**    **Brad** (142), **brad** (44c, 54d, 80b), **brae** (60a, 105b), **brag** (20b, 24a, 32b, 127c), **Bram** (142), **bran** (22a, 22b, 55d, 61d), **bras** (49d), **brat** (26c), **braw** (105a), **bray** (12d, 37c), **Braz.** (236), **brea** (77a), **bred**

(97c), **bree** (105a), **bren** (73d), **br'er** (126a), **Bret** (143), **brew** (29d), **brie** (26b), **brig** (81a, 108b), **brim** (21a), **brio** (33d, 113d, 128d), **Brit.** (236), **brit** (59d), **Brno** (215), **brom-** (92c), **broo** (105a), **Bros.** (236), **brow** (48d, 59d), **bruh** (73b), **brut** (38b, 132c)

_ B R _    **abri** (51a, 108a), **Ebro** (222), **obra** (113a)

_ _ B R    **abbr.** (235), **febr-** (93a), **fibr-** (93a), **Nebr.** (211, 241)

B _ _ R    **Baer** (140), **Bahr** (140), **Bear** (79b), **bear** (40d, 114c, 134c, 230), **beer** (18d, 95d), **bier** (28d, 53d), **birr** (112a, 216), **blur** (62d, 111a), **boar** (60c, 89a, 118d, 132a, 230), **Boer** (10c, 112b), **Bohr** (15c, 33c, 142), **boor** (17a, 38c, 88a, 103c), **br'er** (126a), **buhr** (131c), **Burr** (143, 190), **burr** (94b)

_ _ B S    **albs**, **Babs**, **bibs**, **bubs**, **cabs**, **cobs**, **Cubs** (206), **cubs**, **dabs**, **Debs** (148), **debs**, **dibs** (55d), **dubs**, **ebbs**, **fibs**, **fobs**, **gabs**, **gibs**, **gobs**, **hobs**, **hubs**, **jabs**, **jibs**, **JOBS** (240), **jobs**, **labs**, **mobs**, **nabs**, **nebs**, **nibs**, **nobs** (32a), **nubs**, **orbs**, **pobs** (91c), **pubs**, **rebs**, **ribs**, **robs**, **rubs**, **sibs**, **sobs**, **subs**, **tabs**, **tubs**, **webs**

B _ _ S    **baas**, **Babs**, **bags**, **bans**, **bars**, **bats**, **bays**, **Beas**, **beds**, **bees**, **begs**, **bels**, **Bens**, **Bess** (141), **bets**, **Bevs**, **beys**, **bias** (12c, 35c, 94a), **bibs**, **bids**, **bins**, **bits** (19a), **boas**, **bogs**, **bois** (51b), **boos**, **bops**, **Bors** (102c), **boss** (40c, 116c), **bots**, **bows**, **boys**, **bras** (49d), **Bros.** (236), **bubs**, **buds**, **bugs**, **bums**, **buns**, **burs**, **buss** (68a), **buts**, **buys**, **byes**

_ _ B T    **debt** (71c, 83a)

B _ _ T    **baft** (43b), **baht** (223, 246), **bait** (16b, 41b, 73d, 119c, 123b), **Bapt.** (236), **Bart** (140), **Bart.** (236), **bast** (17b, 45d, 88c, 133c), **batt** (16d), **beat** (17c, 30a, 47c, 100b, 121b, 121c, 131c, 233), **beet** (127c), **belt** (16d, 27b), **bent** (13d, 32a, 55d, 62c), **Bert** (20c, 141), **best** (26d, 30a, 34c, 42b, 85c, 118b), **bhat** (62d), **bhut** (54b), **bitt** (44c), **blat** (20b), **blet** (51d), **B. Lit.** (236), **blot** (115b), **blut** (53d), **boat** (81b, 108b), **Bolt** (142), **bolt** (44c, 47c, 67a, 101c), **boot** (29c, 67b, 124d), **bort** (35c), **bott** (27d), **bout** (30b), **brat** (26c), **Bret** (143), **Brit.** (236), **brit** (59d), **brut** (38b, 132c), **bunt** (17c, 131b), **Burt** (143), **bust** (14c, 17a, 21d, 44a, 58c), **butt** (121d, 132c, 246)

B U _ _    **bual** (132c), **Bubi** (216), **bubo** (85c), **bubs**, **Buck** (23b, 31c, 143), **buck** (34c, 84a), **Budd** (143), **buds**, **buff** (119b, 134b), **bugs**, **buhl** (63a), **buhr** (131c), **bulb** (30d, 126b), **Bulg.** (236), **bulk** (20c, 75b, 129a), **bull** (21b, 86b), **bump** (66a, 66d), **bums**, **buna** (102c), **bund** (40b), **bung** (116a), **bunk** (82a, 110c), **buns**, **bunt** (17c, 131b), **buoy** (26a, 47c), **burd** (105c), **burg** (21a, 57c), **buri** (119b), **Burl** (143), **burl** (68c, 124b), **burn** (62c, 101b), **burp** (18b), **Burr** (143, 190), **burr** (94b), **burs**, **Burt** (143), **bury** (63c), **Bush** (143, 191), **bush** (109a, 119a), **busk** (20c, 31a, 45c), **buss** (68a), **bust** (14c, 17a, 21d, 44a, 58c), **busy** (40d, 83b), **Bute** (64d), **Buto** (198), **buts**, **butt** (121d, 132c, 246), **buyo** (18d), **buys**, **buzz** (79d, 103a, 131d)

_ B U _    **abut** (21a, 75d, 123b), **ebur** (69d)

327

**_ _ B U** **babu** (60a), **Cebu** (64d, 221), **habu** (89c, 103c), **imbu** (51d), **tabu** (48c), **zebu** (21c, 62d, 231)

**B _ _ U** **babu** (60a), **baju** (65b), **Baku** (24b, 213), **baku** (116b, 124a), **Beau** (140), **beau** (117d, 118b), **bleu** (26b, 50a), **Boru** (142)

**B _ _ W** **blew, blow** (42d), **braw** (105a), **brew** (29d), **brow** (48d, 59d)

**B Y _ _** **byes, BYOB** (236), **Byrd** (90d), **byre** (31c)

**_ _ B Y** **Abby** (137), **baby** (26c, 40d, 83c), **gaby** (109c), **goby** (46d, 228), **Roby** (178), **Ruby** (179), **ruby** (19c, 53b), **toby** (11b, 38a, 66d, 79d, 96a)

**B _ _ Y** **baby** (26c, 40d, 83c), **bevy** (16d, 31c, 47c, 232), **body** (56c), **bogy** (13c, 113b), **bony** (110a), **bray** (12d, 37c), **buoy** (26a, 47c), **bury** (63c), **busy** (40d, 83b)

**B _ _ Z** **Baez** (140), **Boaz** (103c, 197), **Braz.** (236), **buzz** (79d, 103a, 131d)

**C A _ _** **caam** (73a), **Caan** (144), **caba** (133d), **cabs, caco-** (92c), **Cade** (192), **cade** (59d, 67c, 88b), **cadi** (13d, 80c), **cads, Caen** (17c), **cafe** (19c), **Cage** (144), **cage** (30a, 40d), **cagy** (31d), **Cain** (9a, 10a, 41a, 68d, 79d, 107a, 144, 197), **cake** (35b), **calf** (134d), **Cali** (215), **calk** (61b), **call** (12d, 15a, 85b, 108d, 117d, 128c, 134b), **calm** (11c, 13c, 15b, 82a, 85b, 89d, 97a, 106d, 111c, 111d, 126c), **calx** (59a, 85d), **came** (132b), **Camp** (144), **camp** (19c, 39d, 127a), **cams, Cana** (46c, 52b), **canc.** (236), **cane** (98a, 114b, 115a, 115b, 117d, 129b), **cans, cant** (62c, 63b, 66a, 70d, 103d, 122a, 122b), **capa** (122c), **cape** (37c, 58d, 74d, 95a), **Caph** (207), **Capp** (144), **caps, Capt.** (236), **Cara** (144), **cara** (65a), **carb-** (92d), **card** (29a, 66d, 87a), **CARE** (236), **care** (13a, 25b, 29d, 59a, 77a, 99a, 123c, 124d, 133d), **cark** (24b, 133d), **Carl** (144), **caro** (65a), **carp** (25b, 32a, 46a, 46c, 96d, 228), **Carr** (144), **cars, cart** (125d, 127c, 129b), **Cary** (144), **casa** (112d), **case** (14b, 30b, 63b, 71a, 82c), **Cash** (144), **cash** (15a, 78a), **cask** (30b), **Caso** (64c), **Cass** (144), **cast** (15a, 73a, 121c, 123b, 232), **cata-** (92c, 92d), **Cath.** (236), **Cato** (101d, 102a, 194), **cats, Catt** (144), **caul** (45c, 84a), **cava** (127d), **cave** (113c, 126b), **cavy** (56d, 101c, 230), **caws, cays**

**_ C A _** **acad.** (235), **hcap.** (239), **-ical** (117a), **NCAA** (241), **RCAF** (242), **scab** (134a), **scad** (24d, 27b, 61b, 65b), **scan** (47c, 73a, 88b, 98a), **scar** (27b, 134a), **scat** (54b, 96d)

**_ _ C A** **alca** (15d, 98a), **arca** (11d, 21b, 99b), **boca** (113a), **caco-** (92c), **ceca** (69b), **Coca** (146), **coca** (28c, 81a), **deca-** (93d), **Ecca** (53c), **esca** (19d, 36a, 55d), **FICA** (238), **Inca** (15b), **jaca** (65b), **juca** (24c), **Luca** (167), **mica** (64b, 77a, 109b), **onca** (246), **orca** (67b), **paca** (25b, 101c), **pica** (53c, 125d), **SPCA** (243), **YMCA** (244), **yuca** (24c), **YWCA** (244)

**C _ _ A** **caba** (133d), **Cana** (46c, 52b), **capa** (122c), **Cara** (144), **cara** (65a), **casa** (112d), **cata-** (92c, 92d), **cava** (127d), **ceca** (69b), **CETA** (236), **chia** (18d, 76c), **cima** (65c), **Coca** (146), **coca** (28c, 81a),

**coda** (28b, 29d, 46a, 234), **COLA** (237), **cola** (82d, 124a), **coma** (71c, 116d, 126a), **Cora** (34d, 126a), **cora** (53b), **coxa** (60b), **Cuba** (64c, 131b, 215), **cura** (113a), **cyma** (37c, 77d)

_ C B _    **ICBM** (239)

C _ _ B    **carb-** (92d), **chub** (46c, 228), **club** (21c, 32c, 75b, 84c, 104a, 111c), **Cobb** (146), **comb** (31d), **crab** (32b, 108a), **crib** (26b, 74c, 91b, 110c), **curb** (100a, 109a)

_ C C _    **acct.** (235), **Ecca** (53c), **ecce** (18b, 69c, 69d), **eccl.** (238)

C _ _ C    **canc.** (236), **Chic** (145), **chic** (111a), **C in C** (236), **circ.** (237), **conc.** (237), **croc.** (237)

_ C D _    **AC/DC** (235)

_ _ C D    **decd.** (237)

C _ _ D    **card** (29a, 66d, 87a), **Chad** (117a, 145, 215), **clad** (37d), **clod** (21a, 37b, 83a, 116d), **coed** (107b), **cold** (53b, 62a), **cond.** (237), **Cord** (146), **cord** (32c, 43b), **crud** (28c, 35a, 36a), **cued**, **curd** (76d)

C E _ _    **Cebu** (64d, 221), **ceca** (69b), **cede** (54c, 55d, 99b, 118b, 129b), **cedi** (216), **cees**, **ceil** (25b), **-cele** (117c), **cell** (32c), **Celt** (22a, 217), **celt** (115d, 123a), **-cene** (117c), **ceno-** (92d), **cent** (30c, 213-224), **cent.** (236), **cepe** (39c), **cere** (18d, 130c), **Cerf** (145), **CERN** (236), **cero** (46d, 67d), **cero-** (93d), **cert.** (236), **cess** (71c, 120a), **cest** (54c), **CETA** (236), **cete** (232), **CETI** (236), **Ceto** (55c, 75d), **Ceyx** (57b)

_ C E _    **-acea** (117c), **aced** (120c), **acer** (74d), **aces**, **acet-** (92c), **iced**, **Icel.** (239), **icer**, **ices**

_ _ C E    **-ance** (117a, 117c), **bice** (20b, 56c, 89a), **boce** (22a, 46b), **dace** (46c, 228), **dice** (52c), **duce** (65a), **ecce** (18b, 69c, 69d), **-ence** (117b), **-esce** (117c), **face** (15a, 30a, 73a, 79d, 118a, 128c), **lace** (47b), **lice** (86c), **Luce** (10a, 29b, 192), **mace** (40c, 82d, 114b, 118d, 129d), **mice** (49c, 100a, 216), **nice** (90b, 109c), **once** (18b, 49a, 61d, 63d), **Pace** (204), **pace** (52a, 113c, 129b), **pice** (62d, 220), **puce** (42a, 96c), **race** (87d, 103a, 114a, 124b), **Rice** (177, 204), **rice** (37d), **sice** (56c), **syce** (56c), **vice** (35a), **vice-** (92d), **voce** (65c, 234)

C _ _ E    **Cade** (192), **cade** (59d, 67c, 88b), **cafe** (19c), **Cage** (144), **cage** (30a, 40d), **cake** (35b), **Cale** (144), **came** (132b), **cane** (98a, 114b, 115a, 115b, 117d, 129b), **cape** (37c, 58d, 74d, 95a), **CARE** (236), **care** (13a, 25b, 29d, 59a, 77a, 99a, 123d, 124d, 133d), **case** (14b, 30b, 63b, 71a, 82c), **cave** (113c, 126b), **cede** (54c, 55d, 99b, 118b, 129b), **-cele** (117c), **-cene** (117c), **cepe** (39c), **cere** (18d, 130c), **cete** (232), **chee** (246), **-cide** (117b), **cine-** (93b), **cite** (97c), **clue** (60b, 117d), **code** (20c, 23d, 27b, 119a), **coke** (28c, 52a, 62d), **Cole** (146), **come** (94d), **Cone** (146), **cone** (53c, 116c, 111d), **cope** (23d, 30b, 30d, 52d, 128a), **CORE** (237), **core** (25c, 41d, 58d), **cote**

329

(19b, 107d, 108a), **cove** (17d, 58a, 130a), **Cree** (11b, 189), **cube** (53c, 111d), **cuke** (32c), **-cule** (117c), **cure** (94c), **cute** (10a, 32c, 116a), **cyme** (47d)

_ _ C F    **UNCF** (243)

C _ _ F    **calf** (134d), **Cerf** (145), **chef** (30c, 50c, 68a), **clef** (80c, 234), **coef.** (237), **coif** (57b), **conf.** (237), **corf** (28c), **cuff** (21b, 60b, 105b, 110b)

_ _ C G    **USCG** (243)

C _ _ G    **chug** (112a), **clog** (20a, 108c), **cong.** (237), **crag** (101b)

C H _ _    **Chad** (117a, 145, 215), **Cham** (224), **chap** (45b, 74c), **char** (104d, 124d, 228), **Chas.** (74d), **chat** (19a, 29d, 119b, 225), **chaw** (122c), **chay** (39b, 98c), **chee** (246), **chef** (30c, 50c, 68a), **chem.** (31b, 236), **cher** (50b), **Chet** (145), **chew** (75b), **chez** (50a), **chia** (18d, 76c), **Chic** (145), **chic** (111a), **ch'ih** (246), **chil-** (93b), **Ch'in** (26d), **Chin.** (236), **chin** (29d), **Chip** (26d), **chip** (55b), **chir-** (93a), **chis**, **chit** (54c, 82c, 88b, 129c), **chol-** (92c), **chol.** (236), **chop** (75c), **Chou** (26d), **chou** (50a), **chow** (37a, 227), **choy** (39b, 98c), **chub** (46c, 228), **chug** (112a), **chum** (15b, 32a, 45b), **chuo** (246)

_ C H _    **ache** (73a, 85d, 134b), **acht** (53d), **achy** (112a), **echo** (12a, 99d, 100b), **Echo** (80d), **echt** (54a), **icho** (54b), **ichu** (12c, 55d), **Ochs** (173)

_ _ C H    **arch** (28a, 41b, 101c), **-arch** (117c), **arch-** (93b), **arch.** (235), **Asch** (139), **Bach** (140), **dich** (54b), **dich-** (93d), **each** (13b), **etch** (14d, 35a), **euch** (54b), **exch.** (238), **Foch** (49c, 153), **hoch** (42c, 53d), **inch** (31d, 79c, 246), **itch** (58a, 64b), **Koch** (53c, 164), **Lech** (165, 213), **loch** (68b, 105b, 130a), **mach** (113c), **Mich.** (210, 240), **much** (67c, 116d), **orch.** (241), **ouch** (42c, 63a), **Rich** (177), **rich** (73d), **such** (131b), **yech** (112a), **yuch** (112a), **Zech.** (244)

C _ _ H    **Caph** (207), **Cash** (144), **cash** (15a, 78a), **Cath.** (236), **ch'ih** (246), **Cobh** (30d), **cosh** (60b), **Cush** (57c, 197)

C I _ _    **ciao** (65a), **-cide** (117b), **cima** (65c), **C in C** (236), **cine-** (93b), **cinq** (50b), **cion** (83c), **cipo** (71c), **circ.** (237), **cist** (115d), **cite** (97c), **cito** (70a), **city** (76c, 126d)

_ C I _    **acid** (119d), **Acis** (52b)

_ _ C I    **asci** (114a), **deci** (120c), **foci** (25c), **fuci** (38d), **loci** (27a)

C _ _ I    **cadi** (13d, 80c), **Cali** (215), **cedi** (216), **CETI** (236)

C _ _ J    **Cluj** (221), **conj.** (237)

_ _ C K    **back** (14c, 59b, 60a, 98a, 115b), **Beck** (140), **beck** (82a), **Bock** (142), **bock** (18a, 70d), **Buck** (23b, 31c, 143), **buck** (34c, 84a), **cock** (26a, 44d, 102b, 103d, 119c, 127b), **deck** (34b, 108b), **Dick**

330

(149, 192), **dick** (35b), **dock** (33a, 68d, 88d, 108b, 112a, 131a), **duck** (16c, 19a, 19b, 23d, 43b, 62a, 109a, 225), **geck** (105b), **guck** (110c), **hack** (24c, 33a, 60b), **heck** (42a), **hick** (134d), **hock** (71b, 87b, 132c), **Jack** (159), **jack** (17a, 24a, 68a, 78a, 97c), **jock** (74c), **keck** (100a), **kick** (21a, 96a), **lack** (34c, 129d), **lick** (18a, 66a, 110d), **lock** (44c, 57b), **luck** (25d), **Mack** (167), **mack** (97c), **Mick** (170), **mock** (35a, 62a, 66b, 100c, 104d, 120a), **muck** (39a), **neck** (64d), **Nick** (172), **nick** (26d, 82c), **nock** (14c, 82c), **pack** (16d, 22c, 105c, 232, 246), **Peck** (174), **peck** (22d, 246), **pick** (27a, 90b), **pock** (62d), **Puck** (107c, 193), **puck** (36b, 55a, 60c, 77b), **rack** (10b, 28b), **reck** (24b), **Rick** (24c, 177), **rick** (58c, 89a, 114b), **Rock** (178), **rock** (118c, 124b), **ruck** (134a), **sack** (30b, 36a, 89b, 90c, 132c), **sick** (126b), **sock** (96a, 116b, 132b), **suck** (9b), **tack** (13d, 15c, 31b, 44c, 80b), **tick** (14a, 20a, 229), **tock** (10c), **tuck** (115c), **wick** (23d), **yuck** (112a)

C _ _ K    **calk** (61b), **cark** (24b, 133d), **cask** (30b), **cock** (26a, 44d, 102b, 103d, 119c, 127b), **conk** (60b, 116b), **Cook** (79a, 104b, 146), **cook** (68a), **Cork** (217), **cork** (90b, 116a, 132c, 133b), **cusk** (46d)

C L _ _    **clad** (37d), **clam** (19c, 77d), **clan** (124b), **clap** (13c, 121d), **clar.** (237), **claw** (26b, 80b, 119b, 126b), **Clay** (146), **clay** (39a, 92a), **clef** (80c, 234), **Cleo** (96d, 146), **clew** (16c, 103b), **Clio** (29b, 80a), **clip** (15c, 44c, 107d), **clod** (21a, 37b, 83a, 116b), **clog** (20a, 108c), **clop** (61a), **clot** (28c, 73c), **clou** (50d), **clow** (47c, 110d), **cloy** (54d, 104b, 118a), **club** (21c, 32c, 75b, 84c, 104a, 111c), **clue** (60b, 117d), **Cluj** (221), **Clym** (14a)

_ C L _    **acle** (64b), **ACLU** (235)

_ _ C L    **eccl.** (238), **encl.** (238), **excl.** (238), **incl.** (239), **NaCL** (111c)

C _ _ L    **call** (12d, 15a, 85b, 108d, 117d, 128c, 134b), **Carl** (144), **caul** (45c, 84a), **ceil** (25b), **cell** (32c), **chil-** (93b), **chol-** (92c), **chol.** (236), **coal** (13a, 40c, 52a), **-coel** (117a), **coil** (32d, 114a, 125c, 132b, 134a), **coll.** (237), **cool** (23b, 82a), **cowl** (78b), **cull** (88d), **curl** (32a, 57b, 72d, 100d, 126b)

C M _ _    **Cmdr.** (237)

_ C M _    **acme** (32c, 87b, 123a, 135a), **RCMP** (242)

C _ _ M    **caam** (73a), **calm** (11c, 13c, 15b, 82a, 85b, 89d, 97a, 106d, 111c, 111d, 126c), **Cham** (224), **chem.** (31b, 236), **chum** (15b, 32a, 45b), **clam** (19c, 77d), **Clym** (14a), **Colm** (146), **comm.** (237), **coom** (28c), **corm** (22c, 115a), **cosm-** (93d), **cram** (116c), **crim.** (237), **culm** (13a, 28c, 56a, 108b, 115b)

_ C N _    **acne** (110a)

C _ _ N    **Caan** (144), **Caen** (17c), **Cain** (9a, 10a, 41a, 68d, 79d, 107a, 144, 197), **CERN** (236), **Ch'in** (26d), **Chin.** (236), **chin** (29d), **cion** (83c), **clan** (124b), **Coen** (146), **Cohn** (146), **coin** (77b), **Conn.** (209, 237), **conn** (35d), **coon** (97a), **corn** (74b, 94b), **cran** (118c), **cten-** (93c)

331

**C O _ _**      **coal** (13a, 40c, 52a), **coat** (52d), **coax** (131b), **Cobb** (146), **Cobh** (30d), **cobs**, **Coca** (146), **coca** (28c, 81a), **cock** (26a, 44d, 102b, 103d, 119c, 127b), **coco** (86a), **coda** (28b, 29d, 46a, 234), **code** (20c, 23d, 27b, 119a), **coed** (107b), **coef.** (237), **-coel** (117a), **Coen** (146), **cogs**, **Cohn** (146), **coho** (103d), **coif** (57b), **coil** (32d, 114a, 125c, 132b, 134a), **coin** (77b), **coir** (28d, 30d, 45c, 102b), **coix** (66c), **coke** (28c, 52a, 62d), **COLA** (237), **cola** (82d, 124a), **cold** (53b, 62a), **Cole** (146), **coll.** (237), **Colm** (146), **Colo.** (209, 237), **colp** (25c), **cols**, **colt** (61b, 100b, 134d, 135a), **coly** (79b), **coma** (71c, 116d, 126a), **comb** (31d), **come** (94d), **comm.** (237), **Como** (68b, 146), **Comp.** (237), **comr.** (237), **conc.** (237), **cond.** (237), **Cone** (146), **cone** (53c, 116c, 111d), **conf.** (237), **cong.** (237), **conj.** (237), **conk** (60b, 116b), **Conn.** (209, 237), **conn** (35d), **cons**, **cont.** (237), **cony** (97a), **Cook** (79a, 104b, 146), **cook** (68a), **cool** (23b, 82a), **coom** (28c), **coon** (97a), **coop** (40d), **Coos** (189), **coos**, **coot** (19a, 38c, 56d, 75a, 83d, 105a, 225), **cope** (23d, 30b, 30d, 52d, 128a), **copr-** (92d), **cops**, **Copt** (39d), **copy** (40c, 62a), **Cora** (34d, 126a), **cora** (53b), **Cord** (146), **cord** (32c, 43b), **CORE** (237), **core** (25c, 41d, 58d), **corf** (28c), **Cork** (217), **cork** (90b, 116a, 132c, 133b), **corm** (22c, 115a), **corn** (74b, 94b), **Corp.** (237), **cosh** (60b), **cosm-** (93d), **cost** (26a, 94b), **cote** (19b, 107d, 108a), **coto** (17b, 75c), **cots**, **Coty** (49d, 147), **coup** (75b, 116c, 120b), **cove** (17d, 58a, 130a), **cowl** (78b), **cows** (21b), **coxa** (60b), **coyo** (16a, 26d), **Cozy** (147), **cozy** (39b, 111b)

**_ C O _**      **acou-** (93a), **ecol.** (238), **E-COM** (238), **econ.** (238), **icon** (62a, 103b), **scob** (120d), **scop** (90c), **Scot** (59d), **Scot.** (242), **scow** (20c, 47b)

**_ _ C O**      **coco** (86a), **fico** (124c, 133d), **loco** (31d, 63b, 90d), **muco-** (93b), **myco-** (93a), **paco** (11d, 109c), **Pico** (100d), **poco** (72c), **Rico** (72c), **soco** (21c), **toco** (123b), **unco** (105b), **Waco** (21d)

**C _ _ O**      **caco-** (92c), **caro** (65a), **Caso** (64c), **Cato** (101d, 102a, 194), **ceno-** (92d), **cero** (46d, 67d), **cero-** (93d), **Ceto** (55c, 75d), **chuo** (246), **ciao** (65a), **cipo** (71c), **cito** (70a), **Cleo** (96d, 146), **Clio** (29b, 80a), **coco** (86a), **coho** (103d), **Colo.** (209, 237), **Como** (68b, 146), **coto** (17b, 75c), **coyo** (16a, 26d), **cryo-** (93a)

**C _ _ P**      **Camp** (144), **camp** (19c, 39d, 127a), **Capp** (144), **carp** (25b, 32a, 46a, 46c, 96d, 228), **chap** (45b, 74c), **Chip** (26d), **chip** (55b), **chop** (75c), **clap** (13c, 121d), **clip** (15c, 44c, 107d), **clop** (61a), **colp** (25c), **Comp.** (237), **coop** (40d), **Corp.** (237), **coup** (75b, 116c, 120b), **crap** (82a, 91b), **crop** (31d, 108d), **Culp** (147), **cusp** (31d, 61a, 89d, 90c, 90d)

**C _ _ Q**      **cinq** (50b)

**C R _ _**      **crab** (32b, 108a), **crag** (101b), **cram** (116c), **cran** (118c), **crap** (82a, 91b), **-crat** (117c), **craw** (32a, 56d, 115c), **Cree** (11b, 189), **crew** (48c, 56c, 81b, 88b, 133d), **crib** (26b, 74c, 91b, 110c), **crim.** (237), **crit.** (237), **croc.** (237), **crop** (31d, 108d), **Crow** (189), **crow** (19b, 19d, 20b, 43c, 225), **crud** (28c, 35a, 36a), **crus** (71b, 107c), **Crux** (207), **crux** (32b, 74b, 112b), **cryo-** (93a)

**_ C R _**  Acre (214), acre (45d, 68d, 246), acro- (93a, 93c), ecru (18b, 22b, 126a)

**_ _ C R**  necr- (92d), picr- (92c)

**C _ _ R**  Carr (144), char (104d, 124d, 228), cher (50b), chir- (93a), clar. (237), Cmdr. (237), coir (28d, 30d, 45c, 102b), comr. (237), copr- (92d), cuir (37c, 50c), cupr- (92d), czar (103c)

**_ _ C S**  abcs (46c), arcs, docs (88d), orcs, Pecs (217), sacs, tics, WACs

**C _ _ S**  cabs, cads, cams, cans, caps, cars, Cass (144), cats, caws, cays, cees, cess (71c, 120a), Chas. (74d), chis, cobs, cogs, cols, cons, Coos (189), coos, cops, cots, cows (21b), crus (71b, 107c), Cubs (206), cubs, cues, cups, curs, cuss (32d, 88a, 118c), cuts

**C T _ _**  cten- (93c)

**_ C T _**  acta (34b, 94d, 98c, 121a), ACTH (235), acts, ecto- (93c), octa- (92d), octo (69c), octo- (92d), WCTU (244)

**_ _ C T**  acct. (235), dict. (237), duct (125a), fact (9d, 35b, 98a), hect- (93a), noct- (93b), pact (10d, 11c, 17b, 20d), Pict (22a), sect (34d, 43d), tact (35d)

**C _ _ T**  cant (62c, 63b, 66a, 70d, 103d, 122a, 122b), Capt. (236), cart (125d, 127c, 129b), cast (15a, 73a, 121c, 123b, 232), Catt (144), Celt (22a, 217), celt (115d, 123a), oent (30c, 213-224), cent. (236), cert. (236), cest (54c), chat (19a, 29d, 119b, 225), Chet (145), chit (54c, 82c, 88b, 129c), cist (115d), clot (28c, 73c), coat (52d), colt (61b, 100b, 134d, 135a), cont. (237), coot (19a, 38c, 56d, 75a, 83d, 105a, 225), Copt (39d), cost (26a, 94b), -crat (117c), crit. (237), cult (106a, 119c), Curt (147), curt (20b, 22a, 108c, 108d), cyst (128a)

**C U _ _**  Cuba (64c, 131b, 215), cube (53c, 111d), Cubs (206), cubs, cued, cues, cuff (21b, 60b, 105b, 110b), cuir (37c, 50c), cuke (32c), -cule (117c), cull (88d), culm (13a, 28c, 56a, 108b, 115b), Culp (147), cult (106a, 119c), cupr- (92d), cups, cura (113a), curb (100a, 109a), curd (76d), cure (94c), curl (32a, 57b, 72d, 100d, 126b), curs, Curt (147), curt (20b, 22a, 108c, 108d), Cush (57c, 197), cusk (46d), cusp (31d, 61a, 89d, 90c, 90d), cuss (32d, 88a, 118c), cute (10a, 32c, 116a), cuts

**_ C U _**  acus (70a, 89b), Ecua. (238), ocul- (92d), Scud (77b), scud (96d, 103a, 118c), scum (62c, 98d, 110c), scup (91c, 228), scut (119a)

**C _ _ U**  Cebu (64d, 221), Chou (26d), chou (50a), clou (50d)

**C _ _ W**  chaw (122c), chew (75b), chow (37a, 227), claw (26b, 80b, 119b, 126b), clew (16c, 103b), clow (47c, 110d), craw (32a, 56d, 115c), crew (48c, 56c, 81b, 88b, 133d), Crow (189), crow (19b, 19d, 20b, 43c, 225)

333

**C _ _ X**    calx (59a, 85d), Ceyx (57b), coax (131b), coix (66c), Crux (207), crux (32b, 74b, 112b)

**C Y _ _**    cyma (37c, 77d), cyme (47d), cyst (128a)

**_ _ C Y**    agcy. (235), -ancy (117b), -ency (117b), ency. (238), lacy (34c), Lucy (192), Macy (167), racy (20a, 113c), secy. (243)

**C _ _ Y**    cagy (31d), Cary (144), cavy (56d, 101c, 230), chay (39b, 98c), choy (39b, 98c), city (76c, 126d), Clay (146), clay (39a, 92a), cloy (54d, 104b, 118a), coly (79b), cony (97a), copy (40c, 62a), Coty (49d, 147), Cozy (147), cozy (39b, 111b)

**C Z _ _**    czar (103c)

**C _ _ Z**    chez (50a)

**D A _ _**    dabs, dace (46c, 228), Dada (14d, 49c), dado (34b, 84d, 87c, 129d), dads, daft (48b), Dahl (147), dail (40a, 64a), dais (41d, 90b), Dale (26d, 147), dale (35d, 98a, 127b), Dali (147), Daly (147), dama (65a, 112d), dame (45b, 54c, 68c, 81d, 122c), damp (33c, 77c, 131b), dams, Dana (147), Dane (67c, 82b, 104c, 147), dang (42a), dank (33b, 77c), Dans, dans (50c), Danu (199), daps, darb (88a), dare (25d, 34c), dark (38d, 54d, 118c), darn (42a, 75d, 83a, 99c), dart (14c, 33d, 68d, 77b, 90c, 95a, 114a, 118c), dash (20a, 96a, 114a, 120b, 128d), data (29c, 63a, 115a), date (33d, 51d), daub (111a), dauw (22d), Dave (148), Davy (148, 193), davy (103b), Dawn (148), dawn (14b, 15d, 33d), days, daze (48a, 116c, 116d)

**_ D A _**    adad (42c), Adah (41c, 197), Adak (64b), Adam (23d, 84d, 107a, 137, 194, 197), Adar (66d, 78c), Adas, adat (74b), D-Day (67a, 82a), Edam (26b, 38d), -idae (117c), Idas (24d), N.Dak. (241), O'Day (173), S.Dak. (242), udal (59c)

**_ _ D A**    adda (110a), Aïda (84b, 97b, 128a), Alda (137), anda (21c, 133b), coda (28b, 29d, 46a, 234), Dada (14d, 49c), edda (59c, 61b, 82a, 103b), Erda (22b, 198), Jada (197), Leda (24d, 59a, 91a, 113b, 125d, 135a, 198), NADA (241), -poda (117c), Roda (81d), Sada (179), sida (30d, 96d), soda (18d, 38a, 111c, 131c), Toda (37d), USDA (243), veda (60a), Vida (185)

**D _ _ A**    Dada (14d, 49c), dama (65a, 112d), Dana (147), data (29c, 63a, 115a), deca- (93d), deka- (93d), Dela. (209), Deva (60a, 221), dika (74c), Dina (149), dita (88c, 124b), diva (84b, 94c), Doha (221), dona (91d), dopa (89a), Dora (30c, 33d, 35c), duma (103a), dura (113c), dyna- (93d)

**_ D B _**    hdbk. (239)

**D _ _ B**    darb (88a), daub (111a), dieb (65b), doob (18c), drab (22b, 26b, 29a, 38c, 43d, 47b), drib (110d), drub (17c, 32c, 42c, 110b), dumb (109b, 113c)

334

**_ _ D C**   AC/DC (235), AFDC (235)

**D _ _ C**   desc. (237), disc (58b, 98c), disc. (237)

**D D _ _**   D-Day (67a, 82a)

**_ D D _**   adda (110a), adds, edda (59c, 61b, 82a, 103b), Eddy (150), eddy (31b, 118d, 131c), odds (10b, 11c, 26a, 95c)

**_ _ D D**   Budd (143), Judd (163), Ladd (165), Mudd (171), Nidd (134d), Redd (176), redd (113b), Ridd (73a), rudd (24b, 46c, 98c), sudd (47c), Todd (183)

**D _ _ D**   dead (69b), decd. (237), deed (9d, 43a, 71a, 122c), died, dowd (107b), duad (85d, 125c), dyad (85d), dyed

**D E _ _**   dead (69b), deaf (125d, 126d), deal (17b, 36a, 36d, 123d), Dean (148), dean (83c), dear (40d), Debs (148), debs, debt (71c, 83a), deca- (93d), decd. (237), deci (120c), deck (34b, 108b), deed (9d, 43a, 71a, 122c), deem (30b, 66d, 121a), deep (9b, 41c, 73c, 94d), deer (25d, 102d, 114b, 230), dees, deft (10a, 14d, 110a), defy (25d), degu (101c), deil (105a), dein (54b), deka- (93d), Dela. (209), dele (23c, 40b, 43a, 94c, 95b, 119b), dell (35d, 127b), deme (56b), Demi (148), demi- (93a), demo (108d, 119c), demy (86b), Dene (189), dene (104a), dens (70b), Dent (149), dent (35a), deny (30c, 36a, 98d), Depp (149), dept. (237), -derm (117c), Dern (149), desc. (237), Dese (216), Desi (149), desk (134c), deus (42d, 69d), Deut. (237), Deva (60a, 221), Devi (109d), dewy (77c), deys

**_ D E _**   Aden (13d, 224), edel (54a), Eden (41a, 82a, 86c, 150), idea (35b, 44b, 82c, 95a, 121b), idee (50c), idem (70a), Iden (192), ideo- (93a), ides (33d, 101d), odea (29d), Oder (100d), odes

**_ _ D E**   aide (10a, 15b, 59b, 106a), bade, Bede (78a, 127d), bide (38d, 99c, 119d, 129b), bode (48d, 91c), Cade (192), cade (59d, 67c, 88b), cede (54c, 55d, 99b, 118b, 129b), -cide (117b), code (20c, 23d, 27b, 119a), dude (27c, 33c, 44b), Erde (22b), fade (35c, 36a, 127b), Gide (49c, 155), hade (53c), hide (29d, 31c, 43a), Hyde (37a), jade (53b, 56c), Jude (13b, 196), lade (24b, 35d, 72d, 76d, 119a), lode (35a, 76b, 84c, 127d), made (31d), Mede (14d, 88a), mode (44c, 74d, 116d, 130c), nide (88c, 232), node (66c, 68c, 90d, 95c, 118c), nude (17b, 126b), onde (51b), -pede (117b), rede (31b, 105a), Ride (177), ride (29b, 66d, 121a), rode (38b), rude (102c, 126a), side (43d, 47b, 69b, 119b), tide (83b), -tude (117b), vide (98d), Wade (185), wade (129b), wide (102a)

**D _ _ E**   dace (46c, 228), Dale (26d, 147), dale (35d, 98a, 127b), dame (45b, 54c, 68c, 81d, 122c), Dane (67c, 82b, 104c, 147), dare (25d, 34c), date (33d, 51d), Dave (148), daze (48a, 116c, 116d), dele (23c, 40b, 43a, 94c, 95b, 119b), deme (56b), Dene (189), dene (104a), Dese (216), dice (52c), dike (40b, 71c), dime (44d), dine (39b), dire (37d, 44d, 45a, 54b, 56a, 120c), dive (34d, 90c), doge (74a, 127d), Dole (58c, 149), dole (91d, 99b, 131a), dome (32d, 102a), done (85c), dope (10b, 38b, 81a), Dore (49c), dore (54b,

89a), **dose** (94a), **dote** (85c), **Dove** (150), **dove** (19a, 89a, 225), **doze** (110b), **duce** (65a), **dude** (27c, 33c, 44b), **Duke** (87d, 150, 194, 201), **duke** (82a), **dune** (84a, 104a), **dupe** (25a, 34a, 48b, 56d, 74d, 118d), **Duse** (64d, 150), **dyne** (48c, 246)

**D _ _ F**    **deaf** (125d, 126d), **doff** (99c, 119a), **duff** (95d)

**_ D G _**    **edge** (10b, 19c, 21a, 21b, 74d, 87d, 100d, 109a, 130c), **edgy** (81b, 100a, 120c)

**_ _ D G**    **bldg.** (236)

**D _ _ G**    **dang** (42a), **diag.** (237), **ding** (62d, 76b), **Doeg** (197), **dong** (224), **Doug** (150), **drag** (30d, 95d), **drug** (81a), **dung** (42d, 74d)

**D H _ _**    **dhai** (76c), **dhak** (39b), **dhal** (11d), **dhow** (69b, 84d)

**D _ _ H**    **dash** (20a, 96a, 114a, 120b, 128d), **dich** (54b), **dich-** (93d), **dish** (76a, 119a), **doth** (128a)

**D I _ _**    **diag.** (237), **dial** (43d), **diam.** (237), **Dian** (198), **Dias** (91d), **Diaz** (76c), **dibs** (55d), **dice** (52c), **dich** (54b), **dich-** (93d), **Dick** (149, 192), **dick** (35b), **dict.** (237), **Dido** (24c, 125d), **dido** (13a, 24a, 52b, 92b), **didy** (35c), **dieb** (65b), **died**, **dies** (69c), **diet** (44b, 65d, 71b), **dieu** (50b), **digs**, **dika** (74c), **dike** (40b, 71c), **Dili** (91d, 217), **dill** (14c, 88d), **dime** (44d), **dims**, **Dina** (149), **dine** (39b), **ding** (62d, 76b), **Dino** (47c), **dins**, **dint** (42d, 92b), **Dion** (149, 195), **Dior** (149), **dios** (112d), **dipl-** (93d), **dips**, **dire** (37d, 44d, 45a, 54b, 56a, 120c), **Dirk** (149), **dirk** (33a), **dirt** (39a, 99c, 104c), **disc** (58b, 98c), **disc.** (237), **dish** (76a, 119a), **disk** (27b), **diss** (75d), **dist.** (237), **dita** (88c, 124b), **diva** (84b, 94c), **dive** (34d, 90c)

**_ D I _**    **adit** (41b, 77a), **Edie** (150), **edit** (20b, 40c, 94a, 98c, 100b), **FDIC** (238), **idio-** (93c), **Odin** (10b, 51c, 133b, 198), **odio** (65a), **Udic** (82b), **XDIV** (244)

**_ _ D I**    **Andi** (25a), **cadi** (13d, 80c), **cedi** (216), **kadi** (13d, 80d), **Lodi** (80d), **ludi** (102a), **medi-** (93c), **Midi** (112b), **nidi** (113c), **nudi-** (93b), **pedi-** (93a), **qadi** (13d, 80d), **Sodi** (197), **wadi** (38b, 83a, 98a, 101a)

**D _ _ I**    **Dali** (147), **deci** (120c), **Demi** (148), **demi-** (93a), **Desi** (149), **Devi** (109d), **dhai** (76c), **Dili** (91d, 217), **doni** (25d), **drei** (54a)

**_ D J _**    **Adja** (214)

**_ _ D J**    **hadj** (89b)

**D _ _ K**    **dank** (33b, 77c), **dark** (38d, 54d, 118c), **deck** (34b, 108b), **desk** (134c), **dhak** (39b), **Dick** (149, 192), **dick** (35b), **Dirk** (149), **dirk** (33a), **disk** (27b), **dock** (33a, 68d, 88d, 108b, 112a, 131a), **dook** (77a), **duck** (16c, 19a, 19b, 23d, 43b, 62a, 109a, 225), **dunk** (35d, 62a), **dusk** (125c), **Dyak** (217, 219)

**_ D L _**    **Idle** (159), **idle** (40c, 60c, 62c, 62d, 63a, 70c, 127a, 130a), **idly**

336

**D _ _ L**    **Dahl** (147), **dail** (40a, 64a), **deal** (17b, 36a, 36d, 123d), **deil** (105a), **dell** (35d, 127b), **dhal** (11d), **dial** (43d), **dill** (14c, 88d), **dipl-** (93d), **doll** (45b, 96a), **dual** (37c, 125c), **duel** (45d), **Dull** (193), **dull** (20b, 28b, 47b, 63b, 66b, 71d, 73c, 126c)

**_ D M _**    **admi** (53b)

**D _ _ M**    **deem** (30b, 66d, 121a), **-derm** (117c), **diam.** (237), **doom** (35b, 44d, 54b), **dorm** (104d), **dram** (38a, 38b, 84a, 92a, 110d, 246), **drum** (80a, 228), **duim** (246)

**_ D N _**    **Edna** (151)

**D _ _ N**    **darn** (42a, 75d, 83a, 99c), **Dawn** (148), **dawn** (14b, 15d, 33d), **Dean** (148), **dean** (83c), **dein** (54b), **Dern** (149), **Dian** (198), **Dion** (149, 195), **Doon** (101a), **Dorn** (149), **Down** (150), **down** (35a, 45a, 232), **duan** (52a), **Dyan** (150)

**D O _ _**    **dock** (33a, 68d, 88d, 108b, 112a, 131a), **docs** (88d), **dodo** (19b, 38c, 225), **Doeg** (197), **doer** (87d), **does**, **doff** (99c, 119a), **doge** (74a, 127d), **dogs**, **dogy** (38c), **Doha** (221), **doit** (38d), **Dole** (58c, 149), **dole** (91d, 99b, 131a), **doll** (45b, 96a), **dolt** (20a, 48b, 109c, 116d), **dome** (32d, 102a), **doms**, **dona** (91d), **done** (85c), **dong** (224), **doni** (25d), **dons** (85d), **don't**, **doob** (18c), **dook** (77a), **doom** (35b, 44d, 54b), **Doon** (101a), **door** (41b, 91c), **dopa** (89a), **dope** (10b, 38b, 81a), **dopp** (32d), **dopy** (71c), **Dora** (30c, 33d, 35c), **Dore** (49c), **dore** (54b, 89a), **dorm** (104d), **Dorn** (149), **dorp** (57c, 128b), **dorr** (54c), **Dors** (149), **dory** (20b, 47b), **dose** (94a), **doss** (18a), **dost** (128a), **dote** (85c), **doth** (128a), **dots**, **Doug** (150), **dour** (54d, 78d, 107b, 117d), **Dove** (150), **dove** (19a, 89a, 225), **dowd** (107b), **Down** (150), **down** (35a, 45a, 232), **doxy** (133b), **doze** (110b), **dozy** (110c)

**_ D O _**    **Edom** (41c, 61d, 64b, 65b), **Idol** (159), **idol** (39d, 44a, 44d, 58d, 62a, 85b, 133d), **odor** (104d, 111a, 115b), **udos**

**_ _ D O**    **Aldo** (137), **Bodo** (69a), **dado** (34b, 84d, 87c, 129d), **Dido** (24c, 125d), **dido** (13a, 24a, 52b, 92b), **dodo** (19b, 38c, 225), **endo-** (94a), **fado** (91d), **Indo-** (93b), **iodo-** (93b), **judo** (65d, 66d), **lido** (65c, 127d), **ludo** (52b), **ordo** (21a, 27a, 92b), **pedo-** (92d, 93a), **redo** (26a, 74b), **sado** (24c, 66a), **to-do** (21b, 22d, 29b, 52c, 115c), **undo** (12d, 41c, 73a, 99b), **Yedo** (122d)

**D _ _ O**    **dado** (34b, 84d, 87c, 129d), **demo** (108d, 119c), **Dido** (24c, 125d), **dido** (13a, 24a, 52b, 92b), **Dino** (47c), **dodo** (19b, 38c, 225), **Dr. No** (20d), **duro** (88b)

**_ _ D P**    **avdp.** (236)

**D _ _ P**    **damp** (33c, 77c, 131b), **deep** (9b, 41c, 73c, 94d), **Depp** (149), **dopp** (32d), **dorp** (57c, 128b), **drip** (72b, 88a), **drop** (44a, 48d, 77a, 84a, 86d, 90b, 90c, 110d, 120a), **dump** (68d, 99d, 126c)

**D R _ _**    **drab** (22b, 26b, 29a, 38c, 43d, 47b), **drag** (30d, 95d), **dram** (38a, 38b, 84a, 92a, 110d, 246), **drat** (42a, 83a), **draw** (11d, 43c, 91d,

123c), **dray** (24c, 114b, 129b), **drei** (54a), **Drew** (150, 201), **drew** (110a), **drey** (114b), **drib** (110d), **drip** (72b, 88a), **Dr. No** (20d), **drop** (44a, 48d, 77a, 84a, 86d, 90b, 90c, 110d, 120a), **drub** (17c, 32c, 42c, 110b), **drug** (81a), **drum** (80a, 228)

_ _ D R  **Cmdr.** (237), **hydr-** (93d), **Sadr** (207)

D _ _ R  **dear** (40d), **deer** (25d, 102d, 114b, 230), **Dior** (149), **doer** (87d), **door** (41b, 91c), **dorr** (54c), **dour** (54d, 78d, 107b, 117d), **dyer**

_ _ D S  **adds**, **AIDS** (235), **aids**, **beds**, **bids**, **buds**, **cads**, **dads**, **duds** (28b, 122d), **Eads** (21d), **ends**, **fads**, **fids**, **gads**, **gods**, **hods**, **kids**, **lads**, **lids**, **muds**, **Neds**, **nods**, **odds** (10b, 11c, 26a, 95c), **pads**, **pods**, **rads**, **Reds** (206), **reds**, **rids**, **rods**, **Sids**, **sods**, **suds** (18a, 48a, 114a), **tads**, **Teds**, **tods**, **wads**, **weds**, **zeds**

D _ _ S  **dabs**, **dads**, **dais** (41d, 90b), **dams**, **Dans**, **dans** (50c), **daps**, **days**, **Debs** (148), **debs**, **dees**, **dens** (70b), **deus** (42d, 69d), **deys**, **Dias** (91d), **dibs** (55d), **dies** (69c), **digs**, **dims**, **dins**, **dios** (112d), **dips**, **diss** (75d), **docs** (88d), **does**, **dogs**, **doms**, **dons** (85d), **Dors** (149), **doss** (18a), **dots**, **dubs**, **duds** (28b, 122d), **dues**, **duos**, **dyes**

_ D T _  **HDTV** (239)

D _ _ T  **daft** (48b), **dart** (14c, 33d, 68d, 77b, 90c, 95a, 114a, 118c), **debt** (71c, 83a), **deft** (10a, 14d, 110a), **Dent** (149), **dent** (35a), **dept.** (237), **Deut.** (237), **dict.** (237), **diet** (44b, 65d, 71b), **dint** (42d, 92b), **dirt** (39a, 99c, 104c), **dist.** (237), **doit** (38d), **dolt** (20a, 48b, 109c, 116d), **don't**, **dost** (128a), **drat** (42a, 83a), **duct** (125a), **duet** (80c, 85d), **dust** (114a)

D U _ _  **duad** (85d, 125c), **dual** (37c, 125c), **duan** (52a), **dubs**, **duce** (65a), **duck** (16c, 19a, 19b, 23d, 43b, 62a, 109a, 225), **duct** (125a), **dude** (27c, 33c, 44b), **duds** (28b, 122d), **duel** (45d), **dues**, **duet** (80c, 85d), **duff** (95d), **Dufy** (49c, 150), **duim** (246), **Duke** (87d, 150, 194, 201), **duke** (82a), **Dull** (193), **dull** (20b, 28b, 47b, 63b, 66b, 71d, 73c, 126c), **duly** (100c, 117a), **duma** (103a), **dumb** (109b, 113c), **dump** (68d, 99d, 126c), **dune** (84a, 104a), **dung** (42d, 74d), **dunk** (35d, 62a), **duos**, **dupe** (25a, 34a, 48b, 56d, 74d, 118d), **dura** (113c), **duro** (88b), **Duse** (64d, 150), **dusk** (125c), **dust** (114a), **duty** (27a, 83a, 119d)

_ D U _  **educ.** (238), **-odus** (117c)

_ _ D U  **kudu** (13a, 230), **pudu** (34b), **Urdu** (60b, 213, 220)

D _ _ U  **Danu** (199), **degu** (101c), **dieu** (50b)

D _ _ W  **dauw** (22d), **dhow** (69b, 84d), **draw** (11d, 43c, 91d, 123c), **Drew** (150, 201), **drew** (110a)

D Y _ _  **dyad** (85d), **Dyak** (217, 219), **Dyan** (150), **dyed**, **dyer**, **dyes**, **dyna-** (93c), **dyne** (48c, 246)

338

**_ D Y _**   idyl (90c, 233)

**_ _ D Y**   Andy (138), body (56c), didy (35c), Eddy (150), eddy (31b, 118d, 131c), Hedy (157), Jody (161), Judy (163), lady (45b, 81d), Rudy (179), tidy (81a, 84c, 111b), tody (19b)

**D _ _ Y**   Daly (147), Davy (148, 193), davy (103b), D-Day (67a, 82a), defy (25d), demy (86b), deny (30c, 36a, 98d), dewy (77c), didy (35c), dogy (38c), dopy (71c), dory (20b, 47b), doxy (133b), dozy (110c), dray (24c, 114b, 129b), drey (114b), Dufy (49c, 150), duly (100c, 117a), duty (27a, 83a, 119d)

**_ D Z _**   adze (122d)

**_ _ D Z**   Lodz (221)

**D _ _ Z**   Diaz (76c)

**E A _ _**   each (13b), Eads (21d), Earl (150), earl (82a), earn (35b, 52a, 76a), ears, ease (10b, 11c, 15b, 29b, 42d, 71b, 77b, 99b, 99d, 100a, 129d), east (84d), easy (43d, 53c, 55c, 77c, 109c, 111c), eats (48b), eaux (51b)

**_ E A _**   bead (17d, 109b), beak (18d, 77d), beam (98a), Bean (140), bean (58c, 60b, 71b, 106b, 127c), Bear (79b), bear (40d, 114c, 134c, 230), Beas, beat (17c, 30a, 47c, 100b, 121b, 121c, 131c, 233), Beau (140), beau (117d, 118b), dead (69b), deaf (125d, 126d), deal (17b, 36a, 36d, 123d), Dean (148), dean (83c), dear (40d), fear (11a, 51c, 86b, 120d), feat (9d, 43a, 124c), gear (13c, 28b, 41b, 85b, 123a), Geat (104c), head (21a, 25d, 26c, 51c, 78a, 94c), heal (32d), heap (17a, 75b, 79a, 89a), hear (59a, 72b), Heat (206), heat (129d), Jean (160), Kean (164), keas, lead (29d, 35d, 56d, 58c, 245), leaf (85b, 90a), Leah (65b, 68b, 197), leak (72b, 84b), leal (73c, 105b), Lean (165), lean (24b, 29b, 98a, 110c, 113b, 121a, 122b), leap (24a, 67a, 232), Lear (30d, 107c, 195), leas, Mead (61a, 170), mead (18a, 37d, 60d), meal (56c, 99c), mean (9a, 16a, 17b, 34d, 76c, 109b, 115c), meat (48b), neaf (47b), Neal (172), neap (121d, 122d, 129b), near (13d, 28b, 81d), neat (10a, 116a, 121d, 124c), peag (129d), peak (11d, 31d, 32c, 59a, 59d, 117d, 135a), peal (100d), pear (51d, 124a), peas, peat (52a, 127c), read (63c, 88b, 116c), real (9d, 116d), ream (18d, 31b, 41a, 86b, 125c), reap (9d, 33a, 58b), rear (10c, 21d, 40d, 41c, 60a, 97c), seal (28b, 44c, 89b, 231), seam (66c, 67a, 128c), Sean (66c, 180), sear (25b, 133a), seas, seat (25d, 63b, 115c), Seau (180), teak (39b, 124a), teal (19a, 20b, 38c, 226), team (32a, 48c, 56c, 85d, 232), tear (68b, 99c), teas, teat (81d), veal (23b, 75c), weak (45a, 62c, 63a), weal (131b, 131c), wean (117a), wear (114a), yeah (10b), yean (68d), year (122b), yeas (129c), zeal (14b, 45c)

**_ _ E A**   -acea (117c), Alea (15b), area (36d, 37b, 45d, 72d, 97d, 99a, 135c), asea (32b, 129c), brea (77a), flea (63b, 229), Gaea (39b, 198), idea (35b, 44b, 82c, 95a, 121b), ilea (73c), itea (118c, 128c), odea (29d), olea (84a), Otea (64c), plea (42d, 92b, 118a), Rhea

(68c, 78d, 89d, 122c, 135c, 177, 198), **rhea** (19b, 26c, 85a, 226),
**Shea** (180), **shea** (22d, 124a), **Thea** (122c), **toea** (221), **urea** (45c),
**uvea** (43c, 64a)

E _ _ A   **Ecca** (53c), **Ecua.** (238), **edda** (59c, 61b, 82a, 103b), **Edna** (151),
**Elba** (64c, 80d), **Elia** (68d, 87c, 151), **Ella** (151), **ella** (113a), **-ella**
(117b), **Elsa** (55c, 72d, 84b, 129c, 151), **-emia** (117a), **Emma** (21b,
151), **Enna** (109a), **Erda** (22b, 198), **Erma** (151), **esca** (19d, 36a,
55d), **esta** (113a), **Etna** (129a), **etna** (58d), **Etta** (152), **-etta** (117b),
**eyra** (65b), **Ezra** (152, 196, 197)

E B _ _   **ebbs**, **ebon** (19d), **Ebro** (222), **ebur** (69d)

_ E B _   **Bebe** (140), **bebe** (50a), **Cebu** (64d, 221), **Debs** (148), **debs**, **debt**
(71c, 83a), **febr-** (93a), **Hebe** (32d, 59c, 135a, 198), **Nebo** (78d,
79a), **Nebr.** (211, 241), **nebs**, **peba** (14b), **Reba** (67c, 176), **rebs**,
**sebi-** (92d), **sebo-** (92d), **Webb** (186), **webs**, **zebu** (21c, 62d, 231)

_ _ E B   **bleb** (20a, 22b, 54c), **dieb** (65b), **Oreb** (197), **pleb** (29b), **Weeb**
(186)

E C _ _   **Ecca** (53c), **ecce** (18b, 69c, 69d), **eccl.** (238), **Echo** (80d), **echo**
(12a, 99d, 100b), **echt** (54a), **ecol.** (238), **E-COM** (238), **econ.**
(238), **ecru** (18b, 22b, 126a), **ecto-** (93c), **Ecua.** (238)

_ E C _   **Beck** (140), **beck** (82a), **ceca** (69b), **deca-** (93d), **decd.** (237), **deci**
(120c), **deck** (34b, 108b), **geck** (105b), **heck** (42a), **hect-** (93a),
**keck** (100a), **Lech** (165, 213), **neck** (64d), **necr-** (92d), **Peck** (174),
**peck** (22d, 246), **Pecs** (217), **reck** (24b), **sect** (34d, 43d), **secy.**
(243), **yech** (112a), **Zech.** (244)

_ _ E C   **Alec** (137), **alec** (12c, 47a, 104b), **avec** (51b), **elec.** (238), **exec.**
(238), **haec** (70a), **OPEC** (241), **spec.** (243)

E _ _ C   **educ.** (238), **EEOC** (238), **elec.** (238), **epic** (59c, 90c), **Eric** (128b,
151), **eruc** (30d, 45d), **exec.** (238)

E D _ _   **Edam** (26b, 38d), **edda** (59c, 61b, 82a, 103b), **Eddy** (150), **eddy**
(31b, 118d, 131c), **edel** (54a), **Eden** (41a, 82a, 86c, 150), **edge**
(10b, 19c, 21a, 21b, 74d, 87d, 100d, 109a, 130c), **edgy** (81b, 100a,
120c), **Edie** (150), **edit** (20b, 40c, 94a, 98c, 100b), **Edna** (151),
**Edom** (41c, 61d, 64b, 65b), **educ.** (238)

_ E D _   **Bede** (78a, 127d), **beds**, **cede** (54c, 55d, 99b, 118b, 129b), **cedi**
(216), **Hedy** (157), **Leda** (24d, 59a, 91a, 113b, 125d, 135d, 198),
**Mede** (14d, 88a), **medi-** (93c), **Neds**, **-pede** (117b), **pedi-** (93a),
**pedo-** (92d, 93a), **Redd** (176), **redd** (113b), **rede** (31b, 105a), **redo**
(26a, 74b), **Reds** (206), **reds**, **Teds**, **veda** (60a), **weds**, **Yedo**
(122d), **zeds**

_ _ E D   **abed** (110b), **aced** (120c), **aged** (12c, 83c, 83d), **aped**, **awed**,
**axed**, **bled** (97d), **bred** (97c), **coed** (107b), **cued**, **deed** (9d, 43a,
71a, 122c), **died**, **dyed**, **eked**, **eyed**, **feed** (82c), **fled**, **Fred** (47c,

340

153), **gled** (42a), **heed** (15c, 25b, 58d, 72b, 83a, 99a), **hied, hoed, hued, iced, lied** (54a, 234), **meed** (100b), **Mr. Ed** (119b), **need** (34d, 42d, 68b, 92a, 129d), **Obed** (103c, 197), **owed, pied** (114a, 127b), **pled, Reed** (176, 204), **reed** (16d, 55d, 75a, 79c, 84d), **rued, seed** (55c, 84d, 85c, 90a, 112b, 113d), **shed** (24d, 70d, 77d, 108a), **she'd** (30c), **sled** (102b), **sned** (73a), **sped, sued, Swed.** (243), **teed, tied, toed, used** (9c, 57a), **vied, weed** (52d)

E _ _ D     **egad** (83a), **eked, emyd** (120c), **Enid** (14d, 23c, 53c, 120c, 151), **Exod.** (238), **eyed**

E E _ _     **eels, eely, EEOC** (238), **Eero** (151)

_ E E _     **beef** (29c, 75c), **been, beep** (112b), **beer** (18d, 95d), **bees, beet** (127c), **cees, deed** (9d, 43a, 71a, 122c), **deem** (30b, 66d, 121a), **deep** (9b, 41c, 73c, 94d), **deer** (25d, 102d, 114b, 230), **dees, feed** (82c), **feel** (56c, 106c, 123b, 134b), **fees, feet** (71b), **geek** (109a), **Geer** (154), **gees, Geez** (41d), **heed** (15c, 25b, 58d, 72b, 83a, 99a), **heel** (55b), **Heep** (33d, 35c), **heer** (134b), **jeep** (127d), **jeer** (120a), **jeez** (42a), **keef** (58b), **Keel** (164), **keel** (108b), **keen** (16a, 45c, 68d, 129b), **keep** (10a, 60c, 94b, 100a, 104c), **keet** (56d), **leek** (59b, 84a, 131b), **leer** (12b, 73a, 110d), **lees** (37d, 106b), **leet** (31c), **meed** (100b), **Meek** (170), **meek** (37a, 53c, 61c, 76d, 77c, 126a), **meet** (9c, 15a, 30a, 40d, 43d, 63c, 103a, 107a), **need** (34d, 42d, 68b, 92a, 129d), **neep** (105b, 125b), **ne'er** (30b, 82c, 107c), **peek** (73a), **Peel** (174), **peel** (43a, 86c), **peen** (57d), **peep** (73a, 87c), **peer** (41b, 73a, 82a), **Reed** (176, 204), **reed** (16d, 55d, 75a, 79c, 84d), **reef** (98d, 104a, 108b), **reek** (43c, 52a, 111a), **reel** (20c, 33b, 113c, 113d, 114b, 114c, 131c, 133a, 233), **Rees** (176), **seed** (55c, 84d, 85c, 90a, 112b, 113d), **seek** (105d), **seel** (20a), **seem** (13c), **seen, seep** (72b, 84b, 87d, 114a), **seer** (95b, 111d, 128c), **sees, teed, teel** (107a), **teem** (9b, 92a, 118c), **-teen** (117b), **Tees** (82b), **tees, veer** (35c, 125b), **vees, Weeb** (186), **weed** (52d), **week** (122b), **weep** (32b, 68d), **zees** (110c)

_ _ E E     **Agee** (137), **akee** (51d, 124a), **alee** (59a, 108a, 132b), **bree** (105a), **chee** (246), **Cree** (11b, 189), **epee** (45b, 118d), **flee** (9b, 41c), **free** (36b, 56a, 73a, 100c, 112b), **ghee** (22d), **glee** (76a, 111d, 234), **idee** (50c), **Klee** (164), **knee** (66c), **ogee** (14a, 77d, 90c), **pree** (105b), **Rhee** (68c, 177), **Smee** (88b), **snee** (33a, 35d, 68a), **Spee** (53c, 55c), **thee** (95b), **tree** (30d, 53b, 133c), **tyee** (26d)

E _ _ E     **ease** (10b, 11c, 15b, 29b, 42d, 71b, 77b, 99b, 99d, 100a, 129d), **ecce** (18b, 69c, 69d), **edge** (10b, 19c, 21a, 21b, 74d, 87d, 100d, 109a, 130c), **Edie** (150), **eine** (53d, 54a), **Eire** (64a), **Elbe** (82b, 216), **Elie** (151), **Elke** (151), **elle** (49d, 51a, 246), **else** (18c, 61d, 85a), **-ence** (117b), **-ense** (117b), **epee** (45b, 118d), **Erde** (22b), **Erie** (23c, 68d, 189), **Erle** (151), **erne** (19a, 39a, 105c, 225), **Erse** (25c, 52a, 64a), **-esce** (117c), **esne** (12c, 106d, 110b, 121b), **esse** (9d, 18b), **Este** (44b, 45b, 64d, 85b), **este** (113a), **etre** (50a), **-ette** (117b), **eure** (54b), **evoe** (16a, 100b), **Eyre** (22a)

E F _ _     **Efik** (69a, 220), **efts**

341

**_ E F _**    **deft** (10a, 14d, 110a), **defy** (25d), **heft** (22c, 131a), **Jeff** (161), **left** (9a, 34d, 91c, 99c), **teff** (10c), **weft** (32b, 121c, 133c)

**_ _ E F**    **atef** (32b, 39d), **beef** (29c, 75c), **chef** (30c, 50c, 68a), **clef** (80c, 234), **coef.** (237), **fief** (45c), **keef** (58b), **lief** (132a), **reef** (98d, 104a, 108b), **tref** (48b, 126a)

**E _ _ F**    **Enif** (207)

**E G _ _**    **egad** (83a), **egal** (50b), **Eger** (40a), **eggs** (85c), **eggy** (134d), **Egil** (82b), **egos**

**_ E G _**    **begs**, **degu** (101c), **kegs**, **legs**, **mega-** (93b), **Megs**, **pega** (46d), **pegs**, **Pegu** (97d), **sego** (22c, 71d), **tegs**, **Vega** (114d, 207), **Wegg** (85a), **yegg** (22d)

**_ _ E G**    **Doeg** (197), **Gheg** (213), **Greg** (156), **Oreg.** (241), **Roeg** (178), **skeg** (67b, 133b)

**_ E H _**    **Jehu** (197), **jehu** (38a), **lehr** (54c, 85c), **peho** (81c), **sehr** (54a), **wehe** (53d)

**E _ _ H**    **each** (13b), **Elah** (67d), **Esth.** (16d, 238), **Etah** (56c, 63d), **etch** (14d, 35a), **euch** (54b), **exch.** (238)

**E I _ _**    **eine** (53d, 54a), **Eire** (64a)

**_ E I _**    **ceil** (25b), **deil** (105a), **dein** (54b), **feis** (64a), **hein** (42c, 49c), **heir** (63a, 71b), **Keir** (164), **Leif** (43a), **leis**, **mein** (26d), **Meir** (170), **Neil** (172), **nein** (54a), **Reid** (176), **rein** (26b, 30c, 100a), **reis** (24a), **Seir** (41c), **seis** (113a), **teil** (72a), **veil** (29d, 36b, 58c, 59d, 75b), **vein** (20a, 116b), **Weil** (186), **Weir** (186), **weir** (33b, 47a), **zein** (30d)

**_ _ E I**    **drei** (54a), **Iwei** (213), **Omei** (22b)

**E _ _ I**    **Eloi** (122b), **equi-** (93c), **etui** (24c, 50a, 51a, 81b, 127b)

**E J _ _**    **ejoo** (45a)

**_ E J _**    **Beja** (82a, 222), **sejm** (91a)

**E K _ _**    **eked**, **ekes**

**_ E K _**    **deka-** (93d), **leks**, **Reki** (16d), **Teke** (215), **weka** (19b, 74d, 81c, 97b)

**_ _ E K**    **Ezek.** (238), **geek** (109a), **leek** (59b, 84a, 131b), **Meek** (170), **meek** (37a, 53c, 61c, 76d, 77c, 126a), **peek** (73a), **reek** (43c, 52a, 111a), **seek** (105d), **trek** (66d, 73a, 123d), **week** (122b)

**E _ _ K**    **Efik** (69a, 220), **Erik** (151), **Ezek.** (238)

**E L _ _**    **Elah** (67d), **Elam** (88a, 108a, 151), **elan** (33d, 41b, 113d, 128d, 135a), **Elba** (64c, 80d), **Elbe** (82b, 216), **elec.** (238), **elem.** (238), **elev.** (238), **Elia** (68d, 87c, 151), **Elie** (151), **Elio** (151), **Elis** (56b),

Eliz. (238), Elke (151), elks, Ella (151), ella (113a), -ella (117b), elle (49d, 51a, 246), ells, Elmo (21a, 87a, 151), elms, elmy, Eloi (122b), Elon (41c, 82b, 201), Elsa (55c, 72d, 84b, 129b, 151), else (18c, 61d, 85a), elul (78c)

_ E L _  Bela (18c, 39c, 140), Belg. (236), Bell (140), bell (22c, 120b), bels, belt (16d, 27b), -cele (117c), cell (32c), Celt (22a, 217), celt (115d, 123a), Dela. (209), dele (23c, 40b, 43a, 94c, 95b, 119b), dell (35d, 127b), eels, eely, Fell (152), fell (33a), felt (42d, 43b, 43d), geld (120a), gels, gelt (78a), held (91d), heli- (93d), Hell (9a, 16a, 34a, 57a, 108a), he'll (30c), Helm (157), helm (108b, 122a), help (10d, 15a, 62b, 117a), jell (111d), kela (246), kelp (64a, 106a), meld (23c, 34b), mell (60d), Mels, melt (72b, 120d), Nell (83d, 172), Pele (58c), pelf (21a, 46a, 100c), Pell (174), pelt (28c, 43a, 57b, 59d), pelu (26c), rely (124d), self (39d, 62d), sell (74d, 87c, 127d), tela (21c, 75d, 130d), tele- (92d, 93d), Tell (14a), tell (13d, 62b, 81a, 99a), telo- (92d), Vela (103c, 208), veld (104c, 112b), Weld (186), weld (38d, 66c, 126c), Welk (186), well (25c, 97c), we'll (30c), welt (100c, 129d, 130c, 131c), Yell (64d), yell (18c, 108d), yelp (12d, 37b)

_ _ E L  Abel (10a, 23a, 107a, 197), -coel (117a), duel (45d), edel (54a), esel (53d), Evel (68a), ezel (67c), feel (56c, 106c, 123b, 134b), fuel (53a), Gael (25c, 105a), goel (16a), heel (55b), Icel. (239), Jael (197), Joel (161, 196, 197), Kael (163), Keel (164), keel (108b), Kiel (23c), koel (32c), myel- (93d), Noel (172), noel (24b, 27a, 111d), Orel (173), Peel (174), peel (43a, 86c), pyel- (93c), reel (20c, 33b, 113c, 113d, 114b, 114c, 131c, 133a, 233), riel (214), seel (20a), tael (71c, 131a), teel (107a)

E _ _ L  Earl (150), earl (82a), eccl. (238), ecol. (238), edel (54a), egal (50b), Egil (82b), elul (78c), Emil (151), encl. (238), enol (120a), esel (53d), et al. (69c, 238), Evel (68a), evil (74c, 109c, 131d, 134c), excl. (238), ezel (67c)

E M _ _  emeu (19b), -emia (117a), Emil (151), emim (54b), emir (13d, 94c, 102d, 125b), emit (36a, 40a, 43c, 47d, 99b, 106c), Emma (21b, 151), Emmy (120b), emus, emyd (120c)

_ E M _  bema (90b, 95d), deme (56b), Demi (148), demi- (93a), demo (108d, 119c), demy (86b), feme (133b), gems, hema- (92c), heme (20a), hemi- (93a), hemo- (92c), hemp (23d, 30d, 45c, 55d, 102b), hems, Kemp (164), Lema (166), memo (82c), nema (39d), Nemo (128a), remi (53b), seme (37c), semi (62c), semi- (93a, 93c), tema (121a, 234), temp. (243), xema (14a, 56d), zemi (45c)

_ _ E M  ahem (15c, 112a), chem. (31b, 236), deem (30b, 66d, 121a), elem. (238), Flem. (238), idem (70a), item (9c, 14d, 35b, 41b, 71a, 72b, 81c, 83a, 86d), Ozem (197), poem (128a), riem (59d), seem (13c), Shem (81d, 197), stem (26b, 95c, 114c, 115d), teem (9b, 92a, 118c), them (95a)

E _ _ M  E-COM (238), Edam (26b, 38d), Edom (41c, 61d, 64b, 65b), Elam (88a, 108a, 151), elem. (238), emim (54b), Enam (66d), exam (120d)

343

**E N _ _**    **Enam** (66d), **-ence** (117b), **encl.** (238), **-ency** (117b), **ency.** (238), **endo-** (94a), **ends, engr.** (238), **Enid** (14d, 23c, 53c, 120c, 151), **Enif** (207), **Enna** (109a), **enol** (120a), **Enos** (9d, 42a, 107a, 151, 197), **enow** (105a), **-ense** (117b), **ento-** (94a), **envy** (34a, 107a), **Enyo** (129d)

**_ E N _**    **bend** (12c, 32d, 125b), **bene** (65c, 70b), **Beni** (214), **beno** (86a), **Bens, bent** (13d, 32a, 55d, 62c), **-cene** (117c), **ceno-** (92d), **cent** (30c, 213-224), **cent.** (236), **Dene** (189), **dene** (104a), **dens** (70b), **Dent** (149), **dent** (35a), **deny** (30c, 36a, 98d), **fend** (44b, 86d, 129d), **fens, Gena** (154), **Gene** (154), **gene** (59c), **Genl.** (239), **gens** (35a), **gent** (45b), **genu** (18c, 69d), **-geny** (117c), **hens** (92a), **Jena** (121d), **keno** (52b), **Kens, Kent** (70d, 195, 202), **Lena** (30b, 52a, 166), **lend** (62b), **Leno** (166), **leno** (43b, 75a), **lens** (54c, 74a, 84c, 98d, 120b), **Lent** (44c, 87c, 106a), **lent** (99c), **mend** (99c), **mene** (57d), **meno** (71b, 233), **-ment** (117b), **menu** (19a, 24c, 29c, 48b, 51a), **nene** (58c), **oeno-** (94a), **Peña** (174), **pend** (16c, 58a), **Penn** (174), **Penn.** (211, 242), **pens, pent** (30a), **rend** (28a), **René** (176), **Reni** (65a, 176), **reni-** (93b), **Reno** (15c, 81c, 113d), **reno-** (93b), **rent** (60b, 60c, 120a, 123b), **send** (36c, 74b, 86d, 91d, 99c, 108b, 123d), **sens** (49c), **sent, tend** (24b, 73a, 77a, 124b), **Tenn.** (212, 243), **teno-** (93d), **tens, tent** (24a, 87b), **vena** (70b), **vend** (74d, 87c, 106c), **veni-** (93d), **veno-** (93d), **vent** (11a, 13b, 40c, 60c, 84b, 85b, 115a), **wend** (54d, 110b, 112a), **wens, went** (34d), **xeno-** (93a), **yeni** (119c), **yens, Zeno** (56b)

**_ _ E N**    **Aden** (13d, 224), **amen** (111b, 128a), **been, B. Gen.** (236), **bien** (51b), **bren** (73d), **Caen** (17c), **Coen** (146), **cten-** (93c), **Eden** (41a, 82a, 86c, 150), **even** (23b, 41b, 42b, 47b, 61d, 67c, 71c, 82a, 111a, 126c, 134c), **Glen** (155), **glen** (35d, 98a, 127b), **G-men** (45a), **Gwen** (156), **Iden** (192), **Kaen** (223), **keen** (16a, 45c, 68d, 129b), **lien** (53a, 71a, 95b), **mien** (13c, 17d, 24c, 34d, 36d, 74d), **omen** (15d, 48c, 48d, 91c, 94a, 109b), **open** (18b, 23c, 49b, 63a, 83b, 85c, 95d, 126a, 126b, 126c), **oven** (61c, 67b), **oxen** (12d, 21b), **peen** (57d), **phen-** (92c), **pien** (14c), **rien** (50d), **seen, Sten** (182), **sten** (73d), **Sven, ta'en** (107c), **-teen** (117b), **then** (10c, 121a), **T-men** (45a, 123d), **when** (96d, 131c), **Wien** (33c), **Wren** (187), **wren** (19a, 226)

**E _ _ N**    **earn** (35b, 52a, 76a), **ebon** (19d), **econ.** (238), **Eden** (41a, 82a, 86c, 150), **elan** (33d, 41b, 113d, 128d, 135a), **Elon** (41c, 82b, 201), **Erin** (64a, 151), **ESPN** (26a), **ethn-** (93c), **Eton** (58b, 65b), **even** (23b, 41b, 42b, 47b, 61d, 67c, 71c, 82a, 111a, 126c, 134c)

**E O _ _**    **eons, -eous** (117a)

**_ E O _**    **aeon** (122b), **EEOC** (238), **geog.** (239), **geol.** (239), **geom.** (239), **jeon** (218), **Keos** (64c), **Leon** (166, 222), **Leos, meow** (25a), **neon** (53a, 71d, 245), **peon** (48c, 76c), **Teos** (64a)

**_ _ E O**    **Cleo** (96d, 146), **ideo-** (93a), **ileo-** (93b), **oleo-** (93b), **rheo-** (92d), **skeo** (47a)

**E _ _ O**    **Ebro** (222), **Echo** (80d), **echo** (12a, 99d, 100b), **ecto-** (93c), **Eero** (151), **ejoo** (45a), **Elio** (151), **Elmo** (21a, 87a, 151), **endo-** (94a), **ento-** (94a), **Enyo** (129d), **ergo** (121a), **Ezio** (152)

**E P _ _**    **epee** (45b, 118d), **epic** (59c, 90c), **Epis.** (238), **epit.** (238), **epos** (41b, 59c, 90c)

**_ E P _**    **cepe** (39c), **Depp** (149), **dept.** (237), **FEPA** (238), **FEPC** (238), **hept-** (93c), **kepi** (58d, 76d), **kept, lept-** (93d), **neph-** (92d), **pepo** (32c, 75d, 96a), **peps, repp** (43b), **reps, seps** (72c, 106d), **Sept.** (78c, 243), **sept** (27d, 64a, 111b), **wept, Zeph.** (244)

**_ _ E P**    **beep** (112b), **deep** (9b, 41c, 73c, 94d), **Heep** (33d, 35c), **jeep** (127d), **keep** (10a, 60c, 94b, 100a, 104c), **neep** (105b, 125b), **peep** (73a, 87c), **prep** (104d), **seep** (72b, 84b, 87d, 114a), **skep** (18a, 60b), **step** (55c, 129b), **weep** (32b, 68d)

**E Q _ _**    **equi-** (93c)

**_ E Q _**    **seqq.** (243)

**_ _ E Q**    **freq.** (238)

**E R _ _**    **eras, erat** (96a, 97c), **Erda** (22b, 198), **Erde** (22b), **ergo** (121a), **ergs, Eric** (128b, 151), **Erie** (23c, 68d, 189), **Erik** (151), **Erin** (64a, 151), **Eris** (14b, 198), **Erle** (151), **Erma** (151), **erne** (19a, 39a, 105c, 225), **erns, Eros** (32d, 132c, 195, 198), **errs, Erse** (25c, 52a, 64a), **erst** (49a), **eruc** (30d, 45d)

**_ E R _**    **aeri-** (92c), **aero-** (92c), **aero.** (235), **aery** (39a), **Berg** (141), **berg** (61b), **berm** (23c, 71a, 108d), **Bern** (9a, 222), **Bert** (20c, 141), **cere** (18d, 130c), **Cerf** (145), **CERN** (236), **cero** (46d, 67d), **cero-** (93c), **cert.** (236), **-derm** (117c), **Dern** (149), **Eero** (151), **fern** (106b), **feru** (30d, 45c), **gerb** (46b), **Gere** (155), **germ** (36b, 61b, 76c), **Hera** (14b, 67c, 135c, 198), **Herb** (158), **herb** (90a, 106b), **herd** (38b, 232), **here** (63d, 101c), **herl** (14d, 17a), **Hero** (70d, 194), **hero** (34d, 95c, 104a), **herr** (53d), **hers** (95a), **ieri** (65c), **jerk** (20a, 38d, 48b, 88a, 95d), **kerb** (109a), **kerf** (33a, 82c), **Kern** (164), **kern** (48c, 101b, 125d), **Kerr** (164), **Lero** (64c), **lerp** (41d), **mere** (17b, 50d, 68b, 84b, 91b, 130a), **merl** (19a, 19d, 226), **mero** (56c, 66b), **Meru** (79a, 218), **Merv** (170), **Nera** (121d), **Nero** (10d, 102a), **pere** (49d, 50b), **peri** (44a, 88a), **peri-** (92c), **perk** (28d, 51c), **pern** (60d), **pero** (112d), **Pers.** (242), **pert** (49a, 62b, 72c, 104b, 114a, 128d), **Peru** (221), **sera** (13a, 47d, 65a), **Serb** (134d), **sere** (37d, 133a), **serf** (20d, 110b), **Seri** (76c), **sero-** (93c), **Sert** (112c), **tera-** (93d), **Teri** (183), **term** (71d, 72a, 80b, 106c, 115c), **tern** (19a, 28c, 56d, 104d, 105d, 118b, 226), **terp** (79a, 94a), **Vera** (185), **verb** (86d), **vers** (51b), **vert** (56c), **vert.** (244), **very** (43c, 78d, 111b), **were, we're** (30c), **werf** (44c), **weri** (16c, 25a), **wert** (128a), **xero-** (92c), **Zero** (188), **zero** (27b, 65d, 73b, 82c, 89d)

**_ _ E R**    **acer** (74d), **Ager** (137), **ager** (69d, 100d, 102a), **Amer.** (235), **amer** (50a), **aper** (28b, 77a), **Auer** (61c, 139), **aver** (10b, 15a, 16c, 34b, 74b, 115a, 118c), **Baer** (140), **beer** (18d, 95d), **bier** (28d, 53d),

**Boer** (10c, 112b), **br'er** (126a), **cher** (50b), **deer** (25d, 102d, 114b, 230), **doer** (87d), **dyer**, **Eger** (40a), **euer** (54b), **ever** (12a, 18b, 62c), **ewer** (66a, 66d, 89c, 131d), **Geer** (154), **gier** (39a), **goer**, **heer** (134b), **hier** (51b), **hier-** (93c), **hoer**, **icer**, **Iser** (40a), **iter** (69d, 101a, 101d), **jeer** (120a), **kier** (19d, 127b), **leer** (12b, 73a, 110d), **ne'er** (30b, 82c, 107c), **Nuer** (222), **Oder** (100d), **omer** (59a), **over** (9b, 9d, 14c, 32a, 87a, 99c), **oyer** (31c), **peer** (41b, 73a, 82a), **Pier** (175), **pier** (21d, 66b, 68d, 131b), **pter-** (94a), **ruer**, **seer** (95b, 111d, 128c), **-ster** (117a, 117b), **suer** (95b), **tier** (46a, 89b, 102c), **user** (10a, 29c, 40c), **uter-** (93d), **veer** (35c, 125b), **vier** (53d)

E _ _ R    **ebur** (69d), **Eger** (40a), **emir** (13d, 94c, 102d, 125b), **engr.** (238), **euer** (54b), **ever** (12a, 18b, 62c), **ewer** (66a, 66d, 89c, 131d)

E S _ _    **Esau** (64b, 65b, 98b, 197), **esca** (19d, 36a, 55d), **-esce** (117c), **esel** (53d), **esne** (12c, 106d, 110b, 121b), **ESPN** (26a), **espy** (106b), **esse** (9d, 18b), **esta** (113a), **Este** (44b, 45b, 64d, 85b), **este** (113a), **Esth.** (16d, 238)

_ E S _    **Bess** (141), **best** (26d, 30a, 34c, 42b, 85c, 118b), **cess** (71c, 120a), **cest** (54c), **desc.** (237), **Dese** (216), **Desi** (149), **desk** (134c), **Fess** (152), **fess** (41c), **-fest** (117b), **gest** (119b), **Hess** (158), **Jess** (161), **jess** (116a), **jest** (17a, 66d), **less** (77b, 82c), **lest** (48d), **mesa** (40b, 59d, 90b, 119a), **mesh** (40d, 63c, 81c, 111b, 130d), **meso-** (93b), **mess** (21b, 26a, 30a, 36c, 67a, 79c, 111b), **ness** (24a, 58d, 95a), **nest** (31c, 100a, 111b, 118c, 232), **peso** (215 - 217, 219, 221, 224), **pest** (82d, 88a, 89d), **resh** (12a), **rest** (16b, 21d, 71b, 80c, 87b, 99b, 99c, 99d, 234), **sess** (111b), **sess.** (243), **Tess** (58a, 183), **test** (23d, 41d, 42b, 124b, 124d), **vest** (28b, 129b), **West** (186), **west** (83b), **zest** (45c, 57c, 99b)

_ _ E S    **Abes**, **aces**, **ages**, **ales**, **Ames** (138), **apes**, **Ares** (13b, 41c, 59b, 75a, 129d, 135c, 198), **ates** (118c), **aves**, **awes**, **axes**, **ayes** (129c), **bees**, **byes**, **cees**, **cues**, **dees**, **dies** (69c), **does**, **dues**, **dyes**, **ekes**, **Eves**, **eves**, **ewes**, **exes**, **eyes**, **fees**, **foes**, **gees**, **GOES** (239), **goes**, **hies**, **hoes**, **hues**, **ices**, **ides** (33d, 101d), **Ikes**, **Ives** (159), **Joes**, **lees** (37d, 106b), **lies**, **lues** (118d), **lyes**, **Maes**, **Moes**, **noes** (81b), **odes**, **ones** (87d), **ores**, **owes**, **oyes** (31c, 32c, 58d), **pies**, **Pres.** (242), **pres** (50d), **pyes**, **Raes**, **Rees** (176), **roes**, **rues**, **sees**, **she's** (30c), **Spes** (198), **sues**, **Tees** (82b), **tees**, **ties**, **toes**, **tres** (42b, 51b, 113a), **Tues.** (243), **uses**, **Utes**, **vees**, **vies**, **woes**, **Yves** (188), **zees** (110c), **Zoes**

E _ _ S    **Eads** (21d), **ears**, **eats** (48b), **ebbs**, **eels**, **efts**, **eggs** (85c), **egos**, **ekes**, **Elis** (56b), **elks**, **ells**, **elms**, **emus**, **ends**, **Enos** (9d, 42a, 107a, 151, 197), **eons**, **-eous** (117a), **Epis.** (238), **epos** (41b, 59c, 90c), **eras**, **ergs**, **Eris** (14b, 198), **erns** (32d, 132c, 195, 198), **errs**, **Evas**, **Eves**, **eves**, **ewes**, **exes**, **eyas** (19b, 58c), **eyes**

E T _ _    **Etah** (56c, 63d), **et al.** (69c, 238), **etat** (51a), **etch** (14d, 35a), **ethn-** (93c), **Etna** (129a), **etna** (58d), **Eton** (58b, 65b), **etre** (50a), **Etta** (152), **-etta** (117b), **-ette** (117b), **etui** (24c, 50a, 51a, 81b, 127b)

_ E T _    **beta** (11d, 106a), **Bete** (215), **bete** (50a), **Beth** (11a, 141), **beth**

346

(12a), **bets**, **CETA** (236), **cete** (232), **CETI** (236), **Ceto** (55c, 75d), **fete** (45c), **geta** (65b, 108c), **gets**, **Getz** (155), **Heth** (197), **jete** (16c), **jeth** (78b), **Jets** (206), **jets**, **Jett** (161), **keta** (37b), **keto-** (93b), **Leto** (13b, 14d, 28d, 88c, 198), **lets**, **Lett** (16d), **meta-** (92d), **mete** (11c, 13d, 91d), **Meth.** (240), **metr-** (94a), **Mets** (206), **Metz** (216), **Neth.** (241), **Nets** (206), **nets**, **Pete** (85a, 174), **Peto** (193), **peto** (129b), **petr-** (93d), **pets**, **rete** (81c, 90b), **rets**, **seta** (22a, 57b, 113c), **Seth** (10a, 42b, 197, 198), **seth** (76a), **Seti** (88c), **sets**, **sett** (87b, 119d), **tete** (50c), **teth** (12a), **veto** (95a), **vets**, **weta** (72d), **wets**, **Yeti** (9b), **zeta** (11d)

_ _ E T  **abet** (10d, 48b, 59b), **acet-** (92c), **beet** (127c), **blet** (51d), **Bret** (143), **Chet** (145), **diet** (44b, 65d, 71b), **duet** (80c, 85d), **feet** (71b), **fret** (22a, 25d, 36d, 42c, 128b, 133d), **hyet-** (93c), **keet** (56d), **laet** (49b), **leet** (31c), **meet** (9c, 15a, 30a, 40d, 43d, 63c, 103a, 107a), **nyet** (81d), **Piet** (175), **piet** (26b, 74b), **poet** (40b), **spet** (17b), **stet** (71c, 94c, 95b), **suet** (44c, 83d), **tret** (130a, 131a), **whet** (39c, 107d)

E _ _ T  **east** (84d), **echt** (54a), **edit** (20b, 40c, 94a, 98c, 100b), **emit** (36a, 40a, 43c, 47d, 99b, 106c), **epit.** (238), **erat** (96a, 97c), **erst** (49a), **etat** (51a), **exit** (71a, 130c)

E U _ _  **euch** (54b), **euer** (54b), **eure** (54b), **eury-** (94a)

_ E U _  **deus** (42d, 69d), **Deut.** (237), **feud** (45c, 96b, 127d), **jeux** (50b), **leuc-** (94a), **leuk-** (94a), **meus** (69d), **neur-** (93b), **neut.** (241), **oeuf** (50b), **Peul** (217, 219, 221), **peur** (50b), **Zeus** (55c, 59c, 198)

_ _ E U  **bleu** (26b, 50a), **dieu** (50b), **emeu** (19b), **lieu** (89d)

E _ _ U  **ecru** (18b, 22b, 126a), **emeu** (19b), **Esau** (64b, 65b, 98b, 197)

E V _ _  **Evas**, **Evel** (68a), **even** (23b, 41b, 42b, 47b, 61d, 67c, 71c, 82a, 111a, 126c, 134c), **ever** (12a, 18b, 62c), **Eves**, **eves**, **evil** (74c, 109c, 131d, 134c), **evoe** (16a, 100b)

_ E V _  **Bevs**, **bevy** (16d, 31c, 47c, 232), **Deva** (60a, 221), **Devi** (109d), **Levi** (13b, 64d, 70d, 197), **levo-** (93b), **levy** (15a, 62b, 120a), **Neva** (100d), **neve** (46c, 54c, 55d, 111b), **nevi** (19c, 77d), **reve** (50b), **revs**, **Seve** (180), **we've** (30c)

_ _ E V  **elev.** (238), **Kiev** (223)

E _ _ V  **elev.** (238)

E W _ _  **ewer** (66a, 66d, 89c, 131d), **ewes**

_ E W _  **dewy** (77c), **hewn** (27a), **hews**, **Jews**, **lewd** (69b, 103d), **mewl** (131c), **mews** (114b), **news** (121d), **Newt** (172), **newt** (39d, 103d, 225) **pews**, **sewn**, **sews**, **Tewa** (189), **yews**

_ _ E W  **anew** (10b, 10c), **blew**, **brew** (29d), **chew** (75b), **clew** (16c, 103b), **crew** (48c, 56c, 81b, 88b, 133d), **Drew** (150, 201), **drew** (110a),

**flew, grew, knew, Llew** (199), **phew** (42c), **plew** (18a), **shew** (128a), **skew** (118c, 125b), **slew** (110c, 118c), **smew** (19a, 38c, 76a, 104c), **spew** (40a), **stew** (20c, 30c), **thew** (79d), **view** (12c, 15a, 42b, 73a, 95b, 104d), **whew** (42c)

E _ _ W    **enow** (105a)

E X _ _    **exam** (120d), **exch.** (238), **excl.** (238), **exec.** (238), **exes, exit** (71a, 130c), **Exod.** (238)

_ E X _    **hexa-** (93c), **next** (81a), **sexi-** (93c), **sext** (23d, 84d, 109d), **sexy** (41c), **text** (86d, 133c)

_ _ E X    **Alex** (137), **AMEX** (235), **apex** (32c, 59a, 59d, 87b, 89b, 123a, 135a), **flex** (18c), **ibex** (54d, 230), **ilex** (60c), **N. Mex.** (241), **obex** (21c)

E _ _ X    **eaux** (51b)

E Y _ _    **eyas** (19b, 58c), **eyed, eyes, eyra** (65b), **Eyre** (22a), **eyry** (39a)

_ E Y _    **beys, Ceyx** (57b), **deys, keys**

_ _ E Y    **ahey** (42c), **drey** (114b), **Frey** (10b, 153, 198), **Grey** (156, 192, 194), **Huey** (159), **Ivey** (159), **Joey** (161), **joey** (67a, 134d), **obey** (29c, 59a, 67b, 10a), **prey** (128b), **sley** (130d), **they** (95a), **trey** (24a, 121c), **Urey** (15c, 184), **whey** (76d)

E _ _ Y    **easy** (43d, 53c, 55c, 77c, 109c, 111c), **Eddy** (150), **eddy** (31b, 118d, 131c), **edgy** (81b, 100a, 120c), **eely** (81b), **eggy** (134d), **elmy, Emmy** (120b), **-ency** (117b), **ency.** (238), **envy** (34a, 107a), **espy** (106b), **eury-** (94a), **eyry** (39a)

E Z _ _    **Ezek.** (238), **ezel** (67c), **Ezio** (152), **Ezra** (152, 196, 197)

_ _ E Z    **Baez** (140), **chez** (50a), **Geez** (41d), **Inez** (37c), **jeez** (42a), **knez** (94c), **oyez** (31c, 32c, 58d), **Suez** (23c)

E _ _ Z    **Eliz.** (238)

F A _ _    **fabe** (55b), **face** (15a, 30a, 73a, 79d, 118a, 128c), **fact** (9d, 35b, 98a), **fade** (35c, 36a, 127b), **fado** (91d), **fads, Fahr.** (238), **fail** (35c, 44a, 48a), **Fain** (152), **fain** (35b, 54c, 133a), **fair** (10a, 17d, 41b, 45c, 62b, 67c), **fait** (9c, 50b), **fake** (45a, 62a, 94b, 107c), **Fala** (44d), **fa-la** (98d), **Falk** (152), **fall** (38b, 57b, 106a), **falx** (102a), **Fama** (103a), **fame** (99c, 99d), **fane** (104a, 120b), **Fang** (193, 216), **fang** (123a), **fans, faon** (44d), **fare** (35c, 48b), **farl** (105b), **farm** (21d, 32a, 55d, 122a), **faro** (24b), **Farr** (152), **fast** (46b, 47c, 96d, 118c, 126d), **fate** (35b, 68a, 73b), **Fats** (152), **Faun** (45d, 133b, 198), **favi** (122a), **fawn** (32a, 34c), **Faye** (152), **Fays, faze** (36a)

_ F A _    **Afar** (41d, 216), **afar** (36d), **Sfax** (223)

_ _ F A    **Kafa** (32d, 216), **sofa** (36d), **tufa** (91c, 129a), **Urfa** (76a)

**F _ _ A**      **Fala** (44d), **fa-la** (98d), **Fama** (103a), **FEPA** (238), **FICA** (238), **fila** (121c), **flea** (63b, 229), **FNMA** (238), **FOIA** (238), **fora** (75a, 101d), **Fula** (216, 217)

**F _ _ B**      **flub** (21b), **forb** (59c), **frib** (35d)

**F _ _ C**      **FDIC** (238), **FEPC** (238), **fisc** (42c, 102c), **floc** (111a)

**F D _ _**      **FDIC** (238)

**_ F D _**      **AFDC** (235)

**F _ _ D**      **feed** (82c), **fend** (44b, 86d, 129d), **feud** (45c, 96b, 127d), **find** (36a), **fled**, **fold** (57d, 90b, 107d), **-fold** (117c), **fond** (10b, 73c), **food** (44b, 56d, 82d, 128b), **Ford** (153, 191, 194), **ford** (129a), **foud** (44c, 74a), **fowd** (44c, 74a), **Fred** (47c, 153), **Fuad** (44c), **fund** (9c, 78a, 100a), **fyrd** (83d)

**F E _ _**      **fear** (11a, 51c, 86b, 120d), **feat** (9d, 43a, 124c), **febr-** (93a), **feed** (82c), **feel** (56c, 106c, 123b, 134b), **fees**, **feet** (71b), **feis** (64a), **Fell** (152), **fell** (33a), **felt** (42d, 43b, 43d), **feme** (133b), **fend** (44b, 86d, 129d), **fens**, **FEPA** (238), **FEPC** (238), **fern** (106b), **feru** (30d, 45c), **Fess** (152), **fess** (41c), **-fest** (117b), **fete** (45c), **feud** (45c, 96b, 127d)

**_ _ F E**      **cafe** (19c), **fife** (48a, 80c), **life** (19a, 57a, 94d), **orfe** (46d, 134b), **rife** (9b, 94b), **safe** (106b, 116c, 127b), **wife** (114a)

**F _ _ E**      **fabe** (55b), **face** (15a, 30a, 73a, 79d, 118a, 128c), **fade** (35c, 36a, 127b), **fake** (45a, 62a, 94b, 107c), **fame** (99c, 99d), **fane** (104a, 120b), **fare** (35c, 48b), **fate** (35b, 68a, 73b), **Faye** (152), **faze** (36a), **feme** (133b), **fete** (45c), **fife** (48a, 80c), **file** (72a, 97d, 99a, 122d), **Fine** (152), **fine** (26d, 34c, 40b, 40d, 79d, 87c, 116d, 233), **fire** (14b, 36a, 36c, 108c), **five** (17c, 88c, 97c), **flee** (9b, 41c), **floe** (61b), **flue** (11a, 26c), **fore** (51c, 108b), **frae** (105a), **free** (36b, 56a, 73a, 100c, 112b), **froe** (28a, 122d, 123a, 130d), **fume** (111a, 116a), **fuse** (75d, 76a), **fuze** (35b), **fyke** (16b)

**_ F F _**      **affy** (18d), **iffy** (26a, 100d), **offs** (32a, 118d)

**_ _ F F**      **baff** (55b), **biff** (60b), **buff** (119b, 134b), **cuff** (21b, 60b, 105b, 110b), **doff** (99c, 119a), **duff** (95d), **gaff** (46d, 47a, 113b), **guff** (16b, 62c, 82a), **Huff** (159), **huff** (47b, 119c), **Jeff** (161), **jiff** (77d), **luff** (48a), **miff** (96b), **Muff** (17b), **muff** (17c, 21b, 22c), **puff** (20a, 74a), **raff** (102d), **riff** (66a, 78c), **ruff** (34d, 37b, 51c), **teff** (10c), **tiff** (96b), **toff** (33c), **tuff** (91c, 129a)

**F _ _ F**      **fief** (45c)

**F _ _ G**      **Fang** (193, 216), **fang** (123a), **flag** (17a, 38a, 41a, 69a, 87b, 114d, 130c, 132a), **flog** (131c), **frog** (17c, 225), **frug** (33b), **fung-** (93a)

**F _ _ H**      **fish** (128d), **Foch** (49c, 153)

**F I _ _**  fiat (34b, 84c), fibr- (93a), fibs, FICA (238), fico (124c, 133d), fids, fief (45c), fife (48a, 80c), figs, Fiji (216), fila (121c), file (72a, 97d, 99a, 122d), fill (83b, 88b, 104b), film (28b, 77b, 121b), fils (51a, 213, 217, 218, 223, 224), find (36a), Fine (152), fine (26d, 34c, 40b, 40d, 79d, 87c, 116d, 233), fink (46a), Finn. (238), fins, fire (14b, 36a, 36c, 108c), firm (29b, 29d, 114b, 126d), firn (54c, 55d, 111b), firs, fisc (42c, 102c), fish (128d), fisk (42c), fist (21c, 57d), fits, fitz (111d), five (17c, 88c, 97c), fizz (39d)

**_ F I _**  Efik (69a, 220)

**_ _ F I**  hi-fi (112b), Safi (220), sufi (88a)

**F _ _ I**  favi (122a), Fiji (216), foci (25c), fuci (38d), Fuji (66a), fuji (65b)

**F _ _ K**  Falk (152), fink (46a), fisk (42c), flak (13a), folk (87d, 124b), fork (13c, 36d, 37a, 119a), funk (10d, 35a, 47b)

**F L _ _**  flag (17a, 38a, 41a, 69a, 87b, 114d, 130c, 132a), flak (13a), flam (38b), flan (32d, 87a), flap (48a, 79c, 89d, 119a, 130c, 132d), flat (42a, 63b, 95a, 95c, 114c, 234), flaw (19d, 34c), flax (72a, 72b), flay (110a, 110b, 116c), flea (63b, 229), fled, flee (9b, 41c), Flem. (238), flew, flex (18c), Flip (153), flip (123b), flit (33d), floc (111a), floe (61b), flog (131c), flop (44a), flor (46a, 108a), flow (14b, 37d, 116b), flub (21b), flue (11a, 26c), fluo- (93a), flux (26a, 47d)

**F _ _ L**  fail (35c, 44a, 48a), fall (38b, 57b, 106a), farl (105b), feel (56c, 106c, 123b, 134b), Fell (152), fell (33a), fill (83b, 88b, 104b), foal (61b), foil (16b, 45b, 76b, 116d, 121d), fool (20b, 22c, 34a, 38d, 61d, 78d, 109c, 116d), foul (9a, 126b), fowl (19b), fuel (53a), full (29c, 99d), furl (101c)

**F _ _ M**  farm (21d, 32a, 55d, 122a), film (28b, 77b, 121b), firm (29b, 29d, 114b, 126d), flam (38b), Flem. (238), foam (51c, 114a), form (44c, 107c, 127a), from (18b, 115a)

**F N _ _**  FNMA (238)

**_ F N _**  Ifni (220)

**F _ _ N**  Fain (152), fain (35b, 54c, 133a), faon (44d), Faun (45d, 133b, 198), fawn (32a, 34c), fern (106b), Finn. (238), firn (54c, 55d, 111b), flan (32d, 87a), Fran (153)

**F O _ _**  foal (61b), foam (51c, 114a), fobs, Foch (49c, 153), foci (25c), foes, fogs, fogy (83d), FOIA (238), foil (16b, 45b, 76b, 116d, 121d), Foix (49c), fold (57d, 90b, 107d), -fold (117c), folk (87d, 124b), fond (10b, 73c), font (17a, 125d), food (44b, 56d, 82d, 128b), fool (20b, 22c, 34a, 38d, 61d, 78d, 109c, 116d), foot (17b, 87b, 246), fops, fora (75a, 101d), forb (59c), Ford (153, 191, 194), ford (129a), fore (51c, 108b), fork (13c, 36d, 37a, 119a), form (44c, 107c, 127a), fort (51c, 116c), foss (36d), foud (44c, 74a), foul (9a, 126b), four (72c, 120d), fowd (44c, 74a), fowl (19b), Foxx (153), foxy (14d, 31d, 132a), Foyt (153)

_ _ F O   **info.** (239)

F _ _ O   **fado** (91d), **faro** (24b), **fico** (124c, 133d), **fluo-** (93a)

F _ _ P   **flap** (48a, 79c, 89d, 119a, 130c, 132d), **Flip** (153), **flip** (123b), **flop** (44a), **frap** (37d, 122a)

F _ _ Q   **freq.** (238)

F R _ _   **frae** (105a), **Fran** (153), **frap** (37d, 122a), **fras**, **frat** (29a), **frau** (54a), **fray** (45d, 49b, 125a), **Fred** (47c, 153), **free** (36b, 56a, 73a, 100c, 112b), **freq.** (238), **fret** (22a, 25d, 36d, 42c, 128b, 133d), **Frey** (10b, 153, 198), **frib** (35d), **frit** (54c), **Friz** (154), **friz** (32d), **froe** (28a, 122d, 123a, 130d), **frog** (17c, 225), **from** (18b, 115a), **frow** (123a), **frug** (33b)

_ F R _   **Afro** (57b), **Afro-** (92c)

_ _ F R   **S. Afr.** (242)

F _ _ R   **Fahr.** (238), **fair** (10a, 17d, 41b, 45c, 62b, 67c), **Farr** (152), **fear** (11a, 51c, 86b, 120d), **febr-** (93a), **fibr-** (93a), **flor** (46a, 108a), **four** (72c, 120d)

_ _ F S   **Alfs**, **oafs**, **offs** (32a, 118d)

F _ _ S   **fads**, **fans**, **Fats** (152), **Fays**, **fees**, **feis** (64a), **fens**, **Fess** (152), **fess** (41c), **fibs**, **fids**, **figs**, **fils** (51a, 213, 217, 218, 223, 224), **fins**, **firs**, **fits**, **fobs**, **foes**, **fogs**, **fops**, **foss** (36d), **fras**, **furs**, **fuss** (21b, 36d, 92a)

_ F T _   **efts**

_ _ F T   **baft** (43b), **daft** (48b), **deft** (10a, 14d, 110a), **gift** (13d, 94a, 119b), **haft** (60a), **heft** (22c, 131a), **left** (9a, 34d, 91c, 99c), **lift** (40b), **loft** (15c, 55b, 129d), **Luft** (167), **Raft** (176), **raft** (47c), **rift** (21d, 47a, 84b, 113d), **sift** (105c, 109b, 132d), **soft** (39b, 74c, 76d), **Taft** (183, 191), **toft** (60d), **tuft** (22c, 28c), **waft** (47c), **weft** (32b, 121c, 133c)

F _ _ T   **fact** (9d, 35b, 98a), **fait** (9c, 50b), **fast** (46b, 47c, 96d, 118c, 126d), **feat** (9d, 43a, 124c), **feet** (71b), **felt** (42d, 43b, 43d), **-fest** (117b), **fiat** (34b, 84c), **fist** (21c, 57d), **flat** (42a, 63b, 95a, 95c, 114c, 234), **flit** (33d), **font** (17a, 125d), **foot** (17b, 87b, 246), **fort** (51c, 116c), **Foyt** (153), **frat** (29a), **fret** (22a, 25d, 36d, 42c, 128b, 133d), **frit** (54c), **fust** (107b)

F U _ _   **Fuad** (44c), **fuci** (38d), **fuel** (53a), **fugu** (65d), **Fuji** (66a), **fuji** (65b), **Fula** (216, 217), **full** (29c, 99d), **fume** (111a, 116a), **fumy** (127b), **fund** (9c, 78a, 100a), **fung-** (93a), **funk** (10d, 35a, 47b), **furl** (101c), **furs**, **fury** (97b, 116a), **fuse** (75d, 76a), **fuss** (21b, 36d, 92a), **fust** (107b), **fuze** (35b), **fuzz** (37c)

_ _ F U   **Gifu** (60d)

F _ _ U   **feru** (30d, 45c), **frau** (54a), **fugu** (65d)

351

**F _ _ W**   flaw (19d, 34c), flew, flow (14b, 37d, 116b), frow (123a)

**F _ _ X**   falx (102a), flax (72a, 72b), flex (18c), flux (26a, 47d), Foix (49c), Foxx (153)

**F Y _ _**   fyke (16b), fyrd (83d)

**_ _ F Y**   affy (18d), defy (25d), Dufy (49c, 150), iffy (26a, 100d)

**F _ _ Y**   flay (110a, 110b, 116c), fogy (83d), foxy (14d, 31d, 132a), fray (45d, 49b, 125a), Frey (10b, 153, 198), fumy (127b), fury (97b, 116a)

**F _ _ Z**   fitz (111d), fizz (39d), Friz (154), friz (32d), fuzz (37c)

**G A _ _**   gabi (119d), gabs, gaby (109c), gads, Gaea (39b, 198), Gael (25c, 105a), gaff (46d, 47a, 113b), gaga (24c, 76a), gage (90b), gags, Gaia (39b), Gail (154), gain (9d, 44d, 83b, 94d, 132b), gait (130c), gala (45c), Gale (154), gale (130d, 132b, 132c), gall (18d, 25d, 64b, 128b), gals, gamb (12d), game (114a), gamo- (93c), Gamp (35c), gamp (125b), gams (71b), gamy (90b, 103d), gang (16d, 32a, 232), gaol (94d), gaon (66c), gape (134b), gaps, garb (28b, 37d), gare (50d, 97b), Garn (154), Garo (69a, 154), GARP (239), Garr (154), gars, Gary (154), gash (33a, 110b), gasp (21d, 86b), gata (107d), gate (15c, 41b, 91c), gats, Gath (88c), gats, GATT (239), gaud (124c, 133d), Gaul (49b), gaur (25a, 62d, 132a, 230), gave, gawk (109c, 114d), Gaya (18d), Gaye (154), gays (60d), Gaza (88c, 216), gaze (114d, 115a)

**_ G A _**   Agag (67c, 104a, 197), agal (18a, 30d), Agao (57c), Agar (137), agar (32c, 106a), agas, Agau (57c), egad (83a), egal (50b), ogam (64b)

**_ _ G A**   alga (105d), biga (125c), gaga (24c, 76a), giga (45d), juga (24c), LPGA (240), mega- (93b), Naga (15a, 69a, 128c), naga (23c, 28c, 60a), Olga (173), pega (46d), raga (80a), Riga (218), ruga (48a, 134a), saga (71b, 104c, 119b), soga (52c), toga (101d), Vega (114d, 207), yoga (14d, 60a), yuga (60a)

**G _ _ A**   Gaea (39b, 198), gaga (24c, 76a), Gaia (39b), gala (45c), gata (107d), Gaya (18d), Gaza (88c, 216), Gena (154), geta (65b, 108c), giga (45d), gila (72c), Gina (155), Giza (113c), Gola (218), gola (33c, 37c, 77d), Goya (112c)

**_ G B _**   Igbo (68c, 220)

**G _ _ B**   gamb (12d), garb (28b, 37d), gerb (46b), Gibb (155), glib (47d, 110c, 111a, 129a), glob (75b), grab (80b, 106c, 111b), grub (35d, 69b), guib (13a)

**_ G C _**   agcy. (235)

**G _ _ D**   gaud (124c, 133d), geld (120a), gild (40b), gird (16d, 18c, 40c,

118b), **glad** (66d), **gled** (42a), **goad** (62c, 114b), **gold** (74a, 134b, 245), **Gond** (62d), **good** (127a, 131a), **grad** (25c), **grad.** (239), **grid** (17c, 90b, 116a)

**G E _ _**    **gear** (13c, 28b, 41b, 85b, 123a), **Geat** (104c), **geck** (105b), **geek** (109a), **Geer** (154), **gees**, **Geez** (41d), **geld** (120a), **gels**, **gelt** (78a), **gems**, **Gena** (154), **Gene** (154), **gene** (59c), **Genl.** (239), **gens** (35a), **gent** (45b), **genu** (18c, 69d), **-geny** (117c), **geog.** (239), **geol.** (239), **geom.** (239), **gerb** (46b), **Gere** (155), **germ** (36b, 61b, 76c), **gest** (119b), **geta** (65b, 108c), **gets**, **Getz** (155)

**_ G E _**    **aged** (12c, 83c, 83d), **Agee** (137), **Ager** (137), **ager** (69d, 100d, 102a), **ages**, **B. Gen.** (236), **Eger** (40a), **ogee** (14a, 77d, 90c)

**_ _ G E**    **auge** (71b), **Cage** (144), **cage** (30a, 40d), **doge** (74a, 127d), **edge** (10b, 19c, 21a, 21b, 74d, 87d, 100d, 109a, 130c), **gage** (90b), **huge** (54b, 62a, 69b), **Inge** (22d, 54d, 88b, 159), **loge** (120d), **luge** (110b), **mage** (74a), **Page** (173, 193, 194), **page** (12d, 41c, 48b, 70d, 107a), **rage** (26d, 74c, 116a, 120b), **sage** (14c, 70d, 77b, 106a, 131b, 132d), **tige** (89b), **urge** (35b, 54d, 63b, 94b), **wage** (103d)

**G _ _ E**    **gage** (90b), **Gale** (154), **gale** (130d, 132b, 132c), **game** (114a), **gaon** (66c), **gape** (134b), **gare** (50d, 97b), **gate** (15c, 41b, 91c), **gave**, **Gaye** (154), **gaze** (114d, 115a), **Gene** (154), **gene** (59c), **Gere** (155), **ghee** (22d), **gibe** (10d, 35a), **Gide** (49c, 155), **gite** (50c), **give** (11c, 13d, 29d, 94a, 95c), **glee** (76a, 111d, 234), **glue** (10a, 115b), **gone** (9b, 34d, 36c), **Gore** (155, 191), **gore** (87c, 88d, 124b), **gyle** (21d), **gyne** (45b), **gyre** (27b), **gyve** (45c, 107b)

**G _ _ F**    **gaff** (46d, 47a, 113b), **golf** (12a), **goof** (28b), **Graf** (135a, 156), **graf** (53d, 81d), **guff** (16b, 62c, 82a), **gulf** (9c, 130a)

**_ G G _**    **eggs** (85c), **eggy** (134d), **oggi** (65c)

**_ _ G G**    **nogg** (11b), **Rigg** (177), **vugg** (25b, 53c, 101b), **Wegg** (85a), **yegg** (22d)

**G _ _ G**    **gang** (16d, 32a, 232), **geog.** (239), **Gheg** (213), **gong** (80a), **Greg** (156), **grig** (32a, 39c, 56a, 72c), **grog** (11a, 72b, 113d)

**G H _ _**    **ghat** (28c, 79b), **ghee** (22d), **Gheg** (213), **ghor** (127b)

**_ G H _**    **agha** (125b)

**_ _ G H**    **high** (108d, 123c), **Hugh** (159), **Magh** (213), **magh** (78b), **nigh** (28b, 81a), **sigh** (21d), **vugh** (25b, 53c, 101b), **yogh** (12c)

**G _ _ H**    **gash** (33a, 110b), **Gath** (88c), **Gish** (155), **gosh** (42a, 53b), **Goth** (120d), **Groh** (156), **gush** (114b, 118a)

**G I _ _**    **Gibb** (155), **gibe** (10d, 35a), **gibs**, **Gide** (49c, 155), **gier** (39a), **gift** (13d, 94a, 119b), **Gifu** (60d), **giga** (45d), **Gigi** (155), **GIGO** (239),

**gigs**, **gila** (72c), **gild** (40b), **gill** (21c, 246), **Gils**, **gilt** (60c, 112b, 134d), **gimp** (124c), **Gina** (155), **gink** (39c), **Gino** (155), **gins**, **gird** (16d, 18c, 40c, 118b), **girl** (45b), **giro** (31d, 65c), **girt** (27b), **Gish** (155), **gist** (74b, 89c), **gite** (50c), **give** (11c, 13d, 29d, 94a, 95c), **Giza** (113c)

_ G I _      **Agib** (13d), **agio** (42c, 48d, 78a, 94a), **Agis** (67d), **Egil** (82b), **TGIF** (243)

_ _ G I      **Gigi** (155), **hagi** (65d), **magi** (88a, 94c, 132d), **oggi** (65c), **ragi** (25c), **sugi** (65b), **vagi** (31d), **Yogi** (187), **yogi** (60a)

G _ _ I      **gabi** (119d), **Gigi** (155), **Gobi** (35a), **goni-** (92c), **gyri** (21c)

G _ _ K      **gawk** (109c, 114d), **geck** (105b), **geek** (109a), **gink** (39c), **gook** (110c), **guck** (110c), **gunk** (110c)

G L _ _      **glad** (66d), **gled** (42a), **glee** (76a, 111d, 234), **Glen** (155), **glen** (35d, 98a, 127b), **glib** (47d, 110c, 111a, 129a), **glim** (23d, 43c), **glob** (75b), **glom** (115a), **glop** (75b), **glos.** (239), **glow** (108a), **glue** (10a, 115b), **glum** (54d, 78d, 112b, 117d), **glut** (42b, 55b, 85c, 104b, 118a)

_ G L _      **Ogle** (173), **ogle** (43c, 71a, 73a), **ugli** (51d), **ugly** (126a)

_ _ G L      **Angl.** (235)

G _ _ L      **Gael** (25c, 105a), **Gail** (154), **gall** (18d, 25d, 64b, 128b), **gaol** (94d), **Gaul** (49b), **Genl.** (239), **geol.** (239), **gill** (21c, 246), **girl** (45b), **goal** (10d, 17c, 40d, 83a, 96c, 104d, 119d), **goel** (16a), **gull** (19a, 28c, 34a, 34c, 68a, 76c, 105c, 118d, 225)

G M _ _      **G-man** (45a), **G-men** (45a)

G _ _ M      **geom.** (239), **germ** (36b, 61b, 76c), **glim** (23d, 43c), **glom** (115a), **glum** (54d, 78d, 112b, 117d), **gram** (76b, 246), **grim** (19d, 54b, 115b), **grum** (54d), **Guam** (64c)

G N _ _      **gnar** (56d), **gnat** (48a, 63b, 76c, 229), **gnaw** (19c, 26c), **gnus**

_ G N _      **Agni** (68c), **igni-** (93a)

_ _ G N      **lign-** (94a), **sign** (74d, 91c, 114c)

G _ _ N      **gain** (9d, 44d, 83b, 94d, 132b), **Garn** (154), **Glen** (155), **glen** (35d, 98a, 127b), **G-man** (45a), **G-men** (45a), **goon** (116c), **gown** (37d), **grin** (111a), **guan** (19b), **Gwen** (156), **Gwyn** (199), **gymn-** (93b)

G O _ _      **goad** (62c, 114b), **goal** (10d, 17c, 40d, 83a, 96c, 104d, 119d), **goas**, **goat** (81a, 102d, 230), **Gobi** (35a), **Gobo** (16d), **gobo** (66a), **gobs**, **goby** (46d, 228), **goel** (16a), **gods**, **goer**, **GOES** (239), **goes**, **Gogo** (17a), **gogo** (111b), **Gola** (218), **gola** (33c, 37c, 77d), **gold** (74a, 134b, 245), **golf** (12a), **Gond** (62d), **gone** (9b, 34d, 36c), gong (80a), goni- (92c), gono- (93c), good (127a, 131a), goof (28b), gook (110c), goon (116c), goop (110c), Gore (155, 191), gore (87c, 88d, 124b), Gort (101b), gory (20a), gosh (42a, 53b), Goth (120d), gout (14d, 113d), govt. (239), gown (37d), Goya (112c)

_ G O _     agog (39a, 42c, 67b), agon (30b, 45c, 56b), egos, Igor (49b, 159)

_ _ G O     Argo (14b, 66a), bago (15a), ergo (121a), GIGO (239), Gogo (17a), gogo (111b), Hugo (49c, 71c, 104d, 159), Iago (44a, 85a, 107c, 195), kago (86a), lago (65a, 112d), logo (22d, 29b), mogo (115d), Pogo (83d, 91d), sago (44b, 86a, 95d, 114d), sego (22c, 71d), Togo (223), zygo- (93c)

G _ _ O     gamo- (93c), Garo (69a, 154), GIGO (239), Gino (155), giro (31d, 65c), Gobo (16d), gobo (66a), Gogo (17a), gogo (111b), gono- (93c), gyno- (92c), gyro- (93a)

_ G P _     OGPU (103c)

G _ _ P     Gamp (35c), gamp (125b), GARP (239), gasp (21d, 86b), gimp (124c), glop (75b), goop (110c), grip (27d, 55d, 60c, 96a, 117d), gulp (20d, 37d, 118b)

G R _ _     grab (80b, 106c, 111b), grad (25c), grad. (239), Graf (135a, 156), graf (53d, 81d), gram (76b, 246), Grau (156), Gray (21a, 41a, 156, 192), gray (60c), Graz (213), grew (156, 192, 194), grid (17c, 90b, 116a), grig (32a, 39c, 56a, 72c), grim (19d, 54b, 115b), grin (111a), grip (27d, 55d, 60c, 96a, 117d), Gris (156), gris (50c), grit (104a), grog (11a, 72b, 113d), Groh (156), Gros (49c), gros (38c, 43d, 109c), grow (15d, 41a, 42d, 43a, 114a, 118c), grub (35d, 69b), grum (54d), Grus (207)

_ G R _     Agra (24c, 119a), agra (64a, 118c), agri. (235), ogre (78b)

_ _ G R     engr. (238), hygr- (94a), Msgr. (241)

G _ _ R     Garr (154), gaur (25a, 62d, 132a, 230), gear (13c, 28b, 41b, 85b, 123a), Geer (154), ghor (127b), gier (39a), gnar (56d), goer, guar (38b, 48c), guhr (39a), Gyor (217)

_ _ G S     bags, begs, bogs, bugs, cogs, digs, dogs, eggs (85c), ergs, figs, fogs, gags, gigs, hags, hogs, hugs, jags, jigs, jogs, jugs, kegs, lags, legs, logs, lugs, Megs, mugs, nags, nogs, pegs, pigs, pugs, rags, rigs, rugs, sags, tags, tegs, togs (28b), tugs, wags, wigs

G _ _ S     gabs, gads, gags, gals, gams (71b), gaps, gars, gats, gays (60d), gees, gels, gems, gens (35a), gets, gibs, gigs, Gils, gins, glos. (239), gnus, goas, gobs, gods, GOES (239), goes, Gris (156), gris (50c), Gros (49c), gros (38c, 43d, 109c), Grus (207), gums, guns, GUTS (239), guts (63a), guys, gyms, gyps

_ G T _     lgth. (240)

**_ _ G T**  M.Sgt. (241), S.Sgt. (243)

**G _ _ T**  gait (130c), GATT (239), Geat (104c), gelt (78a), gent (45b), gest (119b), ghat (28c, 79b), gift (13d, 94a, 119b), gilt (60c, 112b, 134d), girt (27b), gist (74b, 89c), glut (42b, 55b, 85c, 104b, 118a), gnat (48a, 63b, 76c, 229), goat (81a, 102d, 230), Gort (101b), gout (14d, 113d), govt. (239), grit (104a), Guat. (239), gust (20a)

**G U _ _**  Guam (64c), guan (19b), guar (38b, 48c), Guat. (239), guck (110c), guff (16b, 62c, 82a), guhr (39a), guib (13a), gulf (9c, 130a), gull (19a, 28c, 34a, 34c, 68a, 76c, 105c, 118d, 225), gulp (20d, 37d, 118b), gums, gunk (110c), guns, guru (60b), gush (114b, 118a), gust (20a), GUTS (239), guts (63a), guys

**_ G U _**  agua (113a), ague (26c, 45c, 74b, 104b), ogum (64b)

**_ _ G U**  degu (101c), fugu (65d), Pegu (97d)

**G _ _ U**  genu (18c, 69d), Gifu (60d), Grau (156), guru (60b)

**G W _ _**  Gwen (156), Gwyn (199)

**G _ _ W**  glow (108a), gnaw (19c, 26c), grew, grow (15d, 41a, 42d, 43a, 114a, 118c)

**G Y _ _**  gyle (21d), gymn- (93b), gyms, gyne (45b), gyno- (92d), -gyny (117b), Gyor (217), gyps, gyre (27b), gyri (21c), gyro- (93a), gyve (45c, 107b)

**_ _ G Y**  -algy (117c), bogy (13c, 113b), cagy (31d), dogy (38c), edgy (81b, 100a, 120c), eggy (134d), fogy (83d), logy (38c), Nagy (61c, 172), orgy (24b, 100b, 104b), pogy (68d, 75d, 78d)

**G _ _ Y**  gaby (109c), gamy (90b, 103d), Gary (154), -geny (117c), goby (46d, 228), gory (20a), Gray (21a, 41a, 156, 192), gray (60c), Grey (156, 192, 194), -gyny (117b)

**G _ _ Z**  Geez (41d), Getz (155), Graz (213)

**H A _ _**  haab (75b), habu (89c, 103c), hack (24c, 33a, 60b), hade (53c), hadj (89b), haec (70a), haft (60a), hagi (65d), hags, ha-ha (45b, 118a), Hahn (156), hahs (42c), Haid (156), Haig (156), haik (52d), hail (9c, 16a, 56c, 60d, 104a, 127d, 130d), Haim (156), hair (46a), haje (28c, 39d), haji (75c, 89b), hajj (75c, 89b), hake (46d, 228), Hale (12b, 156), hale (112a, 131d), half (77c), Hall (156), hall (31a, 87a), halo (27b, 71d, 81d, 100d), Hals (38d, 156), halt (14c, 25b, 32a, 59d, 87b, 115d), Hama (222), hame (61b), hams, Hana (157), hand (10d, 15a, 59b, 87c, 133d, 246), hang (118b), Hank (157), hank (57b, 109d), Hans (17b, 53d, 67a, 157), Hapi (198), hapi (53b), hapl- (93c), hard (123b), hare (101c, 230), hark (72b), harl (46a, 48a, 59b), harm (33b, 61d, 62a, 63a), harp (80b), Hart (157), hart (34c, 114b), Harz (79b), hash (21b), hasp (44c, 113c), hast (128a), hate (35b, 72d), hath (128a), hats, haud (70a), haul (37c),

356

**have** (20b), **hawk** (19a, 87c, 225), **Hawn** (157), **haws**, **Hays** (157), **haze** (28b, 48a, 77b, 127b), **hazy** (127a)

**_ H A _**    **Ahab** (24a, 66c, 67d, 87d, 197), **Ahaz** (67d, 197), **bhat** (62d), **Chad** (117a, 145, 215), **Cham** (224), **chap** (45b, 74c), **char** (104d, 124d, 228), **Chas.** (74d), **chat** (19a, 29d, 119b, 225), **chaw** (122c), **chay** (39b, 98c), **dhai** (76c), **dhak** (39b), **dhal** (11d), **ghat** (28c, 79b), **Khan** (164), **khan** (10b, 63a, 88a, 94c), **khat** (58b), **phag-** (92d), **Phar.** (242), **shad** (25b, 46d), **shag** (57b, 119c, 122c), **shah** (16c, 88a), **Shak.** (243), **sham** (9d, 34a, 45a, 49b, 77b, 91d, 94b, 109c), **Shan** (62d, 69a, 220), **Shaw** (41a, 43a, 180, 204), **shay** (84a), **Thad** (183), **Thai** (109a, 218, 223), **than** (29b), **Thar** (35a), **thar** (55a), **that** (34d, 95a, 99b), **thaw** (72b), **wham** (110b), **whap** (60b), **what** (96d, 99b)

**_ _ H A**    **agha** (125b), **Akha** (121d), **Doha** (221), **ha-ha** (45b, 118a), **maha** (25d, 69a, 104a), **OSHA** (241), **paha** (60a), **poha** (58c), **taha** (130d), **YMHA** (244), **YWHA** (244)

**H _ _ A**    **ha-ha** (45b, 118a), **Hama** (222), **Hana** (157), **hema-** (92c), **Hera** (14b, 67c, 135c, 198), **hexa-** (93c), **hora** (21a, 33b), **Hova** (219), **hoya** (12c, 15d, 130c), **Hsia** (26d, 38d), **huia** (81c), **hula** (58b), **Hupa** (15b, 189), **hura** (104a), **hyla** (12b, 122c)

**H _ _ B**    **haab** (75b), **Herb** (158)

**H C _ _**    **hcap.** (239)

**H _ _ C**    **haec** (70a), **HUAC** (239)

**H D _ _**    **hdbk.** (239), **HDTV** (239)

**H _ _ D**    **Haid** (156), **hand** (10d, 15a, 59b, 87c, 133d, 246), **hard** (123b), **haud** (70a), **head** (21a, 25d, 26c, 51c, 78a, 94c), **heed** (15c, 25b, 58d, 72b, 83a, 99a), **held** (91d), **herb** (90a, 106b), **herd** (38b, 232), **hied**, **hind** (34b, 37a), **hoed**, **hold** (9c, 15a, 16c, 27d, 67b, 74b, 95b, 100a, 115a, 121a, 234), **Hond.** (239), **Hood** (79b), **hood** (19c, 31c, 52c, 58c), **hued**

**H E _ _**    **head** (21a, 25d, 26c, 51c, 78a, 94c), **heal** (32d), **heap** (17a, 75b, 79a, 89a), **hear** (59a, 72b), **Heat** (206), **heat** (129d), **Hebe** (32d, 59c, 135a, 198), **heck** (42a), **hect-** (93a), **Hedy** (157), **heed** (15c, 25b, 58d, 72b, 83a, 99a), **heel** (55b), **Heep** (33d, 35c), **heer** (134b), **heft** (22c, 131a), **hein** (42c, 49c), **heir** (63a, 71b), **held** (91d), **heli-** (93d), **Hell** (9a, 16a, 34a, 57a, 108a), **he'll** (30c), **Helm** (157), **helm** (108b, 122a), **help** (10d, 15a, 62b, 117a), **hema-** (92c), **heme** (20a), **hemi-** (93a), **hemo-** (92c), **hemp** (23d, 30d, 45c, 55d, 102b), **hems**, **hens** (92a), **hept-** (93c), **Hera** (14b, 67c, 135c, 198), **Herb** (158), **herb** (90a, 106b), **herd** (38b, 232), **here** (63d, 101c), **herl** (14d, 17a), **Hero** (70d, 194), **hero** (34d, 95c, 104a), **herr** (53d), **hers** (95a), **Hess** (158), **Heth** (197), **hewn** (27a), **hews**, **hexa-** (93c)

**_ H E _**    **ahem** (15c, 112a), **ahey** (42c), **chee** (246), **chef** (30c, 50c, 68a), **chem.** (31b, 236), **cher** (50b), **Chet** (145), **chew** (75b), **chez** (50a), ghee (22d), **Gheg** (213), **phen-** (92c), **phew** (42c), **Rhea** (68c, 78d, 89d, 122c, 135c, 177, 198), **rhea** (19b, 26c, 85a, 226), **Rhee** (68c, 177), **rheo-** (92c), **Shea** (180), **shea** (22d, 124a), **shed** (24d, 70d, 77d, 108a), **she'd** (30c), **Shem** (81d, 197), **she's** (30c), **shew** (128a), **Thea** (122c), **thee** (95b), **them** (95a), **then** (10c, 121a), **thew** (79d), **they** (95a), **when** (96d, 131c), **whet** (39c, 107d), **whew** (42c), **whey** (76d)

_ _ H E    **ache** (73a, 85d, 134b), **Ashe** (139), **Oahe** (33b), **wehe** (53d)

H _ _ E    **hade** (53c), **haje** (28c, 39d), **hake** (46d, 228), **Hale** (12b, 156), **hale** (112a, 131d), **hame** (61b), **hare** (101c, 230), **hate** (35b, 72d), **have** (20b), **haze** (28b, 48a, 77b, 127b), **Hebe** (32d, 59c, 135a, 198), **heme** (20a), **here** (63d, 101c), **hide** (29d, 31c, 43a), **hike** (62c), **hire** (40c, 40d, 71b, 99c, 100a), **hive** (18a), **hole** (9c, 13b, 84b, 89c, 109d), **home** (61c, 99d), **hone** (39c, 107d, 131c), **HOPE** (239), **Hope** (158), **hope** (42c), **hose** (115c), **hove** (71d), **Howe** (17c, 63d, 159), **huge** (54b, 62a, 69b), **hule** (21c, 25a, 102c), **Hume** (159, 192), **Hyde** (37a), **hype** (95a)

H _ _ F    **half** (77c), **hoof** (126b), **Huff** (159), **huff** (47b, 119c)

H _ _ G    **Haig** (156), **hang** (118b), **hing** (14d), **hong** (26d), **Hung.** (239), **hung**

H _ _ H    **hash** (21b), **hath** (128a), **Heth** (197), **high** (108d, 123c), **hoch** (42c, 53d), **Hoth** (20a), **Hugh** (159), **hush** (109b)

H I _ _    **hick** (134d), **hide** (29d, 31c, 43a), **hied**, **hier** (51b), **hier-** (93c), **hies**, **hi-fi** (112b), **high** (108d, 123c), **hike** (62c), **Hill** (158), **hill** (17a), **hilt** (57d), **hind** (34b, 37a), **hing** (14d), **hint** (11d, 32c, 33d, 117d, 133a), **hipp-** (93a), **hips**, **hire** (40c, 40d, 71b, 99c, 100a), **Hiss** (158), **hiss** (36a, 112a), **hist.** (239), **hits**, **hive** (18a)

_ H I _    **ahir** (24d), **chia** (18d, 76c), **Chic** (145), **chic** (111a), **ch'ih** (246), **chil-** (93b), **Ch'in** (26d), **Chin.** (236), **chin** (29d), **Chip** (26d), **chip** (55b), **chir-** (93a), **chis**, **chit** (54c, 82c, 88b, 129c), **Ohio** (211), **Phil** (175), **Phil.** (242), **phis**, **Phiz** (35c), **rhin-** (93b), **RHIP** (242), **rhiz-** (93c), **shi'a** (80c), **shim** (71c, 119c, 130d), **shin** (11d, 12a, 71a, 71b, 107c), **ship** (106c, 128a), **shiv** (68a), **thin** (35c, 35d, 53b, 110c), **thio-** (93d), **this** (34d, 95a), **whig** (71c), **whim** (24a, 44b, 82c), **whin** (55c, 101b), **whip** (18a, 47c, 69b, 121b), **whir** (112a), **whit** (122c), **whiz** (88a, 112a)

_ _ H I    **Ishi** (134a), **ophi-** (93d)

H _ _ I    **hagi** (65d), **haji** (75c), **Hapi** (198), **hapi** (53b), **heli-** (93d), **hemi-** (93a), **hi-fi** (112b), **Hopi** (95d, 189)

H _ _ J    **hadj** (89b), **hajj** (75c, 89b)

H _ _ K    **hack** (24c, 33a, 60b), **haik** (52d), **Hank** (157), **hank** (57b, 109d), **hark** (72b), **hawk** (19a, 87c, 225), **hdbk.** (239), **heck** (42a), **hick**

(134d), **hock** (71b, 87b, 132c), **honk** (55b, 112b), **hook** (24d, 27d, 55b), **hulk** (126d), **hunk** (57d, 88d), **husk** (43a, 61c, 106b, 232)

**_ _ H L**    **buhl** (63a), **Dahl** (147), **Kohl** (18c, 164), **kohl** (43c), **Pohl** (175), **Sahl** (179)

**H _ _ L**    **hail** (9c, 16a, 56c, 60d, 104a, 127d, 130d), **Hall** (156), **hall** (31a, 87a), **hapl-** (93c), **harl** (46a, 48a, 59b), **haul** (37c), **heal** (32d), **heel** (55b), **Hell** (9a, 16a, 34a, 57a, 108a), **he'll** (30c), **herl** (14d, 17a), **Hill** (158), **hill** (17a), **howl** (12d, 17d, 32b, 114b), **Hull** (159), **hull** (106b, 108b), **hurl** (121c, 123b), **hyal-** (93a)

**_ H M _**    **ohms**

**H _ _ M**    **Haim** (156), **harm** (33b, 61d, 62a, 63a), **Helm** (157), **helm** (108b, 122a), **Holm** (158), **holm** (60c, 64b, 83a)

**_ H N _**    **ohne** (54a)

**_ _ H N**    **Cohn** (146), **ethn-** (93c), **Hahn** (156), **John** (13b, 18a, 88b, 91b, 107c, 135a, 162, 193, 196), **Kahn** (163)

**H _ _ N**    **Hahn** (156), **Hawn** (157), **hein** (42c, 49c), **hewn** (27a), **hoon** (246), **Horn** (24a), **horn** (13a, 31a, 124d), **hymn** (111d)

**H O _ _**    **hoar** (51c, 131d), **hoax** (34a, 92b), **hobo** (123d, 127a), **hobs, hoch** (42c, 53d), **hock** (71b, 87b, 132c), **hods, hoed, hoer, hoes, hogs, hold** (9c, 15a, 16c, 27d, 67b, 74b, 95b, 100a, 115a, 121a, 234), **hole** (9c, 13b, 84b, 89c, 109d), **Holm** (158), **holm** (60c, 64b, 83a), **holo-** (94a), **Holt** (158), **holt** (30c), **holy** (30b), **home** (61c, 99d), **homo** (69d), **homo-** (93c), **Homs** (222), **Hond.** (239), **hone** (39c, 107d, 131c), **hong** (26d), **honk** (55b, 112b), **Hood** (79b), **hood** (19c, 31c, 52c, 58c), **hoof** (126b), **hook** (24d, 27d, 55b), **hoon** (246), **hoop** (131d), **Hoot** (158), **hoot** (85c), **HOPE** (239), **Hope** (158), **hope** (42d), **Hopi** (95d, 189), **hops** (18a), **hora** (21a, 33b), **Horn** (24a), **horn** (13a, 31a, 124d), **hors** (50d), **hort.** (239), **hose** (115c), **hosp.** (239), **host** (14c, 42a, 79d), **Hoth** (20a), **hour** (122b), **Hova** (219), **hove** (71d), **Howe** (17c, 63d, 159), **howl** (12d, 17d, 32b, 114b), **hoya** (12c, 15d, 130c), **Hoyt** (159)

**_ H O _**    **Ahom** (69a), **ahoy** (57b, 81a), **chol-** (92c), **chol.** (236), **chop** (75c), **Chou** (26d), **chou** (50a), **chow** (37a, 227), **choy** (39b, 98c), **dhow** (69b, 84d), **ghor** (127b), **Khon** (223), **mhos, phon** (73b), **phon-** (93d), **phot** (246), **rhos, shod, shoe** (122b), **shoo** (38a, 54b), **shop** (62d, 100a), **shot** (12b, 70c), **shou** (26d), **show** (9d, 34d, 35a, 36c, 43a, 74c), **Thor** (10b, 76c, 77b, 83b, 121d, 183, 198), **Thos.** (74d), **thos** (65b), **thou** (95b), **whoa** (42c, 115d), **whom** (34d, 96d), **whop** (60b)

**_ _ H O**    **coho** (103d), **Echo** (80d), **echo** (12a, 99d, 100b), **icho** (54b), **moho** (60d), **Otho** (102a), **peho** (81c), **Saho** (32d, 57c, 216), **So-Ho** (73a), **to-ho** (61d)

H _ _ O **halo** (27b, 71d, 81d, 100d), **hemo-** (92c), **Hero** (70d, 194), **hero** (34d, 95c, 104a), **hobo** (123d, 127a), **holo-** (94a), **homo** (69d), **homo-** (93c), **Hugo** (49c, 71c, 104d, 159), **hylo-** (94a), **hypo** (88d)

H _ _ P **harp** (80b), **hasp** (44c, 113c), **hcap.** (239), **heap** (17a, 75b, 79a, 89a), **Heep** (33d, 35c), **help** (10d, 15a, 62b, 117a), **hemp** (23d, 30d, 45c, 55d, 102b), **hipp-** (93a), **hoop** (131d), **hosp.** (239), **hrip** (239), **hump** (95c)

H R _ _ **hrip** (239)

_ H R _ **ihre** (54b), **NHRA** (241), **thru**

_ _ H R **Bahr** (140), **Bohr** (15c, 33c, 142), **buhr** (131c), **Fahr.** (238), **guhr** (39a), **Lahr** (165), **lehr** (54c, 85c), **mohr** (53b), **Ruhr** (53d, 100b), **sehr** (54a), **tahr** (55a)

H _ _ R **hair** (46a), **hear** (59a, 72b), **heer** (134b), **heir** (63a, 71b), **herr** (53d), **hier** (51b), **hier-** (93c), **hoar** (51c, 131d), **hoer, hour** (122b), **hydr-** (93d), **hygr-** (94a)

H S _ _ **Hsia** (26d, 38d)

_ H S _ **AHST** (235)

_ _ H S **hahs** (42c), **Ochs** (173), **rahs**

H _ _ S **hags, hahs** (42c), **Hals** (38d, 156), **hams, Hans** (17b, 53d, 67a, 157), **hats, haws, Hays** (157), **hems, hens** (92a), **hers** (95a), **Hess** (158), **hews, hies, hips, Hiss** (158), **hiss** (36a, 112a), **hits, hobs, hods, hoes, hogs, Homs** (222), **hops** (18a), **hors** (50d), **hubs, hues, hugs, hums, Huns** (15c), **huts**

_ _ H T **acht** (53d), **baht** (223, 246), **echt** (54a)

H _ _ T **haft** (60a), **halt** (14c, 25b, 32a, 59d, 87b, 115d), **Hart** (157), **hart** (34c, 114b), **hast** (128a), **Heat** (206), **heat** (129d), **hect-** (93a), **heft** (22c, 131a), **hept-** (93c), **hilt** (57d), **hint** (11d, 32c, 33d, 117d, 133a), **hist.** (239), **Holt** (158), **holt** (30c), **Hoot** (158), **hoot** (85c), **hort.** (239), **host** (14c, 42a, 79d), **Hoyt** (159), **Hunt** (159), **hunt** (105d), **Hurt** (159), **hurt** (33b, 58a, 62a, 63a, 133d), **hyet-** (93c)

H U _ _ **HUAC** (239), **hubs, hued, hues, Huey** (159), **Huff** (159), **huff** (47b, 119c), **huge** (54b, 62a, 69b), **Hugh** (159), **Hugo** (49c, 71c, 104d, 159), **hugs, huia** (81c), **hula** (58b), **hule** (21c, 25a, 102c), **hulk** (126d), **Hull** (159), **hull** (106b, 108b), **Hume** (159, 192), **hump** (95c), **hums, Hung.** (239), **hung, hunk** (57d, 88d), **Huns** (15c), **Hunt** (159), **hunt** (105d), **Hupa** (15b, 189), **hura** (104a), **hurl** (121c, 123b), **Hurt** (159), **hurt** (33b, 58a, 62a, 63a, 133d), **hush** (109b), **husk** (43a, 61c, 106b, 232), **huts, Hutu** (214, 221)

_ H U _ **bhut** (54b), **chub** (46c, 228), **chug** (112a), **chum** (15b, 32a, 45b), **chuo** (246), **shul** (118d), **shun** (16c, 41c), **shut** (28b), **thud** (20a, 112a), **thug** (52c), **Thur.** (243), **thus** (111b, 121a)

\_ \_ H U    **ichu** (12c, 55d), **Jehu** (197), **jehu** (38a), **kahu** (15d), **Oahu** (64c)

H \_ \_ U    **habu** (89c, 103c), **Hutu** (214, 221)

H \_ \_ V    **HDTV** (239)

\_ H W \_    **YHWH** (244)

H \_ \_ X    **hoax** (34a, 92b)

H Y \_ \_    **hyal-** (93a), **Hyde** (37a), **hydr-** (93d), **hyet-** (93c), **hygr-** (94a), **hyla** (12b, 122c), **hylo-** (94a), **hymn** (111d), **hype** (95a), **hypo** (88d)

\_ H Y \_    **whys**

\_ \_ H Y    **achy** (112a), **ashy** (86a, 129d)

H \_ \_ Y    **hazy** (127a), **Hedy** (157), **holy** (30b), **Huey** (159)

H \_ \_ Z    **Harz** (79b)

I A \_ \_    **Iago** (44a, 85a, 107c, 195), **Ians**, **iamb** (48c), **-iana** (117c), **Iasi** (221)

\_ I A \_    **bias** (12c, 35c, 94a), **ciao** (65a), **diag.** (237), **dial** (43d), **diam.** (237), **Dian** (198), **Dias** (91d), **Diaz** (76c), **fiat** (34b, 84c), **Liam** (166), **Liao** (101a), **liar** (75d), **Lias** (53c), **Piaf** (49d, 100c, 175), **rial** (220), **sial** (85b), **Siam** (120d), **vial** (110d)

\_ \_ I A    **Abia** (104a), **amia** (21b, 79c), **Apia** (91c, 224), **aria** (75d, 111d, 125a, 234), **Asia** (39b), **chia** 18d, 76c), **Elia** (68d, 87c, 151), **-emia** (117a), **FOIA** (238), **Gaia** (39b), **Hsia** (26d, 38d), **huia** (81c), **ilia** (60b, 87c), **inia** (12b, 83b, 110b), **ixia** (30d), **Maia** (59c, 107b, 129c, 198, 207), **obia** (45c), **-opia** (117b, 117c), **shi'a** (80c), **Uria** (197), **-uria** (117b), **USIA** (243)

I \_ \_ A    **-iana** (117c), **idea** (35b, 44b, 82c, 95a, 121b), **ilea** (73c), **ilia** (60b, 87c), **Ilka** (159), **Ilşa** (24c), **Inca** (15b), **inia** (12b, 83b, 110b), **Iona** (25c, 64b, 202), **iota** (11d, 66d, 122c, 131c), **Iowa** (189, 210), **Issa** (216), **itea** (118c, 128c), **ixia** (30d)

I B \_ \_    **Iban** (33d), **ibex** (54d, 230), **ibid.** (70a, 239), **ibis** (19a, 39d, 40a, 129a, 225), **-ible** (117a)

\_ I B \_    **bibb** (75b), **Bibi** (141), **bibi** (62d), **bibl.** (236), **bibs**, **dibs** (55d), **fibr-** (93a), **fibs**, **Gibb** (155), **gibe** (10d, 35a), **gibs**, **jibe** (28d, 29d, 31a), **jibs**, **kibe** (26c), **nibs**, **ribs**, **sibs**

\_ \_ I B    **abib** (59a, 81d), **Agib** (13d), **crib** (26b, 74c, 91b, 110c), **drib** (110d), **frib** (35d), **glib** (47d, 110c, 111a, 129a), **guib** (13a), **stib** (38d)

I \_ \_ B    **iamb** (48c)

361

I C _ _    -ical (117a), ICBM (239), iced, Icel. (239), icer, ices, icho (54b), ichu (12c, 55d), icon (62a, 103b)

_ I C _    bice (20b, 56c, 89a), dice (52c), dich (54b), dich- (93d), Dick (149, 192), dick (35b), dict. (237), FICA (238), fico (124c, 133d), hick (134d), kick (21a, 96a), lice (86c), lick (18a, 66a, 110d), mica (64b, 77a, 109b), mice, Mich. (210, 240), Mick (170), Nice (49c, 100a, 216), nice (90b, 109c), Nick (172), nick (26d, 82c), pica (53c, 125d), pice (62d, 220), pick (27a, 90b), Pico (100d), picr- (92c), Pict (22a), Rice (177, 204), rice (37d), Rich (177), rich (73d), Rick (24c, 177), rick (58c, 89a, 114b), Rico (72c), sice (56c), sick (126b), tick (14a, 20a, 229), tics, vice (35a), vice- (92d), wick (23d)

_ _ I C    -atic (117c), Chic (145), chic (111a), epic (59c, 90c), Eric (128b, 151), FDIC (238), laic (28a, 70c, 82a, 94d, 106b), otic (15d, 39a), saic (71c), Udic (82b)

I D _ _    -idae (117c), Idas (24d), idea (35b, 44b, 82c, 95a, 121b), idee (50c), idem (70a), Iden (192), ideo- (93a), ides (33d, 101d), idio- (93c), Idle (159), idle (40c, 60c, 62c, 62d, 63a, 70c, 127a, 130a), idly, Idol (159), idol (39d, 44a, 44d, 58d, 62a, 85b, 133d), idyl (90c, 233)

_ I D _    Aïda (84b, 97b, 128a), aide (10a, 15b, 59b, 106a), AIDS (235), aids, bide (38d, 99c, 119d, 129b), bids, -cide (117b), Dido (24c, 125d), dido (13a, 24a, 52b, 92b), didy (35c), fids, Gide (49c, 155), hide (29d, 31c, 43a), kids, lido (65c, 127d), lids, Midi (112b), Nidd (134d), nide (88c, 232), nidi (113c), Ridd (73a), Ride (177), ride (29b, 66d, 121a), rids, sida (30d, 96d), side (43d, 47b, 69b, 119b), Sids, tide (83b), tidy (81a, 84c, 111b), Vida (185), vide (98d), wide (102a)

_ _ I D    acid (119d), amid (12b), arid (38b), avid (39a, 41b, 56b, 67b, 135a), Enid (14d, 23c, 53c, 120c, 151), grid (17c, 90b, 116a), Haid (156), ibid. (70a, 239), irid (90a), laid, maid (37b, 54c, 107a), naid (51b), olid (49a, 116c), Ovid (102a), paid (99a), quid (32c, 122c), raid (48c, 62d), Reid (176), Said (91c), said (127c), skid (110c), slid, void (12d, 40c, 82d, 127a)

I _ _ D    ibid. (70a, 239), iced, Irad (197), irid (90a)

I E _ _    ieri (65c)

_ I E _    bien (51b), bier (28d, 53d), dieb (65b), died, dies (69c), diet (44b, 65d, 71b), dieu (50b), fief (45c), gier (39a), hied, hier (51b), hier- (93c), hies, Kiel (23c), kier (19d, 127b), Kiev (223), lied (54a, 234), lief (132a), lien (53a, 71a, 95b), lies, lieu (89d), mien (13c, 17d, 24c, 34d, 36d, 74d), pied (114a, 127b), pien (14c), Pier (175), pier (21d, 66b, 68d, 131b), pies, Piet (175), piet (26b, 74b), riel (214), riem (59d), rien (50d), tied, tier (46a, 89b, 102c), ties, vied, vier (53d), vies, view (12c, 15a, 42b, 73a, 95b, 104d), Wien (33c)

_ _ I E    Abie (81c), amie (50b), Arie (139), brie (26b), Edie (150), Elie (151), Erie (23c, 68d, 189), Ilie (159), Okie (76d), soie (51a)

362

I _ _ E     -ible (117a), -idae (117c), idee (50c), Idle (159), idle (40c, 60c, 62c, 62d, 63a, 70c, 127a, 130a), ihre (54b), Ilie (159), ille (69d), imbe (30d, 45c), Imre (159), Inge (22d, 54d, 88d, 159), in re (29d, 63d, 99a), lole (42a, 59c, 94c), lone (22c, 69b, 73d), ipse (37a, 69d), irae (35c), isle (11a, 64b, 67b)

I F _ _     iffy (26a, 100d), Ifni (220)

_ I F _     biff (60b), fife (48a, 80c), gift (13d, 94a, 119b), Gifu (60d), hi-fi (112b), jiff (77d), life (19a, 57a, 94d), lift (40b), miff (96b), rife (9b, 94b), riff (66a, 78c), rift (21d, 47a, 84b, 113d), sift (105c, 109b, 132d), tiff (96b), wife (114a)

_ _ I F     alif (11d), coif (57b), Enif (207), Leif (43a), naif (126c), TGIF (243), waif (116b)

I _ _ F     IOOF (240)

I G _ _     Igbo (68c, 220), igni- (93a), Igor (49b, 159)

_ I G _     biga (125c), digs, figs, giga (45d), Gigi (155), GIGO (239), gigs, high (108d, 123c), jigs, lign- (94a), nigh (28b, 81a), pigs, Riga (218), Rigg (177), rigs, sigh (21d), sign (74d, 91c, 114c), tige (89b), wigs

_ _ I G     brig (81a, 108b), grig (32a, 39c, 56a, 72c), Haig (156), olig- (93a), orig. (241), prig (85c), swig (37d, 57a), trig (114a, 124c), trig. (31b, 243), twig (21c), whig (71c)

I H _ _     ihre (54b)

_ _ I H     ch'ih (246)

I _ _ H     inch (31d, 79c, 246), itch (58a, 64b)

I I _ _     iiwi (58c)

_ I I _     Riis (177)

I _ _ I     Iasi (221), ieri (65c), Ifni (220), igni- (93a), iiwi (58c), immi (246), Impi (135c), INRI (32b, 239), inti (221), Ishi (134a)

_ I J _     Fiji (216), lija (46a, 70d)

I K _ _     Ikes, ikon (62a)

_ I K _     bike (67a, 127c), dika (74c), dike (40b, 71c), hike (62c), Kiki (164), kiku (27a), like (24b, 109c), Mike (170), mike (12a), Nike (77b, 132c, 198), Niki (172), pika (30c, 72c, 101c, 231), pike (46d, 59d, 90c, 113b, 228), piki (74b), sika (34c, 65d, 231), Sikh (60b), tiki (91a)

_ _ I K     Efik (69a, 220), Erik (151), haik (52d)

I _ _ K     Isak (159)

**I L _ _**     ilea (73c), ileo- (93b), ilex (60c), ilia (60b, 87c), Ilie (159), Ilka (159), ille (69d), ills (124d), illy, Ilsa (24c), Ilus (69a, 124d)

**_ I L _**     ails, bile (26d), bilk (26b, 34a, 34c), Bill (141), bill (17d, 109d), Dili (91d, 217), dill (14c, 88d), Dili (121c), file (72a, 97d, 99a, 122d), fill (83b, 88b, 104b), film (28b, 77d, 121b), fils (51a, 213, 217, 218, 223, 224), gila (72c), gild (40b), gill (21c, 246), Gils, gilt (60c, 112b, 134d), Hill (158), hill (17a), hilt (57d), Jill (161), jilt (99a), kill (31d, 79d, 102d), kiln (16b, 85c), kilo (12a, 76b, 246), kilo- (93d), kilt (105a), lill (16b, 89b, 132b), lilt (72c), Lily (166), lily (47c, 47d), mild (28a, 53c, 77c, 120c), mile (52c, 68c, 246), milk (128d), Mill (170), mill (96d), Milo (171), milo (112a), mils, milt (47a), Nile (81b, 216, 222), oils, oily (44c, 83d, 126a), pile (17a, 58d, 79a), pili- (93a), pill (119a), rile (12d, 64b, 95c, 115c), rill (22a, 31d, 101a, 110d, 116b), silk (43b), Sill (49a), sill (37c, 121c, 132b), silo (48a, 116a), silt (79c, 106b), tile (27d, 46b, 74b, 102a, 120d), till (32c), tilt (23d, 24b, 62c, 72b, 101c), Vila (224), vile (9a, 17b, 46a, 62a, 74c), Vili (83b), wild (18c, 31d, 104c, 126d, 128c), wile (34a), Will (186), will (18c, 35b, 120d, 129a, 133a), Wilt (187), wilt (38a), wily (14d, 31d, 32c, 110c)

**_ _ I L**     anil (38d, 62d), aril (106b), axil (12c), bail (20d, 68b), boil (30c), ceil (25b), chil- (93b), coil (32d, 114a, 125c, 132b, 134a), dail (40a, 64a), deil (105a), Egil (82b), Emil (151), evil (74c, 109c, 131d, 134c), fail (35c, 44a, 48a), foil (16b, 45b, 76b, 116d, 121d), Gail (154), hail (9c, 16a, 56c, 60d, 104a, 127d, 130d), ipil (88c), jail (62b), kail (23a), koil (32c), mail (14c, 76b, 91d), moil (20c, 133d), nail (27d, 44c, 119b, 126b), Neil (172), noil (45d, 68c), pail (30b), Phil (175), Phil. (242), rail (9c, 19a, 30d, 75a, 111d, 123c, 129a, 226), roil (79c, 115c), sail (91c), soil (39a, 114c, 117d, 120d), tail (13c, 25a, 40d, 48b, 89d, 107b, 123c), teil (72a), toil (38b, 124d, 133c, 133d), veil (29d, 36b, 58c, 59d, 75b), wail (32b, 61c, 68d, 114b), Weil (186)

**I _ _ L**     -ical (117a), Icel. (239), Idol (159), idol (39d, 44a, 44d, 58d, 62a, 85b, 133d), idyl (90c, 233), incl. (239), Intl. (239), ipil (88c), ital. (240), it'll (30c)

**I M _ _**     imam (23b, 80c), imbe (30d, 45b), imbu (51d), imit. (239), immi (246), Impi (135c), imps, Imre (159)

**_ I M _**     aims, cima (65c), dime (44d), dims, gimp (124c), Jimi (161), Jims, Lima (27c, 221), lima (12a, 17d), limb (13c, 21c), lime (23b, 27c, 51d, 78d, 124a), limn (35a), limp (47b, 63a, 129b), limy, mime (66b), Mimi (68b, 84b, 95d, 171), Pima (189), pima (31a), pimp (94d), Rima (56c), rima (47a), rime (30a, 51c, 60c), rims, rimu (62a, 98d), rimy, sima (101b), Simi (64c), simp (48b, 109c), Sims (181), time (38d, 41b, 41c, 87d, 100b), Timi (183), Tims, wimp (130c)

**_ _ I M**     Akim (137), alim (120a), brim (21a), crim. (237), duim (246), emim (54b), glim (23d, 43c), grim (19d, 54b, 115b), Haim (156), maim (80d), prim (115b), shim (71c, 119c, 130d), skim (47c, 54d,

364

56a), **Slim** (181), **slim** (110c, 118b), **swim** (37a), **trim** (81a, 84d, 114a, 118b, 121d, 124c), **urim** (103b), **whim** (24a, 44b, 82c)

**I _ _ M**   **ICBM** (239), **idem** (70a), **imam** (23b, 80c), **item** (9c, 14d, 35b, 41b, 71a, 72b, 81c, 83a, 86d)

**I N _ _**   **Inca** (15b), **inch** (31d, 79c, 246), **incl.** (239), **Indo-** (93b), **Inez** (37c), **info.** (239), **Inge** (22d, 54d, 88d, 159), **inia** (12b, 83b, 110b), **init.** (239), **inks**, **inky** (19d, 33d), **inns**, **in re** (29d, 63d, 99a), **INRI** (32b, 239), **Insp.** (239), **Inst.** (239), **inti** (221), **Intl.** (239), **into** (133a)

**_ I N _**   **ain't**, **aine** (51a), **ains**, **bina** (60b), **bind** (122a), **bine** (115b, 128b), **Bing** (141), **bino** (86a), **bins**, **C in C** (236), **cine-** (93b), **cinq** (50b), **Dina** (149), **dine** (39b), **ding** (62d, 76b), **Dino** (47c), **dins**, **dint** (42d, 92b), **eine** (53d, 54a), **find** (36a), **Fine** (152), **fine** (26d, 34c, 40b, 40d, 79d, 87c, 116d, 233), **fink** (46a), **Finn.** (238), **fins**, **Gina** (155), **gink** (39c), **Gino** (155), **gins**, **hind** (34b, 37a), **hing** (14d), **hint** (11d, 32c, 33d, 117d, 133a), **jink** (40b), **jinx** (61a), **kina** (108a, 221), **kind** (112a, 113b, 127b), **kine** (31c), **King** (164, 190), **king** (24a, 26c, 82a), **kink** (31d), **kino** (38d, 57a, 119c, 127b), **Lina** (166), **Lind** (166), **line** (11b, 30d, 46a, 96d, 102c, 116b), **ling** (22c, 46d, 58d, 130b, 228), **link** (30a, 63c, 66c), **lint** (47d), **liny**, **Linz** (33c, 213), **Mina** (223), **mina** (131a), **mind** (29c, 63c, 67b, 73a, 83a, 120c), **mine** (55a, 95a), **Ming** (26d), **mini-** (93c), **mink** (128c, 230), **Minn.** (210, 240), **mint** (14c, 28d, 59b), **minx** (88b), **Nina** (24a, 29a, 172), **nina** (112d), **nine** (17c), **Nino** (172), **nino** (112c), **pina** (29d), **pine** (30a, 42a, 69a, 73a, 124a, 134b), **Ping** (125a), **ping** (76b), **pink** (24b), **pins**, **pint** (54b, 246), **piny**, **rind** (43a, 76d, 87c), **rine** (36d), **Ring** (177), **ring** (16d, 27b, 40c, 40d, 131b, 134a), **rink** (109d, 114a), **sine** (52a, 70b, 96b, 124c), **sing** (129d), **sink** (34b, 60c, 110d), **Sino-** (92d), **sino** (112d), **sins**, **Tina** (183), **tine** (13a, 95a, 123a), **ting** (76b), **tins**, **tint** (29a, 107b), **tiny** (77b, 110d), **vina** (60b), **vine** (28a, 71c), **vini-** (94a), **vino** (72b, 132c), **viny**, **wind** (10d, 28d, 32d, 125c), **wine** (60c, 91c), **wing** (12d, 47c, 48a, 89b, 89d, 232), **wink** (63c, 81d, 106a), **wino** (38b), **wins**, **winy** (128c), **Xing.** (244), **zinc** (20b, 76a, 245), **zing** (32a)

**_ _ I N**   **akin** (67c, 99a), **asin** (78b), **ayin** (12a), **Bain** (140), **bain** (50a), **Cain** (9a, 10a, 41a, 68d, 79d, 107a, 144, 197), **Ch'in** (26d), **Chin.** (236), **chin** (29d), **coin** (77b), **dein** (54b), **Erin** (64a, 151), **Fain** (152), **fain** (35b, 54c, 133a), **gain** (9d, 44d, 83b, 94d, 132b), **grin** (111a), **hein** (42c, 49c), **jain** (60b), **join** (30a, 126c), **juin** (49d), **kain** (74c), **lain** (33a, 75c), **Main** (168), **main** (26c, 29d, 67b, 94c), **mein** (26d), **nein** (54a), **Odin** (10b, 51c, 133b, 198), **Olin** (173), **pain** (10b, 61d), **rain** (92a, 120a, 130d), **rein** (26b, 30c, 100a), **rhin-** (93b), **ruin** (34d, 35b, 62b), **sain** (19d, 32b), **shin** (11d, 12a, 71a, 71b, 107c), **skin** (43a, 59d, 87c, 104c), **spin** (100b, 131c), **thin** (35c, 35d, 53b, 110c), **Trin.** (243), **Tsin** (26d), **twin** (37c, 75b, 125c), **vain** (40c, 63a), **vein** (20a, 116b), **wain** (129b), **whin** (55c, 101b), **zein** (30d)

**I _ _ N**   **Iban** (33d), **icon** (62a, 103b), **Iden** (192), **ikon** (62a), **Iran** (88a,

365

217), **iron** (45b, 45c, 55a, 57c, 74c, 75b, 245), **ISBN** (240), **Ivan** (66c, 103c, 159)

**I O _ _**  **iodo-** (93b), **Iole** (42a, 59c, 94c), **Iona** (25c, 64b, 202), **Ione** (22c, 69b, 73d), **ions**, **IOOF** (240), **iota** (11d, 66d, 122c, 131c), **-ious** (117a), **Iowa** (189, 210)

**_ I O _**  **biol.** (236), **Bion** (56b), **cion** (83c), **Dion** (149, 195), **Dior** (149), **dios** (112d), **Lion** (193), **lion** (94b, 230), **pion** (42b), **riot** (85a, 101c, 125a), **-sion** (117a), **-tion** (117a, 117b), **viol** (80b), **zion** (95a)

**_ _ I O**  **agio** (42c, 48d, 78a, 94a), **Baio** (140), **brio** (33d, 113d, 128d), **Clio** (29b, 80a), **Elio** (151), **Ezio** (152), **idio-** (93c), **odio** (65a), **Ohio** (211), **olio** (36b, 60c, 75d, 77b, 92a), **thio-** (93d), **trio** (80c, 124b), **unio** (80d)

**I _ _ O**  **Iago** (44a, 85a, 107c, 195), **icho** (54b), **ideo-** (93a), **idio-** (93c), **Igbo** (68c, 220), **ileo-** (93b), **Indo-** (93b), **info.** (239), **into** (133a), **iodo-** (93b), **Isao** (159)

**I P _ _**  **ipil** (88c), **ipse** (37a, 69d)

**_ I P _**  **cipo** (71c), **dipl-** (93d), **dips**, **hipp-** (93a), **hips**, **kips**, **Li Po** (26d), **lipo-** (92d), **lips**, **nipa** (15b, 38a, 39b, 86a, 120d), **nips**, **pipe** (80c, 125a, 131c), **pips**, **ripe** (47b, 75b), **rips**, **sipe** (122b), **sips**, **tips**, **VIPs**, **wipe** (123d), **xiph-** (93d), **yipe** (42c), **yips**, **zips**

**_ _ I P**  **blip** (97b), **Chip** (26d), **chip** (55b), **clip** (15c, 44c, 107c), **drip** (72b, 88a), **Flip** (153), **flip** (123b), **grip** (27d, 55d, 60c, 96a, 117d), **hrip** (239), **quip** (66b, 66d, 132d, 133a), **RHIP** (242), **ship** (106c, 128a), **skip** (9b, 56a, 84a, 87a), **slip** (36b, 41c, 52d, 54d, 110c, 126b), **snip** (28a), **trip** (66d, 232), **whip** (18a, 47c, 69b, 121b)

**I _ _ P**  **Insp.** (239)

**I _ _ Q**  **Iraq** (217)

**I R _ _**  **Irad** (197), **irae** (35c), **Iran** (88a, 217), **Iraq** (217), **Iras** (28a, 195), **irid** (90a), **Iris** (159, 195), **iris** (20b, 43c, 85a, 97c), **irks**, **iron** (45b, 45c, 55a, 57c, 74c, 75b, 245), **Irus** (83c)

**_ I R _**  **aire** (64a), **airs** (94b), **airy** (41d, 66a, 71d), **Bird** (141), **bird** (16a), **birl** (72d), **birn** (27d), **birr** (112a, 216), **circ.** (237), **dire** (37d, 44d, 45a, 54b, 56a, 120c), **Dirk** (149), **dirk** (33a), **dirt** (39a, 99c, 104c), **Eire** (64a), **fire** (14b, 36a, 36c, 108c), **firm** (29b, 29d, 114b, 126d), **firn** (54c, 55d, 111b), **firs**, **gird** (16d, 18c, 40c, 118b), **girl** (45b), **giro** (31d, 65c), **girt** (27b), **hire** (40c, 40d, 71b, 99c, 100a), **Kiri** (164), **kiri** (87a), **Kirk** (164), **kirk** (27a, 105a), **lira** (25c, 218, 219, 221, 223, 224), **lire** (50d, 64d), **Mira** (207), **mire** (20c, 39a, 78c, 79c), **Miró** (112c, 171), **MIRV** (240), **NIRA** (241), **pirn** (20c, 98d, 130d), **sire** (18b, 21d, 44d, 48d, 94d, 120c, 122c), **sirs**, **tire** (21a, 42d, 44d, 47b, 131c), **tiro** (18b, 82c), **wire** (30d, 120b), **wiry** (109d)

**_ _ I R**    **abir** (98d), **ahir** (24d), **amir** (10b, 13d), **chir-** (93a), **coir** (28d, 30d, 45c, 102b), **cuir** (37c, 50c), **emir** (13d, 94c, 102d, 125b), **fair** (10a, 17d, 41b, 45c, 62b, 67c), **hair** (46a), **heir** (63a, 71b), **Keir** (164), **lair** (34d, 60c), **loir** (37c), **Meir** (170), **Muir** (11a, 171), **Nair** (37d), **nair** (85a), **noir** (50a, 102c), **pair** (21c, 31b, 90d, 119c, 125c), **Seir** (41c), **soir** (50b), **spir-** (92d), **stir** (10d, 14c, 29b, 36d, 63b, 77b, 79c, 94d, 95a, 115c), **vair** (52c, 114b), **Weir** (186), **weir** (33b, 47a), **whir** (112a), **ymir** (54b)

**I _ _ R**    **icer**, **Igor** (49b, 159), **Isar** (33d, 79d, 100d, 216), **Iser** (40a), **iter** (69d, 101a, 101d), **Ivor** (159), **iyar** (78c), **izar** (52d)

**I S _ _**    **Isak** (159), **Isao** (159), **Isar** (33d, 79d, 100d, 216), **ISBN** (240), **Iser** (40a), **Ishi** (134a), **Isis** (61b, 85a), **isle** (11a, 64b, 67b), **isn't**, **Issa** (216)

**_ I S _**    **bise** (132b), **cist** (115d), **disc** (58b, 98c), **disc.** (237), **dish** (76a, 119a), **disk** (27b), **diss** (75d), **dist.** (237), **fisc** (42c, 102c), **fish** (128d), **fisk** (42c), **fist** (21c, 57d), **Gish** (155), **gist** (74b, 89c), **Hiss** (158), **hiss** (36a, 112a), **hist.** (239), **Kish** (197), **kish** (55d, 104c), **kiss** (22d, 91b), **kist** (105b), **Lisa** (166), **Lise** (166), **Lisi** (166), **lisp** (113c), **liss** (49a), **list** (24d, 41b, 65c, 101c, 102b, 104d, 122a), **misc.** (240), **mise** (10d, 134c), **miso** (65d), **miso-** (93a), **Miss.** (210, 240), **miss** (54c, 108c), **mist** (28b, 38a, 48a, 127b), **nisi** (70b, 126c), **Pisa** (70d), **pisc-** (93a), **pish** (42c), **pisk** (12b), **rise** (62c, 114c), **risk** (52b, 58c, 66b, 127d), **sish** (61b), **Uist** (64d), **visa** (87a), **Visc.** (244), **vise** (60c), **Wisc.** (212, 244), **Wise** (187), **wise** (103b, 111a), **wish** (35b), **wisp** (49b), **wist** (68c)

**_ _ I S**    **Acis** (52b), **Agis** (67d), **Amis** (138), **amis** (50b), **anis**, **Apis** (22c, 40a, 95d, 103b), **atis** (60a), **avis** (69c), **axis** (25c, 34c, 60c), **bois** (51b), **chis**, **dais** (41d, 90b), **Elis** (56b), **Epis.** (238), **Eris** (14b, 198), **feis** (64a), **Gris** (156), **gris** (50c), **ibis** (19a, 39d, 40a, 129a, 225), **Iris** (159, 195), **iris** (20b, 43c, 85a, 97c), **Isis** (61b, 85a), **-itis** (117b), **Kris** (165), **kris** (74b), **leis**, **Lois** (118a), **Luis** (167), **mais** (50a), **nais** (51b, 101a), **obis**, **-osis** (117a), **Otis** (12b, 63d, 173), **phis**, **psis**, **rais** (24a), **reis** (24a), **Riis** (177), **Sais** (39d), **sais** (56c), **seis** (113a), **skis**, **this** (34d, 95a), **Tris** (184), **Uris** (184)

**I _ _ S**    **Ians**, **ibis** (19a, 39d, 40a, 129a, 225), **ices**, **Idas** (24d), **ides** (33d, 101d), **Ikes**, **ills** (124d), **Ilus** (69a, 124d), **imps**, **inks**, **inns**, **ions**, **-ious** (117a), **Iras** (28a, 195), **Iris** (159, 195), **iris** (20b, 43c, 85a, 97c), **irks**, **Irus** (83c), **Isis** (61b, 85a), **-itis** (117b), **Itys** (120c), **Ives** (159)

**I T _ _**    **ital.** (240), **itch** (58a, 64b), **itea** (118c, 128c), **item** (9c, 14d, 35b, 41b, 71a, 72b, 81c, 83a, 86d), **iter** (69d, 101a, 101d), **-itis** (117b), **it'll** (30c), **Itys** (120c)

**_ I T _**    **bite** (26c, 115c), **bito** (10c, 35b, 47a), **bits** (19a), **bitt** (44c), **cite** (97c), **cito** (70a), **city** (76c, 126d), **dita** (88c, 124b), **fits**, **fitz** (111d), **gite** (50c), **hits**, **Kite** (164), **kite** (19a, 58c, 226), **kith** (105a), **kits**, **Kitt** (164), **-lite** (117b, 117c), **Lith.** (240), **-lith** (117c), **litz** (97b), mite (14a, 63b, 64a, 86c, 86d), mitt (17b, 46b, 54d), mitu (32d), Nita (172), nito (45b), nitr- (93b), nits, pita (11d, 25c, 45c), pith (30d, 41d, 51d, 54c, 74b, 75a, 90a, 97c, 120d), pits, Pitt (41a, 175), pity (29b, 87a, 134b), Rita (177), rite (72c), Ritz (177), Sita (97d), site (72d, 76a, 107a), sito- (93a), sits, titi (20b, 71a, 78b, 124a), Tito (183, 134d), tits, vita (69d, 71d), vite (50d), with (11d, 12c), wits, Witt (187)

_ _ I T     adit (41b, 77a), alit (36c, 68d, 107a), bait (16b, 41b, 73d, 119c, 123b), B. Lit. (236), Brit. (236), brit (59d), chit (54c, 82c, 88b, 129c), crit. (237), doit (38d), edit (20b, 40c, 94a, 98c, 100b), emit (36a, 40a, 43c, 47d, 99b, 106c), epit. (238), exit (71a, 130c), fait (9c, 50b), flit (33d), frit (54c), gait (130c), grit (104a), imit. (239), init. (239), knit (126c), lait (50d), nuit (50d), obit. (34a, 52c, 241), omit (40b, 81b, 87a, 110a), quit (9a, 34d, 71a, 99d), skit (108d, 110a), slit (33a), smit (128a), snit (10d, 12c, 47b), spit (90d, 101b), suit (9c, 10a, 31c, 47b, 71a, 85b, 90b, 104b), Swit (182), tait (15d, 60d), twit (88a), unit (77d, 84a), wait (24b, 72a, 99c, 115a, 119d), whit (122c), writ (71a)

I _ _ T     imit. (239), init. (239), Inst. (239), isn't

_ I U _     Niue (64c), Pius (91b)

I _ _ U     ichu (12c, 55d), imbu (51d)

I V _ _     Ivan (66c, 103c, 159), Ives (159), Ivey (159), Ivor (159)

_ I V _     diva (84b, 94c), dive (34d, 90c), five (17c, 88c, 97c), give (11c, 13d, 29d, 94a, 95c), hive (18a), jive (61d, 63b, 66a), kiva (25c, 95d), Kivu (68b), live (38d, 42d), Livy (101d), rive (28a), Siva (91a), viva (73a), vive (73a), vivo (72c, 233)

_ _ I V     shiv (68a), XDIV (244)

_ I W _     biwa (65d), iiwi (58c), kiwi (13d, 19a, 19b, 97d, 226)

I X _ _     ixia (30d)

_ I X _     mixt. (240)

_ _ I X     coix (66c), Foix (49c), -trix (117b)

I _ _ X     ibex (54d, 230), ilex (60c)

I Y _ _     iyar (78c)

I _ _ Y     idly, iffy (26a, 100d), illy, inky (19d, 33d), Ivey (159)

I Z _ _     izar (52d)

_ I Z _     fizz (39d), Giza (113c), Liza (166), Mize (171), size (129a)

_ _ I Z     Ariz. (209, 235), Eliz. (238), Friz (154), friz (32d), Phiz (35c), quiz (42b), rhiz- (93c), whiz (88a, 112a)

368

**I _ _ Z**   Inez (37c)

**J A _ _**   jabs, jaca (65b), Jack (159), jack (17a, 24a, 68a, 78a, 97c), Jada (197), jade (53b, 56c), Jael (197), jags, jail (62b), jain (60b), Jaja (79a), Jake (160), jako (56a), jamb (37c, 109a, 126d), jams, Jamy (194), Jana (80d, 160), Jane (160), Jann (160), Jans, jape (66c), jarl (104c), jars, jass (118d), JATO (240), Java (64c), java (28d), jaws, jays, Jazz (206), jazz (61d, 118d)

**_ J A _**   ajar (84b), Ajax (56b, 120b, 120d, 194)

**_ _ J A**   Adja (214), Baja (23b, 76c), Beja (82a, 222), Jaja (79a), lija (46a, 70d), maja (31d), raja (60a), soja (56c)

**J _ _ A**   jaca (65b), Jada (197), Jaja (79a), Jana (80d, 160), Java (64c), java (28d), Jena (121d), jota (112c), Juba (216), juca (24c), juga (24c), Jura (79b)

**J _ _ B**   jamb (37c, 109a, 126d), Joab (33d, 197)

**J _ _ D**   Joad (55d), Judd (163)

**J E _ _**   Jean (160), jeep (127d), jeer (120a), jeez (42a), Jeff (161), Jehu (197), jehu (38a), jell (111d), Jena (121d), jeon (218), jerk (20a, 38d, 48b, 88a, 95d), Jess (161), jess (116a), jest (17a, 66d), jete (16c), jeth (78b), Jets (206) jets, Jett (161), jeux (50b), Jews

**_ _ J E**   haje (28c, 39d)

**J _ _ E**   jade (53b, 56c), Jake (160), Jane (160), jape (66c), jete (16c), jibe (28d, 29d, 31a), jive (61d, 63b, 66a), joke (66b), José (163), Jove (67c, 198), jube (102a), Jude (13b, 196), Jule (163), June (163), jure (70b), jute (30d, 45c, 102b, 103a)

**J _ _ F**   Jeff (161), jiff (77d)

**J _ _ G**   Jong (163), Jung (95d, 163)

**J _ _ H**   jeth (78b), Josh (163), josh (17a, 6b, 66d, 90d)

**J I _ _**   jibe (28d, 29d, 31a), jibs, jiff (77d), jigs, Jill (161), jilt (99a), Jimi (161), Jims, jink (40b), jinx (61a), jive (61d, 63b, 66a)

**_ _ J I**   Fiji (216), Fuji (66a), fuji (65b), haji (75c), suji (131b)

**J _ _ I**   Jimi (161), joli (50d), Joni (163), Juli (163)

**_ _ J J**   hajj (75c, 89b)

**J _ _ K**   Jack (159), jack (17a, 24a, 68a, 78a, 97c), jerk (20a, 38d, 48b, 88a, 95d), jink (40b), jock (74c), junk (26c, 102d)

**J _ _ L**   Jael (197), jail (62b), jarl (104c), jell (111d), Jill (161), Joel (161, 196, 197), jowl (26b, 35c)

369

**_ _ J M**     sejm (91a)

**J _ _ N**     jain (60b), Jann (160), Jean (160), jéon (218), Joan (161), John (13b, 18a, 88b, 91b, 107c, 135a, 162, 193, 196), join (30a, 126c), Juan (163), juin (49d)

**J O _ _**     Joab (33d, 197), Joad (55d), Joan (161), jobo (60c), JOBS (240), jobs, jock (74c), Jody (161), Joel (161, 196, 197), Joes, Joey (161), joey (67a, 134d), jogs, John (13b, 18a, 88b, 91b, 107c, 135a, 162, 193, 196), join (30a, 126c), joke (66b), joli (50d), Jolo (64d), jolt (20a, 66a, 108b), Jong (163), Joni (163), Jons, Jory (163), José (163), Josh (163), josh (17a, 66b, 66d, 90d), joss (26d, 62c), jota (112c), jots, Jove (67c, 198), jowl (26b, 35c), joys

**_ J O _**     ejoo (45a)

**_ _ J O**     mojo (129c), rojo (113a)

**J _ _ O**     jako (56a), JATO (240), jobo (60c), Jolo (64d), judo (65d, 66d), Juno (67c, 77b, 96d, 195, 199)

**J _ _ P**     jeep (127d), Jump (163), jump (10b, 114d, 127b)

**J _ _ R**     jeer (120a)

**J _ _ S**     jabs, jags, jams, Jans, jars, jass (118d), jaws, jays, Jess (161), jess (116a), Jets (206), jets, Jews, jibs, jigs, Jims, JOBS (240), jobs, Joes, jogs, Jons, joss (26d, 62c), jots, joys, jugs, juts

**J _ _ T**     jest (17a, 66d), Jett (161), jilt (99a), jolt (20a, 66a, 108b), just (41b, 44a, 62b, 76a, 97c, 127c)

**J U _ _**     Juan (163), Juba (216), jube (102a), juca (24c), Judd (163), Jude (13b, 196), judo (65d, 66d), Judy (163), juga (24c), jugs, juin (49d), juju (26b, 45c, 119b), Jule (163), Juli (163), July, Jump (163), jump (10b, 114d, 127b), June (163), Jung (95d, 163), junk (26c, 102d), Juno (67c, 77b, 96d, 195, 199), Jura (79b), jure (70b), jury (31c), just (41b, 44a, 62b, 76a, 97c, 127c), jute (30d, 45c, 102b, 103a), juts

**_ _ J U**     baju (65b), juju (26b, 45c, 119b)

**J _ _ U**     Jehu (197), jehu (38a), juju (26b, 45c, 119b)

**J _ _ X**     jeux (50b), jinx (61a)

**J _ _ Y**     Jamy (194), Jody (161), Joey (161), joey (67a, 134d), Jory (163), Judy (163), July, jury (31c)

**J _ _ Z**     Jazz (206), jazz (61d, 118d), jeez (42a)

**K A _ _**     Kaat (163), kadi (13d, 80d), Kael (163), Kaen (223), Kafa (32d, 216), kago (86a), Kahn (163), kahu (15d), kail (23a), kain (74c),

**kaka** (81c), **kaki** (65d, 81c), **kale** (23a, 78a, 90a, 103d, 127c), **Kali** (109d, 199), **kali** (104a), **kalo** (119d), **Kama** (199), **kama** (60a, 129a), **kame** (60a, 100c), **kami** (65d, 108a), **kana** (66a), **Kane** (163), **Kano** (129c), **Kans.** (210, 240), **Kant** (53d, 163), **kari** (15d), **Karl** (163), **kary-** (93b), **Kate** (107c, 163), **kati** (246), **Kato** (56c), **Kaus** (208), **kava** (18d, 91a), **kavi** (66a), **kawi** (66a), **Kaye** (164), **kayo** (68c), **Kays**

_ K A _  **Akan** (69a, 215, 216), **okas**, **okay** (10b, 13d, 86d, 112a), **skat** (24b), **skaw** (67c)

_ _ K A  **Anka** (138), **deka-** (93d), **dika** (74c), **Ilka** (159), **kaka** (81c), **pika** (30c, 72c, 101c, 231), **roka** (74a, 124a), **sika** (34c, 65d, 231), **taka** (213), **waka** (23d), **weka** (19b, 74d, 81c, 97b)

K _ _ A  **Kafa** (32d, 216), **kaka** (81c), **Kama** (199), **kama** (60a, 129a), **kana** (66a), **kava** (18d, 91a), **kela** (246), **keta** (37b), **kina** (108a, 221), **kiva** (25c, 95d), **koba** (13a, 130b), **Kola** (103c), **kola** (82d), **kora** (130b), **Kuba** (24b), **Kura** (101a)

K _ _ B  **kerb** (109a), **knob** (57d, 82a, 95c)

K _ _ C  **Kroc** (165)

K _ _ D  **kind** (112a, 113b, 127b), **Kurd** (64a, 217)

K E _ _  **Kean** (164), **keas**, **keck** (100a), **keef** (58b), **Keel** (164), **keel** (108b), **keen** (16a, 45c, 68d, 129b), **keep** (10a, 60c, 94b, 100a, 104c), **keet** (56d), **kegs**, **Keir** (164), **kela** (246), **kelp** (64a, 106a), **Kemp** (164), **keno** (52b), **Kens**, **Kent** (70d, 195, 202), **Keos** (64c), **kepi** (58d, 76d), **kept**, **kerb** (109a), **kerf** (33a, 82c), **Kern** (164), **kern** (48c, 101b, 125d), **Kerr** (164), **keta** (37b), **keto-** (93b), **keys**

_ K E _  **akee** (51d, 124a), **eked**, **ekes**, **Ikes**, **skeg** (67b, 133b), **skeo** (47a), **skep** (18a, 60b), **skew** (118c, 125b)

_ _ K E  **bake** (30c, 101b), **bike** (67a, 127c), **cake** (35b), **coke** (28c, 52a, 62d), **cuke** (32c), **dike** (40b, 71c), **Duke** (87d, 150, 194, 201), **duke** (82a), **Elke** (151), **fake** (45a, 62a, 94b, 107c), **fyke** (16b), **hake** (46d, 228), **hike** (62c), **Jake** (160), **joke** (66b), **Lake** (165), **lake** (89a, 130a), **like** (24b, 109c), **Luke** (42a, 167, 196), **make** (13c, 29c, 30c, 40d, 43d, 44c), **Mike** (170), **mike** (12a), **moke** (37c), **Nike** (77b, 132c, 198), **pike** (46d, 59d, 90c, 113b, 228), **poke** (65b, 82d, 96a), **puke** (99a), **rake** (34a, 52d), **sake** (10b, 65d, 131a), **soke** (67c), **suke** (120a), **take** (117a), **Teke** (215), **tuke** (23d, 43b), **tyke** (21c, 26c), **wake** (102c, 123c), **woke**, **yoke** (66c, 232)

K _ _ E  **kale** (23a, 78a, 90a, 103d, 127c), **kame** (60a, 100c), **Kane** (163), **Kate** (107c, 163), **Kaye** (164), **kibe** (26c), **kine** (31c), **Kite** (164), **kite** (19a, 58c, 226), **Klee** (164), **knee** (66c), **koae** (58b), **Kobe** (60d, 218), **Kure** (60d), **Kyle** (165)

K _ _ F  **keef** (58b), **kerf** (33a, 82c)

K _ _ G    **King** (164, 190), **king** (24a, 26c, 82a)

K H _ _    **Khan** (164), **khan** (10b, 63a, 88a, 94c), **khat** (58b), **Khon** (223)

_ K H _    **Akha** (121d)

_ _ K H    **ankh** (32a), **lakh** (84a, 108a), **Sikh** (60b)

K _ _ H    **Kish** (197), **kish** (55d, 104c), **kith** (105a), **Koch** (53c, 164), **koph** (12a)

K I _ _    **kibe** (26c), **kick** (21a, 96a), **kids, Kiel** (23c), **kier** (19d, 127b), **Kiev** (223), **Kiki** (164), **kiku** (27a), **kill** (31d, 79d, 102d), **kiln** (16b, 85c), **kilo** (12a, 76b, 246), **kilo-** (93d), **kilt** (105a), **kina** (108a, 221), **kind** (112a, 113b, 127b), **kine** (31c), **King** (164, 190), **king** (24a, 26c, 82a), **kink** (31d), **kino** (38d, 57a, 119c, 127b), **kips, Kiri** (164), **kiri** (87a), **Kirk** (164), **kirk** (27a, 105a), **Kish** (197), **kish** (55d, 104c), **kiss** (22d, 91b), **kist** (105b), **Kite** (164), **kite** (19a, 58c, 226), **kith** (105a), **kits, Kitt** (164), **kiva** (25c, 95d), **Kivu** (68b), **kiwi** (13d, 19a, 19b, 97d, 226)

_ K I _    **Akim** (137), **akin** (67c, 99a), **Okie** (76d), **skid** (110c), **skim** (47c, 54d, 56a), **skin** (43a, 59d, 87c, 104c), **skip** (9b, 56a, 84a, 87a), **skis, skit** (108d, 110a)

_ _ K I    **Aoki** (139), **kaki** (65d, 81c), **Kiki** (164), **Loki** (10b, 16c, 198), **maki** (71b), **Moki** (95d), **Niki** (172), **piki** (74b), **raki** (11a), **Reki** (16d), **Saki** (95c), **saki** (78b, 231), **tiki** (91a)

K _ _ I    **kadi** (13d, 80d), **kaki** (65d, 81c), **Kali** (109d, 199), **kali** (104a), **kami** (65d, 108a), **kari** (15d), **kati** (246), **kavi** (66a), **kawi** (66a), **kepi** (58d, 76d), **Kiki** (164), **Kiri** (164), **kiri** (87a), **kiwi** (13d, 19a, 19b, 97d, 226), **koli** (24d), **kori** (10b, 60a)

K _ _ K    **keck** (100a), **kick** (21a, 96a), **kink** (31d), **Kirk** (164), **kirk** (27a, 105a), **kook** (39c)

K L _ _    **Klee** (164)

_ K L _    **Okla.** (211, 241), **wkly.** (244)

K _ _ L    **Kael** (163), **kail** (23a), **Karl** (163), **Keel** (164), **keel** (108b), **Kiel** (23c), **kill** (31d, 79d, 102d), **koel** (32c), **Kohl** (18c, 164), **kohl** (43c), **koil** (32c)

K N _ _    **knap** (60a), **knar** (68c), **knee** (66c), **knew, knez** (94c), **knit** (126c), **knob** (57d, 82a, 95c), **knop** (68c), **knot** (76d, 82a, 232), **know** (13a, 16c), **Knox** (49a), **knur** (54d, 68c), **Knut** (33c, 164)

K _ _ N    **Kaen** (223), **Kahn** (163), **kain** (74c), **Kean** (164), **keen** (16a, 45c, 68d, 129b), **Kern** (164), **kern** (48c, 101b, 125d), **Khan** (164), **khan** (10b, 63a, 88a, 94c), **Khon** (223), **kiln** (16b, 85c), **Koln** (100b, 216), **kwan** (246)

372

**K O _ _**   koae (58b), koba (13a, 130b), Kobe (60d, 218), kobo (220), Koch (53c, 164), koel (32c), Kohl (18c, 164), kohl (43c), koil (32c), Koko (73a, 134d), koko (86d), koku (246), Kola (103c), kola (82d), koli (24d), Koln (100b, 216), kolo (48b, 106d), kook (39c), koph (12a), Kops (67b), kora (130b), kori (10b, 60a), Koso (108d), koss (246), koto (66a), kozo (86b)

**_ K O _**   ikon (62a)

**_ _ K O**   jako (56a), Koko (73a, 134d), koko (86d), mako (20b, 107d), Yoko (187)

**K _ _ O**   kago (86a), kalo (119d), Kano (129c), Kato (56c), kayo (68c), keno (52b), keto- (93b), kilo (12a, 76b, 246), kilo- (93d), kino (38d, 57a, 119c, 127b), kobo (220), Koko (73a, 134d), koko (86d), kolo (48b, 106d), Koso (108d), koto (66a), kozo (86b)

**K _ _ P**   keep (10a, 60c, 94b, 100a, 104c), kelp (64a, 106a), Kemp (164), knap (60a), knop (68c), Kulp (165)

**K R _ _**   Kris (165), kris (74b), Kroc (165)

**_ K R _**   Akra (216), okra (57a, 127c)

**K _ _ R**   Keir (164), Kerr (164), kier (19d, 127b), knar (68c), knur (54d, 68c)

**_ _ K S**   arks, asks, auks, elks, inks, irks, leks, oaks, Saks (179), yaks, yuks (70b)

**K _ _ S**   Kans. (210, 240), Kaus (208), Kays, keas, kegs, Kens, Keos (64c), keys, kids, kips, kiss (22d, 91b), kits, Kops (67b), koss (246), Kris (165), kris (74b)

**_ _ K T**   takt (80a, 120b)

**K _ _ T**   Kaat (163), Kant (53d, 163), keet (56d), Kent (70d, 195, 202), kept, khat (58b), kilt (105a), kist (105b), Kitt (164), knit (126c), knot (76d, 82a, 232), Knut (33c, 164), Kurt (165), kyat (220)

**K U _ _**   Kuba (24b, 213), kudu (13a, 230), Kulp (165), Kura (101a), Kurd (64a, 217), Kure (60d), Kurt (165)

**_ K U _**   akua (91a), skua (56d, 65b, 105c)

**_ _ K U**   Baku (24b, 213), baku (116b, 124a), kiku (27a), koku (246), poku (13a, 130b), puku (13a, 130b)

**K _ _ U**   kahu (15d), kiku (27a), Kivu (68b), koku (246), kudu (13a, 230)

**_ K V _**   NKVD (103c)

**K _ _ V**   Kiev (223)

**K W _ _**   kwan (246)

373

**K _ _ W**    **knew, know** (13a, 16c)

**K _ _ X**    **Knox** (49a)

**K Y _ _**    **kyat** (220), **Kyle** (165)

**_ K Y _**    **Skye** (64d, 120d), **skyr** (20d)

**_ _ K Y**    **inky** (19d, 33d), **laky, poky** (110d), **suky** (120a)

**K _ _ Y**    **kary-** (93b)

**K _ _ Z**    **knez** (94c)

**L A _ _**    **laap** (41d), **Labe** (217), **labs, lace** (47b), **lack** (34c, 129d), **lacy** (34c), **Ladd** (165), **lade** (24b, 35d, 72d, 76d, 119a), **lads, lady** (45b, 81d), **laet** (49b), **Iago** (65a, 112d), **lags, Lahr** (165), **laic** (28a, 70c, 82a, 94d, 106b), **laid, lain, lair** (34d, 60c), **lait** (50d), **Lake** (165), **lake** (89a, 130a), **lakh** (84a, 108a), **laky, Lalo** (165), **lalo** (117d), **lama** (22b, 121d), **Lamb** (40b, 165), **lamb** (107d), **lame** (32a, 57c), **lamp** (71d, 73c), **Iams, Lana** (165), **lana** (70b), **Land** (165), **land** (9d, 36b, 120d), **Lane** (165), **lane** (11c, 21b, 116b), **Lang** (165), **lang.** (240), **lank** (121a), **lanx** (102a), **Laos** (218), **Lapp** (82b, 222), **laps, Lara** (23c), **lard** (44c, 50a, 56a, 83d), **lari** (219), **lark** (19a, 51c, 226), **lash** (42d, 47c, 122a, 131c), **lass** (45b, 74b), **last** (30b, 40d, 108c, 130d), **late** (33d, 98b), **lath** (116c), **laud** (57b, 92b, 127d), **lava** (77d, 101b, 129a), **lave** (130a), **lawn** (31a, 43b, 69a, 72a), **laws, lays, laze** (61d), **lazy** (62d)

**_ L A _**    **alae** (132d), **Alai** (103c), **Alan** (137), **alar** (16c, 132d), **Alas.** (209, 235), **alas** (42c, 103b, 133b), **blab** (119d), **blah** (82a, 71d), **blat** (20b), **clad** (37d), **clam** (19c, 77d), **clan** (124b), **clap** (13c, 121d), **clar.** (237), **claw** (26b, 80b, 119b, 126b), **Clay** (146), **clay** (39a, 92a), **Elah** (67d), **Elam** (88a, 108a, 151), **elan** (33d, 41b, 113d, 128d, 135a), **flag** (17a, 38a, 41a, 69a, 87b, 114d, 130c, 132a), **flak** (13a), **flam** (38b), **flan** (32d, 87a), **flap** (48a, 79c, 89d, 119a, 130c, 132d), **flat** (42a, 63b, 95a, 95c, 114c, 234), **flaw** (19d, 34c), **flax** (72a, 72b), **flay** (110a, 110b, 116c), **glad** (66d), **Olaf** (82b, 128b, 173), **olax** (42b), **plan** (13d, 15c, 35b, 76b, 95a, 104d), **plat** (74d, 90b), **play** (51c, 52b, 87d, 91d, 114a), **slab** (88d, 110c), **slag** (28c, 38b, 76b, 105a, 111a, 129a, 130a), **slam** (124c, 131c), **slap** (22c, 98b), **slat** (69b, 133b), **Slav** (14d), **slaw** (28d), **slay** (36c, 79d), **Ulam** (197)

**_ _ L A**    **Alla** (138), **alla** (233), **amla** (39b), **aula** (53d), **Bala** (53c), **Bela** (18c, 39c, 140), **bola** (53a), **COLA** (237), **cola** (82d, 124a), **Dela.** (209), **Ella** (151), **ella** (113a), **-ella** (117b), **Fala** (44d), **fa-la** (98d), **fila** (121c), **Fula** (216, 217), **gala** (45c), **gila** (72c), **Gola** (218), **gola** (33c, 37c, 77d), **hula** (58b), **hyla** (12b, 122c), **kela** (246), **Kola** (103c), **kola** (82d), **Lola** (25b, 75a, 167), **Okla.** (211, 241), **olla** (30c, 36b, 66a, 112c, 113a, 131d), **Oola** (11c), **Pola** (175), **pula** (214), **pyla** (21c), **sala** (112d, 113a), **sola** (11d, 39b, 89c), **tala** (17c), **tela** (21c, 75d, 130d), **tola** (66d, 103a), **tula** (10d, 11d), **Vela** (103c, 208), **Vila** (224), **vola** (111c), **Zola** (49c, 188)

**L _ _ A**   **lama** (22b, 121d), **Lana** (165), **lana** (70b), **Lara** (23c), **lava** (77d, 101b, 129a), **Leda** (24d, 59a, 91a, 113b, 125d, 135a, 198), **Lema** (166), **Lena** (30b, 52a, 166), **lija** (46a, 70d), **Lima** (27c, 221), **lima** (12a, 17d), **Lina** (166), **lira** (25c, 218, 219, 221, 223, 224), **Lisa** (166), **Liza** (166), **Lola** (25b, 75a, 167), **loma** (59d), **LPGA** (240), **Luba** (224), **Luca** (167), **Luna** (89d, 198), **luna** (78d), **Lyra** (58a, 207)

**_ L B _**   **alba** (73c, 75c, 131d), **albs, Elba** (64c, 80d), **Elbe** (82b, 216)

**_ _ L B**   **bulb** (30d, 126b)

**L _ _ B**   **Lamb** (40b, 165), **lamb** (107d), **limb** (13c, 21c), **lobb** (77a)

**_ L C _**   **alca** (15d, 98a)

**_ _ L C**   **talc** (25d, 49c, 77a, 92a, 111b)

**L _ _ C**   **laic** (28a, 70c, 82a, 94d, 106b), **leuc-** (94a)

**_ L D _**   **Alda** (137), **Aldo** (137), **bldg.** (236)

**_ _ L D**   **auld** (105b), **bald** (17b), **bold** (33d), **cold** (53b, 62a), **fold** (57d, 90b, 107d), **-fold** (117c), **geld** (120a), **gild** (40b), **gold** (74a, 134b, 245), **held** (91d), **hold** (9c, 15a, 16c, 27d, 67b, 74b, 95b, 100a, 115a, 121a, 234), **meld** (23c, 34b), **mild** (28a, 53c, 77c, 120c), **mold** (44c, 107c), **sold, told** (99a), **veld** (104c, 112b), **Weld** (186), **weld** (38d, 66c, 126c), **wild** (18c, 31d, 104c, 126d, 128c), **wold** (38d, 126d)

**L _ _ D**   **Ladd** (165), **laid, Land** (165), **land** (9d, 36b, 120d), **lard** (44c, 50a, 56a, 83d), **laud** (57b, 92b, 127d), **lead** (29d, 35d, 56d, 58c, 245), **lend** (62b), **lewd** (69b, 103d), **lied** (54a, 234), **Lind** (166), **load** (10b, 22d, 24b, 119a), **Lord** (167), **lord** (82a), **loud** (115b)

**L E _ _**   **lead** (29d, 35d, 56d, 58c, 245), **leaf** (85b, 90a), **Leah** (65b, 68b, 197), **leak** (72b, 84b), **leal** (73c, 105b), **Lean** (165), **lean** (24b, 29b, 98a, 110c, 113b, 121a, 122b), **leap** (24a, 67a, 232), **Lear** (30d, 107c, 195), **leas, Lech** (165, 213), **Leda** (24d, 59a, 91a, 113b, 125d, 135a, 198), **leek** (59b, 84a, 131b), **leer** (12b, 73a, 110d), **lees** (37d, 106b), **leet** (31c), **left** (9a, 34d, 91c, 99c), **legs, lehr** (54c, 85c), **Leif** (43a), **leis, leks, Lema** (166), **Lena** (30b, 52a, 166), **lend** (62b), **Leno** (166), **leno** (43b, 75a), **lens** (54c, 74a, 84c, 98d, 120b), **Lent** (44c, 87c, 106a), **lent, Leon** (166, 222), **Leos, lept-** (93d), **Lero** (64c), **lerp** (41d), **less** (77b, 82c), **lest** (48d), **Leto** (13b, 14d, 28d, 88c, 198), **lets, Lett** (16d), **leuc-** (94a), **leuk-** (94a), **Levi** (13b, 64d, 70d, 197), **levo-** (93b), **levy** (15a, 62b, 120a), **lewd** (69b, 103d)

**_ L E _**   **Alea** (15b), **Alec** (137), **alec** (12c, 47a, 104b), **alee** (59a, 108a, 132b), **ales, Alex** (137), **bleb** (20a, 22b, 54c), **bled** (97d), **blet** (51d), **bleu** (26b, 50a), **blew, clef** (80c, 234), **Cleo** (96d, 146), **clew** (16c, 103b), **elec.** (238), **elem.** (238), **elev.** (238), **flea** (63b, 229), **fled, flee** (9b, 41c), **Flem.** (238), **flew, flex** (18c), **gled** (42a), **glee**

375

(76a, 111d, 234), **Glen** (155), **glen** (35d, 98a, 127b), **ilea** (73c), **ileo-** (93b), **ilex** (60c), **Klee** (164), **Llew** (199), **olea** (84a), **oleo-** (93b), **plea** (42d, 92b, 118a), **pleb** (29b), **pled**, **plew** (18a), **sled** (102b), **slew** (110c, 118c), **sley** (130d)

**_ _ L E**  **able** (10a, 29c, 96b, 110a), **acle** (64b), **atle** (104a, 119b), **axle** (113c, 131c), **bale** (22c, 232), **bile** (26d), **bole** (27d, 98c, 124b), **Cale** (144), **-cele** (117c), **Cole** (146), **-cule** (117c), **Dale** (26d, 147), **dale** (35d, 98a, 127b), **dele** (23c, 40b, 43a, 94c, 95b, 119b), **Dole** (58c, 149), **dole** (91d, 99b, 131a), **elle** (49d, 51a, 246), **Erle** (151), **file** (72a, 97d, 99a, 122d), **Gale** (154), **gale** (130d, 132b, 132c), **gyle** (21d), **Hale** (12b, 156), **hale** (112a, 131d), **hole** (9c, 13b, 84b, 89c, 109d), **hule** (21c, 25a, 102c), **-ible** (117a), **Idle** (159), **idle** (40c, 60c, 62c, 62d, 63a, 70c, 127a, 130a), **ille** (69d), **lole** (42a, 59c, 94c), **isle** (11a, 64b, 67b), **Jule** (163), **kale** (23a, 78a, 90a, 103d, 127c), **Kyle** (165), **Lyle** (167), **Male** (37d, 219), **male** (53b, 70b, 114b), **mile** (52c, 68c, 246), **Mlle.** (240), **Mole** (69a), **mole** (19b, 22d, 106a, 114d, 230), **mule** (108c, 110d, 131b, 230), **Nile** (81b, 216, 222), **Ogle** (173), **ogle** (43c, 71a, 73a), **orle** (46a, 59b, 108a), **pale** (19d, 86a, 88d, 129d), **Pele** (58c), **pile** (17a, 58d, 79a), **pole** (101c, 113a, 129b, 133b, 246), **pule** (131c), **Pyle** (175), **rale** (21d, 26c, 34a), **rile** (12d, 64b, 95c, 115c), **role** (52a, 86d), **rule** (13b, 35b, 37b, 70b, 118c), **sale** (15c, 17b, 50b, 51a, 123d), **sole** (42c, 46d, 47d, 84b, 87c, 109d, 111d, 228), **tale** (43a, 71b, 103b, 134a), **tele-** (92d, 93d), **tile** (27d, 46b, 74b, 102a, 120d), **tole** (41b, 76b), **tule** (22c, 25a), **Vale** (184), **vale** (44b, 127b), **vile** (9a, 17b, 46a, 62a, 74c), **vole** (75b, 79b, 110b, 111b, 231), **wale** (55c, 100c, 130c, 131b, 131c), **wile** (34a), **Yale** (79b, 101c, 205), **yule** (27a)

**L _ _ E**  **Labe** (217), **lace** (47b), **lade** (24b, 35d, 72d, 76d, 119a), **Lake** (165), **lake** (89a, 130a), **lame** (32a, 57c), **Lane** (165), **lane** (11c, 21b, 116b), **late** (33d, 98b), **lave** (130a), **laze** (61d), **lice** (86c), **life** (19a, 57a, 94d), **like** (24b, 109c), **lime** (23b, 27c, 51d, 78d, 124a), **line** (11b, 30d, 46a, 96d, 102c, 116b), **lire** (50d, 64d), **Lise** (166), **-lite** (117b, 117c), **live** (38d, 42d), **lobe** (70d, 102c), **lode** (35a, 76b, 84c, 127d), **loge** (120d), **Lome** (223), **lone** (109d, 111d), **lope** (39b, 52a, 52b), **lore** (60b, 70d, 71b, 132d), **lose** (48d), **Love** (167), **love** (24b, 120c), **Lowe** (167), **Luce** (10a, 29b, 192), **luge** (110b), **Luke** (42a, 167, 196), **lune** (31d, 58c), **lure** (34b, 41b, 63d, 120c), **lute** (25c, 66a, 80b, 100d), **luxe** (100c), **Lyle** (167), **lyre** (80b, 85a), **-lyse** (117b), **-lyte** (117a), **-lyze** (117b)

**_ L F _**  **Alfs**

**_ _ L F**  **calf** (134d), **golf** (12a), **gulf** (9c, 130a), **half** (77c), **pelf** (21a, 46a, 100c), **self** (39d, 62d), **Wolf** (187, 207), **wolf** (23d, 231)

**L _ _ F**  **leaf** (85b, 90a), **Leif** (43a), **lief** (132a), **loaf** (61d, 73b, 130a), **luff** (48a)

**L G _ _**  **lgth.** (240)

**_ L G _**  **alga** (105d), **-algy** (117c), **Olga** (173)

_ _ L G    **Belg.** (236), **Bulg.** (236)

L _ _ G    **Lang** (165), **lang.** (240), **ling** (22c, 46d, 58d, 130b, 228), **Long** (167), **long** (31d), **lung** (100a, 121b)

L _ _ H    **lakh** (84a, 108a), **lash** (42d, 47c, 122a, 131c), **lath** (116c), **Leah** (65b, 68b, 197), **Lech** (165, 213), **lgth.** (240), **Lith.** (240), **-lith** (117c), **loch** (68b, 105b, 130a), **losh** (40b), **lush** (38b, 73d), **Luth.** (240)

L I _ _    **Liam** (166), **Liao** (101a), **liar** (75d), **Lias** (53c), **lice** (86c), **lick** (18a, 66a, 110d), **lido** (65c, 127d), **lids, lied** (54a, 234), **lief** (132a), **lien** (53a, 71a, 95b), **lies, lieu** (89d), **life** (19a, 57a, 94d), **lift** (40b), **lign-** (94a), **lija** (46a, 70d), **like** (24b, 109c), **lill** (16b, 89b, 132b), **lilt** (72c), **Lily** (166), **lily** (47c, 47d), **Lima** (27c, 221), **lima** (12a, 17d), **limb** (13c, 21c), **lime** (23b, 27c, 51d, 78d, 124a), **limn** (35a), **limp** (47b, 63a, 129b), **limy, Lina** (166), **Lind** (166), **line** (11b, 30d, 46a, 96d, 102c, 116b), **ling** (22c, 46d, 58d, 130b, 228), **link** (30a, 63c, 66c), **lint** (47d), **liny, Linz** (33c, 213), **Lion** (193), **lion** (94b, 230), **Li Po** (26d), **lipo-** (92d), **lips, lira** (25c, 218, 219, 221, 223, 224), **lire** (50d, 64d), **Lisa** (166), **Lise** (166), **Lisi** (166), **lisp** (113c), **liss** (49a), **list** (24d, 41b, 65c, 101c, 102b, 104d, 122a), **-lite** (117b, 117c), **Lith.** (240), **-lith** (117c), **litz** (97b), **live** (38d, 42d), **Livy** (101d), **Liza** (166)

_ L I _    **alif** (11d), **alim** (120a), **alit** (36c, 68d, 107a), **B. Lit.** (236), **blip** (97b), **Clio** (29b, 80a), **clip** (15c, 44c, 107d), **Elia** (68d, 87c, 151), **Elie** (151), **Elio** (151), **Elis** (56b), **Eliz.** (238), **Flip** (153), **flip** (123b), **flit** (33d), **glib** (47d, 110c, 111a, 129a), **glim** (23d, 43c), **ilia** (60b, 87c), **Ilie** (159), **olid** (49a, 116c), **olig-** (93a), **Olin** (173), **olio** (36b, 60c, 75d, 77b, 92a), **slid, Slim** (181), **slim** (110c, 118b), **slip** (36b, 41c, 52d, 54d, 110c, 126b), **slit** (33a)

_ _ L I    **Atli** (15c, 56d, 61c), **Bali** (64c), **Cali** (215), **Dali** (147), **Dili** (91d, 217), **heli-** (93d), **joli** (50d), **Juli** (163), **Kali** (109d, 199), **kali** (104a), **koli** (24d), **Mali** (219), **mali** (24d), **Pali** (22b, 104b, 127c), **pili-** (93a), **puli** (37b, 61c, 227), **soli** (14b), **ugli** (51d), **Vali** (83b), **Vili** (83b)

L _ _ I    **lari** (219), **Levi** (13b, 64d, 70d, 197), **Lisi** (166), **loci** (27a), **Lodi** (80d), **Loki** (10b, 16c, 198), **Loni** (167), **Lori** (167), **Loti** (49c, 95d), **loti** (218), **ludi** (102a), **luni-** (93b), **lwei** (213), **lysi-** (93a)

_ L K _    **Elke** (151), **elks, Ilka** (159)

_ _ L K    **balk** (16b, 89c, 116a), **bilk** (26b, 34a, 34c), **bulk** (20c, 75b, 129a), **calk** (61b), **Falk** (152), **folk** (87d, 124b), **hulk** (126d), **milk** (128d), **Polk** (175, 190), **pulk** (79c), **Salk** (179), **silk** (43b), **sulk** (117d), **talk** (29d, 36a, 113b), **volk** (54a), **walk** (85b), **Welk** (186), **yolk** (128d)

L _ _ K    **lack** (34c, 129d), **lank** (121a), **lark** (19a, 51c, 226), **leak** (72b, 84b), **leek** (59b, 84a, 131b), **leuk-** (94a), **lick** (18a, 66a, 110d), **link** (30a, 63c, 66c), **lock** (44c, 57b), **lonk** (107d), **look** (13c, 15a, 22b, 43d, 106b, 118b, 128c), **luck** (25d), **lurk** (71d, 110b)

377

**L L _ _**    **Llew** (199)

**_ L L _**    **Alla** (138), **alla** (233), **allo-** (93d), **Ally** (138), **ally** (11b, 15b, 29d, 30a, 126c), **Ella** (151), **ella** (113a), **-ella** (117b), **elle** (49d, 51a, 246), **ells, ille** (69d), **ills** (124d), **illy, Mlle.** (240), **olla** (30c, 36b, 66a, 112c, 113a, 131d)

**_ _ L L**    **Ball** (140), **ball** (17b), **Bell** (140), **bell** (22c, 120b), **Bill** (141), **bill** (17d, 109d), **Böll** (142), **boll** (90a, 90c), **bull** (21b, 86b), **call** (12d, 15a, 85b, 108d, 117d, 128c, 134b), **cell** (32c), **coll.** (237), **cull** (88d), **dell** (35d, 127b), **dill** (14c, 88d), **doll** (45b, 96a), **Dull** (193), **dull** (20b, 28b, 47b, 63b, 66b, 71d, 73c, 126c), **fall** (38b, 57b, 106a), **Fell** (152), **fell** (33a), **fill** (83b, 88b, 104b), **full** (29c, 99d), **gall** (18d, 25d, 64b, 128b), **gill** (21c, 246), **gull** (19a, 28c, 34a, 34c, 68a, 76c, 105c, 118d, 225), **Hall** (156), **hall** (31a, 87a), **Hell** (9a, 16a, 34a, 57a, 108a), **he'll** (30c), **Hill** (158), **hill** (17a), **Hull** (159), **hull** (106b, 108b), **it'll** (30c), **jell** (111d), **Jill** (161), **kill** (31d, 79d, 102d), **lill** (16b, 89b, 132b), **loll** (38a, 73b, 98b), **lull** (11c), **mall** (74c, 95a, 108c), **mell** (60d), **Mill** (170), **mill** (96d), **Moll** (171), **moll** (52d), **Mull** (171), **mull** (43b, 91b, 103a, 121b), **Nell** (83d, 172), **null** (82c, 128d), **pall** (28b, 122b, 130d), **Pell** (174), **pill** (119a), **poll** (129c), **pull** (11d, 37d, 123c), **rill** (22a, 31d, 101a, 110d, 116b), **roll** (118c), **sell** (74d, 87c, 127d), **Sill** (49a), **sill** (37c, 121c, 132b), **syll.** (243), **tall** (72d), **Tell** (14a), **tell** (13d, 62b, 81a, 99a), **till** (32c), **toll** (18c, 94b, 100d), **Wall** (193), **wall** (118a), **well** (25c, 97c), **we'll** (30c), **Will** (186), **will** (18c, 35b, 120d, 129a, 133a), **Yell** (64d), **yell** (18c, 108d)

**L _ _ L**    **leal** (73c, 105b), **lill** (16b, 89b, 132b), **loll** (38a, 73b, 98b), **lull** (11c)

**_ L M _**    **Alma** (138), **alma** (32a, 33b), **alms** (26a), **Elmo** (21a, 87a, 151), **elms, elmy**

**_ _ L M**    **balm** (83d, 126a), **calm** (11c, 13c, 15b, 82a, 85b, 89d, 97a, 106d, 111c, 111d, 126c), **Colm** (146), **culm** (13a, 28c, 56a, 108b, 115b), **film** (28b, 77b, 121b), **Helm** (157), **helm** (108b, 122a), **Holm** (158), **holm** (60c, 64b, 83a), **malm** (27d, 72a), **palm** (124a)

**L _ _ M**    **Liam** (166), **loam** (39a, 111c), **loom** (13c, 40c, 57d, 109b, 130d)

**_ L N _**    **ulna** (32c, 20d)

**_ _ L N**    **kiln** (16b, 85c), **Koln** (100b, 216)

**L _ _ N**    **lain, lawn** (31a, 43b, 69a, 72a), **Lean** (165), **lean** (24b, 29b, 98a, 110c, 113b, 121a, 122b), **Leon** (166, 222), **lien** (53a, 71a, 95b), **lign-** (94a), **limn** (35a), **Lion** (193), **lion** (94b, 230), **loan** (17a, 78a), **loin** (33a, 75c), **loon** (19a, 19b, 226), **lorn** (49a), **Lynn** (167), **Lyon** (216)

**L O _ _**    **load** (10b, 22d, 24b, 119a), **loaf** (61d, 73b, 130a), **loam** (39a, 111c), **loan** (17a, 78a), **lobb** (77a), **lobe** (70d, 102c), **lobo** (122a, 133b), **lobs, loch** (68b, 105b, 130a), **loci** (27a), **lock** (44c, 57b),

**loco** (31d, 63b, 90d), **lode** (35a, 76b, 84c, 127d), **Lodi** (80d), **Lodz** (221), **loft** (15c, 55b, 129d), **loge** (120d), **logo** (22d, 29b), **logs**, **logy** (38c), **loin** (33a, 75c), **loir** (37c), **Lois** (118a), **Loki** (10b, 16c, 198), **Lola** (25b, 75a, 167), **loll** (38a, 73b, 98b), **Lolo** (69a, 215), **loma** (59d), **Lome** (223), **lone** (109d, 111d), **Long** (167), **long** (31d), **Loni** (167), **lonk** (107d), **look** (13c, 15a, 22b, 43d, 106b, 118b, 128c), **loom** (13c, 40c, 57d, 109b, 130d), **loon** (19a, 19b, 226), **loop** (27b, 82a), **Loos** (167), **loot** (21a, 58b, 89b, 90c, 103a, 113d), **lope** (39b, 52a, 52b), **lops**, **Lord** (167), **lord** (82a), **lore** (60b, 70d, 71b, 132d), **Lori** (167), **lorn** (49a), **loro** (86d), **lory** (86d), **lose** (48d), **losh** (40b), **loss** (35a, 94d, 130a), **LOST** (240), **lost** (77b, 130a), **Loti** (49c, 95d), **loti** (218), **lots** (26a), **Lott** (167), **loud** (115b), **loup** (50d, 51b, 105c), **lour** (33d, 54d), **lout** (21a, 83a), **Love** (167), **love** (24b, 120c), **Lowe** (167), **lows**

**_ L O _**   **aloe** (10c, 19c, 59b, 59c, 71d, 75c, 90a, 122d), **alop** (38a), **Alou** (138), **alow** (18c, 126a), **blob** (29a, 75b), **bloc** (126c), **blot** (115b), **blow** (42d), **clod** (21a, 37b, 83a, 116d), **clog** (20a, 108c), **clop** (61a), **clot** (28c, 73c), **clou** (50d), **clow** (47c, 110d), **cloy** (54d, 104b, 118a), **Eloi** (122b), **Elon** (41c, 82b, 201), **floc** (111a), **floe** (61b), **flog** (131c), **flop** (44a), **flor** (46a, 108a), **flow** (14b, 37d, 116b), **glob** (75b), **glom** (115a), **glop** (75b), **glos.** (239), **glow** (108a), **Olof** (173), **olor** (118b), **plod** (124d, 129b), **plop** (44a, 130b), **plot** (23a, 30b, 104d, 123c), **plow** (32c, 122a), **ploy** (14d, 116a), **slob** (126d), **sloe** (15b, 19d, 51d, 90b, 132a), **slog** (38b, 124d, 129b), **slop** (48b, 111b), **slot** (12d, 13b, 34c, 84b, 123c), **slow** (34a, 35d, 58a, 110d, 116d)

**_ _ L O**   **allo-** (93d), **Arlo** (139), **bolo** (68a, 130d), **Colo.** (209, 237), **halo** (27b, 71d, 81d, 100d), **holo-** (94a), **hylo-** (94a), **Jolo** (64d), **kalo** (119d), **kilo** (12a, 76b, 246), **kilo-** (93d), **kolo** (48b, 106d), **Lalo** (165), **lalo** (117d), **Lolo** (69a, 215), **malo** (21d, 58c, 72d, 112d), **Milo** (171), **milo** (112a), **orlo** (46a, 90b), **Oslo** (220), **Polo** (127d), **silo** (48a, 116a), **solo** (11d, 14b, 84a), **telo-** (92d), **xylo-** (94a)

**L _ _ O**   **Iago** (65a, 112d), **Lalo** (165), **lalo** (117d), **Leno** (166), **leno** (43b, 75a), **Lero** (64c), **Leto** (13b, 14d, 28d, 88c, 198), **levo-** (93b), **Liao** (101a), **lido** (65c, 127d), **Li Po** (26d), **lipo-** (92d), **lobo** (122a, 133b), **loco** (31d, 63b, 90d), **logo** (22d, 29b), **Lolo** (69a, 215), **loro** (86d), **ludo** (52b)

**L P _ _**   **LPGA** (240)

**_ L P _**   **Alph** (101a), **Alps** (79b), **olpe** (70d, 132c)

**_ _ L P**   **colp** (25c), **Culp** (147), **gulp** (20d, 37d, 118b), **help** (10d, 15a, 62b, 117a), **kelp** (64a, 106a), **Kulp** (165), **palp** (13a, 45a, 123b), **pulp** (51d, 74a, 75b, 86b), **salp** (83b), **yelp** (12d, 37b)

**L _ _ P**   **laap** (41d), **lamp** (71d, 73c), **Lapp** (82b, 222), **leap** (24a, 67a, 232), **lerp** (41d), **limp** (47b, 63a, 129b), **lisp** (113c), **loop** (27b, 82a), **loup** (50d, 51b, 105c), **lump** (17a, 55a, 79a, 118c)

**_ L R _**   **NLRB** (241)

**L _ _ R**  **Lahr** (165), **lair** (34d, 60c), **Lear** (30d, 107c, 195), **leer** (12b, 73a, 110d), **lehr** (54c, 85c), **liar** (75d), **loir** (37c), **lour** (33d, 54d)

**_ L S _**  **also** (12c, 18c, 62c, 78c, 90c, 115b), **Elsa** (55c, 72d, 84b, 129b, 151), **else** (18c, 61d, 85a), **Ilsa** (24c)

**_ _ L S**  **ails, awls, bels, cols, eels, ells, fils** (51a, 213, 217, 218, 223, 224), **gals, gels, Gils, Hals** (38d, 156), **ills** (124d), **Mels, mils, oils, owls, pals, Sols**

**L _ _ S**  **labs, lads, lags, lams, Laos** (218), **laps, lass** (45b, 74b), **laws, lays, leas, lees** (37d, 106b), **legs, leis, leks, lens** (54c, 74a, 84c, 98d, 120b), **Leos, less** (77b, 82c), **lids, lies, lips, liss** (49a), **lobs, logs, Lois** (118a), **Loos** (167), **lops, loss** (35a, 94d, 130a), **lots** (26a), **lows, lues** (118d), **lugs, Luis** (167), **lyes**

**_ L T _**  **Alta.** (235), **alte** (69d), **alti-** (93a), **alto** (113a, 128d), **alto-** (93a)

**_ _ L T**  **belt** (16d, 27b), **Bolt** (142), **bolt** (44c, 47c, 67a, 101c), **Celt** (22a, 217), **celt** (115d, 123a), **colt** (61b, 100b, 134d, 135a), **cult** (106a, 119c), **dolt** (20a, 48b, 109c, 116d), **felt** (42d, 43b, 43d), **gelt** (78a), **gilt** (60c, 112b, 134d), **halt** (14c, 25b, 32a, 59d, 87b, 115d), **hilt** (57d), **Holt** (158), **holt** (30c), **jilt** (99a), **jolt** (20a, 66a, 108b), **kilt** (105a), **lilt** (72c), **malt** (18a), **melt** (72b, 120d), **milt** (47a), **molt** (24d, 107d), **mult-** (93b), **pelt** (28c, 43a, 57b, 59d), **SALT** (242), **salt** (29d, 80b, 94b, 103b, 106a, 111c), **silt** (79c, 106b), **tilt** (23d, 24b, 62c, 72b, 101c), **volt** (40a, 61b, 246), **Walt** (185), **welt** (100c, 129b, 130c, 131c), **Wilt** (187), **wilt** (38a)

**L _ _ T**  **laet** (49b), **lait** (50d), **last** (30b, 40d, 108c, 130d), **leet** (31c), **left** (9a, 34d, 91c, 99c), **Lent** (44c, 87c, 106a), **lent, lept-** (93d), **lest** (48d), **Lett** (16d), **lift** (40b), **lilt** (72c), **lint** (47d), **list** (24d, 41b, 65c, 101c, 102b, 104d, 122a), **loft** (15c, 55b, 129d), **loot** (21a, 58b, 89b, 90c, 103a, 113d), **LOST** (240), **lost** (77b, 130a), **Lott** (167), **lout** (21a, 83a), **Luft** (167), **Lunt** (167), **lust** (34a, 107a)

**L U _ _**  **luau** (58b), **Luba** (224), **Luca** (167), **Luce** (10a, 29b, 192), **luck** (25d), **Lucy** (192), **ludi** (102a), **ludo** (52b), **lues** (118d), **luff** (48a), **Luft** (167), **luge** (110b), **lugs, Luis** (167), **Luke** (42a, 167, 196), **lull** (11c), **lulu** (73a), **lump** (17a, 55a, 79a, 118c), **Luna** (89d, 198), **luna** (78d), **lune** (31d, 58c), **lung** (100a, 121b), **luni-** (93b), **Lunt** (167), **lure** (34b, 41b, 63d, 120c), **lurk** (71d, 110b), **lush** (38b, 73d), **lust** (34a, 107a), **lute** (25c, 66a, 80b, 100d), **Luth.** (240), **luxe** (100c)

**_ L U _**  **alum** (37c, 77a), **alum.** (235), **Blue** (142), **blue** (75d, 112a, 126c), **blur** (62d, 111a), **blut** (53d), **club** (21c, 32c, 75b, 84c, 104a, 111c), **clue** (60b, 117d), **Cluj** (221), **elul** (78c), **flub** (21b), **flue** (11a, 26c), **fluo-** (93a), **flux** (26a, 47d), **glue** (10a, 115b), **glum** (54d, 78d, 112b, 117d), **glut** (42b, 55b, 85c, 104b, 118a), **Ilus** (69a, 124d), **plug** (116a, 133d), **plum** (51d, 124a), **plus** (12c, 62c), **slub** (134b), **slue** (110c, 118c), **slug** (38a, 76b, 116b), **slum** (81b, 99d), **slur** (36c, 40b, 74c, 95b, 123c, 128b), **slut** (133b)

380

**_ _ L U**  ACLU (235), **lulu** (73a), **pelu** (26c), **Sulu** (88c), **sulu** (46a), **tolu** (16d), **Zulu** (12a, 222)

**L _ _ U**  lieu (89d), luau (58b), **lulu** (73a)

**L V _ _**  Lvov (223)

**_ L V _**  Alva (39c), Blvd. (236), ulva (105d)

**L _ _ V**  Lvov (223)

**L W _ _**  lwei (213)

**L _ _ W**  Llew (199)

**_ _ L X**  calx (59a, 85d), falx (102a)

**L _ _ X**  lanx (102a), Lynx (207), lynx (24a, 131d, 230)

**L Y _ _**  lyes, Lyle (167), Lynn (167), Lynx (207), lynx (24a, 131d, 230), Lyon (216), Lyra (58a, 207), lyre (80b, 85a), -lyse (117b), lysi- (93a), -lyte (117a), -lyze (117b)

**_ L Y _**  Clym (14a)

**_ _ L Y**  -ably (117b), Ally (138), ally (11b, 15b, 29d, 30a, 126c), coly (79b), Daly (147), duly (100c, 117a), eely, holy (30b), idly, illy, July, Lily (166), lily (47c, 47d), moly (59b, 132a), oily (44c, 83d, 126a), only (11d, 22d, 42c, 76a, 111d), poly- (93b), rely (124d), ugly (126a), wily (14d, 31d, 32c, 110c), wkly. (244)

**L _ _ Y**  lacy (34c), lady (45b, 81d), laky, lazy (62d), levy (15a, 62b, 120a), Lily (166), lily (47c, 47d), limy, liny, Livy (101d), logy (38c), Lucy (192)

**L _ _ Z**  Linz (33c, 213), litz (97b), Lodz (221)

**M A _ _**  ma'am (74a), maar (129a), mabi (47d, 80b), mace (40c, 82d, 114b, 118d, 129d), mach (113c), Mack (167), mack (97c), Macy (167), made (31d), Maes, mage (74a), Magh (213), magh (78b), magi (88a, 94c, 132d), maha (25d, 69a, 104a), Maia (59c, 107b, 129c, 198, 207), maid (37b, 54c, 107a), mail (14c, 76b, 91d), maim (80d), Main (168), main (26c, 29d, 67b, 94c), mais (50a), maja (31d), make (13c, 29c, 30c, 40d, 43d, 44c), maki (71b), mako (20b, 107d), Male (37d, 219), male (53b, 70b, 114b), Mali (219), mali (24d), mall (74c, 95a, 108c), malm (27d, 72a), malo (21d, 58c, 72d, 112d), malt (18a), mama (44b), mamo (58b), mana (91a), mand (25c), mane (57b), mani (87b), Mann (168), mano (65a), Manx (25c), manx (24d), many (82d), mapo (55a), maps, mara (101c, 230), Marc (168), marc (55d), mare (61a, 82c), Mari (16d), mari (50c), Mark (42a, 102c, 168, 196), mark (10d, 15c, 55c, 96b, 109b, 114c, 133a), marl (27d, 35a, 45c), Marr (168), Mars (89d, 98d, 129d, 199), mars (49d), mart (40c, 74d), maru (65d), Marv (169), Marx (169), Mary (96c, 107c, 169, 197), masa (30d), masc.. (240),

**MASH** (240), **Mash** (197), **mash** (32b, 115d), **mask** (29d, 36b, 37c), **Mass.** (210, 240), **mass** (9c, 10d, 17a, 22c, 53a, 58d, 107a, 129a), **mast** (18a, 90d, 108b, 113a), **mate** (15b, 18d, 26c, 29b, 34c, 85d, 114a, 120a), **math** (116c), **Mats** (169), **Matt** (169, 240), **maty** (62d), **Maud** (131d, 169), **maud** (43b, 56a), **Maui** (64c), **maul** (17c, 57d, 74c), **maws**, **Maya** (134d, 169, 214, 217), **maya** (60a, 130d), **Mayo** (169), **Mays** (169), **maze** (68b), **mazy**

_ M A _    **amah** (74b, 82d, 84d), **amas** (69d), **amat** (69d), **G-man** (45a), **imam** (23b, 80c), **Oman** (220), **Omar** (41c, 78d, 88a, 120c, 173, 197), **T-man** (45a), **Xmas** (27a)

_ _ M A    **Alma** (138), **alma** (32a, 33b), **amma** (9a), **bema** (90b, 95d), **boma** (10c), **cima** (65c), **coma** (71c, 116d, 126a), **cyma** (37c, 77d), **dama** (65a, 112d), **duma** (103a), **Emma** (21b, 151), **Erma** (151), **Fama** (103a), **FNMA** (238), **Hama** (222), **hema-** (92c), **Kama** (199), **kama** (60a, 129a), **lama** (22b, 121d), **Lema** (166), **Lima** (27c, 221), **lima** (12a, 17d), **loma** (59d), **mama** (44b), **Nama** (61c), **nema** (39d), **noma** (52c), **Numa** (102a), **Pima** (189), **pima** (31a), **puma** (24d, 31b, 79a, 231), **Rama** (128c), **Rima** (56c), **rima** (47a), **Roma** (65c, 218), **sama** (80d), **sima** (101b), **soma** (12d, 20c, 62d), **tema** (121a, 234), **USMA** (243), **xema** (14a, 56d), **Yuma** (189), **Zama** (106a)

M _ _ A    **maha** (25d, 69a, 104a), **Maia** (59c, 107b, 129c, 198, 207), **maja** (31d), **mama** (44b), **mana** (91a), **mara** (101c, 230), **masa** (30d), **Maya** (134d, 169, 214, 217), **maya** (60a, 130d), **mega-** (93b), **mesa** (40b, 59d, 90b, 119a), **meta-** (92d), **mica** (64b, 77a, 109b), **Mina** (223), **mina** (131a), **Mira** (207), **Mona** (171), **mona** (56d), **mora** (46b, 48c, 52b, 56d, 65a, 76b, 118b), **moxa** (25b, 26d, 133d), **mura** (65d), **musa** (16d), **muta** (26a, 80d), **Myra** (15a, 171), **myna** (19b)

_ M B _    **ambi-** (92c), **ambo** (95d, 98a), **imbe** (30d, 45c), **imbu** (51d), **umbo** (21a)

_ _ M B    **bomb** (107d, 130c), **comb** (31d), **dumb** (109b, 113c), **gamb** (12d), **iamb** (48c), **jamb** (37c, 109a, 126d), **Lamb** (40b, 165), **lamb** (107d), **limb** (13c, 21c), **numb** (33d, 126b), **tomb** (22d), **womb** (127c)

M _ _ B    **Moab** (66b, 73b, 197)

_ M C _    **YMCA** (244)

_ _ M C    **USMC** (243)

M _ _ C    **Marc** (168), **marc** (55d), **masc.** (240), **misc.** (240)

_ M D _    **Cmdr.** (237)

M _ _ D    **maid** (37b, 54c, 107a), **mand** (25c), **Maud** (131d, 169), **maud** (43b, 56a), **Mead** (61a, 170), **mead** (18a, 37d, 60d), **meed** (100b), **meld** (23c, 34b), **mend** (99c), **mild** (28a, 53c, 77c, 120c), **mind** (29c, 63c, 67b, 73a, 83a, 120c), **mold** (44c, 107c), **mood** (10d, 36c, 122d), **Mr. Ed** (119b), **Mudd** (171)

**M E _ _**    **Mead** (61a, 170), **mead** (18a, 37d, 60d), **meal** (56c, 99c), **mean** (9a, 16a, 17b, 34d, 76c, 109b, 115c), **meat** (48b), **Mede** (14d, 88a), **medi-** (93c), **meed** (100b), **Meek** (170), **meek** (37a, 53c, 61c, 76d, 77c, 126a), **meet** (9c, 15a, 30a, 40d, 43d, 63c, 103a, 107a), **mega-** (93b), **Megs, mein** (26d), **Meir** (170), **meld** (23c, 34b), **mell** (60d), **Mels, melt** (72b, 120d), **memo** (82c), **mend** (99c), **mene** (57d), **meno** (71b, 233), **-ment** (117b), **menu** (19a, 24c, 29c, 48b, 51a), **meow** (25a), **mere** (17b, 50d, 68b, 84b, 91b, 130a), **merl** (19a, 19d, 226), **mero** (56c, 66b), **Meru** (79a, 218), **Merv** (170), **mesa** (40b, 59d, 90b, 119a), **mesh** (40d, 63c, 81c, 111b, 130d), **meso-** (93b), **mess** (21b, 26a, 30a, 36c, 67a, 79c, 111b), **meta-** (92d), **mete** (11c, 13d, 91d), **Meth.** (240), **metr-** (94a), **Mets** (206), **Metz** (216), **meus** (69d), **mewl** (131c), **mews** (114b)

**_ M E _**    **amen** (111b, 128a), **Amer.** (235), **amer** (50a), **Ames** (138), **AMEX** (235), **emeu** (19b), **G-men** (45a), **N.Mex.** (241), **Omei** (22b), **omen** (15d, 48c, 48d, 91c, 94a, 109b), **omer** (59a), **Smee** (88b), **smew** (19a, 38c, 76a, 104c), **T-men** (45a, 123d)

**_ _ M E**    **acme** (32c, 87b, 123a, 135a), **came** (132b), **come** (94d), **cyme** (47d), **dame** (45b, 54c, 68c, 81d, 122c), **deme** (56b), **dime** (44d), **dome** (32d, 102a), **fame** (99c, 99d), **feme** (133b), **fume** (111a, 116a), **game** (114a), **hame** (61b), **heme** (20a), **home** (61c, 99d), **Hume** (159, 192), **kame** (60a, 100c), **lame** (32a, 57c), **lime** (23b, 27c, 51d, 78d, 124a), **Lome** (223), **mime** (66b), **name** (10d, 13c, 28d, 38b, 82a, 122c), **pome** (51d), **rime** (30a, 51c, 60c), **Rome** (13c, 27c, 41d, 218), **same** (36d, 61d), **seme** (37c), **some** (86d, 96b), **tame** (37a, 37b, 53c), **time** (38d, 41b, 41c, 87d, 100b), **tome** (20d, 129a)

**M _ _ E**    **mace** (40c, 82d, 114b, 118d, 129d), **made** (31d), **mage** (74a), **make** (13c, 29c, 30c, 40d, 43d, 44c), **Male** (37d, 219), **male** (53b, 70b, 114b), **mane** (57b), **mare** (61a, 82c), **mate** (15b, 18d, 26c, 29b, 34c, 85d, 114a, 120a), **maze** (68b), **Mede** (14d, 88a), **mene** (57d), **mere** (17b, 50d, 68b, 84b, 91b, 130a), **mete** (11c, 13d, 91d), **mice, Mike** (170), **mike** (12a), **mile** (52c, 68c, 246), **mime** (66b), **mine** (55a, 95a), **mire** (20c, 39a, 78c, 79c), **mise** (10d, 134c), **mite** (14a, 63b, 64a, 86c, 86d), **Mize** (171), **Mlle.** (240), **mode** (44c, 74d, 116d, 130c), **moke** (37c), **mole** (19b, 22d, 106a, 114d, 230), **mope** (22a, 117d), **More** (171), **more** (43c, 56a), **mote** (113b), **moue** (50d, 134c), **move** (10d, 36b, 62b, 125b), **mule** (108c, 110d, 131b, 230), **muse** (52d, 91b, 121b), **mute** (109b, 113c, 232, 234)

**M _ _ F**    **miff** (96b), **Muff** (17b), **muff** (17c, 21b, 22c)

**M _ _ G**    **Ming** (26d)

**M H _ _**    **mhos**

**_ M H _**    **YMHA** (244)

**M _ _ H**    **mach** (113c), **Magh** (213), **magh** (78b), **MASH** (240), **Mash** (197), **mash** (32b, 115d), **math** (116c), **mesh** (40d, 63c, 81c, 111b, 130d),

**Meth.** (240), **Mich.** (210, 240), **Moth** (193), **moth** (22d, 71b, 229), **much** (67c, 116d), **mush** (75b), **myth** (43a, 71b)

**M I _ _**   **mica** (64b, 77a, 109b), **mice**, **Mich.** (210, 240), **Mick** (170), **Midi** (112b), **mien** (13c, 17d, 24c, 34d, 36d, 74d), **miff** (96b), **Mike** (170), **mike** (12a), **mild** (28a, 53c, 77c, 120c), **mile** (52c, 68c, 246), **milk** (128d), **Mill** (170), **mill** (96d), **Milo** (171), **milo** (112a), **mils**, **milt** (47a), **mime** (66b), **Mimi** (68b, 84b, 95d, 171), **Mina** (223), **mina** (131a), **mind** (29c, 63c, 67b, 73a, 83a, 120c), **mine** (55a, 95a), **Ming** (26d), **mini-** (93c), **mink** (128c, 230), **Minn.** (210, 240), **mint** (14c, 28d, 59b), **minx** (88b), **Mira** (207), **mire** (20c, 39a, 78c, 79c), **Miró** (112c, 171), **MIRV** (240), **misc.** (240), **mise** (10d, 134c), **miso** (65d), **miso-** (93a), **Miss.** (210, 240), **miss** (54c, 108c), **mist** (28b, 38a, 48a, 127b), **mite** (14a, 63b, 64a, 86c, 86d), **mitt** (17b, 46b, 54d), **mitu** (32d), **mixt.** (240), **Mize** (171)

**_ M I _**   **amia** (21b, 79c), **amid** (12b), **amie** (50b), **amir** (10b, 13d), **Amis** (138), **amis** (50b), **-emia** (117a), **Emil** (151), **emim** (54b), **emir** (13d, 94c, 102d, 125b), **emit** (36a, 40a, 43c, 47d, 99b, 106c), **imit.** (239), **omit** (40b, 81b, 87a, 110a), **smit** (128a), **ymir** (54b)

**_ _ M I**   **admi** (53b), **Demi** (148), **demi-** (93a), **hemi-** (93a), **immi** (246), **Jimi** (161), **kami** (65d, 108a), **Mimi** (68b, 84b, 95d, 171), **rami** (21c), **remi** (53b), **semi** (62c), **semi-** (93a, 93c), **Simi** (64c), **Timi** (183), **zemi** (45c)

**M _ _ I**   **mabi** (47d, 80b), **magi** (88a, 94c, 132d), **maki** (71b), **Mali** (219), **mali** (24d), **mani** (87b), **Mari** (16d), **mari** (50c), **Maui** (64c), **medi-** (93c), **Midi** (112b), **Mimi** (68b, 84b, 95d, 171), **mini-** (93c), **Moki** (95d), **Muni** (171), **myri-** (93b)

**M _ _ K**   **Mack** (167), **mack** (97c), **Mark** (42a, 102c, 168, 196), **mark** (10d, 15c, 55c, 96b, 109b, 114c, 133a), **mask** (29d, 36b, 37c), **Meek** (170), **meek** (37a, 53c, 61c, 76d, 77c, 126a), **Mick** (170), **milk** (128d), **mink** (128c, 230), **mock** (35a, 62a, 66b, 100c, 104d, 120a), **Monk** (171), **monk** (25c, 51c), **muck** (39a), **murk** (28b, 48a, 77b), **musk** (87d)

**M L _ _**   **Mlle.** (240)

**_ M L _**   **amla** (39b)

**M _ _ L**   **mail** (14c, 76b, 91d), **mall** (74c, 95a, 108c), **marl** (27d, 35a, 45c), **maul** (17c, 57d, 74c), **meal** (56c, 99c), **mell** (60d), **merl** (19a, 19d, 226), **mewl** (131c), **Mill** (170), **mill** (96d), **moil** (20c, 133d), **Moll** (171), **moll** (52d), **Mull** (171), **mull** (43b, 91b, 103a, 121b), **myel-** (93d)

**_ M M _**   **amma** (9a), **ammo** (12b), **Emma** (21b, 151), **Emmy** (120b), **immi** (246)

**_ _ M M**   **comm.** (237)

**M _ _ M**   **ma'am** (74a), **maim** (80d), **malm** (27d, 72a)

384

**_ M N _**   omni- (92d)

**_ _ M N**   gymn- (93b), hymn (111d), limn (35a)

**M _ _ N**   Main (168), main (26c, 29d, 67b, 94c), Mann (168), mean (9a, 16a, 17b, 34d, 76c, 109b, 115c), mein (26d), mien (13c, 17d, 24c, 34d, 36d, 74d), Minn. (210, 240), moan (32b, 112b), Moon (171), moon (33a, 104b), morn (33d), mown, muon (71b)

**M O _ _**   Moab (66b, 73b, 197), moan (32b, 112b), moas, moat (36d), mobs, mock (35a, 62a, 66b, 100c, 104d, 120a), mode (44c, 74d, 116d, 130c), Moes, mogo (115d), moho (60d), mohr (53b), moil (20c, 133d), mojo (129c), moke (37c), Moki (95d), mold (44c, 107c), Mole (69a), mole (19b, 22d, 106a, 114d, 230), Moll (171), moll (52d), molt (24d, 107d), moly (59b, 132a), moms, Mona (171), mona (56d), Monk (171), monk (25c, 51c), mono (61c), mono- (93c), mons (69d, 133d), Mont. (211, 240), mont (50d), mood (10d, 36c, 122d), Moon (171), moon (33a, 104b), Moor (78c, 104b, 219), moor (12c, 15c, 58d, 130a), moos, moot (36d), mope (22a, 117d), mops, mopy (72b), mora (46b, 48c, 52b, 56d, 65a, 76b, 118d), More (171), more (43c, 56a), morn (33d), Moro (171), moro (88c), Mors (34a, 198), Mort (171), Moss (171), moss (71c, 86c, 125a), most (74b, 78c), mote (113b), Moth (193), moth (22d, 71b, 229), moto (79c), mots, Mott (171), moue (50d, 134c), move (10d, 36b, 62b, 125b), mown, mows, moxa (25b, 26d, 133d)

**_ M O _**   à moi (50d), amok (18c, 51b), Amon (67d, 198), Amor (32d, 198), amor (112d), Amos (108a, 138, 196, 197), Amoy (69a), BMOC (236), smog (130d)

**_ _ M O**   ammo (12b), Como (68b, 146), demo (108d, 119c), Elmo (21a, 87a, 151), gamo- (93c), hemo- (92c), homo (63d), homo- (93c), mamo (58b), memo (82c), Nemo (128a), nomo- (92d), Pomo (189), sumo (66a), zymo- (93a)

**M _ _ O**   mako (20b, 107d), malo (21d, 58c, 72d, 112d), mamo (58b), mano (65a), mapo (55a), Mayo (169), memo (82c), meno (71b, 233), mero (56c, 66b), meso- (93b), Milo (171), milo (112a), Miró (112c, 171), miso (65d), miso- (93a), mogo (115d), moho (60d), mojo (129c), mono (61c), mono- (93c), Moro (171), moro (88c), moto (79c), muco- (93b), myco- (93a), myxo- (93b)

**_ M P _**   amph. (235), amps, Impi (135c), imps

**_ _ M P**   bump (66a, 66d), Camp (144), camp (19c, 39d, 127a), Comp. (237), damp (33c, 77c, 131b), dump (68d, 99d, 126c), Gamp (35c), gamp (125b), gimp (124c), hemp (23d, 30d, 45c, 55d, 102b), hump (95c), Jump (163), jump (10b, 114d, 127b), Kemp (164), lamp (71d, 73c), limp (47b, 63a, 129b), lump (17a, 55a, 79a, 118c), pimp (94d), pomp (85a, 85b), pump (108c), ramp (52c, 62c, 110d), RCMP (242), romp (51c), rump (23a, 33a, 75c), samp (55c, 60d, 91c), simp (48b, 109c), sump (25d, 77a), tamp (76d, 85b, 92a, 97d), temp. (243), tump (60a), tymp (19d), vamp (62c, 108c, 233), wimp (130c)

**M R _ _**  Mr. Ed (119b)

**_ M R _**  amra (60c), Imre (159), Omri (67d, 197)

**_ _ M R**  comr. (237)

**M _ _ R**  maar (129a), Marr (168), Meir (170), metr- (94a), mohr (53b), Moor (78c, 104b, 219), moor (12c, 15c, 58d, 130a), Msgr. (241), Muir (11a, 171)

**M S _ _**  Msgr. (241), M.Sgt. (241)

**_ M S _**  Omsk (64b)

**_ _ M S**  aims, alms (26a), arms (130d), bums, cams, dams, dims, doms, elms, gams (71b), gems, gums, gyms, hams, hems, Homs (222), hums, jams, Jims, lams, moms, mums, ohms, Pams, Rams (206), rams, rims, rums, Sams, Sims (181), sums, tams, Tims, Toms, yams

**M _ _ S**  Maes, mais (50a), maps, Mars (89d, 98d, 129d, 199), mars (49d), Mass. (210, 240), mass (9c, 10d, 17a, 22c, 53a, 58d, 107a, 129a), Mats (169), maws, Mays (169), Megs, Mels, mess (21b, 26a, 30a, 36c, 67a, 79c, 111b), Mets (206), meus (69d), mews (114b), mhos, mils, Miss. (210, 240), miss (54c, 108c), moas, mobs, Moes, moms, mons (69d, 133d), moos, mops, Mors (34a, 198), Moss (171), moss (71c, 86c, 125a), mots, mows, muds, mugs, mums, muss (103a)

**M _ _ T**  malt (18a), mart (40c, 74d), mast (18a, 90d, 108b, 113a), Matt (169, 240), meat (48b), meet (9c, 15a, 30a, 40d, 43d, 63c, 103a, 107a), melt (72b, 120d), -ment (117b), milt (47a), mint (14c, 28d, 59b), mist (28b, 38a, 48a, 127b), mitt (17b, 46b, 54d), mixt. (240), moat (36d), molt (24d, 107d), Mont. (211, 240), mont (50d), moot (36d), Mort (171), most (74b, 78c), Mott (171), M.Sgt. (241), mult- (93b), must (55d, 81c, 116c, 132c), mutt (32d, 78a), myst (56b)

**M U _ _**  Muav (53c), much (67c, 116d), muck (39a), muco- (93b), Mudd (171), muds, Muff (17b), muff (17c, 21b, 22c), mugs, Muir (11a, 171), mule (108c, 110d, 131b, 230), Mull (171), mull (43b, 91b, 103a, 121b), mult- (93b), mums, Muni (171), muon (71b), mura (65d), murk (28b, 48a, 77b), musa (16d), muse (52d, 91b, 121b), mush (75b), musk (87d), muss (103a), must (55d, 81c, 116c, 132c), muta (26a, 80d), mute (109b, 113c, 232, 234), mutt (32d, 78a)

**_ M U _**  Amur (101a), emus, smug (29c, 106c), smur (38a), smut (28c, 36a, 90a, 111d)

**_ _ M U**  rimu (62a, 98d)

**M _ _ U**  maru (65d), menu (19a, 24c, 29c, 48b, 51a), Meru (79a, 218), mitu (32d)

**M _ _ V**    **Marv** (169), **Merv** (170), **MIRV** (240), **Muav** (53c)

**M _ _ W**    **meow** (25a)

**M _ _ X**    **Manx** (25c), **manx** (24d), **Marx** (169), **minx** (88b)

**M Y _ _**    **myco-** (93a), **myel-** (93d), **myna** (19b), **Myra** (15a, 171), **myri-** (93b), **myst** (56b), **myth** (43a, 71b), **myxo-** (93b)

**_ M Y _**    **amyl** (114d), **amyl-** (93d), **Amys**, **emyd** (120c)

**_ _ M Y**    **army** (61c), **demy** (86b), **elmy**, **Emmy** (120b), **fumy** (127b), **gamy** (90b, 103d), **Jamy** (194), **limy**, **-nomy** (117c), **rimy**, **-tomy** (117b)

**M _ _ Y**    **Macy** (167), **many** (82d), **Mary** (96c, 107c, 169, 197), **maty** (62d), **mazy**, **moly** (59b, 132a), **mopy** (72b)

**M _ _ Z**    **Metz** (216)

**N A _ _**    **nabs**, **NaCL** (111c), **NADA** (241), **Naga** (15a, 69a, 128c), **naga** (23c, 28c, 60a), **nags**, **Nagy** (61c, 172), **naid** (51b), **naif** (126c), **nail** (27d, 44c, 119b, 126b), **Nair** (37d), **nair** (85a), **nais** (51b, 101a), **Nama** (61c), **name** (10d, 13c, 28d, 38b, 82a, 122c), **Nana** (88b, 135c), **nano-** (92c), **Nans**, **naos** (25b, 104a, 120b), **Napa** (23b, 132c), **napa** (54d, 70d), **nape** (16b, 82d), **naps**, **narc-** (93c), **nard** (75d, 83d), **Nare** (72d), **nark** (63a, 115d), **nary** (82c), **NASA** (241), **Nash** (172), **nasi** (87a), **NASL** (241), **naso-** (93b), **Nast** (172), **Nate** (172), **Natl.** (241), **NATO** (11c, 241), **Nats**, **naut.** (241), **nave** (27a, 131c), **navy** (20a, 47c), **nays** (129c), **nazi** (81a)

**_ N A _**    **anag.** (235), **anak** (54b), **anal** (51c), **anas**, **anat.** (235), **Enam** (66d), **gnar** (56d), **gnat** (48a, 63b, 76c, 229), **gnaw** (19c, 26c), **knap** (60a), **knar** (68c), **Onan** (66d), **snab** (22b, 105a), **snag** (13a, 24d, 60a, 68c, 95a, 122b), **snap** (17b, 21d, 31d, 39b, 44c, 66c), **Unas**, **unau** (110d)

**_ _ N A**    **Anna** (84a, 122d, 138), **anna** (103a), **arna** (22b, 131d), **bina** (60b), **Bona** (79b, 192), **bona** (69d, 70a), **buna** (102c), **Cana** (46c, 52b), **Dana** (147), **Dina** (149), **dona** (91d), **dyna-** (93c), **Edna** (151), **Enna** (109a), **Etna** (129a), **etna** (58d), **Gena** (154), **Gina** (155), **Hana** (157), **-iana** (117c), **Iona** (25c, 64b, 202), **Jana** (80d, 160), **Jena** (121d), **kana** (66a), **kina** (108a, 221), **Lana** (165), **lana** (70b), **Lena** (30b, 52a, 166), **Lina** (166), **Luna** (89d, 198), **luna** (78d), **mana** (91a), **Mina** (223), **mina** (131a), **Mona** (171), **mona** (56d), **myna** (19b), **Nana** (88b, 135c), **Nina** (24a, 29a, 172), **nina** (112d), **Nona** (86c), **Oona** (173), **Peña** (174), **pina** (29d), **Puna** (12c), **puna** (28d, 90b, 132b), **rana** (51c, 60a), **Sa'na** (134c), **Tana** (68b), **Tina** (183), **tuna** (125a, 229), **ulna** (32c, 20d), **USNA** (243), **vena** (70b), **vina** (60b), **Zana** (58a), **zona** (108a)

**N _ _ A**    **NADA** (241), **Naga** (15a, 69a, 128c), **naga** (23c, 28c, 60a), **Nama** (61c), **Nana** (88b, 135c), **Napa** (23b, 132c), **napa** (54d, 70d), **NASA** (241), **NCAA** (241), **nema** (39d), **Nera** (121d), **Neva** (100d), **NHRA**

(241), **Nina** (24a, 29a, 172), **nina** (112d), **nipa** (15b, 38a, 39b, 86a, 120d), **NIRA** (241), **Nita** (172), **NOAA** (241), **noma** (52c), **Nona** (86c), **Nora** (61b, 81d, 172), **nota** (69d), **Nova** (203), **nova** (114d), **Numa** (102a)

_ N B _    **anba** (28a)

N _ _ B    **NLRB** (241), **NTSB** (241), **numb** (33d, 126b)

N C _ _    **NCAA** (241)

_ N C _    **-ance** (117a, 117c), **-ancy** (117b), **-ence** (117b), **encl.** (238), **-ency** (117b), **ency.** (238), **Inca** (15b), **inch** (31d, 79c, 246), **incl.** (239), **onca** (246), **once** (18b, 49a, 61d, 63d), **UNCF** (243), **unco** (105b)

_ _ N C    **banc** (66d), **canc.** (236), **C in C** (236), **conc.** (237), **zinc** (20b, 76a, 245)

N _ _ C    **narc-** (93c)

N D _ _    **N.Dak.** (241)

_ N D _    **anda** (21c, 133b), **Andi** (25a), **Andy** (138), **endo-** (94a), **ends, Indo-** (93b), **onde** (51b), **undo** (12d, 41c, 73a, 99b)

_ _ N D    **Arnd** (53d), **band** (56c, 116b, 232), **bend** (12c, 32d, 125b), **bind** (122a), **Bond** (142), **bond** (10a, 28d, 71d, 72b, 78a, 107b, 118a, 122a), **bund** (40b), **cond.** (237), **fend** (44b, 86d, 129d), **find** (36a), **fond** (10b, 73c), **fund** (9c, 78a, 100a), **Gond** (62d), **hand** (10d, 15a, 59b, 87c, 133d, 246), **hind** (34b, 37a), **Hond.** (239), **kind** (112a, 113b, 127b), **Land** (165), **land** (9d, 36b, 120d), **lend** (62b), **Lind** (166), **mand** (25c), **mend** (99c), **mind** (29c, 63c, 67b, 73a, 83a, 120c), **pend** (16c, 58a), **pond** (91b, 130a), **Rand** (176), **rand** (220, 222), **rend** (28a), **rind** (43a, 76d, 87c), **rynd** (76d), **Sand** (179), **sand** (78d, 109b), **send** (36c, 74b, 86d, 91d, 99c, 108b, 123d), **tend** (24b, 73a, 77a, 124b), **vend** (74d, 87c, 106c), **wand** (90d, 101c, 115b), **wend** (54d, 110b, 112a), **wind** (10d, 28d, 32d, 125c), **yond** (36d)

N _ _ D    **naid** (51b), **nard** (75b, 83d), **need** (34d, 42d, 68b, 92a, 129d), **Nidd** (134d), **NKVD** (103c)

N E _ _    **neaf** (47b), **Neal** (172), **neap** (121d, 122d, 129b), **near** (13d, 28b, 81d), **neat** (10a, 116a, 121d, 124c), **Nebo** (78d, 79a), **Nebr.** (211, 241), **nebs**, **neck** (64d), **necr-** (92d), **Neds**, **need** (34d, 42d, 68b, 92a, 129d), **neep** (105b, 125b), **ne'er** (30b, 82c, 107c), **Neil** (172), **nein** (54a), **Nell** (83d, 172), **nema** (39d), **Nemo** (128a), **nene** (58c), **neon** (53a, 71d, 245), **neph-** (92d), **Nera** (121d), **Nero** (10d, 102a), **ness** (24a, 58d, 95a), **nest** (31c, 100a, 111b, 118c, 232), **Neth.** (241), **Nets** (206), **nets**, **neur-** (93b), **neut.** (241), **Neva** (100d), **neve** (46c, 54c, 55d, 111b), **nevi** (19c, 77d), **news** (121d), **Newt** (172), **newt** (39d, 103d, 225), **next** (81a)

_ N E _    **anew** (10b, 10c), **Inez** (37c), **knee** (66c), **knew**, **knez** (94c), **ones** (87d), **sned** (73a), **snee** (33a, 35d, 68a)

**_ _ N E**    acne (110a), aine (51a), Anne (96b, 107c, 138, 192, 194), a-one (42b, 46c, 123b), Arne (102d, 139), aune (246), bane (58a, 81b, 90d, 102d, 133b), bene (65c, 70b), bine (115b, 128b), bone (46a, 110a), cane (98a, 114b, 115a, 115b, 117d, 129b), -cene (117c), cine- (93b), Cone (146), cone (53c, 116c, 111d), Dane (67c, 82b, 104c, 147), Dene (189), dene (104a), dine (39b), done (85c), dune (84a, 104a), dyne (48c, 246), eine (53d, 54a), erne (19a, 39a, 105c, 225), esne (12c, 106d, 110b, 121b), fane (104a, 120b), Fine (152), fine (26d, 34c, 40b, 40d, 79d, 87c, 116d, 233), Gene (154), gene (59c), gone (9b, 34d, 36c), gyne (45b), hone (39c, 107d, 131c), Ione (22c, 69b, 73d), Jane (160), June (163), Kane (163), kine (31c), Lane (165), lane (11c, 21b, 116b), line (11b, 30d, 46a, 96d, 102c, 116b), Ione (109d, 111d), lune (31d, 58c), mane (57b), mene (57d), mine (55a, 95a), nene (58c), nine (17c), none (82c), ohne (54a), Orne (23a), pane (114c, 114d), pine (30a, 42a, 69a, 73a, 124a, 134b), pone (30d, 66c), René (176), rine (36d), rune (82b), Ryne (179), sane (97d), sine (52a, 70b, 96b, 124c), sone (246), syne (105b), tine (13a, 95a, 123a), Tone (184), tone (9c, 82c, 89c), Tune (184), tune (9c, 10a, 10d, 14b, 58a, 75d, 111d, 116a), Tyne (82b, 184, 223), vane (130d, 132b), vine (28a, 71c), wane (9a, 34b, 69a, 116d), wine (60c, 91c), Zane (188), zone (18c, 36d, 40d, 118b)

**N _ _ E**    name (10d, 13c, 28d, 38b, 82a, 122c), nape (16b, 82d), Nare (72d), Nate (172), nave (27a, 131c), nene (58c), neve (46c, 54c, 55d, 111b), Nice (49c, 100a, 216), nice (90b, 109c), nide (88c, 232), Nike (77b, 132c, 198), Nile (81b, 216, 222), nine (17c), Niue (64c), node (66c, 68c, 90d, 95c, 118c), none (82c), nope (81b), Nore (120d), nose (89d, 95c), note (15c, 71c, 75d, 83b, 95a, 98c, 99c, 122c, 129c, 234), nove (65c), nude (17b, 126b), NYSE (241)

**_ N F _**    info. (239)

**_ _ N F**    conf. (237)

**N _ _ F**    naif (126c), neaf (47b)

**_ N G _**    Angl. (235), engr. (238), Inge (22d, 54d, 88d, 159)

**_ _ N G**    bang (110b), Bing (141), bong (111a), bung (116a), cong. (237), dang (42a), ding (62d, 76b), dong (224), dung (42d, 74d), Fang (193, 216), fang (123a), fung- (93a), gang (16d, 32a, 232), gong (80a), hang (118b), hing (14d), hong (26d), Hung. (239), hung, Jong (163), Jung (95d, 163), King (164, 190), king (24a, 26c, 82a), Lang (165), lang. (240), ling (22c, 46d, 58d, 130b, 228), Long (167), long (31d), lung (100a, 121b), Ming (26d), Pang (125a), pang (85d, 114b, 121c), Ping (125a), ping (76b), Pong (125a), pung (21c, 110c), rang, Ring (177), ring (16d, 27b, 40c, 40d, 131b, 134a), rung (25d, 32b, 115b), sang, sing (129d), song (14b, 61d, 125a), Sung (26d), sung, T'ang (26d), tang (22a, 47b, 135a), ting (76b), tong (26d), tung (83d), uang (100b), USNG (243), vang (57c, 102b), wing (12d, 47c, 48a, 89b, 89d, 232), Wong (187), Xing. (244), yang (134d), zing (32a)

**N _ _ G**    nogg (11b)

**N H _ _**    NHRA (241)

**N _ _ H**    Nash (172), neph-(92d), Neth.(241), nigh (28b, 81a), Noah (68d, 76b, 172, 197)

**N I _ _**    nibs, Nice (49c, 100a, 216), nice (90b, 109c), Nick (172), nick (26d, 82c), Nidd (134d), nide (88c, 232), nidi (113c), nigh (28b, 81a), Nike (77b, 132c, 198), Niki (172), Nile (81b, 216, 222), Nina (24a, 29a, 172), nina (112d), nine (17c), Nino (172), nino (112c), nipa (15b, 38a, 39b, 86a, 120d), nips, NIRA (241), nisi (70b, 126c), Nita (172), nito (45b), nitr- (93b), nits, Niue (64c)

**_ N I _**    anil (38d, 62d), anis (14d, 23c, 53c, 120c), 151), Enif (207), inia (12b, 83b, 110b), init. (239), knit (126c), snip (28a), snit (10d, 12c, 47b), unio (80d), unit (77d, 84a)

**_ _ N I**    Agni (68c), bani (101d), Beni (214), doni (25d), goni- (92c), Ifni (220), igni- (93a), Joni (163), Loni (167), luni- (93b), mani (87b), mini- (93c), Muni (171), omni- (92d), rani (60a, 94c), Reni (65a, 176), reni- (93b), sebi- (92d), Toni (184), Unni (197), veni- (93d), vini- (94a), yeni (119c), Zuni (95d, 189)

**N _ _ I**    nasi (87a), nazi (81a), nevi (19c, 77d), nidi (113c), Niki (172), nisi (70b, 126c), nori (11b, 105d), nudi- (93b)

**_ _ N J**    conj. (237)

**N K _ _**    NKVD (103c)

**_ N K _**    Anka (138), ankh (32a), inks, inky (19d, 33d)

**_ _ N K**    bank (19a, 47c, 91b), bunk (82a, 110c), conk (60b, 116b), dank (33b, 77c), dunk (35d, 62a), fink (46a), funk (10d, 35a, 47b), gink (39c), gunk (110c), Hank (157), hank (57b, 109d), honk (55b, 112b), hunk (57d, 88d), jink (40b), junk (26c, 102d), kink (31d), lank (121a), link (30a, 63c, 66c), lonk (107d), mink (128c, 230), Monk (171), monk (25c, 51c), pink (24b), punk (12a, 123b), rank (27d, 46a, 55c, 72a, 73d, 97c, 116c), rink (109d, 114a), sank, sink (34b, 60c, 110d), sunk, tank (127d), wink (63c, 81d, 106a), Yank (12b), yank (95d)

**N _ _ K**    nark (63a, 115d), N.Dak. (241), neck (64d), Nick (172), nick (26d, 82c), nock (14c, 82c), nook (30d, 100a)

**N L _ _**    NLRB (241)

**_ N L _**    only (11d, 22d, 42c, 76a, 111d)

**_ _ N L**    Genl. (239)

**N _ _ L**    NaCL (111c), nail (27d, 44c, 119b, 126b), NASL (241), Natl. (241), Neal (172), Neil (172), Nell (83d, 172), Noel (172), noel (24b, 27a, 111d), noil (45d, 68c), null (82c, 128d)

**N M _ _**    **N.Mex.** (241)

**_ N M _**    **FNMA** (238)

**N _ _ M**    **Noam** (172), **Norm** (172), **norm** (16a, 86b, 97d, 114d)

**_ N N _**    **Anna** (84a, 122d, 138), **anna** (103a), **Anne** (96b, 107c, 138, 192, 194), **anno** (70b), **Anns**, **Enna** (109a), **inns**, **Unni** (197)

**_ _ N N**    **Bonn** (18b, 216), **Conn.** (209, 237), **conn** (35d), **Finn.** (238), **Jann** (160), **Lynn** (167), **Mann** (168), **Minn.** (210, 240), **Nunn** (173), **Penn** (174), **Penn.** (211, 242), **sunn** (45d), **Tenn.** (212, 243), **Wynn** (187)

**N _ _ N**    **nein** (54a), **neon** (53a, 71d, 245), **noon** (76c), **Norn** (82a), **noun** (86d, 116d), **Nunn** (173)

**N O _ _**    **NOAA** (241), **Noah** (68d, 76b, 172, 197), **Noam** (172), **nobs** (32a), **nock** (14c, 82c), **noct-** (93b), **node** (66c, 68d, 90d, 95c, 118c), **nods**, **Noel** (172), **noel** (24b, 27a, 111d), **noes** (81b), **nogg** (11b), **nogs**, **noil** (45d, 68c), **noir** (50a, 102c), **noma** (52c), **nomo-** (92d), **-nomy** (117c), **Nona** (86c), **none** (82c), **nook** (30d, 100a), **noon** (76c), **nope** (81b), **Nora** (61b, 81d, 172), **Nore** (120d), **nori** (11b, 105d), **Norm** (172), **norm** (16a, 86b, 97d, 114d), **Norn** (82a), **nose** (89d, 95c), **noso-** (92d), **Nosu** (215), **nosy** (63b), **nota** (69d), **note** (15c, 71c, 75d, 83b, 95a, 98c, 99c, 122d, 129c, 234), **noto-** (92c), **noun** (86d, 116d), **nous** (50d, 51b), **Nova** (203), **nova** (114d), **nove** (65c)

**_ N O _**    **anoa** (48d, 85d, 132a, 229), **anon** (10c, 15d, 62a, 94a, 108d, 111d), **anon.** (235), **enol** (120a), **Enos** (9d, 42a, 107a, 151, 197), **enow** (105a), **knob** (57d, 82a, 95c), **knop** (68c), **knot** (76d, 82a, 232), **know** (13a, 16c), **Knox** (49a), **snob** (88a, 111b), **snot** (62c, 88a), **Snow** (181), **snow** (130d)

**_ _ N O**    **anno** (70b), **Arno** (101a, 139), **at. no.** (236), **beno** (86a), **bino** (86a), **Bono** (142), **Brno** (215), **ceno-** (92d), **Dino** (47c), **Dr. No** (20d), **Gino** (155), **gono-** (93c), **gyno-** (92d), **Juno** (67c, 77b, 96d, 195, 199), **Kano** (129c), **keno** (52b), **kino** (38d, 57a, 119c, 127b), **Leno** (166), **leno** (43b, 75a), **mano** (65a), **meno** (71b, 233), **mono** (61c), **mono-** (93c), **nano-** (92c), **Nino** (172), **nino** (112c), **oeno-** (94a), **puno** (132b), **Reno** (15c, 81c, 113d), **reno-** (93b), **Sino-** (92d), **sino** (112d), **Tano** (95d, 189), **teno-** (93d), **tono-** (93c), **tuno** (57c), **veno-** (93d), **vino** (72b, 132c), **wino** (38b), **xeno-** (93a), **Zeno** (56b)

**N _ _ O**    **nano-** (92c), **naso-** (93b), **NATO** (11c, 241), **Nebo** (78d, 79a), **Nemo** (128a), **Nero** (10d, 102a), **Nino** (172), **nino** (112c), **nito** (45b), **nomo-** (92d), **noso-** (92d), **noto-** (92c)

**N _ _ P**    **neap** (121d, 122d, 129b), **neep** (105b, 125b)

**_ _ N Q**    **cinq** (50b)

**_ N R _**     **in re** (29d, 63d, 99a), **INRI** (32b, 239)

**_ _ N R**     **USNR** (244)

**N _ _ R**     **Nair** (37d), **nair** (85a), **near** (13d, 28b, 81d), **Nebr.** (211, 241), **necr-** (92d), **ne'er** (30b, 82c, 107c), **neur-** (93b), **nitr-** (93b), **noir** (50a, 102c), **Nuer** (222)

**_ N S _**     **ansa** (57d), **anse** (50c), **ANSI** (235), **ansu** (13d, 68c), **-ense** (117b), **Insp.** (239), **Inst.** (239)

**_ _ N S**     **ains, Anns, arns, awns, bans, Bens, bins, buns, cans, cons, Dans, dans** (50c), **dens** (70b), **dins, dons** (85d), **eons, erns, fans, fens, fins, gens** (35a), **gins, guns, Hans** (17b, 53d, 67a, 157), **hens** (92a), **Huns** (15c), **ians, inns, ions, Jans, Jons, Kans.** (210, 240), **Kens, lens** (54c, 74a, 84c, 98d, 120b), **mons** (69d, 133d), **Nans, nuns, owns** (91d), **pans, pens, pins, Pons** (49d, 175), **puns, runs, sans** (51b), **sens** (49c), **sins, sons** (83c), **Suns** (206), **suns, tans, tens, tins, tons, tuns, urns, vans, wens, wins, yens**

**N _ _ S**     **nabs, nags, nais** (51b, 101a), **Nans, naos** (25b, 104a, 120b), **naps, Nats, nays** (129c), **nebs, Neds, ness** (24a, 58d, 95a), **Nets** (206), **nets, news** (121d), **nibs, nips, nits, nobs** (32a), **nods, noes** (81b), **nogs, nous** (50d, 51b), **nubs, nuns, nuts**

**N T _ _**     **NTSB** (241), **Nt. Wt.** (241)

**_ N T _**     **anta** (89a, 91c), **ante** (68a, 69c, 90d, 114c), **ante-** (92c), **anth.** (235), **anti** (10c, 84c), **anti-** (92c), **ants, ento-** (94a), **inti** (221), **Intl.** (239), **into** (133a), **on to** (59b), **unto**

**_ _ N T**     **ain't, aunt** (44b, 99b), **bent** (13d, 32a, 55d, 62c), **bunt** (17c, 131b), **cant** (62c, 63b, 66a, 70d, 103d, 122a, 122b), **cent** (30c, 213-224), **cent.** (236), **cont.** (237), **Dent** (149), **dent** (35a), **dint** (42d, 92b), **don't, font** (17a, 125d), **gent** (45b), **hint** (11d, 32c, 33d, 117d, 133a), **Hunt** (159), **hunt** (105d), **isn't, Kant** (53d, 163), **Kent** (70d, 195, 202), **Lent** (44c, 87c, 106a), **lent, lint** (47d), **Lunt** (167), **-ment** (117b), **mint** (14c, 28d, 59b), **Mont.** (211, 240), **mont** (50d), **oont** (23c, 230), **pant** (18a, 21d), **pent** (30a), **pint** (54b, 246), **pont** (50a), **punt** (20b, 47b), **rant** (34b, 58a, 98a, 119b), **rent** (60b, 60c, 120a, 123b), **runt** (12d, 38d), **sent, tent** (24a, 87b), **tint** (29a, 107b), **vent** (11a, 13b, 40c, 60c, 84b, 85b, 115a), **want** (34a, 35b, 68b, 81b, 92a, 133a), **went** (34d), **wont** (9c, 33a, 57a, 92b)

**N _ _ T**     **Nast** (172), **naut.** (241), **neat** (10a, 116a, 121d, 124c), **nest** (31c, 100a, 111b, 118c, 232), **neut.** (241), **Newt** (172), **newt** (39d, 103d, 225), **next** (81a), **noct-** (93b), **Nt. Wt.** (241), **nuit** (50d), **nyet** (81d)

**N U _ _**     **nubs, nude** (17b, 126b), **nudi-** (93b), **Nuer** (222), **nuit** (50d), **null** (82c, 128d), **Numa** (102a), **numb** (33d, 126b), **Nunn** (173), **nuns, nuts**

**_ N U _**     **gnus, knur** (54d, 68c), **Knut** (33c, 164), **onus** (22d, 72d, 83a, 131a), **snub** (62a, 81b, 98b, 109a, 110c), **Snug** (193), **snug** (31c, 122a), **unus** (69c)

_ _ N U    **Danu** (199), **genu** (18c, 69d), **menu** (19a, 24c, 29c, 48b, 51a)

N _ _ U    **Nosu** (215)

_ N V _    **envy** (34a, 107a)

_ _ N X    **jinx** (61a), **lanx** (102a), **Lynx** (207), **lynx** (24a, 131d, 230), **Manx** (25c), **manx** (24d), **minx** (88b)

N _ _ X    **N.Mex.** (241)

N Y _ _    **nyet** (81d), **NYSE** (241)

_ N Y _    **Anya** (139), **Enyo** (129d), **onyx** (23c, 25d, 53b, 106c)

_ _ N Y    **awny**, **bony** (110a), **cony** (97a), **deny** (30c, 36a, 98d), **-geny** (117c), **-gyny** (117b), **liny**, **many** (82d), **piny**, **pony** (26b, 33b, 61a), **puny** (45a, 130c), **tiny** (77b, 110d), **Tony** (184), **viny**, **winy** (128c), **zany** (28b, 38a, 48b, 109c)

N _ _ Y    **Nagy** (61c, 172), **nary** (82c), **navy** (20a, 47c), **-nomy** (117c), **nosy** (63b)

_ _ N Z    **Linz** (33c, 213)

O A _ _    **oafs**, **Oahe** (33b), **Oahu** (64c), **oaks**, **oars**, **oast** (16b, 67b, 85c), **oath** (90b, 111c), **oats**

_ O A _    **boar** (60c, 89a, 118d, 132a, 230), **boas**, **boat** (81b, 108b), **Boaz** (103c, 197), **coal** (13a, 40c, 52a), **coat** (52d), **coax** (131b), **foal** (61b), **foam** (51c, 114a), **goad** (62c, 114b), **goal** (10d, 17c, 40d, 83a, 96c, 104d, 119d), **goas**, **goat** (81a, 102d, 230), **hoar** (51c, 131d), **hoax** (34a, 92b), **Joab** (33d, 197), **Joad** (55d), **Joan** (161), **koae** (58b), **load** (10b, 22d, 24b, 119a), **loaf** (61d, 73b, 130a), **loam** (39a, 111c), **loan** (17a, 78a), **Moab** (66b, 73b, 197), **moan** (32b, 112b), **moas**, **moat** (36d), **NOAA** (241), **Noah** (68d, 76b, 172, 197), **Noam** (172), **road** (31b, 38a, 121b, 130c), **roam** (123d, 129d), **roan** (61a, 98c, 131c), **roar** (12d, 13c), **soak** (9b, 37d, 104b, 115a), **soap** (17c), **soar** (48a), **toad** (17c, 225), **woad** (20a, 38d)

_ _ O A    **anoa** (48d, 85d, 132a, 229), **Aroa** (127d), **proa** (20c, 23d, 74b), **stoa** (29a, 91c), **whoa** (42c, 115d)

O _ _ A    **obia** (45c), **obra** (113a), **octa-** (92d), **odea** (29d), **Okla.**(211, 241), **okra** (57a, 127c), **olea** (84a), **Olga** (173), **olla** (30c, 36b, 66a, 112c, 113a, 131d), **onca** (246), **Oola** (11c), **Oona** (173), **-opia** (117b, 117c), **orca** (67b), **OSHA** (241), **Ossa** (79a, 84a, 121a), **ossa** (20d), **Otea** (64c)

O B _ _    **Obad.** (241), **Obal** (197), **Obed** (103c, 197), **obex** (21c), **obey** (29c, 59a, 67b, 10a), **obia** (45c), **obis**, **obit.** (34a, 52c, 241), **oboe** (58b, 80a, 80c, 133c), **obol** (26b, 83d), **obra** (113a)

_ O B _    **Bobo** (214), **Cobb** (146), **Cobh** (30d), **cobs**, **fobs**, **Gobi** (35a), **Gobo** (16d), **gobo** (66a), **gobs**, **goby** (46d, 228), **hobo** (123d,

127a), **hobs**, **jobo** (60c), **JOBS** (240), **jobs**, **koba** (13a, 130b), **Kobe** (60d, 218), **kobo** (220), **lobb** (77a), **lobe** (70d, 102c), **lobo** (122a, 133b), **lobs**, **mobs**, **nobs** (32a), **pobs** (91c), **Robb** (177), **robe** (52d), **robs**, **Roby** (178), **sobs**, **Tobe** (183), **tobe** (10c), **toby** (11b, 38a, 66d, 79d, 96a)

_ _ O B    **blob** (29a, 75b), **boob** (109c), **BYOB** (236), **doob** (18c), **glob** (75b), **knob** (57d, 82a, 95c), **scob** (120d), **slob** (126d), **snob** (88a, 111b)

O _ _ B    **Oreb** (197)

O C _ _    **Ochs** (173), **octa-** (92d), **octo** (69c), **octo-** (92d), **ocul-** (92d)

_ O C _    **boca** (113a), **boce** (22a, 46d), **Bock** (142), **bock** (18a, 70d), **Coca** (146), **coca** (28c, 81a), **cock** (26a, 44d, 102b, 103d, 119c, 127b), **coco** (86a), **dock** (33a, 68d, 88d, 108b, 112a, 131a), **docs** (88d), **Foch** (49c, 153), **foci** (25c), **hoch** (42c, 53d), **hock** (71b, 87b, 132c), **jock** (74c), **Koch** (53c, 164), **loch** (68b, 105b, 130a), **loci** (27a), **lock** (44c, 57b), **loco** (31d, 63b, 90d), **mock** (35a, 62a, 66b, 100c, 104d, 120a), **nock** (14c, 82c), **noct-** (93b), **pock** (62d), **poco** (72c), **Rock** (178), **rock** (118c, 124b), **sock** (96a, 116b, 132b), **soco** (21c), **tock** (10c), **toco** (123b), **voce** (65c, 234)

_ _ O C    **Apoc.** (235), **bloc** (126c), **BMOC** (236), **croc.** (237), **EEOC** (238), **floc** (111a), **Kroc** (165), **USOC** (244)

O _ _ C    **OPEC** (241), **otic** (15d, 39a)

O D _ _    **O'Day** (173), **odds** (10b, 11c, 26a, 95c), **odea** (29d), **Oder** (100d), **odes**, **Odin** (10b, 51c, 133b, 198), **odio** (65a), **odor** (104d, 111a, 115b), **-odus** (117c)

_ O D _    **bode** (48d, 91c), **Bodo** (69a), **body** (56c), **coda** (28b, 29d, 46a, 234), **code** (20c, 23d, 27b, 119a), **dodo** (19b, 38c, 225), **gods**, **hods**, **iodo-** (93b), **Jody** (161), **lode** (35a, 76b, 84c, 127d), **Lodi** (80d), **Lodz** (221), **mode** (44c, 74d, 116d, 130c), **node** (66c, 68c, 90d, 95c, 118c), **nods**, **-poda** (117c), **pods**, **Roda** (81d), **rode** (38b), **rods**, **soda** (18d, 38a, 111c, 131c), **Sodi** (197), **sods**, **Toda** (37d), **Todd** (183), **to-do** (21b, 22d, 29b, 52c, 115c), **tods**, **tody** (19b)

_ _ O D    **apod** (48c), **clod** (21a, 37b, 83a, 116d), **Exod.** (238), **food** (44b, 56d, 82d, 128b), **good** (127a, 131a), **Hood** (79b), **hood** (19c, 31c, 52c, 58c), **mood** (10d, 36c, 122d), **plod** (124d, 129b), **pood** (246), **prod** (38a, 46a, 54d, 59c, 62c, 63b, 65b, 81b, 82d, 90d, 121d, 126c), **quod** (94d, 96a), **rood** (32a), **shod**, **trod**, **Wood** (187), **wood** (55a)

O _ _ D    **Obad.** (241), **Obed** (103c, 197), **olid** (49a, 116c), **Ovid** (102a), **owed**

O E _ _    **oeno-** (94a), **oeuf** (50b)

394

**_ O E _**  Boer (10c, 112b), coed (107b), coef. (237), -coel (117a), Coen (146), Doeg (197), doer (87d), does, foes, goel (16a), goer, GOES (239), goes, hoed, hoer, hoes, Joel (161, 196, 197), Joes, Joey (161), joey (67a, 134d), koel (32c), Moes, Noel (172), noel (24b, 27a, 111d), noes (81b), poem (128a), poet (40b), Roeg (178), roes, toea (221), toed, toes, woes, Zoes

**_ _ O E**  aloe (10c, 19c, 59b, 59c, 71d, 75c, 90a, 122d), BPOE (236), evoe (16a, 100b), floe (61b), froe (28a, 122d, 123a, 130d), oboe (58b, 80a, 80c, 133c), Otoe (109d, 189), shoe (122b), sloe (15b, 19d, 51d, 90b, 132a)

**O _ _ E**  Oahe (33b), oboe (58b, 80a, 80c, 133c), ogee (14a, 77d, 90c), Ogle (173), ogle (43c, 71a, 73a), ogre (78b), ohne (54a), Okie (76d), olpe (70d, 132c), once (18b, 49a, 61d, 63d), onde (51b), ooze (43c, 72b, 79c, 87d), orfe (46d, 134b), orle (46a, 59b, 108a), Orne (23a), oste (20d), Otoe (109d, 189), Ouse (101a, 134d, 223)

**O F _ _**  offs (32a, 118d)

**_ O F _**  doff (99c, 119a), loft (15c, 55b, 129d), sofa (36d), soft (39b, 74c, 76d), toff (33c), toft (60d)

**_ _ O F**  goof (28b), hoof (126b), IOOF (240), Olof (173), Prof. (242), roof (61c), woof (32b, 37b, 121c, 131a)

**O _ _ F**  oeuf (50b), Olaf (82b, 128b, 173), Olof (173)

**O G _ _**  ogam (64b), ogee (14a, 77d, 90c), oggi (65c), Ogle (173), ogle (43c, 71a, 73a), OGPU (103c), ogre (78b), ogum (64b)

**_ O G _**  bogs, bogy (13c, 113b), cogs, doge (74a, 127d), dogs, dogy (38c), fogs, fogy (83d), Gogo (17a), gogo (111b), hogs, jogs, loge (120d), logo (22d, 29b), logs, logy (38c), mogo (115d), nogg (11b), nogs, Pogo (83d, 91d), pogy (68d, 75d, 78d), soga (52c), toga (101d), Togo (223), togs (28b), yoga (14d, 60a), yogh (12c), Yogi (187), yogi (60a)

**_ _ O G**  agog (39a, 42c, 67b), clog (20a, 108c), flog (131c), frog (17c, 225), geog. (239), grog (11a, 72b, 113d), slog (38b, 124d, 129b), smog (130d)

**O _ _ G**  olig- (93a), Oreg. (241), orig. (241)

**O H _ _**  Ohio (211), ohms, ohne (54a)

**_ O H _**  Bohr (15c, 33c, 142), Cohn (146), coho (103d), Doha (221), John (13b, 18a, 88b, 91b, 107c, 135a, 162, 193, 196), Kohl (18c, 164), kohl (43c), moho (60d), mohr (53b), poha (58c), Pohl (175), So-Ho (73a), to-ho (61d)

**_ _ O H**  Groh (156), pooh (42c)

**O _ _ H**  oath (90b, 111c), opah (22a, 46d), orch. (241), orth- (92d), ouch (42c, 63a)

**O I _ _**    oils, oily (44c, 83d, 126a)

**_ O I _**    boil (30c), bois (51b), coif (57b), coil (32d, 114a, 125c, 132b, 134a), coin (77b), coir (28d, 30d, 45c, 102b), coix (66c), doit (38d), FOIA (238), foil (16b, 45b, 76b, 116d, 121d), Foix (49c), join (30a, 126c), koil (32c), loin (33a, 75c), loir (37c), Lois (118a), moil (20c, 133d), noil (45d, 68c), noir (50a, 102c), roil (79c, 115c), soie (51a), soil (39a, 114c, 117d, 120d), soir (50b), toil (38b, 124d, 133c, 133d), void (12d, 40c, 82d, 127a)

**_ _ O I**    a moi (50d), Eloi (122b)

**O _ _ I**    oggi (65c), Omei (22b), omni- (92d), Omri (67d, 197), ophi- (93d), ossi- (92c)

**_ O J _**    mojo (129c), rojo (113a), soja (56c)

**O K _ _**    okas, okay (10b, 13d, 86d, 112a), Okie (76d), Okla. (211, 241), okra (57a, 127c)

**_ O K _**    Aoki (139), coke (28c, 52a, 62d), joke (66b), Koko (73a, 134d), koko (86d), koku (246), Loki (10b, 16c, 198), moke (37c), Moki (95d), poke (65b, 82d, 96a), poku (13a, 130b), poky (110d), roka (74a, 124a), soke (67c), woke, yoke (66c, 232), Yoko (187)

**_ _ O K**    amok (18c, 51b), book (71c, 129a), Cook (79a, 104b, 146), cook (68a), dook (77a), gook (110c), hook (24d, 27d, 55b), kook (39c), look (13c, 15a, 22b, 43d, 106b, 118b, 128c), nook (30d, 100a), rook (19b, 26c, 32b, 226), sook (23b), took (83b)

**O _ _ K**    Omsk (64b)

**O L _ _**    Olaf (82b, 128b, 173), olax (42b), olea (84a), oleo- (93b), Olga (173), olid (49a, 116c), olig- (93a), Olin (173), olio (36b, 60c, 75d, 77b, 92a), olla (30c, 36b, 66a, 112b, 113a, 131d), Olof (173), olor (118b), olpe (70d, 132c)

**_ O L _**    bola (53a), bold (33d), bole (27d, 98c, 124b), Böll (142), boll (90a, 90c), bolo (68a, 130d), Bolt (142), bolt (44c, 47c, 67a, 101c), COLA (237), cola (82d, 124a), cold (53b, 62a), Cole (146), coll. (237), Colm (146), Colo. (209, 237), colp (25c), cols, colt (61b, 100b, 134d, 135a), coly (79b), Dole (58c, 149), dole (91d, 99b, 131a), doll (45b, 96a), dolt (20a, 48b, 109c, 116d), fold (57d, 90b, 107d), -fold (117c), folk (87d, 124b), Gola (218), gola (33c, 37c, 77d), gold (74a, 134b, 245), golf (12a), hold (9c, 15a, 16c, 27d, 67b, 74b, 95b, 100a, 115a, 121a, 234), hole (9c, 13b, 84b, 89c, 109d), Holm (158), holm (60c, 64b, 83a), holo- (94a), Holt (158), holt (30c), holy (30b), lole (42a, 59c, 94c), joli (50d), Jolo (64d), jolt (20a, 66a, 108b), Kola (103c), kola (82d), koli (24d), Koln (100b, 216), kolo (48b, 106d), Lola (25b, 75a, 167), loll (38a, 73b, 98b), Lolo (69a, 215), mold (44c, 107c), Mole (69a), mole (19b, 22d, 106a, 114d, 230), Moll (171), moll (52d), molt (24d, 107d), moly (59b, 132a), Oola (11c), Pola (175), pole (101c, 113a, 129b,

133b, 246), **Polk** (175, 190), **poll** (129c), **Polo** (127d), **poly-** (93b), **role** (52a, 86d), **roll** (118c), **sola** (11d, 39b, 89c), **sold**, **sole** (42c, 46d, 47d, 84b, 87c, 109d, 111d, 228), **soli** (14b), **solo** (11d, 14b, 84a), **Sols**, **tola** (66d, 103a), **told** (99a), **tole** (41b, 76b), **toll** (18c, 94b, 100d), **tolu** (16d), **vola** (111c), **vole** (75b, 79b, 110b, 111b, 231), **volk** (54a), **volt** (40a, 61b, 246), **wold** (38d, 126d), **Wolf** (187, 207), **wolf** (23d, 231), **yolk** (128d), **Zola** (49c, 188)

_ _ O L    **AWOL** (236), **biol.** (236), **chol-** (92c), **chol.** (236), **cool** (23b, 82a), **ecol.** (238), **enol** (120a), **fool** (20b, 22c, 34a, 38d, 61d, 78d, 109c, 116d), **gaol** (94d), **geol.** (239), **Idol** (159), **idol** (39d, 44a, 44d, 58d, 62a, 85b, 133d), **obol** (26b, 83d), **pool** (52b, 90c, 91b, 130a), **STOL** (243), **tool** (25a, 62b, 127c), **viol** (80b), **VTOL** (244), **wool** (47c), **zool.** (244)

O _ _ L    **Obal** (197), **obol** (26b, 83d), **ocul-** (92d), **opal** (19c, 53b, 54c, 64a), **oral** (79b, 113d, 127c, 128a), **Orel** (173), **oval** (39d, 40b)

O M _ _    **Oman** (220), **Omar** (41c, 78d, 88a, 120c, 173, 197), **Omei** (22b), **omen** (15d, 48c, 48d, 91c, 94a, 109b), **omer** (59a), **omit** (40b, 81b, 87a, 110a), **omni-** (92d), **Omri** (67d, 197), **Omsk** (64b)

_ O M _    **boma** (10c), **bomb** (107d, 130c), **coma** (71c, 116a, 126a), **comb** (31d), **come** (94d), **comm.** (237), **Como** (68b, 146), **Comp.** (237), **comr.** (237), **dome** (32d, 102a), **doms**, **home** (61c, 99d), **homo** (69d), **homo-** (93c), **Homs** (222), **loma** (59d), **Lome** (223), **moms**, **noma** (52c), **nomo-** (92d), **-nomy** (117c), **pome** (51d), **Pomo** (189), **pomp** (85a, 85b), **Rome** (13c, 27c, 41d, 218), **romp** (51c), **soma** (12d, 20c, 62d), **some** (86d, 96b), **tomb** (22d), **tome** (20d, 129a), **Toms**, **-tomy** (117b), **womb** (127c)

_ _ O M    **Ahom** (69a), **atom** (77d, 131c), **boom** (43a, 112a, 113a), **brom-** (92c), **coom** (28c), **doom** (35b, 44d, 54b), **E-COM** (238), **Edom** (41c, 61d, 64b, 65b), **from** (18b, 115a), **geom.** (239), **glom** (115a), **loom** (13c, 40c, 57d, 109b, 130d), **PROM** (29c, 242), **prom** (33b), **room** (25d), **whom** (34d, 96d), **zoom** (23c)

O _ _ M    **ogam** (64b), **ogum** (64b), **ovum** (39d, 69c), **Ozem** (197)

O N _ _    **Onan** (66d), **onca** (246), **once** (18b, 49a, 61d, 63d), **onde** (51b), **ones** (87d), **only** (11d, 22d, 42c, 76a, 111d), **on to** (59b), **onus** (22d, 72d, 83a, 131a), **onyx** (23c, 25d, 53b, 106c)

_ O N _    **a-one** (42b, 46c, 123b), **Bona** (79b, 192), **bona** (69d, 70a), **Bond** (142), **bond** (10a, 28d, 71d, 72b, 78a, 107b, 118a, 122a), **bone** (46a, 110a), **bong** (111a), **Bonn** (18b, 216), **Bono** (142), **bony** (110a), **conc.** (237), **cond.** (237), **Cone** (146), **cone** (53c, 116c, 111d), **conf.** (237), **cong.** (237), **conj.** (237), **conk** (60b, 116b), **Conn.** (209, 237), **conn** (35d), **cons**, **cont.** (237), **cony** (97a), **don't**, **dona** (91d), **done** (85c), **dong** (224), **doni** (25d), **dons** (85d), **eons**, **fond** (10b, 73c), **font** (17a, 125d), **Gond** (62d), **gone** (9b, 34d, 36c), **gong** (80a), **goni-** (92c), **gono-** (93c), **Hond.** (239), **hone** (39c, 107d, 131c), **hong** (26d), **honk** (55b, 112b), **Iona** (25c, 64b,

202), **lone** (22c, 69b, 73d), **ions**, **Jong** (163), **Joni** (163), **Jons**, **lone** (109d, 111d), **Long** (167), **long** (31d), **Loni** (167), **lonk** (107d), **Mona** (171), **mona** (56d), **Monk** (171), **monk** (25c, 51c), **mono** (61c), **mono-** (93c), **mons** (69d, 133d), **Mont.** (211, 240), **mont** (50d), **Nona** (86c), **none** (82c), **Oona** (173), **oont** (23c, 230), **pond** (91b, 130a), **pone** (30d, 66c), **Pong** (125a), **Pons** (49d, 175), **pont** (50a), **pony** (26b, 33b, 61a), **sone** (246), **song** (14b, 61d, 125a), **sons** (83c), **Tone** (184), **tone** (9c, 82c, 89c), **tong** (26d), **Toni** (184), **tono-** (93c), **tons**, **Tony** (184), **Wong** (187), **wont** (9c, 33a, 57a, 92b), **yond** (36d), **zona** (108a), **zone** (18c, 36d, 40d, 118b)

**_ _ O N**   **aeon** (122b), **agon** (30b, 45c, 56b), **Amon** (67d, 198), **anon** (10c, 15d, 62a, 94a, 108d, 111d), **anon.** (235), **aton** (118a), **Avon** (107c), **axon** (81b), **azon** (10b), **Bion** (56b), **boon** (18c, 20a), **cion** (83c), **coon** (97a), **Dion** (149, 195), **Doon** (101a), **ebon** (19d), **econ.** (238), **Elon** (41c, 82b, 201), **Eton** (58b, 65b), **faon** (44d), **gaon** (66c), **goon** (116c), **hoon** (246), **icon** (62a, 103b), **ikon** (62a), **iron** (45b, 45c, 55a, 57c, 74c, 75b, 245), **jeon** (218), **Khon** (223), **Leon** (166, 222), **Lion** (193), **lion** (94b, 230), **loon** (19a, 19b, 226), **Lyon** (216), **Moon** (171), **moon** (33a, 104b), **muon** (71b), **neon** (53a, 71d, 245), **noon** (76c), **Oxon** (85d), **paon** (87b), **peon** (48c, 76c), **phon** (73b), **phon-** (93c), **pion** (42b), **poon** (103d, 124b), **-sion** (117a), **soon** (94a, 108d), **-tion** (117a, 117b), **toon** (74b), **-tron** (117b), **upon** (9b), **zion** (95a), **zoon** (39d)

**O _ _ N**   **Odin** (10b, 51c, 133b, 198), **Olin** (173), **Oman** (220), **omen** (15d, 48c, 48d, 91c, 94a, 109b), **Onan** (66d), **open** (18b, 23c, 49b, 63a, 83b, 85c, 95d, 126a, 126b, 126c), **Oran** (213), **oven** (61c, 67b), **oxen** (12d, 21b), **Oxon** (85d)

**O O _ _**   **Oola** (11c), **Oona** (173), **oont** (23c, 230), **ooze** (43c, 72b, 79c, 87d), **oozy** (106b, 110c)

**_ O O _**   **boob** (109c), **book** (71c, 129a), **boom** (43a, 112a, 113a), **boon** (18c, 20a), **boor** (17a, 38c, 88a, 103c), **boos**, **boot** (29c, 67b, 124d), **Cook** (79a, 104b, 146), **cook** (68a), **cool** (23b, 82a), **coom** (28c), **coon** (97a), **coop** (40d), **Coos** (189), **coos**, **coot** (19a, 38c, 56d, 75a, 83d, 105a, 225), **doob** (18c), **dook** (77a), **doom** (35b, 44d, 54b), **Doon** (101a), **door** (41b, 91c), **food** (44b, 56d, 82d, 128b), **fool** (20b, 22c, 34a, 38d, 61d, 78d, 109c, 116d), **foot** (17b, 87b, 246), **good** (127a, 131a), **goof** (28b), **gook** (110c), **goon** (116c), **goop** (110c), **Hood** (79b), **hood** (19c, 31c, 52c, 58c), **hoof** (126b), **hook** (24d, 27d, 55b), **hoon** (246), **hoop** (131d), **Hoot** (158), **hoot** (85c), **IOOF** (240), **kook** (39c), **look** (13c, 15a, 22b, 43d, 106b, 118b, 128c), **loom** (13c, 40c, 57d, 109b, 130d), **loon** (19a, 19b, 226), **loop** (27b, 82a), **Loos** (167), **loot** (21a, 58b, 89b, 90c, 103a, 113d), **mood** (10d, 36c, 122d), **Moon** (171), **moon** (33a, 104b), **Moor** (78c, 104b, 219), **moor** (12c, 15c, 58d, 130a), **moos**, **moot** (36d), **nook** (30d, 100a), **noon** (76c), **pood** (246), **pooh** (42c), **pool** (52b, 90c, 91b, 130a), **poon** (103d, 124b), **poop** (20c, 34b, 108b), **poor** (28d), **rood** (32a), **roof** (61c), **rook** (19b, 26c, 32b, 226), **room** (25d), **Roos** (53d), **Root** (178), **root** (17b, 17c, 102d), **sook** (23b), **soon** (94a, 108d), **soot** (24a, 28c, 68d), **took**

398

(83b), **tool** (25a, 62b, 127c), **toon** (74b), **toot** (112b), **Wood** (187), **wood** (55a), **woof** (32b, 37b, 121c, 131a), **wool** (47c), **woos, zool.** (244), **zoom** (23c), **zoon** (39d), **zoos, Zoot** (188)

_ _ O O    **broo** (105a), **ejoo** (45a), **shoo** (38a, 54b)

O _ _ O    **octo** (69c), **octo-** (92d), **odio** (65a), **oeno-** (94a), **Ohio** (211), **oleo-** (93b), **olio** (36b, 60c, 75d, 77b, 92a), **on to** (59b), **ordo** (21a, 27a, 92b), **orlo** (46a, 90b), **Oslo** (220), **Otho** (102a), **otro** (112c, 113a), **Otto** (53c, 173), **otto** (65a), **ouzo** (11a)

O P _ _    **opah** (22a, 46d), **opal** (19c, 53b, 54c, 64a), **OPEC** (241), **open** (18b, 23c, 49b, 63a, 83b, 85c, 95d, 126a, 126b, 126c), **ophi-** (93d), **-opia** (117b, 117c), **opts, opus** (29c, 80c, 129a, 133c)

_ O P _    **bops, cope** (23d, 30b, 30d, 52d, 128a), **copr-** (92d), **cops, Copt** (39d), **copy** (40c, 62a), **dopa** (89a), **dope** (10b, 38b, 81a), **dopp** (32d), **dopy** (71c), **fops, HOPE** (239), **Hope** (158), **hope** (42d), **Hopi** (95d, 189), **hops** (18a), **koph** (12a), **Kops** (67b), **lope** (39b, 52a, 52b), **lops, mope** (22a, 117d), **mops, mopy** (72b), **nope** (81b), **Pope** (27c, 175), **pope** (19c, 27a, 91b), **pops, rope** (30d, 69b, 100b), **ropy** (116b), **soph.** (243), **sops, tope** (107d, 229), **topi** (30d, 89c), **topo.** (243), **tops**

_ _ O P    **alop** (38a), **atop** (85c, 126a), **chop** (75c), **clop** (61a), **coop** (40d), **crop** (31d, 108d), **drop** (44a, 48d, 77a, 84a, 86d, 90b, 90c, 110d, 120a), **flop** (44a), **glop** (75b), **goop** (110c), **hoop** (131d), **knop** (68c), **loop** (27b, 82a), **plop** (44a, 130b), **poop** (20c, 34b, 108b), **prop** (118a), **scop** (90c), **shop** (62d, 100a), **slop** (48b, 111b), **stop** (9a, 14c, 17a, 25b, 40d, 57c, 84c, 131d), **trop** (51b, 123a), **whop** (60b)

O R _ _    **oral** (79b, 113d, 127c, 128a), **Oran** (213), **orbs, orca** (67b), **orch.** (241), **orcs, ordo** (21a, 27a, 92b), **Oreb** (197), **Oreg.** (241), **Orel** (173), **ores, orfe** (46d, 134b), **orgy** (24b, 100b, 104b), **orig.** (241), **orle** (46a, 59b, 108a), **orlo** (46a, 90b), **Orne** (23a), **orth-** (92d), **orts** (105c), **oryx** (13a, 231)

_ O R _    **bora** (132b), **bord** (77a), **bore** (23b, 37d, 87d, 121d), **Borg** (142), **Born** (142), **born** (71d, 81a, 81b), **boro** (114a), **Bors** (102c), **bort** (35c), **Boru** (142), **Cora** (34d, 126a), **cora** (53b), **Cord** (146), **cord** (32c, 43b), **CORE** (237), **core** (25c, 41d, 58d), **corf** (28c), **Cork** (217), **cork** (90b, 116a, 132c, 133b), **corm** (22c, 115a), **corn** (74b, 94b), **Corp.** (237), **Dora** (30c, 33d, 35c), **Dore** (49c), **dore** (54b, 89a), **dorm** (104d), **Dorn** (149), **dorp** (57c, 128b), **dorr** (54c), **Dors** (149), **dory** (20b, 47b), **fora** (75a, 101d), **forb** (59c), **Ford** (153, 191, 194), **ford** (129a), **fore** (51c, 108b), **fork** (13c, 36d, 37a, 119a), **form** (44c, 107c, 127a), **fort** (51c, 116c), **Gore** (155, 191), **gore** (87c, 88d, 124b), **Gort** (101b), **gory** (20a), **hora** (21a, 33b), **Horn** (24a), **horn** (13a, 31a, 124d), **hors** (50d), **hort.** (239), **Jory** (163), **kora** (130b), **kori** (10b, 60a), **Lord** (167), **lord** (82a), **lore** (60b, 70d, 71b, 132d), **Lori** (167), **lorn** (49a), **loro** (86d), **lory** (86d), **mora** (46b, 48c, 52b, 56d, 65a, 76b, 118d), **More** (171), **more** (43c, 56a),

**morn** (33d), **Moro** (171), **moro** (88c), **Mors** (34a, 198), **Mort** (171), **Nora** (61b, 81d, 172), **Nore** (120d), **nori** (11b, 105d), **Norm** (172), **norm** (16a, 86b, 97d, 114d), **Norn** (82a), **porc** (50d), **pore** (48c, 84b, 84d), **pork** (55c, 75c), **porn** (79c), **Port.** (242), **port** (58a, 132c), **Rory** (178), **sora** (19a, 97b), **sorb** (13c, 79a, 107a, 110b), **sore** (12d, 106c), **sori** (45b), **sors** (69c), **sort** (27d, 36d, 67c, 106d, 109b, 113b, 127b, 132d), **tora** (13a, 58b), **tore**, **Tori** (184), **tori** (30c), **Torn** (184), **torn** (99c), **toro** (31c, 112c), **torr** (246), **tors**, **tort** (27c, 71a, 134c), **tory** (22a, 30b, 73c), **-vora** (117c), **-vore** (117c), **word** (95a, 120c, 121d), **wore**, **work** (52a, 116c), **worm** (88a), **worn** (107b), **wort** (59b, 92a), **yore** (12c, 23a, 55b, 73a, 83d, 87a, 122b), **York** (41a, 187, 192, 193, 194), **zori** (108c)

_ _ O R  **amor** (112d), **Amor** (32d, 198), **asor** (59a), **-ator** (117c), **boor** (17a, 38c, 88a, 103c), **Dior** (149), **door** (41b, 91c), **flor** (46a, 108a), **ghor** (127b), **Gyor** (217), **Igor** (49b, 159), **Ivor** (159), **Moor** (78c, 104b, 219), **moor** (12c, 15c, 58d, 130a), **odor** (104d, 111a, 115b), **olor** (118b), **poor** (28d), **spor-** (93d), **Thor** (10b, 76c, 77b, 83b, 121d, 183, 198)

O _ _ R  **Oder** (100d), **odor** (104d, 111a, 115b), **olor** (118b), **Omar** (41c, 78d, 88a, 120c, 173, 197), **omer** (59a), **over** (9b, 9d, 14c, 32a, 87a, 99c), **oyer** (31c)

O S _ _  **OSHA** (241), **-osis** (117a), **Oslo** (220), **Ossa** (79a, 84a, 121a), **ossa** (20d), **ossi-** (92c), **oste** (20d)

_ O S _  **bosa** (13d), **bosc** (87b), **bosh** (82a), **bosk** (133b), **bo's'n** (20c, 88b), **boss** (40c, 116c), **cosh** (60b), **cosm-** (93d), **cost** (26a, 94b), **dose** (94a), **doss** (18a), **dost** (128a), **foss** (36d), **gosh** (42a, 53b), **hose** (115c), **hosp.** (239), **host** (14c, 42a, 79d), **José** (163), **Josh** (163), **josh** (17a, 66b, 66d, 90d), **joss** (26d, 62c), **Koso** (108d), **koss** (246), **lose** (48d), **losh** (40b), **loss** (35a, 94d, 130a), **LOST** (240), **lost** (77b, 130a), **Moss** (171), **moss** (71c, 86c, 125a), **most** (74b, 78c), **nose** (89d, 95c), **noso-** (92d), **Nosu** (215), **nosy** (63b), **pose** (9d, 15c, 94b), **posh** (21a, 40b), **Post** (175), **post** (69c, 74b, 81c, 115a), **posy** (82b, 100d), **Rosa** (178), **Rose** (9a, 178), **Ross** (178, 193, 195, 207, 208), **ross** (17b, 119c), **rosy** (54d, 84c), **so-so** (76c, 86d, 122d), **tosh** (82a), **Tosk** (213), **toss** (22c, 47c, 121c)

_ _ O S  **Amos** (108a, 138, 196, 197), **apos.** (235), **boos**, **Bros.** (236), **Coos** (189), **coos**, **dios** (112d), **duos**, **egos** (9d, 42a, 107a, 151, 197), **Enos** (9d, 42a, 107a, 151, 197), **epos** (41b, 59c, 90c), **Eros** (32d, 132c, 195, 198), **glos.** (239), **Gros** (49c), **gros** (38c, 43d, 109c), **Keos** (64c), **Laos** (218), **Leos**, **Loos** (167), **mhos**, **moos**, **naos** (25b, 104a, 120b), **pros**, **rhos**, **Roos** (53d), **Taos** (81c), **Teos** (64a), **Thos.** (74d), **thos** (65b), **twos**, **udos**, **woos**, **zoos**

O _ _ S  **oafs**, **oaks**, **oars**, **oats**, **obis**, **Ochs** (173), **odds** (10b, 11c, 26a, 95c), **odes**, **-odus** (117c), **offs** (32a, 118d), **ohms**, **oils**, **okas**, **ones** (87d), **onus** (22d, 72d, 83a, 131a), **opts**, **opus** (29c, 80c, 129a, 133c), **orbs**, **orcs**, **ores**, **orts** (105c), **-osis** (117a), **Otis** (12b, 63d, 173), **otus** (54b), **ours** (95a), **outs**, **owes**, **owls**, **owns** (91d), **oyes** (31c, 32c, 58d)

**O T _ _**   **Otea** (64c), **Otho** (102a), **otic** (15d, 39a), **Otis** (12b, 63d, 173), **Otoe** (109d, 189), **otro** (112c, 113a), **Otto** (53c, 173), **otto** (65a), **otus** (54b)

**_ O T _**   **both** (122c, 125c), **bots, bott** (27d), **cote** (19b, 107d, 108a), **coto** (17b, 75c), **cots, Coty** (49d, 147), **dote** (85c), **doth** (128a), **dots, Goth** (120d), **Hoth** (20a), **iota** (11d, 66d, 122c, 131c), **jota** (112c), **jots, koto** (66a), **Loti** (49c, 95d), **loti** (218), **lots** (26a), **Lott** (167), **mote** (113b), **Moth** (193), **moth** (22d, 71b, 229), **moto** (79c), **mots, Mott** (171), **nota** (69d), **note** (15c, 71c, 75d, 83b, 95a, 98c, 99c, 122d, 129c, 234), **noto-** (92c), **pots, rota** (25a, 27a, 31c, 101d, 102b), **ROTC** (242), **Rote** (178), **rote** (75d, 99d, 118a), **Roth** (178), **roti** (51a), **rots, sots, tote** (22a, 24c, 86c), **toti-** (94a), **Toto** (37b, 133a), **tots, vota** (102a), **vote** (49b, 128d)

**_ _ O T**   **blot** (115b), **boot** (29c, 67b, 124d), **clot** (28c, 73c), **coot** (19a, 38c, 56d, 75a, 83d, 105a, 225), **foot** (17b, 87b, 246), **Hoot** (158), **hoot** (85c), **knot** (76d, 82a, 232), **loot** (21a, 58b, 89b, 90c, 103a, 113d), **moot** (36d), **phot** (246), **plot** (23a, 30b, 104d, 123c), **Prot.** (242), **riot** (85a, 101c, 125a), **Root** (178), **root** (17b, 17c, 102d), **ryot** (62d), **Scot** (59d), **Scot.** (242), **shot** (12b, 70c), **slot** (12d, 13b, 34c, 84b, 123c), **snot** (62c, 88a), **soot** (24a, 28c, 68d), **spot** (35d, 72d, 79d, 89d, 114c), **stot** (134d), **toot** (112b), **trot** (66c, 85b), **Zoot** (188)

**O _ _ T**   **oast** (16b, 67b, 85c), **obit.** (34a, 52c, 241), **omit** (40b, 81b, 87a, 110a), **oont** (23c, 230), **oust** (35b, 40a, 42b, 96c)

**O U _ _**   **ouch** (42c, 63a), **ours** (95a), **Ouse** (101a, 134d, 223), **oust** (35b, 40a, 42b, 96c), **outs, ouzo** (11a)

**_ O U _**   **aout** (49d), **bout** (30b), **coup** (75b, 116c, 120b), **Doug** (150), **dour** (54d, 78d, 107b, 117d), **-eous** (117a), **foud** (44c, 74a), **foul** (9a, 126b), **four** (72c, 120d), **gout** (14d, 113d), **hour** (122b), **-ious** (117a), **loud** (115b), **loup** (50d, 51b, 105c), **lour** (33d, 54d), **lout** (21a, 83a), **moue** (50d, 134c), **noun** (86d, 116d), **nous** (50d, 51b), **pouf** (48c, 58d, 85a), **pour** (120a), **pout** (117d), **roue** (34a, 97c), **roup** (92a), **rout** (34c, 36c), **roux** (104b), **souk** (17d, 74d), **Soul** (181), **soul** (95d, 113d, 128c), **soup** (75c), **sour** (15b, 119d), **sous** (51b), **tour** (66d), **tous** (49d), **tout** (49d, 95a. 97b), **vous** (51b), **Wouk** (187), **you'd** (30c), **your** (95a)

**_ _ O U**   **abou** (44d), **acou-** (93a), **Alou** (138), **Chou** (26d), **chou** (50a), **clou** (50d), **shou** (26d), **thou** (95b)

**O _ _ U**   **Oahu** (64c), **OGPU** (103c)

**O V _ _**   **oval** (39d, 40b), **oven** (61c, 67b), **over** (9b, 9d, 14c, 32a, 87a, 99c), **Ovid** (102a), **ovum** (39d, 69c)

**_ O V _**   **cove** (17d, 58a, 130a), **Dove** (150), **dove** (19a, 89a, 225), **govt.** (239), **Hova** (219), **hove** (71d), **Jove** (67c, 198), **Love** (167), **love** (24b, 120c), **move** (10d, 36b, 62b, 125b), **Nova** (203), **nova** (114d), **nove** (65c), **rove** (97d, 101a, 129d), **wove**

_ _ O V   **Azov** (19d, 103c), **Lvov** (223), **Prov.** (242)

O W _ _   **owed, owes, owls, owns** (91d)

_ O W _   **Bowe** (142), **bowk** (115a), **bowl** (78d, 119a), **bows, cowl** (78b), **cows** (21b), **dowd** (107b), **Down** (150), **down** (35a, 45a, 232), **fowd** (44c, 74a), **fowl** (19b), **gown** (37d), **Howe** (17c, 63d, 159), **howl** (12d, 17d, 32b, 114b), **Iowa** (189, 210), **jowl** (26b, 35c), **Lowe** (167), **lows, mown, mows, rows, sown, sows, town** (57c, 128b), **tows, vows, wows, yowl** (12d, 32b)

_ _ O W   **alow** (18c, 126a), **avow** (9d, 15a, 16c, 29d, 30a, 34b, 85c), **blow** (42d), **brow** (48d, 59d), **chow** (37a, 227), **clow** (47c, 110d), **Crow** (189), **crow** (19b, 19d, 20b, 43c, 225), **dhow** (69b, 84d), **enow** (105a), **flow** (14b, 37d, 116b), **frow** (123a), **glow** (108a), **grow** (15d, 41a, 42d, 43a, 114a, 118c), **know** (13a, 16c), **meow** (25a), **plow** (32c, 122a), **prow** (20c, 108b, 115b), **scow** (20c, 47b), **show** (9d, 34d, 35a, 36c, 43a, 74c), **slow** (34a, 35d, 58a, 110d, 116d), **Snow** (181), **snow** (130d), **stow** (85b), **trow** (18b)

O X _ _   **oxen** (12d, 21b), **Oxon** (85d)

_ O X _   **coxa** (60b), **doxy** (133b), **Foxx** (153), **foxy** (14d, 31d, 132a), **moxa** (25b, 26d, 133d)

_ _ O X   **Knox** (49a)

O _ _ X   **obex** (21c), **olax** (42b), **onyx** (23c, 25d, 53b, 106c), **oryx** (13a, 231)

O Y _ _   **oyer** (31c), **oyes** (31c, 32c, 58d), **oyez** (31c, 32c, 58d)

_ O Y _   **Boyd** (142), **boys, coyo** (16a, 26d), **Foyt** (153), **Goya** (112c), **hoya** (12c, 15d, 130c), **Hoyt** (159), **joys, Roys, soya** (112c), **soys, toyo** (58b, 65d, 116b), **toys, yoyo** (88a)

_ _ O Y   **ahoy** (57b, 81a), **Amoy** (69a), **buoy** (26a, 47c), **choy** (39b, 98c), **cloy** (54d, 104b, 118a), **ploy** (14d, 116a), **Troy** (184), **troy** (119c, 131a)

O _ _ Y   **obey** (29c, 59a, 67b, 10a), **O'Day** (173), **oily** (44c, 83d, 126a), **okay** (10b, 13d, 86d, 112a), **only** (11d, 22d, 42c, 76a, 111d), **oozy** (106b, 110c), **orgy** (24b, 100b, 104b), **Ozzy** (173)

O Z _ _   **Ozem** (197), **Ozzy** (173)

_ O Z _   **boza** (13d), **bozo** (38d, 88a), **Cozy** (147), **cozy** (39b, 111b), **doze** (110b), **dozy** (110c), **kozo** (86b), **ooze** (43c, 72b, 79c, 87d), **oozy** (106b, 110c)

O _ _ Z   **oyez** (31c, 32c, 58d)

P A _ _   **Paar** (173), **PABA** (86b), **paca** (25b, 101c), **Pace** (204), **pace** (52a, 113c, 129b), **pack** (16d, 22c, 105c, 232, 246), **paco** (11d, 109c),

**pact** (10d, 11c, 17b, 20d), **pads**, **Page** (173, 193, 194), **page** (12d, 41c, 48b, 70d, 107a), **paha** (60a), **paid** (99a), **pail** (30b), **pain** (10b, 61d), **pair** (21c, 31b, 90d, 119c, 125c), **pale** (19d, 86a, 88d, 129d), **Pali** (22b, 104b, 127c), **pall** (28b, 122b, 130d), **palm** (124a), **palp** (13a, 45a, 123b), **pals**, **Pams**, **pane** (114c, 114d), **Pang** (125a), **pang** (85d, 114b, 121c), **pans**, **pant** (18a, 21d), **paon** (87b), **papa** (12a, 44b), **Papp** (173), **paps**, **Para** (18b, 214), **para** (112d, 214, 215, 222, 224), **pard** (24d), **pare** (87c, 98d), **pari-** (92d), **park** (53b, 95d), **parr** (103d, 109d), **pars**, **part** (11c, 43d, 49b, 57b, 91d, 106d), **pass** (13d, 21d, 84a, 85c, 106c), **past** (55b, 60b, 122a), **Pate** (174), **pate** (32b, 58c), **path** (101a, 102c, 130c), **pats**, **patu** (130d), **Paul** (18a, 91b, 174), **pave** (66b), **Pavo** (87b, 207), **pawl** (73d), **pawn** (26c, 60c, 90b), **paws**, **pays**

_ P A _     **apar** (14b), **opah** (22a, 46d), **opal** (19c, 53b, 54c, 64a), **spad** (80b, 89d), **Spam** (73c), **span** (21d, 32a, 38d, 49a, 81d, 85d, 98a, 120a, 120c, 122a, 232), **spar** (21b, 22c, 52a, 77a, 90d, 101c, 108b), **spas**, **spat** (14b, 85d, 96b, 102c), **spay** (115b), **upas** (66a, 90d, 124a)

_ _ P A     **arpa** (65a), **capa** (122c), **dopa** (89a), **FEPA** (238), **Hupa** (15b, 189), **Napa** (23b, 132c), **napa** (54d, 70d), **nipa** (15b, 38a, 39b, 86a, 120d), **papa** (12a, 44b), **pupa** (27a, 28d, 63b), **sapa** (55d), **tapa** (17b, 28b, 43b, 45c, 79d, 86b, 91a)

P _ _ A     **PABA** (86b), **paca** (25b, 101c), **paha** (60a), **papa** (12a, 44b), **Para** (18b, 214), **para** (112d, 214, 215, 222, 224), **peba** (14b), **pega** (46d), **Peña** (174), **pica** (53c, 125d), **pika** (30c, 72c, 101c, 231), **Pima** (189), **pima** (31a), **pina** (29d), **Pisa** (70d), **pita** (11d, 25c, 45c), **plea** (42d, 92b, 118a), **-poda** (117c), **poha** (58c), **Pola** (175), **proa** (20c, 23d, 74b), **pula** (214), **puma** (24d, 31b, 79a, 231), **Puna** (12c), **puna** (28d, 90b, 132b), **pupa** (27a, 28d, 63b), **pyla** (21c)

P _ _ B     **pleb** (29b)

_ P C _     **SPCA** (243)

_ _ P C     **FEPC** (238)

P _ _ C     **pisc-** (93a), **porc** (50d)

P _ _ D     **paid** (99a), **pard** (24d), **pend** (16c, 58a), **pied** (114a, 127b), **pled**, **plod** (124d, 129b), **pond** (91b, 130a), **pood** (246), **prod** (38a, 46a, 54d, 59c, 62c, 63b, 65b, 81b, 82d, 90d, 121d, 126d)

P E _ _     **peag** (129d), **peak** (11d, 31d, 32c, 59a, 59d, 117d, 135a), **peal** (100d), **pear** (51d, 124a), **peas**, **peat** (52a, 127c), **peba** (14b), **Peck** (174), **peck** (22d, 246), **Pecs** (217), **-pede** (117b), **pedi-** (93a), **pedo-** (92d, 93a), **peek** (73a), **Peel** (174), **peel** (43a, 86c), **peen** (57d), **peep** (73a, 87c), **peer** (41b, 73a, 82a), **pega** (46d), **pegs**, **Pegu** (97d), **peho** (81c), **Pele** (58c), **pelf** (21a, 46a, 100c), **Pell** (174), **pelt** (28c, 43a, 57b, 59d), **pelu** (26c), **Peña** (174), **pend** (16c, 58a), **Penn** (174), **Penn.** (211, 242), **pens**, **pent** (30a), **peon** (48c, 76c), **pepo** (32c, 75d, 96a), **peps**, **pere** (49d, 50b), **peri** (44a, 88a),

peri- (92c), perk (28d, 51c), pern (60d), pero (112d), Pers. (242),
pert (49a, 62b, 72c, 104b, 114a, 128d), Peru (221), peso (215,
216, 217, 219, 221, 224), pest (82d, 88a, 89d), Pete (85a, 174),
Peto (193), peto (129b), petr- (93d), pets, Peul (217, 219, 221),
peur (50b), pews

_ P E _ aped, aper (28b, 77a), apes, apex (32c, 59a, 59d, 87b, 89b, 123a,
135a), epee (45b, 118d), OPEC (241), open (18b, 23c, 49b, 63a,
83b, 85c, 95d, 126a, 126b, 126c), spec. (243), sped, Spee (53c,
55c), Spes (198), spet (17b), spew (40a)

_ _ P E cape (37c, 58d, 74d, 95a), cepe (39c), cope (23d, 30b, 30d, 52d,
128a), dope (10b, 38b, 81a), dupe (25a, 34a, 48b, 56d, 74d, 118d),
gape (134b), HOPE (239), Hope (158), hope (42d), hype (95a),
jape (66c), lope (39b, 52a, 52b), mope (22a, 117d), nape (16b,
82d), nope (81b), olpe (70d, 132c), pipe (80c, 125a, 131c), Pope
(27c, 175), pope (19c, 27a, 91b), rape (107b), ripe (47b, 75b), rope
(30d, 69b, 100b), rype (95d), sipe (122b), tape (19a, 98c), tope
(107d, 229), type (27d, 112a, 113b), wipe (123d), yipe (42c)

P _ _ E Pace (204), pace (52a, 113c, 129b), Page (173, 193, 194), page
(12d, 41c, 48b, 70d, 107a), pale (19d, 86a, 88d, 129d), pane (114c,
114d), pare (87c, 98d), Pate (174), pate (32b, 58c), pave (66b),
-pede (117b), Pele (58c), pere (49d, 50b), Pete (85a, 174), pice
(62d, 220), pike (46d, 59d, 90c, 113b, 228), pile (17a, 58d, 79a),
pine (30a, 42a, 69a, 73a, 124a, 134b), pipe (80c, 125a, 131c),
poke (65b, 82d, 96a), pole (101c, 113a, 129b, 133b, 246), pome
(51d), pone (30d, 66c), Pope (27c, 175), pope (19c, 27a, 91b),
pore (48c, 84b, 84d), pose (9d, 15c, 94b), prae (69c), pree (105b),
puce (42a, 96c), puke (99a), pule (131c), pure (9b, 26b, 126a,
126c), Pyle (175), pyre (52c)

P _ _ F pelf (21a, 46a, 100c), Piaf (49d, 100c, 175), pouf (48c, 58d, 85a),
Prof. (242), puff (20a, 74a)

_ P G _ LPGA (240)

P _ _ G Pang (125a), pang (85d, 114b, 121c), peag (129d), phag- (92d),
Ping (125a), ping (76b), plug (116a, 133d), Pong (125a), prig
(85c), pung (21c, 110c)

P H _ _ phag- (92d), Phar. (242), phen- (92c), phew (42c), Phil (175), Phil.
(242), phis, Phiz (35c), phon (73b), phon- (93d), phot (246)

_ P H _ ophi- (93d)

_ _ P H Alph (101a), amph. (235), Caph (207), koph (12a), neph- (92d),
soph. (243), xiph- (93d), Zeph. (244)

P _ _ H path (101a, 102c, 130c), pish (42c), pith (30d, 41d, 51d, 54c, 74b,
75a, 90a, 97c, 120d), pooh (42c), posh (21a, 40b), Ptah (75d,
198), push (38a, 46a, 108d, 121d)

P I _ _ Piaf (49d, 100c, 175), pica (53c, 125d), pice (62d, 220), pick (27a.

90b), **Pico** (100d), **picr-** (92c), **Pict** (22a), **pied** (114a, 127b), **pien** (14c), **Pier** (175), **pier** (21d, 66b, 68d, 131b), **pies**, **Piet** (175), **piet** (26b, 74b), **pigs**, **pika** (30c, 72c, 101c, 231), **pike** (46d, 59d, 90c, 113b, 228), **piki** (74b), **pile** (17a, 58d, 79a), **pili-** (93a), **pill** (119a), **Pima** (189), **pima** (31a), **pimp** (94d), **pina** (29d), **pine** (30a, 42a, 69a, 73a, 124a, 134b), **Ping** (125a), **ping** (76b), **pink** (24b), **pins**, **pint** (54b, 246), **piny**, **pion** (42b), **pipe** (80c, 125a, 131c), **pips**, **pirn** (20c, 98d, 130d), **Pisa** (70d), **pisc-** (93a), **pish** (42c), **pisk** (12b), **pita** (11d, 25c, 45c), **pith** (30d, 41d, 51d, 54c, 74b, 75a, 90a, 97c, 120d), **pits**, **Pitt** (41a, 175), **pity** (29b, 87a, 134b), **Pius** (91b)

_ P I _    **Apia** (91c, 224), **Apis** (22c, 40a, 95d, 103b), **epic** (59c, 90c), **Epis.** (238), **epit.** (238), **ipil** (88c), **-opia** (117b, 117c), **spin** (100b, 131c), **spir-** (92d), **spit** (90d, 101b)

_ _ P I    **Hapi** (198), **hapi** (53b), **Hopi** (95d, 189), **Impi** (135c), **kepi** (58d, 76d), **topi** (30d, 89c), **Tupi** (12b)

P _ _ I    **Pali** (22b, 104b, 127c), **pari-** (92d), **pedi-** (93a), **peri** (44a, 88a), **peri-** (92c), **piki** (74b), **pili-** (93a), **puli** (37b, 61c, 227), **puri** (62d)

P _ _ K    **pack** (16d, 22c, 105c, 232, 246), **park** (53b, 95d), **peak** (11d, 31d, 32c, 59a, 59d, 117d, 135a), **Peck** (174), **peck** (22d, 246), **peek** (73a), **perk** (28d, 51c), **pick** (27a, 90b), **pink** (24b), **pisk** (12b), **pock** (62d), **Polk** (175, 190), **pork** (55c, 75c), **Puck** (107c, 193), **puck** (36b, 55a, 60c, 77b), **pulk** (79c), **punk** (12a, 123b)

P L _ _    **plan** (13d, 15c, 35b, 76b, 95a, 104d), **plat** (74d, 90b), **play** (51c, 52b, 87d, 91d, 114a), **plea** (42d, 92b, 118a), **pleb** (29b), **pled**, **plew** (18a), **plod** (124d, 129b), **plop** (44a, 130b), **plot** (23a, 30b, 104d, 123c), **plow** (32c, 122a), **ploy** (14d, 116a), **plug** (116a, 133d), **plum** (51d, 124a), **plus** (12c, 62c)

_ _ P L    **dipl-** (93d), **hapl-** (93c)

P _ _ L    **pail** (30b), **pall** (28b, 122b, 130d), **Paul** (18a, 91b, 174), **pawl** (73d), **peal** (100d), **Peel** (174), **peel** (43a, 86c), **Pell** (174), **Peul** (217, 219, 221), **Phil** (175), **Phil.** (242), **pill** (119a), **Pohl** (175), **poll** (129c), **pool** (52b, 90c, 91b, 130a), **pull** (11d, 37d, 123c), **purl** (68c), **pyel-** (93c)

P _ _ M    **palm** (124a), **plum** (51d, 124a), **poem** (128a), **pram** (16a, 24c), **prim** (115b), **PROM** (29c, 242), **prom** (33b)

_ _ P N    **ESPN** (26a)

P _ _ N    **pain** (10b, 61d), **paon** (87b), **pawn** (26c, 60c, 90b), **peen** (57d), **Penn** (174), **Penn.** (211, 242), **peon** (48c, 76c), **pern** (60d), **phen-** (92c), **phon** (73b), **phon-** (93d), **pien** (14c), **pion** (42b), **pirn** (20c, 98d, 130d), **plan** (13d, 15c, 35b, 76b, 95a, 104d), **poon** (103d, 124b), **porn** (79c)

P O _ _    **pobs** (91c), **pock** (62d), **poco** (72c), **-poda** (117c), **pods**, **poem** (128a), **poet** (40b), **Pogo** (83d, 91d), **pogy** (68d, 75d, 78d), **poha**

405

(58c), **Pohl** (175), **poke** (65b, 82d, 96a), **poku** (13a, 130b), **poky** (110d), **Pola** (175), **pole** (101c, 113a, 129b, 133b, 246), **Polk** (175, 190), **poll** (129c), **Polo** (127d), **poly-** (93b), **pome** (51d), **Pomo** (189), **pomp** (85a, 85b), **pond** (91b, 130a), **pone** (30d, 66c), **Pong** (125a), **Pons** (49d, 175), **pont** (50a), **pony** (26b, 33b, 61a), **pood** (246), **pooh** (42c), **pool** (52b, 90c, 91b, 130a), **poon** (103d, 124b), **poop** (20c, 34b, 108b), **poor** (28d), **Pope** (27c, 175), **pope** (19c, 27a, 91b), **pops**, **porc** (50d), **pore** (48c, 84b, 84d), **pork** (55c, 75c), **porn** (79c), **Port.** (242), **port** (58a, 132c), **pose** (9d, 15c, 94b), **posh** (21a, 40b), **Post** (175), **post** (69c, 74b, 81c, 115a), **posy** (82b, 100d), **pots**, **pouf** (48c, 58d, 85a), **pour** (120a), **pout** (117d)

_ P O _      **Apoc.** (235), **apod** (48c), **apos.** (235), **BPOE** (236), **epos** (41b, 59c, 90c), **spor-**(93d), **spot** (35d, 72d, 79d, 89d, 114c), **upon** (9b)

_ _ P O      **cipo** (71c), **hypo** (88d), **Li Po** (26d), **lipo-** (92d), **mapo** (55a), **pepo** (32c, 75d, 96a), **topo.** (243), **typo** (41c, 94c), **USPO** (244)

P _ _ O      **paco** (11d, 109c), **Pavo** (87b, 207), **pedo-** (92d, 93a), **peho** (81c), **pepo** (32c, 75d, 96a), **pero** (112d), **peso** (215, 216, 217, 219, 221, 224), **Peto** (193), **peto** (129b), **Pico** (100d), **poco** (72c), **Pogo** (83d, 91d), **Polo** (127d), **Pomo** (189), **puno** (132b), **Puzo** (175), **pyro-** (93a)

_ _ P P      **Capp** (144), **Depp** (149), **dopp** (32d), **hipp-** (93a), **Lapp** (82b, 222), **Papp** (173), **repp** (43b), **typp** (134b), **yapp** (20d)

P _ _ P      **palp** (13a, 45a, 123b), **Papp** (173), **peep** (73a, 87c), **pimp** (94d), **plop** (44a, 130b), **pomp** (85a, 85b), **poop** (20c, 34b, 108b), **prep** (104d), **prop** (118a), **pulp** (51d, 74a, 75b, 86b), **pump** (108c)

_ P Q _      **SPQR** (243)

P R _ _      **prae** (69c), **pram** (16a, 24c), **prat** (23a), **pray** (18c, 41b), **pree** (105b), **prep** (104d), **Pres.** (242), **pres** (50d), **prey** (128b), **prig** (85c), **prim** (115b), **proa** (20c, 23d, 74b), **prod** (38a, 46a, 54d, 59c, 62c, 63b, 65b, 81b, 82d, 90d, 121d, 126d), **Prof.** (242), **PROM** (29c, 242), **prom** (33b), **prop** (118a), **pros**, **Prot.** (242), **Prov.** (242), **prow** (20c, 108b, 115b), **Prut** (33d)

_ P R _      **spry** (9d, 72c, 81d)

_ _ P R      **copr-** (92d), **cupr-** (92d)

P _ _ R      **Paar** (173), **pair** (21c, 31b, 90d, 119c, 125c), **parr** (103d, 109d), **pear** (51d, 124a), **peer** (41b, 73a, 82a), **petr-** (93d), **peur** (50b), **Phar.** (242), **picr-** (92c), **Pier** (175), **pier** (21d, 66b, 68d, 131b), **poor** (28d), **pour** (120a), **pter-** (94a), **purr** (112a)

P S _ _      **psis**

_ P S _      **apse** (12a, 27a, 98b, 106c, 127c), **ipse** (37a, 69d)

_ _ P S **Alps** (79b), **amps, asps, bops, caps, cops, cups, daps, dips, fops, gaps, gyps, hips, hops** (18a), **imps, kips, Kops** (67b), **laps, lips, lops, maps, mops, naps, nips, paps, peps, pips, pops, pups, raps, reps, rips, saps, seps** (72c, 106d), **sips, sops, sups, taps, tips, tops, tups, USPS** (244), **VIPs, yaps, yips, zips**

P _ _ S **pads, pals, Pams, pans, paps, pars, pass** (13d, 21d, 84a, 85c, 106c), **pats, paws, pays, peas, Pecs** (217), **pegs, pens, peps, Pers.** (242), **pets, pews, phis, pies, pigs, pins, pips, pits, Pius** (91b), **plus** (12c, 62c), **pobs** (91c), **pods, Pons** (49d, 175), **pops, pots, Pres.** (242), **pres** (50d), **pros, pubs, pugs, puns, pups, puss** (24d), **puts, pyes**

P T _ _ **Ptah** (75d, 198), **pter-** (94a)

_ P T _ **opts**

_ _ P T **Bapt.** (236), **Capt.** (236), **Copt** (39d), **dept.** (237), **hept-** (93c), **kept, lept-** (93d), **rapt** (9b, 41a), **Sept.** (78c, 243), **sept** (27d, 64a, 111b), **supt.** (243), **wept**

P _ _ T **pact** (10d, 11c, 17b, 20d), **pant** (18a, 21d), **part** (11c, 43d, 49b, 57b, 91d, 106d), **past** (55b, 60b, 122a), **peat** (52a, 127c), **pelt** (28c, 43a, 57b, 59d), **pent** (30a), **pert** (49a, 62b, 72c, 104b, 114a, 128d), **pest** (82d, 88a, 89d), **phot** (246), **Pict** (22a), **Piet** (175), **piet** (26b, 74b), **pint** (54b, 246), **Pitt** (41a, 175), **plat** (74d, 90b), **plot** (23a, 30b, 104d, 123c), **poet** (40b), **pont** (50a), **Port.** (242), **port** (58a, 132c), **Post** (175), **post** (69c, 74b, 81c, 115a), **pout** (117d), **prat** (23a), **Prot.** (242), **Prut** (33d), **punt** (20b, 47b), **putt** (55b)

P U _ _ **pubs, puce** (42a, 96c), **Puck** (107c, 193), **puck** (36b, 55a, 60c, 77b), **pudu** (34b), **puff** (20a, 74a), **pugs, puke** (99a), **puku** (13a, 130b), **pula** (214), **pule** (131c), **puli** (37b, 61c, 227), **pulk** (79c), **pull** (11d, 37d, 123c), **pulp** (51d, 74a, 75b, 86b), **puma** (24d, 31b, 79a, 231), **pump** (108c), **Puna** (12c), **puna** (28d, 90b, 132b), **pung** (21c, 110c), **punk** (12a, 123b), **puno** (132b), **puns, punt** (20b, 47b), **puny** (45a, 130c), **pupa** (27a, 28d, 63b), **pups, pure** (9b, 26b, 126a, 126c), **puri** (62d), **purl** (68c), **purr** (112a), **push** (38a, 46a, 108d, 121d), **puss** (24d), **puts, putt** (55b), **Puzo** (175)

_ P U _ **Apus** (207), **opus** (29c, 80c, 129a, 133c), **spud** (92a), **spun, spur** (46a, 54d, 62c, 63c, 95a)

_ _ P U **OGPU** (103c)

P _ _ U **patu** (130d), **Pegu** (97d), **pelu** (26c), **Peru** (221), **poku** (13a, 130b), **pudu** (34b), **puku** (13a, 130b)

P _ _ V **Prov.** (242)

P _ _ W **phew** (42c), **plew** (18a), **plow** (32c, 122a), **prow** (20c, 108b, 115b)

P Y _ _ **pyel-** (93c), **pyes, pyla** (21c), **Pyle** (175), **pyre** (52c), **pyro-** (93a)

407

_ _ P Y   **copy** (40c, 62a), **dopy** (71c), **espy** (106b), **mopy** (72b), **ropy** (116b)

P _ _ Y   **piny**, **pity** (29b, 87a, 134b), **play** (51c, 52b, 87d, 91d, 114a), **ploy** (14d, 116a), **pogy** (68d, 75d, 78d), **poky** (110d), **poly-** (93b), **pony** (26b, 33b, 61a), **posy** (82b, 100d), **pray** (18c, 41b), **prey** (128b), **puny** (45a, 130c)

P _ _ Z   **Phiz** (35c)

Q A _ _   **qadi** (13d, 80d)

Q _ _ D   **quad** (29a), **quid** (32c, 122c), **quod** (94d, 96a)

Q _ _ G   **quag** (20c)

Q _ _ I   **qadi** (13d, 80d)

Q _ _ P   **quip** (66b, 66d, 132d, 133a)

_ _ Q Q   **seqq.** (243)

_ _ Q R   **SPQR** (243)

Q _ _ T   **quit** (9a, 34d, 71a, 99d)

Q U _ _   **quad** (29a), **quag** (20c), **quay** (68d, 88d, 131b), **quid** (32c, 122c), **quip** (66b, 66d, 132d, 133a), **quit** (9a, 34d, 71a, 99d), **quiz** (42b), **quod** (94d, 96a)

_ Q U _   **aqua** (20b, 70b), **aqui** (112d), **equi-** (93c)

Q _ _ Y   **quay** (68d, 88d, 131b)

Q _ _ Z   **quiz** (42b)

R A _ _   **raad** (15a, 40a, 112b, 121d), **RAAF** (242), **Rabe** (176), **Rabi** (15c, 88d), **rabi** (78b), **race** (87d, 103a, 114a, 124b), **rack** (10b, 28b), **racy** (20a, 113c), **rads**, **Raes**, **raff** (102d), **Raft** (176), **raft** (47c), **raga** (80a), **rage** (26d, 74c, 116a, 120b), **ragi** (25c), **rags**, **rahs**, **raid** (48c, 62d), **rail** (9c, 19a, 30d, 75a, 111d, 123c, 129a, 226), **rain** (92a, 120a, 130d), **rais** (24a), **raja** (60a), **rake** (34a, 52d), **raki** (11a), **rale** (21d, 26c, 34a), **Rama** (128c), **rami** (21c), **ramp** (52c, 62c, 110d), **Rams** (206), **rams** (51c, 60a), **rana** (51c, 60a), **Rand** (176), **rand** (220, 222), **rang**, **rani** (60a, 94c), **rank** (27d, 46a, 55c, 72a, 73d, 97d, 116c), **rant** (34b, 58a, 98a, 119b), **rape** (107b), **raps**, **rapt** (9b, 41a), **rare** (83b, 104c, 126a, 126d), **rase** (34d), **rash** (98b, 110a), **rasp** (46a, 56a, 105c, 122d), **rata** (46a), **rate** (13d, 27d, 30b, 41d, 42a, 55c, 66d, 94b, 97d, 107a, 127b), **rath** (99d), **RATO** (242), **rats**, **Raul** (176), **rave** (34b, 58a, 119b), **Ravi** (176), **raya** (85a), **rays**, **raze** (34d, 35b, 36c, 71c), **razz** (59a)

_ R A _   **Arab** (104b, 213, 217, 218, 219, 221, 222, 223, 224), **Arab.** (235), **Arad** (221), **arad** (65b), **Aral** (103c), **Aram** (108a, 118d, 139), **Aran**

(52b, 64c), **Aras**, **Brad** (142), **brad**.(44c, 54d, 80b), **brae** (60a, 105b), **brag** (20b, 24a, 32b, 127c), **Bram** (142), **bran** (22a, 22b, 55d, 61d), **bras** (49d), **brat** (26c), **braw** (105a), **bray** (12d, 37c), **Braz.** (236), **crab** (32b, 108a), **crag** (101b), **cram** (116c), **cran** (118c), **crap** (82a, 91b), **-crat** (117c), **craw** (32a, 56d, 115c), **drab** (22b, 26b, 29a, 38c, 43d, 47b), **drag** (30d, 95d), **dram** (38a, 38b, 84a, 92a, 110d, 246), **drat** (42a, 83a), **draw** (11d, 43c, 91d, 123c), **dray** (24c, 114b, 129b), **eras**, **erat** (96a, 97c), **frae** (105a), **Fran** (153), **frap** (37d, 122a), **fras**, **frat** (29a), **frau** (54a), **fray** (45d, 49b, 125a), **grab** (80b, 106c, 111b), **grad** (25c), **grad.** (239), **Graf** (135a, 156), **graf** (53d, 81d), **gram** (76b, 246), **Grau** (156), **Gray** (21a, 41a, 156, 192), **gray** (60c), **Graz** (213), **Irad** (197), **irae** (35c), **Iran** (88a, 217), **Iraq** (217), **Iras** (28a, 195), **oral** (79b, 113d, 127c, 128a), **Oran** (213), **prae** (69c), **pram** (16a, 24c), **prat** (23a), **pray** (18c, 41b), **tram** (124c), **trap** (24c, 24d, 41a, 54b, 55b, 101b, 111b), **tray** (98b, 104a, 107a), **Ural** (103c), **uran** (78a), **WRAF** (244), **wrap** (19a, 28a, 41b), **Wray** (187), **x-ray** (12a, 75c, 88d)

_ _ R A   **Agra** (24c, 119a), **agra** (64a, 118c), **Akra** (216), **amra** (60c), **aura** (10d, 36d, 39d, 40b, 57c, 100d), **Bara** (140), **bora** (132b), **Cara** (144), **cara** (65a), **Cora** (34d, 126a), **cora** (53b), **cura** (113a), **Dora** (30c, 33d, 35c), **dura** (113c), **eyra** (65b), **Ezra** (152, 196, 197), **fora** (75a, 101d), **Hera** (14b, 67c, 135c, 198), **hora** (21a, 33b), **hura** (104a), **Jura** (79b), **kora** (130b), **Kura** (101a), **Lara** (23c), **lira** (25c, 218, 219, 221, 223, 224), **mara** (101c, 230), **Mira** (207), **mora** (46b, 48c, 52b, 56d, 65a, 76b, 118d), **mura** (65d), **Myra** (15a, 171), **Nera** (121d), **NHRA** (241), **NIRA** (241), **Nora** (61b, 81d, 172), **obra** (113a), **okra** (57a, 127c), **Para** (18b, 214), **para** (112d, 214, 215, 222, 224), **Sara** (179, 215), **sera** (13a, 47d, 65a), **sora** (19a, 97b), **sura** (68c, 86a), **Tara** (104d), **tara** (45b, 64a), **tera-** (93d), **tora** (13a, 58b), **Tyra** (184), **vara** (72a), **Vera** (185), **vera** (105c), **-vora** (117c)

R _ _ A   **raga** (80a), **raja** (60a), **Rama** (128c), **rana** (51c, 60a), **rata** (46a), **raya** (85a), **Reba** (67c, 176), **Rhea** (68c, 78d, 89d, 122c, 135c, 177, 198), **rhea** (19b, 26c, 85a, 226), **Riga** (218), **Rima** (56c), **rima** (47a), **Rita** (177), **Roda** (81d), **roka** (74a, 124a), **Roma** (65c, 218), **Rosa** (178), **rota** (25a, 27a, 31c, 101d, 102b), **ruga** (48a, 134a), **rusa** (104a)

_ R B _   **orbs**

_ _ R B   **barb** (47a, 89a, 90c, 95a), **carb-** (92d), **curb** (100a, 109a), **darb** (88a), **forb** (59c), **garb** (28b, 37d), **gerb** (46b), **Herb** (158), **herb** (90a, 106b), **kerb** (109a), **NLRB** (241), **Serb** (134d), **sorb** (13c, 79a, 107a, 110b), **verb** (86d)

R _ _ B   **Robb** (177)

R C _ _   **RCAF** (242), **RCMP** (242)

_ R C _   **arca** (11d, 21b, 99b), **arch** (28a, 41b, 101c), **-arch** (117c), **arch-** (93b), **arch.** (235), **arcs**, **orca** (67b), **orch.** (241), **orcs**

**_ _ R C**  circ. (237), **Marc** (168), **marc** (55d), **narc-** (93c), **porc** (50d)

**R _ _ C**  **ROTC** (242)

**_ R D _**  **Erda** (22b, 198), **Erde** (22b), **ordo** (21a, 27a, 92b), **Urdu** (60b, 213, 220)

**_ _ R D**  **Bard** (200), **bard** (14c, 16b, 90c), **Bird** (141), **bird** (16a), **bord** (77a), **burd** (105c), **Byrd** (90d), **card** (29a, 66d, 87a), **Cord** (146), **cord** (32c, 43b), **curd** (76d), **Ford** (153, 191, 194), **ford** (129a), **fyrd** (83d), **gird** (16d, 18c, 40c, 118b), **hard** (123b), **herd** (38b, 232), **Kurd** (64a, 217), **lard** (44c, 50a, 56a, 83d), **Lord** (167), **lord** (82a), **nard** (75b, 83d), **pard** (24d), **sard** (24b, 25d, 53b, 84c, 106c, 115d), **surd** (30b, 82d), **Ward** (186), **ward** (27c, 35a, 67b), **word** (95a, 120c, 121d), **Yard** (187), **yard** (40d, 69a, 113a, 246)

**R _ _ D**  **raad** (15a, 40a, 112b, 121d), **raid** (48c, 62d), **Rand** (176), **rand** (220, 222), **read** (63c, 88b, 116c), **Redd** (176), **redd** (113b), **Reed** (176, 204), **reed** (16d, 55d, 75a, 79c, 84d), **Reid** (176), **rend** (28a), **Ridd** (73a), **rind** (43a, 76d, 87c), **road** (31b, 38a, 121b, 130c), **rood** (32a), **rudd** (24b, 46c, 98c), **rued**, **rynd** (76d)

**R E _ _**  **read** (63c, 88b, 116c), **real** (9d, 116d), **ream** (18d, 31b, 41a, 86b, 125c), **reap** (9d, 33a, 58b), **rear** (10c, 21d, 40d, 41c, 60a, 97c), **Reba** (67c, 176), **rebs**, **reck** (24b), **Redd** (176), **redd** (113b), **rede** (31b, 105a), **redo** (26a, 74b), **Reds** (206), **reds**, **Reed** (176, 204), **reed** (16d, 55d, 75a, 79c, 84d), **reef** (98d, 104a, 108b), **reek** (43c, 52a, 111a), **reel** (20c, 33b, 113c, 113d, 114b, 114c, 131c, 133a, 233), **Rees** (176), **Reid** (176), **rein** (26b, 30c, 100a), **reis** (24a), **Reki** (16d), **rely** (124d), **remi** (53b), **rend** (28a), **René** (176), **Reni** (65a, 176), **reni-** (93c), **Reno** (15c, 81c, 113d), **reno-** (93b), **rent** (60b, 60c, 120a, 123b), **repp** (43b), **reps**, **resh** (12a), **rest** (16b, 21d, 71b, 80c, 87b, 99b, 99c, 99d, 234), **rete** (81c, 90b), **rets**, **reve** (50b), **revs**

**_ R E _**  **area** (36d, 37b, 45d, 72d, 97d, 99a, 135c), **Ares** (13b, 41c, 59b, 75a, 129d, 135c, 198), **brea** (77a), **bred** (97c), **bree** (105a), **bren** (73d), **br'er** (126a), **Bret** (143), **brew** (29d), **Cree** (11b, 189), **crew** (48c, 56c, 81b, 88b, 133d), **drei** (54a), **Drew** (150, 201), **drew** (110a), **drey** (114b), **Fred** (47c, 153), **free** (36b, 56a, 73a, 100c, 112b), **freq.** (238), **fret** (22a, 25d, 36d, 42c, 128b, 133d), **Frey** (10b, 153, 198), **Greg** (156), **grew**, **Grey** (156, 192, 194), **Mr. Ed** (119b), **Oreb** (197), **Oreg.** (241), **Orel** (173), **ores**, **pree** (105b), **prep** (104d), **Pres.** (242), **pres** (50d), **prey** (128b), **tree** (30d, 53b, 133c), **tref** (48b, 126a), **trek** (66d, 73a, 123d), **tres** (42b, 51b, 113a), **tret** (130a, 131a), **trey** (24a, 121c), **urea** (45c), **Urey** (15c, 184), **Wren** (187), **wren** (19a, 226)

**_ _ R E**  **Aare** (18c, 100b), **Acre** (214), **acre** (45d, 68d, 246), **aire** (64a), **bare** (36a, 40c, 43a, 76a, 116b, 127a), **bore** (23b, 37d, 87d, 121d), **byre** (31c), **CARE** (236), **care** (13a, 25b, 29d, 59a, 77a, 99a, 123d, 124d, 133d), **cere** (18d, 130c), **CORE** (237), **core** (25c, 41d, 58d), **cure** (94c), **dare** (25d, 34c), **dire** (37d, 44d, 45a, 54b, 56a, 120c), **Dore**

410

(49c), **dore** (54b, 89a), **Eire** (64a), **etre** (50a), **eure** (54b), **Eyre** (22a), **fare** (35c, 48b), **fire** (14b, 36a, 36c, 108c), **fore** (51c, 108b), **gare** (50d, 97b), **Gere** (155), **Gore** (155, 191), **gore** (87c, 88d, 124b), **gyre** (27b), **hare** (101c, 230), **here** (63d, 101c), **hire** (40c, 40d, 71b, 99c, 100a), **ihre** (54b), **Imre** (159), **in re** (29d, 63d, 99a), **jure** (70b), **Kure** (60d), **lire** (50d, 64d), **lore** (60b, 70d, 71b, 132d), **lure** (34b, 41b, 63d, 120c), **Lyra** (58a, 207), **lyre** (80b, 85a), **mare** (61a, 82c), **mere** (17b, 50d, 68b, 84b, 91b, 130a), **mire** (20c, 39a, 78c, 79c), **More** (171), **more** (43c, 56a), **Nare** (72d), **Nore** (120d), **ogre** (78b), **pare** (87c, 98d), **pere** (49d, 50b), **pore** (48c, 84b, 84d), **pure** (9b, 26b, 126a, 126c), **pyre** (52c), **rare** (83b, 104c, 126a, 126d), **rire** (50c), **sere** (37d, 133a), **sire** (18b, 21d, 44d, 48d, 94d, 120c, 122c), **sore** (12d, 106c), **sure** (10b, 99b, 106b, 126d), **tare** (128b, 131a), **tire** (21a, 42d, 44d, 47b, 131c), **tore** (71a, 88c, 218), **-vore** (117c), **ware** (76a), **were**, **we're** (30c), **wire** (30d, 120b), **wore**, **yore** (12c, 23a, 55b, 73a, 83d, 87a, 122b)

**R _ _ E**   **Rabe** (176), **race** (87d, 103a, 114a, 124b), **rage** (26d, 74c, 116a, 120b), **rake** (34a, 52d), **rale** (21d, 26c, 34a), **rape** (107b), **rare** (83b, 104c, 126a, 126d), **rase** (34d), **rate** (13d, 27d, 30b, 41d, 42a, 55c, 66d, 94b, 97d, 107a, 127b), **rave** (34b, 58a, 119b), **raze** (34d, 35b, 36c, 71c), **rede** (31b, 105a), **René** (176), **rete** (81c, 90b), **reve** (50b), **Rhee** (68c, 177), **Rice** (177, 204), **rice** (37d), **Ride** (177), **ride** (29b, 66d, 121a), **rife** (9b, 94b), **rile** (12d, 64b, 95c, 115c), **rime** (30a, 51c, 60c), **rine** (36d), **ripe** (47b, 75b), **rire** (50c), **rise** (62c, 114c), **rite** (72c), **rive** (28a), **robe** (52d), **rode** (38b), **role** (52a, 86d), **Rome** (13c, 27c, 41d, 218), **rope** (30d, 69b, 100b), **Rose** (9a, 178), **Rote** (178), **rote** (75d, 99d, 118a), **roue** (34a, 97c), **rove** (97d, 101a, 129d), **Rube** (179), **rube** (31b, 103c, 134d), **rude** (102c, 126a), **rule** (13b, 35b, 37b, 70b, 118c), **rune** (82b), **ruse** (60c, 62b, 116a), **Ryne** (179), **rype** (95d)

**_ R F _**   **orfe** (46d, 134b), **Urfa** (76a)

**_ _ R F**   **Cerf** (145), **corf** (28c), **kerf** (33a, 82c), **serf** (20d, 110b), **surf** (21d), **turf** (87b, 111c, 118b), **werf** (44c), **zarf** (28d, 32d, 114d)

**R _ _ F**   **RAAF** (242), **raff** (102d), **RCAF** (242), **reef** (98d, 104a, 108b), **riff** (66a, 78c), **roof** (61c), **ruff** (34d, 37b, 51c)

**_ R G _**   **Argo** (14b, 66a), **ergo** (121a), **ergs**, **orgy** (24b, 100b, 104b), **urge** (35b, 54d, 63b, 94d)

**_ _ R G**   **Berg** (141), **berg** (61b), **Borg** (142), **burg** (21a, 57c), **surg.** (243)

**R _ _ G**   **rang**, **Rigg** (177), **Ring** (177), **ring** (16d, 27b, 40c, 40d, 131b, 134a), **Roeg** (178), **rung** (25d, 32b, 115b)

**R H _ _**   **Rhea** (68c, 78d, 89d, 122c, 135c, 177, 198), **rhea** (19b, 26c, 85a, 226), **Rhee** (68c, 177), **rheo-** (92d), **rhin-** (93b), **RHIP** (242), **rhiz-** (93c), **rhos**

**R _ _ H**   **rash** (98b, 110a), **rath** (99d), **resh** (12a), **Rich** (177), **rich** (73d),

411

**Roth** (178), **Rush** (179), **rush** (114a), **Ruth** (80d, 179, 196, 197), **ruth** (29b, 89c)

**R I _ _**    **rial** (220), **ribs**, **Rice** (177, 204), **rice** (37d), **Rich** (177), **rich** (73d), **Rick** (24c, 177), **rick** (58c, 89a, 114b), **Rico** (72c), **Ridd** (73a), **Ride** (177), **ride** (29b, 66d, 121a), **rids**, **riel** (214), **riem** (59d), **rien** (50d), **rife** (9b, 94b), **riff** (66a, 78c), **rift** (21d, 47a, 84b, 113d), **Riga** (218), **Rigg** (177), **rigs**, **Riis** (177), **rile** (12d, 64b, 95c, 115c), **rill** (22a, 31d, 101a, 110d, 116b), **Rima** (56c), **rima** (47a), **rime** (30a, 51c, 60c), **rims**, **rimu** (62a, 98d), **rimy** (43a, 76d, 87c), **rind** (43a, 76d, 87c), **rine** (36d), **Ring** (177), **ring** (16d, 27b, 40c, 40d, 131b, 134a), **rink** (109d, 114a), **riot** (85a, 101c, 125a), **ripe** (47b, 75b), **rips**, **rire** (50c), **rise** (62c, 114c), **risk** (52b, 58c, 66b, 127d), **Rita** (177), **rite** (72c), **Ritz** (177), **rive** (28a)

**_ R I _**    **aria** (75d, 111d, 125a, 234), **arid** (38b), **Arie** (139), **aril** (106b), **Ariz.** (209, 235), **brie** (26b), **brig** (81a, 108b), **brim** (21a), **brio** (33d, 113d, 128d), **Brit.** (236), **brit** (59d), **crib** (26b, 74c, 91b, 110c), **crim.** (237), **crit.** (237), **drib** (110d), **drip** (72b, 88a), **Eric** (128b, 151), **Erie** (23c, 68d, 189), **Erik** (151), **Erin** (64a, 151), **Eris** (14b, 198), **frib** (35d), **frit** (54c), **Friz** (154), **friz** (32d), **grid** (17c, 90b, 116a), **grig** (32a, 39c, 56a, 72c), **grim** (19d, 54b, 115b), **grin** (111a), **grip** (27d, 55d, 60c, 96a, 117d), **Gris** (156), **gris** (50c), **grit** (104a), **hrip** (239), **irid** (90a), **Iris** (159, 195), **iris** (20b, 43c, 85a, 97c), **Kris** (165), **kris** (74b), **orig.** (241), **prig** (85c), **prim** (115b), **trig** (114a, 124c), **trig.** (31b, 243), **trim** (81a, 84d, 114a, 118b, 121d, 124c), **Trin.** (243), **trio** (80c, 124b), **trip** (66d, 232), **Tris** (184), **-trix** (117b), **Uria** (197), **-uria** (117b), **urim** (103b), **Uris** (184), **writ** (71a)

**_ _ R I**    **abri** (51a, 108a), **aeri-** (92c), **agri.** (235), **Bari** (10a, 218), **buri** (119b), **gyri** (21c), **ieri** (65c), **INRI** (32b, 239), **kari** (15d), **Kiri** (164), **kiri** (87a), **kori** (10b, 60a), **lari** (219), **Lori** (167), **Mari** (16d), **mari** (50c), **myri-** (93b), **nori** (11b, 105d), **Omri** (67d, 197), **pari-** (92d), **peri** (44a, 88a), **peri-** (92c), **puri** (62d), **ruri** (69c), **sari** (52d, 60a), **Seri** (76c), **sori** (45b), **Teri** (183), **Tori** (184), **tori** (30c), **vari** (71b), **weri** (16c, 25a), **Yuri** (188), **zori** (108c)

**R _ _ I**    **Rabi** (15c, 88d), **rabi** (78b), **ragi** (25c), **raki** (11a), **rami** (21c), **rani** (60a, 94c), **Ravi** (176), **Reki** (16d), **remi** (53b), **Reni** (65a, 176), **reni-** (93b), **roti** (51a), **ruri** (69c)

**_ R K _**    **arks**, **irks**

**_ _ R K**    **bark** (12d, 37b), **cark** (24b, 133d), **Cork** (217), **cork** (90b, 116a, 132c, 133b), **dark** (38d, 54d, 118c), **Dirk** (149), **dirk** (33a), **fork** (13c, 36d, 37a, 119a), **hark** (72b), **jerk** (20a, 38d, 48b, 88a, 95d), **Kirk** (164), **kirk** (27a, 105a), **lark** (19a, 51c, 226), **lurk** (71d, 110b), **Mark** (42a, 102c, 168, 196), **mark** (10d, 15c, 55c, 96b, 109b, 114c, 133a), **murk** (28b, 48a, 77b), **nark** (63a, 115d), **park** (53b, 95d), **perk** (28d, 51c), **pork** (55c, 75c), **Sark** (26a, 64b), **Turk** (85a, 217), **Turk.** (243), **work** (52a, 116c), **York** (41a, 187, 192, 193, 194)

**R _ _ K**    **rack** (10b, 28b), **rank** (27d, 46a, 55c, 72a, 73d, 97d, 116c), **reck**

(24b), **reek**(43c, 52a, 111a), **Rick**(24c, 177), **rick**(58c, 89a, 114b), **rink** (109d, 114a), **risk** (52b, 58c, 66b, 127d), **Rock** (178), **rock** (118c, 124b), **rook** (19b, 26c, 32b, 226), **ruck** (134a), **rusk** (21d)

_ R L _     **Arlo** (139), **Erle** (151), **orle** (46a, 59b, 108a), **orlo** (46a, 90b)

_ _ R L     **birl** (72d),**Burl** (143),**burl** (68c,124b),**Carl** (144),**curl** (32a, 57b, 72d, 100d,126b),**Earl** (150),**earl** (82a), **farl** (105b), **furl** (101c), **girl** (45b), **harl** (46a, 48a, 59b), **herl** (14d, 17a), **hurl** (121c, 123b), **jarl** (104c), **Karl** (163), **marl** (27d, 35a, 45c), **merl** (19a, 19d, 226), **purl** (68c)

R _ _ L     **rail** (9c, 19a, 30d, 75a, 111d, 123c, 129a, 226), **Raul** (176), **real** (9d, 116d), **reel** (20c, 33b, 113c, 113d, 114b, 114c, 131c, 133a, 233), **rial** (220), **riel** (214), **rill** (22a, 31d, 101a, 110d, 116b), **roil** (79c, 15c), **roll** (118c), **ryal** (83d)

_ R M _     **arms** (130d), **army** (61c), **Erma** (151)

_ _ R M     **barm** (134b), **berm** (23c, 71a, 108d), **corm** (22c, 115a), **-derm** (117c), **dorm** (104d), **farm** (21d, 32a, 55d, 122a), **firm** (29b, 29d, 114b, 126d), **form** (44c, 107c, 127a), **germ** (36b, 61b, 76c), **harm** (33b, 61d, 62a, 63a), **Norm** (172), **norm** (16a, 86b, 97d, 114d), **term** (71d, 72a, 80b, 106c, 115c), **warm** (10b, 58d, 120c), **worm** (88a), **wurm** (54c)

R _ _ M     **ream** (18d, 31b, 41a, 86b, 125c), **riem** (59d), **roam** (123d, 129d), **room** (25d)

_ R N _     **arna** (22b, 131d), **Arnd** (53d), **Arne** (102d, 139), **Arno** (101a, 139), **arns**, **Brno** (215), **Dr. No** (20d), **erne** (19a, 39a, 105c, 225), **erns**, **Orne** (23a), **urns**

_ _ R N     **barn** (116a), **Bern** (9a, 222), **birn** (27d), **Born** (142), **born** (71d, 81a, 81b), **burn** (62c, 101b), **CERN** (236), **corn** (74b, 94b), **darn** (42a, 75d, 83a, 99c), **Dern** (149), **Dorn** (149), **earn** (35b, 52a, 76a), **fern** (106b), **firn** (54c, 55d, 111b), **Garn** (154), **Horn** (24a), **horn** (13a, 31a, 124d), **Kern** (164), **kern** (48c, 101b, 125d), **lorn** (49a), **morn** (33d), **Norn** (82a), **pern** (60d), **pirn** (20c, 98d, 130d), **porn** (79c), **tarn** (68b, 79b, 91b, 130a), **tern** (19a, 28c, 56d, 104d, 105d, 118b, 226), **Torn** (184), **torn** (99c), **turn** (12c, 100b, 102b, 108a, 125c, 127c, 132b), **warn** (11b, 25b), **worn** (107b), **yarn** (43a, 114b, 119b, 133c)

R _ _ N     **rain** (92a, 120a, 130d), **rein** (26b, 30c, 100a), **rhin-** (93b), **rien** (50d), **roan** (61a, 98c, 131c), **ruin** (34d, 35b, 62b), **Ryan** (179), **Ryun** (179)

R O _ _     **road** (31b, 38a, 121b, 130c), **roam** (123d, 129d), **roan** (61a, 98c, 131c), **roar** (12d, 13c), **Robb** (177), **robe** (52d), **robs**, **Roby** (178), **Rock** (178), **rock** (118c, 124b), **Roda** (81d), **rode** (38b), **rods**, **Roeg** (178), **roes**, **roil** (79c, 115c), **rojo** (113a), **roka** (74a, 124a), **role** (52a, 86d), **roll** (118c), **Roma** (65c, 218), **Rome** (13c, 27c, 41d, 218), **romp** (51c), **rood** (32a), **roof** (61c), **rook** (19b, 26c, 32b,

413

226), **room** (25d), **Roos** (53d), **Root** (178), **root** (17b, 17c, 102d), **rope** (30d, 69b, 100b), **ropy** (116b), **Rory** (178), **Rosa** (178), **Rose** (9a, 178), **Ross** (178, 193, 195, 207, 208), **ross** (17b, 119c), **rosy** (54d, 84c), **rota** (25a, 27a, 31c, 101d, 102b), **ROTC** (242), **Rote** (178), **rote** (75d, 99d, 118a), **Roth** (178), **roti** (51a), **rots, roue** (34a, 97c), **roup** (92a), **rout** (34c, 36c), **roux** (104b), **rove** (97d, 101a, 129d), **rows, Roys**

_ R O _   **Aroa** (127d), **brom-** (92c), **broo** (105a), **Bros.** (236), **brow** (48d, 59d), **croc.** (237), **crop** (31d, 108d), **Crow** (189), **crow** (19b, 19d, 20b, 43c, 225), **drop** (44a, 48d, 77a, 84a, 86d, 90b, 90c, 110d, 120a), **Eros** (32d, 132c, 195, 198), **froe** (28a, 122d, 123a, 130d), **frog** (17c, 225), **from** (18b, 115a), **frow** (123a), **grog** (11a, 72b, 113d), **Groh** (156), **Gros** (49c), **gros** (38c, 43d, 109c), **grow** (15d, 41a, 42d, 43a, 114a, 118c), **iron** (45b, 45c, 55a, 57c, 74c, 75b, 245), **Kroc** (165), **proa** (20c, 23d, 74b), **prod** (38a, 46a, 54d, 59c, 62c, 63b, 65b, 81b, 82d, 90d, 121d, 126d), **Prof.** (242), **PROM** (29c, 242), **prom** (33b), **prop** (118a), **pros, Prot.** (242), **Prov.** (242), **prow** (20c, 108b, 115b), **trod, -tron** (117b), **trop** (51b, 123a), **trot** (66c, 85b), **trow** (18b), **Troy** (184), **troy** (119c, 131a)

_ _ R O   **acro-** (93a, 93c), **aero-** (92c), **aero.** (235), **Afro** (57b), **Afro-** (92c), **baro-** (93c), **boro** (114a), **caro** (65a), **cero** (46d, 67d), **cero-** (93d), **duro** (88b), **Ebro** (222), **Eero** (151), **faro** (24b), **Garo** (69a, 154), **giro** (31d, 65c), **gyro-** (93a), **Hero** (70d, 194), **hero** (34d, 95c, 104a), **Lero** (64c), **loro** (86d), **mero** (56c, 66b), **Miró** (112c, 171), **Moro** (171), **moro** (88c), **Nero** (10d, 102a), **otro** (112c, 113a), **pero** (112d), **pyro-** (93a), **sero-** (93c), **taro** (14d, 39c, 52a, 90d, 102b, 114d, 125a), **tiro** (18b, 82c), **toro** (31c, 112c), **Tyro** (81b), **tyro** (12b, 18b, 82c), **xero-** (92d), **Yuro** (188), **Zero** (188), **zero** (27b, 65d, 73b, 82c, 89d)

R _ _ O   **RATO** (242), **redo** (26a, 74b), **Reno** (15c, 81c, 113d), **reno-** (93b), **rheo-** (92d), **Rico** (72c), **rojo** (113a)

_ R P _   **arpa** (65a)

_ _ R P   **AARP** (235), **burp** (18b), **carp** (25b, 32a, 46a, 46c, 96d, 228), **Corp.** (237), **dorp** (57c, 128b), **GARP** (239), **harp** (80b), **lerp** (41d), **tarp** (23d, 130b), **terp** (79a, 94a), **warp** (30b, 121c, 125c)

R _ _ P   **ramp** (52c, 62c, 110d), **rasp** (46a, 56a, 105c, 122d), **RCMP** (242), **reap** (9d, 33a, 58b), **repp** (43b), **RHIP** (242), **romp** (51c), **roup** (92a), **RSVP** (242), **rump** (23a, 33a, 75c)

_ R R _   **errs**

_ _ R R   **birr** (112a, 216), **Burr** (143, 190), **burr** (94b), **Carr** (144), **dorr** (54c), **Farr** (152), **Garr** (154), **herr** (53d), **Kerr** (164), **Marr** (168), **parr** (103d, 109d), **purr** (112a), **torr** (246)

R _ _ R   **rear** (10c, 21d, 40d, 41c, 60a, 97c), **roar** (12d, 13c), **ruer, Ruhr** (53d, 100b)

414

**R S _ _**   RSVP (242)

**_ R S _**   Erse (25c, 52a, 64a), erst (49a), Ursa (17d)

**_ _ R S**   airs (94b), bars, Bors (102c), burs, cars, curs, Dors (149), ears, errs, firs, furs, gars, hers (95a), hors (50d), jars, Mars (89d, 98d, 129d, 199), mars (49d), Mors (34a, 198), oars, ours (95a), pars, Pers. (242), sirs, sors (69c), tars, tors, vers (51b), wars

**R _ _ S**   rads, Raes, rags, rahs, rais (24a), Rams (206), rams, raps, rats, rays, rebs, Reds (206), reds, Rees (176), reis (24a), reps, rets, revs, rhos, ribs, rids, rigs, Riis (177), rims, rips, robs, rods, roes, Roos (53d), Ross (178, 193, 195, 207, 208), ross (17b, 119c), rots, rows, Roys, rubs, rues, rugs, rums, runs, Russ (179), Russ. (242), ruts

**_ R T _**   Arta (56d), Arte (139), arts, arty, orth- (92d), orts (105c), Srta. (243)

**_ _ R T**   Bart (140), Bart. (236), Bert (20c, 141), bort (35c), Burt (143), cart (125d, 127c, 129b), cert. (236), Curt (147), curt (20b, 22a, 108c, 108d), dart (14c, 33d, 68d, 77b, 90c, 95a, 114a, 118c), dirt (39a, 99c, 104c), fort (51c, 116c), girt (27b), Gort (101b), Hart (157), hart (34c, 114b), hort. (239), Hurt (159), hurt (33b, 58a, 62a, 63a, 133d), Kurt (165), mart (40c, 74d), Mort (171), part (11c, 43d, 49b, 57b, 91d, 106d), pert (49a, 62b, 72c, 104b, 114a, 128d), Port. (242), port (58a, 132c), Sart (64a), Sert (112c), sort (27d, 36d, 67c, 106d, 109b, 113b, 127b, 132d), tart (87a, 112b), tort (27c, 71a, 134c), vert (56c), vert. (244), Wart (193), wart (95c), wert (128a), wort (59b, 92a), yurt (78a)

**R _ _ T**   Raft (176), raft (47c), rant (34b, 58a, 98a, 119b), rapt (9b, 41a), rent (60b, 60c, 120a, 123b), rest (16b, 21d, 71b, 80c, 87b, 99b, 99c, 99d, 234), rift (21d, 47a, 84b, 113d), riot (85a, 101c, 125a), Root (178), root (17b, 17c, 102d), rout (34c, 36c), runt (12d, 38d), rust (31a, 85d, 90a), ryot (62d)

**R U _ _**   Rube (179), rube (31b, 103c, 134d), rubs, Ruby (179), ruby (19c, 53b), ruck (134a), rudd (24b, 46c, 98c), rude (102c, 126a), Rudy (179), rued, ruer, rues, ruff (34d, 37b, 51c), ruga (48a, 134a), rugs, Ruhr (53d, 100b), ruin (34d, 35b, 62b), rule (13b, 35b, 37b, 70b, 118c), rump (23a, 33a, 75c), rums, rune (82b), rung (25d, 32b, 115b), runs, runt (12d, 38d), ruri (69c), ruru (81c), rusa (104a), ruse (60c, 62b, 116a), Rush (179), rush (114a), rusk (21d), Russ (179), Russ. (242), rust (31a, 85d, 90a), Ruth (80d, 179, 196, 197), ruth (29b, 89c), ruts

**_ R U _**   arui (13b), arum (32c, 71d, 114d), bruh (73b), brut (38b, 132c), crud (28c, 35a, 36a), crus (71b, 107c), Crux (207), crux (32b, 74b, 112b), drub (17c, 32c, 42c, 110b), drug (81a), drum (80a, 228), eruc (30d, 45d), frug (33b), grub (35d, 69b), grum (54d), Grus (207), Irus (83c), Prut (33d), true (9d, 15d, 31a, 42b, 44a, 73c, 111b), Truk (24b), urus (15d, 85c, 132a, 227, 231)

_ _ R U    **Boru** (142), **ecru** (18b, 22b, 126a), **feru** (30d, 45c), **guru** (60b), **maru** (65d), **Meru** (79a, 218), **Peru** (221), **ruru** (81c), **thru**

R _ _ U    **rimu** (62a, 98d), **ruru** (81c)

_ R V _    **ARVN** (235), **urva** (78a)

_ _ R V    **Marv** (169), **Merv** (170), **MIRV** (240)

_ _ R X    **Marx** (169)

R _ _ X    **roux** (104b)

R Y _ _    **ryal** (83d), **Ryan** (179), **rynd** (76d), **Ryne** (179), **ryot** (62d), **rype** (95d), **Ryun** (179)

_ R Y _    **aryl** (14b), **oryo-** (93a), **oryx** (13a, 231)

_ _ R Y    **aery** (39a), **airy** (41d, 66a, 71d), **awry** (15a, 32a, 125c, 134c), **bury** (63c), **Cary** (144), **dory** (20b, 47b), **eury-** (94a), **eyry** (39a), **fury** (97b, 116a), **Gary** (154), **gory** (20a), **Jory** (163), **jury** (31c), **kary-** (93b), **lory** (86d), **Mary** (96c, 107c, 169, 197), **nary** (82c), **Rory** (178), **spry** (9d, 72c, 81d), **tory** (22a, 30b, 73c), **vary** (26a, 35c, 77c), **very** (43c, 78d, 111b), **wary** (25b, 128b, 130a), **wiry** (109d)

R _ _ Y    **racy** (20a, 113c), **rely** (124d), **rimy**, **Roby** (178), **ropy** (116b), **Rory** (178), **rosy** (54d, 84c), **Ruby** (179), **ruby** (19c, 53b), **Rudy** (179)

_ _ R Z    **Harz** (79b)

R _ _ Z    **razz** (59a), **rhiz-** (93c), **Ritz** (177)

S A _ _    **saal** (53d), **Saar** (49c, 78d, 101a), **saba** (45d, 88c), **Sabe** (67b), **sack** (30b, 36a, 89b, 90c, 132c), **sacs**, **Sada** (179), **sado** (24c, 66a), **Sadr** (207), **safe** (106b, 116c, 127b), **Safi** (220), **S.Afr.** (242), **saga** (71b, 104c, 119b), **sage** (14c, 70d, 77b, 106a, 131b, 132d), **sago** (44b, 86a, 95d, 114d), **sags**, **Sahl** (179), **Saho** (32d, 57c, 216), **saic** (71c), **Said** (91c), **said** (127c), **sail** (91c), **sain** (19d, 32b), **Sais** (39d), **sais** (56c), **sake** (10b, 65d, 131a), **Saki** (95c), **saki** (78b, 231), **Saks** (179), **sala** (112d, 113a), **sale** (15c, 17b, 50b, 51a, 123d), **Salk** (179), **salp** (83b), **SALT** (242), **salt** (29d, 80b, 94b, 103b, 106a, 111c), **sama** (80d), **same** (36d, 61d), **samp** (55c, 60d, 91c), **Sams**, **Sa'na** (134c), **Sand** (179), **sand** (78d, 109b), **sane** (97d), **sang, sank, sans** (51b), **sapa** (55d), **saps, Sara** (179, 215), **sard** (24b, 25d, 53b, 84c, 106c, 115d), **sari** (52d, 60a), **Sark** (26a, 64b), **Sart** (64a), **sash** (18c, 37c, 54c, 132b), **Sask.** (242), **sass** (16b, 62c), **sate** (28b, 54d, 56a, 118a), **Sati** (96d, 109d, 198), **SATs** (29a), **Sauk** (49b, 56c, 189), **Saul** (67d, 87a, 179, 197), **-saur** (117b), **save** (42b, 67b, 84b, 94b, 126c), **sawn, saws, saya** (88c), **says**

_ S A _    **asap** (62a, 235), **Asas, ASAT** (235), **Esau** (64b, 65b, 98b, 197), **Isak** (159), **Isao** (159), **Isar** (33d, 79d, 100d, 216), **tsar** (103c), **USAF** (243), **usar** (11b, 17b, 62d)

**_ _ S A**  ansa (57d), bosa (13d), casa (112d), Elsa (55c, 72d, 84b, 129b, 151), Ilsa (24c), Issa (216), Lisa (166), masa (30d), mesa (40b, 59d, 90b, 119a), musa (16d), NASA (241), Ossa (79a, 84a, 121a), ossa (20d), Pisa (70d), Rosa (178), rusa (104a), Susa (40a), Ursa (17d), vasa (38c, 128a), visa (87a)

**S _ _ A**  saba (45d, 88c), Sada (179), saga (71b, 104c, 119b), sala (112d, 113a), sama (80d), Sa'na (134c), sapa (55d), Sara (179, 215), saya (88c), sera (13a, 47d, 65a), seta (22a, 57b, 113c), Shea (180), shea (22d, 124a), shi'a (80c), sida (30d, 96d), sika (34c, 65d, 231), sima (101b), Sita (97d), Siva (91a), skua (56d, 65b, 105c), soda (18d, 38a, 111c, 131c), sofa (36d), soga (52c), soja (56c), sola (11d, 39b, 89c), soma (12d, 20c, 62d), sora (19a, 97b), soya (112c), SPCA (243), Srta. (243), stoa (29a, 91c), sura (68c, 86a), Susa (40a), Suva (128d, 216)

**_ S B _**  ISBN (240)

**_ _ S B**  NTSB (241)

**S _ _ B**  scab (134a), scob (120d), Serb (134d), slab (88d, 110c), slob (126d), slub (134b), snab (22b, 105a), snob (88a, 111b), snub (62a, 81b, 98b, 109a, 110c), sorb (13c, 79a, 107a, 110b), stab (15c, 68a, 88d), stib (38d), stub (121d, 122c), swab (57c, 78c, 134b)

**S C _ _**  scab (134a), scad (24d, 27b, 61b, 65b), scan (47c, 73a, 88b, 98a), scar (27b, 134a), scat (54b, 96d), scob (120d), scop (90c), Scot (59d), Scot. (242), scow (20c, 47b), Scud (77b), scud (96d, 103a, 118c), scum (62c, 98d, 110c), scup (91c, 228), scut (119a)

**_ S C _**  Asch (139), asci (114a), esca (19d, 36a, 55d), -esce (117c), USCG (243)

**_ _ S C**  bosc (87b), desc. (237), disc (58b, 98c), disc. (237), fisc (42c, 102c), masc. (240), misc. (240), pisc- (93a), Visc. (244), Wisc. (212, 244)

**S _ _ C**  saic (71c), spec. (243)

**S D _ _**  S.Dak. (242)

**_ S D _**  USDA (243)

**S _ _ D**  Said (91c), said (127c), Sand (179), sand (78d, 109b), sard (24b, 25d, 53b, 84c, 106c, 115d), scad (24d, 27b, 61b, 65b), Scud (77b), scud (96d, 103a, 118c), seed (55c, 84d, 85c, 90a, 112b, 113d), send (36c, 74b, 86d, 91d, 99c, 108b, 123d), shad (25b, 46d), shed (24d, 70d, 77d, 108a), she'd (30c), shod, skid (110c), sled (102b), slid, sned (73a), sold, spad (80b, 89d), sped, spud (92a), stad (112b), stud (23a, 44c, 74c, 84d, 126d), sudd (47c), sued, surd (30b, 82d), Swed. (243)

417

**S E _ _**    **seal** (28b, 44c, 89b, 231), **seam** (66c, 67a, 128c), **Sean** (66c, 180), **sear** (25b, 133a), **seas**, **seat** (25d, 63b, 115c), **Seau** (180), **sebi-** (92d), **sebo-** (92d), **sect** (34d, 43d), **secy.** (243), **seed** (55c, 84d, 85c, 90a, 112b, 113d), **seek** (105d), **seel** (20a), **seem** (13c), **seen**, **seep** (72b, 84b, 87d, 114a), **seer** (95b, 111d, 128c), **sees**, **sego** (22c, 71a), **sehr** (54a), **Seir** (41c), **seis** (113a), **sejm** (91a), **self** (39d, 62d), **sell** (74d, 87c, 127d), **seme** (37c), **semi** (62c), **semi-** (93a, 93c), **send** (36c, 74b, 86d, 91d, 99c, 108b, 123d), **sens** (49c), **sent**, **seps** (72c, 106d), **Sept.** (78c, 243), **sept** (27d, 64a, 111b), **seqq.** (243), **sera** (13a, 47d, 65a), **Serb** (134d), **sere** (37d, 133a), **serf** (20d, 110b), **Seri** (76c), **sero-** (93c), **Sert** (112c), **sess** (111b), **sess.** (243), **seta** (22a, 57b, 113c), **Seth** (10a, 42b, 197, 198), **seth** (76a), **Seti** (88c), **sets**, **sett** (87b, 119d), **Seve** (180), **sewn**, **sews**, **sexi-** (93c), **sext** (23d, 84d, 109c), **sexy** (41c)

**_ S E _**    **asea** (32b, 129c), **esel** (53d), **Iser** (40a), **used** (9c, 57a), **user** (10a, 29c, 40c), **uses**

**_ _ S E**    **anse** (50c), **apse** (12a, 27a, 98b, 106c, 127c), **asse** (49b), **base** (9a, 41d, 49a, 62a, 73c, 92b, 102b, 102d), **bise** (132b), **case** (14b, 30b, 63b, 71a, 82c), **Dese** (216), **dose** (94a), **Duse** (64d, 150), **ease** (10b, 11c, 15b, 29b, 42d, 71b, 77b, 99b, 99d, 100a, 129d), **else** (18c, 61d, 85a), **-ense** (117b), **Erse** (25c, 52a, 64a), **esse** (9d, 18b), **fuse** (75d, 76a), **hose** (115c), **ipse** (37a, 69d), **José** (163), **Lise** (166), **lose** (48d), **-lyse** (117b), **mise** (10d, 134c), **muse** (52d, 91b, 121b), **nose** (89d, 95c), **NYSE** (241), **Ouse** (101a, 134d, 223), **pose** (9d, 15c, 94b), **rase** (34d), **rise** (62c, 114c), **Rose** (9a, 178), **ruse** (60c, 62b, 116a), **vase** (30b, 47d), **vise** (60c), **Wise** (187), **wise** (103b, 111a)

**S _ _ E**    **Sabe** (67b), **safe** (106b, 116c, 127b), **sage** (14c, 70d, 77b, 106a, 131b, 132d), **sake** (10b, 65d, 131a), **sale** (15c, 17b, 50b, 51a, 123d), **same** (36d, 61d), **sane** (97d), **sate** (28b, 54d, 56a, 118a), **save** (42b, 67b, 84b, 94b, 126c), **seme** (37c), **sere** (37d, 133a), **Seve** (180), **shoe** (122b), **sice** (56c), **side** (43d, 47b, 69b, 119b), **sine** (52a, 70b, 96b, 124c), **sipe** (122b), **sire** (18b, 21d, 44d, 48d, 94d, 120c, 122c), **site** (72d, 76a, 107a), **size** (129a), **Skye** (64d, 120d), **sloe** (15b, 19d, 51d, 90b, 132a), **slue** (110c, 118c), **Smee** (88b), **snee** (33a, 35d, 68a), **soie** (51a), **soke** (67c), **sole** (42c, 46d, 47d, 84b, 87c, 109d, 111d, 228), **some** (86d, 96b), **sone** (246), **sore** (12d, 106c), **Spee** (53c, 55c), **suke** (120a), **sure** (10b, 99b, 106b, 126d), **syce** (56c), **syne** (105b)

**S F _ _**    **Sfax** (223)

**S _ _ F**    **self** (39d, 62d), **serf** (20d, 110b), **surf** (21d)

**_ S G _**    **Msgr.** (241), **M.Sgt.** (241), **S.Sgt.** (243)

**S _ _ G**    **sang**, **shag** (57b, 119c, 122c), **sing** (129d), **skeg** (67b, 133b), **slag** (28c, 38b, 76b, 105a, 111a, 129a, 130a), **slog** (38b, 124d, 129b), **slug** (38a, 76b, 116b), **smog** (130d), **smug** (29c, 106c), **snag** (13a, 24d, 60a, 68c, 95a, 122b), **Snug** (193), **snug** (31c, 122a), **song**

(14b, 61d, 125a), **stag** (34c, 52b, 76a), **Sung** (26d), **sung, surg.** (243), **swag** (115c), **swig** (37d, 57a)

**S H _ _**  **shad** (25b, 46d), **shag** (57b, 119c, 122c), **shah** (16c, 88a), **Shak.** (243), **sham** (9d, 34a, 45a, 49b, 77b, 91d, 94b, 109c), **Shan** (62d, 69a, 220), **Shaw** (41a, 43a, 180, 204), **shay** (84a), **Shea** (180), **shea** (22d, 124a), **shed** (24d, 70d, 77d, 108a), **she'd** (30c), **Shem** (81d, 197), **she's** (30c), **shew** (128a), **shi'a** (80c), **shim** (71c, 119c, 130d), **shin** (11d, 12a, 71a, 71b, 107c), **ship** (106c, 128a), **shiv** (68a), **shod, shoe** (122b), **shoo** (38a, 54b), **shop** (62d, 100a), **shot** (12b, 70c), **shou** (26d), **show** (9d, 34d, 35a, 36c, 43a, 74c), **shul** (118d), **shun** (16c, 41c), **shut** (28b)

**_ S H _**  **Ashe** (139), **ashy** (86a, 129d), **Ishi** (134a), **OSHA** (241)

**_ _ S H**  **bash** (60b, 86d), **bosh** (82a), **Bush** (143, 191), **bush** (109a, 119a), **Cash** (144), **cash** (15a, 78a), **cosh** (60b), **Cush** (57c, 197), **dash** (20a, 96a, 114a, 120b, 128d), **dish** (76a, 119a), **fish** (128d), **gash** (33a, 110b), **Gish** (155), **gosh** (42a, 53b), **gush** (114b, 118a), **hash** (21b), **hush** (109b), **Josh** (163), **josh** (17a, 66b, 66d, 90d), **Kish** (197), **kish** (55d, 104c), **lash** (42d, 47c, 122a, 131c), **losh** (40b), **lush** (38b, 73d), **MASH** (240), **Mash** (197), **mash** (32b, 115d), **mesh** (40d, 63c, 81c, 111b, 130d), **mush** (75b), **Nash** (172), **pish** (42c), **posh** (21a, 40b), **push** (38a, 46a, 108d, 121d), **rash** (98b, 110a), **resh** (12a), **Rush** (179), **rush** (114a), **sash** (18c, 37c, 54c, 132b), **sish** (61b), **tosh** (82a), **tush** (23a), **Wash** (82b), **Wash.** (212), **wash** (14d), **wish** (35b)

**S _ _ H**  **sash** (18c, 37c, 54c, 132b), **Seth** (10a, 42b, 197, 198), **seth** (76a), **shah** (16c, 88a), **sigh** (21d), **Sikh** (60b), **sish** (61b), **soph.** (243), **such** (131b)

**S I _ _**  **sial** (85b), **Siam** (120d), **sibs, sice** (56c), **sick** (126b), **sida** (30d, 96d), **side** (43d, 47b, 69b, 119b), **Sids, sift** (105c, 109b, 132d), **sigh** (21d), **sign** (74d, 91c, 114c), **sika** (34c, 65d, 231), **Sikh** (60b), **silk** (43b), **Sill** (49a), **sill** (37c, 121c, 132b), **silo** (48a, 116a), **silt** (79c, 106b), **sima** (101b), **Simi** (64c), **simp** (48b, 109c), **Sims** (181), **sine** (52a, 70b, 96b, 124c), **sing** (129d), **sink** (34b, 60c, 110d), **Sino-** (92d), **sino** (112d), **sins, -sion** (117a), **sipe** (122b), **sips, sire** (18b, 21d, 44d, 48d, 94d, 120c, 122c), **sirs, sish** (61b), **Sita** (97d), **site** (72d, 76a, 107a), **sito-** (93a), **sits, Siva** (91a), **size** (129a)

**_ S I _**  **Asia** (39b), **asin** (78b), **Hsia** (26d, 38d), **Isis** (61b, 85a), **-osis** (117a), **psis, Tsin** (26d), **USIA** (243)

**_ _ S I**  **ANSI** (235), **assi** (60c), **Desi** (149), **lasi** (221), **Lisi** (166), **lysi-** (93a), **nasi** (87a), **nisi** (70b, 126c), **ossi-** (92c)

**S _ _ I**  **Safi** (220), **Saki** (95c), **saki** (78b, 231), **sari** (52d, 60a), **Sati** (96d, 109d, 198), **sebi-** (92d), **semi** (62c), **semi-** (93a, 93c), **Seri** (76c), **Seti** (88c), **sexi-** (93c), **Simi** (64c), **Sodi** (197), **soli** (14b), **sori** (45b), **sufi** (88a), **sugi** (65b), **suji** (131b)

419

**S _ _ J**    subj. (243)

**S K _ _**    skat (24b), skaw (67c), skeg (67b, 133b), skeo (47a), skep (18a, 60b), skew (118c, 125b), skid (110c), skim (47c, 54d, 56a), skin (43a, 59d, 87c, 104c), skip (9b, 56a, 84a, 87a), skis, skit (108d, 110a), skua (56d, 65b, 105c), Skye (64d, 120d), skyr (20d)

**_ S K _**    asks

**_ _ S K**    bask (46d, 73d, 80b, 128d, 228), bosk (133b), busk (20c, 31a, 45c), cask (30b), cusk (46d), desk (134c), disk (27b), dusk (125c), fisk (42c), husk (43a, 61c, 106b, 232), mask (29d, 36b, 37c), musk (87d), Omsk (64b), pisk (12b), risk (52b, 58c, 66b, 127d), rusk (21d), Sask. (242), task (115c), Tosk (213), tusk (46d, 65c, 123a)

**S _ _ K**    sack (30b, 36a, 89b, 90c, 132c), Salk (179), sank, Sark (26a, 64b), Sask. (242), Sauk (49b, 56c, 189), S.Dak. (242), seek (105d), Shak. (243), sick (126b), silk (43b), sink (34b, 60c, 110d), soak (9b, 37d, 104b, 115a), sock (96a, 116b, 132b), sook (23b), souk (17d, 74d), suck (9b), sulk (117d), sunk, SWAK (243)

**S L _ _**    slab (88d, 110c), slag (28c, 38b, 76b, 105a, 111a, 129a, 130a), slam (124c, 131c), slap (22c, 98b), slat (69b, 133b), Slav (14d), slaw (28d), slay (36c, 79d), sled (102b), slew (110c, 118c), sley (130d), slid, Slim (181), slim (110c, 118b), slip (36b, 41c, 52d, 54d, 110c, 126b), slit (33a), slob (126d), sloe (15b, 19d, 51d, 90b, 132a), slog (38b, 124d, 129b), slop (48b, 111b), slot (12d, 13b, 34c, 84b, 123c), slow (34a, 35d, 58a, 110d, 116d), slub (134b), slue (110c, 118c), slug (38a, 76b, 116b), slum (81b, 99d), slur (36c, 40b, 74c, 95b, 123c, 128b), slut (133b)

**_ S L _**    isle (11a, 64b, 67b), Oslo (220)

**_ _ S L**    NASL (241)

**S _ _ L**    saal (53d), Sahl (179), sail (91c), Saul (67d, 87a, 179, 197), seal (28b, 44c, 89b, 231), seel (20a), sell (74d, 87c, 127d), shul (118d), sial (85b), Sill (49a), sill (37c, 121c, 132b), soil (39a, 114c, 117d, 120d), Soul (181), soul (95d, 113d, 128c), STOL (243), syll. (243)

**S M _ _**    Smee (88b), smew (19a, 38c, 76a, 104c), smit (128a), smog (130d), smug (29c, 106c), smur (38a), smut (28c, 36a, 90a, 111d)

**_ S M _**    USMA (243), USMC (243)

**_ _ S M**    cosm- (93d), Tasm. (243)

**S _ _ M**    scum (62c, 98d, 110c), seam (66c, 67a, 128c), seem (13c), sejm (91a), sham (9d, 34a, 45a, 49b, 77b, 91d, 94b, 109c), Shem (81d, 197), shim (71c, 119c, 130d), Siam (120d), skim (47c, 54d, 56a), slam (124c, 131c), Slim (181), slim (110c, 118b), slum (81b, 99d), Spam (73c), stem (26b, 95c, 114c, 115d), stum (55d, 100b, 132c), swam, swim (37a), swum

**S N _ _**  **snab** (22b, 105a), **snag** (13a, 24d, 60a, 68c, 95a, 122b), **snap** (17b, 21d, 31d, 39b, 44c, 66c), **sned** (73a), **snee** (33a, 35d, 68a), **snip** (28a), **snit** (10d, 12c, 47b), **snob** (88a, 111b), **snot** (62c, 88a), **Snow** (181), **snow** (130d), **snub** (62a, 81b, 98b, 109a, 110c), **Snug** (193), **snug** (31c, 122a)

**_ S N _**  **esne** (12c, 106d, 110b, 121b), **isn't**, **USNA** (243), **USNG** (243), **USNR** (244)

**_ _ S N**  **assn.** (236), **bo's'n** (20c, 88b)

**S _ _ N**  **sain** (19d, 32b), **sawn**, **scan** (47c, 73a, 88b, 98a), **Sean** (66c, 180), **seen**, **sewn**, **Shan** (62d, 69a, 220), **shin** (11d, 12a, 71a, 71b, 107c), **shun** (16c, 41c), **sign** (74d, 91c, 114c), **-sion** (117a), **skin** (43a, 59d, 87c, 104c), **soon** (94a, 108d), **sown** (21d, 32a, 38d, 49a, 81d, 85d, 98a, 120a, 120c, 122a, 232), **spin** (100b, 131c), **spun**, **Stan** (181), **Sten** (182), **sten** (73d), **stun** (108b, 116c), **sunn** (45d), **Svan** (25a), **Sven** (19a, 28c, 226), **swan** (19a, 28c, 226)

**S O _ _**  **soak** (9b, 37d, 104b, 115a), **soap** (17c), **soar** (48a), **sobs**, **sock** (96a, 116b, 132b), **soco** (21c), **soda** (18d, 38a, 111c, 131c), **Sodi** (197), **sods**, **sofa** (36d), **soft** (39b, 74c, 76d), **soga** (52c), **So-Ho** (73a), **soie** (51a), **soil** (39a, 114c, 117d, 120d), **soir** (50b), **soja** (56c), **soke** (67c), **sola** (11d, 39b, 89c), **sold**, **sole** (42c, 46d, 47d, 84b, 87c, 109d, 111d, 228), **soli** (14b), **solo** (11d, 14b, 84a), **Sols**, **soma** (12d, 20c, 62d), **some** (86d, 96b), **sone** (246), **song** (14b, 61d, 125a), **sons** (83c), **sook** (23b), **soon** (94a, 108d), **soot** (24a, 28c, 68d), **soph.** (243), **sops**, **sora** (19a, 97b), **sorb** (13c, 79a, 107a, 110b), **sore** (12d, 106c), **sori** (45b), **sors** (69c), **sort** (27d, 36d, 67c, 106d, 109b, 113b, 127b, 132d), **so-so** (76c, 86d, 122d), **sots**, **souk** (17d, 74d), **Soul** (181), **soul** (95d, 113d, 128c), **soup** (75c), **sour** (15b, 119d), **sous** (51b), **sown**, **sows**, **soya** (112c), **soys**

**_ S O _**  **asor** (59a), **USOC** (244)

**_ _ S O**  **also** (12c, 18c, 62c, 78c, 90c, 115b), **Caso** (64c), **Koso** (108d), **meso-** (93b), **miso** (65d), **miso-** (93a), **naso-** (93b), **noso-** (92d), **peso** (215, 216, 217, 219, 221, 224), **so-so** (76c, 86d, 122d), **vaso-** (92c)

**S _ _ O**  **sado** (24c, 66a), **sago** (44b, 86a, 95d, 114d), **Saho** (32d, 57c, 216), **sebo-** (92d), **sego** (22c, 71d), **sero-** (93c), **shoo** (38a, 54b), **silo** (48a, 116a), **Sino-** (92d), **sino** (112d), **sito-** (93a), **skeo** (47a), **soco** (21c), **So-Ho** (73a), **solo** (11d, 14b, 84a), **so-so** (76c, 86d, 122d), **sumo** (66a)

**S P _ _**  **spad** (80b, 89d), **Spam** (73c), **span** (21d, 32a, 38d, 49a, 81d, 85d, 98a, 120a, 120c, 122a, 232), **spar** (21b, 22c, 52a, 77a, 90d, 101c, 108b), **spas**, **spat** (14b, 85d, 96b, 102c), **spay** (115b), **SPCA** (243), **spec.** (243), **spcd**, **Spee** (53c, 55c), **Spes** (198), **spet** (17b), **spew** (40a), **spin** (100b, 131c), **spir-** (92d), **spit** (90d, 101b), **spor-** (93d), **spot** (35d, 72d, 79d, 89d, 114c), **SPQR** (243), **spry** (9d, 72c, 81d), **spud** (92a), **spun**, **spur** (46a, 54d, 62c, 63c, 95a)

**_ S P _**   asps, ESPN (26a), espy (106b), USPO (244), USPS (244)

**_ _ S P**   cusp (31d, 61a, 89d, 90c, 90d), gasp (21d, 86b), hasp (44c, 113c), hosp. (239), Insp. (239), lisp (113c), rasp (46a, 56a, 105c, 122d), WASP (244), wasp (63b, 229), wisp (49b)

**S _ _ P**   salp (83b), samp (55c, 60d, 91c), scop (90c), scup (91c, 228), seep (72b, 84b, 87d, 114a), ship (106c, 128a), shop (62d, 100a), simp (48b, 109c), skep (18a, 60b), skip (9b, 56a, 84a, 87a), slap (22c, 98b), slip (36b, 41c, 52d, 54d, 110c, 126b), slop (48b, 111b), snap (17b, 21d, 31d, 39b, 44c, 66c), snip (28a), soap (17c), soup (75c), step (55c, 129b), stop (9a, 14c, 17a, 25b, 40d, 57c, 84c, 131d), sump (25d, 77a), swap (123c)

**S _ _ Q**   seqq. (243)

**S R _ _**   Srta. (243)

**_ _ S R**   USSR (244)

**S _ _ R**   Saar (49c, 78d, 101a), Sadr (207), S.Afr. (242), -saur (117b), scar (27b, 134a), sear (25b, 133a), seer (95b, 111d, 128c), sehr (54a), Seir(41c), skyr(20d), slur (36c, 40b, 74c, 95b, 123c, 128b), smur (38a), soar (48a), soir (50b), sour (15b, 119d), spar (21b, 22c, 52a, 77a, 90d, 101c, 108b), spir- (92d), spor- (93d), SPQR (243), spur (46a, 54d, 62c, 63c, 95a), star (15b, 73c), -ster (117a, 117b), stir (10d, 14c, 29b, 36d, 63b, 77b, 79c, 94d, 95a, 115c), suer (95b)

**S S _ _**   S.Sgt. (243)

**_ S S _**   asse (49b), assi (60c), assn. (236), asst. (236), esse (9d, 18b), Issa (216), Ossa (79a, 84a, 121a), ossa (20d), ossi- (92c), USSR (244)

**_ _ S S**   Bess (141), boss (40c, 116c), buss (68a), Cass (144), cess (71c, 120a), cuss (32d, 88a, 118c), diss (75d), doss (18a), Fess (152), fess (41c), foss (36d), fuss (21b, 36d, 92a), Hess (158), Hiss (158), hiss (36a, 112a), jass (118d), Jess (161), jess (116a), joss (26d, 62c), kiss (22d, 91b), koss (246), lass (45b, 74b), less (77b, 82c), liss (49a), loss (35a, 94d, 130a), Mass. (210, 240), mass (9c, 10d, 17a, 22c, 53a, 58d, 107a, 129a), mess (21b, 26a, 30a, 36c, 67a, 79c, 111b), Miss. (210, 240), miss (54c, 108c), Moss (171), moss (71c, 86c, 125a), muss (103a), ness (24a, 58d, 95a), pass (13d, 21d, 84a, 85c, 106c), puss (24d), Ross (178, 193, 195, 207, 208), ross (17b, 119c), Russ (179), Russ. (242), sass (16b, 62c), sess (111b), sess. (243), TASS (81c, 112b), Tess (58a, 183), toss (22c, 47c, 121c)

**S _ _ S**   sacs, sags, Sais (39d), sais (56c), Saks (179), Sams, sans (51b), saps, sass (16b, 62c), SATs (29a), saws, says, seas, sees, seis (113a), sens (49c), seps (72c, 106d), sess (111b), sess. (243), sets, sews, she's (30c), sibs, Sids, Sims (181), sins, sips, sirs, sits, skis, sobs, sods, Sols, sons (83c), sops, sors (69c), sots,

**sous** (51b), **sows**, **soys**, **spas**, **Spes** (198), **Stus**, **subs**, **suds** (18a, 48a, 114a), **sues**, **sums**, **Suns** (206), **suns**, **sups**

S T _ _    **stab** (15c, 68a, 88d), **stad** (112b), **stag** (34c, 52b, 76a), **Stan** (181), **star** (15b, 73c), **stat** (15c, 114a), **-stat** (117c), **stat.** (243), **stay** (34c, 57c, 95b, 99c, 102b, 119d, 128c, 129b), **stem** (26b, 95c, 114c, 115d), **Sten** (182), **sten** (73d), **step** (55c, 129b), **-ster** (117a, 117b), **stet** (71c, 94c, 95b), **stew** (20c, 30c), **stib** (38d), **stir** (10d, 14c, 29b, 36d, 63b, 77b, 79c, 94d, 95a, 115c), **stoa** (29a, 91c), **STOL** (243), **stop** (9a, 14c, 17a, 25b, 40d, 57c, 84c, 131d), **stot** (134d), **stow** (85b), **stub** (121d, 122c), **stud** (23a, 44c, 74c, 84d, 126d), **stum** (55d, 100b, 132c), **stun** (108b, 116c), **Stus**, **Styx** (26b, 57a)

_ S T _    **Asta** (37b, 81d, 121b), **Asti** (65a, 132c), **astr-** (93d), **esta** (113a), **Este** (44b, 45b, 64d, 85b), **este** (113a), **Esth.** (16d, 238), **oste** (20d), **USTA** (244)

_ _ S T    **AHST** (235), **asst.** (236), **bast** (17b, 45d, 88c, 133c), **best** (26d, 30a, 34c, 42b, 85c, 118b), **bust** (14c, 17a, 21d, 44a, 58c), **cast** (15a, 73a, 121c, 123b, 232), **cest** (54c), **cist** (115d), **cost** (26a, 94b), **cyst** (128a), **dist.** (237), **dost** (128a), **dust** (114a), **east** (84d), **erst** (49a), **fast** (46b, 47c, 96d, 118c, 126d), **-fest** (117b), **fist** (21c, 57d), **fust** (107b), **gest** (119b), **gist** (74b, 89c), **gust** (20a), **hast** (128a), **hist.** (239), **host** (14c, 42a, 79d), **Inst.** (239), **jest** (17a, 66d), **just** (41b, 44a, 62b, 76a, 97c, 127c), **kist** (105b), **last** (30b, 40d, 108c, 130d), **lest** (48d), **list** (24d, 41b, 65c, 101c, 102b, 104d, 122a), **LOST** (240), **lost** (77b, 130a), **lust** (34a, 107a), **mast** (18a, 90d, 108b, 113a), **mist** (28b, 38a, 48a, 127b), **most** (74b, 78c), **must** (55d, 81c, 116c, 132c), **myst** (56b), **Nast** (172), **nest** (31c, 100a, 111b, 118c, 232), **oast** (16b, 67b, 85c), **oust** (35b, 40a, 42b, 96c), **past** (55b, 60b, 122a), **pest** (82d, 88a, 89d), **Post** (175), **post** (69c, 74b, 81c, 115a), **rest** (16b, 21d, 71b, 80c, 87b, 99b, 99c, 99d, 234), **rust** (31a, 85d, 90a), **test** (23d, 41d, 42b, 124b, 124d), **Uist** (64d), **vast** (61c, 62a), **vest** (28b, 129b), **wast** (128a), **West** (186), **west** (83b), **wist** (68c), **zest** (45c, 57c, 99b)

S _ _ T    **SALT** (242), **salt** (29d, 80b, 94b, 103b, 106a, 111c), **Sart** (64a), **scat** (54b, 96d), **Scot** (59c), **Scot.** (242), **scut** (119a), **seat** (25d, 63b, 115c), **sect** (34d, 43d), **sent**, **Sept.** (78c, 243), **sept** (27d, 64a, 111b), **Sert** (112c), **sett** (87b, 119d), **sext** (23d, 84d, 109d), **shot** (12b, 70c), **shut** (28b), **sift** (105c, 109b, 132d), **silt** (79c, 106b), **skat** (24b), **skit** (108d, 110a), **slat** (69b, 133b), **slit** (33a), **slot** (12d, 13b, 34c, 84b, 123c), **slut** (133b), **smit** (128a), **smut** (28c, 36a, 90a, 111d), **snit** (10d, 12c, 47b), **snot** (62c, 88a), **soft** (39b, 74c, 76d), **soot** (24a, 28c, 68d), **sort** (27d, 36d, 67c, 106d, 109b, 113b, 127b, 132d), **spat** (14b, 85d, 96b, 102c), **spet** (17b), **spit** (90d, 101b), **spot** (35d, 72d, 79d, 89d, 114c), **S.Sgt.** (243), **stat** (15c, 114a), **-stat** (117c), **stat.** (243), **stet** (71c, 94c, 95b), **stot** (134d), **suet** (44c, 83d), **suit** (9c, 10a, 31c, 47b, 71a, 85b, 90b, 104b), **supt.** (243), **SWAT** (243), **swat** (20a, 28b, 116b), **Swit** (182)

S U _ _    **subj.** (243), **subs**, **such** (131b), **suck** (9b), **sudd** (47c), **suds** (18a, 48a, 114a), **sued**, **suer** (95b), **sues**, **suet** (44c, 83d), **Suez** (23c),

**sufi** (88a), **sugi** (65c), **suit** (9c, 10a, 31c, 47b, 71a, 85b, 90b, 104b), **suji** (131b), **suke** (120a), **suky** (120a), **sulk** (117d), **Sulu** (88c), **sulu** (46a), **sumo** (66a), **sump** (25d, 77a), **sums**, **Sung** (26d), **sung**, **sunk**, **sunn** (45d), **Suns** (206), **suns**, **sups**, **supt.** (243), **sura** (68c, 86a), **surd** (30b, 82d), **sure** (10b, 99b, 106b, 126d), **surf** (21d), **surg.** (243), **Susa** (40a), **susu** (20a), **Suva** (128d, 216)

_ S U _     **tsun** (246), **usus** (69c, 70b)

_ _ S U     **ansu** (13d, 68c), **Nosu** (215), **susu** (20a), **Zasu** (188)

S _ _ U     **Seau** (180), **shou** (26d), **Sulu** (88c), **sulu** (46a), **susu** (20a)

S V _ _     **Svan** (25a), **Sven**

_ S V _     **RSVP** (242)

S _ _ V     **shiv** (68a), **Slav** (14d)

S W _ _     **swab** (57c, 78c, 134b), **swag** (115c), **SWAK** (243), **swam**, **swan** (19a, 28c, 226), **swap** (123c), **SWAT** (243), **swat** (20a, 28b, 116b), **sway** (29b, 37b, 63a, 67c, 76d, 79c, 85a, 130c, 133a), **Swed.** (243), **swig** (37d, 57a), **swim** (37a), **Swit** (182), **swum**

S _ _ W     **scow** (20c, 47b), **Shaw** (41a, 43a, 180, 204), **shew** (128a), **show** (9d, 34d, 35a, 36c, 43a, 74c), **skew** (118c, 125b), **skaw** (67c), **slaw** (28d), **slew** (110c, 118c), **slow** (34a, 35d, 58a, 110d, 116d), **smew** (19a, 38c, 76a, 104c), **Snow** (181), **snow** (130d), **spew** (40a), **stew** (20c, 30c), **stow** (85b)

S _ _ X     **Sfax** (223), **Styx** (26b, 57a)

S Y _ _     **syce** (56c), **syll.** (243), **syne** (105b)

_ _ S Y     **busy** (40d, 83b), **easy** (43d, 53c, 55c, 77c, 109c, 111c), **nosy** (63b), **posy** (82b, 100d), **rosy** (54d, 84c)

S _ _ Y     **secy.** (243), **sexy** (41c), **shay** (84a), **slay** (36c, 79d), **sley** (130d), **spay** (115b), **spry** (9d, 72c, 81d), **stay** (34c, 57c, 95b, 99c, 102b, 119d, 128c, 129b), **suky** (120a), **sway** (29b, 37b, 63a, 67c, 76d, 79c, 85a, 130c, 133a)

S _ _ Z     **Suez** (23c)

T A _ _     **Taal** (10c, 69a, 112b), **tabs**, **tabu** (48c), **tack** (13d, 15c, 31b, 44c, 80b), **tact** (35d), **tads**, **tael** (71c, 131a), **ta'en** (107c), **Taft** (183, 191), **tags**, **taha** (130d), **tahr** (55a), **tail** (13c, 25a, 40d, 48b, 89d, 107b, 123c), **tait** (15d, 60d), **taka** (213), **take** (117a), **takt** (80a, 120b), **tala** (17c), **talc** (25d, 49c, 77a, 92a, 111b), **tale** (43a, 71b, 103b, 134a), **talk** (29d, 36a, 113b), **tall** (72d), **tame** (37a, 37b, 53c), **tamp** (76d, 85b, 92a, 97d), **tams**, **Tana** (68b), **T'ang** (26d), **tang** (22a, 47b, 135a), **tank** (127d), **Tano** (95d, 189), **tans**, **Taos** (81c),

424

**tapa** (17b, 28b, 43b, 45c, 79d, 86b, 91a), **tape** (19a, 98c), **taps**, **Tara** (104d), **tara** (45b, 64a), **tare** (128b, 131a), **tarn** (68b, 79b, 91b, 130a), **taro** (14d, 39c, 52a, 90d, 102b, 114d, 125a), **tarp** (23d, 130b), **tars**, **tart** (87a, 112b), **task** (115c), **Tasm.** (243), **TASS** (81c, 112b), **ta-ta** (44b), **tats, tatu** (14b), **taur-** (92c), **taus, taut** (120c, 122a), **tawa** (81c), **taws, taxi** (95d)

_ T A _    **atap** (86a), **Etah** (56c, 63d), **et al.** (69c, 238), **etat** (51a), **ital.** (240), **Ptah** (75d, 198), **stab** (15c, 68a, 88d), **stad** (112b), **stag** (34c, 52b, 76a), **Stan** (181), **star** (15b, 73c), **stat** (15c, 114a), **-stat** (117c), **stat.** (243), **stay** (34c, 57c, 95b, 99c, 102b, 119d, 128c, 129b), **Utah** (212), **utas** (40a)

_ _ T A    **acta** (34b, 94d, 98c, 121a), **Alta.** (235), **anta** (89a, 91c), **Arta** (56d), **Asta** (37b, 81d, 121b), **atta** (70c), **beta** (11d, 106a), **cata-** (92c, 92d), **CETA** (236), **data** (29c, 63a, 115a), **dita** (88c, 124b), **esta** (113a), **Etta** (152), **-etta** (117b), **gata** (107d), **geta** (65b, 108c), **iota** (11d, 66d, 122c, 131c), **jota** (112c), **keta** (37b), **meta-** (92d), **muta** (26a, 80d), **Nita** (172), **nota** (69d), **octa-** (92d), **pita** (11d, 25c, 45c), **rata** (46a), **Rita** (177), **rota** (25a, 27a, 31c, 101d, 102b), **seta** (22a, 57b, 113c), **Sita** (97d), **Srta.** (243), **ta-ta** (44b), **USTA** (244), **vita** (69d, 71d), **vota** (102a), **weta** (72c), **zeta** (11d)

T _ _ A    **taha** (130d), **taka** (213), **tala** (17c), **Tana** (68b), **tapa** (17b, 28b, 43b, 45c, 79d, 86b, 91a), **Tara** (104d), **tara** (45b, 64a), **ta-ta** (44b), **tawa** (81c), **tela** (21c, 75d, 130d), **tema** (121a, 234), **tera-** (93d), **Tewa** (189), **Thea** (122c), **Tina** (183), **Toda** (37d), **toea** (221), **toga** (101d), **tola** (66d, 103a), **tora** (13a, 58b), **tuba** (80a, 86a), **tufa** (91c, 129a), **tula** (10d, 11d), **tuna** (125a, 229), **Tyra** (184)

T _ _ B    **tomb** (22d)

_ T C _    **etch** (14d, 35a), **itch** (58a, 64b)

_ _ T C    **ROTC** (242)

T _ _ C    **talc** (25d, 49c, 77a, 92a, 111b)

T _ _ D    **teed, tend** (24b, 73a, 77a, 124b), **Thad** (183), **thud** (20a, 112a), **tied, toad** (17c, 225), **Todd** (183), **toed, told** (99a), **trod**

T E _ _    **teak** (39b, 124a), **teal** (19a, 20b, 38c, 226), **team** (32a, 48c, 56c, 85d, 232), **tear** (68b, 99c), **teas, teat** (81d), **Teds, teed, teel** (107a), **teem** (9b, 92a, 118c), **-teen** (117b), **Tees** (82b), **tees, teff** (10c), **tegs, teil** (72a), **Teke** (215), **tela** (21c, 75d, 130d), **tele-** (92d, 93d), **Tell** (14a), **tell** (13d, 62b, 81a, 99a), **telo-** (92d), **tema** (121a, 234), **temp.** (243), **tend** (24b, 73a, 77a, 124b), **Tenn.** (212, 243), **teno-** (93d), **tens, tent** (24a, 87b), **Teos** (64a), **tera-** (93d), **Teri** (183), **term** (71d, 72a, 80b, 106c, 115c), **tern** (19a, 28c, 56d, 104d, 105d, 118b, 226), **terp** (79a, 94a), **Tess** (58a, 183), **test** (23d, 41d, 42b, 124b, 124d), **tete** (50c), **teth** (12a), **Tewa** (189), **text** (86d, 133c)

_ T E _    **atef** (32b, 39d), **ates** (118c), **cten-** (93c), **itea** (118c, 128c), **item** (9c, 14d, 35b, 41b, 71a, 72b, 81c, 83a, 86d), **iter** (69d, 101a, 101d),

425

**Otea** (64c), **pter-** (94a), **stem** (26b, 95c, 114c, 115d), **Sten** (182), **sten** (73d), **step** (55c, 129b), **-ster** (117a, 117b), **stet** (71c, 94c, 95b), **stew** (20c, 30c), **uter-** (93d), **Utes**

_ _ T E    **alte** (69d), **ante** (68a, 69c, 90d, 114c), **ante-** (92c), **Arte** (139), **bate** (119c), **Bete** (215), **bete** (50a), **bite** (26c, 115c), **Bute** (64d), **cete** (232), **cite** (97c), **cote** (19b, 107d, 108a), **cute** (10a, 32c, 116a), **date** (33d, 51d), **dote** (85c), **Este** (44b, 45b, 64d, 85b), **este** (113a), **-ette** (117b), **fate** (35b, 68a, 73b), **fete** (45c), **gate** (15c, 41b, 91c), **gite** (50c), **hate** (35b, 72d), **jete** (16c), **jute** (30d, 45c, 102b, 103a), **Kate** (107c, 163), **Kite** (164), **kite** (19a, 58c, 226), **late** (33d, 98b), **-lite** (117b, 117c), **lute** (25c, 66a, 80b, 100d), **-lyte** (117a), **mate** (15b, 18d, 26c, 29b, 34c, 85d, 114a, 120a), **mete** (11c, 13d, 91d), **mite** (14a, 63b, 64a, 86c, 86d), **mote** (113b), **mute** (109b, 113c, 232, 234), **Nate** (172), **note** (15c, 71c, 75d, 83b, 95a, 98c, 99c, 122d, 129c, 234), **oste** (20d), **Pate** (174), **pate** (32b, 58c), **Pete** (85a, 174), **rate** (13d, 27d, 30b, 41d, 42a, 55c, 66d, 94b, 97d, 107a, 127b), **rete** (81c, 90b), **rite** (72c), **Rote** (178), **rote** (75d, 99d, 118a), **sate** (28b, 54d, 56a, 118a), **site** (72d, 76a, 107a), **teto** (50c), **tote** (22a, 24c, 86c), **vite** (50d), **vote** (49b, 128d), **yate** (41d)

T _ _ E    **take** (117a), **tale** (43a, 71b, 103b, 134a), **tame** (37a, 37b, 53c), **tape** (19a, 98c), **tare** (128b, 131a), **Teke** (215), **tele-** (92d, 93d), **tete** (50c), **thee** (95b), **tide** (83b), **tige** (89b), **tile** (27d, 46b, 74b, 102a, 120d), **time** (38d, 41b, 41c, 87d, 100b), **tine** (13a, 95a, 123a), **tire** (21a, 42d, 44d, 47b, 131c), **Tobe** (183), **tobe** (10c), **tole** (41b, 76b), **tome** (20d, 129a), **Tone** (184), **tone** (9c, 82c, 89c), **tope** (107d, 229), **tore** (22a, 24c, 86c), **tree** (30d, 53b, 133c), **true** (9d, 15d, 31a, 42b, 44a, 73c, 111b), **tube** (33c, 89c, 117a), **-tude** (117b), **tuke** (23d, 43b), **tule** (22c, 25a), **Tune** (184), **tune** (9c, 10a, 10d, 14b, 58a, 75d, 111d, 116a), **tyee** (26d), **tyke** (21c, 26c), **Tyne** (82b, 184, 223), **type** (27d, 112a, 113b), **Tyre** (71a, 88c, 218)

T _ _ F    **teff** (10c), **TGIF** (243), **tiff** (96b), **toff** (33c), **tref** (48b, 126a), **tuff** (91c, 129a), **turf** (87b, 111c, 118b)

T G _ _    **TGIF** (243)

T _ _ G    **T'ang** (26d), **tang** (22a, 47b, 135a), **thug** (52c), **ting** (76b), **tong** (26d), **trig** (114a, 124c), **trig.** (31b, 243), **tung** (83d), **twig** (21c)

T H _ _    **Thad** (183), **Thai** (109a, 218, 223), **than** (29b), **Thar** (35a), **thar** (55a), **that** (34d, 95a, 99b), **thaw** (72b), **Thea** (122c), **thee** (95b), **them** (95a), **then** (10c, 121a), **thew** (79d), **they** (95a), **thin** (35c, 35d, 53b, 110c), **thio-** (93d), **this** (34d, 95a), **Thor** (10b, 76c, 77b, 83b, 121d, 183, 198), **Thos.** (74d), **thos** (65b), **thou** (95b), **thru**, **thud** (20a, 112a), **thug** (52c), **Thur.** (243), **thus** (111b, 121a)

_ T H _    **ethn-** (93c), **Otho** (102a)

_ _ T H    **ACTH** (235), **anth.** (235), **auth.** (236), **Bath** (41a, 112c), **bath** (35d, 88d, 125a, 246), **Beth** (11a, 141), **beth** (12a), **both** (122c, 125c), **Cath.** (236), **doth** (128a), **Esth.** (16d, 238), **Gath** (88c), **Goth**

426

(120d), **hath** (128a), **Heth** (197), **Hoth** (20a), **jeth** (78b), **kith** (105a), **lath** (116c), **lgth.** (240), **Lith.** (240), **-lith** (117c), **Luth.** (240), **math** (116c), **Meth.** (240), **Moth** (193), **moth** (22d, 71b, 229), **myth** (43a, 71b), **Neth.** (241), **oath** (90b, 111c), **orth-** (92d), **path** (101a, 102c, 130c), **pith** (30d, 41d, 51d, 54c, 74b, 75a, 90a, 97c, 120d), **rath** (99d), **Roth** (178), **Ruth** (80d, 179, 196, 197), **ruth** (29b, 89c), **Seth** (10a, 42b, 197, 198), **seth** (76a), **teth** (12a), **with** (11d, 12c)

**T _ _ H**   **teth** (12a), **tosh** (82a), **tush** (23a)

**T I _ _**   **tick** (14a, 20a, 229), **tics**, **tide** (83b), **tidy** (81a, 84c, 111b), **tied**, **tier** (46a, 89b, 102c), **ties**, **tiff** (96b), **tige** (89b), **tiki** (91a), **tile** (27d, 46b, 74b, 102a, 120d), **till** (32c), **tilt** (23d, 24b, 62c, 72b, 101c), **time** (38d, 41b, 41c, 87d, 100b), **Timi** (183), **Tims**, **Tina** (183), **tine** (13a, 95a, 123a), **ting** (76b). **tins**, **tint** (29a, 107b), **tiny** (77b, 110d), **-tion** (117a, 117b), **tips**, **tire** (21a, 42d, 44d, 47b, 131c), **tiro** (18b, 82c), **titi** (20b, 71a, 78b, 124a), **Tito** (183, 134d), **tits**

**_ T I _**   **-atic** (117c), **atis** (60a), **-itis** (117b), **otic** (15d, 39a), **Otis** (12b, 63d, 173), **stib** (38d), **stir** (10d, 14c, 29b, 36d, 63b, 77b, 79c, 94d, 95a, 115c)

**_ _ T I**   **·alti-** (93a), **anti** (10c, 84c), **anti-** (92c), **Asti** (65a, 132c), **CETI** (236), **inti** (221), **kati** (246), **Loti** (49c, 95d), **loti** (218), **roti** (51a), **Sati** (96d, 109d, 198), **Seti** (88c), **titi** (20b, 71a, 78b, 124a), **toti-** (94a), **Yeti** (9b)

**T _ _ I**   **taxi** (95d), **Teri** (183), **Thai** (109a, 218, 223), **tiki** (91a), **Timi** (183), **titi** (20b, 71a, 78b, 124a), **Toni** (184), **topi** (30d, 89c), **Tori** (184), **tori** (30c), **toti-** (94a), **Tupi** (12b)

**T _ _ K**   **tack** (13d, 15c, 31b, 44c, 80b), **talk** (29d, 36a, 113b), **tank** (127d), **task** (115c), **teak** (39b, 124a), **tick** (14a, 20a, 229), **tock** (10c), **took** (83b), **Tosk** (213), **trek** (66d, 73a, 123d), **Truk** (24b), **tuck** (115c), **Turk** (85a, 217), **Turk.** (243), **tusk** (46d, 65c, 123a)

**_ T L _**   **atle** (104a, 119b), **Atli** (15c, 56d, 61c), **it'll** (30c)

**_ _ T L**   **Intl.** (239), **Natl.** (241)

**T _ _ L**   **Taal** (10c, 69a, 112b), **tael** (71c, 131a), **tail** (13c, 25a, 40d, 48b, 89d, 107b, 123c), **tall** (72d), **teal** (19a, 20b, 38c, 226), **teel** (107a), **teil** (72a), **Tell** (14a), **tell** (13d, 62b, 81a, 99a), **till** (32c), **toil** (38b, 124d, 133c, 133d), **toll** (18c, 94b, 100d), **tool** (25a, 62b, 127c)

**T M _ _**   **T-man** (45a), **T-men** (45a, 123d)

**T _ _ M**   **Tasm.** (243), **team** (32a, 48c, 56c, 85d, 232), **teem** (9b, 92a, 118c), **term** (71d, 72a, 80b, 106c, 115c), **them** (95a), **tram** (124c), **trim** (81a, 84d, 114a, 118b, 121d, 124c)

**_ T N _**   **at. no.** (236), **Etna** (129a), **etna** (58d)

_ _ T N    **attn.** (236)

T _ _ N    **ta'en** (107c), **tarn** (68b, 79b, 91b, 130a), **-teen** (117b), **Tenn.** (212, 243), **tern** (19a, 28c, 56d, 104d, 105d, 118b, 226), **than** (29b), **then** (10c, 121a), **thin** (35c, 35d, 53b, 110c), **-tion** (117a, 117b), **T-man** (45a), **T-men** (45a, 123d), **toon** (74b), **Torn** (184), **torn** (99c), **town** (57c, 128b), **Trin.** (243), **-tron** (117b), **Tsin** (26d), **tsun** (246), **tuan** (74c), **turn** (12c, 100b, 102b, 108a, 125c, 127c, 132b), **twin** (37c, 75b, 125c)

T O _ _    **toad** (17c, 225), **Tobe** (183), **tobe** (10c), **toby** (11b, 38a, 66d, 79d, 96a), **tock**(10c), **toco** (123b), **Toda** (37d), **Todd** (183), **to-do** (21b, 22d, 29b, 52c, 115c), **tods**, **tody** (19b), **toea** (221), **toed**, **toes**, **toff** (33c), **toft** (60d), **toga** (101d), **Togo** (223), **togs** (28b), **to-ho** (61d), **toil** (38b, 124d, 133c, 133d), **tola** (66d, 103a), **told** (99a), **tole** (41b, 76b), **toll** (18c, 94b, 100d), **tolu** (16d), **tomb** (22d), **tome** (20d, 129a), **Toms**, **-tomy** (117b), **Tone** (184), **tone** (9c, 82c, 89c), **tong** (26d), **Toni** (184), **tono-** (93c), **tons**, **Tony** (184), **took** (83b), **tool** (25a, 62b, 127c), **toon** (74b), **toot** (112b), **tope** (107d, 229), **topi** (30d, 89c), **topo.** (243), **tops**, **tora** (13a, 58b), **tore**, **Tori** (184), **tori** (30c), **Torn** (184), **torn** (99c), **toro** (31c, 112c), **torr** (246), **tors**, **tort** (27c, 71a, 134c), **tory** (22a, 30b, 73c), **tosh** (82a), **Tosk** (213), **toss** (22c, 47c, 121c), **tote** (22a, 24c, 86c), **toti-** (94a), **Toto** (37b, 133a), **tots**, **tour** (66d), **tous** (49d), **tout** (49d, 95a, 97b), **tows**, **town** (57c, 128b), **toyo** (58b, 65d, 116b), **toys**

_ T O _    **atom** (77d, 131c), **aton** (118a), **atop** (85c, 126d), **-ator** (117c), **Eton** (58b, 65b), **Otoe** (109d, 189), **stoa** (29a, 91c), **STOL** (243), **stop** (9a, 14c, 17a, 25b, 40d, 57c, 84c, 131d), **stot** (134d), **stow** (85b), **VTOL** (244)

_ _ T O    **alto** (113a, 128d), **alto-** (93a), **atto-** (93c), **auto** (24a), **bito** (10c, 35b, 47a), **Buto** (198), **Cato** (101d, 102a, 194), **Ceto** (55c, 75d), **cito** (70a), **coto** (17b, 75c), **ecto-** (93c), **ento-** (94a), **into** (133a), **JATO** (240), **Kato** (56c), **keto-** (93b), **koto** (66a), **Leto** (13b, 14d, 28d, 88c, 198), **moto** (79c), **NATO** (11c, 241), **nito** (45b), **noto-** (92c), **octo** (69c), **octo-** (92d), **on to** (59b), **Otto** (53c, 173), **otto** (65a), **Peto** (193), **peto** (129b), **RATO** (242), **sito-** (93a), **Tito** (183, 134d), **Toto** (37b, 133a), **unto**, **veto** (95a)

T _ _ O    **Tano** (95d, 189), **taro** (14d, 39c, 52a, 90d, 102b, 114d, 125a), **telo-** (92d), **teno-** (93d), **thio-** (93d), **tiro** (18b, 82c), **Tito** (183, 134d), **toco** (123b), **to-do** (21b, 22d, 29b, 52c, 115c), **Togo** (223), **to-ho** (61d), **tono-** (93c), **topo.** (243), **toro** (31c, 112c), **Toto** (37b, 133a), **toyo** (58b, 65d, 116b), **trio** (80c, 124b), **tuno** (57c), **typo** (41c, 94c), **Tyro** (81b), **tyro** (12b, 18b, 82c)

T _ _ P    **tamp** (76d, 85b, 92a, 97d), **tarp** (23d, 130b), **temp.** (243), **terp** (79a, 94a), **trap** (24c, 24d, 41a, 54b, 55b, 101b, 111b), **trip** (66d, 232), **trop** (51b, 123a), **tump** (60a), **tymp** (19d), **typp** (134b)

T R _ _    **tram** (124c), **trap** (24c, 24d, 41a, 54b, 55b, 101b, 111b), **tray** (98b, 104a, 107a), **tree** (30d, 53b, 133c), **tref** (48b, 126a), **trek** (66d, 73a,

123d), **tres** (42b, 51b, 113a), **tret** (130a, 131a), **trey** (24a, 121c), **trig** (114a, 124c), **trig.** (31b, 243), **trim** (81a, 84d, 114a, 118b, 121d, 124c), **Trin.** (243), **trio** (80c, 124b), **trip** (66d, 232), **Tris** (184), **-trix** (117b), **trod, -tron** (117b), **trop** (51b, 123a), **trot** (66c, 85b), **trow** (18b), **Troy** (184), **troy** (119c, 131a), **true** (9d, 15d, 31a, 42b, 44a, 73c, 111b), **Truk** (24b)

_ T R _     **etre** (50a), **otro** (112c, 113a)

_ _ T R     **astr-** (93d), **metr-** (94a), **nitr-** (93b), **petr-** (93d)

T _ _ R     **tahr** (55a), **taur-** (92c), **tear** (68b, 99c), **Thar** (35a), **thar** (55a), **Thor** (10b, 76c, 77b, 83b, 121d, 183, 198), **Thur.** (243), **tier** (46a, 89b, 102c), **torr** (246), **tour** (66d), **tsar** (103c)

T S _ _     **tsar** (103c), **Tsin** (26d), **tsun** (246)

_ T S _     **NTSB** (241)

_ _ T S     **acts, ants, arts, bats, bets, bits** (19a), **bots, buts, cats, cots, cuts, dots, eats** (48b), **efts, Fats** (152), **fits, gats, gets, GUTS** (239), **guts** (63a), **hats, hits, huts, Jets** (206), **jets, jots, juts, kits, lets, lots** (26a), **Mats** (169), **Mets** (206), **mots, Nats, Nets** (206), **nets, nits, nuts, oats, opts, orts** (105c), **outs, pats, pets, pits, pots, puts, rats, rets, rots, ruts, SATs** (29a), **sets, sits, sots, tats, tits, tots, vats, vets, WATS** (244), **wets, wits**

T _ _ S     **tabs, tads, tags, tams, tans, Taos** (81c), **taps, tars, TASS** (81c, 112b), **tats, taus, taws, teas, Teds, Tees** (82b), **tees, tegs, tens, Teos** (64a), **Tess** (58a, 183), **this** (34d, 95a), **Thos.** (74d), **thos** (65b), **thus** (111b, 121a), **tics, ties, Tims, tins, tips, tits, tods, toes, togs** (28b), **Toms, tons, tops, tors, toss** (22c, 47c, 121c), **tots, tous** (49d), **tows, toys, tres** (42b, 51b, 113a), **Tris** (184), **tubs, Tues.** (243), **tugs, tuns, tups, 'twas** (30b, 107c), **twos, Tyus** (184)

_ T T _     **atta** (70c), **attn.** (236), **atto-** (93c), **Attu** (64b), **atty.** (236), **Etta** (152), **-etta** (117b), **-ette** (117b), **Otto** (53c, 173), **otto** (65a)

_ _ T T     **batt** (16d), **bitt** (44c), **bott** (27d), **butt** (121d, 132c, 246), **Catt** (144), **GATT** (239), **Jett** (161), **Kitt** (164), **Lett** (16d), **Lott** (167), **Matt** (169, 240), **mitt** (17b, 46b, 54d), **Mott** (171), **mutt** (32d, 78a), **Pitt** (41a, 175), **putt** (55b), **sett** (87b, 119d), **Watt** (63d, 186), **watt** (129a, 246), **Witt** (187)

T _ _ T     **tact** (35d), **Taft** (183, 191), **tait** (15d, 60d), **takt** (80a, 120b), **tart** (87a, 112b), **taut** (120c, 122a), **teat** (81d), **tent** (24a, 87b), **test** (23d, 41d, 42b, 124b, 124d), **text** (86d, 133c), **that** (34d, 95a, 99b), **tilt** (23d, 24b, 62c, 72b, 101c), **tint** (29a, 107b), **toft** (60d), **toot** (112b), **tort** (27c, 71a, 134c), **tout** (49d, 95a, 97b), **tret** (130a, 131a), **trot** (66c, 85b), **tuft** (22c, 28c), **twit** (88a)

T U _ _     **tuan** (74c), **tuba** (80a, 86a), **tube** (33c, 89c, 117a), **tubs, tuck** (115c), **-tude** (117b), **Tues.** (243), **tufa** (91c, 129a), **tuff** (91c,

129a), **tuft** (22c, 28c), **tugs**, **tuke** (23d, 43b), **tula** (10d, 11d), **tule** (22c, 25a), **tump** (60a), **tuna** (125a, 229), **Tune** (184), **tune** (9c, 10a, 10d, 14b, 58a, 75d, 111d, 116a), **tung** (83d), **tuno** (57c), **tuns**, **Tupi** (12b), **tups**, **turf** (87b, 111c, 118b), **Turk** (85a, 217), **Turk.** (243), **turn** (12c, 100b, 102b, 108a, 125c, 127c, 132b), **tush** (23a), **tusk** (46d, 65c, 123a), **tutu** (16d, 110a)

_ T U _    **atua** (91a), **etui** (24c, 50a, 51a, 81b, 127b), **otus** (54b), **stub** (121d, 122c), **stud** (23a, 44c, 74c, 84d, 126d), **stum** (55d, 100b, 132c), **stun** (108b, 116c), **Stus**

_ _ T U    **Attu** (64b), **Hutu** (214, 221), **mitu** (32d), **patu** (130d), **tatu** (14b), **tutu** (16d, 110a), **vatu** (224), **WCTU** (244)

T _ _ U    **tabu** (48c), **tatu** (14b), **thou** (95b), **thru**, **tolu** (16d), **tutu** (16d, 110a)

_ _ T V    **HDTV** (239)

T W _ _    **'twas** (30b, 107c), **Tway** (184), **twig** (21c), **twin** (37c, 75b, 125c), **twit** (88a), **twos**

_ T W _    **at. wt.** (236), **Nt. Wt.** (241)

T _ _ W    **thaw** (72b), **thew** (79d), **trow** (18b)

T _ _ X    **-trix** (117b)

T Y _ _    **tyee** (26d), **tyke** (21c, 26c), **tymp** (19d), **Tyne** (82b, 184, 223), **type** (27d, 112a, 113b), **typo** (41c, 94c), **typp** (134b), **Tyra** (184), **Tyre** (71a, 88c, 218), **Tyro** (81b), **tyro** (12b, 18b, 82c), **Tyus** (184)

_ T Y _    **Itys** (120c), **Styx** (26b, 57a)

_ _ T Y    **arty**, **atty.** (236), **city** (76c, 126d), **Coty** (49d, 147), **duty** (27a, 83a, 119d), **maty** (62d), **pity** (29b, 87a, 134b)

T _ _ Y    **they** (95a), **tidy** (81a, 84c, 111b), **tiny** (77b, 110d), **toby** (11b, 38a, 66d, 79d, 96a), **tody** (19b), **-tomy** (117b), **Tony** (184), **tory** (22a, 30b, 73c), **tray** (98b, 104a, 107a), **trey** (24a, 121c), **Troy** (184), **troy** (119c, 131a), **Tway** (184)

_ _ T Z    **fitz** (111d), **Getz** (155), **litz** (97b), **Metz** (216), **Ritz** (177)

U A _ _    **uang** (100b)

_ U A _    **bual** (132c), **duad** (85d, 125c), **dual** (37c, 125c), **duan** (52a), **Fuad** (44c), **Guam** (64c), **guan** (19b), **guar** (38b, 48c), **Guat.** (239), **HUAC** (239), **Juan** (163), **luau** (58b), **Muav** (53c), **quad** (29a), **quag** (20c), **quay** (68d, 88d, 131b), **tuan** (74c), **Yüan** (26d, 78a), **yuan** (215)

_ _ U A    **agua** (113a), **akua** (91a), **aqua** (20b, 70b), **atua** (91a), **Ecua.** (238), **roue** (34a, 97c), **skua** (56d, 65b, 105c)

430

**U _ _ A**    **ulna**(32c, 20d), **ulva**(105d), **urea**(45c), **Urfa**(76a), **Uria**(197), **-uria** (117b), **Ursa** (17d), **urva** (78a), **USDA** (243), **USIA** (243), **USMA** (243), **USNA** (243), **USTA** (244), **uvea** (43c, 64a)

**_ U B _**    **aube** (11a), **Bubi** (216), **bubo** (85c), **bubs**, **Cuba** (64c,131b,215), **cube** (53c, 111d), **Cubs** (206), **cubs**, **dubs**, **hubs**, **Juba** (216), **jube** (102a), **Kuba** (24b), **Luba** (224), **nubs**, **pubs**, **Rube** (179), **rube** (31b, 103c, 134d), **rubs**, **Ruby** (179), **ruby** (19c, 53b), **subj.** (243), **subs**, **tuba** (80a, 86a), **tube** (33c, 89c, 117a), **tubs**

**_ _ U B**    **chub** (46c, 228), **club** (21c, 32c, 75b, 84c, 104a, 111c), **daub** (111a), **drub** (17c, 32c, 42c, 110b), **flub** (21b), **grub** (35d, 69b), **slub** (134b), **snub** (62a, 81b, 98b, 109a, 110c), **stub** (121d, 122c)

**_ U C _**    **Buck** (23b, 31c, 143), **buck** (34c, 84a), **duce** (65a), **duck** (16c, 19a, 19b, 23d, 43b, 62a, 109a, 225), **duct** (125a), **euch** (54b), **fuci** (38d), **guck** (110c), **juca** (24c), **Luca** (167), **Luce** (10a, 29b, 192), **luck** (25d), **Lucy** (192), **much** (67c, 116d), **muck** (39a), **muco-** (93b), **ouch** (42c, 63a), **puce** (42a, 96c), **Puck** (107c, 193), **puck** (36b, 55a, 60c, 77b), **ruck** (134a), **such** (131b), **suck** (9b), **tuck** (115c), **yuca** (24c), **yuch** (112a), **yuck** (112a)

**_ _ U C**    **educ.** (238), **eruc** (30d, 45d), **leuc-** (94a)

**U _ _ C**    **Udic** (82b), **USMC** (243), **USOC** (244)

**U D _ _**    **udal** (59c), **Udic** (82b), **udos**

**_ U D _**    **Budd** (143), **buds**, **dude** (27c, 33c, 44b), **duds** (28b, 122d), **Judd** (163), **Jude** (13b, 196), **judo** (65d, 66d), **Judy** (163), **kudu** (13a, 230), **ludi** (102a), **ludo** (52b), **Mudd** (171), **muds**, **nude** (17b, 126b), **nudi-** (93b), **pudu** (34b), **rudd** (24b, 46c, 98c), **rude** (102c, 126a), **Rudy** (179), **sudd** (47c), **suds** (18a, 48a, 114a), **-tude** (117b)

**_ _ U D**    **baud** (120b), **crud** (28c, 35a, 36a), **feud** (45c, 96b, 127d), **foud** (44c, 74a), **gaud** (124c, 133d), **haud** (70a), **laud** (57b, 92b, 127d), **loud** (115b), **Maud** (131d, 169), **maud** (43b, 56a), **Scud** (77b), **scud** (96d, 103a, 118c), **spud** (92a), **stud** (23a, 44c, 74c, 84d, 126d), **thud** (20a, 112a), **you'd** (30c)

**U _ _ D**    **used** (9c, 57a)

**_ U E _**    **Auer** (61c, 139), **cued**, **cues**, **duel** (45d), **dues**, **duet** (80c, 85d), **euer** (54b), **fuel** (53a), **hued**, **hues**, **Huey** (159), **lues** (118d), **Nuer** (222), **rued**, **ruer**, **rues**, **sued**, **suer** (95b), **sues**, **suet** (44c, 83d), **Suez** (23c), **Tues.** (243)

**_ _ U E**    **ague** (26c, 45c, 74b, 104b), **Blue** (142), **blue** (75d, 112a, 126c), **clue** (60b, 117d), **flue** (11a, 26c), **glue** (10a, 115b), **moue** (50d, 134c), **Niue** (64c), **slue** (110c, 118c), **true** (9d, 15d, 31a, 42b, 44a, 73c, 111b)

**U _ _ E**    **urge** (35b, 54d, 63b, 94d)

**_ U F _**  buff (119b, 134b), cuff (21b, 60b, 105b, 110b), duff (95d), Dufy (49c, 150), guff (16b, 62c, 82a), Huff (159), huff (47b, 119c), luff (48a), Luft (167), Muff (17b), muff (17c, 21b, 22c), puff (20a, 74a), ruff (34d, 37b, 51c), sufi (88a), tufa (91c, 129a), tuff (91c, 129a), tuft (22c, 28c)

**_ _ U F**  oeuf (50b), pouf (48c, 58d, 85a)

**U _ _ F**  UNCF (243), USAF (243)

**U G _ _**  ugli (51d), ugly (126a)

**_ U G _**  auge (71b), bugs, fugu (65d), huge (54b, 62a, 69b), Hugh (159), Hugo (49c, 71c, 104d, 159), hugs, juga (24c), jugs, luge (110b), lugs, mugs, pugs, ruga (48a, 134a), rugs, sugi (65b), tugs, vugg (25b, 53c, 101b), vugh (25b, 53c, 101b), yuga (60a)

**_ _ U G**  chug (112a), Doug (150), drug (81a), frug (33b), plug (116a, 133d), slug (38a, 76b, 116b), smug (29c, 106c), Snug (193), snug (31c, 122a), thug (52c)

**U _ _ G**  uang (100b), USCG (243), USNG (243)

**_ U H _**  buhl (63a), buhr (131c), guhr (39a), Ruhr (53d, 100b)

**_ _ U H**  bruh (73b)

**U _ _ H**  Utah (212)

**U I _ _**  Uist (64d)

**_ U I _**  cuir (37c, 50c), duim (246), guib (13a), huia (81c), juin (49d), Luis (167), Muir (11a, 171), nuit (50d), quid (32c, 122c), quip (66b, 66d, 132d, 133a), quit (9a, 34d, 71a, 99d), quiz (42b), ruin (34d, 35b, 62b), suit (9c, 10a, 31c, 47b, 71a, 85b, 90b, 104b)

**_ _ U I**  aqui (112d), arui (13b), equi- (93c), etui (24c, 50a, 51a, 81b, 127b), Maui (64c)

**U _ _ I**  ugli (51d), Unni (197)

**_ U J _**  Fuji (66a), fuji (65b), juju (26b, 45c, 119b), suji (131b)

**_ _ U J**  Cluj (221)

**_ U K _**  auks, cuke (32c), Duke (87d, 150, 194, 201), duke (82a), Luke (42a, 167, 196), puke (99a), puku (13a, 130b), suke (120a), suky (120a), tuke (23d, 43b), yuks (70b)

**_ _ U K**  leuk- (94a), Sauk (49b, 56c, 189), souk (17d, 74d), Truk (24b), Wouk (187)

**U L _ _**  Ulam (197), ulna (32c, 20d), ulva (105d)

432

**_ U L _**    **aula** (53d), **auld** (105b), **bulb** (30d, 126b), **Bulg.** (236), **bulk** (20c, 75b, 129a), **bull** (21b, 86b), **-cule** (117c), **cull** (88d), **culm** (13a, 28c, 56a, 108b, 115b), **Culp** (147), **cult** (106a, 119c), **Dull** (193), **dull** (20b, 28b, 47b, 63b, 66b, 71d, 73c, 126c), **duly** (100c, 117a), **Fula** (216, 217), **full** (29c, 99d), **gulf** (9c, 130a), **gull** (19a, 28c, 34a, 34c, 68a, 76c, 105c, 118d, 225), **gulp** (20d, 37d, 118b), **hula** (58b), **hule** (21c, 25a, 102c), **hulk** (126d), **Hull** (159), **hull** (106b, 108b), **Jule** (163), **Juli** (163), **July**, **Kulp** (165), **lull** (11c), **lulu** (73a), **mule** (108c, 110d, 131b, 230), **Mull** (171), **mull** (43b, 91b, 103a, 121b), **mult-** (93b), **null** (82c, 128d), **pula** (214), **pule** (131c), **puli** (37b, 61c, 227), **pulk** (79c), **pull** (11d, 37d, 123c), **pulp** (51d, 74a, 75b, 86b), **rule** (13b, 35b, 37b, 70b, 118c), **sulk** (117d), **Sulu** (88c), **sulu** (46a), **tula** (10d, 11d), **tule** (22c, 25a), **yule** (27a), **Zulu** (12a, 222)

**_ _ U L**    **azul** (112c), **caul** (45c, 84a), **elul** (78c), **foul** (9a, 126b), **Gaul** (49b), **haul** (37c), **maul** (17c, 57d, 74c), **ocul-** (92d), **Paul** (18a, 91b, 174), **Peul** (217, 219, 221), **Raul** (176), **Saul** (67d, 87a, 179, 197), **shul** (118d), **Soul** (181), **soul** (95d, 113d, 128c), **waul** (114b)

**U _ _ L**    **udal** (59c), **Ural** (103c)

**U M _ _**    **umbo** (21a)

**_ U M _**    **bump** (66a, 66d), **bums**, **duma** (103a), **dumb** (109b, 113c), **dump** (68d, 99d, 126c), **fume** (111a, 116a), **fumy** (127b), **gums**, **Hume** (159, 192), **hump** (95c), **hums**, **Jump** (163), **jump** (10b, 114d, 127b), **lump** (17a, 55a, 79a, 118c), **mums**, **Numa** (102a), **numb** (33d, 126b), **puma** (24d, 31b, 79a, 231), **pump** (108c), **rump** (23a, 33a, 75c), **rums**, **sumo** (66a), **sump** (25d, 77a), **sums**, **tump** (60a), **Yuma** (189)

**_ _ U M**    **alum** (37c, 77a), **alum.** (235), **arum** (32c, 71d, 114d), **Baum** (85d, 140), **chum** (15b, 32a, 45b), **drum** (80a, 228), **glum** (54d, 78d, 112b, 117d), **grum** (54d), **ogum** (64b), **ovum** (39d, 69c), **plum** (51d, 124a), **scum** (62c, 98d, 110c), **slum** (81b, 99d), **stum** (55d, 100b, 132c), **swum**

**U _ _ M**    **Ulam** (197), **urim** (103b)

**U N _ _**    **Unas**, **unau** (110d), **UNCF** (243), **unco** (105b), **undo** (12d, 41c, 73a, 99b), **unio** (80d), **unit** (77d, 84a), **Unni** (197), **unto**, **unus** (69c)

**_ U N _**    **aune** (246), **aunt** (44b, 99b), **buna** (102c), **bund** (40b), **bung** (116a), **bunk** (82a, 110c), **buns**, **bunt** (17c, 131b), **dune** (84a, 104a), **dung** (42d, 74d), **dunk** (35d, 62a), **fund** (9c, 78a, 100a), **fung-** (93a), **funk** (10d, 35a, 47b), **gunk** (110c), **guns**, **Hung.** (239), **hung**, **hunk** (57d, 88d), **Huns** (15c), **Hunt** (159), **hunt** (105d), **June** (163), **Jung** (95d, 163), **junk** (26c, 102d), **Juno** (67c, 77b, 96d, 195, 199), **Luna** (89d, 198), **luna** (78d), **lune** (31d, 58c), **lung** (100a, 121b), **luni-** (93b), **Lunt** (167), **Muni** (171), **Nunn** (173), **nuns**, **Puna** (12c), **puna** (28d, 90b, 132b), **pung** (21c, 110c), **punk** (12a, 123b), **puno** (132b), **puns**, **punt** (20b, 47b), **puny** (45a, 130c), **rune**

(82b), **rung** (25d, 32b, 115b), **runs, runt** (12d, 38d), **Sung** (26d), **sung, sunk, sunn** (45d), **Suns** (206), **suns, tuna** (125a, 229), **Tune** (184), **tune** (9c, 10a, 10d, 14b, 58a, 75d, 111d, 116a), **tung** (83d), **tuno** (57c), **tuns, Zuni** (95d, 189)

**_ _ U N**   **Faun** (45d, 133b, 198), **noun** (86d, 116d), **Ryun** (179), **shun** (16c, 41c), **spun, stun** (108b, 116c), **tsun** (246)

**U _ _ N**   **upon** (9b), **uran** (78a)

**_ U O _**   **buoy** (26a, 47c), **duos, muon** (71b), **quod** (94d, 96a)

**_ _ U O**   **chuo** (246), **fluo-** (93a)

**U _ _ O**   **umbo** (21a), **unco** (105b), **undo** (12d, 41c, 73a, 99b), **unio** (80d), **unto, USPO** (244)

**U P _ _**   **upas** (66a, 90d, 124a), **upon** (9b)

**_ U P _**   **cupr-** (92d), **cups, dupe** (25a, 34a, 48b, 56d, 74d, 118d), **Hupa** (15b, 189), **pupa** (27a, 28d, 63b), **pups, sups, supt.** (243), **Tupi** (12b), **tups**

**_ _ U P**   **coup** (75b, 116c, 120b), **loup** (50d, 51b, 105c), **roup** (92a), **scup** (91c, 228), **soup** (75c), **yaup** (119b)

**U R _ _**   **Ural** (103c), **uran** (78a), **Urdu** (60b, 213, 220), **urea** (45c), **Urey** (15c, 184), **Urfa** (76a), **urge** (35b, 54d, 63b, 94d), **Uria** (197), **-uria** (117b), **urim** (103b), **Uris** (184), **urns, Ursa** (17d), **urus** (15d, 85c, 132a, 227, 231), **urva** (78a)

**_ U R _**   **aura** (10d, 36d, 39d, 40b, 57c, 100d), **burd** (105c), **burg** (21a, 57c), **buri** (119b), **Burl** (143), **burl** (68c, 124b), **burn** (62c, 101b), **burp** (18b), **Burr** (143, 190), **burr** (94b), **burs, Burt** (143), **bury** (63c), **cura** (113a), **curb** (100a, 109a), **curd** (76d), **cure** (94c), **curl** (32a, 57b, 72d, 100d, 126b), **curs, Curt** (147), **curt** (20b, 22a, 108c, 108d), **dura** (113c), **duro** (88b), **eure** (54b), **eury-** (94a), **furl** (101c), **furs, fury** (97b, 116a), **guru** (60b), **hura** (104a), **hurl** (121c, 123b), **Hurt** (159), **hurt** (33b, 58a, 62a, 63a, 133d), **Jura** (79b), **jure** (70b), **jury** (31c), **Kura** (101a), **Kurd** (64a, 217), **Kure** (60d), **Kurt** (165), **lure** (34b, 41b, 63d, 120c), **lurk** (71d, 110b), **mura** (65d), **murk** (28b, 48a, 77b), **ours** (95a), **pure** (9b, 26b, 126a, 126c), **puri** (62d), **purl** (68c), **purr** (112a), **ruri** (69c), **ruru** (81c), **sura** (68c, 86a), **surd** (30b, 82d), **sure** (10b, 99b, 106b, 126d), **surf** (21d), **surg.** (243), **turf** (87b, 111c, 118b), **Turk** (85a, 217), **turn** (12c, 100b, 102b, 108a, 125c, 127c, 132b), **wurm** (54c), **Yuri** (188), **Yuro** (188), **yurt** (78a)

**_ _ U R**   **Amur** (101a), **azur** (50a), **blur** (62d, 111a), **dour** (54d, 78d, 107b, 117d), **ebur** (69d), **four** (72c, 120d), **gaur** (25a, 62d, 132a, 230), **hour** (122b), **knur** (54d, 68c), **lour** (33d, 54d), **neur-** (93b), **peur** (50b), **pour** (120a), **-saur** (117b), **slur** (36c, 40b, 74c, 95b, 123c, 128b), **smur** (38a), **sour** (15b, 119d), **spur** (46a, 54d, 62c, 63c, 95a), **taur-** (92c), **Thur.** (243), **tour** (66d), **your** (95a)

434

**U _ _ R**   usar (11b, 17b, 62d), user (10a, 29c, 40c), USNR (244), USSR (244), uter- (93d)

**U S _ _**   USAF (243), usar (11b, 17b, 62d), USCG (243), USDA (243), used (9c, 57a), user (10a, 29c, 40c), uses, USIA (243), USMA (243), USMC (243), USNA (243), USNG (243), USNR (244), USOC (244), USPO (244), USPS (244), USSR (244), USTA (244), usus (69c, 70b)

**_ U S _**   Bush (143, 191), bush (109a, 119a), busk (20c, 31a, 45c), buss (68a), bust (14c, 17a, 21d, 44a, 58c), busy (40d, 83b), Cush (57c, 197), cusk (46d), cusp (31d, 61a, 89d, 90c, 90d), cuss (32d, 88a, 118c), Duse (64d, 150), dusk (125c), dust (114a), fuse (75d, 76a), fuss (21b, 36d, 92a), fust (107b), gush (114b, 118a), gust (20a), hush (109b), husk (43a, 61c, 106b, 232), just (41b, 44a, 62b, 76a, 97c, 127c), lush (38b, 73d), lust (34a, 107a), musa (16d), muse (52d, 91b, 121b), mush (75b), musk (87d), muss (103a), must (55d, 81c, 116c, 132c), Ouse (101a, 134d, 223), oust (35b, 40a, 42b, 96c), push (38a, 46a, 108d, 121d), puss (24d), rusa (104a), ruse (60c, 62b, 116a), Rush (179), rush (114a), rusk (21d), Russ (179), Russ. (242), rust (31a, 85d, 90a), Susa (40a), susu (20a), tush (23a), tusk (46d, 65c, 123a)

**_ _ U S**   acus (70a, 89b), Apus (207), avus (69d), crus (71b, 107c), deus (42d, 69d), emus, -eous (117a), gnus, Grus (207), Ilus (69a, 124d), -ious (117a), Irus (83c), Kaus (208), meus (69d), nous (50d, 51b), -odus (117c), onus (22d, 72d, 83a, 131a), opus (29c, 80c, 129a, 133c), otus (54b), Pius (91b), plus (12c, 62c), sous (51b), Stus, taus, thus (111b, 121a), tous (49d), Tyus (184), unus (69c), urus (15d, 85c, 132a, 227, 231), usus (69c, 70b), vous (51b), Zeus (55c, 59c, 198)

**U _ _ S**   udos, Unas, unus (69c), upas (66a, 90d, 124a), Uris (184), urns, urus (15d, 85c, 132a, 227, 231), uses, USPS (244), usus (69c, 70b), utas (40a), Utes

**U T _ _**   Utah (212), utas (40a), uter- (93d), Utes

**_ U T _**   auth. (236), auto (24a), Bute (64d), Buto (198), buts, butt (121d, 132c, 246), cute (10a, 32c, 116a), cuts, duty (27a, 83a, 119d), GUTS (239), guts (63a), huts, Hutu (214, 221), jute (30d, 45c, 102b, 103a), juts, lute (25c, 66a, 80b, 100d), Luth. (240), muta (26a, 80d), mute (109b, 113c, 232, 234), mutt (32d, 78a), nuts, outs, puts, putt (55b), Ruth (80d, 179, 196, 197), ruth (29b, 89c), ruts, tutu (16d, 110a)

**_ _ U T**   abut (21a, 75d, 123b), aout (49d), bhut (54b), blut (53d), bout (30b), brut (38b, 132c), Deut. (237), glut (42b, 55b, 85c, 104b, 118a), gout (14d, 113d), Knut (33c, 164), lout (21a, 83a), naut. (241), neut. (241), pout (117d), Prut (33d), rout (34c, 36c), scut (119a), shut (28b), slut (133b), smut (28c, 36a, 90a, 111d), taut (120c, 122a), tout (49d, 95a, 97b)

**U _ _ T**   Uist (64d), unit (77d, 84a)

435

**U _ _ U**    **unau** (110d), **Urdu** (60b, 213, 220)

**U V _ _**    **uvea** (43c, 64a)

**_ U V _**    **Suva** (128d, 216)

**_ _ U W**    **dauw** (22d)

**_ U X _**    **luxe** (100c)

**_ _ U X**    **Crux** (207), **crux** (32b, 74b, 112b), **eaux** (51b), **flux** (26a, 47d), **jeux** (50b), **roux** (104b), **Vaux** (192, 195), **vaux** (49c)

**_ U Y _**    **buyo** (18d), **buys, guys**

**U _ _ Y**    **ugly** (126a), **Urey** (15c, 184)

**_ U Z _**    **buzz** (79d, 103a, 131d), **fuze** (35b), **fuzz** (37c), **ouzo** (11a), **Puzo** (175)

**V A _ _**    **vagi** (31d), **vain** (40c, 63a), **vair** (52c, 114b), **Vale** (184), **vale** (44b, 127b), **Vali** (83b), **vamp** (62c, 108c, 233), **vane** (130d, 132b), **vang** (57c, 102b), **vans, vara** (72a), **vari** (71b), **vary** (26a, 35c, 77c), **vasa** (38c, 128a), **vase** (30b, 47d), **vaso-** (92c), **vast** (61c, 62a), **vats, vatu** (224), **Vaux** (192, 195), **vaux** (49c)

**_ V A _**    **Avar** (25a, 82b), **Avas, Evas, Ivan** (66c, 103c, 159), **oval** (39d, 40b), **Svan** (25a)

**_ _ V A**    **Alva** (39c), **cava** (127d), **Deva** (60a, 221), **diva** (84b, 94c), **Hova** (219), **Java** (64c), **java** (28d), **kava** (18d, 91a), **kiva** (25c, 95d), **lava** (77d, 101b, 129a), **Neva** (100d), **Nova** (203), **nova** (114d), **Siva** (91a), **Suva** (128d, 216), **ulva** (105d), **urva** (78a), **viva** (73a)

**V _ _ A**    **vara** (72a), **vasa** (38c, 128a), **veda** (60a), **Vega** (114d, 207), **Vela** (103c, 208), **vena** (70b), **Vera** (185), **vera** (105c), **Vida** (185), **Vila** (224), **vina** (60b), **visa** (87a), **vita** (69d, 71d), **viva** (73a), **vola** (111c), **-vora** (117c), **vota** (102a)

**V _ _ B**    **verb** (86d)

**V _ _ C**    **Visc.** (244)

**_ V D _**    **avdp.** (236)

**_ _ V D**    **Blvd.** (236), **NKVD** (103c)

**V _ _ D**    **veld** (104c, 112b), **vend** (74d, 87c, 106c), **vied, void** (12d, 40c, 82d, 127a)

**V E _ _**    **veal** (23b, 75c), **veda** (60a), **veer** (35c, 125b), **vees, Vega** (114d, 207), **veil** (29d, 36b, 58c, 59d, 75b), **vein** (20a, 116b), **Vela** (103c, 208), **veld** (104c, 112b), **vena** (70b), **vend** (74d, 87c, 106c), **veni-**

(93d), **veno-** (93d), **vent** (11a, 13b, 40c, 60c, 84b, 85b, 115a), **Vera** (185), **vera** (105c), **verb** (86d), **vers** (51b), **vert** (56c), **vert.** (244), **very** (43c, 78d, 111b), **vest** (28b, 129b), **veto** (95a) **vets**

**_ V E _**   **avec** (51b), **aver** (10b, 15a, 16c, 34b, 74b, 115a, 118c), **aves**, **Evel** (68a), **even** (23b, 41b, 42b, 47b, 61d, 67c, 71c, 82a, 111a, 126c, 134c), **ever** (12a, 18b, 62c), **Eves**, **eves**, **Ives** (159), **Ivey** (159), **oven** (61c, 67b), **over** (9b, 9d, 14c, 32a, 87a, 99c), **Sven**, **uvea** (43c, 64a), **Yves** (188)

**_ _ V E**   **cave** (113c, 126b), **cove** (17d, 58a, 130a), **Dave** (148), **dive** (34d, 90c), **Dove** (150), **dove** (19a, 89a, 225), **five** (17c, 88c, 97c), **gave**, **give** (11c, 13d, 29d, 94a, 95c), **gyve** (45c, 107b), **have** (20b), **hive** (18a), **hove** (71d), **jive** (61d, 63b, 66a), **Jove** (67c, 198), **lave** (130a), **live** (38d, 42d), **Love** (167), **love** (24b, 120c), **move** (10d, 36b, 62b, 125b), **nave** (27a, 131c), **neve** (46c, 54c, 55d, 111b), **nove** (65c), **pave** (66b), **rave** (34b, 58a, 119b), **reve** (50b), **rive** (28a), **rove** (97d, 101a, 129d), **save** (42b, 67b, 84b, 94b, 126c), **Seve** (180), **vive** (73a), **wave** (48a, 83b, 100d, 118c, 126b), **we've** (30c), **wove**

**V _ _ E**   **Vale** (184), **vale** (44b, 127b), **vane** (130d, 132b), **vase** (30b, 47d), **vice** (35a), **vice-** (92d), **vide** (98d), **vile** (9a, 17b, 46a, 62a, 74c), **vine** (28a, 71c), **vise** (60c), **vite** (50d), **vive** (73a), **voce** (65c, 234), **vole** (75b, 79b, 110b, 111b, 231), **-vore** (117c), **vote** (49b, 128d)

**V _ _ G**   **vang** (57c, 102b), **vugg** (25b, 53c, 101b)

**V _ _ H**   **vugh** (25b, 53c, 101b)

**V I _ _**   **vial** (110d), **vice** (35a), **vice-** (92d), **Vida** (185), **vide** (98d), **vied**, **vier** (53d), **vies**, **view** (12c, 15a, 42b, 73a, 95b, 104d), **Vila** (224), **vile** (9a, 17b, 46a, 62a, 74c), **Vili** (83b), **vina** (60b), **vine** (28a, 71c), **vini-** (94a), **vino** (72b, 132c), **viny**, **viol** (80b), **VIPs**, **visa** (87a), **Visc.** (244), **vise** (60c), **vita** (69d, 71d), **vite** (50d), **viva** (73a), **vive** (73a), **vivo** (72c, 233)

**_ V I _**   **avid** (39a, 41b, 56b, 67b, 135a), **avis** (69c), **evil** (74c, 109c, 131d, 134c), **Ovid** (102a)

**_ _ V I**   **Devi** (109c), **favi** (122a), **kavi** (66a), **Levi** (13b, 64d, 70d, 197), **nevi** (19c, 77d), **Ravi** (176)

**V _ _ I**   **vagi** (31d), **Vali** (83b), **vari** (71b), **veni-** (93d), **Vili** (83b), **vini-** (94a)

**V _ _ K**   **volk** (54a)

**V _ _ L**   **veal** (23b, 75c), **veil** (29d, 36b, 58c, 59d, 75b), **vial** (110d), **viol** (80b), **VTOL** (244)

**_ _ V N**   **ARVN** (235)

**V _ _ N**   **vain** (40c, 63a), **vein** (20a, 116b)

**V O _ _**  voce(65c, 234), void(12d, 40c, 82d, 127a), vola(111c), vole (75b, 79b, 110b, 111b, 231), volk (54a), volt (40a, 61b, 246), -vora (117c), -vore (117c), vota (102a), vote (49b, 128d), vous (51b), vows

**_ V O _**  Avon (107c), avow (9d, 15a, 16c, 29d, 30a, 34b, 85c), evoe (16a, 100b), Ivor (159), Lvov (223)

**_ _ V O**  levo- (93b), Pavo (87b, 207), vivo (72c, 233)

**V _ _ O**  vaso- (92c), veno- (93d), veto (95a), vino (72b, 132c), vivo (72c, 233)

**_ _ V P**  RSVP (242)

**V _ _ P**  vamp (62c, 108c, 233)

**V _ _ R**  vair (52c, 114b), veer (35c, 125b), vier (53d)

**_ _ V S**  Bevs, revs

**V _ _ S**  vans, vats, vees, vers (51b), vies, VIPs, vous (51b), vows

**V T _ _**  VTOL (244)

**_ _ V T**  govt. (239)

**V _ _ T**  vast (61c, 62a), vent (11a, 13b, 40c, 60c, 84b, 85b, 115a), vert (56c), vert. (244), vest (28b, 129b), volt (40a, 61b, 246)

**V U _ _**  vugg (25b, 53c, 101b), vugh (25b, 53c, 101b)

**_ V U _**  avus (69d), ovum (39d, 69c)

**_ _ V U**  Kivu (68b)

**V _ _ U**  vatu (224)

**V _ _ W**  view (12c, 15a, 42b, 73a, 95b, 104d)

**V _ _ X**  Vaux (192, 195), vaux (49c)

**_ _ V Y**  bevy (16d, 31c, 47c, 232), cavy (56d, 101c, 230), Davy (148, 193), davy (103b), envy (34a, 107a), levy (15a, 62b, 120a), Livy (101d), navy (20a, 47c), wavy (126b)

**V _ _ Y**  vary (26a, 35c, 77c), very (43c, 78d, 111b), viny

**W A _ _**  WAAC (244), WAAF (244), Waco (21d), WACs, Wade (185), wade (129b), wadi (38b, 83a, 98a, 101a), wads, waft (47c), wage (103d), wags, waif (116b), wail (32b, 61c, 68d, 114b), wain (129b), wait (24b, 72a, 99c, 115a, 119d), waka (23d), wake (102c, 123c), wale (55c, 100c, 130c, 131b, 131c), walk (85b), Wall (193), wall (118a),

438

Walt (185), wand (90d, 101c, 115b), wane (9a, 34b, 69a, 116d), want (34a, 35b, 68b, 81b, 92a, 133a), Ward (186), ward (27c, 35a, 67b), ware (76a), warm (10b, 58d, 120c), warn (11b, 25b), warp (30b, 121c, 125c), wars, Wart (193), wart (95c), wary (25b, 128b, 130a), Wash (82b), Wash. (212), wash (14d), WASP (244), wasp (63b, 229), wast (128a), WATS (244), Watt (63d, 186), watt (129a, 246), waul (114b), wave (48a, 83b, 100d, 118c, 126b), wavy (126b), wawl (114b), waxy, ways

_ W A _    away (9b, 55b, 59b, 83c), kwan (246), swab (57c, 78c, 134b), swag (115c), SWAK (243), swam, swan (19a, 28c, 226), swap (123c), SWAT (243), swat (20a, 28b, 116b), sway (29b, 37b, 63a, 67c, 76d, 79c, 85a, 130c, 133a), 'twas (30b, 107c), Tway (184)

_ _ W A    biwa (65d), Iowa (189, 210), tawa (81c), Tewa (189)

W _ _ A    waka (23d), weka (19b, 74d, 81c, 97b), weta (72d), whoa (42c, 115d)

W _ _ B    Webb (186), Weeb (186), womb (127c)

W C _ _    WCTU (244)

_ W C _    YWCA (244)

W _ _ C    WAAC (244), Wisc. (212, 244)

_ _ W D    bawd (22a), dowd (107b), fowd (44c, 74a), lewd (69b, 103d)

W _ _ D    wand (90d, 101c, 115b), Ward (186), ward (27c, 35a, 67b), weed (52d), Weld (186), weld (38d, 66c, 126c), wend (54d, 110b, 112a), wild (18c, 31d, 104c, 126d, 128c), wind (10d, 28d, 32d, 125c), woad (20a, 38d), wold (38d, 126d), Wood (187), wood (55a), word (95a, 120c, 121d)

W E _ _    weak (45a, 62c, 63a), weal (131b, 131c), wean (117a), wear (114a), Webb (186), webs, weds, Weeb (186), weed (52d), week (122b), weep (32b, 68d), weft (32b, 121c, 133c), Wegg (85a), wehe (53d), Weil (186), Weir (186), weir (33b, 47a), weka (19b, 74d, 81c, 97b), Weld (186), weld (38d, 66c, 126c), Welk (186), well (25c, 97c), we'll (30c), welt (100c, 129b, 130c, 131c), wend (54d, 110b, 112a), wens, went (34d), wept, were, we're (30c), werf (44c), weri (16c, 25a), wert (128a), West (186), west (83b), weta (72d), wets, we've (30c)

_ W E _    awed, awes, ewer (66a, 66d, 89c, 131d), ewes, Gwen (156), Iwei (213), owed, owes, Swed. (243)

_ _ W E    Bowe (142), Howe (17c, 63d, 159), Lowe (167)

W _ _ E    Wade (185), wade (129b), wage (103d), wake (102c, 123c), wale (55c, 100c, 130c, 131b, 131c), wane (9a, 34b, 69a, 116d), ware (76a), wave (48a, 83b, 100d, 118c, 126b), wehe (53d), were, we're

439

(30c), we've (30c), wide (102a), wife (114a), wile (34a), wine (60c, 91c), wipe (123d), wire (30d, 120b), Wise (187), wise (103b, 111a) woke, wore, wove

**W _ _ F**    WAAF (244), waif (116b), werf (44c), Wolf (187, 207), wolf (23d, 231), woof (32b, 37b, 121c, 131a), WRAF (244)

**W _ _ G**    Wegg (85a), whig (71c), wing (12d, 47c, 48a, 89b, 89d, 232), Wong (187)

**W H _ _**    wham (110b), whap (60b), what (96d, 99b), when (96d, 131c), whet (39c, 107d), whew (42c), whey (76d), whig (71c), whim (24a, 44b, 82c), whin (55c, 101b), whip (18a, 47c, 69b, 121b), whir (112a), whit (122c), whiz (88a, 112a), whoa (42c, 115d), whom (34d, 96d), whys

**_ W H _**    YWHA (244)

**_ _ W H**    YHWH (244)

**W _ _ H**    Wash (82b), Wash. (212), wash (14d), wish (35b), with (11d, 12c)

**W I _ _**    wick (23d), wide (102a), Wien (33c), wife (114a), wigs, wild (18c, 31d, 104c, 126d, 128c), wile (34a), Will (186), will (18c, 35b, 120d, 129a, 133a), Wilt (187), wilt (38a), wily (14d, 31d, 32c, 110c), wimp (130c), wind (10d, 28d, 32d, 125c), wine (60c, 91c), wing (12d, 47c, 48a, 89b, 89d, 232), wink (63c, 81d, 106a), wino (38b), wins, winy (128c), wipe (123d), wire (30d, 120b), wiry (109d), Wisc. (212, 244), Wise (187), wise (103b, 111a), wish (35b), wisp (49b), wist (68c), with (11d, 12c), wits, Witt (187)

**_ W I _**    swig (37d, 57a), swim (37a), Swit (182), twig (21c), twin (37c, 75b, 125c), twit (88a)

**_ _ W I**    iiwi (58c), kawi (66a), kiwi (13d, 19a, 19b, 97d, 226)

**W _ _ I**    wadi (38b, 83a, 98a, 101a), weri (16c, 25a)

**W K _ _**    wkly. (244)

**_ _ W K**    bowk (115a), gawk (109c, 114d), hawk (19a, 87c, 225)

**W _ _ K**    walk (85b), weak (45a, 62c, 63a), week (122b), Welk (186), wick (23d), wink (63c, 81d, 106a), work (52a, 116c), Wouk (187)

**_ W L _**    awls, owls

**_ _ W L**    bawl (18c, 129b, 134b), bowl (78d, 119a), cowl (78b), fowl (19b), howl (12d, 17d, 32b, 114b), jowl (26b, 35c), mewl (131c), pawl (73d), wawl (114b), yawl (20b, 103b), yowl (12d, 32b)

**W _ _ L**    wail (32b, 61c, 68d, 114b), Wall (193), wall (118a), waul (114b), wawl (114b), weal (131b, 131c), Weil (186), well (25c, 97c), we'll (30c), Will (186), will (18c, 35b, 120d, 129a, 133a), wool (47c)

440

**W _ _ M**    **warm** (10b, 58d, 120c), **wham** (110b), **whim** (24a, 44b, 82c), **whom** (34d, 96d), **worm** (88a), **wurm** (54c)

**_ W N _**    awns, awny, owns (91d)

**_ _ W N**    **Dawn** (148), **dawn** (14b, 15d, 33d), **Down** (150), **down** (35a, 45a, 232), **fawn** (32a, 34c), **gown** (37d), **Hawn** (157), **hewn** (27a), **lawn** (31a, 43b, 69a, 72a), **mown**, **pawn** (26c, 60c, 90b), **sawn**, **sewn**, **sown**, **town** (57c, 128b), **yawn** (21a)

**W _ _ N**    **wain** (129b), **warn** (11b, 25b), **wean** (117a), **when** (96d, 131c), **whin** (55c, 101b), **Wien** (33c), **worn** (107b), **Wren** (187), **wren** (19a, 226), **Wynn** (187)

**W O _ _**    **woad** (20a, 38d), **woes**, **woke**, **wold** (38d, 126d), **Wolf** (187, 207), **wolf** (23d, 231), **womb** (127c), **Wong** (187), **wont** (9c, 33a, 57a, 92b), **Wood** (187), **wood** (55a), **woof** (32b, 37b, 121c, 131a), **wool** (47c), **woos**, **word** (95a, 120c, 121d), **wore**, **work** (52a, 116c), **worm** (88a), **worn** (107b), **wort** (59b, 92a), **Wouk** (187), **wove**, **wows**

**_ W O _**    AWOL (236), twos

**W _ _ O**    Waco (21d), wino (38b)

**_ _ W P**    yawp (12d, 119b)

**W _ _ P**    **warp** (30b, 121c, 125c), **WASP** (244), **wasp** (63b, 229), **weep** (32b, 68d), **whap** (60b), **whip** (18a, 47c, 69b, 121b), **whop** (60b), **wimp** (130c), **wisp** (49b), **wrap** (19a, 28a, 41b)

**W R _ _**    **WRAF** (244), **wrap** (19a, 28a, 41b), **Wray** (187), **Wren** (187), **wren** (19a, 226), **writ** (71a)

**_ W R _**    awry (15a, 32a, 125c, 134c)

**W _ _ R**    **wear** (114a), **Weir** (186), **weir** (33b, 47a), **whir** (112a)

**_ _ W S**    bows, caws, cows (21b), haws, hews, jaws, Jews, laws, lows, maws, mews (114b), mows, news (121d), paws, pews, rows, saws, sews, sows, taws, tows, vows, wows, yaws, yews

**W _ _ S**    WACs, wads, wags, wars, WATS (244), ways, webs, weds, wens, wets, whys, wigs, wins, wits, woes, woos, wows

**_ _ W T**    at. wt. (236), Newt (172), newt (39d, 103d, 225), Nt. Wt. (241)

**W _ _ T**    **waft** (47c), **wait** (24b, 72a, 99c, 115a, 119d), **Walt** (185), **want** (34a, 35b, 68b, 81b, 92a, 133a), **Wart** (193), **wart** (95c), **wast** (128a), **Watt** (63d, 186), **watt** (129a, 246), **weft** (32b, 121c, 133c), **welt** (100c, 129b, 130c, 131c), **went** (34d), **wept**, **wert** (128a), **West** (186), **west** (83b), **what** (96d, 99b), **whet** (39c, 107d), **whit** (122c), **Wilt** (187), **wilt** (38a), **wist** (68c), **Witt** (187), **wont** (9c, 33a, 57a, 92b), **wort** (59b, 92a), **writ** (71a)

W U _ _     **wurm** (54c)

_ W U _     **swum**

W _ _ U     **WCTU** (244)

W _ _ W     **whew** (42c)

W Y _ _     **Wynn** (187)

_ W Y _     **Gwyn** (199)

_ _ W Y     **dewy** (77c)

W _ _ Y     **wary** (25b, 128b, 130a), **wavy** (126b), **waxy**, **whey** (76d), **wily** (14d, 31d, 32c, 110c), **winy** (128c), **wiry** (109d), **wkly.** (244), **Wray** (187)

W _ _ Z     **whiz** (88a, 112a)

_ X A _     **exam** (120d)

_ _ X A     **coxa** (60b), **hexa-** (93c), **moxa** (25b, 26d, 133d)

X _ _ A     **xema** (14a, 56d)

_ X C _     **exch.** (238), **excl.** (238)

X D _ _     **XDIV** (244)

X E _ _     **xema** (14a, 56d), **xeno-** (93a), **xero-** (92d)

_ X E _     **axed**, **axes**, **exec.** (238), **exes**, **oxen** (12d, 21b)

_ _ X E     **luxe** (100c)

X _ _ G     **Xing.** (244)

X _ _ H     **xiph-** (93d)

X I _ _     **Xing.** (244), **xiph-** (93d)

_ X I _     **axil** (12c), **axis** (25c, 34c, 60c), **exit** (71a, 130c), **ixia** (30d)

_ _ X I     **sexi-** (93c), **taxi** (95d)

_ X L _     **axle** (113c, 131c)

X M _ _     **Xmas** (27a)

_ X O _     **axon** (81b), **Exod.** (238), **Oxon** (85d)

_ _ X O     **myxo-** (93b)

X _ _ O     **xeno-** (93a), **xero-** (92d), **xylo-** (94a)

X R _ _     **x-ray** (12a, 75c, 88d)

X _ _ S     **Xmas** (27a)

_ _ X T     **mixt.** (240), **next** (81a), **sext** (23d, 84d, 109d), **text** (86d, 133c)

X _ _ V     **XDIV** (244)

_ _ X X     **Foxx** (153)

X Y _ _     **xylo-** (94a)

_ _ X Y     **doxy** (133b), **foxy** (14d, 31d, 132a), **sexy** (41c), **waxy**

X _ _ Y     **x-ray** (12a, 75c, 88d)

Y A _ _     **yaks**, **Yale** (79b, 101c, 205), **yams**, **yang** (134d), **Yank** (12b), **yank** (95d), **yapp** (20d), **yaps**, **Yard** (187), **yard** (40d, 69a, 113a, 246), **yarn** (43a, 114b, 119b, 133c), **yate** (41d), **yaup** (119b), **yawl** (20b, 103b), **yawn** (21a), **yawp** (12d, 119b), **yaws**, **Yazd** (217)

_ Y A _     **ayah** (62d, 82d), **dyad** (85d), **Dyak** (217, 219), **Dyan** (150), **eyas** (19b, 58c), **hyal-** (93a), **iyar** (78c), **kyat** (220), **ryal** (83d), **Ryan** (179)

_ _ Y A     **Anya** (139), **Baya** (215), **baya** (130d), **Gaya** (18d), **Goya** (112c), **hoya** (12c, 15d, 130c), **Maya** (134d, 169, 214, 217), **maya** (60a, 130d), **raya** (85a), **saya** (88c), **soya** (112c)

Y _ _ A     **YMCA** (244), **YMHA** (244), **yoga** (14d, 60a), **yuca** (24c), **yuga** (60a), **Yuma** (189), **YWCA** (244), **YWHA** (244)

_ Y C _     **myco-** (93a), **syce** (56c)

_ Y D _     **Hyde** (37a), **hydr-** (93d)

_ _ Y D     **Boyd** (142), **emyd** (120c)

Y _ _ D     **Yard** (187), **yard** (40d, 69a, 113a, 246), **Yazd** (217), **yond** (36d), **you'd** (30c)

Y E _ _     **yeah** (10b), **yean** (68d), **year** (122b), **yeas** (129c), **yech** (112a), **Yedo** (122d), **yegg** (22d), **Yell** (64d), **yell** (18c, 108d), **yelp** (12d, 37b), **yeni** (119c), **yens**, **Yeti** (9b), **yews**

_ Y E _     **ayes** (129c), **byes**, **dyed**, **dyer**, **dyes**, **eyed**, **eyes**, **hyet-** (93c), **lyes**, **myel-** (93d), **nyet** (81d), **oyer** (31c), **oyes** (31c, 32c, 58d), **oyez** (31c, 32c, 58d), **pyel-** (93c), **pyes**, **tyee** (26d)

_ _ Y E     **Faye** (152), **Gaye** (154), **Kaye** (164), **Skye** (64d, 120d)

Y _ _ E     **Yale** (79b, 101c, 205), **yate** (41d), **yipe** (42c), **yoke** (66c, 232), **yore** (12c, 23a, 55b, 73a, 83d, 87a, 122b), **yule** (27a)

_ Y G _    **hygr-** (94a), **zygo-** (93c)

Y _ _ G    **yang** (134d), **yegg** (22d)

Y H _ _    **YHWH** (244)

Y _ _ H    **yeah** (10b), **yech** (112a), **YHWH** (244), **yogh** (12c), **yuch** (112a)

Y I _ _    **yipe** (42c), **yips**

_ Y I _    **ayin** (12a)

Y _ _ I    **yeni** (119c), **Yeti** (9b), **Yogi** (187), **yogi** (60a), **Yuri** (188)

_ Y K _    **fyke** (16b), **tyke** (21c, 26c)

Y _ _ K    **Yank** (12b), **yank** (95d), **yolk** (128d), **York** (41a, 187, 192, 193, 194), **yuck** (112a)

_ Y L _    **gyle** (21d), **hyla** (12b, 122c), **hylo-** (94a), **Kyle** (165), **Lyle** (167), **pyla** (21c), **Pyle** (175), **syll.** (243), **xylo-** (94a)

_ _ Y L    **amyl** (114d), **amyl-** (93d), **aryl** (14b), **idyl** (90c, 233)

Y _ _ L    **yawl** (20b, 103b), **Yell** (64d), **yell** (18c, 108d), **yowl** (12d, 32b)

Y M _ _    **YMCA** (244), **YMHA** (244), **ymir** (54b)

_ Y M _    **cyma** (37c, 77d), **cyme** (47d), **gymn-** (93b), **gyms**, **hymn** (111d), **tymp** (19d), **zymo-** (93a)

_ _ Y M    **Clym** (14a)

_ Y N _    **dyna-** (93c), **dyne** (48c, 246), **gyne** (45b), **gyno-** (92d), **-gyny** (117b), **Lynn** (167), **Lynx** (207), **lynx** (24a, 131d, 230), **myna** (19b), **rynd** (76d), **Ryne** (179), **syne** (105b), **Tyne** (82b, 184, 223), **Wynn** (187)

_ _ Y N    **Gwyn** (199)

Y _ _ N    **yarn** (43a, 114b, 119b, 133c), **yawn** (21a), **yean** (68d), **Yüan** (26d, 78a), **yuan** (215)

Y O _ _    **yoga** (14d, 60a), **yogh** (12c), **Yogi** (187), **yogi** (60a), **yoke** (66c, 232), **Yoko** (187), **yolk** (128d), **yond** (36d), **yore** (12c, 23a, 55b, 73a, 83d, 87a, 122b), **York** (41a, 187, 192, 193, 194), **you'd** (30c), **your** (95a), **yowl** (12d, 32b), **yoyo** (88a)

_ Y O _    **BYOB** (236), **Gyor** (217), **Lyon** (216), **ryot** (62d)

_ _ Y O    **buyo** (18d), **coyo** (16a, 26d), **cryo-** (93a), **Enyo** (129d), **kayo** (68c), **Mayo** (169), **toyo** (58b, 65d, 116c), **yoyo** (88a)

Y _ _ O    **Yedo** (122d), **Yoko** (187), **yoyo** (88a), **Yuro** (188)

_ Y P _    **gyps, hype** (95a), **hypo** (88d), **rype** (95d), **type** (27d, 112a, 113b), **typo** (41c, 94c), **typp** (134b)

Y _ _ P    **yapp** (20d), **yaup** (119b), **yawp** (12d, 119b), **yelp** (12d, 37b)

_ Y R _    **Byrd** (90d), **byre** (31c), **eyra** (65b), **Eyre** (22a), **eyry** (39a), **fyrd** (83d), **gyre** (27b), **gyri** (21c), **gyro-** (93a), **Lyra** (58a, 207), **lyre** (80b, 85a), **Myra** (15a, 171), **myri-** (93b), **pyre** (52c), **pyro-** (93a), **Tyra** (184), **Tyre** (71a, 88c, 218), **Tyro** (81b), **tyro** (12b, 18b, 82c)

_ _ Y R    **skyr** (20d)

Y _ _ R    **year** (122b), **ymir** (54b), **your** (95a)

_ Y S _    **cyst** (128a), **-lyse** (117b), **lysi-** (93a), **myst** (56b), **NYSE** (241)

_ _ Y S    **Amys, bays, beys, boys, buys, cays, days, deys, Fays, gays** (60d), **guys, Hays** (157), **Itys** (120c), **jays, joys, Kays, keys, lays, Mays** (169), **nays** (129c), **pays, rays, Roys, says, soys, toys, ways, whys**

Y _ _ S    **yaks, yams, yaps, yaws, yeas** (129c), **yens, yews, yips, yuks** (70b), **Yves** (188)

_ Y T _    **-lyte** (117a), **myth** (43a, 71b)

_ _ Y T    **Foyt** (153), **Hoyt** (159)

Y _ _ T    **yurt** (78a)

Y U _ _    **Yüan** (26d, 78a), **yuan** (215), **yuca** (24c), **yuch** (112a), **yuck** (112a), **yuga** (60a), **yuks** (70b), **yule** (27a), **Yuma** (189), **Yuri** (188), **Yuro** (188), **yurt** (78a)

_ Y U _    **Ryun** (179), **Tyus** (184)

Y V _ _    **Yves** (188)

_ Y V _    **gyve** (45c, 107b)

Y W _ _    **YWCA** (244), **YWHA** (244)

_ Y X _    **myxo-** (93b)

_ _ Y X    **Ceyx** (57b), **onyx** (23c, 25d, 53b, 106c), **oryx** (13a, 231), **Styx** (26b, 57a)

_ Y Z _    **-lyze** (117b)

Z A _ _    **Zama** (106a), **Zana** (58a), **Zane** (188), **zany** (28b, 38a, 48b, 109c), **zarf** (28d, 32d, 114d), **Zasu** (188)

_ Z A _    **azan** (80c), **czar** (103c), **izar** (52d)

445

_ _ Z A     **boza** (13d), **Gaza** (88c, 216), **Giza** (113c), **Liza** (166)

Z _ _ A     **Zama** (106a), **Zana** (58a), **zeta** (11d), **Zola** (49c, 188), **zona**(108a)

Z _ _ C     **zinc** (20b, 76a, 245)

_ _ Z D     **Yazd** (217)

Z E _ _     **zeal** (14b, 45c), **zebu** (21c, 62d, 231), **Zech.** (244), **zeds, zees** (110c), **zein** (30d), **zemi** (45c), **Zeno** (56b), **Zeph.** (244), **Zero** (188), **zero** (27b, 65d, 73b, 82c, 89d), **zest** (45c, 57c, 99b), **zeta** (11d), **Zeus** (55c, 59c, 198)

_ Z E _     **Ezek.** (238), **ezel** (67c), **Ozem** (197)

_ _ Z E     **adze** (122d), **daze** (48a, 116c, 116d), **doze** (110b), **faze** (36a), **fuze** (35b), **gaze** (114d, 115a), **haze** (28b, 48a, 77b, 127b), **laze** (61d), **-lyze** (117b), **maze** (68b), **Mize** (171), **ooze** (43c, 72b, 79c, 87d), **raze** (34d, 35b, 36c, 71c), **size** (129a)

Z _ _ E     **Zane** (188), **zone** (18c, 36d, 40d, 118b)

Z _ _ F     **zarf** (28d, 32d, 114d)

Z _ _ G     **zing** (32a)

Z _ _ H     **Zech.** (244), **Zeph.** (244)

Z I _ _     **zinc** (20b, 76a, 245), **zing** (32a), **zion** (95a), **zips**

_ Z I _     **Ezio** (152)

_ _ Z I     **nazi** (81a)

Z _ _ I     **zemi** (45c), **zori** (108c), **Zuni** (95d, 189)

Z _ _ L     **zeal** (14b, 45c), **zool.** (244)

Z _ _ M     **zoom** (23c)

Z _ _ N     **zein** (30d), **zion** (95a), **zoon** (39d)

Z O _ _     **Zoes, Zola** (49c, 188), **zona** (108a), **zone** (18c, 36d, 40d, 118b), **zool.** (244), **zoom** (23c), **zoon** (39d), **zoos, Zoot** (188), **zori**(108c)

_ Z O _     **azon** (10b), **Azov** (19d, 103c)

_ _ Z O     **bozo** (38d, 88a), **kozo** (86b), **ouzo** (11a), **Puzo** (175)

Z _ _ O     **Zeno** (56b), **Zero** (188), **zero** (27b, 65d, 73b, 82c, 89d), **zygo-** (93c), **zymo-** (93a)

_ Z R _     **Ezra** (152, 196, 197)

Z _ _ S    **zeds, zees** (110c), **Zeus** (55c, 59c, 198), **zips, Zoes, zoos**

Z _ _ T    **zest** (45c, 57c, 99b), **Zoot** (188)

Z U _ _    **Zulu** (12a, 222), **Zuni** (95d, 189)

_ Z U _    **azul** (112c), **azur** (50a)

Z _ _ U    **Zasu** (188), **zebu** (21c, 62d, 231), **Zulu** (12a, 222)

Z Y _ _    **zygo-** (93c), **zymo-** (93a)

_ _ Z Y    **Cozy** (147), **cozy** (39b, 111b), **dozy** (110c), **hazy** (127a), **lazy** (62d), **mazy, oozy** (106b, 110c), **Ozzy** (173)

Z _ _ Y    **zany** (28b, 38a, 48b, 109c)

_ Z Z _    **Ozzy** (173)

_ _ Z Z    **buzz** (79d, 103a, 131d), **fizz** (39d), **fuzz** (37c), **Jazz** (206), **jazz** (61d, 118d), **razz** (59a)